Pattern Recognition
Using Neural Networks

Pattern Recognition Using Neural Networks

Theory and Algorithms for Engineers and Scientists

Carl G. Looney
Computer Science Department
University of Nevada

New York   Oxford
OXFORD UNIVERSITY PRESS
1997

OXFORD UNIVERSITY PRESS

Oxford   New York
Athens   Auckland   Bangkok   Bogota   Bombay
Buenos Aires   Calcutta   Cape Town   Dar es Salaam   Delhi
Florence   Hong Kong   Istanbul   Karachi
Kuala Lumpur   Madras   Madrid   Melbourne
Mexico City   Nairobi   Paris   Singapore
Taipei   Tokyo   Toronto

and associated companies in

Berlin   Ibadan

Library of Congress Cataloging-in-Publication Data
Looney, Carl G.
    Pattern recognition using neural networks : theory and algorithms
for engineers and scientists / by Carl G. Looney.
        p.   cm.
    Includes bibliographical references and index.
    ISBN 0-19-507920-5 (cloth)
    1. Pattern recognition systems.   2. Neural networks (Computer
science)   I. Title.
TK7882.P3L66   1996
006.4—dc20   96-29042
                                                       CIP

Printing (last digit):   9 8 7 6 5 4 3 2 1

Printed in the United States of America
on acid-free paper

To the major candles in my life:
my wife Laurette,
my son Erin Claude, and
my daughter Adrianne

Contents

Part I. *Fundamentals of Pattern Recognition*

Part II. Introductory Neural Networks

Part III. *Advanced Fundamentals of Neural Networks*

Chapter 5. Acceleration and Stabilization of Supervised Gradient Training of MLPs   155

Chapter 6. Supervised Training via Strategic Search   206

List of Tables

Preface

The goals of this practical *algorithmic approach* are to expose in a readable fashion the

- **(i)** standard decision-theoretic methods of pattern recognition
- **(ii)** applicable parts of contemporary artificial neural network methodology
- **(iii)** engineering of features, data, and network architectures
- **(iv)** applications of artificial neural networks to recognition and classification

Feedforward artificial neural networks (FANNs) include the multiple-layered percep-trons (MLPs), functional link nets (FLNs), and radial basis function networks (RBFNs). The Hornik–Stinchcombe–White theorem establishes that all of these FANNs are sufficiently powerful to perform nonlinear pattern discrimination, which means that any failures are *not* attributable to the neural network paradigm. Instead, failure is due to *inadequate training*, *inappropriate architecture* for the problem at hand, or the *noise power*, *nonseparability* of the feature data (*inappropriate data and feature engineering*). This work also addresses the related problems of feature extraction, data engineering, architectural design, training and testing techniques, and the effects of algorithmic parameters, all of which are necessary for the successful use of FANNs for pattern recognition. We cover in depth FANNs that must have supervised training, but also expose the algorithmic machinations of feature maps and learning vector quantization networks that are useful clustering (self-organzing) paradigms. We also present the recurrent, or feedback, neural networks of Amari and Hopfield because of their potential as stochastic automata.

A Neural Network Weltanschauung

FANNs are especially well suited to the operational decisionmaking of pattern recognition and to the learning that is classification. We cover the more useful and applicable algorithms that are most easily implementable in computer programs to solve real-world problems in recognition and classification. The great majority of researchers who use artificial neural networks implement the feedforward type, and MLPs in particular.

The gradient training of MLPs encounters multiple local minima and other problematic behavior, unfortunately. The problems encountered in the use of backpropagation as a new tool led to some mistrust of MLPs by 1990, although the failures were actually due to one or more of the problems mentioned above. Researchers in large-scale highly nonlinear optimization problems forsook such first-order gradient (steepest descent) methods in the 1960s because of their problematic behavior. The training of a sizable MLP on data that are not linearly separable presents the same type of optimization problem. There are, however, some algorithms and architectures that are more stable, robust, and powerful. For MLPs, these include strategic search, Fahlman's cascade correlation, and modified gradient methods such as conjugate gradient directions. For RBFNs, the *quick-training* and *full-training* algorithms are very effective, and these extend also to FLNs. FANNs are, in fact, extremely powerful tools that will be heavily used in the future, especially in recognition and other decision-making, forecasting, and signal processing and in the modeling of complex nonlinear systems by fitting such networks to nonlinear data.

The Concert-goers

The intended readership for this work consists of scientists and engineers, graduate students, well-prepared seniors, and researchers in areas that use pattern recognition and classification to glean knowledge from data. With an assumed background in a technical/scientific area, a reader should find ample tools within this volume for successful applications to various decision problems. There already exist numerous books that present good overviews of neural networks, as well as many books that recount the ancient times (1940s and 1950s) and the middle ages (1960s through early 1980s) of neural computing. We deliberately avoid rehashing the multitudinous approaches of lesser current practical use. We omit the usual "pie-in-the-sky" hyperbole ad nauseam, as well as sophistry and obfuscation. Instead, we analyze the internals of the network "black boxes" so readers can understand and use them judiciously to perform recognition.

Prelude in C Major

Chapter 0 introduces the basic concepts of pattern recognition and classification. Chapter 1 reviews a representative sample of useful linear decision theoretic methods of pattern recognition. For the sake of completeness, Chapter 2 briefly introduces the syntactic, or structural, approach to pattern recognition. FANNs are introduced in Chapter 3 as (i) multiple-layered perceptrons, (ii) functional link networks, and (iii) radial basis function networks. This chapter also introduces (a) self-organizing feature maps, (b) learning vector quantization networks, and (c) the recurrent, or feedback, type of neural network of Amari and Hopfield.

Chapter 4 covers the supervised training of feedforward networks via a particular type of gradient method know as *error backpropagation*. This is currently the most heavily used algorithm for training MLPs, FLNs, and RBFNs for applications. We derive the backpropagation algorithm for MLPs in complete detail for the cases of a single hidden layer and two hidden layers of neurons as well as for both unipolar and bipolar sigmoidal activation functions. We then derive the backpropagation type of training for RBFNs (which extend to FLNs). Chapter 4 also discusses the selection of unique output target vectors for identifying the classes. Appendix 4 provides an analysis of gradient methods for training that exposes the inherent problems and also presents a short review of vector calculus with intuitive chain rules.

Chapter 5 provides methods for overcoming the problematic behavior of gradient training for MLPs. The *fullpropagation* (FP) gradient algorithm given there trades off greater memory requirements for greater efficiency by training on all exemplar input vectors concurrently instead of one at a time as does backpropagation. FP is significantly faster than the epochal and batch modes of BP. Important techniques are provided that stabilize and speed up the training. Appendix 5 describes the Fahlman–Lebiere method of *cascade correlation*.

Chapter 6 discusses the training of MLPs via strategic search algorithms that avoids the divergent behavior and the local minimum trap of gradient methods. These are particularly useful for difficult learning problems and for large networks. Random optimization is the simplest and most basic type of search, but we also discuss quadratic, cubic, and quartic search in random directions, as well as evolutionary search with genetic algorithms. Strategic search may be used in an initial stage to obtain a reasonably good weight set in a region of low error values from which to start a gradient descent.

Chapter 7 provides advanced methods for functional link networks, radial basis function networks, self-organizing feature maps, and learning vector quantization networks. The *quick-training* and *full-training* algorithms for RBFNs are given there. Some of the new techniques include the so-called fuzzy logic, so a short introduction is included. Some of these techniques, however, can be done quantitatively without any mention of fuzzy logic per se. The self-organizing networks perform clustering as do the basic pattern recognition algorithms from Chapter 1.

Chapter 8 covers recurrent (Amari–Hopfield) neural networks. These single-layer feedback networks were not actually trained in the original algorithms. Instead, the weights were taken to be feature correlations that remained fixed while the outputs were fed back as inputs until the outputs attained stable states (attractors). We include some recent techniques from the literature that allow the partial training of Hopfield networks so as to gain a larger number of stable states. This allows more classes to be recognized with fewer than the usual unwieldy number of neurodes (a major weakness of Hopfield networks). We feel that more theory is needed to reach the full potential of these stochastic automata.

Chapter 9 analyzes the neural network "black box" to aid in the engineering of an appropriate network architecture for a given task. It discusses the two diametrically opposed philosophies of architectural adjustment, which are as follows: (i) Start with a large network and prune neurons while continuing the training; or (ii) start with a small network and add neurons while continuing the training. It also discusses the important topic of validation of the training and the verification of the final neural network as a model of the system that generated the training data.

Chapter 10 presents topics in feature engineering, which is a critical part of pattern recognition that is often overlooked or given less than satisfactory coverage. While the usual coverage of this topic is theoretical and not very useful, we follow certain theoretical aspects with practical approximative techniques. This chapter discusses the independence, correlation, selection, ordering, and weighting of features. Chapter 10 also discusses data engineering, which is the design of transformations on the data to obtain more robust training of greater generalizability.

Chapter 11 compares the results of various training algorithms for FANNs and shows the effects of various parameters and techniques used in the training. For example, back-propagation is compared with fullpropagation; and the effects of momentum, learning rates, and other parameters are explored with computer runs. Chapter 12 covers some applications of pattern recognition. From a virtually unlimited arena of such applications, we present a few that are illustrative and informative.

Maps of Two Treks to Nirvana

The following two outlines are suggested as the possible tracks: (i) pattern recognition or (ii) applied feedforward artificial neural networks. However, other tracks are possible for special purposes.

a. Track 1: Pattern Recognition with Artificial Neural Networks

Chapter 0 (Basic Concepts of Pattern Recognition); Chapter 1 (Decision-Theoretic Algorithms); Chapter 2 (Structural Pattern Recognition); Chapter 3 (Artificial Neural Network Structures); Chapter 4 (Supervised Training via Error Backpropagation: Derivations); Chapter 5 (Acceleration and Stabilization of Gradient Supervised Training of MLPs); Chapter 6 (Supervised Training via Strategic Search); Chapter 7 (Advances in Network Algorithms for Recognition); Chapter 9 (Neural Engineering and Testing of FANNs); Chapter 10 (Feature and Data Engineering); and Chapter 12 (Pattern Recognition Applications). The progression is

$$0 \to 1 \to 2 \to 3 \to 4 \to 5 \to 6 \to 7 \to 9 \to 10 \to 12$$

b. Track 2: Applied Artificial Neural Networks

Chapter 0 (Basic Concepts of Pattern Recognition); Chapter 3 (Artificial Neural Network Structures); Chapter 4 (Supervised Training via Error Backpropagation: Derivations); Chapter 5 (Acceleration and Stabilization of Gradient Supervised Training of FANNs); Chapter 6 (Supervised Training via Strategic Search); Chapter 7 (Advances in Network Algorithms for Recognition); Chapter 8 (Recurrent Networks); Chapter 9 (Neural Engineering and Testing of FANNs); Chapter 10 (Feature and Data Engineering); and Chapter 11 (Some Comparative Studies of Feedforward Artificial Neural Networks). In this case, the chapter progression is

$$0 \to 3 \to 4 \to 5 \to 6 \to 7 \to 8 \to 9 \to 10 \to 11$$

Acknowledgments

I sincerely appreciate the award of my sabbatical by Dr. Robert Hoover, Vice President for Academic Affairs, University of Nevada (Reno), who is now President of the University of Idaho. I thank Professor Dave Brown, Chairman of Computer Science, University of Alabama (Tuscaloosa) for the accommodations during my visit there, especially the private office and computer facilities. While it is necessary to severely cut the list, I must, however, mention my two major mathematical mentors: Professor Bob Tompson and the late Professor E. M. Beesley, both of whom taught at the University of Nevada (Reno) from the 1950s into the 1980s and whom both coincidentally received their Ph.D.s at Brown University. I also thank Milton Fuller, President, Solid State Farms, 500 Winchester Drive, Reno, NV 89506 (biomedical and electronic research and development), for financial support during part of the composition of this material.

Carl G. Looney
Reno

Pattern Recognition
Using Neural Networks

Part I

Fundamentals of Pattern Recognition

Chapter 0

Basic Concepts of Pattern Recognition

The goal of this chapter is to introduce the concepts of grouping objects into classes and recognizing sample objects as belonging to classes.

0.1. Patterns and Classification as Knowledge

The concept of *pattern* is universal in intelligence and discovery. For example, we perceive the colored lines on the walls of the caves at Lascaux, France, painted in prehistoric times, as mammals of prey. Artists of today put colored beads on walls to form symbols or pictures. More technically, the phase angle differences over time at the two ends of a drive shaft of a large marine engine contains patterns of torsion that can reveal the performance of particular cylinders. The patterns in biological data contain knowledge, if only we can discover it. Discrimination of signal patterns allows personal identification by voice, handwriting, fingerprints, facial images, and so on, as well as the recognition of speech, written characters, and scenes in images. It also includes the identification of military targets based on radar, infrared, and/or video images. Patterns exist in high-frequency electromagnetic scans of body chemicals and other organic chemicals, including DNA.

Possibilities abound in geologic, climatic, meteorologic, personality, cultural, historical, spectral, electromagnetic, and other data, as well as from microscopic images of cells to macroscopic images of regions of the earth obtained from satellite scans and radio telescope images of galaxies. There remains only for the researcher in some area to glean the essentials and begin to explore the classification and recognition of patterns in data that will lead to discoveries of associations and cause–effect relationships. The concept of *classification* involves the learning of likenesses and differences of patterns that are abstractions of instances of objects in a population of nonidentical objects. The associations between patterns and their causes are the bricks from which the wall of scientific knowledge is built. An example is the classification of life forms by the Swedish physician Carl von Linne (1707–1778), known by his Latinized name of Carolus Linnaeus, which made possible Darwin's generalized law of evolution.

0.2. The Goal and Some Waypoints

The main goal of this volume is to clearly expose the fundamentals of pattern recognition and the applicable new tool of feedforward artificial neural networks (FANNs). While this work is not intended to be an evolutionary or comprehensive treatise on artificial neural networks, it contains ample material on the theoretical and applicable aspects of most useful models. FANNs are powerful tools for pattern recognition and classification. We take the algorithmic approach because it is more useful for the necessary implementations of methods and techniques as computer programs. We include some classical algorithms for completeness; cover in detail many neural network algorithms that are practical, efficient, and robust for recognition; and discuss their relative performances on certain data sets and the tradeoffs involved. The coverage also includes feature engineering and network architecture. We apply FANNs to real-world classification problems, discuss modifications to produce self-organizing operation, and provide a stimulating variety of applications.

0.3. What Are the Pattern Recognition and Classification Problems?

Recognition versus Classification

Humans recognize the faces of friends in a crowd, characters and words on the printed page, the voices of acquaintances, favorite melodies, the scent of fresh strawberries, textures of tree bark, patterns of weave in cloth, the shape of leaves, contextual meaning in word phrases, and so forth. Other mammals are also excellent recognizers. The senses preprocess signals such as sound or light waves that have been modulated—that is, transformed in some fashion by interaction with an object that impressed information on them. The preprocessed modulated signals are then mapped into a decision that equates to recognition of the object. Such processing detects (discriminates) subtle differences in the modulation of the signals to perform recognition. A *pattern* will be taken to be a primitive here, in that we agree on its meaning without being required to define it (in terms of yet other words whose definitions would then be required in terms of others, and so on, until a circular definition is reached as required by a finite language).

When it is determined that an object from a population P belongs to a known subpopulation S, we say that *pattern recognition* is done. The recognition of an individual object as a unique singleton class is called *identification*. *Classification* is the process of grouping objects together into *classes* (subpopulations) according to their perceived likenesses or similarities. The subject area of pattern recognition includes both classification and recognition and belongs to the broader field of *machine intelligence*—that is, the study of how to make machines learn and reason to make decisions, as do humans.

Learning is done by a system when it records its experience into internal system changes that cause its behavior to be changed (see Nilsson, 1965). It is an anti-entropic process that accumulates and concentrates experience into internal modifications of a system. Humans learn from experience by accumulating rules in various forms such as associations, tables, inequalities, equations, relationships, data structures, logical implications, and so on. Classification is a form of learning which induces from antecedent attributes the classes that are consequents. On the other hand, *reasoning* is a process of applying general rules, equations, relationships, and so on, to an initial collection of data, facts, and so on, to deduce a result or decision. Recognition is a form of reasoning, while classification is a form of learning.

The Recognition Process

Figure 0.1 depicts subpopulations $S_1,...,S_4$ of a population P of nonidentical objects, along with the processing that recognizes a sample object. An object's *attributes* are sensed or measured to yield a *pattern vector* that is transformed into a reduced set of *features*, and the object is recognized from its features by the recognizer. Let $\{m_i: i = 1,..., P\}$ be variables for pattern measurements to be made on objects selected from P. A *feature extractor T* transforms the pattern vector $\mathbf{m} = (m_1,..., m_P)$ into a *feature vector* $\mathbf{x} = (x_1,..., x_N) = T(\mathbf{m})$. A *pattern recognizer* is a system to which a feature vector is given as input, and which operates on the feature vector to produce an output that is the unique *identifier* (name, number, codeword, vector, string, etc.) associated with the class to which the object belongs. In a larger sense, each individual object is an *atomic class* (i.e., has no subclasses), so that recognition includes *identification*. The pattern recognition process given above may be *concrete* in that the recognition is based on measurements of physical attributes. In the world of ideas, patterns are based upon the attributes of concepts and mental models, which is *abstract* pattern recognition. We are more concerned here with concrete, rather than abstract, pattern recognition, but the distinction is blurred and is one of degree.

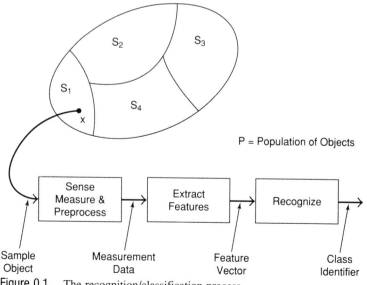

Figure 0.1.   The recognition/classification process.

More formally, let there be given a population P of nonidentical objects where each is represented by an N_0-dimensional pattern vector of measurements (or string of symbols or, more generally, a data structure). These are usually converted to a set of N-dimensional feature vectors. Thus we may consider P to be a set of N-dimensional feature vectors. Further, suppose that P is partitioned into unknown equivalence classes $S_1,..., S_K$. The *classification problem* (see Pavel, 1989) is: Decide whether or not multiple feature vectors belong to the same or different equivalence classes. The *recognition problem* is: Decide whether or not any given sample feature vector is equivalent to an *exemplar* (prototypical, archetypical, representative, template) vector, or set of such exemplar vectors, that represents a class.

Example 0.1. Optical Character Recognition

This set of data is taken from a project to recognize handwritten digits so that machines can automatically read ZIP codes. Each digit must be written in a rectangular box printed on an envelope. Prototypes of the digits 0, 1,..., 9 are written on the bottom right of the envelope as a guide to the writer. Suppose that our scanner can sense 256 different shades of gray from 0 (black) to 255 (white) for each *pixel* (picture element, or dot in an image). The preprocessor converts all gray levels below a threshold value of 127 into 0 (black) and everything from 127 to 255 into 1 (white), so that a single bit (0 or 1) represents a pixel. The rectangle for each digit contains 16 pixel rows by 14 pixel columns, for a total of 224 pixels, where each is 0 or 1 for black or white, respectively. A pattern vector consists of 224 values from the alphabet {0,1}, arranged into 16 rows of 14 columns each. Figure 0.2 shows a rectangle of 224 pixels with a handwritten digit that is an exemplar for the number seven. The pixel values for the preprocessed image of the "7" shown in Figure 0.2 are shown in Table 0.1.

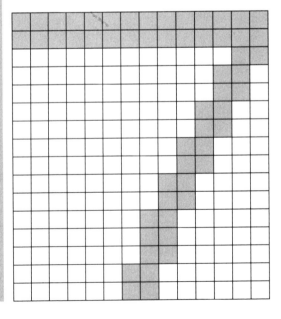

Figure 0.2.   A digit in a 16 × 14 pixel box.

Table 0.1.
The Pixel Values for the Digit "7"

1	1	1	1	1	1	1	1	1	1	1	1	1	1
1	1	1	1	1	1	1	1	1	1	1	1	1	1
0	0	0	0	0	0	0	0	0	0	0	0	1	1
0	0	0	0	0	0	0	0	0	0	0	1	1	0
0	0	0	0	0	0	0	0	0	0	0	1	1	0
0	0	0	0	0	0	0	0	0	0	1	1	0	0
0	0	0	0	0	0	0	0	0	0	1	1	0	0
0	0	0	0	0	0	0	0	0	1	1	0	0	0
0	0	0	0	0	0	0	0	0	1	1	0	0	0
0	0	0	0	0	0	0	0	1	1	0	0	0	0
0	0	0	0	0	0	0	0	1	1	0	0	0	0
0	0	0	0	0	0	0	1	1	0	0	0	0	0
0	0	0	0	0	0	0	1	1	0	0	0	0	0
0	0	0	0	0	0	0	1	1	0	0	0	0	0
0	0	0	0	0	0	1	1	0	0	0	0	0	0
0	0	0	0	0	0	1	1	0	0	0	0	0	0

We start at the top left and number the rows from 0 to 15 and then number the columns from 0 to 13. To reduce the number of attributes, we use only the rows numbered 1, 4, 7, 8, 11, and 14 and use only columns numbered 1, 4, 6, 7, 9, and 12. Starting from the top left (in the first row), we count the number of *changes* from black to white and from white to black while moving across the row. The selected six rows make up the first six measurements $m_1,..., m_6$. Next, we count the number of changes in the six selected columns to obtain six more measurements $m_7,..., m_{12}$. The reason that we count the changes rather than the number of black pixels is that the width of the written lines vary, and we want to avoid performing *skeletonization*—that is, reducing each character to medial lines of only one pixel in width. If characters are slightly rotated, the attributes may be affected somewhat, so the classification/recognition processor must be robust.

Each character box is *registered* by starting the top row on at least one black pixel, and the leftmost column must also contain at lease one black pixel. Thus the character is pushed against the top and to the left side of the character box. No changes are counted on a row or column that contains only white or only black pixels. Table 0.2 shows the 10 raw vectors of

Table 0.2.
The Attribute Vectors for Optical Character
Recognition of Digits

Digit	Count of pixel changes
0	(4, 3, 3, 2, 2, 4; 2, 3, 2, 2, 3, 2)
1	(2, 2, 2, 2, 2, 2; 0, 0, 0, 0, 2, 0)
2	(2, 1, 1, 2, 2, 1; 1, 2, 4, 4, 4, 3)
3	(0, 2, 2, 2, 2, 2; 0, 3, 3, 4, 7, 4)
4	(4, 4, 3, 0, 2, 2; 0, 3, 2, 2, 0, 2)
5	(2, 2, 4, 1, 1, 2; 2, 4, 4, 4, 4, 3)
6	(2, 2, 2, 3, 2, 2; 2, 5, 4, 4, 4, 4)
7	(0, 2, 2, 2, 2, 2; 1, 1, 2, 2, 3, 1)
8	(1, 3, 1, 1, 3, 3; 0, 7, 4, 4, 4, 4)
9	(4, 4, 3, 6, 2, 2; 0, 4, 3, 4, 5, 1)

12 attributes each. We convert these to features in this case by dividing each attribute by 8 to standardize them to fall between 0 and 1. The feature vector for "7" is $\mathbf{x}^{(7)} = (0, 2/8, 2/8, 2/8, 2/8, 2/8; 1/8, 1/8, 2/8, 2/8, 3/8, 1/8)$, which is unique among all 10 feature vectors. More than just uniqueness is required, however. The feature vector must not be too *similar* (too close) to any of the feature vectors for other digits lest moderate noise on the pixel values cause an error in recognition.

0.4. Approaches to Recognition and Classification

A Taxonomy of Methodologies

Recognition and classification methodologies can be categorized, although there is some overlap. The first category is the historical area, called *statistical pattern recognition*. It arose when R. A. Fisher (see Fisher, 1936) was asked to help classify objects (skulls) into sub-populations. His approach used measurements of attributes such as width and width-to-height ratios and the empirical distributions of the attribute values to classify the patterns by making overall statistical decisions. Because of natural fluctuations of the values that are measured, and measurement errors to a lesser extent, the feature values appear to have random components. Therefore, there is an estimation (Fisher, 1925) subproblem in any pattern recognition problem. Statistical pattern recognition is a subarea of the decision-theoretic one.

A more recent type of decisionmaking is based on the concept of strings of symbols selected from an alphabet. Such strings can be considered to be sentences in a grammar of correctly constructed sentences, where the construction is constrained by a set of rules called *productions*. Sentences arise from particular internal structures in the patterns. If an object's structural attributes can be transformed into a sentence in a grammar, then it is recognized as belonging to the class associated with that grammar. If not, it belongs to another class. Such classification is called *syntactic* (or *structural*) *pattern recognition* (syntax refers to sentence structure). Chapter 2 introduces this approach. A generalization is *stochastic syntactic pattern recognition* (see Tou and Gonzalez, 1974; or Fu, 1982a), where the probabilities of the occurrence of characters in a string are considered and the decision is based on the greatest probability of a sentence belonging to a grammar. Table 0.3 shows one breakdown of pattern recognition.

A modern approach to pattern recognition uses FANNs (Fausett, 1994; Fu, 1994; Zurada, 1992). A FANN is a nonlinear mapping T on an N-dimensional cube into an M-dimensional cube: $T:[a, b]^N \rightarrow [a, b]^M$, that is, $(x_1,..., x_N) \rightarrow (y_1,..., y_M)$, where $a \leq x_n, y_n \leq b$. The standard N-cube $[0,1]^N$ is often used in practice, or the bipolar N-cube $[-1,1]^N$ may also be used. A related area is fuzzy mappings, because the interval $[0,1]$ is the set of values for fuzzy logic. Fuzzy mappings are also used for pattern recognition (see Bezdek and Pal, 1992).

Automatic Pattern Recognition and Classification

An *automated pattern recognition system* is an operational system that minimally contains (i) an input subsystem that accepts sample pattern vectors and (ii) a decisionmaker subsystem that decides the *classes* (*types*, *categories*, *kinds*, *varieties*, etc.) to which an input pattern vector belongs. If it also *classifies*, then it has a learning mode in which it learns a set of classes of the population from a sample of pattern vectors; that is, it partitions the population into the subpopulations that are the classes. Automated pattern recognition systems use computers that

Table 0.3.
A Taxonomy of Pattern Recognition Methods

Decision-theoretic
  Statistical
    Parametric, Nonparametric Methods, Bayesian Estimation
  Graph-theoretic
  Rule-based
    Binary logical rules
    Fuzzy logical rules
Structural/syntactic
  Automata
    Deterministic
    Stochastic
  Hopfield recurrent neural networks
  Bidirectional associative maps
Associative mappings (neural and fuzzy mappings)
  Feedforward neural networks
    Multiple layered perceptrons
    Functional link nets
    Radial basis function networks
  Self-organizing networks
    Self-organizing feature maps
    Fuzzy c-means clustering algorithms
    Fuzzy self-organizing maps
    Adaptive resonance theory
  Hybrid networks
    Learning vector quantization networks
    Probabilistic neural networks
    Fuzzy associative maps
    Fuzzy learning vector quantization networks

execute programs of instructions to implement mathematical algorithms. Some of the application tasks to be performed include: (i) optical character recognition, or recognition of characters from images of printed characters; (ii) recognition of spoken words from features that are gleaned from sampled voice signals; (iii) recognition of biochemicals from features extracted from spectra of samples of blood, hair, and tissue, and so on; (iv) recognition of defective parts on a factory production line; (v) recognition of patterns in physiological signals such as EKG (electrocardiogram) and EMG (electromyogram); (vi) recognition of parts and their orientation by a computer vision system in an assembly plant; (vii) recognition of individual finger prints; (viii) recognition in food processing plants of complex system states that are associated with corrective control actions; (ix) recognition of targets from features gleaned from satellite photographs, radar reflections, sonar returns, and/or infrared images; and (x) recognition of cancer cells from features gleaned from objects (blobs) in microscopic images of Pap smears. Application possibilities exist everywhere we look.

0.5. Features and Their Distributions

Features as Nonredundant Attributes

For a given population P of objects, an *attribute* is a variable m that takes on a real measured value. A *feature* is either an attribute or a function of one or more attributes. These include such values as those obtained by integration of accelerometer values, Fourier transformations of transduced signals, width-to-length ratios, logarithms of products, conversions of coordinate systems or dimensions, estimates of parameters from data, and so on. Features must be *observable*, in that they can either be measured, obtained as a function of measured variables, or estimated from measured values of correlated variables.

Ideally, the set of features used in a classification decision should also be statistically *independent*, in that none of the features can be determined by a function of other features in the set, or estimated from them because of correlation. This would provide zero redundancy. For example, if a subspecies of grasshopper were to be examined, two features might be width at the widest part of the body and length. These are independent if one cannot be predicted from the other. In this case, the features consisting of width and the ratio of width to length could also be used in place of width and length. Note that the ratio could not be made without both of the original two measurements and so the ratio contains information other than width. Width, length, and ratio are not independent, however; that is, they include redundancy of information. The three variables provide only two degrees of freedom.

In general, a pattern vector of attributes is converted to a *feature vector* of lower dimension that contains all of the essential information of the pattern. This often eliminates a substantial amount of redundancy (see Example 0.2 below). Thus a feature vector $\mathbf{x} = (x_1,..., x_N)$ is to be associated with each object selected from P. The recognition decision for an object is based on the processing of its feature vector. Feature vectors from the same class, however, are also different. Typically, the differences come from three sources: (i) noise, which includes measurement and other random errors; (ii) bias (systemic error) in the measuring instruments, data acquisition system, and preprocessing system; and (iii) the natural variation between the objects within the same classes due to unknown variations of operators that create the objects. The latter variations cannot be predicted for individual objects, so they also appear to be random according to some probability distribution. For example, the size within a subspecies of grasshopper may vary greatly depending upon the amount of food available, the mineral content of the food, the weather, and so forth. The size between subspecies is different (in an average sense), due to such things as preferences for plants, but there may be overlapping effects due to a combination of known and unknown operators. Therefore, size alone may not be sufficient to classify the insects into subspecies. There is an assumed or empirically derived distribution of actual values for each feature, which is a random variable X that assumes a value $X = x$ for each sampled object taken as an experiment.

Example 0.2.   Data Compression as Elimination of Redundancy

Consider an image on a video monitor that has 800×600 pixels (picture elements, or dots). If each pixel requires eight bits to allow 256 shades of gray, then the image file requires 480,000 bytes of data. When one stores a library of images, some form of data compression is helpful. One method is called *JPEG compression*. The differences in the consecutive pixel values are used to keep the numbers smaller on the average. These are then transformed by a two-dimensional *discrete cosine transform* (DCT), which is the real part of the two-dimensional discrete Fourier transform, into two dimensions of spatial frequency power. The frequencies at low power can be eliminated from the transform data, which often allows a

480,000-byte image file to be stored in about 50,000 bytes. This nonredundant data represents the image and can be decoded by taking the inverse DCT and adding the pixel differences. The decoded image is virtually the same as the original image in most cases, although there is obviously some loss. Another commonly used compression technique is the *Limpel–Ziv–Welsh (LZW) algorithm*, which builds a code table of strings on the fly in both the compression and decompression modes. Compuserve implements a version of this in their images (*.GIF files).

Probability Distributions of Features

The probability distributions of different subpopulations for any single feature X may overlap as shown in Figure 0.3. Here, $f_1(x)$ and $f_2(x)$ are the probability density functions for the feature random variables $X = X^{(1)}$ and $X = X^{(2)}$ for Classes 1 and 2, respectively. Because this occurs for multiple features, the evidence must be built up in some fashion so that the total weight of evidence will favor the correct class. There are many ways to do this, but classical statistical pattern recognition (i) compares the probabilities for classes over all features and (ii) uses *similarity measures* in some averaging process.

0.6. Object Separation in Feature Space

The *feature space* for a population of objects with N features is taken to be the N-dimensional Euclidean vector space E^N, although it is sometimes taken to be the N-dimensional cube $[0,1]^N$ (or more generally $[a, b]^N$). To illustrate the separation of feature vectors that rep-

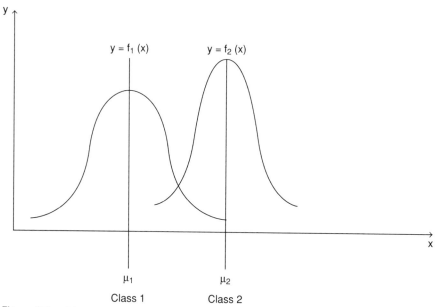

Figure 0.3.   Distributions of a feature for two classes.

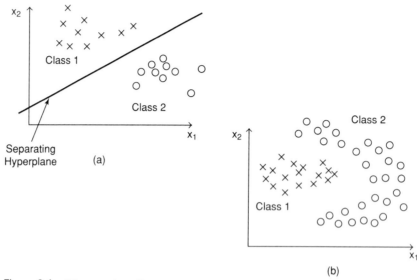

Figure 0.4.   Linear and nonlinear separation in feature space with (a) linear separability and (b) non-linear separability.

resent a population P, let there be two features x_1 and x_2, so the feature space is the plane. Suppose also that the objects fall into the two subpopulations S_1 and S_2. In Figure 0.4(a), it is clear that a straight line separates the samples as shown. Figure 0.4(b), however, shows sample feature vectors from two classes that cannot be separated by any straight line. The lesson to be learned from this is that classes of feature vectors cannot always be separated linearly—that is, by a line or linear subspace that may be translated by a numerical value.

In general, let P be a population with N-dimensional feature space that contains two classes (subpopulations). Any translation of an $(N - 1)$-dimensional linear subspace L of E^N by the fixed vector $\mathbf{v}$, designated by $H = L + \mathbf{v}$, is called a *hyperplane* of N-dimensional space. In Figure 0.4(a), the hyperplane H is a line. If a hyperplane H in feature space exists such that all feature vectors from one class S_1 are on one side of H, while all of the feature vectors of the other class S_2 are on the other side of H, then we say that S_1 and S_2 are *linearly separable* and are *linearly separated* by H. In such a case, we need only to evaluate the hyperplane equation at an input feature vector $\mathbf{x}$ in order to determine on which side of H the vector falls. But a recognition system must first learn (determine) such a hyperplane H, if one exists.

If several classes can be separated two at a time by hyperplanes, then they are called *pairwise linearly separable*, and the decision can be made by checking to determine on which side of each separating hyperplane a feature vector falls. Figure 0.5 displays this situation, where H_{ij} linearly separates Classes i and j. A given vector must be checked against H_{12}, H_{23}, and H_{13} to determine to which class it belongs.

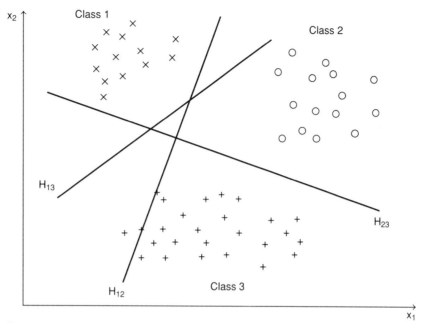

Figure 0.5.   Multilinear separation.

0.7. Training and Operational Modes

Modes

There are two distinct modes of processes that a pattern recognition system executes on the feature vectors of a population of objects. The second is the *operational* mode where the system maps each input feature vector into the output vector that represents the class decision. This decisionmaking is *recognition*. Before a system can do this, however, it must have first learned the classes of feature vectors through a process that partitions the set of feature vectors. This is *classification*, which involves *training*, or *machine learning*.

Supervised Training and Self-Organizing Learning

Categories of machine learning are (i) *supervised training* and (ii) *self-organization* (also called *unsupervised training*). In the supervised training mode, each of a sample of Q feature vectors is fed to the system, along with its known class identifier as the desired output vector, and the system learns to map the input feature vector into the desired class identifier.

In the self-organizing mode of classification, a system performs both training and operational processes on any input feature vector. The sample feature vectors are fed to the system in some sequence, and every time an input feature vector is not mapped to an identifier for a class already learned—that is, is not put into some class already learned—the system establishes a new class, assigns a unique identifier to that class, and adjusts its parameters to map the feature vector into that identifier. This is done in the stronger self-organizing processes such as the ISODATA algorithm (see the next chapter). In the weaker self-organizing algorithms, the number K of classes must be given and all sample feature vectors are squeezed into those K classes. This is done in the k-means algorithm (see the next chapter).

In either supervised or unsupervised training, the system determines one or more prototypical, archetypical, template, representative, central, and so on, vectors as idealized model(s) for each class. After training, the system is ready for operational use, although some testing should be done first to verify the training. In the operational mode, each incoming feature vector is compared via some measure of likeness to the exemplar vector(s) for each class, and a decision is made according to greatest similarity (least dissimilarity) between the input feature vector and the exemplar(s). Typical algorithms for a single pass of training are stated below for a given sample of Q exemplar feature vectors.

A High-Level Algorithm for Learning by Training

Step 1. /Arrange Q pairs of exemplar input $\mathbf{x}^{(q)}$ and output target $\mathbf{t}^{(k(q))}$ vectors in random order/
randomize order of $\{(\mathbf{x}^{(q)}, \mathbf{t}^{(k(q))}): q = 1,..., Q\}$ /random q ordering/

Step 2. For $q = 1$ to Q do
read the qth input/output pair of vectors $(\mathbf{x}^{(q)}, \mathbf{t}^{(k(q))})$
adjust system parameters to associate $\mathbf{t}^{(k(q))}$ with $\mathbf{x}^{(q)}$ /Map $\mathbf{x}^{(q)}$ into target $\mathbf{t}^{(k(q))}$/

A High-Level Algorithm for Self-Organizing Learning (Single Pass)

Step 1. /Randomize order of Q pairs of exemplar input vectors/
randomize order of $(\mathbf{x}^{(q)}, \mathbf{t}^{(k(q))})$;

Step 2. $K \leftarrow 1$; class(1) $\leftarrow 1$;   /Assign $\mathbf{x}^{(1)}$ to Class 1/

Step 3. For $q = 2$ to Q do   /For K current classes/
read input vector $\mathbf{x}^{(q)}$;
class_set = false;
for $k = 1$ to K do
if $\mathbf{x}^{(q)}$ is similar to C_k, then   /If $\mathbf{x}^{(q)}$ is in Class k/
class(q) = k; class_set = true;   /assign* qth input vector to Class k/
if class_set = false, then   /else make new class $K + 1$/
$K \leftarrow K + 1$; class(q) = K;   /and assign qth input vector to Class $K + 1$/
* By class(q) = k we mean that $\mathbf{x}^{(q)}$ is assigned to Class k.

0.8. The Concept of Clustering as the Learning of Classes

Clusters

In the self-organizing mode, the process of grouping feature vectors into classes is called *clustering*. The terminology comes from the appearance of an incoming sequence of feature vectors which arrange themselves into *clusters*—that is, groups of points that are closer to each other and their own centers rather than to the centers of other groups. When a feature vector is input to the system, its distances to the existing cluster representatives is determined, and it is either assigned to the cluster with minimal distance or taken to be a representative of a new cluster. Hierarchical strategies have also been proposed, where hierarchical implies that a complex pattern is described as a collection of simpler subpatterns, down through possibly many levels of subpatterns with their subclusters.

Fu's Generalized Clustering Algorithm

According to K. S. Fu (1982b), clustering consists of the four steps given below that use (a) a *similarity measure*, (b) a *distinctness test* on the clusters, (c) a *repartitioning method* that improves the value of the measure of similarity, and (d) a *stopping rule*.

Step 1. *Partition* the sample set $S = \{\mathbf{x}^{(1)},..., \mathbf{x}^{(Q)}\}$ of Q sample feature vectors into **K** trial subsets (clusters) via an appropriate similarity (or dissimilarity) criterion (such as distance from the center of the cluster)

Step 2. *Test* the partition to determine whether or not the K trial clusters are sufficiently dissimilar between clusters and similar within clusters.

Step 3. *Stop* if stopping criterion is met (no clusters have changed).

Step 4. *Repartition* S (merge clusters that are too similar, break up those that are too dissimilar within, or otherwise reassign the vectors to clusters), change K accordingly, and go to Step 2.

0.9. Classical Linear Separation

Linear separation, called *linear discrimination*, is best demonstrated with examples. The two examples given below invoke linear separation implicitly and explicitly, respectively.

Example 0.3. **Two Clusters in the Plane**

Let $\mathbf{X} = (X_1, X_2)$ be a feature vector of random variables that assumes a feature vector (x_1, x_2) for each object drawn from a population P as a sampling experiment. Suppose that five objects are selected from P at random and that the feature vector instances are

$$\mathbf{x}^{(1)} = (2.0,\ 3.6), \quad \mathbf{x}^{(2)} = (2.2,\ 4.0), \quad \mathbf{x}^{(3)} = (4.8,\ 1.0),$$
$$\mathbf{x}^{(4)} = (3.0,\ 5.0), \quad \text{and} \quad \mathbf{x}^{(5)} = (5.2,\ 2.0)$$

Figure 0.6 shows these feature vectors in the plane. We separate these vectors into two classes by taking the Euclidean distances between all pairs of points, and then arrange them in a 5 × 5 symmetric matrix of distance entries $d(i, j)$ from point i to point j, $1 \le i, j \le 5$, where $d(i, j) = [(x_1^{(i)} - x_1^{(j)})^2 + (x_2^{(i)} - x_2^{(j)})^2]^{1/2}$. From this we select a threshold τ midway between the minimal and maximal distances. All point pairs that have a distance less than τ are put into the same class. If we do not obtain two classes, then we decrease the threshold τ and try again. When we arrive at an appropriate threshold, we obtain two classes. In this example, Class 1 contains $\mathbf{x}^{(1)}$, $\mathbf{x}^{(2)}$, and $\mathbf{x}^{(4)}$, while Class 2 contains $\mathbf{x}^{(3)}$ and $\mathbf{x}^{(5)}$. We assumed here that we knew a priori that there were two classes.

The vector average of a class is the vector of componentwise averages over that class. For this example, $\boldsymbol{\mu}^{(1)} = (\mu_1^{(1)}, \mu_2^{(1)}) = (2.4, 4.2)$ for Class 1, and $\boldsymbol{\mu}^{(2)} = (\mu_1^{(2)}, \mu_2^{(2)}) = (5.0, 1.5)$ for Class 2. If we take the mean-squared error between the vectors in a class and the center of that class, we find that the classes shown minimize that error over any other grouping into classes. Thus we do not repartition. The classification algorithm has learned two classes, and it is now ready to run in the operational mode. When a *novel* feature vector (one that was not used in training) is input to the system, the system will compute the distances from the new vector $\mathbf{x}^{(\text{new})}$ to the class representative vectors $\boldsymbol{\mu}^{(1)}$ and $\boldsymbol{\mu}^{(2)}$, and will make the class membership decision according to the minimal distance (greatest similarity).

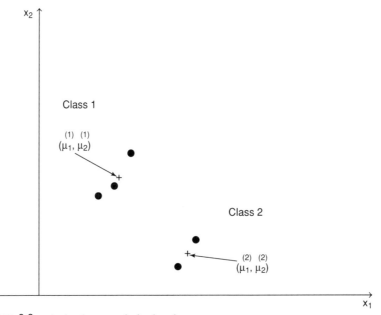

Figure 0.6. A simple example in the plane.

Example 0.4.   Linear Separation of Two Clusters in the Plane

A variation on the above example is to put a line L through the two representative points $\boldsymbol{\mu}^{(1)} = (\mu_1^{(1)}, \mu_2^{(1)}) = (2.4, 4.2)$ and $\boldsymbol{\mu}^{(2)} = (\mu_1^{(2)}, \mu_2^{(2)}) = (5.0, 1.5)$ for the two classes and then construct a perpendicular bisector (hyperplane H) of the line segment between these points. Let $\mathbf{w} = (w_1, w_2)$ be the point where the line L intersects H, and let $\mathbf{h} = (h_1, h_2)$ be any point on the separating hyperplane H, as shown by Figure 0.7. Note that the segment of L along $\boldsymbol{\mu}^{(2)}$ to $\boldsymbol{\mu}^{(1)}$ is perpendicular to H if and only if L is perpendicular to the line through $\mathbf{h}$ and $\mathbf{w}$. Thus $(\boldsymbol{\mu}^{(1)} - \boldsymbol{\mu}^{(2)}) \perp (\mathbf{h} - \mathbf{w})$.

The perpendicularity of two vectors $\mathbf{x}$ and $\mathbf{y}$ (denoted by $\mathbf{x} \perp \mathbf{y}$) is equivalent to their *dot product* being zero, that is, to $\mathbf{x} \circ \mathbf{y} = 0$. From Figure 0.7, $(\boldsymbol{\mu}^{(1)} - \boldsymbol{\mu}^{(2)}) \circ (\mathbf{h} - \mathbf{w}) = 0$. Then

$$(\boldsymbol{\mu}^{(1)} - \boldsymbol{\mu}^{(2)}) \circ \mathbf{h} = (\boldsymbol{\mu}^{(1)} - \boldsymbol{\mu}^{(2)}) \circ \mathbf{w} \tag{0.1}$$

By writing $\boldsymbol{\mu}^{(1)} - \boldsymbol{\mu}^{(2)} = (\mu_1^{(1)} - \mu_1^{(2)}, \mu_2^{(1)} - \mu_2^{(2)})$ and taking the midpoint $\mathbf{w} = \boldsymbol{\mu}^{(1)} + (1/2)(\boldsymbol{\mu}^{(2)} - \boldsymbol{\mu}^{(1)}) = (3.7, 2.86)$, we can substitute these into Equation (0.1) to obtain a linear equation for H of the form

$$ah_1 + bh_2 + c = 0 \tag{0.2a}$$

$$ax_1 + bx_2 + c = d \tag{0.2b}$$

Equation (0.2a) becomes $-2.6h_1 + 2.7h_2 + 1.925 = 0$. Substituting any point $\mathbf{h} = (h_1, h_2)$ in H, including $\mathbf{h} = \mathbf{w}$, satisfies this equation. Note that all points (x_1, x_2) on one side of

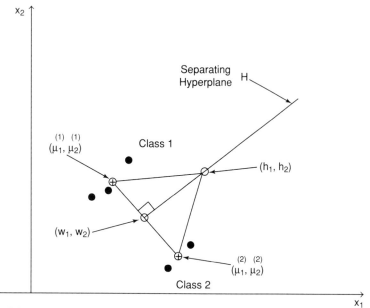

Figure 0.7.   Separation via hyperplane.

H cause the left-hand side of Equation (0.2b) to be positive ($-2.6x_1 + 2.7x_2 + 1.925 \geq 0$), while points on the other side of H cause it to be negative ($-2.6x_1 + 2.7x_2 + 1.925 \geq 0$). These regions are known as the *positive* (*right*) and *negative* (*left*) half-spaces, respectively. We can move H closer to, or farther from, $\boldsymbol{\mu}^{(1)}$, while keeping it perpendicular to the line through $\boldsymbol{\mu}^{(1)}$ and $\boldsymbol{\mu}^{(2)}$, by merely adding or subtracting a constant $d > 0$ to the right-hand side of Equation (0.2b), which yields the form $ah_1 + bh_2 + c = d$, and then arrange this into the form $ah_1 + bh_2 + (c - d) = 0$.

Figure 0.8 displays an analogous separating hyperplane H in three-dimensional space. Generally, a sample of Q feature vectors in N-dimensional space may or may not be separable by an $(N - 1)$-dimensional hyperplane. But if so, then linear discrimination is achievable by finding such a hyperplane (Fisher, 1925, 1936).

0.10. Similarity in Feature Space

Measures of Similarity

Henceforth, we identify each object in a population P by its N-dimensional feature vector $\mathbf{x} = (x_1,..., x_N)$ and refer to feature vectors, rather than objects, in P. The components of $\mathbf{x} = (x_1,..., x_N)$ are real values that are outcomes of experiments that draw and measure objects from P

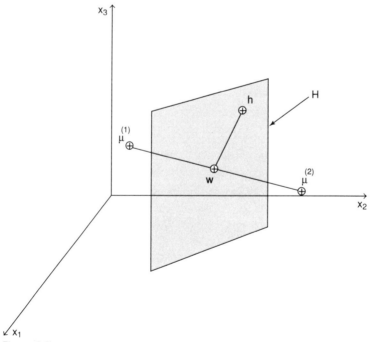

Figure 0.8. Hyperplane separation in three-dimensional space.

to form pattern vectors and then extract features from the pattern vectors. Therefore, a vector $\mathbf{X} = (X_1,..., X_N)$ of random variables assumes a feature vector $\mathbf{X} = \mathbf{x}$ as an experimental outcome, where $X_n = x_n$ for $1 \leq n \leq N$. Given a random sample of feature vectors, $\mathbf{S} = \{\mathbf{x}^{(1)},..., \mathbf{x}^{(Q)})\}$, from P, where each qth sample vector is denoted by $\mathbf{x}^{(q)} = (x_1^{(q)},..., x_N^{(q)})$, the tasks are to (i) operate on S with a process to cluster the sample feature vectors in S into K classes $\{S_1,..., S_K\}$ and (ii) use these learned classes to operate on future input feature vectors to make decisions as to their classes. These processes are classification and recognition, respectively. The learning of classes may be in either supervised training or self-organizing mode.

During the learning, it is necessary to consider how much alike any two different feature vectors $\mathbf{x}$ and $\mathbf{y}$ are. Any measure of the degree of likeness (closeness) is called a *similarity measure*. Distance functions that give the distance $d(\mathbf{x}, \mathbf{y})$ between $\mathbf{x}$ and $\mathbf{y}$ are the most useful of these. The Euclidean distance, denoted by $\|\mathbf{x} - \mathbf{y}\|_2$, is the most commonly used similarity measure, where a lower value (the vectors being closer together) implies greater similarity. These are sometimes called *dissimilarity* measures because a greater distance means greater dissimilarity. Formally, the Euclidean distance between two vectors $\mathbf{x}$ and $\mathbf{y}$ is defined by their root sum-squared error

$$\|\mathbf{x} - \mathbf{y}\|_2 = \{\textstyle\sum_{(n=1, N)}(x_n - y_n)^2\}^{1/2} \qquad (0.3)$$

Each class may be represented by one (or more) exemplar, or prototypical, vector(s) that forms a centralized idealization of what vectors in that class should be. Given any input feature vector $\mathbf{x}$, the k_0 that minimizes $\|\mathbf{x} - \mathbf{z}^{(k)}\|_2$ over all K class exemplars $\{\mathbf{z}^{(k)}\}$, for the various classes, also minimizes the distance by assigning $\mathbf{x}$ to Class k_0 when

$$\|\mathbf{x} - \mathbf{z}^{(k_0)}\|_2 = \min_k \{\|\mathbf{x} - \mathbf{z}^{(k)}\|_2\}$$

The *sum-squared error* (SSE) within a cluster with center $\mathbf{z}^{(k)}$ is the sum of the distances squared between the member points in the cluster and $\mathbf{z}^{(k)}$, which is

$$\sigma^2(k) = \textstyle\sum_{(x \in \text{Cluster}(k))}(\|\mathbf{x} - \mathbf{z}^{(k)}\|_2)^2 \qquad (0.4)$$

Other distance measures may also be used (see Figure 0.9). Some other useful norms are (i) the *city block* norm (see Therrien, 1989; or Batchelor, 1978)

$$\|\mathbf{x} - \mathbf{y}\|_1 = \textstyle\sum_{(n=1, N)}|x_n - y_n| \qquad (0.5)$$

which is the total of the componentwise distances; (ii) the *Tchebyshev* (*supremum* or *maximum*) norm

$$\|\mathbf{x} - \mathbf{y}\|_\infty = \sup_{(n=1, N)}|x_n - y_n| \qquad (0.6)$$

which is the maximum of the componentwise distances; and (iii) the *Mahalanobis distance* (see Bow, 1984; or Tou and Gonzalez, 1974)

$$\|\mathbf{x} - \boldsymbol{\mu}\|_M = \{(\mathbf{x} - \boldsymbol{\mu})^t C^{-1}(\mathbf{x} - \boldsymbol{\mu})\}^{1/2} \qquad (0.7)$$

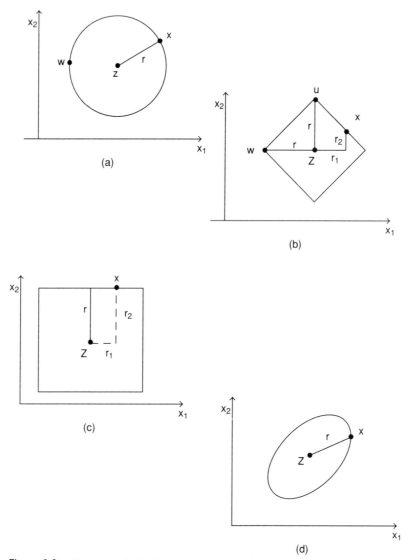

Figure 0.9. Norms as similarity measures and their r-hyperballs with (a) Euclidean Norm, (b) City Block Norm, (c) Supremum Norm, and (d) Mahalanobis Distance.

where $\boldsymbol{\mu}$ is the vector of averaged components for a subpopulation, C^{-1} is the inverse covariance matrix for that subpopulation, and $(\mathbf{x} - \boldsymbol{\mu})^t$ is the transpose of $(\mathbf{x} - \boldsymbol{\mu})$. The latter norm weights the component distances according to a priori importance based on the componentwise mean-squared error of what would otherwise be a Euclidean distance (where C is the identity matrix of variances on the diagonal and zero elsewhere).

Now consider the space of all vectors of the form $\mathbf{x} = (x_1,..., x_N)$, where each component x_n takes on a value from a binary alphabet $\{0,1\}$. Examples in the six-dimensional cube $\{0,1\}^6$ are $\mathbf{x} = (100010)$ and $\mathbf{y} = (001011)$. The *Hamming distance* between $\mathbf{x}$ and $\mathbf{y}$ is

$$d_H(\mathbf{x}, \mathbf{y}) = \Sigma_{(i=1, 6)}|x_n - y_n| \tag{0.8}$$

which is just the count of the number of components in which $\mathbf{x}$ and $\mathbf{y}$ are different. For the case given here, $\mathbf{x} = (100010)$ and $\mathbf{y} = (001011)$ have distance $d_H(\mathbf{x}, \mathbf{y}) = 3$ because they differ in three components. The set of all vectors $\mathbf{x}$ that have a distance of 1 from $\mathbf{y}$ is just the set of vectors that differ from y in only a single component (they occupy adjacent vertices of the 6-cube $[0,1]^6$).

A *hypersphere* centered on some vector $\mathbf{z}$ with radius r in N-dimensional space is a set of the form $S = \{\mathbf{x}: \|\mathbf{x} - \mathbf{z}\| = r\}$, for some distance function $d(\mathbf{x}, \mathbf{z}) = \|\mathbf{x} - \mathbf{z}\|$. A *hyperball* is a hypersphere along with all points on the same side as the center—that is, $\{\mathbf{x}: \|\mathbf{x} - \mathbf{z}\| \leq r\}$. Figure 0.9 shows hyperballs in the plane centered on the vector $\mathbf{z}$ with radius r, for the various distances, in the plane. In Figure 0.9(b), the vector point $\mathbf{x}$ has radius $r = r_1 + r_2$, while, for example, $\mathbf{w}$ and $\mathbf{u}$ also have distances of r from $\mathbf{z}$. In Figure 0.9(c), $\mathbf{x}$ has distance $r = \max\{|x_1 - z_1|, |x_2 - z_2|\} = r_2$ from $\mathbf{z}$. Figure 0.9(d) shows the distance $r = \{c_{11}(x_1 - z_1)^2 + c_{12}(x_1 - z_1)(x_2 - z_2) + c_{22}(x_2 - z_2)^2\}^{1/2}$, between $\mathbf{z}$ and $\mathbf{x}$, where $c_{12} = c_{21} = \sigma_{12}$ is the covariance and c_{11} and c_{22} are the variances σ_1^2 and σ_2^2, respectively. The axes could be rotated to form an ellipse along new major and minor axes. The Mahalanobis distance provides a weighted average that allows elongated hyperballs—that is, *ellipsoids*. These could be useful, but the weightings must be determined a priori.

Convexity and Cluster Separation

Other *hypersolids* such as hyperellipsoids or hypercylinders may also be used to separate classes in N-dimensional space. Hyperballs and other hypersolids of interest have an important property. A subset C of E^N (N-dimensional Euclidean space) is *convex* if and only if for every pair of points $\mathbf{c}_1$ and $\mathbf{c}_2$ in C, the entire line segment $L_{12} = \{\alpha\mathbf{c}_1 + (1 - \alpha)\mathbf{c}_2: 0 \leq \alpha \leq 1\}$ is also contained in C. Any vector $\mathbf{z} = \alpha\mathbf{c}_1 + (1 - \alpha)\mathbf{c}_2$ is called a *convex combination* of $\mathbf{c}_1$ and $\mathbf{c}_2$. Thus a convex set C contains all convex combinations of all pairs of points in C. Figure 0.10 shows two convex sets and a nonconvex set. If any line segment between two points in a set contains points not in that set, then the set is not convex. A vector space with a norm (distance function) is called a *normed vector space*.

Proposition 0.1: Disjoint closed convex sets in a normed vector space can be separated by hyperplanes.

Proof: Closed sets contain all of their boundary points. For disjoint closed convex sets C and D, take the minimum distance $\delta = \min\{\|\mathbf{c} - \mathbf{d}\|_2 : \mathbf{c} \in C \text{ and } \mathbf{d} \in D\}$. Because C and D are closed and the distance function is continuous, two points $\mathbf{c}_0$ and $\mathbf{d}_0$ exist in C and D, respectively, such that $\delta = \|\mathbf{c}_0 - \mathbf{d}_0\|_2$. We put a line through these points and take its perpendicular bisecting hyperplane. It is obvious that all points in C are on one side of this hyperplane, and that all points in D are on the other side to preserve the perpendicularity and minimum distance (Figure 0.8 elucidates this if we let $\boldsymbol{\mu}^{(1)}$ and $\boldsymbol{\mu}^{(2)}$ re-

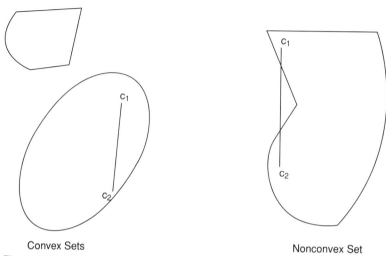

Convex Sets   Nonconvex Set

Figure 0.10.   A convex set and a nonconvex set.

place $\mathbf{c}_0$ and $\mathbf{d}_0$, respectively, and take closed balls centered on $\boldsymbol{\mu}^{(1)}$ and $\boldsymbol{\mu}^{(2)}$, respectively, that contain all points in their respective clusters). Thus clusters in side disjoint convex hypersolids are linearly separable.

The *convex hull* of a set $D \subset E^N$ is the set $D^{CH} = \{\alpha \mathbf{d}^{(1)} + (1 - \alpha)\mathbf{d}^{(2)} : \mathbf{d}^{(1)}, \mathbf{d}^{(2)} \in D,$ $0 \le \alpha \le 1\}$ of all convex combinations of vectors in D. D^{CH*} is the *closure* of the convex hull of D, which includes all of the boundary points of D^{CH}. If C_k is the kth cluster of a collection of K clusters and if the K clusters have closed convex hulls that are disjoint, then the clusters can be pairwise linearly separated via hyperplanes. Feature vectors in the same convex set which is disjoint from other convex clusters are similar. See Section 4a.1 of Appendix 4a for further discussion of convexity. In E^N, a hyperplane satisfies $\alpha_1 x_1 + \dots + a_N x_N = c$ for a constant c.

0.11. Three Easy Pieces: Principles for Clustering

The Nearest-Neighbor Principle

For completeness, we state three well-known principles concerning clusters: the nearest neighbor, the best mean square estimate of the center of a cluster, and an optimal assignment to clusters. Let $C_1, \dots, C_K$ be K clusters of feature vectors. Given a new feature vector $\mathbf{x}^{(q)}$, the task is to assign it to one of the K clusters. The most basic method is to find the distance $d(\mathbf{x}^{(q)}, C_k)$ between $\mathbf{x}^{(q)}$ and the kth cluster C_k, which is the minimal distance

$$d(\mathbf{x}^{(q)}, C_k) = \min\{\|\mathbf{x}^{(q)} - \mathbf{x}\| : \mathbf{x} \in C_k\}$$

In other words, this is the minimal distance between $\mathbf{x}^{(q)}$ and vectors $\mathbf{x}$ in C_k.

Although this is a natural way to assign feature vectors to existing clusters, it can yield long stringy clusters that are quite large. There is a better way to assign feature vectors to clusters that requires finding a representative vector for each cluster to use in place of the distance $d(\mathbf{x}^{(q)}, C_k)$. Such a representative vector should be located in a central position in the cluster so as to minimize the overall sum-squared error between the representative vector and the feature vectors in the cluster. The next principle allows us to find such a representative vector for each cluster.

The Principle of Optimal Representation

Given a cluster $S_k = \{\mathbf{x}^{(1)},..., \mathbf{x}^{(M)}\}$, we would like to estimate a center $\mathbf{z}^{(k)}$ for it. In the case of a single dimension, we have real numbers $x^{(1)},..., x^{(M)}$, generated by a random variable X. We estimate a center $\mathbf{z}$ to minimize the sum of the squared distances, that is, the sum-squared error

$$e^2 = \sum_{(m=1, M)} |\mathbf{x}^{(m)} - \mathbf{z}|^2$$

by setting the derivative to zero for any component:

$$de/dz = 2\sum_{(m-1, M)}(x^{(m)} - z) = 0$$

Thus we can solve for z via

$$\sum_{(m=1, M)} x^{(m)} = \sum_{(m=1, M)} z = Mz, \qquad z = (1/M)\sum_{(m=1, M)} x^{(m)}$$

Therefore, z turns out to be the *sample mean* of the numbers $x^{(1)},..., x^{(M)}$ in S_k. In the vector case of $\mathbf{x}^{(m)} = (x_1^{(m)},..., x_N^{(m)})$, the vectors $\mathbf{x}^{(1)},..., \mathbf{x}^{(M)}$ have an average that is the vector of the average components. For the center $\mathbf{z} = (z_1,..., z_N)$, the average nth component of $\mathbf{z}$ is

$$z_n = (1/M)\sum_{(m=1, M)} x_n^{(m)}$$

for each $n = 1,..., N$, so

$$\mathbf{z} = (z_1,..., z_N) \tag{0.9}$$

There is nothing that limits the center of a cluster to a single representative vector. A set of multiple vectors may be used as a "center" for any cluster.

The Minimum Distance Assignment Principle

Again let $C_1,..., C_K$ be K clusters of feature vectors. Given a new feature vector $\mathbf{x}^{(q)}$, the task is to assign it to one of the K clusters. For each cluster C_k, we take $\mathbf{z}^{(k)} = (z_1^{(k)},..., z_N^{(k)})$ to be the average of all of the feature vectors in the cluster. According to the principle of optimal representation given above, $\mathbf{z}^{(k)}$ provides the minimal sum-squared error. Therefore, we take the averages of clusters as their representatives, or prototypes (models), of the clusters.

We assign the new vector $\mathbf{x}^{(q)}$ to the cluster C_k such that the distance from $\mathbf{x}^{(q)}$ to the representative $\mathbf{z}^{(k)}$ for C_k is the minimum over all K clusters. In other words, for

$$d_{\min} = \min_{1 \leq k \leq K}\{D(\mathbf{x}^{(q)}, C_k)\} = \min_{1 \leq k \leq K}\{\|\mathbf{x}^{(q)} - \mathbf{z}^{(k)}\|\}$$

where the $\mathbf{z}^{(k)}$ are the representatives for the clusters C_k.

0.12. Linear Discriminant Networks

The processes of classification (training) and recognition (decisionmaking) is naturally connected to network graphs that model their behavior. We have seen that an N-dimensional feature space is separated into two half-spaces by the hyperplane H determined by a *discriminant* function of Equation (0.2b) of the form

$$D(\mathbf{x}) = w_1 x_1 + w_2 x_2 + \cdots + w_N x_N + w_{N+1} = 0 \qquad (0.10)$$

Each feature vector $\mathbf{x} = (x_1,..., x_N)$ satisfies one of

$$D(\mathbf{x}) > 0, \qquad D(\mathbf{x}) = 0, \qquad D(\mathbf{x}) < 0$$

Those that satisfy the first inequality belong to the right half-space, while those that satisfy the third one belong to the left half-space. The remaining feature vectors satisfy Equation (0.10) and thus belong to the hyperplane H.

The hyperplane can be reoriented by adjusting the weights $\mathbf{w} = (w_1,...,w_{N+1})$. For convenience, we put $\mathbf{x}$ into $(N + 1)$-dimensional space by putting its $(N + 1)$st component at 1; that is, put $\mathbf{x} = (x_1,..., x_N,1)$, so we can write

$$D(\mathbf{x}) = \textstyle\sum_{(n=1,\ N)} w_n x_n = \mathbf{w}^t \mathbf{x} = 0 \qquad (0.11)$$

where the superscript t denotes the transpose ($\mathbf{w}^t\mathbf{x} = \mathbf{w} \circ \mathbf{x}$, the *dot product*). Figure 0.11 shows the network model for the decisionmaking process. The inputs are linearly combined with the weights by multiplication and then summed to obtain $y = D(\mathbf{x})$. Then y is put through the thresholder, where it is converted to the output $z = 1$ if $y \geq 0$ or to $z = -1$ if $y < 0$. The class identifier is z.

Figure 0.12 presents a multilinear network that uses two summing nodes that put out the two linear discriminant values $y_1 = D_1(\mathbf{x})$ and $y_2 = D_2(\mathbf{x})$ that are fed into the threshold functions to yield the final outputs z_1 and z_2. These two values provide us with the combinations $\mathbf{z} = (z_1, z_2)$ that can be one of

$$(1,1), \quad (1,-1), \quad (-1,1), \quad (-1,-1)$$

While z_1 determines which half-space for hyperplane H_1 the input feature vector falls in, z_2 determines in which half-space for hyperplane H_2 the feature vector falls. Together, the output vector (z_1, z_2) determines which one of four regions $\mathbf{x}$ lies in. These regions are the in-

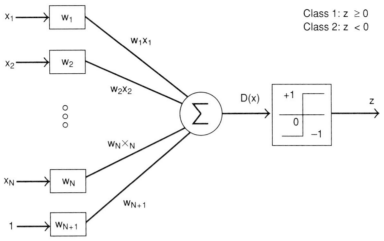

Figure 0.11. A linear discriminant network.

tersections of the two half-spaces determined by H_1, with the two half-spaces determined by H_2. Figure 0.13 shows four regions in two-dimensional feature space that are determined by H_1 and H_2. The regions are enumerated by a number in a circle. Region 1 at the top is the intersection of the left half-space for H_1 and the right half-space for H_2. The other regions are the intersections of other combinations of left and right half-spaces for H_1 and H_2.

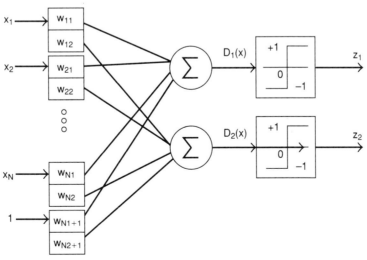

Figure 0.12. A multilinear discriminant network.

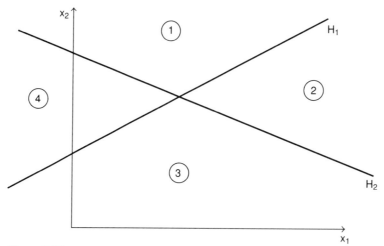

Figure 0.13.   Intersections of half-spaces determine by two hyperplanes.

0.13. Notes

The linear discriminant network is actually an early type of artificial neuron, called a *perceptron*. The multilinear discriminant network is a layer of perceptrons. For K summing nodes and a threshold function for each, these partition the feature space into regions that are the intersections of $2K$ half-spaces. Each of these intersections is convex and so there is linear separation of the regions. By adjusting the weights and the thresholds of the discriminant functions $D_k(\mathbf{x})$, these regions can be manipulated but remain convex. The feature vectors fall into these regions, so proper training to adjust the weights appropriately will adjust the regions to contain groups of feature vectors as clusters. These discrimination networks will be revisited in Chapter 3.

Some early reference books on pattern recognition are Chen (1973), Duda and Hart (1973), Fukanaga (1972), Patrick (1972), and Fu (1976). Later ones include Fu (1982b), Bow (1984), Therrien (1989), and Fukanaga (1990). For artificial neural networks, see Fu (1994), Fausett (1994), Haykin (1994), Hecht-Nielsen (1990), Kosko (1992), and Zurada (1992). For fuzzy pattern recognition, see Bezdek and Pal (1992).

Exercises

0.1. Put the appropriate numbers into Equation (0.1) for the example in the text that is shown in Figure 0.6, and verify the equation that results from Equation (0.2b). Check that the points for Class 1 fall on one side of H and the points for Class 2 fall on the other side of H.

0.2. Find a point $\mathbf{w}$ and derive Equations (0.2b) for N-dimensional feature vectors so that any point $(x_1,..., x_N)$ on the hyperplane H satisfies $a_1 x_1 + \cdots + a_N x_N + c = 0$, and H separates the feature space E^N into two parts, each of which contains the feature vectors of one class.

0.3. Suppose that two clusters of sample feature vectors are separated by a hyperplane, but during operation we encounter feature vectors that are unacceptably far from either of the two class averages, so that we suspect a third class exists. What should be done? Should we reassign vectors to new classes?

0.4. A set $S = \{(0,0), (1,0), (0,1), (1,1)\}$ of points in the plane is to be classified so that $(0,0)$ and $(1,1)$ belong to one class, and $(1,0)$ and $(0,1)$ belong to a second class. Graph the points in the plane. Can the classes be separated with hyperplanes? Average the points in each class. Can the averages be separated linearly? Can the classes be separated nonlinearly? If so, show how to do it.

0.5. A set C of vectors is said to be *convex* if it satisfies the property that for every $\mathbf{x}$ and $\mathbf{y}$ in C, the vector $\mathbf{z} = \alpha\mathbf{x} + (1 - \alpha)\mathbf{y}$ is also in C, for $0 \le \alpha \le 1$ ($\mathbf{z} = \alpha\mathbf{x} + (1 - \alpha)\mathbf{y}$ is called a *convex combination* of $\mathbf{x}$ and $\mathbf{y}$). Show that a hyperball (a sphere and its interior in N-dimensions) in N-dimensional Euclidean space is convex.

0.6. Show that any two hyperballs in Euclidean N-dimensional space that are disjoint may be separated by a hyperplane. Let their centers be $\mathbf{z}^{(1)}$ and $\mathbf{z}^{(2)}$ and find an equation for the required hyperplane H.

0.7. Show that three disjoint hyperballs in N-dimensional Euclidean space can be pairwise linearly separated. Discuss how this can be used in pattern recognition.

0.8. Consider a sequence $\{\mathbf{x}^{(1)},..., \mathbf{x}^{(Q)}\}$ of feature vectors for a population P of objects. We are to create a process of self-organizing learning to learn K classes. Start with $K = 1$ and assign $\mathbf{x}^{(1)}$ to Class 1 via class(1) = 1. Choose the representative vector $\mathbf{z}^{(1)} = \mathbf{x}^{(1)}$. Next, assign $\mathbf{x}^{(2)}$ to Class 1 by class(2) = 1 if $\mathbf{x}^{(2)}$ is close to $\mathbf{z}^{(1)}$, or else create a new class with representative $\mathbf{z}^{(2)} = \mathbf{x}^{(2)}$ and put class(2) = 2. Write an algorithm that continues in this manner to assign Q input feature vectors to K classes with centers at $\mathbf{z}^{(1)},..., \mathbf{z}^{(K)}$. Does it satisfy Fu's algorithm? Why?

0.9. In Exercise 0.8 above, how would you implement Fu's general algorithm to check the clusters for distinctness and repartition if necessary (consider new cluster centers that better represent the clusters and then reassign all vectors to the cluster to whose centers they are closest)?

0.10. Let there be N features and two classes. Consider each nth feature as the outcome of a random trial where the feature value may be in Class 1 with probability $p_1(n)$ or in Class 2 with probability $p_2(n)$. For the N trials (each feature outcome is a trial), what is the probability that the feature vector belongs to Class 1 (consider the different feature trials to be independent)?

0.11. In the binary unit cube $\{0,1\}^6$, find the unit hypersphere and unit ball about the vector $\mathbf{0} = (0,0,0,0,0,0)$ using the Hamming distance.

0.12. Find the point in $\{0,1\}^3$ that is farthest away from $(0,0,0)$ in Hamming distance. Find the point that is farthest away from $(0,1,1)$. Sketch the cube $\{0,1\}^3$. Either prove or disprove the following conjecture: The point farthest from $(x_1, x_2,..., x_N)$ in $\{0,1\}^N$ is the point $(y_1, y_2,..., y_N)$, where for each n, y_n is the *complement* of x_n. Is the farthest point unique?

0.13. Suppose that two clusters of feature vectors in Euclidean N-space are contained in two N-dimensional ellipsoids that are disjoint but have different orientations with respect to their major and minor axes. Are the clusters linearly separable?

0.14. How may two clusters that are not linearly separable be separated in some nonlinear fashion (see Figure 0.4(b) for a hint)?

References

Batchelor, B. G. (1978), Classification and data analysis in vector spaces, in *Pattern Recognition*, edited by B. G. Batchelor, Plenum Press, NY, 67–116.

Bow, Sing-Tze (1984), *Pattern Recognition*, Marcel Dekker, New York.

Bezdek, J., and Pal, S. K., editors (1992), *Fuzzy Models for Pattern Recognition*, IEEE Press, New York.

Chen, C. H. (1973), *Statistical Pattern Recognition*, Hayden, Washington, D.C.

Duda, R. O., and Hart, P. E. (1973), *Pattern Classification and Scene Analysis*, Wiley, New York.

Fausett, Laurene (1994), *Fundamentals of Neural Networks*, Prentice-Hall, Englewood Cliffs, NJ.

Fisher, R. A. (1925), Theory of statistical estimation, *Proceedings of the Cambridge Philosophical Society*, vol. 22, 700.

Fisher, R. A. (1936), The use of multiple measurements in taxonomic problems, *Ann. Eugenics*, vol. 7, part II, 179–188.

Fu, K. S. (1976), Introduction, in *Digital Pattern Recognition*, edited by K. S. Fu, Springer-Verlag, Berlin, 1–14.

Fu, K. S. (1982a), *Syntactic Pattern Recognition with Applications*, Prentice-Hall, Englewood Cliffs, NJ.

Fu, K. S. (1982b), Introduction, in *Applications of Pattern Recognition*, edited by K. S. Fu, CRC Press, Boca Raton, FL, 1–13.

Fu, LiMin (1994), *Neural Networks in Computer Intelligence*, McGraw-Hill, New York.

Fukanaga, K., (1972), *Introduction to Statistical Pattern Recognition*, Academic Press, New York.

Fukanaga, K. (1990), *Introduction to Statistical Pattern Recognition*, 2nd edition, Academic Press, New York.

Haykin, S. (1994), *Neural Networks*, Macmillan, New York.

Hecht-Nielsen, R. (1990), *Neurocomputing*, Addison-Wesley, Reading, MA.

Kosko, B. (1992), *Neural Networks and Fuzzy Systems*, Prentice-Hall, Englewood Cliffs, NJ.

Nilsson, J. J. (1965), *Learning Machines*, McGraw-Hill, New York.

Pavel, Monique (1989), *Fundamentals of Pattern Recognition*, Marcel Dekker, New York.

Patrick, E. A. (1972), *Fundamentals of Pattern Recognition*, Prentice-Hall, Englewood Cliffs, NJ.

Therrien, C. W. (1989), *Decision, Estimation, and Classification*, Wiley, New York.

Tou, J. T., and Gonzalez, R. C. (1974), *Pattern Recognition Principles*, Addison-Wesley, Reading, MA.

Zurada, J. M. (1992), *Artificial Neural Systems*, West Publishing, St. Paul, MN.

Chapter 1

Decision-Theoretic Algorithms

The goal of this chapter is to survey some important decision theoretic algorithms for classification and recognition.

1.1. Assignment via the *k*-Nearest-Neighbors Rule

Suppose that a sample of Q feature vectors $S = \{\mathbf{x}^{(q)}: q = 1,..., Q\}$ has been grouped into J clusters $C_1,..., C_J$. For any *novel* feature vector $\mathbf{x}$ (not one of the $\mathbf{x}^{(q)}$ in S), the task is to assign $\mathbf{x}$ to a cluster, and thus recognize it as belonging to a class. An older method is to find the distance from $\mathbf{x}$ to each of its k nearest neighbors, say $\mathbf{x}^{(q(1))},..., \mathbf{x}^{(q(k))}$, for some fixed $k > 0$. Let

$$d_m = d(\mathbf{x}, \mathbf{x}^{(q(m))}) = \left\| \mathbf{x} - \mathbf{x}^{(q(m))} \right\|$$

be such a distance for each $m = 1,..., k$. We allow each d_m to vote for the cluster j to which $\mathbf{x}^{(q(m))}$ belongs. The cluster C_j with the majority vote wins and $\mathbf{x}$ is assigned to that cluster. Figure 1.1 shows the situation where a new feature vector is assigned to Class 1 based on the 7-nearest-neighbor rule. The vote for Class 1 is 4 to 3 over Class 2.

In the case of a voting tie, the assignment can be decided at random (Cover and Wagner, 1976). Ties in the distance have probability of zero, theoretically; but for a computer of finite precision, it is positive but still too small to be of concern. We may also use the sum of the distances from $\mathbf{x}$ to the nearest neighbors in the clusters (that have tied votes) to break the tie: The cluster with the minimum summed distance wins.

The *advantage* of this assignment procedure is simplicity. The *disadvantages* are that it requires previous organization of the clusters and it ignores the fact that a cluster usually has a central region where the feature vectors fall more frequently than outside of this region.

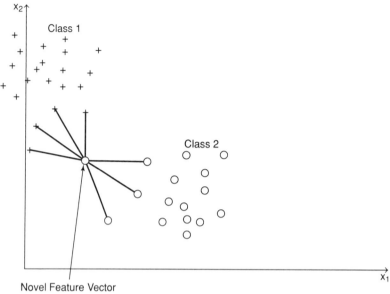

x_2

Class 1

Class 2

Novel Feature Vector

x_1

Figure 1.1. Seven nearest neighbors.

From Figure 1.1 it can be seen that the assignment is not necessarily the best (a single out-lier can decide the vote). *In practice*, we would use this method only for nonlinearly sepa-rated clusters, and the neighbors in each particular cluster would be representatives from a core—that is, a central region of that cluster. In that case, a distance to neighbors in a clus-ter would be the summed distance to the neighbors in the core for that cluster.

1.2. Basic Clustering: The *k*-Means Algorithm

A High-Level Description of the Self-Organizing Process

The *k-means algorithm* (MacQueen, 1967) self-organizes to create clusters. It can be found in Bow (1984), Tou and Gonzalez (1974), and Duda and Hart (1973, p. 201). It uses a sam-ple of feature vectors $S = \{\mathbf{x}^{(1)},..., \mathbf{x}^{(Q)}\}$ from a population P, but requires the number K of clusters to be given, $K < Q$. The process begins by assigning the first K sample feature vec-tors $\mathbf{x}^{(1)},..., \mathbf{x}^{(K)}$ to be centers $\mathbf{z}^{(1)},..., \mathbf{z}^{(K)}$, respectively, for the K clusters, so the ordering of the sample should be randomized. The algorithm then assigns each of the remaining $Q - K$ sample feature vectors $\mathbf{x}^{(K+1)},..., \mathbf{x}^{(Q)}$ to the cluster to whose center it is closest in *Euclidean* distance, that is, by the *minimum distance assignment principle* from the previous chapter. Then, the sample feature vectors for each kth cluster, in turn, are averaged to determine a new cluster center $\mathbf{z}^{(k)}$ for each kth cluster, which is the *principle of optimal representation* from the previous chapter. Next, each of the Q sample feature vectors is again assigned to the class to whose new representative center it is closest. This loop of generating new cen-ters by averaging each cluster and then reassigning all vectors by minimum distance to the new centers is repeated until no clusters change further, in which case the algorithm is done. This realizes Fu's generalized algorithm of Section 0.8.

The mean-squared error σ_k^2 for each fixed class k is

$$\sigma_k^2 = (1/n(k))\sum_{\{q:\ \text{class}(q)=k\}}\left\|\mathbf{x}^{(q)} - \mathbf{z}^{(k)}\right\|_2^2 \tag{1.1}$$

It is an *intraset* measure for each cluster, where $n(k)$ is the number of sample vectors currently assigned to the kth cluster. The total mean squared error

$$\sigma_T^2 = \sum_{\{k=1,K\}}\sigma_k^2 \tag{1.2}$$

is a measure of the total clustering that is to be minimized over the number K of clusters.

The Class Assignment Index Function

To assign the sample feature vectors to clusters, a sequence $\{\mathbf{x}^{(1)},...,\mathbf{x}^{(Q)}\}$ of sample feature vectors is input, one vector $\mathbf{x}^{(q)}$ at a time, and processed to assign it to one of the K clusters $C_1,...,C_K$. K cluster representatives are established during the initialization. The assignment is recorded by the *class assignment index function* class$(q) = k$ to indicate that $\mathbf{x}^{(q)}$ has been assigned to the kth cluster C_k. In the algorithm below, $\mathbf{\textit{z}}$ is the updated version of $\mathbf{z}$. By $n(k) = p$ we mean that the number of input vectors assigned to Class k is p.

The *k*-Means Clustering Algorithm

Inputs: {randomly ordered sample of feature vectors $S = \{\mathbf{x}^{(1)},...,\mathbf{x}^{(Q)}\}$; and the number K of clusters}

Outputs: {clusters $C_1,...,C_K$ given by class assignment index class$(q) = k$; number of vectors $n(k)$ in each C_k; center $\mathbf{z}^{(k)}$ of each cluster C_k; the variance (mean squared error) σ_k^2 of the kth cluster for each $k = 1,...,K$; and the total mean squared error σ_T^2 defined above}

Step 1: /Put the first K sample vectors as initial centers/
for $k = 1$ to K do $\mathbf{z}^{(k)} \leftarrow \mathbf{x}^{(k)}$; $n(k) \leftarrow 0$;   /Initialize cluster centers/

Step 2: /Assign each sample vector to the cluster with nearest center/
for $q = 1$ to Q do   /For each sample feature vector/
$d_{\min} \leftarrow 999999.9$ /initialize minimum distance/
for $k = 1$ to K do
if $\left\|\mathbf{x}^{(q)} - \mathbf{z}^{(k)}\right\| < d_{\min}$, then   /Find minimum distance to a center/
$d_{\min} \leftarrow \left\|\mathbf{x}^{(q)} - \mathbf{z}^{(k)}\right\|$; $k_{\min} \leftarrow k$;
class$(q) \leftarrow k_{\min}$;   /Assign qth vector to $k_{\min}$th class/
$n(k_{\min}) \leftarrow n(k_{\min}) + 1$;   /Update number of vectors in $k_{\min}$th/
/class/

Step 3: /Compute new average as new center for each cluster C_k/
    for $k = 1$ to K do   /Compute K new centers/
      $\mathbf{z}^{(k)} \leftarrow [1/n(k)]\sum_{\{q:\ \text{class}(q)=k\}} \mathbf{x}^{(q)}$ /Average over kth cluster/
      $\sigma_k^2 \leftarrow [1/n(k)]\sum_{\{q:\ \text{class}(q)=k\}} \left\| \mathbf{x}^{(q)} - \mathbf{z}^{(k)} \right\|_2^2$

                               /Mean-squared error of each class/
      $\sigma_T^2 \leftarrow \sum_{(k=1,\ K)} \sigma_k^2$ /Total (overall) sum-squared error/

Step 4: /If any center has changed, then iterate, else terminate/
    change_flag $\leftarrow$ FALSE
    for $k = 1$ to K do   /Record any change/
      if $\left\| \mathbf{z}^{(k)} - \mathbf{z}^{(k)} \right\|_2 > 0.0005$ then change_flag $\leftarrow$ TRUE
    if change_flag = TRUE, then   /If any change were made/
      for $k = 1$ to K do $\mathbf{z}^{(k)} \leftarrow \mathbf{z}^{(k)}$;   /then update centers/
      goto Step 2   /and repeat process/
    else stop

The *advantages* of this method are its simplicity, efficiency, and self-organization, as well as its minimization of the mean square error (see the principle of optimal representation in the first chapter). The *disadvantages* are as follows: (i) K must be provided (so the self-organization is not total), and K is seldom known a priori; (ii) it is a linearly separating method, because as the clusters must be in disjoint hyperballs; and (iii) there is no known proof of convergence (Bow, 1984), although it has been observed to always work well for data that exhibits clusters that are not too close to each other.

In practice, we make several runs with different K values, and the K that yields the minimum total sum squared error is selected. Some related algorithms use the nearest neighbor, or k nearest neighbors (see Mizoguchi and Kakusho, 1978) of a feature vector for cluster assignment. It is also possible to use a "core" set of multiple central vectors to represent each cluster and take the distances from a vector $\mathbf{x}$ to each such representative and sum them to obtain a "total distance" to the center of a cluster.

Example 1.1.   An Example of *k*-Means Classification

Given the sample of feature vectors $S = \{(2,1), (3,1), (2,4), (3,2), (2,3), (1,3)\} = \{\mathbf{x}^{(1)},...,\mathbf{x}^{(6)}\}$, use the k-means algorithm to classify it into $K = 2$ classes. We select the first two sample vectors as initial centers

$$\mathbf{z}^{(1)} = \mathbf{x}^{(1)} = (2,1), \qquad \mathbf{z}^{(2)} = \mathbf{x}^{(2)} = (3,1)$$

Next, we assign each sample feature vector that is closest to $\mathbf{z}^{(1)}$ to Class 1, and similarly for $\mathbf{z}^{(2)}$, to obtain

$$C_1 = \{(2,1), (2,4), (2,3), (1,3)\} = \{\mathbf{x}^{(1)}, \mathbf{x}^{(3)}, \mathbf{x}^{(5)}, \mathbf{x}^{(6)}\},$$

$$C_2 = \{(3,1), (3,2)\} = \{\mathbf{x}^{(2)}, \mathbf{x}^{(4)}\}$$

as shown in Figure 1.2. For example, the distance from $(3,2)$ to $\mathbf{z}^{(1)}$ is $d((3,2),(2,1)) = [(3 -$

$2)^2 + (2 - 1)^2]^{1/2} = \sqrt{2}$, while the distance from (3,2) to $\mathbf{z}^{(2)}$ is $d((3,2),(3,1)) = [(3 - 3)^2 + (2 - 1)^2]^{1/2} = 1$. Therefore, (3,2) belongs to C_2 with center $\mathbf{z}^{(2)}$. These initial clusters are shown inside ellipses.

Upon averaging each cluster, we obtain the new optimal centers

$$\mathbf{z}^{(1)} = ((2 + 2 + 2 + 1)/4, (1 + 4 + 3 + 3)/4) = (1.75, 2.75),$$

$$\mathbf{z}^{(2)} = ((3 + 3)/2, (1 + 2)/2) = (3.0, 1.5)$$

as shown in Figure 1.2 by the cross-hair squares. By reassigning the input sample feature vectors, we obtain

$$C_1 = \{(2,1), (3,2), (3,1)\} = \{\mathbf{x}^{(1)}, \mathbf{x}^{(2)}, \mathbf{x}^{(4)}\}$$

$$C_2 = \{(1,3), (2,4), (2,3)\} = \{\mathbf{x}^{(3)}, \mathbf{x}^{(5)}, \mathbf{x}^{(6)}\}$$

The cluster centers change upon averaging to become

$$\mathbf{z}^{(1)} = ((2 + 3 + 3)/3, (1 + 2 + 1)/3) = (2.66, 1.33)$$

$$\mathbf{z}^{(2)} = ((1 + 2 + 2)/3, (3 + 4 + 3)/3) = (1.66, 3.33)$$

When we reassign the sample feature vectors based on the last two cluster centers, the clusters do not change and so we are done.

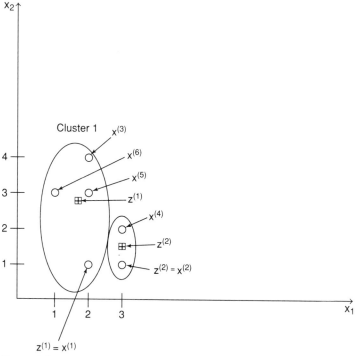

Figure 1.2. Clustering by the k-means self-organizing algorithm.

1.3. A Distance Threshold Clustering Algorithm

The High-Level Description of Threshold Clustering

This algorithm fully self-organizes (Bow, 1984, p. 104) and determines the number K of clusters. A sample of feature vectors $S = \{\mathbf{x}^{(1)},..., \mathbf{x}^{(Q)}\}$ is presented to the system, one vector at a time. K starts with the initial value $K = 1$. For any current K, the K classes are designated by $C_1,..., C_K$, and for each of these there is a center (representative, exemplar, prototype, or archetypical) vector designated by $\mathbf{z}^{(k)}$, $1 \le k \le K$. A *threshold* τ and *proportion* p must be given by the user.

To start, put $K \leftarrow 1$ and $\mathbf{z}^{(1)} \leftarrow \mathbf{x}^{(1)}$. As each of the Q sample feature vectors $\mathbf{x}^{(q)}$ is read, the Euclidean distance $d(\mathbf{x}^{(q)}, \mathbf{z}^{(k)})$ is computed from it to each cluster center representative $\mathbf{z}^{(k)}$ ($k = 1,..., K$). If the minimum distance from $\mathbf{x}^{(q)}$ to a center is to $\mathbf{z}^{(k*)}$ and $d(\mathbf{x}^{(q)}, \mathbf{z}^{(k*)}) < p\tau$, then $\mathbf{x}^{(q)}$ is assigned to C_{k*}. If this distance is greater than τ, then $\mathbf{x}^{(q)}$ is taken to be the center $\mathbf{z}^{(K+1)}$ for a new cluster C_{K+1}. After all Q samples $\mathbf{x}^{(q)}$ in S have been processed, each cluster C_k is averaged to obtain a new cluster center $\mathbf{z}^{(k)}$. The process of assigning sample feature vectors to new centers in the above given fashion and then averaging the clusters to obtain new centers is iterated until the clusters C_k become stable in the sense that no changes occur on the last iteration. Figure 1.3 shows the use of p and τ. To update the statistics in the algorithm, we use a recursive principle that is given after the next algorithm.

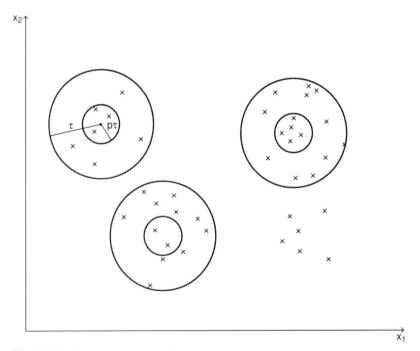

Figure 1.3.   Proportional thresholding.

The Threshold Clustering Algorithm

Inputs: {the randomly ordered sample $S = \{\mathbf{x}^{(1)},..., \mathbf{x}^{(Q)}\}$ of feature vectors; a threshold value τ, and a proportion p, where $0 < p < 1$}.

Outputs: {the number of classes K; the classes C_k as provided by the index function $\text{class}(q) = k$; the number $n(k)$ of feature vectors in each kth class ($1 \le k \le K$); the centers $\mathbf{z}^{(k)}$ of each class; the variance σ_k^2 of each class ($\sigma_k^2 = (1/n(k))\sum_{\{q:\,\text{class}(q)=k\}}\|\mathbf{x}^{(q)} - \mathbf{z}^{(k)}\|^2$ for each $k = 1,..., K$); and the total mean-squared error $\sigma_T^2 = \sum_{(k=1,\,K)}\sigma_k^2$}

Step 1: /Put first sample as center of first cluster/
$K \leftarrow 1$; $\mathbf{z}^{(1)} \leftarrow \mathbf{x}^{(1)}$; class (1) $\leftarrow$ 1;　　　　/$\mathbf{z}^{(1)} \equiv$ center of Cluster 1/

Step 2: /Assign vectors to classes C_k by minimum distance; when threshold is met,/
/compute new statistics/
/repeat　　　　　　　　　　　　　　　　/Do until *stop* remains true/
stop $\leftarrow$ TRUE;
　for $k = 1$ to K, $n(k) \leftarrow 0$;　　　　/Zero out number of vectors in class k/
　for $q = 1$ to Q　　　　　　　　　/For each qth sample vector/
　　$d_{\min} \leftarrow 999999.9$;
　　for $k = 1$ to K　　　　　　　　/find minimum distance to center/
　　　if $\|\mathbf{x}^{(q)} - \mathbf{z}^{(k)}\| < d_{\min}$, then $d_{\min} \leftarrow \|\mathbf{x}^{(q)} - \mathbf{z}^{(k)}\|$; $k_{\min} \leftarrow k$;
　　if $d_{\min} > \tau$, then　　　　　　/If threshold exceeded/
　　　$K \leftarrow K + 1$; $\mathbf{z}^{(K)} \leftarrow \mathbf{x}^{(q)}$;　　/then add new class center/
　　　class(q) $\leftarrow K$;　　　　　/Put $\mathbf{x}^{(q)}$ in new class/
　　　$n(K) \leftarrow n(K) + 1$;　　　　/Update count/
　　if $d_{\min} < p\tau$, then　　　　　/If close to a center/
　　　assign class(q) $\leftarrow k_{\min}$;　　/assign $\mathbf{x}^{(q)}$ to existing class $C_{k\min}$/
　　　$n(k_{\min}) \leftarrow n(k_{\min}) + 1$;　　/Increment number of vectors in this/
　　　　　　　　　　　　　　　　/class/
　　　call **Update_Statistics**($k_{\min}$);　/Call function to update cluster $k_{\min}$/
　　　　　　　　　　　　　　　　/statistics/
　for $k = 1$ to K　　　　　　　　/Check to see if any class changed/
　　if $\|\mathbf{z}^{(k)} - \mathbf{z}^{(k)}\| > 0.0005$ then　/If there is any approximate change/
　　　stop $\leftarrow$ FALSE;　　　　　/then repeat, else stop/
until stop = TRUE;

The Principle of Recursive Averaging

The function **Update_Statistics( )** uses a principle described next. Let $\{r_1,..., r_K\}$ be a sequence of real numbers that we are given, one at a time, for computing the current average. Then

$$\mu_1 = r_1$$

$$\mu_2 = (1/2)r_1 + (1/2)r_2 = (1/2)\mu_1 + (1/2)r_2$$

$$\mu_3 = (1/3)r_1 + (1/3)r_2 + (1/3)r_3 = (2/3)(1/2)r_1 + (2/3)(1/2)r_2 + (1/3)r_3$$

$$= (2/3)\mu_2 + (1/3)r_3$$

.   .   .

.   .   .

.   .   .

$$\mu_k = (1/k)r_1 + (1/k)r_2 + \cdots + (1/k)r_k = \cdots = [(k-1)/k]\mu_{k-1} + (1/k)r_k$$

We use this type of averaging in the Update_Statistics algorithm explained below.

The Procedure Update_Statistics

This is called with the parameter k to update the statistics recursively for the cluster C_k each time a new assignment is made to it. The new mean center vectors $\mathbf{z}^{(k)}$ and the vector $\boldsymbol{\sigma}(k)^2$, where $\boldsymbol{\sigma}(k)^2 = ((\sigma_1(k))^2,\ldots, (\sigma_N(k))^2)$, of mean-squared error components for the clusters C_k are updated recursively as given below for $k = 1,\ldots, K$.

Step 1.   /Recursively compute new average vector as center of C_k/
$$\mathbf{z}^{(k)} \leftarrow [(n(k) - 1)\mathbf{z}^{(k)} + \mathbf{x}^{(q)}]/n(k)$$

Step 2.   /Recursively compute new mean-squared error vector (componentwise)/
$$(\boldsymbol{\sigma}(k))^2 \leftarrow [(n(k) - 1)(\boldsymbol{\sigma}(k))^2 + (\mathbf{x}^{(q)} - \mathbf{z}^{(k)})^2]/n(k)$$

The *advantages* of this method are computational efficiency and a high level of self-organization because it determines K. The *disadvantages* are as follows: (i) The clusters must be contained within disjoint hyperballs (actual classes of feature vectors may be long, narrow, and curved); (ii) the clustering is dependent upon the order of presentation of the sample feature vectors; (iii) the results are strongly dependent upon the values of p and τ that were chosen a priori; (iv) the method is limited to pattern classes that are linearly separable; and (v) it is possible that not all sample feature vectors will be assigned.

In practice, the algorithm should be rerun multiple times with $p = 0.5$ (unless there is available a priori information that indicates otherwise) and for different values τ. The solution with the lowest total variance over all classes (the sum of the variances for the clusters) should be selected, provided that all feature vectors have been assigned to classes. It is useful to vary p at this point to minimize the mean-squared error (variance). Figure 1.4 displays feature vectors that are not capable of being contained in separating hyperballs and that are therefore not linearly separable. Thus they are not amenable to this and similar methods.

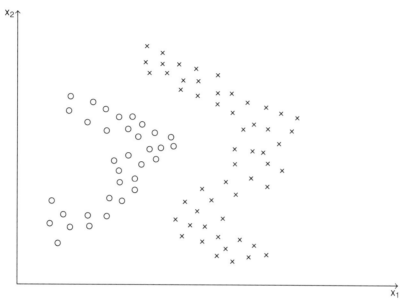

Figure 1.4. Patterns that are not separable by hyperballs.

Example 1.2.   Applying the Threshold Clustering Algorithm

We take the sample points given in Example 1.1. Putting $p = 0.5$ and $\tau = 2.9$, we assign $\mathbf{z}^{(1)} = \mathbf{x}^{(1)} = (2,1)$. The point $\mathbf{x}^{(2)}$ is within the distance $p\tau = 1.45$ of $\mathbf{z}^{(1)}$ so we assign it to Class 1 via class(2) = 1. Because $\mathbf{x}^{(3)}$ has distance greater than $\tau = 2.9$, we create Class 2 with $K = 2$, put $\mathbf{z}^{(2)} = \mathbf{x}^{(3)}$, and assign class(3) = 2. Next, $\mathbf{x}^{(4)}$ is closer to $\mathbf{z}^{(1)}$ than to $\mathbf{z}^{(2)}$ and within a distance of $p\tau = 1.45$ so we assign it via class(4) = 1. Continuing, we obtain class(5) = 2 and class(6) = 2. Thus the first round of clustering provides $C_1 = \{\mathbf{x}^{(1)}, \mathbf{x}^{(2)}, \mathbf{x}^{(4)}\}$ and $C_2 = \{\mathbf{x}^{(3)}, \mathbf{x}^{(5)}, \mathbf{x}^{(6)}\}$. Upon taking the average vectors of each class, we obtain the new centers which are the same as those obtained in Example 1.1. The clusters do not change further.

1.4. The Batchelor–Wilkins Maximin-Distance Self-Organizing Algorithm

A High-Level Description of Maximin Distance

This algorithm completely self-organizes, which includes the determination of K. Again, $S = \{\mathbf{x}^{(1)},..., \mathbf{x}^{(Q)}\}$ is a sample of randomly ordered feature vectors to be used in the unsupervised training (Batchelor and Wilkins, 1969). A proportion p $(0 < p < 1)$ is used in the decision making, and must be given. Without a priori knowledge, we may use $p = 0.5$.

    The algorithm assigns $\mathbf{x}^{(1)}$ as the center $\mathbf{z}^{(1)}$ for the first cluster. It next finds the maximum distance: $\max\{\|\mathbf{x}^{(q)} - \mathbf{z}^{(1)}\|: q > 1\}$. The $\mathbf{x}^{(q)}$ that yields this maximum distance is then assigned as $\mathbf{z}^{(2)}$. Next, for each q such that $\mathbf{x}^{(q)}$ has not been assigned as a center, the pairs of distances $(\|\mathbf{x}^{(q)} - \mathbf{z}^{(1)}\|, \|\mathbf{x}^{(q)} - \mathbf{z}^{(2)}\|)$ are compared and the minimum of each pair is saved as $d_{\min}{}^{(q)}$. The maximum of these minima, $d_{\max}$, equals $\max\{d_{\min}{}^{(q)}: \mathbf{x}^{(q)}$ is not a center$\}$, and the corresponding feature vector is denoted as $\mathbf{x}^{(q*)}$. If this maximum distance, say $d_{\max} = \|\mathbf{x}^{(q*)} - \mathbf{z}^{(2)}\|$, is greater than the proportion p times the average value of the distances between the centers, that is, satisfies $\|\mathbf{x}^{(q*)} - \mathbf{z}^{(2)}\| > p\|\mathbf{z}^{(2)} - \mathbf{z}^{(1)}\|$, then $\mathbf{z}^{(3)} = \mathbf{x}^{(q*)}$ is the new center, else this subprocess terminates at $K = 2$ with centers $\mathbf{z}^{(1)}$ and $\mathbf{z}^{(2)}$ only.

If appropriate, this process is repeated again to find another center $\mathbf{z}^{(K+1)}$. For each feature vector $\mathbf{x}^{(q)}$ that has not been assigned as a center, its distances to the three centers $\mathbf{z}^{(1)}$, $\mathbf{z}^{(2)}$, and $\mathbf{z}^{(3)}$ are compared and the minimum distance is saved as $d_{\min}{}^{(q)}$. From the resulting set of minimum distances, the maximum one is determined, and the feature vector $\mathbf{x}^{(q**)}$ that yields the maximum, say, from $\mathbf{z}^{(1)}$, is the candidate for a new center. If this maximum distance $\|\mathbf{x}^{(q**)} - \mathbf{z}^{(1)}\|$ is greater than the proportion p times the average distance between centers

$$\|\mathbf{x}^{(q**)} - \mathbf{z}^{(1)}\| > p[\|\mathbf{z}^{(2)} - \mathbf{z}^{(1)}\| + \|\mathbf{z}^{(3)} - \mathbf{z}^{(2)}\| + \|\mathbf{z}^{(1)} - \mathbf{z}^{(3)}\|]/3$$

then $\mathbf{x}^{(q**)}$ is assigned as the center $\mathbf{z}^{(4)}$, else the process of finding new centers for clusters terminates at $K = 3$.

When the process terminates with K centers $\mathbf{z}^{(1)},..., \mathbf{z}^{(K)}$, then the remaining unassigned feature vectors in the sample S are assigned to the clusters via minimum distance, that is, each such $\mathbf{x}^{(q)}$ is assigned to cluster C_k if it is closest the center $\mathbf{z}^{(k)}$ for C_k.

Figure 1.5 shows the maximin procedure. The vectors $\mathbf{z}^{(1)}$, $\mathbf{z}^{(2)}$, and $\mathbf{z}^{(3)}$ are the assigned centers thus far, and $\mathbf{x}^{(q)}$ and $\mathbf{x}^{(q+1)}$ are feature vectors that are unassigned thus far. Each of these unassigned vectors has a distance (as shown in the figure) to each of the centers, and the minimum distance shown is recorded. Here, the two minimum distances are $\|\mathbf{x}^{(q)} - \mathbf{z}^{(1)}\|$ and $\|\mathbf{x}^{(q+1)} - \mathbf{z}^{(3)}\|$. The maximum of these two is then taken, which in the figure is the latter distance $d_{\max} = \|\mathbf{x}^{(q+1)} - \mathbf{z}^{(3)}\|$. At this point, this distance is compared with the average of all of the pairwise distances between the centers, and if $d_{\max}$ is greater than p times this average, then $\mathbf{x}^{(q+1)}$ would be assigned as the next center. Otherwise, no center is determined,

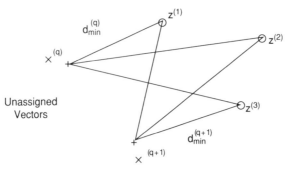

Figure 1.5. The maximin process.

Unassigned Vectors

Assigned Centers

and so further iterations would not find a new center either. In this case, all unused feature vectors are then assigned via minimum distance to the cluster to whose center it is closest.

The Maximin-Distance Algorithm

Inputs: {sample sequence $S = \{\mathbf{x}^{(1)},..., \mathbf{x}^{(Q)}\}$; and proportion p $(0 < p < 1)$}

Outputs: {number K of classes; classes $C_1,..., C_K$ given by the class assignment index $class(q) = k$ that designates that $\mathbf{x}^{(q)}$ is assigned to cluster C_k; cluster centers denoted by the index function $cc(q) = k$ to denote that $x^{(q)}$ is the center of cluster C_k; and $n(k) = $ number of vectors in the kth cluster C_k}

Step 1: /Assign first sample vector as first cluster center, zero out assignment indices/
   for $q = 1$ to Q do $cc(q) \leftarrow 0$;   /Zero out cluster center/
                    /assignments/
   $\mathbf{z}^{(1)} \leftarrow \mathbf{x}^{(1)}$; $\mathbf{K} \leftarrow 1$; $cc(1) \leftarrow 1$; $class(1) \leftarrow 1$; /Assign first cluster center/

Step 2: /Find feature vector farthest from center $\mathbf{z}^{(1)}$/
   $d_{\max} = 0.0$;
   for $q = 2$ to Q do   /Find second cluster center/
    if $\left\| \mathbf{x}^{(q)} - \mathbf{z}^{(1)} \right\| > d_{\max}$, then
     $d_{\max} \leftarrow \left\| \mathbf{x}^{(q)} - \mathbf{z}^{(1)} \right\|$; $q_{\max} \leftarrow q$; /Find maximum distance vector/
   $K \leftarrow K + 1$; $\mathbf{z}^{(K)} \leftarrow \mathbf{x}^{(q_{\max})}$; $cc(q_{\max}) \leftarrow K$; /Assign and index cluster center/
   $class(q_{\max}) \leftarrow K$; $n(K) \leftarrow 1$;   /Update all indices and counts/

Step 3: /Compute minimum distance for each unclassified sample vector/
   /and find new cluster center if appropriate/
   repeat   /Do until no new center found/
    $d_{\max} \leftarrow 0.0$; $d_{\min} \leftarrow 999999.9$; /Initialize maximum, minimum/
    $cluster\_found \leftarrow$ TRUE;   /Repeat loop criterion/
    for $q = 1$ to Q /Find all noncenters/
     if $cc(q) = 0$ then   /If $\mathbf{x}^{(q)}$ is not a center/
      for $k = 1$ to K /then check its distances/
       $d[q, k] \leftarrow \left\| \mathbf{x}^{(q)} - \mathbf{z}^{(k)} \right\|$; /Find distance to each/
                 /cluster center $\mathbf{z}^{(k)}$/
      if $d[q, k] < d_{\min}$, then   /Take minimum over $\mathbf{z}^{(k)}$/
       $d_{\min} \leftarrow d[q,k]$;   /Save min. distance/
       $k_{\min} \leftarrow k$;   /and its index/
     if $d_{\min} > d_{\max}$, then   /Then take maximum/
      $d_{\max} \leftarrow d_{\min}$; $k_{\max} \leftarrow k_{\min}$; /and save its index/
    $average \leftarrow 0.0$;   /Initialize sum of distances/
    for $k = 1$ to $K - 1$ /Take average of distances/
     for $k1 = k + 1$ to K /between all pairs of centers/
      $average \leftarrow average + \left\| \mathbf{z}^{(k)} - \mathbf{z}^{(k1)} \right\|$; /Sum for averaging/
    $average \leftarrow average/K$;   /Take average/

if $d_{max} > (p)(\text{average})$, then	/If larger distance, get new/
	/center/
$K \leftarrow K + 1; \text{cc}(k_{max}) \leftarrow K;$	/for new cluster/
$\text{class}(k_{max}) \leftarrow K; \mathbf{z}^{(K)} \leftarrow \mathbf{x}^{(kmax)};$	/Update class assignment, center/
else	
cluster_found $\leftarrow$ FALSE;	/Else no cluster center found/
if cluster_found $\equiv$ TRUE then	
call **Assign_Vectors**;	/Assign all feature vectors to/
	/clusters/
until cluster_found $\equiv$ FALSE;	/Repeat until no center found/

The procedure **Assign_Vectors**( ) assigns each of the sample vectors $\mathbf{x}^{(1)},..., \mathbf{x}^{(Q)}$ to the center among $\mathbf{z}^{(1)},..., \mathbf{z}^{(K)}$ to which it is closest and need not be listed here (see Step 2 of the k-means algorithm).

The *advantages* of this heuristic algorithm are as follows: (i) It determines K; (ii) it self-organizes; and (iii) it is efficient for small-to-medium numbers of classes. The *disadvantages* are as follows: (a) The proportion p must be given; (b) the ordering of the samples influences the clustering; (c) the value of p influences the clustering; d) the separation is linear; (e) the cluster centers are not recomputed to better represent the classes; (f) there is no measure of how good the clustering is; and (g) an outlier can upset the process. *In practice*, we suggest that the process be run for several values of p and the mean-squared error $\sigma_k^2 = (1/n(k))\sum_{\{q:\text{class}(q) = k\}}\|\mathbf{x}^{(q)} - \mathbf{z}^{(k)}\|^2$ be computed for each kth cluster ($k = 1,..., K$) and then summed over all classes k to obtain the total mean-squared error. The value of p that provides the lowest total mean-squared error is an optimal one. The *final clusters should be averaged* to obtain a new center and all sample vectors reassigned via minimum distance to the new centers.

1.5. The ISODATA

The High-Level Description of ISODATA

The *Iterative Self-Organizing Data Analysis Technique (Algorithm)* is like the k-means algorithm, except that it incorporates some heuristics (rules-of-thumb) gleaned from experience (Ball and Hall, 1965, 1966, 1967) to aid in the realization of Fu's high-level algorithm. Many modifications may be made, but we present here a basic version. For other descriptions, see Therrien (1989, p. 218), Bow (1984, p. 114), or Tou and Gonzalez (1974).

Let K be an approximate number of clusters desired, K_c be the initial current number of clusters, and $S = \{\mathbf{x}^{(1)},..., \mathbf{x}^{(Q)}\}$ be the randomly ordered sample of Q N-dimensional feature vectors for training, and let $C_1,..., C^{K_c}$ denote the K_c current clusters with respective centers $\mathbf{z}^{(1)},..., \mathbf{z}^{(K_c)}$. We also need the parameters to be used in the heuristic rules for merging and splitting current clusters. Let n_{min} be the minimum number of feature vectors allowed in a cluster (else it is eliminated and the vectors assigned to other clusters). We use a standard deviation threshold parameter σ_{split} against which to test a cluster. If the standard deviation $\sigma_n(k)$ of any fixed nth component over all vectors in the kth cluster is larger than σ_{split}, then we split that center into two centers that differ from the previous one only in the nth component. The two new centers use the nth components $z_n^{(k)} + \sigma_n(k)$ and $z_n^{(k)} - \sigma_n(k)$ for the two new centers, respectively. The parameter d_L is the *lumping threshold* for the distance between centers of clusters for *lumping* (merging) two clusters whose centers are too close: If the centers of a pair of clusters are closer than d_L, then that pair is lumped into a single cluster. Only pairs of clusters may be lumped. Further, on any one iteration, only L_{max} pairs of lumpings are allowed.

A higher-level description follows.

1. Assign the first K_c samples as cluster centers via $\mathbf{z}^{(k)} \leftarrow \mathbf{x}^{(k)}$ ($k = 1,..., K_c$). Input estimated K.

2. Assign all sample vectors to clusters according to each one's minimum distance to a center.

3. Eliminate clusters that contain less than n_{min} feature vectors and assign those vectors to the other clusters via minimum distance to cluster centers. Decrease K_c accordingly.

4. Compute a new cluster center as the average of all feature vectors in each kth cluster, where $\mathbf{z}^{(k)} = [1/n(k)]\sum_{\{class(q) = k\}}\mathbf{x}^{(q)}$ and $n(k)$ is the number of feature vectors in the kth cluster. Compute the new mean-squared error (variance)

$$\sigma_k^2 = (1/n(k))\sum_{(r=1, N)}\sum_{(class(q)=k)}(z_r^{(k)} - x_r^{(q)})^2$$

within each kth cluster and add them over all clusters to get the total mean-squared error over all clusters.

5. For each kth cluster, compute the mean-squared error $\sigma_n^2(k)$ of each nth component x_n over that cluster and find the maximum $\sigma_{n*}^2(k)$ component mean-squared error within cluster k for over $n = 1,..., N$, where the index $n*$ is for the maximum component.

6. If there are not enough clusters ($K_c < K/2$) and this is not the last iteration, then if $\sigma_{max}(k) > \sigma_{split}$ for any cluster k, split that cluster into two clusters by splitting the center into two centers that differ only in the component where the maximum difference occurred (the two new centers have the $n*$th components $z_{n*} + \sigma_{max}(k)$ and $z_{n*} - \sigma_{max}(k)$ and all other components are the same). Increment K_c. Now reassign the feature vectors based on minimum distance to one of these cluster centers.

7. If this is an even iteration and $K_c > 2K$, then compute all distances $D_{ij} = d(\mathbf{z}^{(i)}, \mathbf{z}^{(j)})$ between cluster centers $\mathbf{z}^{(i)}$ and $\mathbf{z}^{(j)}$ ($1 \le i < j \le K_c$). If a distance satisfies $D_{ij} < d_L$, then lump (merge) the ith and jth clusters into a single cluster (if number of lumpings has not exceeded L_{max}). Decrement K_c.

8. Update the iteration number ($i \leftarrow i + 1$). If $i > I$, then stop, else go to Step 2 above.

An ISODATA Algorithm

Inputs: {randomly ordered sample feature vectors $S = \{\mathbf{x}^{(1)},..., \mathbf{x}^{(Q)}\}$; initial current number K_c of clusters; approximate desired number K of clusters; maximum standard deviation threshold σ_{split} for splitting clusters; minimum distance threshold parameter d_L for lumping a pair of clusters; minimum number n_{min} of feature vectors that a cluster must have without being eliminated; maximum number of cluster pairs L_{max} that can be lumped in an iteration; and maximum number of iterations I}

Outputs: {current number of clusters K_c; the clusters C_k given by the classification assignment index function class$(q) = k$ (for $\mathbf{x}^{(q)} \in C_k$); and number $n(k)$ of vectors in the kth cluster}

Step 1: /Initialize iteration number and parameters/
    $i \leftarrow 0$; input K, K_c, I, d_L, σ_{split};   /Initialize parameters/
    for $q = 1$ to Q do
        cc$(q) \leftarrow 0$;   /Initialize cluster change assignment/
        class$(q) \leftarrow 0$;   /Initialize assignment index/
        for $k = 1$ to $2K + 1$ do $n(k) \leftarrow 0$;   /Initialize number vectors per cluster/

Step 2: /Assign first K_c sample vectors as cluster centers/
    for $k = 1$ to K_c do
        $\mathbf{z}^{(k)} \leftarrow \mathbf{x}^{(k)}$;   /Assign K_c centers/
        class$(k) \leftarrow k$;   /Record assignments/

Step 3: /Assign feature vectors to clusters via minimum distance, check for change/
    change_cluster $\leftarrow$ FALSE;   /Set no change to start/
    for $q = 1$ to Q do   /For each sample feature vector $\mathbf{x}^{(q)}$/
        $d_{min} \leftarrow 999999.9$;   /find minimum distance to a center/
        for $k = 1$ to K_c do   /over all K_c current centers/
            if $\left\| \mathbf{x}^{(q)} - \mathbf{z}^{(k)} \right\|_2 < d_{min}$, then
                $d_{min} \leftarrow \left\| \mathbf{x}^{(q)} - \mathbf{z}^{(k)} \right\|_2$;
                $k_{min} \leftarrow k$;   /Assign via minimum distance/
        cc$(q) \leftarrow k_{min}$; $n(k_{min}) \leftarrow n(k_{min}) + 1$;   /Set assignment, update count/
        if cc$(q) \neq$ class(q), then
            change_cluster $\leftarrow$ TRUE;   /Check for cluster change/
    if change_cluster $\equiv$ FALSE, then stop;   /and stop if no changes/
    for $q = 1$ to Q do class$(q) \leftarrow$ cc(q);   /Update assignments indices/

Step 4: /Eliminate clusters with less than n_{min} vectors, renumber, update number of clusters/
    for $k = 1$ to K_c do   /Check all current clusters/
        if $n(k) < n_{min}$, then   /If number of vectors in cluster k is too/
                /small/

            for $r = k + 1$ to K_c do   /then eliminate it and adjust indices/
                $n(r - 1) \leftarrow n(r)$, $\mathbf{z}^{(r-1)} \leftarrow \mathbf{z}^{(r)}$;
            for $q = 1$ to Q do
                if class$(q) > k$, then
                    class$(q) \leftarrow$ class$(q) - 1$;   /Close-up assignments to clusters/
            $K_c \leftarrow K_c - 1$;   /Reduce current number of clusters K_c/

Step 5: /Compute new centers of all clusters/
for $k = 1$ to K_c do
  $\mathbf{z}^{(k)} \leftarrow (1/n(k))\sum_{\{q:\text{class}(q)\ =\ k\}}\mathbf{x}^{(q)};$ /Component averages form new center/

Step 6: /Compute new mean-square error for each cluster/
for $k = 1$ to K_c do
  $D_k \leftarrow (1/n(k))\sum_{\{q:\text{class}(q)\ =\ k\}}\left\|\mathbf{x}^{(q)} - \mathbf{z}^{(k)}\right\|_2^2;$

Step 7: /Compute total mean-squared error and maximum component variance for each cluster/

$D_{\text{total\_ave}} \leftarrow (1/Q)\sum_{(k=1,K_c)}n(k)D_k;$ /Total mean-squared error over all/
                          /clusters/

for $k = 1$ to K_c do   /For each kth cluster/
  $s_{\max} \leftarrow 0.0;\ \text{sum} \leftarrow 0.0;$ /compute variance over all N/
                          /components/

    for $n = 1$ to N do   /For each fixed component n/
      for $q = 1$ to Q do   /sum squares over all vectors in cluster/
                          /k/

        if class$(q) = k$, then sum $\leftarrow$ sum $+ [x_n^{(q)} - z_n^{(k)}]^2;$
      sum $\leftarrow$ sum$/n(k);$ /Take average component sum-squared/
                          /error/

      if sum $\geq s_{\max}$, then   /Find maximum standard deviation/
                          /from $s_{\max}$/

        $s_{\max} \leftarrow$ sum;
        $\sigma_{\max}(k) \leftarrow \sqrt{(\text{sum})};\ n_{\max} \leftarrow n;$ /Get maximum standard deviation and/
                          /index for max./

Step 8: /Check for performing splitting or lumping of clusters/
if $i \geq$ I, then   /If last iteration/
  $d_L \leftarrow 0;$ goto Step 10;   /then do not split, but may lump/
if $(K_c \leq K/2)$, then goto Step 9;   /If not enough clusters then try to split/
if (i is even AND $K_c \geq 2K$)   /If too many clusters, try to lump/
  then goto Step 10;

Step 9: /Check and split cluster into two clusters if conditions are met/
split $\leftarrow$ FALSE;
for $k = 1$ to K_c do   /If maximum component $\sigma_{\max}(k)$ is too large/

    if $\sigma_{\max}(k) > \sigma_{\text{split}}$, then   /then split if there are enough vectors/
                          /for 2 clusters and the mean-squared/
                          /error is large, or if too few clusters/

    if $(n(k) > 2n_{\min} + 1)$ AND $D_k > D_{\text{total\_ave}})$ OR $(K_c < K/2)$ then
      split $\leftarrow$ TRUE; $K \leftarrow K + 1;$
        $z_{n_{\max}}^{(k)} \leftarrow z_{n_{\max}}^{(k)} -$ /Split on offending component/
                $(1/2)\sigma_{\max}(k);$
        $z_{n_{\max}}^{(K)} \leftarrow z_{n_{\max}}^{(K)} +$ /into 2 clusters/
                $(1/2)\sigma_{\max}(k);$
    if split = TRUE then goto Step 3;   /If split, go back to reassign vectors/

Step 10: /Compute distances between all pairs of cluster centers, lump if too close/
/Compare each distance with d_L, set lump flag to TRUE if less than d_L/
for $k = 1$ to $K_c - 1$ do
    for $r = k + 1$ to K_c do   /For all pairs of clusters (k, r)/
        $D_{rk} \leftarrow \left\| \mathbf{z}^{(r)} - \mathbf{z}^{(k)} \right\|_2$;   /test distance between centers/
        if $D_{rk} < d_L$, then $L[r, k] \leftarrow$ TRUE;   /against d_L and record/
        else $L[r, k] \leftarrow$ FALSE;   /results for lumping/

Step 11: /Find smallest one of distances D_{rk} less than d_L and lump the two clusters/
/Repeat until either $L_{\max}$ lumpings are done or no more distances are less than d_L/
count $\leftarrow 0$ /Count is no. of lumpings done/
repeat   /which cannot exceed L/
    $d_{\min} \leftarrow 999999.9$; empty $\leftarrow$ TRUE;   /Initialize parameters/
    for $k = 1$ to $K_c - 1$ do   /for all pairs of clusters/
        for $r = k + 1$ to K_c do
            if $L[r, k] =$ TRUE, then   /If distance $< d_L$, then find minimum/
                if $D_{rk} < d_{\min}$, then   /of distances less than d_L/
                    $d_{\min} \leftarrow D_{rk}$;
                    empty $\leftarrow$ FALSE;   /If lump indicated, queue not empty/
                    $r^* \leftarrow r$; $k^* \leftarrow k$;   /Save minimum indices/
        if empty $=$ FALSE, then   /Procedure lumps minimum pair/
            Lump(r^*, k^*);
        $L[r^*, k^*] \leftarrow$ FALSE;   /Erase lump indicator/
        count $\leftarrow$ count $+ 1$;   /Update lumpings count, repeat until/
    until (empty $=$ TRUE) OR   /empty or until $L_{\max}$ lumpings done/
        (count $\geq L_{\max}$)

Step 12: /Do another iteration or else stop/
if $i < I$, then $i \leftarrow i + 1$; goto Step 3;   /Update iteration number/
else stop;   /and stop if enough iterations/

The Procedure Lump(r^*, k^*)

/Lump cluster pair C_{r^*}, C_{k^*} together, update clusters/
$k^* = \min\{r^*, k^*\}$; $r^* = \max\{r^*, k^*\}$;   /Use lowest index for lumped cluster/
$n(k^*) \leftarrow n(k^*) + n(r^*)$;   /Number of vectors in new cluster/
$\mathbf{z}^{(k^*)} \leftarrow (1/n(k^*))[n(r^*)\mathbf{z}^{(r^*)} + n(k^*)\mathbf{z}^{(k^*)}]$;   /Average center of new cluster/
for $q = 1$ to Q do   /Update assignment index function/
  if class$(q) = r^*$, then class$(q) \leftarrow k^*$;   /by assigning to new cluster/
$K_c \leftarrow K_c - 1$; $n(r^*) \leftarrow 0$; $\mathbf{z}^{(r^*)} \leftarrow \mathbf{0}$ /Update indices/
for $k = r^*$ to K_c do
  $n(k) \leftarrow n(k + 1)$; $z^{(k)} \leftarrow z^{(k+1)}$;
  for $q = 1$ to K_c do if class $(q) = k$
    then class$(q) \leftarrow k - 1$;

The *advantages* of the powerful ISODATA are its self-organizing capability, its great flexibility in eliminating clusters that are too small, its ability to divide clusters with feature vectors that are too dissimilar, and its ability to lump clusters that are sufficiently similar. But it suffers from the following *disadvantages*: (i) It is linear in that the data must be linearly separable into hyperballs (long narrow or curving classes would not be properly clustered, which is a flaw in minimal distances assignment); (ii) it is difficult to know a priori what the parameters K, n_{min}, d_L, σ_{split}, n_{min}, and L_{max} should be (choosing them is an art, based on experience, as well as a science); (iii) the performance is highly dependent upon the user-given parameters; (iv) for large data sets and large numbers of clusters, the computation for pairwise distances and the lumping and splitting functions are less efficient than other linear separation methods; and (v) convergence is unknown, although it appears to work well for nonoverlapping clusters.

In practice, this algorithm would be run multiple times with different values for K and other parameters and the clustering with the minimal total sum-squared error would be selected. This algorithm shows the power of heuristic rules. There is ample opportunity for modifications.

1.6. Extensions of ISODATA-Type Methods

Some Extensions to ISODATA

Procedures may be added to the ISODATA, k-means algorithm, and other similar algorithms to measure the performance and to choose the number K of clusters automatically. The DYNOC algorithm (Tou, 1979) used a *performance measure* $\phi(K_c) = \min\{D_{jk}\}/\max\{D_{kk}\}$, where these mean-squared errors are (i) $D_{kk} = \{(1/n(k))\sum_{\{q:class(q) = k\}}\|\mathbf{x}^{(q)} - \mathbf{z}^{(k)}\|^2\}^{1/2}$ (within clusters) and (ii) $D_{jk} = \sum_{(n=1, N)}[z_n^{(j)} - z_n^{(k)}]^2\}^{1/2}$ (between cluster centers). The maximum of $\phi(K_c)$ coincides with optimal clustering and optimality of K_c. This measure can be computed just before splitting or lumping. There is also an extended method by Davies and Bouldin (1979). We are most intrigued by the method of Diday.

Diday's Dynamic Clusters

The *dynamic clusters method* (Diday, 1973) employs multiple centers, called *cores*, for each cluster instead of a single one. Figure 1.6 demonstrates the situation where E_k is the core of the cluster C_k ($k = 1, 2$). Let the number of clusters K be given, perhaps by some other algorithm. We start with (i) the tuple $C = (C_1,..., C_K)$ of given disjoint clusters, (ii) an initial tuple of *cores* $E^{(0)} = (E_1^{(0)},..., E_K^{(0)})$, which are initially singletons (sets with only a single element), and (iii) the number N_k of vectors desired in the core E_k for C_k, $k = 1,..., K$.

The clustering problem is then to find the set of cores E and assign the sample feature vectors to them to obtain the clusters C to minimize the measure

$$\delta(C, E) = \sum_{(\mathbf{x} \in C_k)} \sum_{(\mathbf{z} \in E_k)} \|\mathbf{x} - \mathbf{z}\| \tag{1.3}$$

over all $\mathbf{x} \in C_k$ and all $\mathbf{z} \in E_k$, for each $k = 1,..., \mathbf{K}$. Let

$$D(\mathbf{x}, E_k) = \sum_{(\mathbf{z} \in E_k)} \|\mathbf{x} - \mathbf{z}\| = \|\mathbf{x} - E_k\|$$

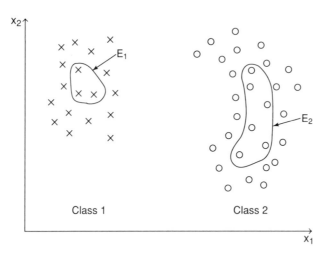

Figure 1.6. Dynamic clusters.

A procedure to do this consists of choosing N_k feature vectors $\mathbf{x}^{(q)}$ from C_k to put into E_k to minimize the function

$$D^{(k)} = D(\mathbf{x}, E_k)/\sum_{(r=1, K)}D(\mathbf{x}, E_r) \qquad (1.4)$$

such that $C_j \cap C_k = \varnothing$. The algorithm is stated below, where I is the given number of iterations, K is the number of clusters desired, $S = \{\mathbf{x}^{(1)},..., \mathbf{x}^{(Q)}\}$ is the sample of feature vectors, $e(q) = k$ assigns $x^{(q)}$ to core E_k, and class$(q) = k$ assigns $\mathbf{x}^{(q)}$ to class k.

A Dynamic Clustering Algorithm

Inputs: {the sample vectors $\{\mathbf{x}^{(1)},..., \mathbf{x}^{(Q)}\}$; the number of clusters K; and N_k for each $k = 1,..., K$ (the number of points to be in the core E_k of the kth cluster C_k)}

Outputs: {the cores E_k as assigned by the index function $e(q) = k$ if $\mathbf{x}^{(q)} \in E_k$; clusters C_k, $k = 1,..., K$, as assigned by class$(q) = k$ for $\mathbf{x}^{(q)}$ in C_k}

Step 1: /Assign first K sample vectors as centers, assign vectors via minimum distance/
$\qquad i \leftarrow 0;$
$\qquad$ for $k = 1$ to K do assign $\mathbf{z}^{(k)} \leftarrow \mathbf{x}^{(k)};$ $\qquad$ /Assign first K centers/
$\qquad$ for $q = 1$ to Q do
$\qquad\qquad$ if $\mathbf{x}^{(q)}$ is nearest $\mathbf{z}^{(k)}$, $\qquad\qquad$ /Assign to clusters by minimum/
$\qquad\qquad$ then class$(q) \leftarrow k;$ $\qquad\qquad$ /distance/

Step 2: /Select multicenter cores for all clusters/
$\qquad$ for $k = 1$ to K do $\qquad\qquad\qquad$ /For each kth cluster, select the core E_k/

for $r = 1$ to N_k /Select N_k vectors for E_k/
    select new $\mathbf{x}^{(r)}$ from C_k;   /Random selection of E_k, assign $\mathbf{x}^{(r)}$/
    $e(r) \leftarrow k$;   /to core E_k/

Step 3: /Assign feature vectors to cluster via minimal distance to cores/
    for $k = 1$ to K do $D^{(k)} \leftarrow 0$;   /Initialize each cluster mean-squared/
                                                                /error/

    for $q = 1$ to Q do   /For each $\mathbf{x}^{(q)}$, assign by minimum/
                                                                  /distance/

        $d_{min} \leftarrow \left\| \mathbf{x}^{(q)} - E_1 \right\|_2$ /Initialize minimum distance to core/
        for $k = 2$ to K do   /For each class k, get closest core to $\mathbf{x}^{(q)}$/
          if $\left\| \mathbf{x}^{(q)} - E_k \right\|_2 < d_{min}$, then
              $k_{min} \leftarrow k$; $d_{min} \leftarrow \left\| \mathbf{x}^{(q)} - E_k \right\|_2$;   /Save index and minimum distance/
        class$(q) \leftarrow k_{min}$;   /Assign $\mathbf{x}^{(q)}$ to class k_{min}/
        $D^{(kmin)} \leftarrow D^{(kmin)} + d_{min}$;

Step 4: /Reselect new E_k for each $k = 1,..., K$ until $D^{(k)}$ is minimized/
    repeat   /Repeat process until change remains/
                                                                      /FALSE/

        change $\leftarrow$ FALSE;   /Assume no change in clusters/
        for $k = 1$ to K do
          reselect new $\mathscr{E}_k$ from C_k;   /Select *new* core randomly from current/
                                                                        /cluster/

          compute $\mathscr{D}^{(k)}$;   /Compute *new* mean-squared error of/
                                                                       /kth cluster/

          if $\mathscr{D}^{(k)} < D^{(k)}$, then   /If error has decreased, then/
             $D^{(k)} \leftarrow \mathscr{D}^{(k)}$; $E_k \leftarrow \mathscr{E}_k$;   /update cores and errors/
             change $\leftarrow$ TRUE;   /Core has changed, so prevent/
                                                                            /stopping/

    until change = FALSE;

Step 5: /Update iteration number and repeat loop or stop/
    $i \leftarrow i + 1$
      if $i > I$, then stop else goto Step 3   /Quit if I iterations are done/

The *advantage* of this method is that the separation need not be linear because the hypersolid clusters need not be hyperballs (they may be elongated and curved). *Disadvantages* are that a strategy for selecting the cores must be determined and programmed; for large numbers of feature vectors and classes, this becomes computationally complex. The clustering is not independent of the order in which the sample feature vectors are presented. This algorithm is similar to the k-means algorithm and the ISODATA, except that the cores are not singletons. *In practice*, one of the previous clustering methods may be used to obtain an initial clustering, and then this algorithm may be used starting at Step 2 above. Cores may be selected by a random draw, or each cluster may be partitioned into subclusters and the centers of the subclusters may be used as cores.

1.7. Graph-Theoretic Algorithms

A High-Level Description

The performances of all algorithms thus far depend upon the order in which the sample feature vectors are presented. Graph-theoretic methods consider all distances simultaneously in the beginning and avoid order dependence. The basic algorithm presented below is equivalent to minimal spanning tree methods for graphs, although we need not cover that theory (see Bow, 1984). Let $S = \{\mathbf{x}^{(1)},..., \mathbf{x}^{(Q)}\}$ be a given sample of Q feature vectors. For any distance threshold $\tau > 0$, we form the *graph similarity matrix M* by: computing the distance $d_{ij} = \|\mathbf{x}^{(i)} - \mathbf{x}^{(j)}\|$ for all i and j ($i \leq j$); and if $d_{ij} < \tau$, then put $m_{ij} = 1$, else put $m_{ij} = 0$. Thus the similarity matrix M contains 0s and 1s, which depend upon the threshold τ (different values of τ yield different similarity matrices). Of course, the diagonal entries are all 1s because each feature vector has distance to itself that is less than any $\tau > 0$. A high-level description follows.

Column searching is a recursive process that comes back to the remaining rows in each column after it has run out of rows for the current column. When no more columns remain for searching, all vectors have been found to assign to the current class number. Next, it updates the cluster number, finds a new vector that has not been assigned, and begins the column searching again on the column number for that vector. The algorithm terminates when there are no more vectors that have not been assigned. In the next example, we search by rows instead; the algorithm that follows uses column search.

Example 1.3. Graph-Theoretic Clustering

Consider the similarity matrix in Table 1.1. The *i*th row contains the entry 1 in the *j*th column for each vector $\mathbf{x}^{(j)}$ that is within the threshold distance τ from $\mathbf{x}^{(i)}$. Starting with the first row ($i = 1$), we see that there are 1s under the columns for the vectors $\mathbf{x}^{(1)}$, $\mathbf{x}^{(6)}$, and

Table 1.1.
An Example Similarity Matrix

Row	Column											
	01	02	03	04	05	06	07	08	09	10	11	12
01	1	0	0	0	0	1	0	1	0	0	0	0
02	0	1	0	0	0	0	0	0	0	1	0	0
03	0	0	1	0	0	0	0	0	0	0	0	1
04	0	0	0	1	0	0	0	1	1	0	0	0
05	0	0	0	0	1	0	0	0	1	0	0	0
06	1	0	0	0	0	1	0	1	0	0	0	0
07	0	0	0	0	0	0	1	0	0	1	1	0
08	1	0	0	1	0	1	0	1	0	0	0	0
09	0	0	0	1	1	0	0	0	1	0	0	0
10	0	1	0	0	0	0	1	0	0	1	1	0
11	0	0	0	0	0	0	1	0	0	1	1	0
12	0	0	1	0	0	0	0	0	0	0	0	1

$\mathbf{x}^{(8)}$. We put them into the first cluster by assigning class(1) = class(6) = class(8) = 1. We push (the indices for) $\mathbf{x}^{(6)}$ and $\mathbf{x}^{(8)}$ onto a search stack. We pop (the index for) $\mathbf{x}^{(6)}$ from the search stack and then examine the sixth row to find no 1s other than under $j = 1, j = 6$ and $j = 8$, which already belong to clusters. Next, we pop $\mathbf{x}^{(8)}$ from the search stack and examine the eighth row. It contains the entry 1 under columns $j = 1, j = 4$, and $j = 8$, so we push $\mathbf{x}^{(4)}$ onto the search stack and assign it to the first cluster via class(4) = 1. Upon popping 4 and examining the fourth row, we find a 1 at $j = 4, j = 8$, and $j = 9$, whereupon we push $\mathbf{x}^{(9)}$ onto the search stack and make the assignment class(9) = 1. We pop $\mathbf{x}^{(9)}$ from the search stack and check the ninth row to find 1s in columns $j = 4, j = 5$, and $j = 9$. Thus we push $\mathbf{x}^{(5)}$ to the search stack and make the assignment class(5) = 1. When we pop $\mathbf{x}^{(5)}$ and examine the fifth row, we find 1s under columns $j = 5$ and $j = 9$, but these vectors were already assigned. The search stack is empty. Thus the first cluster is $C_1 = \{\mathbf{x}^{(1)}, \mathbf{x}^{(4)}, \mathbf{x}^{(5)}, \mathbf{x}^{(6)}, \mathbf{x}^{(8)}, \mathbf{x}^{(9)}\}$.

We update the cluster number from 1 to 2 because class(2) = 0 ($\mathbf{x}^{(2)}$ has not yet been assigned to a cluster) and examine the second row. Because it contains entries of 1 under $j = 2$ and $j = 10$, we assign $\mathbf{x}^{(2)}$ and $\mathbf{x}^{(10)}$ to the second cluster via class(2) = class(10) = 2 and push $\mathbf{x}^{(10)}$ onto the search stack. After popping $\mathbf{x}^{(10)}$ from the stack, we find 1s in the tenth row under columns $j = 2, j = 7, j = 10$, and $j = 11$. Thus we push $\mathbf{x}^{(7)}$ and $\mathbf{x}^{(11)}$ onto the search stack and make the assignments class(7) = class(11) = 2. In turn, we pop $\mathbf{x}^{(7)}$ and $\mathbf{x}^{(11)}$ from the stack and find no entries of 1 for vectors that have not already been assigned. Thus $C_2 = \{\mathbf{x}^{(2)}, \mathbf{x}^{(7)}, \mathbf{x}^{(10)}, \mathbf{x}^{(11)}\}$. We next update the cluster number to 3 because $\mathbf{x}^{(3)}$ has not yet been assigned to a cluster. The third row contains 1s under $j = 3$ and $j = 12$, so we put $\mathbf{x}^{(3)}$ and $\mathbf{x}^{(12)}$ into the third cluster via class(3) = class(12) = 3 and push $\mathbf{x}^{(12)}$ onto the search stack. Upon popping $\mathbf{x}^{(12)}$ and checking the twelfth row, we find no new entries.

We now check to find that all rows have been processed, so there are no more clusters to be formed. Thus we have found the following three clusters: $\{\mathbf{x}^{(1)}, \mathbf{x}^{(4)}, \mathbf{x}^{(5)}, \mathbf{x}^{(6)}, \mathbf{x}^{(8)}, \mathbf{x}^{(9)}\}$, $\{\mathbf{x}^{(2)}, \mathbf{x}^{(7)}, \mathbf{x}^{(10)}, \mathbf{x}^{(11)}\}$, and $\{\mathbf{x}^{(3)}, \mathbf{x}^{(12)}\}$. We have obtained three trial clusters.

An Algorithm for the Graph Similarity Matrix Method

Inputs: {a sample $S = \{\mathbf{x}^{(1)},..., \mathbf{x}^{(Q)}\}$; and a threshold $\tau > 0$}

Outputs: {number of clusters K; clusters C_k, $k = 1,..., K$, denoted by the assignment class(q) = k}

Step 1: /Initialize parameters/
       input τ,   /Enter threshold τ/
       for $q = 1$ to Q do class(q) $\leftarrow$ 0;   /Initialize class assignments to 0/

Step 2: /Compute similarity matrix M/
       for $i = 1$ to Q do
          for $j = i$ to Q do
            $d_{ij} \leftarrow \|x^{(i)} - x^{(j)}\|_2$ /Compute distances, using symmetry of/
                                                               /matrix/

if $d_{ij} < \tau$, then $m_{ij} \leftarrow 1$; $m_{ji} \leftarrow 1$;
else $m_{ij} \leftarrow 0$; $m_{ji} \leftarrow 0$;

Step 3: /Recursive checking procedure inside repeat loop/

$k \leftarrow 1$;	/Initialize class number/
class(1) $\leftarrow 1$; $j \leftarrow 1$;	/Assign vector 1 to class 1/
repeat	
Check_column(j, k);	/Call recursive function to assign by/
	/columns/
$k \leftarrow k + 1$;	/Update class number/
next_col $\leftarrow$ **Get_next_column**( );	/Get next unchecked column/
until next_col $= 0$;	

The functions **Check_column**(*j,k*) and **Get_next_column**( ) are straightforward and are given below. **Check_column**(*j,k*) is recursive, and it calls itself repeatedly until it exhausts the connectivity starting from some row.

Procedure Check_column(j, k):

for $i = 1$ to Q do	/Check row numbers greater than column/
	/number/
if $m_{ij} = 1$ and class(i) $= 0$ then	/If close enough, then assign the new/
class(i) $\leftarrow k$;	/vector to the current class and use the/
Check-column(j, k);	/row as a column to search: Depth First/
	/Search/

Procedure Get_next_column( ):

key_col $\leftarrow 0$;	/Initialize next unassigned vector to 0/
for $q = 1$ to Q do	/If qth vector has not been assigned/
if class(q) $= 0$ then	/then it is a candidate for next column/
	/search/
key_col $\leftarrow q$; exit loop;	/Get out of loop when unassigned vector/
	/found/
return key_col;	

The *advantages* of this method are as follows: (i) It self-organizes fully by determining K; (ii) nonlinear separation is possible (clusters may be long and curved, for example); and (iii) the order of presentation of sample vectors has no effect. The *disadvantages* are as follows: (i) For large sample sets, the similarity matrix becomes large (a sample size of $Q = 1,000$ requires entries of 1,000,000, or at least 500,000 when half of the symmetric matrix is used); (ii) it is possible that two or more classes may be put into a single cluster because there may be a sequence of feature vectors that are close to each other but that contain two or more classes; and (iii) the threshold τ must be picked without a priori knowledge. The memory requirements could be reduced somewhat, but there remains the need to break large clusters into smaller ones.

In practice, this method can be used with various values of τ to obtain a possibly non-linear classification that minimizes the total distance that is the sum of distance sums of all pairs of vectors within each cluster. It could also be used to obtain results to feed into an algorithm such as the dynamic clusters algorithm.

1.8. Bayesian Decisionmaking

Probability and Estimation

Decisionmaking involves *estimation*—that is, selecting a value r for an unknown parameter R based on (i) measured values that contain random errors, (ii) a priori or empirical probability distributions for the outcomes of R, (iii) other estimated values that are correlated to R, and (iv) functions of one or more of the above. For our purposes, we want to know what the probabilities are that, given a feature vector $\mathbf{x}$, it belongs to Class k. A standard approach of decision theory is to minimize the probability of making an incorrect classification.

We recall some fundamentals. Two random variables (rv's) A and B are *independent* if and only if the outcome of one does not affect the outcome of the other. In that case the *conditional probability* of A given B satisfies $P(A|B) = P(A)$ and also $P(B|A) = P(B)$. Upon restricting the set of elementary events S to the subset B, we formally define the *probability of A given the occurrence of B* to be $P(A|B) = [P(A \cap B)/P(S)]/[P(B)/P(S)] = P(A \cap B)/P(B)$. Similarly, $P(B|A) = P(A \cap B)/P(A)$. Independence therefore implies that $P(A \cap B) = P(A|B)P(B)) = P(A)P(B)$, while *dependence* means that $P(A \cap B) = P(A|B)P(B)$ (and $P(A \cap B) = P(B \cap A) = P(B|A)P(A)$). When A and B are independent, their joint *probability density function* (pdf) satisfies $f_{AB}(a,b) = f_A(a)f_B(b)$, because of derivatives of the cumulative joint probability $F_{AB}(a,b) = P(A \le a$ and $B \le b) = $ [by independence] $P(A \le a)P(B \le b) = F_A(a)F_B(b)$. This implies, upon taking the expected value operation $E[-]$, that

$$E[AB] = E[A]E[B] \tag{1.5}$$

A collection $\{A_i: i \in I\}$ of rv's is independent if and only if every subcollection $\{A_j: j \in J \subset I\}$ satisfies $P(\cap_J A_j) = \Pi_J P(A_j)$, so the joint pdf is $\Pi_J f_j(a_j)$. If A and B are dependent rv's, then the *conditional pdf* of A given B is $f_{A|B}(a|b) = f_{AB}(a,b)/f_B(b)$. This provides the approximate probability (area under the curve over an increment) $f_{A|B}(a|b)\Delta a = P(A \in (a,a + \Delta a)|B = b)$. Generalizations follow the form $f_{ABC|DE}(a,b,c|d,e) = f_{ABCDE}(a,b,c,d,e)/f_{DE}(d,e)$ with analogous approximative interpretation.

The *covariance* of A and B is

$$\sigma_{AB}^2 = E[(A - \mu_A)(B - \mu_B)] \tag{1.6}$$

$$\sigma_{AB}^2 = \iint (a - \mu_A)(b - \mu_B)f_{AB}(a,b)dadb \quad \text{(continuous form)} \tag{1.7}$$

where μ_A is the expected value $E[A]$, and so on. This is the expected value of the product of the variations of the rv's about their means and is a measure of how much A and B go together (same signs) or oppose each other (different signs) and by how much, on the average.

Now let $C_1,..., C_K$ be K classes (subpopulations) of a population P of feature vectors. Given a randomly drawn feature vector $\mathbf{x}$, $P(C_k|\mathbf{x})$ is the probability that $\mathbf{x}$ is from the class C_k, given that the vector $\mathbf{x}$ occurred as the outcome of a random selection. While such probabilities are not known directly, Bayes' result allows their reformulation via

$$P(C_k|\mathbf{x}) = P(\mathbf{x}|C_k)P(C_k)/P(\mathbf{x}) \qquad (1.8)$$

[from $P(C_k|\mathbf{x})P(\mathbf{x}) = P(C_k \cap \mathbf{x}) = P(\mathbf{x}|C_k)P(C_k)$]. $P(C_k)$ is the a priori probability of the occurrence of C_k, while $P(\mathbf{x}|C_k)$ is the a posteriori probability for the particular $\mathbf{x}$ having been drawn from C_k.

Now let $X_1,..., X_N$ be N independent random variables. The *likelihood function* to estimate a parameter α from the outcomes $x_1,..., x_N$ of the N random variables is

$$L(\alpha;x_1,..., x_N) \equiv f_1(x_1;\alpha)f_2(x_2;\alpha) \cdot \cdots \cdot f_N(x_N;\alpha) \qquad (1.9)$$

where $f_n(x_n;\alpha)$ is the pdf for X_n given the parameter α. The *Fisher maximal likelihood estimate* of the parameter is the value of the parameter $\alpha = \alpha^\sim$ such that $\alpha^\sim$ maximizes the likelihood function at $(X_1,..., X_N) = x_1,..., x_N)$. To solve for α at the maximal value of $L(\alpha;x_1,..., x_N)$, we set the derivative of $d\{L(\alpha;x_1,..., x_N)\}/d\alpha$ to zero and solve for $\alpha = \alpha^\sim$. The same maximizing value may be obtained by taking the logarithm $\ln[L(\alpha;x_1,..., x_N)]$ and setting its derivative to zero (the logarithm function is strictly monotonic increasing and thus has the same maximizing value for α). Therefore we put

$$d\{\ln[L(\alpha;x_1,..., x_N)]\}/d\alpha = 0 \qquad (1.10)$$

and solve for α.

As an example of an estimate, suppose that we want to estimate the probability p of success from N random trials, where each trial has probability p of success. Suppose the N trials are run and there are k successes out of N. The binomial probability of k successes out of N independent trials is

$$P(k,N) = N!/[k!(N - k)!]p^k(1 - p)^{N-k}$$

The natural logarithm of this is

$$\{\ln(N!) - \ln[k!(N - k)!]\} + k \ln(p) + (N - k)\ln(1 - p)$$

Upon setting the derivative of this (with respect to the parameter p) to zero, we obtain

$$k(1/p) + (N - k)[-1/(1 - p)] = 0$$

$$k/p = (N - k)/(1 - p), \qquad k(1 - p) = (N - k)p$$

$$k - kp = Np - kp, \qquad k = Np, \qquad p^\sim = k/N$$

In a similar fashion, it can be shown that for N independent outcomes $x_1,..., x_N$ of a Gaussian random variable X, the maximal likelihood estimate for the mean μ is

$$\mu^\sim = (1/N)\sum_{(n=1, N)}x_n$$

Other parameters may be estimated similarly, such as the variance σ^2 of a Gaussian random variable.

Decision Rules

First, let there be two classes C_1 and C_2. A feature vector $\mathbf{x}$ is selected, and we want to know whether it is from C_1 or C_2, where $P(C_1) + P(C_2) = 1$ (it is certain to be drawn from one of the two classes). The *decision rule* is as follows:

$$\text{IF } P(C_1|\mathbf{x}) > P(C_2|\mathbf{x}), \text{ THEN } C_1, \text{ ELSE } C_2 \qquad (1.11)$$

By Equation (1.8), $P(C_1|\mathbf{x}) = P(\mathbf{x}|C_1)P(C_1)/P(\mathbf{x})$ and $P(C_2|\mathbf{x}) = P(\mathbf{x}|C_2)P(C_2)/P(\mathbf{x})$. Thus the rule is

$$\text{IF } P(\mathbf{x}|C_1)P(C_1)/P(\mathbf{x}) > P(\mathbf{x}|C_2)P(C_2)/P(\mathbf{x}), \text{ THEN } C_1, \text{ ELSE } C_2$$

Upon eliminating $P(\mathbf{x})$ on both sides and dividing appropriately, we obtain the *Bayes decision rule*:

$$\text{IF } P(\mathbf{x}|C_1)/P(\mathbf{x}|C_2) > P(C_2)/P(C_1), \text{ THEN } C_1, \text{ ELSE } C_2 \qquad (1.12)$$

The left-hand ratio of Equation (1.11) is the *likelihood ratio* $L(\mathbf{x}) = P(\mathbf{x}|C_1)/P(\mathbf{x}|C_2)$, and the rule is called the *likelihood ratio test*. The value $\tau_{21} = P(C_2)/P(C_1)$ is called the *likelihood threshold* and is assumed to be known a priori (but if not, it can be learned empirically or determined from a priori distributions).

The *probabilities of error* in making a decision are $P(C_2|\mathbf{x})$ when $\mathbf{x} \in C_1$ or $P(C_1|\mathbf{x})$ when $\mathbf{x} \in C_2$. These are the conditional probabilities of choosing the wrong class given $\mathbf{x}$, as shown in Figure 1.7 for the case of a single feature x. The shaded part is the conditional probability of error. We choose the decision threshold τ to be the value (shown in Figure 1.7(a)) that minimizes the probability of error over x. It can be seen from Figure 1.7(b) that if τ were moved, then the error area would be greater. Thus the minimum pdf of the error is $P_E(x) = \min \{P(C_1|x), P(C_2|x)\}$ at each x. Upon applying Bayes' results, this general case becomes

$$P_E(\mathbf{x}) = \min \{P(\mathbf{x}|C_1)P(C_1), P(\mathbf{x}|C_2)P(C_2)\} \qquad (1.13)$$

Now let there be $K > 2$ classes denoted $C_1,..., C_K$. One approach is to do a sequence of pairwise likelihood ratio tests starting with C_1 and C_2, using Inequality (1.12). The winner of each of these tests would then be tested against the next C_k, and so on, until all but one class had been eliminated. Another method is to assign a loss value $L(i, j)$ for the situation where

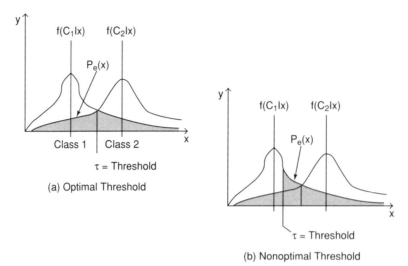

Figure 1.7. The error probability density function of a single feature.

$\mathbf{x}$ is classified in C_i but belongs to C_j. Because there is no loss due to correct classification, we assign $L(i, i) = 0$, but $L(i, j) > 0$ for $j \neq i$. The *conditional expected loss* incurred when assigning $\mathbf{x}$ is

$$R_i(\mathbf{x}) = \sum_{(j=1, K)} L(i, j)P(C_j|\mathbf{x}) \tag{1.14}$$

Using Equation (1.8) and dividing out $P(\mathbf{x})$, this becomes

$$R_i(\mathbf{x}) = \sum_{(j=1, K)} L(i, j)P(\mathbf{x}|C_j)P(C_j) \tag{1.15}$$

where we may use the simplest loss function $L(i, i) = 0$, $L(i, j) = 1$ for $i \neq j$.

The *Bayesian classifier rule* is as follows: when given that $\mathbf{x}$ occurred (as a sample feature vector), compute $R_i(\mathbf{x})$ for $i = 1,..., \mathbf{K}$, and assign $\mathbf{x}$ to C_{k*} where $R_{k*}(\mathbf{x})$ is the minimal conditional expected loss. The values $P(C_k)$ can be estimated by random sampling, determination of the classes, and recording the frequency of occurrence of each class; or they may be known from other information about the population and the proportions of its subpopulations. For further descriptions, see Bow (1984), Duda and Hart (1973), Pao (1989), Therrien (1989), and Tou and Gonzalez (1974). For estimation of the conditional probability density functions, see Therrien (1989, pp. 125–129), or Batchelor (1978).

An *advantage* of Bayesian methods is that the probability of error can be found for each decision. This point should not be overlooked because a decision doesn't mean much unless there is some measure of how good it is. However, their *disadvantages* include the need for certain a priori information or assumptions that may not be available. The a priori distributions $P(C_k)$ over the classes $C_1,..., C_K$, as well as the conditional probabilities $P(\mathbf{x}|C_k)$, must be known, estimated, or assumed, which often presents a difficult task with inappropriate distributions being used. But even if these probabilities are available, statistical methods are essentially linear, which is an insurmountable defect for many difficult classification problems. As we shall see in Chapter 12, a recognizer may also be used as a model of a process where vectors are input and mapped into output vectors or real values. Useful models are usually highly nonlinear, and thus statistical methods such as multiple linear regression are not suitable. We will see that neural networks are especially useful as models.

1.9. Supervised Classification via Minimum Sum Squared Error

Mappings That Minimize the Sum-Squared Error

Suppose that the sample feature vectors $S = \{\mathbf{x}^{(1)},..., \mathbf{x}^{(Q)}\}$ are to be used to train a linear transformation to map any feature vector $\mathbf{x}^{(q)}$ into a vector $\mathbf{y}^{(k)}$ that is an identifier for a class C_k. An example is the mapping $\mathbf{x}^{(q)} \rightarrow \mathbf{y}^{(k)}$ into the nearest center $\mathbf{y}^{(k)}$. This requires supervised training when the user knows the output identifier vector $\mathbf{y}^{(k)}$ into which each sample (exemplar) input feature vector $\mathbf{x}^{(q)}$ must map. A linear transformation of finite-dimensional spaces can be represented by a matrix M, denoted by

$$M\mathbf{x} = \mathbf{y} \qquad (1.16)$$

where $\mathbf{x} = (x_1,..., x_N)$ is the input feature vector, $\mathbf{y} = (y_1,..., y_J)$ is an output vector that represents a class, and M is a $J \times N$ matrix with $N \geq J$.

Given M and $\mathbf{y}$, then $N > J$ implies infinitely many solutions $\mathbf{x}$ to Equation (1.15). Upon multiplying each side of Equation (1.16) by the transpose of the matrix, the square $N \times N$ linear system

$$M^t M\mathbf{x} = M^t\mathbf{y} \qquad (1.17)$$

results. If $M^t M$ is not singular, then a solution $\mathbf{x}$ can be found. One solution method uses the *pseudo-inverse* $M^\# = (M^t M)^{-1}M^t$ and premultiplies each side of Equation (1.17) by $(M^t M)^{-1}$ (or Equation (1.16) by $M^\#$) to obtain

$$\mathbf{x} = (M^t M)^{-1}(M^t M)\mathbf{x} = (M^t M)^{-1}M^t\mathbf{y} = M^\#\mathbf{y}$$

This useful technique solves for an unknown $\mathbf{x}$, however, when M is known. In our usual recognition situation, we know $\mathbf{x}$ and $\mathbf{y}$, but not the mapping M. We seek to find a mapping of input vectors into identifiers.

Now we start a new derivation. We are given Q sample feature vectors $\mathbf{x}^{(q)} = (x_1^{(q)},..., x_N^{(q)})$ and a single output real value $y^{(q)}$ for each q that identifies a class. Figure 1.8 demonstrates the situation. Upon arranging the input features into a matrix X as rows, X then becomes an $N \times Q$ matrix of input values. A set of weights $\mathbf{w} = (w_1,..., w_N)$ then performs the linear mapping

$$y^{(q)} = \sum_{(n=1, N)} x_n^{(q)} w_n \qquad (1.18)$$

The weights $w_1,..., w_N$ shown in the figure map each input vector $\mathbf{x}^{(q)}$ into an output

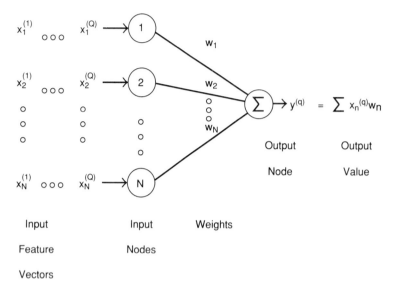

$x_1^{(1)}$ o o o $x_1^{(Q)}$ → ① w_1

$x_2^{(1)}$ o o o $x_2^{(Q)}$ → ② w_2

Σ → $y^{(q)}$ = $\sum x_n^{(q)} w_n$

w_N

Output   Output

Node   Value

$x_N^{(1)}$ o o o $x_N^{(Q)}$ → ⓝ

Input   Input   Weights

Feature   Nodes

Vectors

Figure 1.8.   Training a linear classifier via minimum mean-squared error.

value for a class. Therefore, the weight vector $\mathbf{w} = (w_1,..., w_N)$ must be found (learned) so that it maps the inputs $\mathbf{x}$ into the identifying real value $y^{(q)}$ for the qth class. The algorithm of Widrow–Hoff (Widrow and Hoff, 1960) trains a linear recognizer by minimizing the total sum-squared error function E to obtain the weight vector $\mathbf{w}$. The total sum-squared error (SSE) function to be minimized by adjusting the weights is

$$E(\mathbf{w}) = \|X^t\mathbf{w} - \mathbf{y}\|^2 = \textstyle\sum_{(q=1,Q)} (\sum_{(n=1,\,N)} [x_n^{(q)} w_n - y^{(q)}]^2 \qquad (1.19)$$

The minimization starts with an initial weight vector $\mathbf{w}^{(0)}$ and then moves from any current point $\mathbf{w}^{(r)}$ in the direction $-\nabla E(\mathbf{w}^{(r)})$ of *steepest descent* to find the next approximation $\mathbf{w}^{(r+1)}$ to the solution. In place of Newton's method of the Hessian matrix of second partial derivatives, we use a *step size*, or *learning rate*, $\rho^{(r)}$ on each descent step. This step size must eventually decrease toward zero to achieve convergence as $r \to \infty$. Once the minimizing weight vector $\mathbf{w}_{\min}$ is found, the recognizer/classifier has *learned* classes and is ready for the operational mode. In the operational mode, any input feature vector $\mathbf{x}^{(q)}$ is mapped by $\mathbf{w}_{\min}$ into a y-value that is closest to a $y^{(k)}$ that represents a class, and the input feature vector is thereby classified as belonging to Class k.

This method does not find an exact unique solution (one exists when $N = Q$ and X is nonsingular), usually. However, it finds a solution that minimizes the total sum-squared error. If we were to divide the sum-squared error by Q, then it would be the mean-squared error. The method of minimum mean-squared error was initiated by Gauss circa 1795 and published by both him (Gauss, 1809) and Legendre (Legendre, 1810). It has been heavily used in many fields in recent decades to obtain MMSE (minimum mean-squared error) and SSE (sum-squared error) solutions. The SSE $\sum_{(j=1,\,J)}(z_j - y_j)^2$, the MSE (mean-squared error) $(1/J)\sum_{(j=1,\,J)}(z_j - y_j)^2$, and the RMSE (root mean-squared error) $\{(1/J)\sum_{(j=1,\,J)}(z_j - y_j)^2\}^{1/2}$ are all related in that the minimization of one minimizes the others.

A Minimum Sum-Squared Error Algorithm

Inputs: {sample feature vectors $\{\mathbf{x}^{(1)},..., \mathbf{x}^{(Q)}\}$; output vector $\mathbf{y} = (y^{(1)},..., y^{(Q)})$, where the ouput $y^{(q)}$ is the numerical class identifier; an initial vector $\mathbf{w}^{(0)}$ of weights; number of iterations I; and initial stepsize $\rho^{(0)}$}

Outputs: {weight vector $\mathbf{w}^{(j)}$ at ith iteration that approximates the required transformation}

Step 1: /Initialize the iteration number/
  $r \leftarrow 0$; input I;

Step 2: /Compute the sum-squared error and new weights in the direction of steepest descent/
  $E(\mathbf{w}) \leftarrow \|X^t\mathbf{w} - \mathbf{y}\|^2$
  $\mathbf{w} \leftarrow \mathbf{w} - \rho\nabla E(\mathbf{w})$

Step 3: /Update iteration number and stepsize ρ/
  $r \leftarrow r + 1$;
  $\rho \leftarrow \text{Stepsize}(\rho)$; /Function to adjust stepsize/
  if $(r > I)$ or $(\|\mathbf{w} - \mathbf{w}\|_2 < \in)$, then stop
  else goto Step 2

Note that whether or not the input feature vectors $\{\mathbf{x}^{(q)}\}$ are actually linearly separable, this learning method will attempt to linearly separate them, and so errors may result. The output of this network may be thresholded, as shown in Figure 1.9 (Fu, 1982), in which case

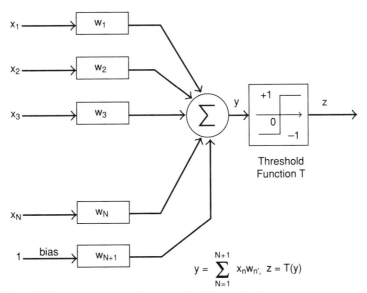

$$y = \sum_{N=1}^{N+1} x_n w_{n'}, \quad z = T(y)$$

Figure 1.9. A linear classifier network with threshold.

it recognizes an input feature vector as being in Class 1 or Class 2, respectively, by outputting a value of -1 or 1. If there were n thresholded outputs, each with the same inputs as shown in the figure and its own set of weights, then the recognizer would be able to linearly separate 2^n different classes according to the binary combination of n output components. Note that there is an extra input of 1 in Figure 1.9, which is multiplied by the weight w_{N+1} that sets the threshold. This is the c value in the linear equation for the separating hyperplane of Equation (0.2b), which takes the general form

$$w_1 x_1 + \cdots + w_N x_N + w_{N+1} = 0 \tag{1.20}$$

The incoming x_{N+1} value is always 1, and the weight w_{N+1} can be changed to an appropriate value.

Exercises

1.1. Write a step-by-step algorithm in pseudo-language for the k-means algorithm. Use a flow chart to lay out the steps for a better understanding of the process. How can one check to determine whether or not it is converging?

1.2. Develop a computational way to measure the convergence of the k-means algorithm [consider the change in the total sum-squared error or the changes in the centers].

1.3. In the threshold clustering algorithm, add rules to vary τ and p so that all sample feature vectors will be assigned to classes in a way that will tend to minimize the sum-squared or mean-squared error?

1.4. Draw a flow chart to map out the intricacies of the Batchelor–Wilkins maximin algorithm. Convert it into a complete detailed algorithm.

1.5. Write a computer program that implements the k-means algorithm. Execute it on the following data: (2.1, 1.2), (2.5, 2.2), (3.3, 2.4), (4.1, 1.1), (4.8, 0.5), (5.3, 1.0), (2.9, 3.0), (4.5, 1.2), (2.1, 3.0), (2.5, 3.4). Now execute it on the data in the reverse order. Are the number of iterations the same? Plot the clusters in the plane.

1.6. Map out the ISODATA algorithm completely with a detailed flow chart.

1.7. Modify the ISODATA algorithm so some of the parameters adjust themselves to make the classification better according to minimum total mean-squared error.

1.8. Describe a modification to the k-means algorithm that permits K to be determined automatically.

1.9. Describe in detail, an algorithm analogous to the k-means algorithm, but instead of computing new centers using averages, find new centers using medians. A median center of a cluster will be a vector that has components that are the componentwise medians. What advantages does this k-medians algorithm have over the k-means? Would this center minimize the mean-squared error over a cluster?

1.10. Make a modified k-means algorithm flow chart to permit elongated clusters rather than the usual hyperballs.

1.11. Write a computer program to implement the *dynamic clusters* method and run it with the data from Exercise 1.5 above. Use $N_1 = N_2 = \cdots = N_K = 3$ for the number of vectors in each core. How do the results compare with the results of Exercise 1.5? Plot the points in the plane for the clusters and show the cores.

1.12. The feature vectors $\mathbf{x}^{(1)} = (0,0)$, $\mathbf{x}^{(2)} = (0,1)$, $\mathbf{x}^{(3)} = (1,0)$, and $\mathbf{x}^{(4)} = (1,1)$ are to be classified such that the first three are to map into $y^{(1)} = 0$ and the last one is to map into $y^{(2)} = 1$. Set up a linear classifier such as is shown in Figure 1.9 and find the weights (w_1, w_2) to perform the mapping. Now use a threshold that outputs either 0 or 1. Draw a unit square graph with a grid of 0.2 squares and plot on each grid crossing point an "o" or "x" to signify whether that point belongs to Class 1 or Class 2, respectively. Explain the results.

1.13. Plot the following feature vectors in the plane: (1,6), (2,7), (2,6), (3,4), (3,3), (2,3), (2,5), (2,4), (1,5), (1,4), (8,6), (8,5), (7,4), (7,5), (5,1), (6,2), (6,7), (7,2), 7,3), (8,3), (8,4), (6,1), (7,7), (7,1). Connect all points with lines that are within a distance of τ from each other, for a suitable value of τ. How many clusters are obtained? What are the advantages of this method? What are some disadvantages? Must the clusters fall into disjoint hyperballs? How close should vectors in different clusters be permitted to be to each other (or does this matter)?

1.14. A similarity matrix for a sampled set of features and a given threshold τ is given below. Go through the graph similarity matrix algorithm step-by-step and determine the clusters.

| | | | Column | | | |
Row	1	2	3	4	5	6
1	1	0	1	1	0	0
2	0	1	0	0	0	1
3	1	0	1	0	0	0
4	1	0	0	1	1	0
5	0	0	0	1	1	0
6	0	1	0	0	0	1

1.15. Use a graph-theoretic algorithm to cluster a sample of feature vectors, and then invent a method for choosing a core of two or three vectors from each cluster. Then reassign the feature vectors to clusters via minimum sum of distances to the core vectors. What are its advantages and disadvantages?

1.16. Let it be given that empirical studies have shown (from sampling) that an object drawn from a population has probability $P(C_1) = 0.7$ of being from Class 1. A decision is to be made as to the class from a single feature component x. The probability distributions for both classes are Gaussian, with respective means and standard deviations of $\mu_1 = 5$ and $\sigma_1 = 3$, and $\mu_2 = 12$ and $\sigma_2 = 2$. Suppose that an x is selected at random, and its feature value is $x = 9$. Sketch the probability function for an error in the classification. Classify the object using a Bayesian decision rule.

References

Ball, G. H., and Hall, D. J. (1965), ISODATA, A Novel Method of Data Analysis and Pattern Classification, Stanford Research Institute Technical Report (NTIS AD699616), Stanford, CA.

Ball, G. H., and Hall, D. J. (1966), ISODATA: an iterative method of multivariate data analysis and pattern classification, *Proceedings of the IEEE International Communications Conference*, Philadelphia.

Ball, G. H., and Hall, D. J. (1967), A clustering technique for summarizing multivariate data, *Behav. Sci.*, vol. 12, 153–155.

Batchelor, B. G. (1978), Classification and data analysis in vector spaces, in *Pattern Recognition*, edited by B. G. Batchelor, Plenum, New York, pp. 67–116.

Batchelor, B. G., and Wilkins, B. R. (1969), Method for location of clusters of patterns to initialize a learning machine, *Electron. Lett.*, vol. 5, no. 20, 481–483.

Bow, Sing-Tze (1984), *Pattern Recognition*, Marcel Dekker, New York.

Cover, T. M., and Wagner, T. J. (1976), Topics in statistical pattern recognition, in *Digital Pattern Recognition*, edited by K. S. Fu, Springer-Verlag, Berlin, 15–46.

Davies, D. L., and Bouldin, D. W. (1979), A cluster separation measure, *IEEE Trans. Pattern Anal. Mach. Intell.*, vol. 1, no. 2, 224–227.

Diday, E. (1973), The dynamic clusters method in non-hierarchical clustering, *Int. J. Comput. Inf. Sci.*, vol. 2, no. 1, 61–68.

Duda, R. O., and Hart, P. E. (1973), *Pattern Classification and Scene Analysis*, Wiley, New York.

Fu, K. S. (1982), Introduction, page 1–13, in *Applications of Pattern Recognition*, edited by K. S. Fu, CRC Press, Boca Raton, FL.

Gauss, K. F. (1809), *Theoria Motus Corporum Coelestium in Sectionibus Conicus Solem Ambientum*, F. Perthes & I. H. Besser, Hamburg (translation: Dover, New York, 1963).

Legendre, A. M. (1810), Methodes des mondres quares, pour trouver le milieu le plus probable entre les resultats de differences observations, *Mem. Inst. France*, 149–154.

MacQueen, J. (1967), Some methods for classification and analysis of multivariate data, *Proc. 5th Berkeley Symposium on Probability and Statistics*, University of California Press, Berkeley.

Mizoguchi, R., and Kakusho, O. (1978), Hierarchical clustering algorithm based on k-nearest neighbors, *4th International Joint Conference on Pattern Recognition*, Kyoto, Japan, 314–316.

Pao, Yoh-Han (1989), *Adaptive Pattern Recognition and Neural Networks*, Addison-Wesley, Reading, MA.

Therrien, C. W. (1989), *Decision, Estimation, and Classification*, Wiley, New York.

Tou, J. T. (1979), DYNOC—a dynamic optimal cluster seeking technique, *Int J. Comput. Inf. Sci.*, vol. 8, no. 6, 541–547.

Tou, J. T., and Gonzalez, R. C. (1974), *Pattern Recognition Principles*, Addison-Wesley, Reading, MA.

Widrow, B., and Hoff, M. E. (1960), *Western Electric Show and Convention Record*, IRE, part 4, 96–104.

Chapter 2

Structural Pattern Recognition

This chapter provides an introduction to the syntactic approach to pattern recognition, which is elegant and has great potential.

2.1. Structure in Objects

Decision-theoretic methods are essentially linear and rely on quantitative measurements. To demonstrate that these are not always sufficient, we pose an example (Miclet, 1986). Suppose that approximate equilateral triangles and squares of various sizes and locations in the plane are to be classified and, further, that the base is always horizontal, as shown in Figure 2.1. Only the boundary is to be considered, and because of the variable size, it is clear that metrics are not useful here, but the structure is critical. Starting at the right side of the base, a circumlocution reveals that there are either two oblique angles or two pairs of parallel lines that are mutually perpendicular, and that all lines are about the same length. The structure, rather than the metrics, determine the classes in this example. The plan is to extract the structure and record it in some way so it can be compared to that of other objects for the purpose of classification. The task is to code the structure as symbols, concatenate the symbols into strings (sentences) in some order, and then compare the strings in some manner to determine when two are equivalent or different. Standard references for structural pattern recognition are (Fu, 1974; Fu, 1982).

2.2. Alphabets and Strings

An *alphabet* is a finite set Z of symbols, called *letters*, which we designate here by *a,b,c*, and so on. A *string* over Z is a finite ordered list of letters from Z that is formed as follows: (i) Letters from Z may be *concatenated*—that is, placed side by side horizontally; (ii) any

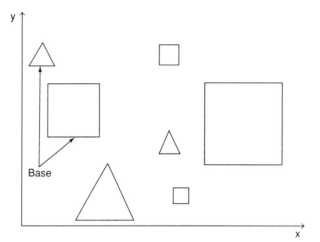

Figure 2.1. Classes of triangles and squares.

letter in Z may be used any number of times; (iii) other strings may be concatenated; and (iv) the *empty string* $\emptyset$ that consists of no letters is also a valid string. Strings over Z are also called *sentences*. The set of all strings over Z is designated by Z^*. Two strings x and y in Z^* may be concatenated to form the new string xy or yx. The string y is a *substring* of the string x whenever $x = uyv$, where u and v are strings (possibly the empty string). We call u a *prefix* string and v a *suffix* string of y with respect to x. The *length* of a string x is the number of letters it contains, denoted by $|x|$.

Example 2.1. String Concatenations

Let $Z = \{a, b\}$, $x = abaaabba$, and $y = aab$. Then $|x| = 8$, $|y| = 3$, y is a substring of x, $u = aba$ is a prefix of y, and $v = ba$ is a suffix of y. The strings of all concatenations of x and y are: $xy = abaaabbaaab$ and $yx = aabababaaabba$.

Classification requires that the structural features of an object be represented as letters in some order that is a blueprint, or template, for the object. Any two strings x and y must be comparable according to some measure. Such comparison may merely check to see that x and y are equal—that is, have the same letters in the same positions (and thus have the same length also). It is sometimes necessary to know whether one string is a substring of another one. For such algorithms, see Miclet (1986), Boyer and Moore (1977), or Findler and van Leeuwen (1979).

2.3. Languages and Grammars

Any subset $L \subset Z^*$ of sentences, where Z^* is the set of all strings (sentences) over the alphabet Z, is called a *language* over the alphabet Z. Two sets of strings L and M may also be elementwise concatenated via $LM = \{xy: x \in L, y \in M\}$. For any set of strings $L \subset Z^*$, we make the following definitions: (i) $L^o = \{\varnothing\}$ (the empty string set); (ii) $L^1 = L$; (iii) $L^2 = LL$; (iv) $L^n = LL^{n-1}$; (v) $L^* = \cup_{(n=0,\infty)} L^n$; and (vi) $L^+ = \cup_{(n=1,\infty)} L^n$.

A *grammar* is a tuplet $\mathbf{G} = (Z, V, S, P)$, where Z is an alphabet of letters and V is an auxiliary alphabet of letter-valued variables. S is the *start* variable from V and P is a set of *production rules* that determines the construction of sentences, which includes intermediate "strings" composed of letters and letter valued variables. The rules provide a means of constructing strings from letters (from Z) and letter-valued variables (from V). S must be used to start any such string. A sentence cannot contain any letter-valued variables from V, so they must all be replaced with letters in intermediate "strings" according to rules in P. For this reason, we call the variables in V the *nonterminals* and call the letters from Z the *terminals*. Because sentences can have only terminals, P must have at least one rule that maps each nonterminal into only terminals. P must also have at least one starting rule that maps S into some other string of terminals and nonterminals. We use uppercase letters such as A, B, and so on, to designate nonterminals (variables) in V, and we use lowercase letters such as a, b, c, and so on, to denote letters (terminals) in the alphabet Z. We use Greek letters α, β, and so on, to designate *intermediary* strings of terminals (letters) and nonterminals (variables).

Example 2.2. Tou–Gonzalez Productions

Let $Z = \{a, b\}$, $V = \{S\}$, and $P = \{S \rightarrow aSb, S \rightarrow ab\}$. Then the grammar $\mathbf{G} = \{Z, V, S, P\}$ generates a language $L = L(\mathbf{G})$ according to P (Tou and Gonzalez, 1974). The intermediary strings that contain nonterminals as well as terminals have the form (i) aSb, (ii) $a(aSb)b = a^2Sb^2$, and (iii) a^nSb^n, $n \geq 1$. These are formed from the first production rule in P according to the mappings $S \rightarrow aSb$, $aSb \rightarrow a(aSb)b$, and so on. The second production rule in P allows the formation of sentences in L of the form (i) $S \rightarrow ab$, (ii) $aSb \rightarrow a(ab)b = a^2b^2$, and (iii) $a^{n-1}Sb^{n-1} \rightarrow a^nb^n$, $n \geq 2$. Thus the language $L(\mathbf{G})$ over Z generated by the grammar $\mathbf{G}$ contains only sentences of the form a^nb^n, $n \geq 1$.

Example 2.3. Sentence Construction

Let $\mathbf{G} = \{Z, V, S, P\}$, where $Z = \{a, b\}$, $V = \{A, S\}$, and $P = \{S \rightarrow aS, S \rightarrow bA, bA \rightarrow bbA, A \rightarrow a\}$, as given in Miclet (1986). An examination of the rules shows that the intermediary strings generated by $\mathbf{G}$ are (i) aS, (ii) bA, (iii) aaS, (iv) bbA, (v) a^nS, $n \geq 1$, (vi) b^nA, $n \geq 1$, and (vii) a^nbA, $n \geq 1$. Upon applying the last rule that takes nonterminals into terminals, we obtain the following sentences: (i) $aS \rightarrow abA \rightarrow aba$; (ii) $S \rightarrow bA \rightarrow ba$; (iii) $S \rightarrow aS \rightarrow a(aS) \rightarrow \cdots \rightarrow a^nS \rightarrow a^nbA \rightarrow a^nba$, $n \geq 1$; and (iv) $S \rightarrow bA \rightarrow b(bA) \rightarrow \cdots \rightarrow b^nA \rightarrow b^na$, $n \geq 1$. Figure 2.2 shows the construction of all sentences in the language over $\mathbf{G}$, denoted $L(\mathbf{G})$.

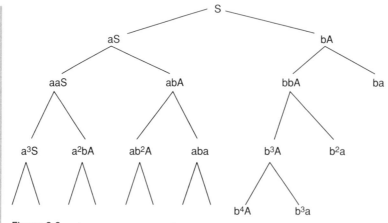

Figure 2.2. A sentence construction tree.

Example 2.4. A Generated Language

The production rules are given by Miclet (1986) to be $P = \{S \rightarrow aSBA, S \rightarrow abA, AB \rightarrow BA, bB \rightarrow bb, bA \rightarrow bc, cA \rightarrow cc, aB \rightarrow ab\}$, where $Z = \{a, b, c\}$, and $V = \{A,B,S\}$. The application of the rules yields, for example: $S \rightarrow aSBA \rightarrow aabABA \rightarrow aabBAA \rightarrow aabbAA \rightarrow aabbcA \rightarrow aabbcc$. All sentences generated are of the form $a^n b^n c^n$, $n \geq 1$, and so the language generated by **G** is $L(\mathbf{G}) = \{a^n b^n c^n : n \geq 1\}$. A structural interpretation can be made, as shown in Figure 2.3, where a, b, and c represent horizontal, upward oblique, and downward oblique lines, respectively, that are multiples of some basic unit.

In the *Chomsky hierarchy*, a grammar $\mathbf{G} = \{Z, V, S, P\}$ is *regular* whenever its production rules have the forms $A \rightarrow aB$ and/or $A \rightarrow a$, for any nonterminals (variables) $A, B \in V$ and any terminal (letter) $a \in Z$. In this case, $L(\mathbf{G})$ is said to be a *regular language*. For example (Miclet, 1986), let $Z = \{a, b\}$, $V = \{S, A\}$, and $P = \{S \rightarrow aS, S \rightarrow bA, A \rightarrow bA, A \rightarrow a\}$. Then $S \rightarrow aS \rightarrow a(aS) \rightarrow aabA \rightarrow aab(bA) \rightarrow aabba$. Continuing, we obtain all sentence forms $a^m b^n a$, $m \geq 0$, $n \geq 1$.

A *context-free* grammar is a grammar where the production rules in P have the form $A \rightarrow \alpha$, where A is any nonterminal in V and α is any intermediary string of terminals and nonterminals or terminals; that is, $\alpha \in (Z \cup V)^*$. The variable A may be replaced by a string regardless of its position or situation in a string, and hence the name follows. A *context-sensitive* grammar has productions of the form $\alpha_1 A \alpha_2 \rightarrow \alpha_1 \beta \alpha_2$, where α_1, α_2, and β are any intermediary strings of terminals and nonterminals in $(Z \cup V)^*$ or sentences of terminals. Here it is seen that the variable A cannot be replaced by a string unless it is in the proper context—that is, between α_1 and α_2. This means that for any production $\alpha \rightarrow \beta$, the number of symbols in β cannot be less than that of α. In other words, there can be no rules that reduce the length of a string from the combined alphabet $Z \cup V$.

An *unrestricted* grammar has productions of the form $\alpha \rightarrow \beta$ for any strings α and β of

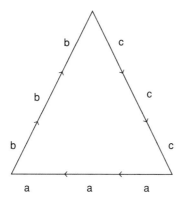

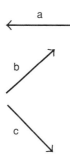

Figure 2.3. Structural interpretation of equilateral triangles.

terminals and nonterminals. Such a grammar is also called *recursively enumerable*. The largest class is unrestricted. The hierarchy is as follows: regular $\subset$ context-free $\subset$ context sensitive $\subset$ unrestricted.

Example 2.2 is a context-free grammar $\mathbf{G} = \{Z, V, S, P\}$, where $Z = \{a, b\}$, $V = \{S\}$, and the productions are $P = \{S \rightarrow ab, S \rightarrow aSb\}$. As we saw above, $L(\mathbf{G}) = \{a^n b^n : n \geq 1\}$.

2.4. Syntactic Pattern Recognition

The word "syntactic" is an adjective that pertains to the noun "sentence" that we know from English grammar. To help us formulate the syntactic pattern recognition problem, we suppose that the objects in a population have features that can be put into a one-to-one correspondence with the letters, or terminals, in an alphabet Z. Then each pattern can be considered to be a sentence in Z^*.

Let S_1 and S_2 be two classes of objects; further, let the objects in S_1 be represented by sentences in $L_1 = L(\mathbf{G}_1)$ (generated by $\mathbf{G}_1$). Similarly, let objects in S_2 be represented by sentences in $L_2 = L(\mathbf{G}_2)$. When an object is processed and converted into a representative sentence x of terminals (letters) representing structural features, it is checked, in turn, against $L(\mathbf{G}_k)$ for both $k = 1$ and $k = 2$. The feature sentence x is parsed to determine to which class it belongs. One way to parse the sentences is to use a finite state machine $L(\mathbf{G})$—that is, a finite automaton—to decide.

2.5. **Automata and Recognizers**

A *finite automaton* (or *finite state machine*) is a machine with memory that stores a state s_k, receives input letters, changes its state as a function of the current state and the current input, and outputs a letter. Figure 2.4 presents a block diagram of an automaton. The abstracted machine consists of a tuple $(Z, Q, \delta, \tau, q_0, Q_f)$, where Z is the alphabet of input/output letters, Q is the set of (memory) *states*, q_0 is the *initial state*, $Q_f \subset Q$ is the set of *final states*, δ is the *transition function* $\delta{:}ZxQ \rightarrow Q$ that maps an input letter and current state into a new state, and τ is the *output function* $\tau{.}QxZ \rightarrow Z$ that assigns an output letter that is dependent upon the current state and the input letter.

When the output is omitted, then we call the automaton a *finite state recognizer* (Kohavi, 1978). If the input is omitted, then the machine is called a *finite state generator*. From here forward, we are concerned with finite state recognizers. A sentence enters the automaton from the left, one letter at each discrete tick of a clock. The machine starts in the initial state q_0, but each time a letter enters the machine, the state changes. After having read in an entire sentence, the machine may be in a final state, in which case we say the machine *accepts* the sentence; or it may be in any other state, in which case we say that the machine *rejects* the sentence. If the machine accepts a sentence, then it classifies it as belonging to the class that the machine recognizes.

A *state transition diagram* is a graph that depicts the states as nodes, the long arrows as transitions, or changes of states, and a short arrow entering the initial state. Figure 2.5 presents a state transition diagram that describes a machine with four states, $s_1,..., s_4$. The letter attached to each transition arrow is the letter that entered the machine as input to cause the transition from the previous state to the new state. It is convenient to think of the sentence as being a sequence of letters stored on a tape that is read by a read-head. The hatched nodes in the figure represent the final, or accepting, states, while both the initial state s_1 and the remaining s_3 are rejecting states.

Let α designate an automaton that is a finite state recognizer. The set of sentences that α accepts make up a language $L(\alpha)$. There is a direct correspondence between a regular grammar and a finite state automaton: (i) $A \rightarrow aB$ corresponds to a transition from state s_A

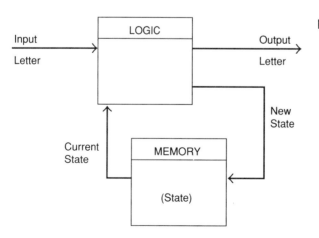

Figure 2.4.   An automaton.

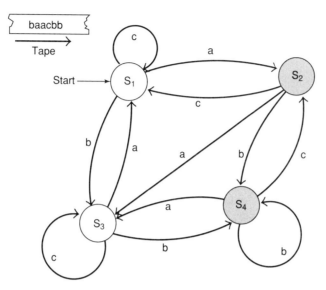

Figure 2.5. A state transition diagram.

to state s_B upon being currently in state s_A and receiving the letter a as input; and (ii) $A \rightarrow$ a corresponds to a transition from state s_A to a final state $s_F \in Q_f$ (Q_f is the set of final states).

Example 2.5.   State Transition Diagram with Reject State

Define the grammar $\mathbf{G} = (Z,V,S,P)$, where $Z = \{a,b,c\}$, $V = \{S,A\}$, and $P = \{S \rightarrow aS, S \rightarrow bA, A \rightarrow bA, A \rightarrow aA, A \rightarrow c\}$. Then $L(\mathbf{G})$ is a regular language. The state transition diagram for the corresponding finite state recognizer is given in Figure 2.6. Note that there was no rule that covered the arrival of letter c as input while the system was in state S. We have therefore specified a reject state G (or s_G) from which there is no return. F (or s_F) is the final state that accepts (or recognizes) an input sentence.

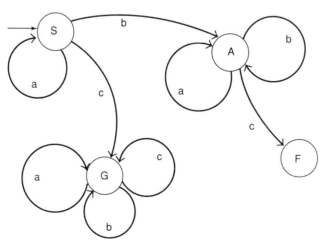

Figure 2.6. An automaton for an example of a regular grammar.

We consider only automata for which all states are accessible and for which all transitions are specified; that is, the transition function $\delta(a,q)$ defines a state in Q for every *configuration* $(a,q) \in ZxQ$. If an automaton is not completely specified, we can always adjoin a nonfinal state s_G, known as the *garbage state* (Miclet, 1986), and complete the specification by defining (i) $\delta(a,q) = s_G$ for all unspecified configurations (a, q) and (ii) $\delta(x, s_G) = s_G$ for all $x \in Z$.

The concept of automaton can be extended. Automata of the form $\mathbf{G} = (Z, Q, \delta, \tau, q_0, Q_f)$ as described above are called *deterministic* automata. If δ is allowed to become a multivalued mapping, the resulting structure is called a *nondeterministic* automaton. This means that for at least one or more configurations $(a,q) \in ZxQ$, the value $\delta(a,q)$ is set valued. For example, $\delta(a,q) = \{q_1, q_2, q_3\}$, which is depicted in Figure 2.7. This means that there may be *ambiguous* strings—that is, strings that can be accepted in more than one way (there are multiple transition paths). Automata derived from regular languages need not be deterministic, which means that there may be ambiguous strings.

2.6. Stochastic Automata

A *stochastic grammar* is a tuple $\mathbf{G}_s = (Z, V, S, P, \mathbf{p})$, where Z is the alphabet of letters (terminals), V is a set of variables (nonterminals), S is the starting nonterminal in V, P is a set of production rules $\{R_1, ..., R_N\}$, and $\mathbf{p} = (p_1, ..., p_N)$ is a vector of probabilities such that p_n is the probability that rule R_n is applied. A *stochastic language* $L_s = L(\mathbf{G}_s)$ is the set of all sentences generated by a stochastic grammar $\mathbf{G}_s$. A probability $p(x)$ is associated with each sentence $x \in L_s$, so $L_s = \{(x, p(x)): x \in L(\mathbf{G}_s)$ and $p(x)$ is the probability of x being generated$\}$. The rules in a stochastic grammar are written with the probability indicated on the right of the arrow; for example, $A \rightarrow (p) aB$.

Example 2.6. A Stochastic Language

Let $Z = \{a,b\}$, $V = \{S\}$, and $P = \{S \rightarrow (p)\ aSb, S \rightarrow (1 - p)\ ab\}$, as given by Tou and Gonzalez (1974). Then the intermediary strings in $(Z \cup V)^*$ have the form aSb, $a(aSb)b = a^2Sb^2$, and a^nSb^n. The probabilities are, respectively, p, p^2, and p^n $(n \geq 1)$. It is clear that the sentences in L_s have the form $(a^nb^n, p^{n-1}(1 - p))$. This follows from $a^{n-1}Sb^{n-1} \rightarrow (1 - p)\ a^nb^n$.

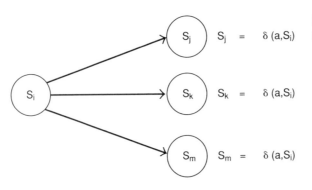

Figure 2.7. A multivalued transition function.

$S_j = \delta(a,S_i)$

$S_k = \delta(a,S_i)$

$S_m = \delta(a,S_i)$

A *stochastic finite automaton* is a tuple $\boldsymbol{\alpha}_s = (Z, Q, M, \mathbf{p}_o, Q_f)$, where Z is the alphabet, Q is the set of states, $Q_f \subset Q$ is a set of final states, $\mathbf{p}_o$ is an initial set of probabilities for the initial state, and M is a probability mapping that takes the form of an $N \times N$ matrix of probabilities. $M(a) = [m_{ij}(a)]$, where $m_{ij}(a)$ is the probability of a transition from state s_i to s_j upon receiving the letter a as input. Obviously, $M(\varnothing) = I_N$ (the $N \times N$ identity matrix), where $\varnothing$ is the empty sentence. It follows that $M(xy) = M(x)M(y)$ for sentences x and y. The stochastic language accepted by $\boldsymbol{\alpha}_s$ is $L(\boldsymbol{\alpha}_s) = \{(x, p(x)): x \in Z^* \text{ and } p(x) = \mathbf{p}_o M(x) > 0\}$. When x is ambiguous, then $p(x) = \sum_i p^{(i)}(x)$, where $p^{(i)}(x)$ is the probability of forming x in one particular way.

A fundamental result (see Miclet, 1986) is that *every stochastic regular grammar can be associated with a stochastic finite automaton that accepts the same language.* To arrive at the associated automaton, we add two states: (i) a final state F (s_F) that corresponds to production rules of the form $A \rightarrow a$ and (ii) a garbage state G (denoted s_G) for which probabilities must be established so as to make the matrix M a stochastic matrix (rows sum to 1). The probabilities can be learned from frequencies of occurrence (see Tou and Gonzalez, 1974) as sampled over a finite time interval.

2.7. Generating Grammars for Classes: Grammatical Inference

Grammatical inference is a process of determining a grammar **G** from a set I of exemplar sentences. The concept originated in Chomsky (1957) and was further developed in Chomsky (1965). Learning classes from a sample of patterns is the most difficult part of syntactical pattern recognition. Given a finite sample I of strings of letters from an alphabet Z, the inference problem is to find a grammar **G** that will accept I—that is, $I \subset L(\mathbf{G})$. Fu and Booth (1975) and Gold (1978) address this problem, as does Miclet (1986). Tou and Gonzalez (1974) also provide an algorithm due to Feldman. There are almost always a very large number of grammars that contain I. A major problem is that the different classes may overlap, so that multiple grammars (or automata) that recognize different classes would accept the same sentence. A distance function may be used to determine the distance between a sentence and the regular grammars, and a classification may be made via minimal distance (see Miclet, 1986). Figure 2.8 shows the inference process.

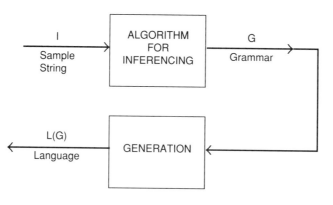

Figure 2.8. Grammatical inference.

Example 2.7.   Possible Grammars for *I* = **{***ab***}**

Given the single sentence *ab* from *Z* = {*a,b*}, any of the following production rule sets form a grammar whose language contains that sentence (Fu, 1994, p. 382).

$$P_1: \qquad S \rightarrow ab$$

$$P_2: \qquad S \rightarrow AB, A \rightarrow a, B \rightarrow b$$

$$P_3: \qquad S \rightarrow Ab, A \rightarrow a$$

$$P_4: \qquad S \rightarrow aB, B \rightarrow b$$

The simplest (minimal) set of productions is {P_1} and this generates a minimal grammar.

A useful method of grammatical inference on a sample of strings *I* is the *maximal canonical grammar*, MCG(*I*), which infers a grammar with language *L*(**G**) = *I* (see the next example).

Example 2.8.   A Maximal Canonical Grammar

Let a sample of strings be *I* = {*ab, abc, abbc, bbcb*}. The MCG(*I*) is represented by the maximal canonical automaton on *I*, MCA(*I*), as displayed in Figure 2.9. The final states are s_2, s_5, s_9, and s_{13}.

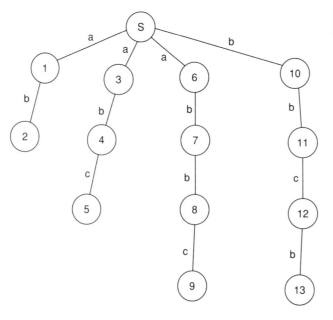

Figure 2.9.   A maximal canonical automaton.

A sample of strings I is structurally complete with respect to a grammar $\mathbf{G} = (Z, V, S, P)$ whenever (i) $I \subset L(\mathbf{G})$, (ii) I is over alphabet Z, and (iii) every rule in P is used at least once in the generation of strings in I. The grammatical inference problem can be stated as follows: (a) Find $\mathbf{G}$ such that $I \subset L(\mathbf{G})$; and (ii) I is structurally complete with respect to $\mathbf{G}$.

Proposition: (Miclet, 1979). A necessary and sufficient condition for an automaton $\boldsymbol{\alpha}$ to be the solution of the inference problem of $I \subset L(\mathbf{G})$ and for I to be structurally complete with respect to $\mathbf{G}$ is that $\boldsymbol{\alpha}$ be derived from the MCA(I). The number of solutions when I contains N elements is the number of partitions of N elements (for $N = 20$, this is about 10^{15}, which necessitates the use of heuristic methods).

According to (Fu, 1994), grammatical inference can be viewed as search through the rule space of all context-free grammars for a grammar that is consistent with the training instances I. Gold (1967) proved that if a program is given an infinite sequence of *positive* examples (sentences that are known to belong to a language), then the program cannot determine a grammar for the correct context-free language in any given finite time. On the one hand, there is the universal language that contains all possible sentences, while on the other hand there is the minimal language that contains all of the exemplar sentences seen thus far.

Exercises

2.1. Let $P = \{S \rightarrow aS, S \rightarrow bA, A \rightarrow bA, A \rightarrow a\}$, $Z = \{a, b\}$, and $V = \{S, A\}$. Find all sentences that the language $L(\mathbf{G})$ generated by $\mathbf{G} = \{Z, V, S, P\}$ contains. Is $L(\mathbf{G})$ regular?

2.2. Is a context-free grammar also a regular grammar? Is a regular grammar also a context-free grammar? Justify with a valid argument.

2.3. The sentence $x = baacbb$ is shown on the tape in Figure 2.5. Starting from s_1, where the first letter is read (b is read first, then a, another a, then c, followed by b and b). Trace through the transitions and determine whether or not the sentence is accepted by the automaton. Now read the sentence in reverse order and determine whether or not this is accepted. Now break the sentence in the middle and exchange the halves to obtain $cbbbaa$. Is this accepted by the automaton?

2.4. In Example 2.6, $L_s = \{(a^n b^n, p^{n-1}(1 - p))\}$. For $p > 0$, find the limit of the probability as $n \rightarrow \infty$.

2.5. A stochastic automaton has alphabet $Z = \{a, b\}$, set of variables $V = \{S, A, B\}$, and stochastic production rules $P = \{S \rightarrow (1)\ bA, A \rightarrow (0.8)\ aB, A \rightarrow (0.2)\ b, B \rightarrow (0.3)\ a, B \rightarrow (0.7)\ bS\}$. Add a final state F and garbage state G, put $Q = \{S, A, B, F, G\}$, and take the initial probability distribution $\mathbf{p}_o = (1,0,0,0,0)$. Note that $p_S = 1$, $p_A = 0,...,$ $p_G = 0$, initially. Find the stochastic matrix function for the sentences a, b, and ab; determine $M(a)$, $M(b)$, $M(ab)$, and $M(ba)$.

2.6. Let $\{ab, abc, abbc\}$ be a sample I of strings that denote structural features in objects. Either find a regular grammar **G** such that $L(\mathbf{G})$ accepts these strings (i.e., $I \subset L(\mathbf{G})$), or show that none exists.

References

Boyer, R. S., and Moore, J. S. (1977), A fast string searching algorithm, *ACM Commun.*, vol. 20, no. 10, 762–772.

Chomsky, N. (1957), *Syntactic Structures*, Mouton, The Hague.

Chomsky, N. (1965), *Aspects of the Theory of Syntax*, MIT Press, Cambridge, MA.

Findler, N. V., and van Leeuwen, J. (1979), A family of similarity measures between two strings, *IEEE Trans. Pattern Anal. Mach. Intell.*, vol. 1, no. 1, 116–118.

Fu, K. S. (1982), *Syntactic Pattern Recognition with Applications*, Prentice-Hall, Englewood Cliffs, NJ.

Fu, K. S. (1974), *Syntactical Methods in Pattern Recognition*, Academic Press, New York.

Fu, K. S., and Booth, T. L. (1975), Grammatical inference: introduction and survey, Part 2, *IEEE Trans. Syst. Man Cybern.*, vol. 5, no. 4, 409–423.

Fu, LiMin (1994), *Neural Networks Comput. Intell.*, McGraw-Hill, New York.

Gold, E. (1967), Language identification in the limit, *Inf. Control*, vol. 16, 447–474.

Gold, E. M. (1978), Complexity of automaton identification from given data, *Inf. Control*, 37, 302–320.

Gonzalez, R. C., and Thomason, M. G. (1978), *Syntactic Pattern Recognition: An Introduction*, Addison-Wesley, Reading, MA.

Kohavi, Z. (1978), *Switching and Finite Automata Theory*, 2nd edition, McGraw-Hill, New York.

Miclet, L. (1979), Regular inference with a tail clustering method, *IEEE Trans. Syst. Man Cybern.*, vol. 9, 737–743.

Miclet, L. (1986), *Structural Methods in Pattern Recognition*, Springer-Verlag, New York.

Tou, J. T., and Gonzalez, R. C. (1974), *Pattern Recognition Principles*, Addison-Wesley, Reading, MA.

Part II

Introductory Neural Networks

Chapter 3

Artificial Neural Network Structures

This chapter has the goal of introducing the concepts of multiple-layered perceptrons, functional link nets, radial basis function networks, self-organizing maps, learning vector quantization networks, and recurrent networks.

3.1. The McCulloch–Pitts Neuron

The McCulloch–Pitts model of an *artificial neuron* (McCulloch and Pitts, 1943) was a first attempt by biophysicists to invent a synthetic neural device. It modeled the functioning of a biological neuron according to what was then "known" about neurons. Figure 3.1 shows the scheme. The input values of 1 (*excitors*) and -1 (*inhibitors*) for the x_n were thought to be analogous to synaptic inputs, and an output of either 1 or -1 for y was *activated*, depending upon whether or not the sum s of the inputs exceeded the threshold value T.

The input lines were called *synaptic* inputs, and inputs led to the activation of an output y. However, this model contained no mechanism for learning other than setting the threshold. For our purposes, the inputs are the features, and the output is the class identifier. While this model is weak, it evolved into powerful networks, as later sections show. For historical aspects, see Hecht-Nielsen (1990), Kosko (1992), Wasserman (1989), and Zurada (1992).

3.2. Hebbian Neurons and Activation Functions

Adjustable Synaptic Weights

D. Hebb postulated a principle for a learning process (Hebb, 1949) at the cellular level: If Neuron A is stimulated repeatedly by Neuron B at times when Neuron A is active, then Neuron A will become more sensitive to stimuli from Neuron B (the correlation principle). While Hebb did not write any equations, the Hebbian learning principle became philosoph-

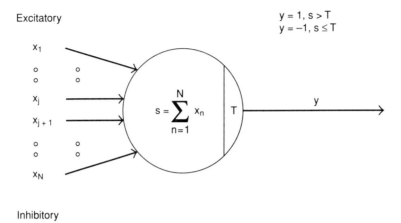

INPUTS   PROCESSING   OUTPUT
Figure 3.1.   The McCulloch–Pitts neuronal model.

ically influential. It implicitly involves adjustments of the strengths of the synaptic inputs, which led to the incorporation of *adjustable synaptic weights* on the input lines to excite or inhibit incoming signals.

Figure 3.2 incorporates adjustable synaptic weights (knobs) on the input lines. An input vector $\mathbf{x} = (x_1,..., x_N)$, considered to be a column matrix vector, is linearly combined with the weight vector $\mathbf{w} = (w_1,..., w_N)$ via the inner (dot) product to form the sum

$$s = \sum\nolimits_{(n=1,\ N)} w_n x_n = \mathbf{w}^t\ \mathbf{x} \tag{3.1}$$

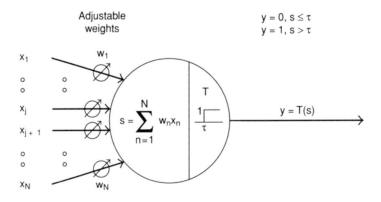

INPUTS   PROCESSING   OUTPUT
Figure 3.2.   A neuron with Hebbian learning ability.

If the sum s is greater than the given threshold τ, then the output y is 1, else it is 0. This *threshold function* is *unipolar* in that it puts out the nonnegative values of 0 or 1 (or 0 or V for some voltage V) and complies with the formerly presumed two-valued all-or-nothing principle of biological neurons. Neurons that use the *bipolar* threshold functions with output values of -1 or 1 (or $-V$ or V for some voltage V) are nowadays called *McCulloch–Pitts* neurons. For further discussion of *thresholded gates*, see Kohavi (1978) or Lewis and Coates (1967). These gates have binary inputs and a single binary output, and there is a method of solution to determine the input combinations to yield a desired output. We do not cover these because of their limitation to linear discrimination logic.

Thresholds and Other Activation Functions

Although threshold functions were the original *activation functions* $y = f(s)$ that map a sum s into the proper range of output values, these discrete-valued functions have given way to continuously differentiable activation functions so that gradient methods can be used to solve for weights that map an input feature vector $\mathbf{x} = (x_1,..., x_N)$ into its desired output identifier (*target*) vector $\mathbf{t} = (t_1,..., t_M)$ that represents a class. Figure 3.3 presents four activation functions. The top two are the unipolar and bipolar thresholds, respectively. For the unipolar threshold, $y = 1$ if $s \geq \tau$, else $y = 0$. The bipolar threshold satisfies: $y = 1$ if $s \geq \tau$, else $y = -1$. The bottom two are continuously differentiable unipolar and bipolar activation functions known as *sigmoid* ("S"), or *logistic*, functions. The first one is the *unipolar sigmoid* that has the form

$$y = 1/[1 + \exp(-\alpha(s - b))] \tag{3.2}$$

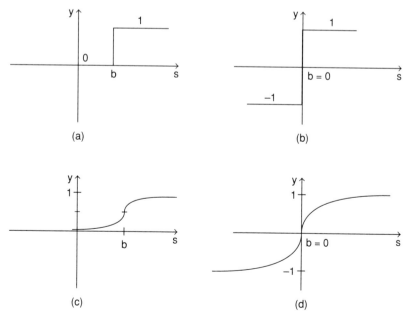

Figure 3.3.   Some activation functions.

for a sum s given by Equation (3.1), where α is the decay (growth) *rate*, b is the *bias* that shifts the function center to where e^0 occurs (at $s = b$), where the output is the midvalue $y = \frac{1}{2}$. Thus b is the s-axis center of asymmetry of $f(s)$.

The second activation function in the lower figure is the *bipolar sigmoid*. It is found from the unipolar sigmoid by translating to the left by b, dilating by 2, and then shifting down 1. It has the form

$$y = 2f(s + b) - 1 = 2\{1/[1 + \exp(-\alpha s)]\} - 1 = [1 - \exp(-\alpha s)]/[1 + \exp(-\alpha s)] \quad (3.3)$$

In Parts (b) and (d) of Figure 3.3, the bipolar functions are shown in the usual situation with $\tau = 0$. The bipolar sigmoid function has an alternate form, derived via

$$f(s) = \frac{1 - \exp(-\alpha s)}{1 + \exp(-\alpha s)} = \frac{\exp(\alpha s/2)[1 - \exp(-\alpha s)]}{\exp(\alpha s/2)[1 + \exp(-\alpha s)]} = \frac{[\exp(\alpha s/2 - \exp(-\alpha s/2)]/2}{[\exp(\alpha s/2 + \exp(-\alpha s/2)]/2}$$

$$= \frac{\sinh(\alpha s/2)}{\cosh(\alpha s/2)} = \tanh(\alpha s/2) \quad (3.4)$$

For bipolar activations, the threshold is $\tau = 0$ on the s-axis, so no bias term is required. This makes bipolar activations more desirable because b is not known apriori and must be adjusted during training. The rate α ($\alpha > 0$) also provides another parameter that can be used in training the network (see Chapters 6 and 7). For larger α, the sigmoid activation functions are very steep and can approximate the threshold functions as closely as desired.

3.3. Snark and the Mark I Perceptron

According to Murphy (1990), Marvin Minsky and Dean Edmond built an analog *synthetic brain* at Harvard in the Summer of 1951 to test Hebb's learning theory. Called *Snark*, the machine used 300 vacuum tubes, 40 control knobs (variable resistors that served as memory) for synaptic weight settings, clutches to adjust the control knobs, motors, and a gyropilot to move the clutches. This first synthetic brain learned to run a maze, which was at the time considered to be a standard test of synthetic intelligence (Bernstein, 1981). It did this in spite of connection failures, which demonstrated fault tolerance.

The world's first working (linear) neural computer was built by Rosenblatt, Wightman, and Martin in 1957 at the Cornell Aeronautics Laboratory (Rosenblatt, 1958), under the sponsorship of the Office of Naval Research. The input signals were provided by a 20×20 array of cadmium sulfide photocell sensors, along with an 8×8 array of servomotor driven potentiometers, which were the adjustable synaptic weights. It was named the *Mark I Perceptron*. Floodlights illuminated a board on which characters were mounted. The stimuli were input to the perceptron and if the response were wrong, then the weights were adjusted. No adjustments were made if the response were correct, so no new learning occurred in that situation. Figure 3.4 displays the perceptron model.

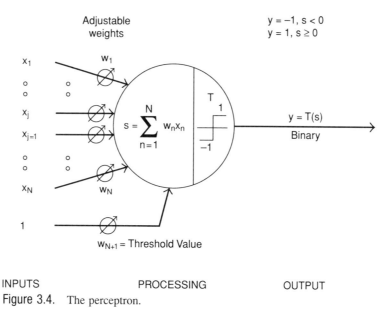

INPUTS   PROCESSING   OUTPUT

Figure 3.4.   The perceptron.

3.4. A Single Perceptron as Linear Discriminator

The Perceptron as Hyperplane Separator

Consider a perceptron as shown in Figure 3.4. The input vector $\mathbf{x} = (x_1,..., x_N)$ is linearly combined with the weights to obtain $s = w_1 x_1 + \cdots + w_N x_N - b$, where b is the threshold. Then s is activated by a threshold function $T(-)$ to produce the output $y = T(s) = 1$ when $s \geq 0$, else $y = T(s) = -1$. The set of all input vectors $\mathbf{x}$ such that $\mathbf{x} \rightarrow s = w_1 x_1 + \cdots + w_N x_N - b = 0$ forms a hyperplane H in the input vector space. H partitions the feature vector space into right and left *half spaces* H^+ and H^- such that

$$w_1 x_1 + \cdots + w_N x_N > b \implies \mathbf{x} \in H^+$$

$$w_1 x_1 + \cdots + w_N x_N < b \implies \mathbf{x} \in H^-$$

Example 3.1.   A Perceptron Discriminator

Figure 3.5 shows a hyperplane and half-spaces H^+ and H^- in two-dimensional space that are determined by a simple perceptron. The weights $\{w_n\}$ may be properly adjusted to separate two given linearly separable classes (clusters) so the classes belong to different half-spaces. In this case, when a sample vector $\mathbf{x}$ is fed to the perceptron, the activated output will be $y = 1$ to designate one class, or $y = -1$ to designate the other class. Let the weights for H be $w_1 = 2$ and $w_2 = -1$, with $b = 0$ so that $2x_1 - x_2 = 0$ determines H (the points $(0,0)$ and $(1,2)$ belong to H). The feature vector $\mathbf{x} = (x_1, x_2) = (2, 3)$ is summed into $s =$

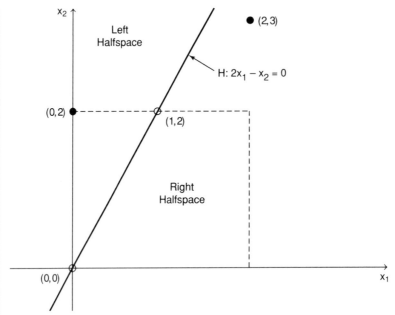

Figure 3.5.   A hyperplane and two half-spaces in two-dimensional feature space.

$2(2) - 1(3) = 1 > 0$, so that the activated output is $y = T(1) = 1$. Thus we see that $(2,3)$ is in the right half-space H^+. On the other hand, the vector $\mathbf{x} = (x_1, x_2) = (0,2)$ activates the output $y = T(2(0) - 1(2)) = T(-1) = -1$, which indicates that $(0,2)$ is in the left half-space H^-. The figure shows these points.

3.5. A Layer of Perceptrons

Multiple Separation Properties

The architecture for a network that consists of a *layer* of M perceptrons is shown in Figure 3.6. An input feature vector $\mathbf{x} = (x_1,..., x_N)$ is input to the network via the set of N branching nodes. The lines fan out at the branching nodes so that each perceptron receives an input from each component of $\mathbf{x}$. At each neuron, the lines fan in from all of the input (branching) nodes. Each incoming line is weighted with a *synaptic coefficient* (weight parameter) from the set $\{w_{nm}\}$, where w_{nm} weights the line from the nth component x_n coming into the mth perceptron.

Each of the M perceptrons in the layer partitions the feature space into two half-spaces so the layer partitions the feature space into $2M$ half-spaces. Each half-space is a convex set and thus the intersections of the $2M$ half-spaces form convex regions. Figure 3.7 shows these regions for the hyperplanes of $M = 4$ perceptrons in a layer as (see Figure 3.6). The maximum number of convex regions that could possibly occur is $K = 2^M$ (an upper bound), while the minimum number of such convex regions for M noncoinciding hyperplanes is $K = M + 1$. The latter case occurs when the M hyperplanes are parallel and $M + 1$ is thus a greatest

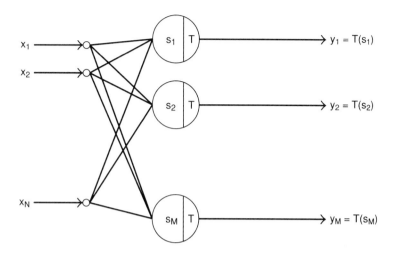

N Inputs   M Perceptrons   M Outputs

Figure 3.6.   A network of one layer of perceptrons.

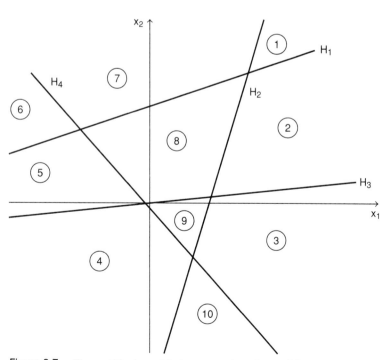

Figure 3.7.   The partitioning of feature space by a layer of four perceptrons.

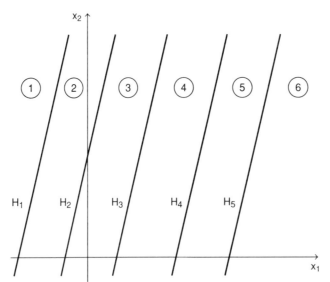

Figure 3.8. Partitioning of feature space by parallel hyperplanes.

lower bound. This parallel case is shown in Figure 3.8 for $M = 5$. These cases do not occur in practice on substantial-sized networks. The expected value $[2^M + (M + 1)]/2$ (approximately 2^{M-1} for $M > 4$) is an a priori estimate of the number of convex regions determined by the intersections of M hyperplanes.

The adjustment of the weights provides the required convex regions that contain the desired multilinearly separable classes. The weight adjustment process is the *training* part (or *learning* by the network) that rotates and translates the hyperplanes. For a feature vector **x** to belong to a certain convex region, it must be in a particular combination of half-spaces; that is, it must satisfy ANDed conditions of the hyperplane equations.

Example 3.2.   Attempt at Classification of Two-Bit Parity with a Single Perceptron

Consider the 4 feature vectors and the corresponding desired outputs of single values given in Table 3.1. This association of input/outputs is also known as the *XOR logic function*, or *2-bit parity*. We will attempt to train a perceptron to correctly recognize the inputs. An even number of 1's in the input feature vector means the network must put out 0. An odd number of 1's as input must yield an output of 1.

Table 3.1.
The Two-Bit Parity Data

Input Vector	Output Value
(0,0)	0
(0,1)	1
(1,0)	1
(1,1)	0

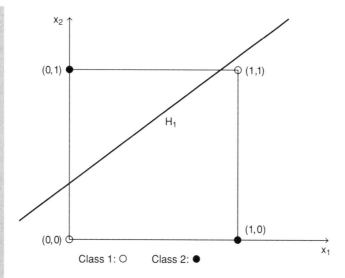

Figure 3.9. A partition of the XOR feature space with a single perceptron.

The 2-bit parity problem specifies $N = 2$ inputs, $M = 1$ outputs, and $Q = 4$ sample vector (input/output) pairs for training, and $K = 2$ classes (*even* and *odd*). However, we see from Figure 3.9 that a single hyperplane cannot separate the four feature vectors into the required two classes, no matter how it is oriented (rotated and translated) by the weights.

The Minsky–Papert Example

The failure of a single layer of perceptrons to be able to learn XOR logic is the famous 1960s example of Minsky and Papert (see Minsky and Papert, 1988) that diminished interest in perceptrons and other artificial neurons for two decades. One layer of perceptrons provides only linear separation. It is known nowadays that the addition of another layer can form a network that is a powerful general nonlinear model that can learn to map multiple inputs to multiple outputs with very small errors. Other types of neural networks, such as Pao's functional link networks and Kohonen's self-organizing feature maps (Sections 3.10 and 3.12), use a single layer of neurons that are not perceptrons, but which can separate classes nonlinearly.

3.6. Feedforward Networks of Layered Neurons

Multiple-Layered Perceptrons

The power of a single neuron can be greatly amplified by using multiple neurons in a network of layered connectionist architecture, as displayed in Figure 3.10. Such a *multiple-layered perceptron* (MLP) is also called a *feedforward artificial neural network* and abbreviated to FANN. The modifier "feedforward" distinguishes it from feedback (recursive) networks. On the left is the layer of inputs, or *branching*, nodes, which are not artificial neu-

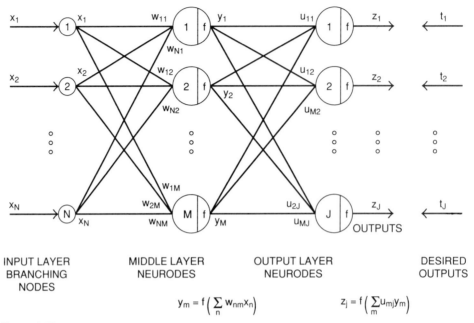

Figure 3.10.   A two-layered feedforward artificial neural network.

$$y_m = f\left(\sum_n w_{nm}x_n\right) \qquad z_j = f\left(\sum_m u_{mj}y_m\right)$$

rons. The *hidden layer* (the *middle* layer here) contains neural nodes, as does the *output layer* on the right. This is the *architecture* of a two-layered NN (so called because there are two layers of neuronal units).

Neural networks may also have multiple hidden layers for the sake of extra power in learning to separate nonlinearly separable classes. The Hornik–Stinchcombe–White theorem, given in Section 3.9, states that a layered artificial neural network with two layers of neurons is sufficient to approximate as closely as desired any piecewise continuous map of a closed bounded subset of a finite-dimensional space into another finite-dimensional space, *provided* that there are sufficiently many neurons in the single hidden layer. There is no theoretical need to use more than two layers of neurons, which would (a) increase the computational complexity and instability in training and (b) slow down the operation because the extra layers cause delays in processing (the idea is that the neurons in a single layer are to process in parallel, while the different layers process sequentially). But extra layers can prevent the necessity of using an excessive number of neurons in a single hidden layer (see Chapter 10) to achieve highly nonlinear classification.

Example 3.3.   Classification of Two-Bit Parity with Two Layers of Perceptrons

Figure 3.11 presents a FANN with two hidden neurons and another neuron in the separate output layer. We take $w_{11} = -1$, $w_{21} = 1$, $w_{12} = -1$, $w_{22} = 1$, $b_1 = \frac{1}{2}$ and $b_2 = -\frac{1}{2}$, so that the result is two parallel hyperplanes that yield three convex regions as shown in Figure 3.12. The hyperplanes are determined by

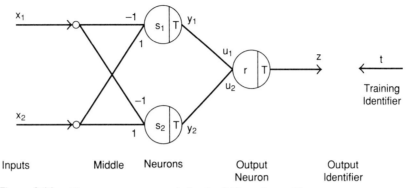

Figure 3.11. The perceptron network for the 2-bit parity problem.

$$w_{11}x_1 + w_{21}x_2 = -1(x_1) + 1(x_2) = \tfrac{1}{2}, \, w_{12}x_1 + w_{22}x_2 = -1(x_1) + 1(x_2) = -\tfrac{1}{2}$$

The threshold at the first neuron in the hidden layer yields $T_1(s) = 0$ if $s < \tfrac{1}{2}$, else $T_1(s) = 1$. The threshold at the second hidden neuron yields $T_2(s) = 1$ if $s \geq -\tfrac{1}{2}$, else $T_2(s) = 0$. This forces the results listed in Table 3.2, where we use 0.1 for 0 and 0.9 for 1 (this is the usual procedure in using neural networks, because 0 and 1 have special properties that inhibit gradient training).

The four sets of above outputs yield the three unique vectors $(y_1, y_2) = (0, 1)$, $(y_1, y_2) = (1, 1)$, and $(y_1, y_2) = (0, 0)$ that identify the three linearly separable regions shown in Figure 3.12. We see from the figure that Regions 1 and 3 make up the odd parity (Class 2), while Region 3 is even parity (Class 1). We saw in Example 3.1 that a network of a single layer cannot output the two correct classes, no matter how we orient the hyperplanes via transla-

Table 3.2.
The Hidden Layer Mapping

Region 2 $[(x_1, x_2) = (0.1, 0.1)]$:

$-1(0.1) + 1(0.1) = 0.0 < \tfrac{1}{2} \Rightarrow y_1 = 0$
$-1(0.1) + 1(0.1) = 0.0 > -\tfrac{1}{2} \Rightarrow y_2 = 1$

Region 1 $[(x_1, x_2) = (0.1, 0.9)]$:

$-1(0.1) + 1(0.9) = 0.8 > \tfrac{1}{2} \Rightarrow y_1 = 1$
$-1(0.1) + 1(0.9) = 0.8 > -\tfrac{1}{2} \Rightarrow y_2 = 1$

Region 3 $[(x_1, x_2) = (0.9, 0.1)]$:

$-1(0.9) + 1(0.1) = -0.8 < \tfrac{1}{2} \Rightarrow y_1 = 0$
$-1(0.9) + 1(0.1) = -0.8 < -\tfrac{1}{2} \Rightarrow y_2 = 0$

Region 2 $[(x_1, x_2) = (0.9, 0.9)]$:

$-1(0.9) + 1(0.9) = 0.0 < \tfrac{1}{2} \, y_1 \Rightarrow = 0$
$-1(0.9) + 1(0.9) = -0.0 > -\tfrac{1}{2} \Rightarrow y_2 = 1$

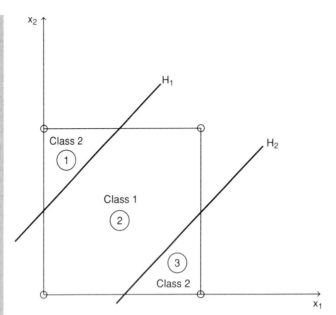

Figure 3.12.   The partitioning of the 2-bit parity feature space with two perceptron layers.

tion and rotation. In all cases of noncoincidental hyperplanes, we obtain three or four convex regions (the lower and upper bounds, respectively).

To show that the network with a second layer of perceptrons can learn the nonlinearly separable classes of even and odd parity (XOR logic), we take the new weights at the single output neuron to be $u_1 = -1$ and $u_2 = 1$ in Figure 3.11. These weight the lines on which y_1 and y_2 enter the output neuron (perceptron). Using the hyperplane $z = u_1 y_1 + u_2 y_2 = 0$, we need to map $\mathbf{y} = (1,1)$ and $\mathbf{y} = (0,0)$ into the same class, Class 1, as shown in Figure 3.12. Because

$$\mathbf{y} = (1,1) \rightarrow (-1)(1) + (1)(1) = 0 = z$$

$$\mathbf{y} = (0,0) \rightarrow (-1)(0) + (1)(0) = 0 = z$$

this is done by $u_1 = -1$ and $u_2 = 1$. Table 3.3 shows the complete mappings $(x_1, x_2) \rightarrow (y_1, y_2) \rightarrow z$. The threshold $z = T_3(r)$ in the output layer satisfies $T_3(r) = 1$ if $r < \frac{1}{2}$, else $T_3(r) = 0$, where $r = u_1 y_1 + u_2 y_2$.

Table 3.3.
The Two-Bit Parity Mapping by Two Layers of Perceptrons

(x_1, x_2)		(y_1, y_2)		r	$z = T(r)$	Class
(0,0)	$\rightarrow$	(0,1)	$\rightarrow$	$-1(0) + 1(1) = 1$	0	1
(0,1)	$\rightarrow$	(1,1)	$\rightarrow$	$-1(1) + 1(1) = 0$	1	2
(1,0)	$\rightarrow$	(0,0)	$\rightarrow$	$-1(0) + 1(0) = 0$	1	2
(1,1)	$\rightarrow$	(0,1)	$\rightarrow$	$-1(0) + 1(1) = 1$	0	1

Thus we can now see that $\mathbf{x}^{(1)} = (0,0)$ and $\mathbf{x}^{(4)} = (1,1)$ map into the output identifier $z = 0$ that denotes even parity and that $\mathbf{x}^{(2)} = (0,1)$ and $\mathbf{x}^{(3)} = (1,0)$ map into the output identifier $z = 1$ that designates odd parity. Thus the two simple layers of perceptrons have learned a highly nonlinear function. Slightly larger networks can learn 3-bit or 5-bit parity (or more generally, the n-bit parity problem). Upon adjusting the weights in some orderly process, much more complicated functions can be learned that will perform recognition.

Why Are Activation Functions Needed?

One may be tempted to omit any type of thresholding function, which sigmoids are, de facto. Without such an activation function, there would remain only a linear sum rather than a decision as to which half-space an input vector belongs. We refer to Figure 3.10 here. Consider a vector of such sums $\mathbf{s} = W^T\mathbf{x}$, where W is the weight matrix whose first column is the weight set at the first hidden neurode, the second column is the weight set at the second hidden neurode, and so on, $\mathbf{x} = (x_1,..., x_N)$ is the vector of inputs, and the superscript T denotes the matrix transpose. Suppose that the components of $\mathbf{s}$ were to remain linear sums—that is, there were no activations functions. Then the components of $\mathbf{s}$ would be passed directly to the output layer and used to form new sums at each output neurode of the form $\mathbf{r} = U^T\mathbf{s}$.

Thus the situation would be

$$\mathbf{x} \rightarrow \mathbf{s} = W^T\mathbf{x} \rightarrow \mathbf{r} = U^T\mathbf{s} = U^TW^T\mathbf{x} = (U^TW^T)\mathbf{x} = V\mathbf{x}$$

where $V = U^TW^T$ is a matrix product. Therefore, the outputs of the two layers of neurodes would be a vector of sums obtained by multiplying $\mathbf{x}$ by a single matrix V, which also performs a linear mapping. This is equivalent to a single linear function, a matrix V, operating on the input vector $\mathbf{x}$. Thus we conclude that the sigmoid functions, which act as a threshold activation, are necessary to obtain a nonlinear "warping" that pushes the output values toward the binary decision values 0 or 1 (see Chapter 9 for an explanation of why the MLP type of FANN works). It is easily seen that the above argument extends to any number of layers of neurodes without activation functions.

3.7. The Operation of Multiple-Layered Perceptrons

Inputs and Hidden Layer Activations

Henceforth, we will refer to neurons in a layered neural network as *neurodes* (neural nodes), which is common terminology in the 1990s to distinguish them from biological neurons which behave quite differently. We refer to Figure 3.10 in the following discussion. A feature vector $\mathbf{x} = (x_1,..., x_N)$ that represents a pattern enters the input layer on the left with each component x_n entering one and only one input node. From each nth input (branching) node, the nth component x_n fans out to each of the M neurodes in the middle layer. Thus each mth hidden (middle) neurode has a fan-in of all N input components (features). As each x_n enters the mth neurode of the hidden layer, it is modified via multiplication by the *synaptic weight* w_{nm} for that connection line. All resulting products $w_{nm}x_n$ at the mth hidden neurode are summed over n to yield

$$s_m = \sum_{(n=1, N)} w_{nm}x_n \qquad (\mathbf{s} = W^T\mathbf{x}) \tag{3.5}$$

and $y_m = f_m(s_m)$ is the activated output.

W is the matrix of weights and W^T is its transpose, so that Equation (3.5) provides all of the sums. Such sums are ideally computed concurrently (in parallel) at the middle neurodes (each neurode is conceptualized to be a processor). Each mth middle neurode processes the sum s_m via $s_m \rightarrow y_m = f(s_m)$ to activate the output y_m from that neurode, so the vector $\mathbf{y} = (y_1,..., y_M)$ is put out from the hidden layer of M neurodes. The output from each of these neurodes also branches out to each of the J neurodes.

Output Layer Activations

At each of the J neurodes in the output layer, there are M incoming lines (one from each of the M neurodes in the hidden layer). Each carries a value y_m that then undergoes multiplication by the synaptic weight u_{mj} on the line from the mth middle neurode to the jth output neurode to yield the product $u_{mj}y_m$ at the jth output neurode. These M values are then summed at the jth neurode to obtain

$$r_j = \sum_{(m=1, M)} u_{mj}y_m \tag{3.6}$$

This sum is processed by the jth output neurode via $r_j \rightarrow z_j = f_j(r_j)$ to activate the output value z_j. The output layer of neurodes therefore puts out the vector $\mathbf{z} = (z_1,..., z_J)$. In a trained NN, such output vectors are codewords that represent classes of feature vectors to which the input $\mathbf{x}$ belongs. Thus the overall network operation $\mathbb{N}$ is the mapping

$$\mathbb{N}: \mathbf{x} \rightarrow \mathbf{z} \qquad (\mathbb{N}: (x_1,..., x_N) \rightarrow (z_1,..., z_J)) \tag{3.7}$$

The network map $\mathbb{N}$ from N-dimensional space to J-dimensional space consists of (i) a linear combination of the input vector followed by a nonlinear activation, which is followed by another stage of linear combination and nonlinear activation.

The Ranges for Data and Weights

The two-layered FANN architectures use standardized (normalized) input component values that fall between 0 and 1 when the unipolar activations are used. The synaptic weights are initially selected at random between -1 and 1, or between -0.5 and 0.5 to prevent certain bottlenecks in training (to be explained in Chapter 6). However, during steepest descent training the weights may move to a larger range $[-a, a]$, where $a > 1$, which is not desirable but may be necessary on the way to an approximate solution. The linear sums at the hidden and output layers of neurodes are contracted by the activation functions, which are also called *squashing functions* because they squash the sums s_m and r_j into the intervals $[0,1]$ or $[-1,1]$. They were called "transfer functions" in the 1980s, but we avoid this terminology that has an alternate meaning in systems theory. Thus a feedforward neural network is a mapping for unipolar activations per

$$\mathbb{N}: \quad [0,1]^N \rightarrow [0,1]^J \qquad \text{(unipolar activations)} \tag{3.8a}$$

When bipolar activation functions are used, the sums s_m at the hidden neurodes and r_j at the output neurodes may be negative as well as positive. In this case, the inputs may satisfy $-1 < x_n < 1$, so that

$$\mathbb{N}: \quad [-1,1]^N \rightarrow [-1,1]^J \qquad \text{(bipolar activations)} \tag{3.8b}$$

3.8. MLPs as Pattern Recognizers

Operation and Training Modes

Recall that a pattern recognizer is a system that maps any input feature vector $\mathbf{x}^{(q)}$ from class k of a population P into the output identifier vector $\mathbf{z}^{(k(q))}$ for Class k. A trained MLP maps input vectors into output vectors, $\mathbf{x} \rightarrow \mathbf{z}$, and has the following important properties: (i) It is nonlinear, and (ii) it is *stable* in the sense that if $\mathbb{N}: \mathbf{x}^{(q)} \rightarrow \mathbf{z}^{(k(q))}$ and $\mathbf{x}$ is close to $\mathbf{x}^{(q)}$, then $\mathbf{x}$ maps into a vector $\mathbf{z}$ that is close to $\mathbf{z}^{(k(q))}$; that is, small errors map into small errors. It may also map a vector $\mathbf{x}^*$ that is far from $\mathbf{x}^{(q)}$ into one that is close to $\mathbf{z}^{(k(q))}$ (many-to-one mappings). In fact, a NN is a nonlinear interpolator and extrapolator. We need only adjust the weights appropriately to train a NN to map exemplar feature vectors from classes into the desired class identifier output vectors, or to approximate functions from $\mathbf{R}^N$ to $\mathbf{R}^J$.

To use an MLP as a pattern recognizer, we need to (i) obtain a sample of Q feature vectors $S = \{\mathbf{x}^{(1)},..., \mathbf{x}^{(Q)}\}$ that contains one or more exemplars for each of K classes, (ii) invent a set of K dissimilar output identifier (*target*) vectors $\{\mathbf{t}^{(1)},..., \mathbf{t}^{(K)}\}$ for the K classes and pair one identifier with each input exemplar to form exemplar input/output pairs $\{(\mathbf{x}^{(q)}, \mathbf{t}^{(k(q))})\}$, and (iii) adjust the hidden weights $\{w_{nm}: n = 1,..., N, m = 1,..., M\}$ and output weights $\{u_{mj}: m = 1,..., M, j = 1,..., J\}$ until all exemplar input vectors are mapped into the correct identifiers. The distance between each *actual* output $\mathbf{z}^{(q)}$ and target output identifier $\mathbf{t}^{(k(q))}$ is the error of classification, $\|\mathbf{z}^{(q)} - \mathbf{t}^{(k(q))}\|$, and it must be less than the distance from $\mathbf{z}^{(q)}$ to any other (incorrect) training vector $\mathbf{t}^{(p)}$; that is, $\|\mathbf{z}^{(q)} - \mathbf{t}^{(k(q))}\| < \|\mathbf{z}^{(q)} - \mathbf{t}^{(p)}\|$ for all $p \neq k$. The *total sum-squared error* is $E = \|\mathbf{z}^{(1)} - \mathbf{t}^{(k(1))}\| + \cdots + \|\mathbf{z}^{(Q)} - \mathbf{t}^{(k(Q))}\|$. The *partial sum-squared error* for any exemplar input $\mathbf{x}^{(q)}$ is $E^{(q)} = \|\mathbf{z}^{(q)} - \mathbf{t}^{(k(q))}\|$. Thus

$$E = \sum_{(q=1, Q)} \|\mathbf{z}^{(k(q))} - \mathbf{t}^{(k)}\|^2 = \sum_{(q=1, Q)} E^{(q)} \tag{3.9}$$

We write SSE for "sum-squared error" hereafter.

Training as Iterative Weight Adjustments: A General Algorithm

The third step given above involves difficulties, although obtaining the exemplar data may be expensive and time-consuming. Because the MLP is a nonlinear map, there is no way to solve analytically (in closed form) for the weights that produce the best (in some sense) mapping of input to output vectors. Therefore, we must use an *iterative* method that implements the following generalized algorithm.

Step 1: Draw initial weight set $\{w_{11}{}^{(0)},..., w_{NM}{}^{(0)}, u_{11}{}^{(0)},..., u_{MJ}{}^{(0)}\}$ randomly on iteration 0, put $r \leftarrow 0$.

Step 2: On the $(r + 1)$st iteration, update the rth weight set $(w_{11}{}^{(r)},..., w_{NM}{}^{(r)}, u_{11}{}^{(r)},..., u_{MJ}{}^{(r)})$ to the $(r + 1)$st weight set $(w_{11}{}^{(r+1)},..., w_{NM}{}^{(r+1)}, u_{11}{}^{(r+1)},..., u_{MJ}{}^{(r+1)})$ according to some strategy that causes the total SSE E to decrease.

Step 3: If a stopping criterion is met, then stop; else go to Step 2 above.

There may be multiple exemplar feature vectors for any of the K classes, which means that different exemplar input feature vectors for the kth class must have the same identifier as target output vector. The weight adjustment continues until all inputs are mapped approximately to the target (identifier) outputs.

Once the supervised training approximately minimizes the total SSE function E, the NN can be used in the operational mode to map feature vectors from the population P, from which the training sample S originated, into target class identifiers for the various classes of the population. This is recognition. It requires that a classification of a sample from P has been done by prior supervised training of the neural network over the adequate representative sample P (the exemplars). The different task of unsupervised classification of a population P requires the NN to perform self-organization to cluster a sample of feature vectors into classes. We address the questions of how to do the training in the sequel chapters. Self-organizing NNs are discussed in Section 3.12 and Chapter 7.

3.9. The Hornik–Stinchcombe–White Theorem and the MLP Model

What the Theorem States

In the mid-1980s many researchers felt that while *standard* MLPs with a single hidden layer were powerful, those with two or more hidden layers would be even more powerful. Many papers applied MLPs with extra hidden layers to problems in engineering, hoping to obtain better results. Various squashing functions other than sigmoids were also used. Hornik et al. (1989, p. 362) answered the questions as to how many layers were actually necessary and what activation functions could be used. Their result established the following result (reworded for our purposes here):

> A feedforward artificial neural network with two layers of neurodes and nonconstant nondecreasing activation function at each hidden neurode can approximate any piecewise continuous function from a closed bounded subset of Euclidean N-dimensional space to Euclidean J-dimensional space with any prespecified accuracy, **provided** that sufficiently many neurodes be used in the single hidden layer.

The theorem that was proved by Hornik et al. holds for Borel measurable functions on compact sets, which includes all continuous and piecewise continuous functions (with finitely or countably many discontinuities on sets of zero "volume") on closed bounded subsets. This is a powerful theoretical result, but the proviso concerning sufficiently many hidden layer neurodes must be heeded.

> **Principle 3.1:** The Hornik–Stinchcombe–White theorem establishes that for any mapping problem, which includes recognition and classification, the failure of a feedforward artificial neural network to learn the mapping task can be attributed to the fault of the architecture (the training) or to the stochastic nature or inappropriateness of the data, but not to the FANN paradigm.

Why Multiple Hidden Layers Are Sometimes Used

Some researchers feel that although a single hidden layer is sufficient from a theoretical viewpoint, a large number of neurodes may be required in the hidden layer for an MLP with a large number of nonlinearly separable classes. To keep the number of hidden neurodes down, they sometimes use an extra hidden layer of neurodes. While we cover NNs with a single hidden layer in the next four chapters, we extend them to multiple hidden layers in Chapters 4 and 9. Section 9.4 makes clear how extra hidden layers can be more efficient in training and modeling highly nonlinear mappings with a large number of nonlinearly separable classes. The total number of weights and neurons can be reduced significantly.

Architectural Practicality

Chapter 9 addresses neural engineering, which includes network architecture. Here, we mention a few basics to fulfill certain needs for discussions prior to that chapter. For an NN with a single hidden layer of M neurodes, there remains the question of how many neurodes are enough. We posit the following rules for now and leave the analysis for consideration in Chapter 9. The number of features N in the input feature vectors is determined separately from data considerations. Let K be the number of classes to be separated. We must find the number M of middle neurodes and the number J of output neurodes. We can let $J = K$ for small K, so that there can be one high output component z_j for each class (the other output components are low). For larger K, we take $J = \log_2(K)$ (from $K = 2^J$), so there is a unique combination of high and low values for each class identifier. The number of output nodes can be any $J \geq 1$, but small J avoids extra computational complexity. Some applications need only a single output, which can be high or low to identify two classes. But even so, two outputs can more easily learn and are more robust.

Recall from Section 3.5 that a hidden layer of M neurons yields M hyperplanes that partition the feature space into a number of convex regions that is between $M + 1$ and 2^M with an expected value of approximately 2^{M-1}. We take the number of neurodes in the hidden layer to be $M = K$, so that we expect K hyperplanes to yield approximately 2^{K-1} convex sets in the feature space. Groups of these ANDed convex regions can be effectively joined (ORed) at the output layer to form the K nonconvex regions for the K classes that are nonlinearly separable. In case that $M = K$ hidden neurodes do not train properly on a few tries, then we must change the architecture of the NN. This usually would mean that we add or prune hidden neurodes to obtain a better partition of the feature space by the hidden layer into convex sets to be joined into nonconvex classes by the output layer. Chapter 9 discusses the aspects of neural engineering, which concerns the design of an MLP architecture.

A popular heuristic rule is that the number of neurodes in the hidden layer should be small to train cleanly (more neurodes than are actually needed cause extraneous noise and weight drift). We must qualify that. The number of hidden neurodes in an MLP must be sufficiently large to map to the accuracy required. We shall see in later chapters that there are two opposing concepts for finding a near-optimal architecture: (i) Start the training with a larger number of hidden neurodes than is necessary, train and prune neurodes that do not contribute significantly, and then train further; or (ii) start with a small number of neurodes and add new ones as necessary during training and then train further after each such addition.

3.10. Functional Link Nets

Pao's Functional Link Nets

An MLP type of FANN needs two layers of neurons to be able to separate nonlinearly separable classes of feature vectors in N-dimensional feature space ($\mathbf{R}^N$). Let C_1 and C_2 be two classes in $\mathbf{R}^N$ that are not linearly separable. If we could adjoin another feature dimension so the new feature space becomes $\mathbf{R}^{N+1}$, and if we could use values of x_{N+1} of, say, 0 for Class 1 and 1 for Class 2, then some classes could be separated in $\mathbf{R}^{N+1}$ by a hyperplane of dimension N via a threshold of $x_{N+1} = \frac{1}{2}$. Figure 3.13 shows the situation. More extra dimensions would allow even more linear separating power in higher-dimensional feature space of the original nonlinearly separable classes. While we could add the new dimensional values to the training vectors, we would not know what new values to adjoin to novel feature vectors from unknown classes. Thus it appears that the embedding principle for linear separation of otherwise nonlinearly separable classes is a dead end. There is, however, a way to do it.

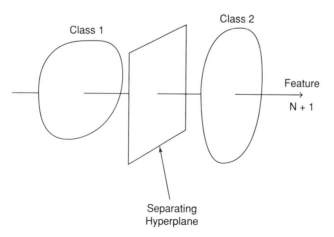

Figure 3.13. Separation in a higher-dimensional space.

Figure 3.14. A second-order tensor functional link network.

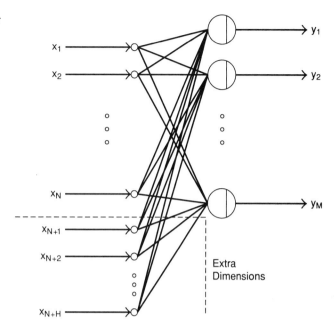

The *functional link net* (FLN), created by Pao (1989), automatically provides extra dimensions and values for the dimensions adjoined to the feature vectors. It creates new dimensions by defining functions of the old features to obtain the new features of the form $x_{N+1} = f_1(\mathbf{x}),..., x_{N+H} = f_H(\mathbf{x})$. In the *tensor* model, he uses

$$x_{N+1} = x_2 x_1,\ x_{N+2} = x_3 x_1,\ ...,\ x_{N+H} = x_N x_{N-1} \qquad (3.10)$$

Higher-order tensor models can be used. For example, we could add $x_{N+H+1} = x_1 x_2 x_3$, $x_{N+H+2} = x_1 x_2 x_4$, and so on, to the above. Usually, the second-order terms add sufficiently many new dimensions (features) to allow linear separation of classes that were not linearly separable in $\mathbf{R}^N$. Figure 3.14 shows the second-order tensor situation. Other models use orthonormal basis functions, polynomials, or other functions of features to obtain the new adjoined features (see Chapter 7). FLNs are also a type of FANN.

Example 3.4.   Two-Bit Parity with a Functional Link Net

Consider the XOR logic (2-bit parity) function. The data are shown in Table 3.4 for the two-dimensional feature space and the three-dimensional feature space that has the second-order feature $x_3 = x_1 x_2$ adjoined. Figure 3.15 shows the two-dimensional XOR data embedded in three-dimensional feature space with the new three-dimensional values given by $x_3 = x_1 x_2$. Zurada (1992) uses -1 and 1 in place of 0 and 1, respectively, for a simpler separation. The functional link network for XOR logic is shown in Figure 3.16.

Table 3.4.
Two-Bit Parity in Two- and Three-Dimensional Feature Space

x_1	x_2	Two-Bit Parity	x_1	x_2	x_3	Two-Bit Parity
0	0	0	0	0	0	0
0	1	1	0	1	0	1
1	0	1	1	0	0	1
1	1	0	1	1	1	0

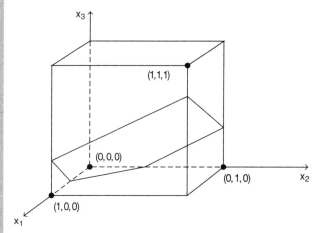

Figure 3.15. Linear separation of 2-bit parity data in three dimensions.

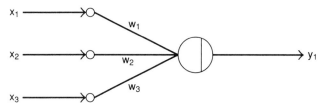

Figure 3.16. Functional link net for 2-bit parity.

A Functional Link Net Algorithm

The functional link nets use only a single layer of neurodes. In the case of XOR logic, a single extra dimension is sufficient. The extra-dimensional features must be sufficiently numerous to separate out the number K of nonlinearly separable classes because of the single layer of neurodes. The training is done by backpropagation (see Chapter 4), which is the gradient method of steepest descent. A high-level algorithm follows, where $y_m = h_m(-)$ is a unipolar sigmoid (sigmoids are not necessary, as is discussed in Chapter 7).

Step 1: Put r ← 0 (iteration number) and draw initial set of weights $\{w_{nm}^{(0)}\}$ at random from $[-0.5, 0.5]$

Step 2: Update network outputs for $q = 1,..., Q$ and $m = 1,..., M$ via
$$y_m^{(q)} \leftarrow f(\textstyle\sum_{(n=1, N+H)} w_{nm} x_n^{(q)})$$

Step 3: Update weights based on minimizing the SSE E for $n = 1,..., N + H$ and $m = 1,..., M$ by
$$w_{nm}^{(r+1)} \leftarrow w_{nm}^{(r)} + \eta\{\textstyle\sum_{(q=1,Q)}(t_m^{k(q)} - y_m^{(q)})y_m^{(q)}(1 - y_m^{(q)})x_n$$
$$/w_{nm}^{(r+1)} \leftarrow w_{nm}^{(r)} - \eta\{\partial E/\partial w_{nm}\}/$$

Step 4: $r \leftarrow r + 1$
if $r \geq I$ then stop   else go to Step 2

The *advantages* of functional link nets are that for a small number N of features they are trainable very quickly and are simple. The *disadvantage* is that for a large number N of features, the number of extra features may be large, even for a second-order tensor model. In this case, there are $N(N - 1)$ extra features to adjoin, which brings the total to $N + N(N - 1) = N[1 + N - 1] = N^2$. For $N = 20$, this would result in $N + H = 400$ features. *In practice*, we add a few tensor features $x_j x_n$ and train and then add one at a time and train, iteratively, until the network separates all K classes appropriately.

Polynomial Separation of Feature Space

A generalization of the linear separation of a feature space by hyperplanes is the nonlinear separation of feature space by polynomials, whose surfaces in the feature space are *hypersurfaces*. Instead of

$$w_1 x_1 + \cdots + w_N x_N = b$$

we could just as well use

$$w_1 x_1^2 + w_2 x_2^2 + \cdots + w_N x_N^2 + w_{N+1} x_2 x_1 + \cdots + w_{N+P} x_N x_{N-1} = b$$

In the feature space $\mathbf{R}^N$, for example, $w_1 x_1^2 + \cdots + w_N x_N^2 = b^2$ determines a *hyperellipsoid surface* that separates the feature space into an *inside part* and an *outside part*. For $N = 2$ and $w_1 = w_2$, this would be a circle that partitions the plane into inside and outside regions. By translating via $x_n - a_n$, we can put such surfaces anywhere. For different weights and using all second-order terms such as x_n^2 and $x_n x_p$, various surfaces can be used to partition the feature space (paraboloids, hyperboloids, and ellipsoids).

3.11. Radial Basis Function Networks

Radial Basis Functions

A new and extremely powerful type of feedforward artificial neural network is the *radial basis function* (RBF) network, which differs strongly from the MLP in the activation functions and how they are used. An RBF network contains the following: (i) an input layer of branching nodes, one for each feature component, just as does an MLP; (ii) a hidden layer of neurodes where each neurode has a special type of activation function centered on the center vector of a cluster or subcluster in the feature space so that the function has a non-negligible response for input vectors close to its center; and (iii) an output layer of neurodes that sum the outputs from the hidden neurodes, that is, the output layer neurodes use a linear activation function. Figure 3.17 presents a general RBF network. A bias b_j at each output neurode assures nonzero mean values of the sums

$$r_j = u_{1j}y_1 + \cdots + u_{Mj}y_M + b_j \tag{3.11}$$

The most common RBFs are $\mathbf{x} \to y_1 = f_1(\mathbf{x};\mathbf{v}^{(1)}),..., \mathbf{x} \to y_M = f_M(\mathbf{x};\mathbf{v}^{(M)})$, where

$$y_m = f_m(\mathbf{x};\mathbf{v}^{(m)}) = \exp[-\|\mathbf{x} - \mathbf{v}^{(m)}\|^2/(2\sigma_m^2)], \qquad m = 1,..., M \tag{3.12}$$

with center at $\mathbf{v}^{(m)}$. Note that y_m is a maximum when $\mathbf{x} = \mathbf{v}^{(m)}$. We usually use a hidden neurode for each exemplar input feature vector $\mathbf{x}^{(q)}$, $q = 1,..., Q$, so we put $M \leftarrow Q$ in this case. The *center vector* $\mathbf{v}^{(m)} = (v_1^{(m)},..., v_N^{(m)})$ at the mth hidden neurode has N components to match the input feature vector. The parameter σ_m in Equation (3.12) is used to control the spread of the radial basis function so that its values decrease more slowly or more rapidly as $\mathbf{x}$ moves away from the center vector $\mathbf{v}^{(m)}$—that is, as $\|\mathbf{x} - \mathbf{v}^{(m)}\|$ increases.

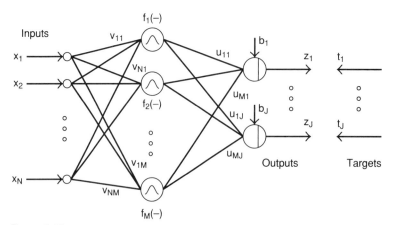

Figure 3.17.   A general RBF network.

Figure 3.18. A radial basis
function on the planar feature
space.

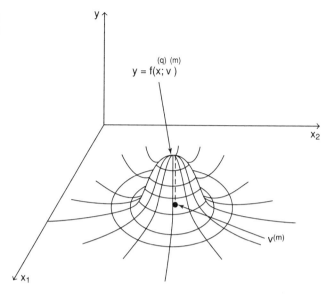

Figure 3.18 shows an RBF on the plane, Figure 3.19 shows a slice of an RBF at the mth
neurode for which the horizontal axis is the distance $\|\mathbf{x} - \mathbf{v}^{(m)}\|$. The region in the feature
space where $f_m(\mathbf{x};\mathbf{v}^{(m)})$ is high is called the *receptive field* of that neurode (Wasserman, 1993),
as shown in Figure 3.19. The activated values y_m are summed to yield a network output z_j
shown in Figure 3.17 and determined by either of

$$z_j = [\textstyle\sum_{(m=1, M)} u_{mj}y_m] / [\textstyle\sum_{(m=1, M)} y_m] \tag{3.13}$$

Figure 3.19. An RBF slice.

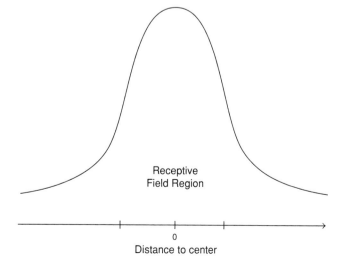

$$z_j = (1/M)[\sum_{(m=1, M)} u_{mj} y_m] \tag{3.14}$$

(to squash the output values).

Each RBF is influential only on its receptive field, which is a small region of the feature space as shown in Figure 3.19. The important regions of the feature space where exemplars are clustered are covered jointly by the M RBFs that are centered on the clusters of exemplar feature vectors that represent subclasses. Other RBFs are sometimes used, but they must respond only to small regions of feature space. According to the Hornik–Stinchcombe–White theorem, the activation functions can be any nonconstant nondecreasing functions. This and results by Poggio and Girosi (1990) and Hartman et al. (1990) prove that RBF networks are universal approximators.

The training consists of (i) assigning each neurodal parametric vector $\mathbf{v}^{(m)}$ a unique exemplar vector $\mathbf{x}^{(q)}$ ($\mathbf{v}^{(m)} \leftarrow \mathbf{x}^{(q)}$), (ii) selecting a parameter σ_m for the spread of the receptive field, (iii) drawing an initial weight set $\{u_{mj}^{(0)}\}$ for the output layer of neurodes, and (iv) performing supervised training of the weights $\{u_{mj}\}$ in the output layer to force the total SSE E to decrease as much as possible, where

$$E = \sum_{(q=1, Q)} \sum_{(j=1, J)} (z_j^{(q)} - t_j^{(q)})^2 \tag{3.15}$$

Because this is supervised training, rather than self-organizing clustering, the corresponding sample of exemplar pairs of input feature vectors and output *target* (identifier) vectors $\{(\mathbf{x}^{(q)}, \mathbf{t}_{(q)})\}$ must be given.

There are different paradigms for RBF networks that determine how the training is done (Wasserman, 1993). In the simplest cases, the weights $\{v_n^{(m)}\}$ at the hidden neurodes and $\{u_m\}$ at the output neurode remain fixed (no training is required). In the second and more flexible model, we train only the weights $\{u_m\}$ at the output neurode. The third and most flexible model requires the training of all weights, centers, and other parameters. Each RBF depends on its center $\mathbf{v}^{(m)}$ where it takes its maximum value and is activated by any input $\mathbf{x}$ near $\mathbf{v}^{(m)}$. It has essentially no response when $\mathbf{x}$ is far from $\mathbf{v}^{(m)}$.

Each RBF $f_m(-; \mathbf{v}^{(m)})$ responds to the small convex region (receptive field) of the feature space; that is, $f_m(\mathbf{x}^{(q)}; \mathbf{v}^{(m)})$ is high only when $\mathbf{x}^{(q)}$ is close to the neurodal center $\mathbf{v}^{(m)}$. A large number of these functions cover either the feature space or the subclasses in the feature space with their receptive fields, so that the output layer of neurodes can OR (join) certain of them together into nonconvex (nonlinearly separable) class regions. Therefore, there must be a sufficiently large number of RBFs to cover all of the subclasses that are linearly separable. Figure 3.20 shows a portion of two-dimensional feature space covered by RBFs.

It has been shown in Bianchini et al. (1995) that whenever the classes in feature space are separable by hyperspheres, the SSE function E for training the RBF networks has no local minima. That is a great simplification. When we train on the weights $\{u_{mj}\}$, we notice the high speed at which steepest descent converges. The minimum is global.

The Quick Training Algorithm

For this particular algorithm, we randomly draw the initial weights $\{u_{mj}^{(0)}\}$ at the neurodes in the output layer and then adjust them by the method of steepest descent (see Chapter 4

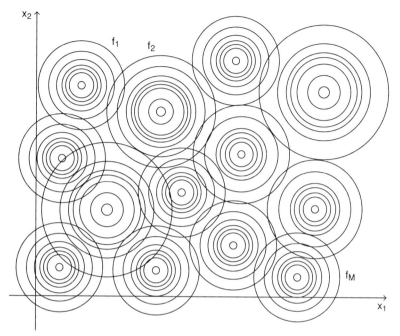

Figure 3.20. RBF contour curves in the plane.

for a derivation of steepest descent, and see Chapter 7 for more details on RBF networks). The method uses the negative gradient $-\nabla E = -(\partial E/\partial u_{11},..., \partial E/\partial u_{MJ})$. The neurode's center vectors (the neurodal center) $\{\mathbf{v}^{(m)}\}$ are set equal to the exemplar $\{\mathbf{x}^{(q)}\}$ so there are Q neurodes in the hidden layer.

Step 1: /Use the given Q input exemplar vectors $\{\mathbf{x}^{(q)}\}$ as centers and input parameters/
        input Q; $M \leftarrow Q$;   /$M = Q$ hidden neurodes/
        for $m = 1$ to M do $\mathbf{v}^{(m)} \leftarrow \mathbf{x}^{(m)}$;   /Assign exemplars as neurode centers/
        input I; $i \leftarrow 1$;   /I is no. of iterations wanted/
        $E \leftarrow 99999.9$; $\epsilon \leftarrow 0.0001$;   /Assign initial TSSE E, ϵ for stopping/
        $\eta_1 \leftarrow 1.0$;   /Input initial learning rate/

Step 2: /Initialize weights at the neurodes in the output layer/
        for $m = 1$ to M do
            for $j = 1$ to J do
                $u_{mj} \leftarrow \text{random}(0,1) - 0.5$;   /Uniform random numbers in $[-0.5, 0.5]$/

Step 3: /Compute a single spread parameter/
        $\sigma \leftarrow 1/(2M)^{1/N}$;   /Compute spread parameter σ and/
        for $m = 1$ to M do $\sigma_m \leftarrow \sigma$;   /put $\sigma_m = \sigma$ at each mth neurode/

Step 4: /Compute $y_m^{(q)} = f_m(\mathbf{x}^{(q)}; \mathbf{v}^{(m)})$, $m = 1,...$, M for each input exemplar feature/
/vector $\mathbf{x}^{(q)}$/

for $q = 1$ to Q do   /For each qth exemplar input vector/
  for $m = 1$ to M do   /and all mth hidden neurode centers/
                                                      /compute output $y_m^{(q)}$ at mth hidden neurode/
     if $q = m$, then $y_m^{(q)} \leftarrow 1$;   /For $\mathbf{x}^{(q)} = \mathbf{v}^{(m)}$, $y_m^{(q)} = \exp(0) = 1$/
     else $y_m^{(q)} \leftarrow \exp(-\|\mathbf{x}^{(q)}$ /else compute $y_m^{(q)}$ values/
              $- \mathbf{v}^{(m)}\|^2/(2\sigma^2_m))$;

Step 5: /Update output values $z_j^{(q)}$ of output neurodes for $j = 1,...$, J and $q = 1,...$, Q/
for $q = 1$ to Q do   /For each exemplar vector $\mathbf{x}^{(q)}$/
  for $j = 1$ to J do   /and each output node/
    $z_j^{(q)} \leftarrow (1/M)\sum_{(m=1, M)}$ /update outputs of output layer/
       $\times u_{mj}y_m^{(q)}$;
$E_{\text{new}} = \sum_{(q=1, Q)}\sum_{(j=1, J)}$ /Compute new total SSE/
    $\times [t_j^{(k(q))} - z_j^{(q)}]^2$;
if $E_{\text{new}} < E$, then $\eta_1 \leftarrow \eta_1*1.04$;   /If lower error, make η_1 slightly larger/
else $\eta_1 \leftarrow \eta_1*0.92$;   /Otherwise, make smaller step/
$E \leftarrow E_{\text{new}}$;   /Update current total SSE value for E/

Step 6: /Adjust weights $\{u_{mj}\}$ in the neurodes of the output layer according to steepest/
/descent/
for $m = 1$ to M do   /For each weight u_{mj}/
  for $j = 1$ to J do   /use steepest descent update/
    $u_{mj} \leftarrow u_{mj} + (2\eta_1/M)\sum_{(q=1, Q)}(t_j^{(k(q))} - z_j^{(q)})y_m^{(q)}$;

Step 7: /Stop or repeat training of $\{u_{mj}\}$/
if $(i \geq \mathrm{I})$ or $(E < \epsilon)$, then stop;   /Stop on $i \geq I$, or if error less than ϵ/
else $i \leftarrow i + 1$; go to Step 5;   /Note: don't repeat Step 4 here, y_m values are/
/fixed/

The *quick training* algorithm adjusts only the output weights $\{u_{mj}\}$. There is a hidden neurode for each exemplar input $\mathbf{x}^{(q)}$, which may be too many for large Q. If $Q > 200$ or so, then we use a smaller M and use the *full training* algorithm given in Chapter 7. It uses $M < Q$, draws the M centers at random, and then adjusts them via steepest descent as well as the output layer weights.

The *advantages* of RBF networks using the *quick training* algorithm are that they are simple and train extremely quickly (up to 1000 times faster than backpropagation), they have no local minima, and they have reduced sensitivity to the order of the presentation of the training exemplars. Their *disadvantages* are that for large datasets (large Q) the *full training* algorithm must be used, which requires more hidden neurodes than MLPs and thus more time for the trained network working in operational mode. They often require a large number of hidden neurodes for good approximation of functions.

In practice, we use RBF networks for classification and recognition where a moderate number K of classes is involved, and especially where the dimension N of the feature space may be large (Fu, 1994, p. 96). We usually put $M = cK$ and assign to each $\mathbf{v}^{(m)}$ an exemplar from a different subclass. For nonlinear separation, we need a feature vector from each of the cK linearly separable subclasses, so we can put $M = Q$ if we have a sufficiently large sample of size Q. MLPs with sigmoids provide better results for many large problems where Q or K is large. Consider training on medical data with $Q = 10,000$ exemplar input vectors, which may need only a few hidden neurodes with MLPs (there may be only two classes). We could use the k-means clustering algorithm to arrive at K small clusters so we can use $M = K$ hidden neurodes. For practical reasons, we should make a large number of small clusters for nonlinear separation (complex nonconvex classes can be composed of a number of small convex clusters). Advanced methods start with fewer hidden neurodes, drawn randomly, and adjust their centers while adjusting the weights of the neurodes in the output layer. Chapter 7 reviews some of these methods. Section 7.7 presents the *full training* algorithm for RBFs.

3.12. Self-Organizing Feature Maps and Learning Vector Quantification

Kohonen's Basic Network Concept

A *Kohonen* network (Kohonen, 1988) contains a single layer of neurodes in addition to an input layer of branching nodes. There are M neurodes in the neural layer and each has a parametric weight vector $\mathbf{v}^{(m)}$ of dimension N, which is the same as the dimension of the input feature vectors $\mathbf{x}^{(q)} = (x_1^{(q)},..., x_N^{(q)})$, where $q = 1,..., Q$. Figure 3.21 displays a Kohonen network, which is also called a *self-organizing feature map* (SOFM). The weight vectors $\mathbf{v}^{(1)},...,$ $\mathbf{v}^{(M)}$ are randomly initialized in the feature space at the beginning. One exemplar input vector $\mathbf{x}^{(q)}$ is selected from the sample and put into the network and the squared distances between $\mathbf{x}^{(q)}$ and each $\mathbf{v}^{(m)}$, $m = 1,..., M$ are computed by

$$D_{qm} = D_{qm}(\mathbf{x}^{(q)},\mathbf{v}^{(m)}) = \sum_{(n=1, N)}(x_n^{(q)} - v_n^{(m)})^2 \tag{3.16}$$

Figure 3.21. A Kohonen network.

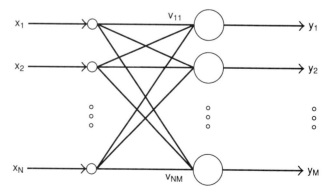

The minimum distance D_{qm*} is then determined to obtain the neurode $m*$ that is the *winner* over the other neurodes. From this point onward, there are different strategies. In the *winner-take-all* strategy, the winning neurode updates its parametric weight vector via

$$\mathbf{v}^{(m*)} = \mathbf{v}^{(m*)} + \eta(\mathbf{x}^{(q)} - \mathbf{v}^{(m*)}) \qquad (3.17)$$

where η is the *step gain* (or *learning rate*). All other neurodes keep their old values.

Another strategy is to update *positively* (*reinforce*, or *reward*) all neurodes that are close to the winning neurode and to update *negatively* (*extinguish*, or *punish*) all of those neurodes that are farther away from the winner. This process is also known as *lateral inhibition*. Figure 3.22 shows a slice across one dimension of the feature space of the lateral inhibition function, where distance is $\|\mathbf{x} - \mathbf{v}^{(m)}\|$ on the horizontal axis. Because of the shape of this function, it is called the "Mexican sombrero." The reinforcement region is gradually reduced over the iterations of unsupervised learning.

When a vector $\mathbf{x}$ is presented to a Kohonen network, the dot product $y_m = \mathbf{x} \cdot \mathbf{v}^{(m)}$ is computed as output from each mth neurode ($m = 1,..., M$). When $\mathbf{x}$ and $\mathbf{v}^{(m)}$ are closest, then their correlation $\mathbf{x} \cdot \mathbf{v}^{(m)}$ is greatest so the neurode $m*$ with the greatest correlation wins. The neurodes may also be arranged in a two-dimensional or one-dimensional array. In the former case, square neighborhoods are centered on the winning neurode so that all neurodes inside that square are reinforced, while all neurodes outside of that neighborhood are extinguished (Kohonen, 1982). Figure 3.23 shows these neighborhoods.

A Self-Organizing Feature Map Algorithm

A higher-level algorithm for a basic SOFM algorithm is given below, where there are M neurodes in a single layer and the *winner-take-all* strategy is used.

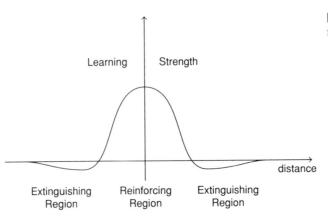

Figure 3.22. Lateral inhibition function.

Learning | Strength

Extinguishing Region   Reinforcing Region   Extinguishing Region

distance

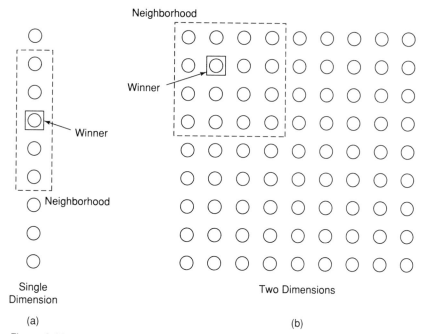

Figure 3.23. Neighborhoods of winning neurodes.

Step 1: Randomize the order of $\{\mathbf{x}^{(q)}\}$; $q \leftarrow 1$;
for $m = 1$ to M do
for $n = 1$ to N do
$v_n^{(m)} \leftarrow \text{random}(0,1)$ /Draw random weights/

Step 2: Draw exemplar $\mathbf{x}^{(q)}$ from the exemplar set;

Step 3: For $m = 1$ to M do
compute distance D_{qm};   /Distance between $\mathbf{x}^{(q)}$ and each $\mathbf{v}^{(m)}$/
find $\mathbf{v}^{(m*)}$ with minimum distance D_{qm*} /Minimize $\|\mathbf{x}^{(q)} - \mathbf{v}^{(m)}\|^2$/

Step 4: Update neurode $m*$ via
$\mathbf{v}^{(m*)} \leftarrow \mathbf{v}^{(m*)} + \eta_1(\mathbf{x}^{(q)} - \mathbf{v}^{(m*)})$ /Reinforce-reward/
and update all neurodes $m \neq m*$ via
$\mathbf{v}^{(m)} \leftarrow \mathbf{v}^{(m)} - \eta_2(\mathbf{x}^{(q)} - \mathbf{v}^{(m)})$ /Extinguish-punish/

Step 5: If stop criterion satisfied then stop
else $q \leftarrow q + 1$; if $q > Q$, then $q = q - Q$;
goto Step 2

The Learning Vector Quantization Algorithm

This method originated in Linde et al. (1980) and Gray (1984) as a tool for image data compression. These networks are similar to the SOFMs described above except that the single layer of neurodes uses target output vectors $\mathbf{t}^{(q)}$ to correspond with the input exemplars $\mathbf{x}^{(q)}$; that is, it trains in the supervised mode rather than in the unsupervised (self-organizing) mode. Thus the target (identifier) vectors must be available to determine if the winner is correct. Figure 3.24 displays such a network. Each mth neurode contains a center vector $\mathbf{v}^{(m)}$, $m = 1,..., M$.

The *learning vector quantization* algorithm was adapted by (Kohonen, 1986, 1988) for pattern recognition. When a feature vector $\mathbf{x}$ is presented to the network, the values $y_m = \mathbf{x} \cdot \mathbf{v}^{(m)}$ are computed, $m = 1,..., M$. Of these M neurodal outputs, only a single one puts out a high value to denote Class m^* as the class to which the input vector $\mathbf{x}$ belongs. The winner is reinforced, provided that it is correct upon testing against the targets, or else it is extinguished. The high-level algorithm is given here.

Step 1: Initialize M neurode centers by putting them equal to first M exemplar input feature vectors;
$q \leftarrow 1; i \leftarrow 1;$ /Set exemplar no. and iteration no./

Step 2: for $m = 1,..., M$ do $y_m^{(q)} \leftarrow \mathbf{x}^{(q)} \cdot \mathbf{v}^{(m)}$
find winning neurode m* by greatest value $y_{m^*}^{(q)}$;

Step 3: If $y_{m^*}^{(q)}$ is high for correct target component of $\mathbf{t}^{(k(q))}$ then
$\mathbf{v}^{(m^*)} \leftarrow \mathbf{v}^{(m^*)} + \eta(\mathbf{x}^{(q)} - \mathbf{v}^{(m^*)})$ /Reinforce/
else $\mathbf{v}^{(m^*)} \leftarrow \mathbf{v}^{(m^*)} - \eta(\mathbf{x}^{(q)} - \mathbf{v}^{(m^*)})$ /Extinguish/

Step 4: If $q < Q$, then $q \leftarrow q + 1$ and go to Step 2;
else $q = 1; i \leftarrow i + 1;$

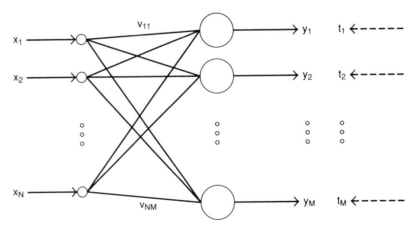

Figure 3.24.   A learning vector quantization network.

> if $i > I$ then stop
> else $\eta \leftarrow f(\eta)$; go to step 2;   /$f(\text{—})$ is a decreasing function/

3.13. The Amari–Hopfield Recurrent Neural Networks

The Amari Model

Shun-ichi Amari published an *NN* model in 1977 that established a new perspective (Amari, 1977). This model, which has feedback (whence the name *recurrent*), is shown in Figure 3.25. While there is only a single layer of neurodes in the architecture, the feedback loops have the effect of providing an unlimited number of layers: one for each feedback loop through the single layer. Amari had long been associated with networks of thresholding gates (Amari, 1971, 1972), but this new model, which was derived from the McCulloch–Pitts model, was a precursor of the Hopfield network that in 1982 revived intense interest in NNs (Hopfield, 1982).

The initial inputs, shown in the figure as $\mathbf{x} = (x_1,..., x_N)$, are put directly to the neurodes without any fan out and become the initial outputs $\mathbf{y} = (y_1^{(0)},..., y_N^{(0)})$ at time $t = 0$. The outputs then feed back to branching nodes where they fan out to each of the neurodes. Thus each neurode now receives the N feedback inputs $y_1^{(0)},..., y_N^{(0)}$ simultaneously in a synchronous fashion. On the $(r + 1)$st feedback loop (iteration), the neurodes have just put out $\mathbf{y} = (y_1^{(r)},..., y_N^{(r)})$ at time $t = r$, which are fed back and fanned out to the neurodes. Each nth neurode now computes its next output by means of a set of synaptic weights $\{w_{pn}\}$ ($1 \leq$

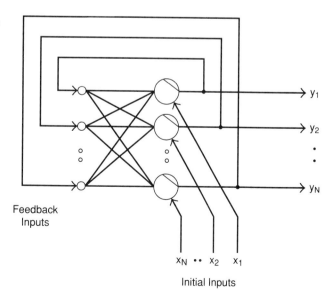

Figure 3.25. The Amari recurrent model.

Feedback
Inputs

x_N •• x_2 x_1

Initial Inputs

$p \leq N$, $1 \leq n \leq N$), a set of thresholds $\{\tau_n\}$, and a threshold function $f(-) = \text{sgn}(-)$. The new output value at the nth neurode is

$$y_n^{(r+1)} = f(s) = f(\textstyle\sum_{(p=1,\ N)} w_{pn}[y_n^{(r)} - \tau_n]) \qquad (3.18)$$

where $f(-)$ is the threshold function

$$f(s) = 1, \quad \text{if } s \geq 0; \qquad f(s) = 0, \quad \text{if } s < 0$$

(the *all-or-none* principle).

The *system state* at time $t = r$ is the tuple $\mathbf{y}^{(r)} = (y_1^{(r)},..., y_N^{(r)})$ of 0s and 1s. If the network converges over the iterative feedback loops to a *stable state* where $\mathbf{y}^{(r+1)} = \mathbf{y}^{(r)}$ for $r > r_0$ for some r_0, then this fixed state is the identifier corresponding to the feature vector $\mathbf{x}$ that was input initially. The nth neuron also feeds back its value $y_n^{(r)}$ to the nth neuron (i.e., to itself), but this tends to have a dominating effect after a number of iterations. Studies show that when convergence to a stable state occurs, it is quicker than other similar recurrent networks. Unfortunately, convergence need not occur.

The Hopfield Model

The Hopfield discrete network is a variation on that of Amari (Hopfield, 1982). Figure 3.26 presents the model. At the branch nodes on the left, the feedback lines fan out to all neurodes *except* the ones from which they came as outputs. In other words no neurode feeds back to itself. Another change from the Amari network is that random variables $I_1,..., I_N$, that are models to account for noise, jitter and delay, feed into each neurode. The inputs $x_1,..., x_N$ form the initial state $(y_1^{(0)},..., y_N^{(0)})$ of the network as before. The weights on the fan-out

Figure 3.26. The Hopfield model.

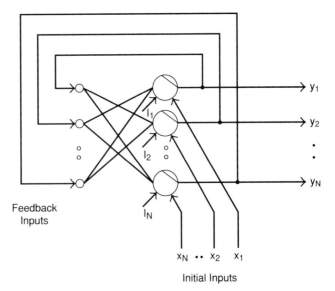

Feedback Inputs

$x_N \cdot\cdot x_2 \quad x_1$

Initial Inputs

lines from the feedback branching nodes are denoted by w_{ij} (on the line from the ith neurode to the jth neurode), where $w_{jj} = 0$ for all j. On the $(r + 1)$st feedback loop, the output $(y_1^{(r)},..., y_N^{(r)})$ is processed by summing the weighted feedback values $w_{ij}y_i^{(r)}$, adding on a random value $I_j = i_j$, and then subtracting a threshold value τ_j. The resulting values are summed and then passed through a *sign* function (bipolar threshold) defined by $f(s) = 1$ if $s \geq 0$, else $f(s) = -1$. The computed output value at the nth neurode is then

$$y_n^{(r+1)} = f(\textstyle\sum_{(i=1,\,N)}[w_{ij}y_i^{(r)}] + I_j - \tau_j) \tag{3.19}$$

The updated outputs are actually computed *asynchronously* in *random order*. Only a single neurode activates an output on each update, so only a single feedback input changes on each feedback loop. However, the firing (activation) of a single neurode affects the changing of all neurodal output values at whatever future times they fire. See Zurada (1992, p. 255) for further discussion. Chapter 8 covers the conditions sufficient for convergence of Hopfield networks.

3.14. Recurrent Artificial Neural Networks as Pattern Recognizers

Recurrent artificial NNs operate very differently from the feedforward NNs that must be trained to map input exemplar feature vectors into desired output identifiers. Recurrent networks were originally not trained, but were only tested to determine the attractor states to which initially given input vectors converged, if any. Through evolutionary research, it was discovered that a symmetric weight matrix is sufficient for convergence (see Chapter 8).

The process is as follows: (i) Compute the weights once from the exemplar input feature vectors as correlation of the initial inputs to obtain a symmetric weight matrix and (ii) test the network weights on the exemplar feature vectors to determine the state (identifier) to which each input vector converges. *Recurrent convergence* occurs when all neurodes have fired in any order without changing the state of the network. After training and collecting the identifier states for each exemplar input feature vector, a novel feature vector $\mathbf{x}$ is input as the initial vector $\mathbf{y}^{(0)} = \mathbf{x}$ in the operational mode. A number of recursions take place until the network converges to a stable output vector (such that $\mathbf{y}^{(r+k)} = \mathbf{y}^{(r)}$ for all $k \geq 0$ and all neurons have fired). Then $\mathbf{y}^{(r)}$ is an identifier for the class to which $\mathbf{x}$ belongs (in which case we say that the network *recognizes* $\mathbf{x}$). The network is a type of noisy automaton that is limited to recognition (no generation).

Hopfield NNs are so intellectually appealing that researchers continue to study them and improve on their training, even though they require a large number of neurons compared to the number of classes (attractor states) and take considerably more time to compute recursively when compared to feedforward artificial neural networks.

Exercises

3.1. Set up an MLP with two inputs, two hidden neurodes in a single hidden layer, and a single neurode in the output layer. Use the unipolar sigmoid as activation function.

Write out the complete sum-squared error function E over $K = 2$ classes of exemplar inputs and their associated desired outputs. Expand E as a composition of all of the functions from the inputs to the outputs, including all weights and sigmoids. The final formulation $E(w_{11},..., w_{NM}, u_{11},..., u_{MJ})$ is the sum-squared error function of the weights.

3.2. Use the method of steepest descent to establish an algorithm for training the weights of an MLP with two input nodes, two middle neurodes and a single output neurode, to recognize two classes ($K = 2$). Starting with an initially randomly drawn set of weights, solve for the weights by adding increments to the current weights over many iterations: Take the partial derivatives of E with respect to each of the $NM + MJ = 6$ weights $\{w_{11}, w_{21}, w_{12}, w_{22}, u_{11}, u_{21}\}$ to obtain $\{\partial E/\partial w_{nm}, \partial E/\partial u_{mj}\}$ and update the new weights on each training iteration by moving in the direction of the negative gradients—that is, by adding an increment to each weight that is a small constant times the negative partial derivatives.

3.3. Implement the algorithm for the MLP of Exercise 3.2 in a computer program. Use it to perform 2-bit even parity, where the inputs (x_1, x_2) take on the combinations $(0, 0)$, $(0, 1)$, $(1, 0)$, $(1, 1)$, with the single output taking the value 0 for an even number of 1s or 1 for an odd number of 1s. Test it to see how it works, using 0.1 for 0 and 0.9 for 1.

3.4. Use four middle neurodes in Exercise 3.3 and train on 2-bit even parity. Test the performance of the trained MLP. Train it on odd parity, also, where the outputs are the complements of even parity.

3.5. Consider a single neuron with two inputs and one output, using a bipolar hyperbolic tangent activation function. Now use the inverse hyperbolic tangent function to map a desired output y_1 backward (inversely) into a linear sum s_1 of weighted inputs. Repeat for a second desired (training) output y_2 (there are two classes) to obtain s_2. Now consider the two linear equations in two unknowns w_1 and w_2. Based on this, justify or contradict the following statement: A single neurode with sigmoid activation is capable only of linear separation of two classes.

3.6. Does the conclusion on linear separability in Exercise 3.5 hold for threshold activation functions? Use hyperplanes to complete the argument, rather than an inverse activation function.

3.7. Write an algorithm that trains an MLP on a sample of input and output data $\{x^{(1)},..., x^{(Q)}, t^{(1)},..., t^{(Q)}\}$ by the method of steepest descent on the sum-squared error function over all input/output samples.

3.8. Write an algorithm that trains an MLP by selecting weights randomly between -1 and 1 and keeping each weight that causes the sum-squared error $E = E(w_{11},..., w_{NM}, u_{11},..., u_{MJ})$ to decrease (throw away those that don't). Use unipolar sigmoids.

3.9. Write a computer program that implements the method steepest descent for training an FLN (functional link net).

3.10. Write a computer program that implements the random search training algorithm from Exercise 3.8.

3.11. Develop an algorithm and write a program to train an RBF network using steepest descent.

3.12. Repeat Exercise 3.11 using random search.

3.13. Write a program to simulate the Amari recurrent neural network with four neurodes. Use the following initial values of inputs: (0, 0, 0, 1), (0, 1, 1, 0), (1, 0, 1, 0), and (1, 1, 0, 1). For the weights, use the initial values $w_{ij} = x_i x_j$. Do any of these inputs converge?

3.14. Use a Hopfield RNN on 2-bit parity, except in this case use four input components. The first two components are the inputs to the 2-bit parity function and the third component is the output of the product of the first two components. The fourth component is to be carried, but may have no meaning unless it is given one (Aleksander et al. 1990). Experiment with the fourth input bit. Can the Hopfield network learn XOR?

3.15. Run a Hopfield RNN in a synchronous mode where all of the neurodes update simultaneously. Try to teach it the XOR function. Report the results.

3.16. Modify the algorithm in Exercise 3.8 above for training an MLP that: (i) draws an initial set of weights randomly from -1 to 1 and computes the SSE (sum-squared error); (ii) adjusts the weights at the hidden neurodes by drawing new ones at random, computing the total SSE, and keeping these new weights if the SSE decreased or else discarding them and putting the previous ones back in if the SSE increased; and (iii) adjusts the weights at the output layer of neurodes according to the same scheme as for the hidden layer. Use bipolar sigmoid activation functions.

3.17. It is desired to design an MLP to recognize the 10 digits 0, 1, ... , 9 based on a feature vector of $N = 12$ feature components for each digit. Choose M and J. Discuss and justify your choices.

3.18. In Exercise 3.17, which type of FANN (MLP, FLN, or RBFN) would be best for this digit recognition task? Justify your answer. Would your answer still hold if the number of features were increased to 100?

3.19. Design an algorithm that could learn to map input feature vectors for the digits into the correct identifier vectors for the digits, where the identifiers are to have 10 components (a single jth component is to go high when the input belongs to the jth digit class). State the algorithm in a brief form of English (a high-level pseudo-language for outlining programs).

3.20. Draw a recurrent network such that $N = 2$ neurodes feed back to all neurodes. Use the weight set {1, 1, -1, 1}. Start with input $\mathbf{x} = (0,1)$ and make a chart of all the current and next state values. Try starting with other vectors $\mathbf{x}$ where all component values must be one of 0 or 1. Do any of these input vectors converge? Do any of them cycle through a fixed path of states (repeating the same sequence)?

3.21. What are the differences between *k*-means clustering and the Kohonen SOFM process? Is one more powerful than the other? What are the tradeoffs?

3.22. Argue that the radial basis function networks can either perform nonlinear separation or cannot.

3.23. Show that a functional link net can perform 3-bit parity (determine whether or not there is an even or odd number of 1s out of three bits as input). If so, what is the minimal number of extratensor features that must be added to separate the even and odd classes?

3.24. Train a radial basis function network to perform 3-bit parity. What is the smallest number of hidden neurodes required? Would you rate this network as a fast learner?

References

Aleksander, I., and H. Morton (1990), *An Introduction to Neural Computing*, Chapman and Hall, London.

Amari, S. (1971), Characteristics of randomly connected threshold-element networks and network systems, *Proc. IEEE*, vol. 59, 35–47.

Amari, S. (1972), Learning patterns and pattern sequences by self-organizing nets of threshold elements, *IEEE Trans. Comput.*, vol. 21, 1197–1206.

Amari, S. (1977), Neural theory of association and concept formation, *Biol. Cybern.*, vol. 26, 175–185.

Bernstein, J. (1981), Profiles: AI, Marvin Minsky, *The New Yorker*, Dec. 14, 50–126.

Bianchini, M., Frasconi, P., Gori, M. (1995), Learning without local minima in radial basis function networks, *IEEE Trans. Neural Networks*, vol. 6, no. 3, 749–756.

Fu, LiMin (1994), *Neural Networks in Computer Intelligence*, McGraw-Hill, New York.

Gray, R. M. (1984), Vector quantization, *IEEE ASSP*, vol. 1, 4–29.

Hartman, E. J., Keeler, J. D., and Kowalski, J. M. (1990), Layered neural networks with Gaussian hidden units as universal approximators, *Neural Comput.*, vol. 2, no. 2, 210–215.

Hebb, Donald (1949), *The Organization of Behavior*, Wiley, New York.

Hecht-Nielsen, R. (1990), *Neurocomputing*, Addison-Wesley, Reading, MA.

Hopfield, J. J. (1982), Neural networks and physical systems with emergent collective computational abilities, *Proc. Natl. Acad. Sci. USA*, vol. 79, 2554–2558.

Hornik, K., Stinchcombe, M., and White, H. (1989), Multilayer feedforward networks are universal approximators, *Neural Networks*, vol. 2, no. 5, 359–366.

Kohavi, Z (1978), *Switching and Finite Automata Theory*, McGraw-Hill, New York.

Kohonen, T. (1982), Self-organized formation of topologically correct feature maps, *Biol. Cybern.*, vol. 43, 59–69.

Kohonen, T. (1986), *Learning Vector Quantization for Pattern Recognition*, Technical Report TKK-F-A601, Helsinki University of Technology, Finland.

Kohonen, T. (1988), *Self-Organization and Associative Memory*, Springer-Verlag, New York.

Kosko, Bart (1992), *Neural Networks and Fuzzy Systems*, Prentice-Hall, Englewood Cliffs, NJ.

Lewis, P. M., and Coates, C. L. (1967), *Threshold Logic*, Wiley, New York.

Linde, Y., Buzo, A., and Gray, R. M. (1980), An algorithm for vector quantizer design, *IEEE Trans. Commun.*, vol. 28, 84–95.

McCulloch, W. S., and Pitts, W. (1943), A logical calculus of the ideas immanent in nervous activity, *Bull. of Math. Biophys.*, vol. 5, 115–133.

Minsky, M. L., and Papert, S. A. (1988), *Perceptrons, Expanded Edition*, MIT Press, Cambridge, MA.

Murphy, John H (1990), The quest for synthetic intelligence, *Proceedings of the 1990 Workshop on Neural Networks*, Auburn, AL, NASA/Soc. Computer Simulation, 16–43.

Pao, Y. H. (1989), *Adaptive Pattern Recognition and Neural Networks*, Addison-Wesley, Reading, MA.

Poggio, T, and Girosi, F. (1990), Networks for approximating and learning, *Proc. IEEE*, vol. 78, 1481–1497.

Rosenblatt, F. (1958), The perceptron: a probabilistic model for information storage and organization in the brain, *Psychol. Review*, vol. 654, 386–408.

Wasserman, P. D. (1989), *Neural Computing*, Van Nostrand Reinhold, New York.

Wasserman, P. D. (1993), *Advanced Methods in Neural Computing*, Van Nostrand Reinhold, New York.

Zurada, J. M. (1992), *Artificial Neural Networks*, West Publishing, St. Paul, MN.

Chapter 4

Supervised Training via Error Backpropagation: Derivations

This chapter derives the error backpropagation algorithm in detail for various cases of MLPs and also for FLNs and RBFNs.

4.1. A Closer Look at the Supervised Training Problem

Some Fundamental Questions

T his chapter derives the gradient descent formulation for training a multiple-layered perceptron (MLP) network in the epochal mode of backpropagation (BP). Chapters 5 and 6 cover fine points and other formulations for better training and performance. We continue to refer to the artificial neural nodes as *neurodes* to distinguish them from biological neurons, which are very different.

The supervised training of an MLP requires (i) a sample of Q exemplar input feature vectors $\{\mathbf{x}^{(q)}\}_{q=1, Q}$ and an associated set of exemplar output target vectors $\{\mathbf{t}^{(k)}: k = 1,...,$ $K\}$ to form the set $\{(\mathbf{x}^{(q)}, \mathbf{t}^{(k(q))}): q = 1,..., Q\}$ of Q exemplar pairs, (ii) the selection of an initial synaptic weight set $\{w_{nm}^{(0)}, u_{mj}^{(0)}: 1 \le n \le N, 1 \le m \le M, 1 \le j \le J\}$; and (iii) the repetitive adjusting of the current weights by some method to force each of the input exemplar feature vectors to be mapped closer to its correct output target vector that identifies a class in the input space. More than one exemplar feature vector of the sample $\{\mathbf{x}^{(1)},..., \mathbf{x}^{(Q)}\}$ may map to a single identifier $\mathbf{t}^{(k)} = \mathbf{t}^{(k(q))}$ for each of the K classes ($K \le Q$). The weights $\{w_{nm}\}$ at the neurodes in the hidden layer and the weights $\{u_{mj}\}$ at the neurodes in the output layer are "knobs" to be adjusted to define a correct mapping of input feature vectors to their output class identifiers. A correct mapping takes each sample input vector $\mathbf{x}^{(q)}$ from the kth class into an output vector $\mathbf{z}^{(q)}$ that is closer to the target $\mathbf{t}^{(k(q))}$ than to the identifier $\mathbf{t}^{(p)}$ of any pth class, $p \neq k$. This means that $\left\| \mathbf{z}^{(q)} - \mathbf{t}^{(k(q))} \right\|$ must be very small for each q.

If this were all that there is to it, it would be a simple process, provided that we had a strategy that would adjust the weights properly. Unfortunately, the MLP *architecture* must be designed properly for the particular dataset to assure that the network will learn robustly and will be reasonably efficient. The main questions in designing the architecture and then training the MLP are listed below.

1. How many layers of neurodes should we use?

2. How many input nodes should we use?

3. How many neurodes in the hidden layers should we use?

4. How many neurodes should we use in the output layer?

5. What should the target (identifier) vectors be?

6. How do we proceed to train the MLP?

7. How can we test to determine whether or not the MLP is properly trained?

8. How do we select parameters (such as η), and speed up and improve the training?

9. What should be the range of the weights and the network inputs and outputs?

Some Answers

Answer 1 is provided by the Hornik–Stinchcombe–White result (Hornik et al., 1989) given in Section 3.9, which states that a hidden layer and an output of layer of neurodes are sufficient, provided that there are enough neurodes in the hidden layer. To reduce a large number of neurodes in some situations, we may use two hidden layers (see Chapter 9 on neural engineering), but this is not necessary. There is also the question of what effects an extra layer of neurodes in the middle can have. Is the training faster? Is the learning better? How do the answers to these questions depend upon the linearity or nonlinearity of the data? We discuss these neural engineering issues in Chapter 9, and we make actual tests in Chapters 11 and 12 to see what the results are. For now, we prefer to use a single hidden layer to avoid new difficulties, although we also derive the backpropagation iterative training equations for the case of two hidden layers.

Answer 2 can be given tentatively. The number N of input nodes must be the number N of features in the feature vectors, so that once a set of features is chosen, their number N is fixed. Chapter 10 discusses feature and data engineering. The pattern attributes of a population may be mapped to one of many possible sets of features of various sizes, but we assume here that this has already been done and that N is given and fixed. Answer 3 on the number of neurodes in the hidden layer(s) is difficult. A lot of research from different approaches has been done to find an answer. We provide answers in Chapter 9. For now, we use $M = 2K$ for a small number K of classes (for, say, $K = 2$ to 8) up to $M = K/2^p$ for larger K (say, $M = 128/2^3 = 16$ or $M = 512/2^4 = 32$). This allows from $M + 1$ to 2^M (lower and upper bounds) convex regions in the feature space. Groups of these can be joined into nonconvex classes by the output neurodes (see Chapter 9).

Answer 4 gives the number J of output neurodes that depends on the resolution required (the number K of classes) and gives the representation encoding scheme to be used. We may take $J = \log_2 K$ (from $K = 2^J$), which permits 2^J combinations of high and low (1 and 0) outputs of the J components. This is discussed in Section 4.7. Answer 5, on how to select the J target vectors, is also given in Section 4.7 and may be chosen from the 2^J combinations of high and low. It is usual practice to employ 0.9 for 1 and 0.1 for 0 (see Section 4.7) because standard MLPs cannot put out 0s and 1s unless the weights become infinite. Answer 6 on the training of an MLP is given in Chapters 4, 5, and 6. The methods are steepest descent, accelerated gradient methods such as conjugate gradients, and strategic search methodologies that include polynomial line search. There appears to be no single algorithm that is best overall for all datasets, so we need multiple methods.

Answer 7, which tells whether or not the training is satisfactory, is given in Chapter 9, which also outlines the way to perform validation and verification testing for acceptance of the MLP training and the model (network architecture). This involves using a *training* subset of the sample of exemplar pairs and two other disjoint *test* subsets that are to be used for validation and verification but not for training. When there are sufficiently many exemplars, we may select 25% of them at random to save for validation, choose another 15% at random to serve as the final verification, and use the remaining 60% for training. Under training, the training sum-squared error $E_{60\%}$ decreases, as does the testing sum-squared error $E_{25\%}$, which is computed after each small segment of training. When $E_{25\%}$ stops decreasing and begins to increase, then we stop the training because it is specializing on the training data and is becoming less accurate on novel data from the same population.

Answer 8, on the question of how to select parameters and speed up the training, is dealt with in Chapters 5 and 6 (also see Looney (1996)). These are mainly optimization techniques. For now we may put $\eta = 0.25$. Answer 9, on the range of the weights, is perhaps the easiest to answer for practical purposes. While the initial weights may be drawn from the interval $[-0.5, 0.5]$, the training may require that some weights move out into the interval $[-b, b]$, for some $b \geq 1$. We want to avoid weight drift, however, where certain weights become large in magnitude and other weights compensate with opposite signs to cancel out its affects. Ideally, the final weights should be in $[-1,1]$ because the inputs and outputs do not exceed 1 in magnitude and the activation functions squash the summed values r_m and s_j to within unit magnitude. In computational practice, though, the weights may be allowed to wander slightly. The range of the input features and outputs is typically taken to be $[0,1]$ for unipolar activation functions and $[-1,1]$ for bipolar ones (see Section 4.7).

Backpropagation with a single hidden layer is derived for both unipolar and bipolar inputs and activation functions in Section 4.4. An algorithm is presented in Section 4.5. It is also derived for two hidden layers with both unipolar and bipolar sigmoid activation functions in Section 4.4.

4.2. The Minimum Sum-Squared Error Methodology

The Network as an Input/Output Mapping

An MLP that has a single hidden layer is shown in Figure 4.1. There are N input branching nodes, M hidden neurodes, and J output neurodes. The weights on the input lines of the middle and output neurodes are designated by $\{w_{nm}\}$ and $\{u_{mj}\}$, respectively. The activation functions for the middle and output layers are, respectively, $h(-)$ and $g(-)$, as shown in

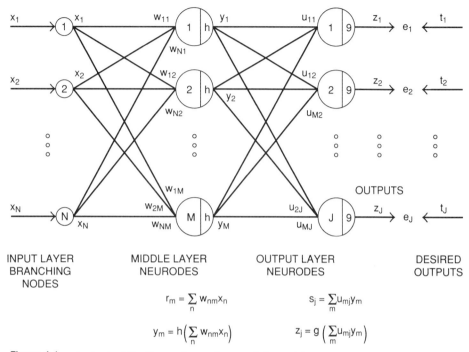

$$r_m = \sum_n w_{nm} x_n \qquad\qquad s_j = \sum_m u_{mj} y_m$$

$$y_m = h\left(\sum_n w_{nm} x_n\right) \qquad z_j = g\left(\sum_m u_{mj} y_m\right)$$

Figure 4.1. A standard feedforward neural network for training.

Figure 4.2. Both of the sigmoids at the hidden and output layer should be of the same type, either unipolar or bipolar. Figure 4.1 uses bipolar sigmoids because it has no $(N+1)$st weight that is the bias input, shown in Figure 3.4. The sigmoids are defined in Equations (3.2) and (3.3).

Figure 4.2. Standard and extended sigmoid functions with (a) Standard Sigmoid and (b) Extended Sigmoid.

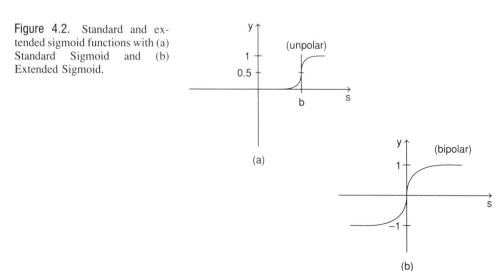

Let there be a sample of Q exemplar vectors $\{\mathbf{x}^{(1)},..., \mathbf{x}^{(Q)}\}$ from K classes ($K \leq Q$). There may be multiple exemplars for certain classes. For each exemplar $\mathbf{x}^{(q)}$ there is an associated *target* output vector $\mathbf{t}^{(k)} = \mathbf{t}^{(k(q))}$ that identifies its class number $k = k(q)$. The problem is to train the MLP by adjusting the weights $\mathbf{w} = (w_{11},..., w_{NM})$ and $\mathbf{u} = (u_{11},..., u_{MJ})$ as shown in Figure 4.1 until each exemplar $\mathbf{x}^{(q)}$ is mapped into an output $\mathbf{z}^{(q)}$ that is very close to $\mathbf{t}^{(k)} = \mathbf{t}^{(k(q))}$. In cases of multiple input exemplars for the same class, the same target vector is associated with each such input exemplar feature vector. If $\mathbf{x}^{(q_1)} \neq \mathbf{x}^{(q_2)}$ are two different exemplars for Class k, then $\mathbf{t}^{(k(q_1))} = \mathbf{t}^{(k(q_2))}$ because $k(q_1) = k(q_2)$.

A neural network is a *black box*—that is, an input/output system for which we need not know the inner workings. This contrasts with an expert rule-based system where every logical implication is known in a set of rules that provides explanation of the partial steps (Looney, 1993). After we train an MLP, it merely maps inputs to outputs with no explanations of its behavior. MLPs are easy to use, however, and can be quickly trained on datasets, whereas even a modest expert system requires several man-months or man-years of development.

The Total Sum-Squared Error Function E

To force each actual output $\mathbf{z}^{(q)}$ toward the correct output target $\mathbf{t}^{(k(q))}$, we adjust the weights so as to minimize the *total sum-squared error* (TSSE) E between the targets $\{\mathbf{t}^{(k(q))}: k = 1,..., K\}$ and the actual outputs $\{\mathbf{z}^{(q)}: q = 1,..., Q\}$, over all Q exemplars. The TSSE is defined via the Euclidean distance to be

$$E = \Sigma_{(q=1, Q)}\|\mathbf{t}^{(q)} - \mathbf{z}^{(q)}\|^2 \tag{4.1a}$$

The *total mean-squared error* (TMSE) is

$$\text{TMSE} = [1/(QJ)]E \tag{4.1b}$$

The *partial sum-squared errors* (PSSEs) with respect to a single exemplar input/output pair $(\mathbf{x}^{(q)}, \mathbf{t}^{(k(q))})$ is designated by $E^{(q)}$ and defined via

$$E^{(q)} = \Sigma_{(j=1, J)}(t_j^{(q)} - z_j^{(q)})^2 \tag{4.1c}$$

Likewise, the *partial mean-squared error* (PMSE) is

$$\text{PMSE} = (1/J)E^{(q)} \tag{4.1d}$$

We consider $E = E(\mathbf{w}, \mathbf{u})$ to be a function of the weights $\mathbf{w} = (w_{11},..., w_{NM})$ and $\mathbf{u} = (u_{11},..., u_{MJ})$. The general minimum MSE methodology was invented and used independently by Gauss (1809) and Legendre (1810) in the late 1790s. $E = E(\mathbf{w}, \mathbf{u})$ is defined (refer to Figure 4.1) in detail by

$$E(\mathbf{w}, \mathbf{u}) = \Sigma_{(q=1, Q)}\|\mathbf{t}^{(q)} - \mathbf{z}^{(q)}\|^2$$
$$= \Sigma_{(q=1, Q)}(\Sigma_{(j=1, J)}[t_j^{(q)} - z_j^{(q)}]^2) = \Sigma_{(q=1, Q)}(\Sigma_{(j=1, J)}[t_j^{(q)} - g(s_j^{(q)})]^2)$$
$$= \Sigma_{(q=1,Q)}(\Sigma_{(j=1, J)}[t_j^{(q)} - g(\Sigma_{(m=1, M)}u_{mj}y_m^{(q)}))]^2)$$

$$= \sum_{(q=1, Q)} (\sum_{(j=1, J)} [t_j^{(q)} - g(\sum_{(m=1, M)} u_{mj} h(r_m^{(q)})])^2)$$

$$= \sum_{(q=1, Q)} (\sum_{(j=1, J)} [t_j^{(q)} - g(\sum_{(m=1, M)} u_{mj} h(\sum_{(n=1, N)} w_{nm} x_n^{(q)}))])^2) \qquad (4.2)$$

where $h(-)$ and $g(-)$ are sigmoidal activation functions, respectively, for the hidden and output layers.

The function $E(\mathbf{w}, \mathbf{u})$ is a nonnegative continuously differentiable function on the weight space, which is $[-b, b]^{NM+MJ}$ $(b \geq 1)$, which is a finite-dimensional closed bounded domain that is complete and thus compact. Therefore, $E(\mathbf{w}, \mathbf{u})$ assumes its minimizing point $(\mathbf{w}^*, \mathbf{u}^*)$ in the weight domain. This doesn't mean that the sum-squared error E will be zero at the solution weight set $(\mathbf{w}^*, \mathbf{u}^*)$, but only that E will assume its minimum value there on the given weight domain. If the target vectors $\{\mathbf{t}^{(k)}\}$ are chosen judiciously to be far apart and if the exemplars for different classes are not too close, then the minimum mapping will successfully recognize the input feature vectors by mapping them to their class identifiers.

To solve for the minimizing weight set $(\mathbf{w}^*, \mathbf{u}^*)$, we use the necessary conditions

$$\partial E(\mathbf{w}^*, \mathbf{u}^*)/\partial w_{nm} = 0, \qquad \partial E(\mathbf{w}^*, \mathbf{u}^*)/\partial u_{mj} = 0 \qquad (4.3)$$

We cannot solve these nonlinear equations in closed form, but can approximate the solution $(\mathbf{w}^*, \mathbf{u}^*)$ iteratively with steepest descent. The next section discusses this method and derives an algorithm by means of chain rules (see Appendix 4 for an intuitive review of chain rules and vector calculus).

4.3. Linear Gradient Descent

To find a local minimum w_{locmin} for a nonlinear real valued function $y = f(w)$, we put

$$df(w)/dw = 0 \qquad (4.4)$$

and solve for $w = w_{\text{locmin}}$. However, in the general case of nonlinear $f(-)$ we can only find an approximate solution w_{approx} to w_{locmin} by iterative methods. Starting from some initial point $w^{(0)}$, we move a step in the *direction of steepest descent* to $w^{(1)} = w^{(0)} - df(w^{(0)})/dw$, which is opposite to the direction of steepest ascent. Note that the direction is either positive or negative along the w-axis. Figure 4.3 shows the first step. For the iterative $(r + 1)$st step, we have

$$w^{(r+1)} = w^{(r)} - \eta(df(w^{(r)})/dw) \qquad (4.5)$$

The *step gain* $\eta > 0$ amplifies or attenuates the step size. If the step were too large, then it would move past the local minimum w_{locmin}, while if it were too small, a large number of steps might not yet reach the local minimum. The difficult problem of setting a proper step gain η is addressed in Chapter 5. The step gain is called the *learning rate* in the literature on neural network training.

In Figure 4.4, where $y = f(w_1, w_2)$, the gradient is the vector of partial derivatives

$$\nabla f(w_1, w_2) = (\partial f(w_1, w_2)/\partial w_1, \partial f(w_1, w_2)/\partial w_2) \qquad (4.6)$$

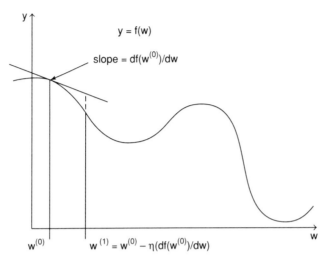

Figure 4.3. Approximating a local minimum.

A function $y = f(w_1,..., w_P)$ of several variables can be locally minimized in an analogous manner. The iterative updates to approximate a solution in the general case are

$$(w_1,..., w_P) \leftarrow (w_1,..., w_P) - \eta \left(\frac{\partial f(w_1,..., w_P)}{\partial w_1} ,..., \frac{\partial f(w_1,..., w_P)}{\partial w_P} \right) \tag{4.7}$$

In vector form, where $\mathbf{w} = (w_1,..., w_P)$, the gradient vector of partial derivatives is

$$\mathbf{w}^{(r+1)} = \mathbf{w}^{(r)} - \eta \nabla f(\mathbf{w}^{(r)}) \tag{4.8}$$

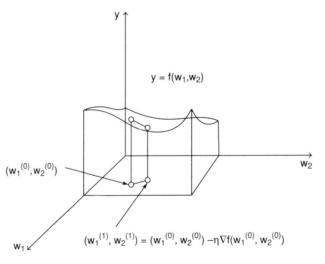

Figure 4.4. Two-dimensional steepest descent.

The normalization of $\nabla f(\mathbf{w}^{(r)})$ to unit length would change η. Usually, η is permitted to adapt to absorb any normalizing factors (see Chapter 5). Equation (4.8) is linear in $\mathbf{w}$ and provides a *piecewise linear* approximation for an adjustment to move $\mathbf{w}^{(r)}$ toward a local minimum. Appendix 4 derives Newton's second-order method and the method of conjugate directions for finding local minima.

4.4. Derivation of Error Backpropagation

Partial Sum-Squared Errors

The architecture of the standard feedforward MLP, shown in Figure 4.1, has N components in the input feature vectors, M neurodes in the middle layer, and J neurodes in the output layer. We assume that there is a sample of Q exemplar input feature vectors paired with K output training vectors. Multiple input exemplar vectors for a class must each map to the same output target vector that identifies that class. For example, if $\mathbf{x}^{(q_1)}$ and $\mathbf{x}^{(q_2)}$ are from the same kth class, then both map to $\mathbf{t}^{(k(q_1))} = \mathbf{t}^{(k(q_2))} = \mathbf{t}^{(k)}$.

The total sum-squared error (total SSE) E is the sum of all of the squared errors over all J output components and over all Q exemplar pairs, where the individual squared errors are $e_j^{(k)} = (t_j^{(k)} - z_j^{(k(q))})^2$. The total SSE can be decomposed into a sum of partial sum-squared errors

$$E = E^{(1)} + \cdots + E^{(Q)} \tag{4.9}$$

of which each summand is the SSE over a single qth exemplar pair.

$$E^{(q)} = \sum_{(j=1,\,J)} e_j^{(q)} = \sum_{(j=1,\,J)} [t_j^{(k(q))} - g(\sum_{(m=1,\,M)} u_{mj} h(\sum_{(n=1,\,N)} w_{nm} x_n^{(q)}))]^2 \tag{4.10a}$$

In the derivation for the steepest descent on $E^{(q)}$ that follows, we suppress the superscript "(q)" for convenience. We derive the *error backpropagation* algorithm for any single qth fixed exemplar pair, based on the PSSE function

$$E^{(q)} = E^{(q)}(\mathbf{w}, \mathbf{u}) = \sum_{(j=1,\,J)} (t_j - z_j)^2 \quad (= \sum_{(j=1,\,J)} (t_j^{(q)} - z_j^{(q)})^2, \text{ fixed } q) \tag{4.10b}$$

The sigmoids are unipolar; that is,

$$h(r_m) = 1/[1 + \exp(-\alpha_1 r_m + b_1)], \qquad g(s_j) = 1/[1 + \exp(-\alpha_2 s_j + b_2)] \tag{4.10c}$$

are activation functions at the hidden and output layers, respectively. In the derivation that follows, b_i is a bias ($i = 1, 2$), α_i is the *rate factor* in the exponential, and r and s are the sums of the products of weights times the incoming line values (see Figure 4.1).

Iterative approximation may take a generalized Newtonian, or *quasi-Newton*, form (see Linz, 1979, p. 146). The simplest of these is the steepest descent linearization

$$\mathbf{w}^{(r+1)} = \mathbf{w}^{(r)} - \eta[\nabla E(\mathbf{w}^{(r)})] = \mathbf{w}^{(r)} + \Delta\mathbf{w} \tag{4.11a}$$

$$\mathbf{u}^{(r+1)} = \mathbf{u}^{(r)} - \eta[\nabla E(\mathbf{u}^{(r)})] = \mathbf{u}^{(r)} + \Delta\mathbf{u} \tag{4.11b}$$

for updating the weights **w** at the hidden neurodes, and **u** at the output neurodes, respectively, on the $(r + 1)$st iteration. Upon taking each weight individually, we obtain the formulas

$$w_{nm}{}^{(r+1)} = w_{nm}{}^{(r)} - \eta(\partial E(\mathbf{w}^{(r)}, \mathbf{u}^{(r)})/\partial w_{nm}) \qquad (4.12a)$$

$$u_{mj}{}^{(r+1)} = u_{mj}{}^{(r)} - \eta(\partial E(\mathbf{w}^{(r)}, \mathbf{u}^{(r)})/\partial u_{mj}) \qquad (4.12b)$$

We now derive the backpropagation training equations to minimize the PSSE function $E^{(q)}$ for any fixed qth exemplar pair $(\mathbf{x}^{(q)}, \mathbf{t}^{(q)})$. We suppress the q notation for convenience. Appendix 4 explains intuitively the chain rules that we use.

The Derivation of Backpropagation with Unipolar Sigmoids

We first derive the computational formula for the weights $\{u_{mj}\}$ at the output neurodes by (i) applying the chain rule repeatedly to the partial derivative in Equation (4.12b), (ii) using

$$s_j = \textstyle\sum_{(m=1, M)} u_{mj} y_m \qquad (4.13)$$

as the sum at the jth output neurode, and (iii) using $g(s_j) = [1 + \exp(-s_j + b)]^{-1}$ as the unipolar activation function. We need not include α_i in the derivation (see Equation (4.10c)) because any constant multiplier can be absorbed into the step gain η. We also use b for the b_i for notational convenience. The derivation is done on the PSSE $E^{(q)}$, which is denoted by E (q is suppressed) for notational convenience.

The derivation for the u_{mj} increment is

$$\partial E/\partial u_{mj} = (\partial E/\partial s_j)(\partial s_j/\partial u_{mj}) \qquad \{\text{note: } s_j = s_j(u_{mj}), \text{ functionally}\}$$

$$= [(\partial E/\partial z_j)(\partial z_j/\partial s_j)](\partial s_j/\partial u_{mj}) \qquad \{\text{note: } z_j = g(s_j), \text{ functionally}\}$$

$$= [(\partial/\partial z_j)(\textstyle\sum_{(p=1, J)}(t_p - z_p)^2)(\partial/\partial s_j)g(s_j)][\partial s_j/\partial u_{mj}] \qquad \{\text{note: } p \text{ is a dummy variable for } j\}$$

$$= [2(-1)(t_j - z_j)(g'(s_j)][\partial/\partial u_{mj}\textstyle\sum_{(r=1, M)}y_r u_{rj}] \qquad \{\text{note: } (\partial/\partial s_j)g(s_j) = g'(s_j), r \text{ is a dummy for } m\}$$

$$= [(-2)(t_j - z_j)g'(s_j)][y_m] \qquad \{\text{note: } \partial/\partial u_{mj}[\textstyle\sum_{(q=1, M)}y_q u_{qj}] = y_m\}$$

$$= -2(t_j - z_j)g'(s_j)y_m \qquad (4.14)$$

But the sigmoid activation function $g(-)$ has derivative

$$g'(s_j) = (d/ds_j)g(s_j) = (d/ds_j)[1 + \exp(-s_j + b)]^{-1}$$

$$= (-1)[1 + \exp(-s_j + b)]^{-2}\exp(-s_j + b)(-1)$$

$$= [1 + \exp(-s_j + b)]^{-2}[\exp(-s_j + b)] \qquad \{\text{note: } z_j = [1 + \exp(-s_j + b)]^{-1}\}$$

$$= [z_j]^2[1 + \exp(-s_j + b) - 1] \qquad \{\text{note: add } (1 - 1) \text{ to rightmost factor}\}$$

$$= [z_j]^2[1/z_j - 1] = [z_j]^2[(1 - z_j)/z_j] = z_j(1 - z_j)$$

so that

$$g'(s_j) = z_j(1 - z_j) \tag{4.15}$$

Now we substitute Equation (4.15) back into Equation (4.14) to obtain

$$\partial E/\partial u_{mj} = -2(t_j - z_j)z_j(1 - z_j)y_m \tag{4.16}$$

Substituting Equation (4.16) into Equation (4.12b) provides the update on the $(r + 1)$st iteration as

$$u_{mj}^{(r+1)} = u_{mj}^{(r)} + \eta(t_j - z_j)z_j(1 - z_j)y_m \tag{4.17}$$

where the 2 has been absorbed into the step gain η.

Second, we derive the weight increments $\{w_{nm}\}$ at the middle neurodes by: (i) applying the chain rule repeatedly to the partial derivation in (4.12a), (ii) using

$$r_m = \sum_{(n=1,\,N)} w_{nm} x_n \tag{4.18}$$

for the sums, and (iii) using the hidden layer activation function $h(r_m) = 1/[1 + \exp(-r_m + b)]$ and derivative $h'(r_m) = y_m(1 - y_m)$. The previous remark about omitting α in the derivation holds here also. Then

$$
\begin{aligned}
\partial E/\partial w_{nm} &= (\partial E/\partial r_m)(\partial r_m/\partial w_{nm}) && \{\text{note: } r_m = \textstyle\sum_{(n=1,\,N)} w_{nm} x_n\} \\[4pt]
&= [(\partial E/\partial y_m)(\partial y_m/\partial r_m)](\partial r_m/\partial w_{nm}) && \{\text{note: } E = E(y_m)\} \\[4pt]
&= [(\partial/\partial y_m)(\textstyle\sum_{(j=1,\,J)}(t_j - z_j)^2) && \{\text{note: } y_m = h(r_m)\} \\
&\quad \times (\partial/\partial r_m)y_m][\partial r_m/\partial w_{nm}] \\[4pt]
&= (\partial/\partial y_m)(\textstyle\sum_{(j=1,\,J)}(t_j - z_j)^2)[(\partial/\partial r_m)h(r_m)] \\
&\quad \times [(\partial/\partial w_{nm})(\textstyle\sum_{(n=1,\,N)} x_n w_{nm})] \\[4pt]
&= (\partial/\partial y_m)(\textstyle\sum_{(j=1,\,J)}(t_j - z_j)^2)[h'(r_m)][x_n] && \{\text{note: } (\partial/\partial w_{nm})(\textstyle\sum x_n w_{nm}) = x_n\} \\[4pt]
&= (\partial/\partial y_m)[E(\mathbf{s}(y_m))][h'(r_m)][x_n] && \{\text{note: } E = E(\mathbf{s}(y_m)) = E(s_1(y_m),...,\,s_J(y_m))\} \\[4pt]
&= \{\textstyle\sum_{(j=1,\,J)}(\partial E/\partial s_j)(\partial s_j/\partial y_m)\}[h'(r_m)][x_n] && \{\text{note: pass } \partial/\partial y_m \text{ to inside of summation}\} \\[4pt]
&= \{\textstyle\sum_{(j=1,\,J)}(\partial/\partial s_j)\textstyle\sum_{(p=1,\,J)}(t_p - z_p)^2 && \{\text{note: use chain rule, full sum above}\} \\
&\quad \times (\partial s_p/\partial y_m)\}[h'(r_m)][x_n] \\[4pt]
&= \{\textstyle\sum_{(j=1,\,J)}(2)(t_j - z_j)(-1)g'(s_j) && \{\text{note: p is a dummy, } \partial z_j/\partial s_j = g'(s_j)\} \\
&\quad \times [\partial s_j/\partial y_m]\}[h'(r_m)][x_n] \\[4pt]
&= \{\textstyle\sum_{(j=1,\,J)}(-2)(t_j - z_j)[g'(s_j)] && \{\text{note: } s_j = \textstyle\sum_{(i=1,\,M)} y_i u_{ij}\} \\
&\quad \times [(\partial/\partial y_m)\textstyle\sum_{(i=1,\,M)} y_i u_{ij}]\}[h'(r_m)][x_n] \\[4pt]
&= \{\textstyle\sum_{(j=1,\,J)}(-2)(t_j - z_j)[z_j(1 - z_j)][u_{mj}]\} && \{\text{note: i is a dummy for } m \text{ above}\} \\
&\quad \times [h'(r_m)][x_n] \\[4pt]
&= \{\textstyle\sum_{(j=1,\,J)}(-2)(t_j - z_j)[z_j(1 - z_j)]u_{mj}\} && \{\text{note: } g'(s_j) = z_j(1 - z_j) \text{ from above}\} \\
&\quad \times [y_m(1 - y_m)][x_n] && \{\text{note: } h'(r_m) = y_m(1 - y_m) \text{ analogously}\}
\end{aligned}
$$

Therefore

$$\partial E/\partial w_{nm} = \{\textstyle\sum_{(j=1, J)}(-2)(t_j - z_j)[z_j(1 - z_j)]u_{mj}\}[y_m(1 - y_m)]x_n \tag{4.19}$$

Upon substituting Equation (4.19) into (4.12a), and absorbing the 2 into η, we obtain the computational formula on the $(r + 1)$st iteration, which is

$$w_{nm}^{(r+1)} = w_{nm}^{(r)} + \eta\{\textstyle\sum_{(j=1, J)}(t_j - z_j)[z_j(1 - z_j)]u_{mj}^{(r)}[y_m(1 - y_m)]x_n\} \tag{4.20}$$

Note that Equation (4.20) sums the differences $(t_j - z_j)$ over all $j = 1,..., J$ output neurodes. This is intuitive because each output difference affects all weights w_{nm} at the hidden layer, whereas a single difference affects a single node in the output layer.

The original backpropagation (BP) algorithm uses Equations (4.17) and (4.20) to update each weight for a fixed qth exemplar input/output pair (Rumelhart et al., 1986). This constitutes one iteration (training all weights on a single exemplar pair $(\mathbf{x}^{(q)}, \mathbf{t}^{(k(q))})$ to minimize $E^{(q)}$). BP repeats this for each qth exemplar pair until all Q PSSEs $E^{(q)}$ have been used in training. This entire process over each PSSE one time constitutes an *epoch*. A single epoch takes a minimizing step over each of the PSSE functions $E^{(1)},..., E^{(Q)}$ and on each such partial $E^{(q)}$, all of the weights are adjusted. Thus a single epoch adjusts each weight Q times. A large number I of epochs may be required for training (each weight is adjusted QI times).

To recapitulate, the unipolar learning equations for each qth exemplar (q is not suppressed) are

$$u_{mj} \leftarrow u_{mj} + \eta_1(t_j^{(q)} - z_j^{(q)})z_j^{(q)}(1 - z_j^{(q)})y_m^{(q)} \tag{4.21a}$$

$$w_{nm} \leftarrow w_{nm} + \eta_2\{\textstyle\sum_{(j=1, J)}(t_j^{(q)} - z_j^{(q)})[z_j^{(q)}(1 - z_j^{(q)})]u_{mj}\}[y_m^{(q)}(1 - y_m^{(q)})]x_n^{(q)} \tag{4.21b}$$

Backpropagation with Bipolar Sigmoids

Many researchers now use the bipolar sigmoid in place of the unipolar one to eliminate the bias b as a source of error and computational need (see Chapter 6). The derivation is the same except for the derivatives of $h(r_m)$ and $g(s_j)$, which now become the derivatives of the bipolar sigmoids, denoted here by $H(r_m)$ and $G(s_j)$. Let

$$z = G(s) = 2\{1/[1 + \exp(-\alpha s)]\} - 1 \tag{4.22a}$$

whose rational form is

$$z = G(s) = [1 + \exp(-\alpha s)]/[1 - \exp(-\alpha s)] \tag{4.22b}$$

From Equation (4.22a), we obtain

$$dz/ds = G'(s) = 2\alpha[1 + \exp(-\alpha s)]^{-2}(\exp(-\alpha s)) \tag{4.23}$$

Upon adding 1 to each side of Equation (4.22a), we obtain

$$(1 + z) = 2/[1 + \exp(-\alpha s)] \tag{4.24}$$

We solve for $\exp(-\alpha s)$ from Equation (4.24) by

$$\exp(-\alpha s) = 2/(1 + z) - 1 = (1 - z)/(1 + z) \tag{4.25a}$$

Similarly, we use Equation (4.24) to solve for $1 + \exp(-\alpha s)$ by

$$1 + \exp(-\alpha s) = 2/(1 + z) \tag{4.25b}$$

The substitutions for $\exp(-\alpha s)$ and $1 + \exp(-\alpha s)$ from Equations (4.25a,b) into Equation (4.23) yields

$$
\begin{aligned}
dz/ds = G'(s) &= 2\alpha[1 + \exp(-\alpha s)]^{-2}[\exp(-\alpha s)] \\
&= 2\alpha[(1 + z)^2/2^2][(1 - z)/(1 + z)] \\
&= \alpha(1 + z)(1 - z)/2
\end{aligned} \tag{4.26}
$$

The omission of α (it will be absorbed by the step gain η) yields the result

$$G'(s) = (1 + z)(1 - z)/2 \tag{4.27a}$$

Analogously, the bipolar sigmoid at the hidden neurodes has derivative

$$H'(r) = (1 + y)(1 - y)/2 \tag{4.27b}$$

The bipolar update formulas come from substituting Equations (4.27a,b) into the computational formulas of Equations (4.21a,b), respectively, to obtain (using the PSSE $E^{(q)}$)

$$u_{mj} \leftarrow u_{mj} + \eta_1(t_j^{(q)} - z_j^{(q)})[(1 + z_j^{(q)})(1 - z_j^{(q)})/2]y_m^{(q)} \tag{4.28a}$$

$$
\begin{aligned}
w_{nm} \leftarrow w_{nm} + \eta_2 \{ \textstyle\sum_{(j=1, J)}(t_j^{(q)} - z_j^{(q)})[(1 + z_j^{(q)})(1 - z_j^{(q)})/2]u_{mj} \} \\
\times [(1 + y_m^{(q)})(1 - y_m^{(q)})/2]x_n^{(q)}
\end{aligned} \tag{4.28b}
$$

Paul Werbos used backpropagation for regression analysis (Werbos, 1974). A similar stochastic approximation had previously been used by Robbins and Monro (1951). A recent book (Werbos, 1994) discusses the history and development of backpropagation. The books by Fu (1994), Kosko (1992), Hecht-Nielsen (1990), and Wasserman (1989) provide historical notes, while Fausett (1994) and Zurada (1992) are also good references. Chapter 6 discusses a more efficient method, called *conjugate gradient directions*, for accelerated gradient minimization. Quasi-Newton methods (Parker, 1982) are second-order methods that converge more rapidly, but they require more computation per iterative step.

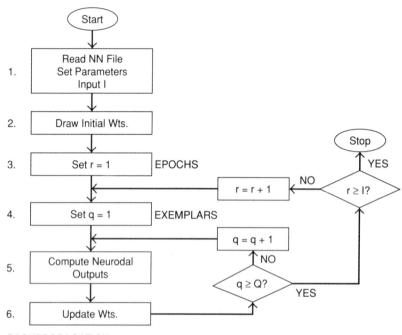

Figure 4.5. A backpropagation flow chart.

4.5. The Basic Backpropagation Algorithm

A High-Level Description of Backpropagation

The flow chart of Figure 4.5 presents a higher-level description of the most basic form of BP. In the first step, the MLP architecture is read from a file, the parameters are set (α's, b's for unipolar sigmoids, and η), and the number I of epochs is accepted from the keyboard. The MLP file consists of the number N of inputs, the number M of hidden layer neurodes, the number J of output neurodes, the number Q of exemplars, and the Q exemplar pairs $\{(\mathbf{x}^{(q)}, \mathbf{t}^{(k(q))}: q = 1,..., Q\}$ of exemplar input feature vectors and output target vectors.

The second step randomly draws NM initial weights $\{w_{nm}^{(0)})$ for the hidden neurodes and MJ initial weights $\{u_{mj}^{(0)}\}$ for the output neurodes (between -0.5 and 0.5 for unipolar or bipolar sigmoids). The third step sets the current epoch number to be $r = 1$, while the fourth step sets the current exemplar number to be $q = 1$. The fifth step performs all summing and activations at the hidden and output layers. These values are then used in the sixth step to compute the weight increments Δw_{nm} for each weight $w_{nm}^{(r)}$ and Δu_{mj} for $u_{mj}^{(r)}$ and then add them to the current weights to obtain the new weights $w_{nm}^{(r+1)}$ and $u_{mj}^{(r+1)}$.

At this point, the test ($q \geq Q$?) is made. If it is false, then q is incremented by $q \leftarrow q + 1$ and the process returns to the fifth step. If it is true, then an *epoch* has been completed, so the test ($r \geq I$?) is made. If false, then r is incremented via $r \leftarrow r + 1$ and the process returns to the fourth step for another epoch or else the process terminates (I epochs have been completed). The updated weights are computed from the computational formulas of Equations (4.21a,b) or (4.28a,b). These are sometimes written in the form of incremental weights as

$$u_{mj}^{(r+1)} = u_{mj}^{(r)} + \Delta u_{mj}, \ w_{nm}^{(r+1)} = w_{nm}^{(r)} + \Delta w_{nm} \quad (4.29)$$

A Backpropagation Algorithm

Inputs: {number of input nodes N; number of middle neurodes M; number of output neurodes J; number of exemplar vectors Q; number of identifiers (classes) K; the exemplar vectors $\{\mathbf{x}^{(q)}\}$ and paired identifier vectors $\{\mathbf{t}^{(k(q))}\}$; number of epochs I; and biases b_i and decay rates α_i ($i = 1, 2$)}

Outputs: {the weights $\mathbf{w} = (w_{11}, w_{21},..., w_{NM})$ and $\mathbf{u} = (u_{11}, u_{21},..., u_{MJ})$ and the total SSE E}

Step 1: /Input N, M, J, Q, exemplar input vectors and corresponding identifiers $\{\mathbf{x}^{(q)}, \mathbf{t}^{(q)}\}$ and I/

    read MLP file;   /Data is stored in file/

    input I;   /Input no. epochs desired from/

                                     /keyboard/

Step 2: /Set parameters α_1, b_1, α_2, b_2, η/

    $b_1 \leftarrow N/2.0$; $b_2 \leftarrow M/2.0$;   /For bipolar sigmoids these are zero/

    $\alpha_1 \leftarrow 2.4$; $\alpha_2 \leftarrow 2.4$; $\eta_1 \leftarrow 0.4$;   /Parameters may differ from these/

    $\eta_2 \leftarrow 0.25$;

Step 3: /Generate initial weights randomly between -0.5 and 0.5/

    for $m = 1$ to M do

        for $n = 1$ to N do   /Draw uniform(0,1), shift down $-\frac{1}{2}$/

            $w_{nm} \leftarrow$ **Random**( ) $- 0.5$;

        for $j = 1$ to J do   /Draw uniform(0,1), shift down $-\frac{1}{2}$/

            $u_{mj} \leftarrow$ **Random**( ) $- 0,5$;

Step 4: /Adjust all weights via steepest descent method/

    for $r = 1$ to I do   /Do I epochs/

        for $q = 1$ to Q do   /with each over all Q exemplar pairs/

            Update_NN( );   /Call procedure to update MLP/

            for $m = 1$ to M do   /Update MJ u_{mj}'s and NM w_{nm}'s/

                for $j = 1$ to J do   /For each m, sum over J outputs/

                  $u_{mj}^{(r+1)} \leftarrow u_{mj}^{(r)} + \eta\{(t_j^{(q)} - z_j^{(q)})[z_j^{(q)}(1 - z_j^{(q)})]y_m^{(q)}\}$;

                for $n = 1$ to N do   /For each n, m sum over J outputs/

                  $w_{nm}^{(r+1)} \leftarrow w_{nm}^{(r)} + \eta\{\sum_{(j=1, J)}(t_j^{(q)} - z_j^{(q)})[z_j^{(q)}(1 - z_j^{(q)})]u_{mj}^{(r)}\}$

                    $x[y_m^{(q)}(1 - y_m^{(q)})][x_n^{(q)}]$

The function **Random**( ) draws a uniform random weight value in the interval $[0,1]$. Early researchers restricted the initial weight set to magnitudes in $[-0.5,0,5]$ because it was thought that the deeper local minima are close to the origin. Current research on this has mixed results. We note that during the training, some weights move away from the origin. Fahlman (1988) found that the initial intervals $[-1,1]$ and $[-2,2]$ yielded results that were just as good on his datasets as did the interval $[-0.5,0.5]$, while McCormack and Doherty (1993) used $[-5, 5]$ when training on certain datasets. The function **Update_NN**( ) puts the qth exemplar input vector through the network to update all of the $y_m^{(q)}$ and $z_j^{(q)}$ values put out by neurodes.

The *advantages* of BP and the MLP type of FANNs are as follows: (i) The learning is somewhat independent of the order in which the exemplar feature vectors are presented, (ii) the architecture can be manipulated for better results (see Chapter 9 on neural engineering), and (iii) the operational mode can be performed with parallel processors. The *disadvantages* are as follows: (i) The training may converge to a local minimum that is shallow so that the learning is not robust; (ii) the step gain (learning rate) cannot be predicted in advance and may be either too small, so that too many steps are required to converge, or too large, so that the process oscillates instead of converging; (iii) the derivatives approach zero so the computed steps are essentially zero, in which case a large number of steps does not move the weight point much; (iv) the gradient provides only a linear approximation to the actual local direction of steepest descent and the approximate directions may change drastically from to step to step; (v) upon changing the value of one or more weights, the PSSEs $E^{(q)}$ are changed as a function of the other weights, which is the *moving target* effect (*thrashing* occurs during each epoch, where a step to minimize $E^{(q)}$ tends to increase some other $E^{(p)}$); and (vi) the network may overtrain on the presented feature vectors and become too specialized and unable to accurately recognize novel vectors.

The first problem (local minima) was demonstrated in a simple example by Gori and Tesi (1992) on nonlinearly separable patterns and showed that BP becomes stuck in a local minimum on a FANN that contained a single hidden layer. We may train an MLP many times from different initial weight points and keep the weight set that yields the lowest total SSE E. This would appear to be a fruitful strategy for dealing with shallow undesirable local minima. However, the lowest SSE does not necessarily provide the best learning, as was observed by Rumelhart (1986) and sometimes indicates specialization (see Section 9.3).

The second problem of no a priori information about the learning rate η requires a strategy for adjusting it on the way to the minimum. It should be sufficiently large on the early iterations, but as the process descends into the well of a local minimum, η must be decreased appropriately. One of the early methods was the *delta-bar-delta* method (Jacobs, 1988), which we discuss in the next chapter. The third problem is *saturation*, where a sigmoid derivative $h'(r_m)$ or $g'(s_j)$ approaches zero, which causes the weight increments $-\eta \nabla E(\mathbf{w}, \mathbf{u})$ to become essentially zero unless the learning rate (step gain) $\eta = \eta^{(r)}$ increases enormously to compensate.

The fourth problem of oscillating directions of steepest descent can be handled by smoothing. This was first done by Rumelhart et al. (1986) with a "momentum" term (see Chapter 5) that performs the required smoothing. The fifth problem of a moving target is a fact of life with MLPs. When any weights are changed, $E(\mathbf{w}, \mathbf{u})$ becomes a different function on the remaining weights. The next chapter discusses this further. The problem of overtraining can be handled by testing during training and afterwards, as discussed in Section 9.8.

In practice, however, convergence takes place often, especially with small to moderate-sized MLPs. When it does not, it may converge on another training run from a different initial weight set, or it may require a change in the MLP architecture. An adaptive step gain can improve the rate of convergence, as we will see in Chapter 5. The more accurate Newtonian formulations use second-order approximations of the SSE function E that may include the Hessian matrix of second-order mixed partial derivatives (discussed in Appendix 4 and Chapter 5). Parker used second-order quasi-Newtonian methods to train MLPs (Parker, 1982). Conjugate gradient methods offer a tradeoff between BP and second-order Newton or quasi-Newton methods in that they converge more rapidly than BP but use significantly less computation than the quasi-Newton and Newton methods.

4.6. Extending Backpropagation to Two Hidden Layers

The Extended Architecture

Figure 4.6 shows an MLP with two hidden layers. The input/output training pairs $\{(\mathbf{x}^{(q)}, \mathbf{t}^{(k(q))}): q = 1,..., Q\}$ are given and the initial weights $\{\mathbf{v}^{(0)}, \mathbf{w}^{(0)}, \mathbf{u}^{(0)}\}$ are drawn randomly from $[-0.5,0.5]^{LN+NM+MJ}$. The situation is the same as for a single hidden layer in that the exemplar feature vectors are paired with the desired identifier codewords that represent the classes. Chapter 9 provides more information on designing extended MLPs.

Backpropagation for Two Hidden Layers with Unipolar Sigmoids

We first derive the computational formulas for updating the weights via steepest descent in an extended BP algorithm. For specificity, we use the unipolar sigmoids. We suppress the index q of the PSSE $E^{(q)}$, as we did above. The partial derivatives

$$\partial E/\partial v_{nl}, \quad \partial E/\partial w_{lm}, \quad \partial E/\partial u_{mj}$$

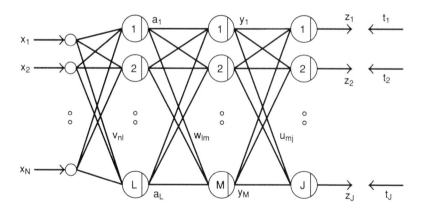

$$p_l = \sum_n x_n v_{nl}, \; r_m = \sum_l a_l w_{lm}, \; s_j = \sum_m y_m u_{mj}$$

$$a_l = f(p_l), \; y_m = h(r_m), \; z_j = g(s_j)$$

Figure 4.6. The extended MLP architecture.

are to be used in the weight updates

$$v_{nl}^{(r+1)} = v_{nl}^{(r)} - \eta \partial E(v_{nl}, w_{lm}, u_{mj})/\partial v_{nl} \qquad (4.30a)$$

$$w_{lm}^{(r+1)} = w_{lm}^{(r)} - \eta \partial E(v_{nl}, w_{lm}, u_{mj})/\partial w_{lm} \qquad (4.30b)$$

$$u_{mj}^{(r+1)} = u_{mj}^{(r)} - \eta \partial E(v_{nl}, w_{lm}, u_{mj})/\partial u_{mj} \qquad (4.30c)$$

From Figure 4.6, we see that the output layer has all of the same parameter names and indices, so we can use Equation (4.21a) for the increments on u_{mj}, which is

$$u_{mj}^{(r+1)} = u_{mj}^{(r)} + \eta(t_j - z_j)z_j(1 - z_j)y_m \qquad (4.31)$$

The hidden layer adjacent to the output layer is the second hidden layer. The difference in the variable designations here from those used to derive Equation (4-21b) is that the inputs to these hidden neurodes are $\mathbf{a} = (a_1,..., a_L)$ instead of $\mathbf{x} = (x_1,..., x_N)$. Upon making these changes in Equation (4.21b), we obtain

$$w_{lm}^{(r+1)} = w_{lm}^{(r)} + \eta\{\textstyle\sum_{(j=1,\,J)}(t_j - z_j)[z_j(1 - z_j)]u_{mj}\}[y_m(1 - y_m)]a_l \qquad (4.32)$$

The derivation of the weight updates at the first hidden layer is more tedious and uses different nomenclature of variables and indices. We omit the column of notes here, and suppress the q subscripts for the exemplar number and use the power of chain rules. But first, we describe $E = E(v_{nl}, w_{lm}, u_{mj})$ as a function of its weights and intermediate variables by

$$\begin{aligned} E = E(v_{nl}, w_{lm}, u_{mj}) &= \textstyle\sum_{(j=1,\,J)}(t_j - z_j)^2 = \textstyle\sum_{(j=1,\,J)}(t_j - g(s_j))^2 \\ &= \textstyle\sum_{(j=1,\,J)}(t_j - g(\textstyle\sum_{(m=1,\,M)}u_{mj}y_m))^2 = \textstyle\sum_{(j=1,\,J)}(t_j - g(\textstyle\sum_{(m=1,\,M)}u_{mj}h(r_m)))^2 \\ &= \textstyle\sum_{(j=1,\,J)}(t_j - g(\textstyle\sum_{(m=1,\,M)}u_{mj}h(\textstyle\sum_{(m=1,\,M)}w_{lm}a_l)))^2 \\ &= \textstyle\sum_{(j=1,\,J)}(t_j - g(\textstyle\sum_{(m=1,\,M)}u_{mj}h(\textstyle\sum_{(l=1,\,L)}w_{lm}f(p_l))))^2 \\ &= \textstyle\sum_{(j=1,\,J)}(t_j - g(\textstyle\sum_{(m=1,\,M)}u_{mj}h(\textstyle\sum_{(l=1,\,L)}w_{lm}f(\textstyle\sum_{(n=1,\,N)}v_{nl}x_n))))^2 \qquad (4.33a) \end{aligned}$$

It is obvious from Figure 4.6 and less obvious from Equation (4.33a) that each weight v_{nl} at the first hidden layer is affected not only by every difference $(t_j - z_j)$ at the output layer, but also by every neurode in the second hidden layer. Thus we need to sum the total error adjustments of all $j = 1,..., J$ and over all $m = 1,..., M$. We first derive the gradient of the SSE with respect to v_{nl} over a single jth output and a single mth neurode in the first hidden layer. Thus we use

$$E_{mj} = ((t_j - g(u_{mj}h(\textstyle\sum_{(l=1,\,L)}w_{lm}f(\textstyle\sum_{(n=1,\,N)}v_{nl}x_n))))^2 \qquad (4.33b)$$

From Equation (4.33b) it is easy to write down the chain rule in terms of dependent variables that start at the output layer and work backward to the first hidden layer, which leads to the partial derivative

$$\partial E_{mj}/\partial v_{nl} = (\partial E_{mj}/\partial z_j)(\partial z_j/\partial v_{nl}) = (\partial E_{mj}/\partial z_j)(\partial z_j/\partial s_j)(\partial s_j/\partial v_{nl})$$

$$= (\partial E_{mj}/\partial z_j)(\partial z_j/\partial s_j)(\partial s_j/\partial y_m)(\partial y_m/\partial v_{nl})$$

$$= (\partial E_{mj}/\partial z_j)(\partial z_j/\partial s_j)(\partial s_j/\partial y_m)(\partial y_m/\partial r_m)(\partial r_m/\partial v_{nl})$$

$$= (\partial E_{mj}/\partial z_j)(\partial z_j/\partial s_j)(\partial s_j/\partial y_m)(\partial y_m/\partial r_m)(\partial r_m/\partial a_l)(\partial a_l/\partial v_{nl})$$

$$= (\partial E_{mj}/\partial z_j)(\partial z_j/\partial s_j)(\partial s_j/\partial y_m)(\partial y_m/\partial r_m)(\partial r_m/\partial a_l)(\partial a_l/\partial p_l)(\partial p_l/\partial v_{nl})$$

$$= [(-2)\{(t_j - z_j)][g'(s_j)]u_{mj}\}[h'(r_m)][w_{lm}f'(p_l)][x_n] \qquad (4.34a)$$

Because we are using unipolar sigmoids, their derivatives all have the same form of $\theta(1 - \theta)$. Substituting into Equation (4.34a) and absorbing the 2 in η, we obtain the $(r + 1)$st iterate

$$v_{nl}{}^{(r+1)} = v_{nl}{}^{(r)} + \eta\{(t_j - z_j)[z_j(1 - z_j)]u_{mj}\}[y_m(1 - y_m)]w_{lm}a_l(1 - a_l)x_n \quad (4.34b)$$

Now we sum over all such parts for $j = 1,..., J$ and $m = 1,..., M$ to obtain the final update

$$v_{nl}{}^{(r+1)} = v_{nl}{}^{(r)} + \eta\{\textstyle\sum_{(j=1, J)}(t_j - z_j)z_j(1 - z_j) \\ \times [\textstyle\sum_{(m=1, M)}u_{mj}y_m(1 - y_m)w_{lm}]a_l(1 - a_l)x_n\} \qquad (4.35)$$

Recapitulating for easy reference, the case of unipolar sigmoids for extended backpropagation yields

$$u_{mj} \leftarrow u_{mj} + \eta(t_j - z_j)z_j(1 - z_j)y_m \qquad (4.36)$$

$$w_{lm} \leftarrow w_{lm} + \eta\{\textstyle\sum_{(j=1, J)}(t_j - z_j)z_j(1 - z_j)u_{mj}\}[y_m(1 - y_m)]a_l \qquad (4.37)$$

$$v_{nl} = v_{ln} + \eta\{\textstyle\sum_{(j=1, J)}(t_j - z_j)z_j(1 - z_j)[\textstyle\sum_{(m=1, M)}u_{mj}y_m(1 - y_m)w_{lm}]a_l(1 - a_l)x_n\} \quad (4.38)$$

Equations (4.36), (4.37) and (4.38) coincide with those of Rogers and Kabrisky (1993).

Backpropagation for Two Hidden Layers with Bipolar Sigmoids

If, on the other hand, we use the bipolar sigmoids where the derivatives of the sigmoids have the form $(1 + \theta)(1 - \theta)/2$, then the weight updates are

$$u_{mj} \leftarrow u_{mj} + \eta(t_j - z_j)[(1 + z_j)(1 - z_j/2)]y_m \qquad (4.39)$$

$$w_{lm} \leftarrow w_{lm} + \eta\{\textstyle\sum_{(j=1, J)}(t_j - z_j)[(1 + z_j)(1 - z_j)/2]u_{mj}\}[(1 + y_m)(1 - y_m)/2]a_l \qquad (4.40)$$

$$v_{nl} \leftarrow v_{nl} + \eta\{\textstyle\sum_{(j=1, J)}(t_j - z_j)[(1 + z_j)(1 - z_j)/2] \\ \times [\textstyle\sum_{(j=1, J)}u_{mj}[(1 + y_m)(1 - y_m)/2]w_{lm}][(1 + a_l)(1 - a_l)/2]x_n]\} \quad (4.41)$$

4.7. Selecting the Output Target Vectors for Training

Identifiers as Codewords

The requirement here is to design a set of identifiers $\{\mathbf{t}^{(k(q))}: q = 1,..., Q\}$ to be paired with the input exemplar feature vectors $\{\mathbf{x}^{(q)}\}_{q=1,\,Q}$. Any output $t_j^{(k(q))}$, to be matched approximately by a computed $z_j^{(q)} = g(s_j^{(q)})$ at the jth output neurode, must be in the range of the activation function $g(-)$ that squashes the sums $s^{(q)}$ into an interval such as $[0,1]$ (unipolar) or $[-1,1]$ (bipolar). The vectors $\mathbf{t}^{(k(q))}$ are usually binary encoded codewords with values from a binary alphabet such as $\{0,1\}$ or $\{-1,1\}$ to produce identifiers such as $\mathbf{t}^{(1)} = (1,0,0,1,1)$ or its bipolar equivalent $(1,-1,-1,1,1)$. The output neurodes cannot actually attain values of 0 or 1 (unipolar case), or -1 or 1 (bipolar case), which are the limiting cases as the weighted sums r_m or s_j go to plus or minus infinity. Therefore we use values such as 0.1 and 0.9 or -0.9 and 0.9. The number J of components in the identifiers must be selected according to the resolution required, and the resolution is directly dependent upon the number K of classes needed. A single output can be given a number of discrete values such as 0.1, 0.3, 0.5, 0.7, and 0.9. Five output target vectors could be specified for $J = 2$, for example, as $(0.1,0.1)$, $(0.1,0.9)$, $(0.9,0.1)$, $(0.9,0.9)$, and $(0.5,0.5)$, while 2^3 are possible here.

The design goal is to separate the input feature vectors without error, so we should select the identifier codewords to be as different as possible. Rather than putting values of a single output variable close together, we should put them far apart. Thus we would not use 0.4 and 0.6 when we could use 0.1 and 0.9. The basic idea here is that appropriately trained weights will push each exemplar feature vector component up or down to fit a particular target identifier (combination of high and low values) to distinguish the different classes from each other.

We have seen in Chapter 3 that the M hidden neurodes partition the feature space into a set of convex regions determined by a set of M hyperplanes. We will see in Chapter 9 that the output layer of neurodes can join combinations of these subclass regions together into classes that are not convex nor linearly separable. The particular regions depend upon the weights $\{w_{nm}\}$ and $\{u_{mj}\}$ that respectively partition and join (two sets are joined by taking their union).

Error Detecting and Error Correcting Identifiers

Ideally, the identifiers of the classes should be sufficiently well separated for error correcting, or at least error detecting. We may choose each component of an identifier to be a symbol from a binary alphabet $\{0,1\}$ or $\{-1,1\}$. The binary alphabet used depends upon which sigmoid activation function is used: (i) unipolar, in which case we use $\{0,1\}$; or (ii) bipolar, where we use $\{-1,1\}$. The *Hamming distance* between two J-symbol identifier *codewords* is the number of positions (components or symbols) in which the codewords are different. For example, the Hamming distance between $(1,1,0,0,1)$ and $(1,0,1,0,1)$ is 2 (they differ in the second and third positions).

If we choose K identifiers for K classes such that the Hamming distance between each pair of them is at least 3, then a single error in the mapping can be corrected. The output vector in error is closer to its correct identifier than to any other codeword and is thus recognized correctly, because it differs in only one position from the correct codeword but differs in at least two positions from any other codeword. But error correction comes with a cost. If the number of classes K is large, then J will need to be significantly larger to select K codewords that differ pairwise by a Hamming distance of 3 or more, so that there will be many output neurodes. This increases the number of weights to be trained and thus increases the complexity of computation both in training and in recognition.

For single error detection, the pairs of identifier codewords must be at least a Hamming distance of 2 from each other. A single error will result in a codeword that is not an identifier and that exposes the error. Error detection and correction require that each output component be changed to either the high value or the low value, whichever it is closest to.

A reasonable tradeoff between the extremes of the error correction and single output is to use the number of outputs J, where $2^{J-1} < K \leq 2^J$ (for K classes needed). The use of $J = 8$ output neurodes and a binary alphabet, for example, allows $K = 2^8 = 256$ unique class identifiers. The input components are better left with continuous (analog) values that contain finer information than discretized values. In case the $\mathbf{x}^{(q)}$ are discretized, the resolution should be high (a large number of discrete values) so that less information will be lost.

4.8. Convergence, Parameters, and Critical Values

Why Output Target Components Can Be Neither 0 nor 1

Suppose we use the unipolar sigmoid activation function at an output neurode where the desired (training) output is 1. Then

$$z_j = 1 / [1 + \exp(-\alpha(s_j - b))] = 1$$

This means that $\exp(-\alpha s_j + b) = 0$, so that $s_j = \infty$. If the desired output is

$$z_j = 1 / [1 + \exp(-\alpha(s_j - b))] = 0$$

then $[1 + \exp(-\alpha(s_j - b))] = \pm \infty$, so that $s_j = \mp \infty$.

Similarly, if the bipolar equations are set to ± 1 via

$$z_j = [1 - \exp(-\alpha(s_j - b))] / [1 + \exp(-\alpha(s_j - b))] = 1$$

then $-\exp(-\alpha(s_j - b)) = \exp(-\alpha(s_j - b))$, which means that $\exp(-\alpha(s_j - b)) = 0$, so that $s_j = \infty$. If

$$z_j = [1 - \exp(-\alpha(s_j - b))] / [1 + \exp(-\alpha(s_j - b))] = -1$$

then $[1 - \exp(-\alpha(s_j - b))] = -[1 + \exp(-\alpha(s_j - b))]$, so that $1 = -1$, unless $s_j = -\infty$.

The conclusion is that we never put the desired output vector components at 0 or 1 (unipolar) or at -1 or 1 (bipolar). We often use 0.1 for 0 and 0.9 for 1 to make comparative runs, but in practice, we prefer to use 0.2 for 0 and 0.8 for 1 (unipolar), or -0.8 for -1 and 0.8 for 1 (bipolar). This causes less saturation and quicker convergence. It also helps prevent weight drift.

How Important Are Biases, Exponential Rates, and Learning Rates?

Chapter 5 discusses training on biases b_1 and b_2 and exponential rates α_1 and α_2, which can be done via

$$b_p \leftarrow b_p - \eta_p(\partial E/\partial b_p), \quad \alpha_r \leftarrow \alpha_r - \eta_r(\partial E/\partial \alpha_r), \qquad p, r = 1,2 \qquad (4.42)$$

Such adjustments can lower the TSSE E. The derivatives given in Equations (4.42) are derived in Chapter 5, but it is often best to fix these to avoid the moving target effect. For large α_i, the sigmoid derivatives are near zero for some neurodes and the convergence virtually halts. We may take: $N/2 \le b_1 \le 1.2N/2$, $M/1 \le b_2 \le 1.2M/2$. The step gains (learning rates) η must be adapted as the training progresses for satisfactory convergence speed (see Section 5.3)

What Do the Error Functions Look Like?

To plot slices of the graphs of the SSE E, we suboptimize E with respect to a set of exemplar training pairs $\{(\mathbf{x}^{(q)}, \mathbf{t}^{(q)}): q = 1,..., Q\}$ from a small dataset. Next, we hold all values of the suboptimal weight set fixed except for a single pair (w_{nm}, u_{mj}) at a time, where the values n, m, and j are randomly selected from 1 to, respectively, N, M, and J. We increment both w_{nm} and u_{mj} from -2.5 to 2.5 by $\Delta = 0.007812$ in Figures 4.7 through 4.11, which display graphs of slices of the SSE function E as described above. Appendix 11 describes the datasets.

The slice of Figure 4.7 (Blood10 dataset) has two local minima in the weight domain of the slice. Both are fairly deep, but one is definitely deeper than the other. The slice shown in Figure 4.8 (on the Digit12 dataset) has two minima with slightly greater differences in the deepness, while Figure 4.9 (on the Rotate9 dataset) has an even greater difference between the two minima. These slices with two minima are essentially quartic—that is, can be fit by a quartic polynomial.

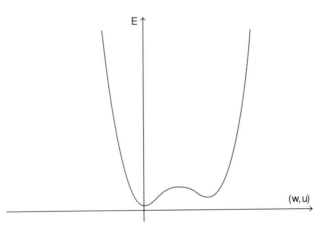

Figure 4.7. A slice of the SSE for the Blood10 dataset.

Figure 4.8. A Digit12 slice.

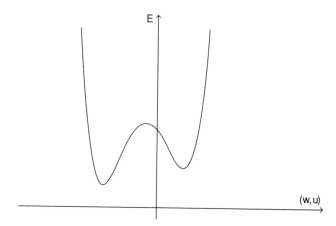

Figure 4.10 (on the Ten5ten dataset) has a single minimum, but it is not a true quadratic. It behaves more like a quartic and there may be another local minimum off the graph to the right. The slice in Figure 4.11 (on the Parity3 dataset) is different in that it has both a very shallow and a very deep local minimum. It is clear that a solution stuck in the shallow minimum would be unsatisfactory. We note that all of the curves approximate either quadratic or quartic polynomials (none have linear, cubic, or quintic form).

It can be observed from Figures 4.8 through 4.11 that on the one hand there can be multiple global minima, or at least multiple deep minima that are approximately global, but that on the other hand, there are shallow local minima that would be bad solutions. When the training process falls into a shallow minimum during gradient descent, it becomes trapped there and the local minimum becomes a solution that may be very unsatisfactory.

Figure 4.9. A Rotate9 slice.

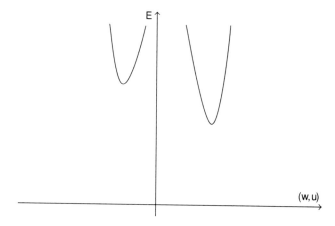

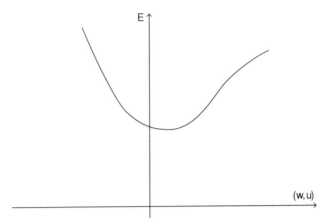

Figure 4.10.   A Ten5ten slice.

4.9. The Slickpropagation Algorithms

The Hornik–Stinchcombe–White Theorem (Hornik et al., 1989) does *not* require sigmoid activation functions. Leaving the sigmoids in the hidden layer, we may take the averaging function $g(s_j)$ at each output neurode to simply the computation (see Figure 4.1 and Equations (4.10c)). Thus we replace

$$g(s_j) = 1/[1 + \exp(-\alpha s_j + b)] \tag{4.43}$$

with the new activation function

$$f(s_j) = (1/J)s_j \tag{4.44}$$

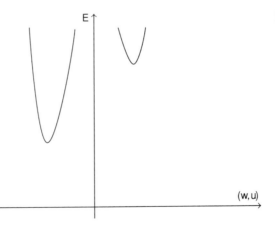

Figure 4.11.   A Parity3 slice.

This not only reduces the volume of computation, but eliminates much of the convoluted ridges and valleys from the surface of the error function E. Perhaps the greatest benefit is that it prevents any saturation at the output layer because the derivative is not too close to zero, as we see from

$$\mathbf{f}'(s_j) = (1/J) \tag{4.45}$$

It also permits the target output components to take the value 0 or 1 (or -1 or 1).

Upon substitution of Equation (4.45) into Equations (4.21a,b) with $1/J$ into the learning rate, the formulas for *slickpropagation* (**SP** or *slickprop*) with unipolar sigmoids at the hidden layer become

$$u_{mj} \leftarrow u_{mj} + (\eta_1/J)(t_j^{(q)} - z_j^{(q)})y_m^{(q)} \tag{4.46a}$$

$$w_{nm} \leftarrow w_{nm} + (\eta_2/J)\{\textstyle\sum_{(j=1, J)}(t_j^{(q)} - z_j^{(q)})u_{mj}\}[y_m^{(q)}(1 - y_m^{(q)})]x_n^{(q)} \tag{4.46b}$$

Similarly, the SP algorithms that use bipolar sigmoids in the single hidden layer that are given in Equations (4.28a,b) now become

$$u_{mj} \leftarrow u_{mj} + (\eta_1/J)(t_j^{(q)} - z_j^{(q)})]y_m^{(q)} \tag{4.47a}$$

$$w_{nm} \leftarrow w_{nm} + (\eta_2/J)\{\textstyle\sum_{(j=1, J)}(t_j^{(q)} - z_j^{(q)})u_{mj}\}[(1 + y_m^{(q)})(1 - y_m^{(q)})/2]x_n^{(q)} \tag{4.47b}$$

For extended MLPs with two hidden layers with unipolar sigmoids, Equations (4.36) to (4.38) become

$$u_{mj} \leftarrow u_{mj} + (\eta_1/J)(t_j - z_j)y_m \tag{4.48a}$$

$$w_{lm} \leftarrow w_{lm} + (\eta_2/J)\{\textstyle\sum_{(j=1, J)}(t_j - z_j)u_{mj}\}[y_m(1 - y_m)]a_l \tag{4.48b}$$

$$v_{nl} \leftarrow v_{ln} + (\eta_3/J)\{\textstyle\sum_{(j=1, J)}(t_j - z_j)[\textstyle\sum_{(m=1, M)}u_{mj}y_m(1 - y_m)w_{lm}]a_l(1 - a_l)x_n\} \tag{4.48c}$$

Likewise, the extended MLPs with two hidden layers with bipolar sigmoids become

$$u_{mj} \leftarrow u_{mj} + (\eta_1/J)(t_j - z_j)y_m \tag{4.49a}$$

$$w_{lm} \leftarrow w_{lm} + (\eta_2/J)\{\textstyle\sum_{(j=1, J)}(t_j - z_j)u_{mj}\}[(1 + y_m)(1 - y_m)/2]a_l \tag{4.49b}$$

$$v_{nl} \leftarrow v_{nl} + (\eta_3/J)\{\textstyle\sum_{(j=1, J)}(t_j - z_j)[\textstyle\sum_{(j=1, J)}u_{mj} \\ \times [(1 + y_m)(1 - y_m)/2]w_{lm}][(1 + a_l)(1 - a_l)/2]x_n]\} \tag{4.49c}$$

4.10. Derivations for FLNs and RBFNs

Functional link networks use the N input features $x_1,..., x_N$ and additionally create H new features from these via

$$x_{N+1} = f_1(x_1,..., x_N),..., x_{N+H} = f_H(x_1,..., x_N) \tag{4.50}$$

The first N features are treated linearly in the single layer of neurodes (see Figure 3.14) whose activations are either unipolar or bipolar sigmoids. Once we compute the new feature inputs from Equations (4.50), we obtain

$$E = \sum_{(q=1,\,Q)}\sum_{(j=1,\,J)} (t_j^{(q)} - y_j^{(q)})^2 = \sum_{(q=1,\,Q)}\sum_{(j=1,\,J)} (t_j^{(q)} - h(r_j^{(q)}))^2$$
$$= \sum_{(q=1,\,Q)}\sum_{(j=1,\,J)} (t_j^{(q)} - h(\sum_{(n=1,\,N)} w_{nj}x_n^{(q)} + \sum_{(n=N+1,N+H)} w_{nj}f_n(-)))^2 \qquad (4.51)$$

Thus the partial derivatives for steepest descent have the form

$$\partial E/\partial w_{nj} = 2\sum_{(q=1,\,Q)}(t_j^{(q)} - y_j^{(q)})(-1)\,[\partial y_j^{(q)}/\partial r_j^{(q)}][\partial r_j^{(q)}/\partial w_{nj}]$$
$$= -2\sum_{(q=1,\,Q)}(t_j^{(q)} - y_j^{(q)})h'(r_j^{(q)})x_n^{(q)}$$
$$\text{(or replace } x_n^{(q)} \text{ with } f_{n-H}(-) \text{ for } n > N) \qquad (4.52)$$

The FLN update algorithm for unipolar sigmoid $h(-)$ is therefore

$$w_{nj} \leftarrow w_{nj} + 2\eta\sum_{(q=1,\,Q)}(t_j^{(q)} - y_j^{(q)})\,[y_j^{(q)}(1 - y_j^{(q)})]x_n^{(q)}$$
$$\text{(or replace } x_n^{(q)} \text{ with } f_{n-H}(-)) \qquad (4.53)$$

The FLN update algorithm for bipolar sigmoid $h(-)$ is

$$w_{nj} \leftarrow w_{nj} + \eta\sum_{(q=1,\,Q)} (t_j^{(q)} - y_j^{(q)})\,[(1 + y_j^{(q)})(1 - y_j^{(q)})]x_n^{(q)}$$
$$\text{(where } x_n^{(q)} \text{ is replaced with } f_{n-H}(-) \text{ if } n > N) \qquad (4.54)$$

Radial basis function networks adjust the weights (see Figure 3.17) u_{mj} at the output layer via steepest descent. There are no sigmoid activation functions at the output layer. From

$$E = \sum_{(q=1,\,Q)}\sum_{(j=1,\,J)}(t_j^{(q)} - z_j^{(q)})^2$$
$$= \sum_{(q=1,\,Q)}\sum_{(j=1,\,J)}(t_j^{(q)} - (1/M)\sum_{(m=1,\,M)}y_m^{(q)}u_{mj})^2 \qquad (4.55)$$

we determine the partial derivatives to have the form

$$\partial E/\partial u_{mj} = (\partial E/\partial z_j^{(q)})(\partial z_j^{(q)}/\partial u_{mj}) = (-2/M)\sum_{-(q=1,\,Q)}(t_j^{(q)} - z_j^{(q)})y_m^{(q)} \qquad (4.56)$$

The RBFN weight updates at the output layer neurodes have the form

$$u_{mj} \leftarrow u_{mj} + (2\eta/M)\sum_{(q=1,\,Q)}(t_j^{(q)} - z_j^{(q)})y_m^{(q)} \qquad (4.57)$$

The neurodal centers $\{\mathbf{v}^{(m)}: m = 1,..., M\}$ at the hidden neurodes may be trained via steepest descent also, where

$$E = \sum_{(q=1,\,Q)}\sum_{(j=1,\,J)} (t_j^{(q)} - (1/M)\sum_{(m=1,\,M)}y_m^{(q)}u_{mj})^2$$
$$= \sum_{(q=1,\,Q)}\sum_{(j=1,\,J)} (t_j^{(q)} - (1/M)\sum_{(m=1,\,M)}f'(\mathbf{x}^{(q)})u_{mj})^2$$

Thus

$$\partial E/\partial v_n^{(m)} = (\partial E/\partial z_j^{(q)})(\partial z_j^{(q)}/\partial y_m^{(q)})(\partial y_m^{(q)}/\partial v_n^{(m)}) \tag{4.58}$$

$$\partial E/\partial v_n^{(m)} = (-2/M)\sum_{(q=1, Q)} (t_j^{(q)} - z_j^{(q)})$$
$$\times (1/\sigma^2)u_{mj}y_m^{(q)}[\sum_{(n=1, N)}(x_n^{(q)} - v_n^{(m)})] \tag{4.59}$$

The RBFN updates for the hidden neurode centers are therefore

$$v_n^{(m)} \leftarrow v_n^{(m)} + (2\eta/M)\sum_{(q=1, Q)} (t_j^{(q)} - z_j^{(q)})(1/\sigma^2)u_{mj}y_m^{(q)}[\sum_{(n=1, N)}(x_n^{(q)} - v_n^{(m)})] \tag{4.60}$$

Exercises

4.1. Derive the specific iterative approximation formulas for steepest descent for an MLP with $N = 2$, $M = 2$, and $J = 1$. Use the unipolar sigmoid activation function. Write out all sums and differentiate term-by-term.

4.2. Equation (4.15) is the derivative of the unipolar sigmoid $g(s_j)$. Find the derivative of the bipolar sigmoid directly from $G(s) = 2g(s + b) - 1$.

4.3. Repeat Exercise 4.1, but this time use the bipolar sigmoid for the activation functions.

4.4. Equation (4.19) contains the substitution $h'(r_m) = y_m(1 - y_m)$ for the unipolar sigmoid function. Find the derivative directly for the bipolar sigmoid function $H(r_m) = \tanh(\alpha r/2)$ from Equation (3.4).

4.5. Write an algorithm for training an MLP with two hidden layers that uses steepest descent at the last two layers and random search on the weights at the first hidden layer.

4.6. Write a simple computer program that implements supervised training of MLPs using the method of steepest descent with unipolar sigmoids (use the backpropagation algorithm that trains on a single exemplar pair at a time).

4.7. Use the program written in Exercise 4.6 above to train a MLP to perform XOR logic (2-bit parity). Use four middle neurodes on one training run, but use only two on another run. Make an even/odd map of the results on $[0,1] \times [0,1]$ by testing all points (x_1, x_2) where the values of x_1 and x_2 assume multiples of 0.1 from 0 to 1. Compare the results for the two different runs.

4.8. Use the program written in the sixth exercise above and the XOR data to analyze via simulation the errors at the output components of $\mathbf{z}$ when the errors ϵ_1 on the single input component x_1 have been chosen from a uniform distribution on [0.0, 0.25]. Compute sample means and variances of the outputs.

4.9. Suppose that an MLP has been trained to map an input vector $\mathbf{x} = (x_1,..., x_N)$ into an output vector $\mathbf{z} = (z_1,..., z_J)$ that approximates some $\mathbf{t} = (t_1,..., t_J)$ closely. Let an error ϵ_1 with uniform distribution on [0.0,0.25] be added to the first component of the exemplar vector $\mathbf{x}$. Analyze the error at the different components of the mapped output $\mathbf{z}$ due to ϵ_1 on x_1.

4.10. Use the process of Exercise 4.9 to analyze what happens when Gaussian random error is added to one input feature vector component. For a large number of input components with uniformly distributed errors, what is the net effect at each output z_j? Consider the Central Limit Theorem from statistics.

4.11. Let $\mathbf{v}^{(r+1)} = \mathbf{v}^{(r)} - \eta\nabla E(\mathbf{v}^{(r)})$ be an iterative step to minimize the sum-squared error $E(\mathbf{v})$ on the vector of all weights $\mathbf{v} = (\mathbf{w}, \mathbf{u})$ of an MLP. Consider the modification $\mathbf{v}^{(r+1)} = \beta\mathbf{v}^{(r)} + (1 - \beta)[\mathbf{v}^{(r)} - \eta\nabla E(\mathbf{v}^{(r)})]$, where β satisfies $0 < \beta < 1$, and η is taken to be 1.0. Analyze the effect.

4.12. Analyze the effect (see Exercise 4.11) of using $\mathbf{v}^{(r+1)} = \mathbf{v}^{(r)} + \beta\mathbf{v}^{(r-1)} - (1 - \beta)\eta\nabla E(\mathbf{v}^{(r)})$, where β satisfies $0 < \beta < 1$. How will this affect the convergence?

4.13. Consider an MLP with two hidden layers. The last two layers on the right have their weights updated as derived in the text. Derive in complete detail the formulation for updating the weights of the first hidden layer that is adjacent to the input branching layer.

4.14. Modify the linearization $\mathbf{v}^{(r+1)} = \mathbf{v}^{(r)} - \eta\nabla E(\mathbf{v}^{(r)})$ by adding a *momentum* term of the form $\mu^{(r)}\mathbf{v}^{r-1}$, where $0 < \mu < 1$. Discuss the ramifications of this strategy.

4.15. Analyze the effects on $\nabla E(\mathbf{v}^{(r)})$ of random errors on the exemplars $\{\mathbf{x}^{(k)}\}$? Discuss and justify your conclusions.

4.16. Modify the program developed in Exercise 4.6 above so that it uses bipolar sigmoids. Compare the convergence rates on XOR logic between unipolar and bipolar versions (be sure to use bipolar data). Make at least 12 runs and compare the average behavior (each run draws a different initial weight set at random).

4.17. Write a flow chart similar to the one given in Figure 4.5, but for training on all exemplars simultaneously in a full steepest descent on $E(\mathbf{w}, \mathbf{u})$. Now write out the complete algorithm.

4.18. Modify the program developed in Exercise 4.16 above so that it trains on all exemplars simultaneously. Run it on the XOR logic function and compare with BP (backpropagation). Try different step gains from 0.05 to 2.0 and note the convergence behavior.

4.19. Show that the bipolar sigmoid functions have maximal slope when the weights are all zero. Can the initial weights be selected to be all zeros to obtain a faster rate of convergence? Explain. State the analogous case for unipolar sigmoid activation functions.

4.20. What is the effect on the weight increments when the weights are in a region where the sigmoid of a neurode has essentially zero slope (consider the update formula for the weights at that neurode)? What about a region where the slope is large?

4.21. Write out a training algorithm where the second-order Newton method is used—that is, where the Hessian matrix of second order partial derivatives is used to obtain a more accurate descent step.

4.22. Take the partial derivative with respect to the exponential rate α of the sum-squared error function E. Work out an equation using $\partial E / \partial \alpha$ to be used in a modification of the BP algorithm (see Zurada, 1992).

4.23. Design the output identifiers for $K = 4$ classes so that a single error can be detected.

4.24. Design the output identifiers for $K = 4$ classes so that a single error can be corrected.

4.25. Take the partial derivative of E with respect to the bias b and include it in the BP algorithm for supervised training as an extra weight on an extra line where the constant 1 is always input.

4.26. Suppose that an MLP is trained to recognize K classes from a sample of Q exemplar pairs ($K \leq Q$). Further, suppose that during operation of the MLP it were discovered that while the MLP could recognize every exemplar input vector, it would sometimes incorrectly recognize novel input vectors that were very close to one of the known exemplars. Explain why this may occur. Give a strategy that could be taken to reduce this undesirable behavior.

4.27. Suppose we copy the exemplar set $\{x^{(1)},..., x^{(Q)}\}$ to a set $\{x^{(Q + 1)},..., x^{(2Q)}\}$. Now suppose that we add a moderate level of Gaussian noise onto the components of the second set and then use the combined set to train an MLP. What would be the effect on the specialization of the learning? Justify your arguments.

4.28. Under backpropagation training, the weight increments $-\eta(\partial E^{(q)}/\partial v_{ps})$ become arbitrarily close to zero as the updated weights $\{v_{ps}\}$ approach a local minimum because $\partial E / \partial v_{ps} \rightarrow 0$. This causes BP to converge at an excruciatingly slow rate as it nears a local minimum because the weight increments also approach zero. Find a method to speed up convergence in the vicinity of a local minimum.

4.29. Suppose that we use 50% of the exemplars to train an MLP to reduce the SSE E_T. After a few epochs of training, let us put the other 50% of the exemplars (that were not used in the training) through the network and compute that SSE as E_N. We repeat this process in a loop. Is it possible that at some point E_N will stop decreasing and begin to increase, even though E_T continues to decrease? What can we infer from this in terms of specialization?

4.30. Describe a method that does not use the gradients to arrive at weights that reduce the total SSE to a reasonably low value [consider drawing random numbers in some fashion].

4.31. Would you use an MLP of size N–M–J = 2–200–1 to train on XOR logic? Why not? What can be inferred from this?

4.32. Suppose that we want to train an MLP on a set of Q exemplar pairs by using gradients. We want to use all of the Q exemplar pairs simultaneously (fullpropagation). However, we are using a computer that does not have sufficient memory for all Q exemplar pairs (Q is very large). Describe an algorithm where a portion of these (say $Q/4$) exemplar pairs are used on each weight updating, consecutively, until all of the Q exemplars have been used. Compare this with backpropagation. Which is the most efficient?

4.33. Derive $\partial E/\partial \alpha_1$ and $\partial E/\partial \alpha_2$ for unipolar and bipolar sigmoid activations functions.

4.34. Derive $2E/\partial b_1$ and $\partial E/\partial b_2$ for unipolar sigmoid activation functions.

4.35. Find the equations for updating the decay rates α_1 and α_1, and also for updating the biases b_1 and b_2 for unipolar sigmoid activation functions.

4.36. Show that for $z_j = g(s_j) = [1 - \exp(-\alpha_2 s_j + b_2)] / [1 + \exp(-\alpha_2 s_j + b_2)]$, it either is or isn't possible that $z_j = -1$.

4.37. Make a copy of your BP program for Problem 4.6 and then modify it to implement SP (slickpropagation). Test it on 2-bit parity (XOR logic) and 3-bit parity. Is it quicker than BP? Why?

4.38. Consider an MLP network that has a single hidden layer. Modify the SP algorithm by substituting activations at the hidden neurodes such that their derivatives will not go to zero.

References

Fahlman, S. E. (1988), *An Empirical Study of Learning Speed in Backpropagation*, Technical Report CMU-CS-88-162, Carnegie Mellon University, Pittsburgh.

Fausett, Laurene (1994), *Fundamentals of Neural Networks*, Prentice-Hall, Englewood Cliffs, NJ.

Fu, LiMin (1994), *Neural Networks in Computer Intelligence*, McGraw-Hill, New York.

Gauss, Karl Frederick (1809), *Theoria Motus Corporum Coelestium in Sectionibus Conicus Solem Ambientum*, F. Perthes and I. H. Besser, Hamburg (translation: Dover, New York, 1963).

Gori, M., and Tesi, A. (1992), On the problem of local minima in backpropagation, *IEEE Trans. Pattern Anal. Mach. Intell.*, vol. 14, 76–86.

Hecht-Nielsen, R. (1990), *Neurocomputing*, Addison-Wesley, Reading, MA.

Hornik, K., Stinchcombe, M., and White, H. (1989), Multilayer feedforward networks are universal approximators, *Neural Networks*, vol. 2, no. 5, 359–366.

Jacobs, R. A. (1988), Increased rates of convergence through learning rate adaptation, *Neural Networks*, vol. 1, 95–307.

Kosko, B. (1992), *Neural Networks and Fuzzy Systems*, Prentice-Hall, Englewood Cliffs, NJ.

Legendre, A. M. (1810), Méthodes des mondres quarrés, pour trouver le milieu le plus probable entre les résultats de différentes observations, *Mem. Inst. France*, 149–154.

Linz, Peter (1979), *Theoretical Numerical Analysis*, Wiley-Interscience, New York.

Looney, C. (1993), Neural networks as expert systems, *J. Expert Syst. Appl.*, vol. 6, no. 2, 129–136.

Looney, C. (1996), Advances in feedforward neural networks: demystifying knowledge acquiring black boxes, *IEEE Trans. Knowl. and Data Eng.*, vol. 8, no. 2, 211–226.

McCormack, C., and Doherty, J. (1993), Neural network super architectures, *Proc. 1993 Int. Conf. Neural Networks, Nagoya*, 301–304.

Parker, D. B. (1982), *Learning Logic*, Invention Report S81-64, File 1, Office of Technology Licensing, Stanford University.

Robbins, H., and Monro, S. (1951), A stochastic approximation method, *Ann. Math. Stat.*, vol. 22, 400–407.

Rogers, S. K., and Kabrisky, M. (1993), *An Introduction to Biological and Artificial Neural Networks for Pattern Recognition*, SPIE Optical Engineering Press, Bellingham, WA.

Rumelhart, D., Hinton, G., and Williams, R. (1986), Learning internal representations by error propagation, appeared in *Parallel Distributed Processing*: *Explorations in the Microstructure of Cognition*, vol. 1, edited by Rumelhart and McClelland, MIT Press, Cambridge, 318–362.

Stornetta, W. S., and Huberman, B. A. (1987), An improved three-layer backpropagation algorithm, *Proc. First IEEE Int. Conf. Neural Networks*, San Diego, vol. 2, 637–643.

Wasserman, P. D. (1989), *Neural Computing*, Van Nostrand Reinhold, New York.

Werbos, P. J. (1994), *The Roots of Backpropagation*, Wiley, New York.

Werbos, P. J. (1974), *Beyond regression: New Tools for Prediction and Analysis in the Behavioral Sciences*, Ph.D. thesis in Applied Mathematics, Harvard University.

Zurada, M. (1992), *Artificial Neural Systems*, West Publishing, St. Paul, MN.

Appendix 4a

Local Minima and Convexity

4a.1. Convexity and Quasi-Convex Functions

The N-dimensional Euclidean space E^N is the set of N-tuples $E^N = \{\mathbf{x} = (x_1, ..., x_N): x_n$ is real, $1 \leq n \leq N\}$ equipped with the Euclidean *norm* (distance measure) as defined on all N-tuples in E^N via

$$\|\mathbf{x}\| = [x_1{}^2 + \cdots + x_N{}^2]^{1/2} \tag{4a.1}$$

$$\|\mathbf{x}^{(1)} - \mathbf{x}^{(2)}\| = [(x_1{}^{(1)} - x_1{}^{(2)})^2 + \cdots + (x_N{}^{(1)} - x_N{}^{(2)})^2]^{1/2} \tag{4a.2}$$

A *convex* subset C of N-dimensional Euclidean space E^N satisfies the following: For any pair of vectors $\mathbf{c}_1$ and $\mathbf{c}_2$ in C, all points $\alpha \mathbf{c}_1 + (1 - \alpha)\mathbf{c}_2$ on the line segment between $\mathbf{c}_1$ and $\mathbf{c}_2$ also belong to C for all α such that $0 \leq \alpha \leq 1$. In other words, C contains all lines between all pairs of points (vectors). It must have a boundary that is flat or curves "inward" (toward its interior). It cannot contain any "dents" or niches where a line segment from a point on one side of the dent to a point on the other side of the dent could pass outside of the set. Figure 4a.1 shows convex and nonconvex sets in the plane. See Himmelblau (1972), Mital (1976), or Fletcher (1980) for convex optimization.

Proposition 4a.1: Balls in E^N of the form $B_\tau = \{\mathbf{x} \in E^N: \|\mathbf{x}\| \leq \tau\}$ are convex.

Proof: Let $\mathbf{x}_1$ and $\mathbf{x}_2$ be any points in B_τ and let $\mathbf{x}_0 = \alpha \mathbf{x}_1 + (1 - \alpha)\mathbf{x}_2$ be any point on the line segment from $\mathbf{x}_1$ to $\mathbf{x}_2$. By the triangle inequality and the property that $\|\beta \mathbf{x}\| = |\beta| \|\mathbf{x}\|$, we have that

Figure 4a.1. Convex and non-convex sets in the plane.

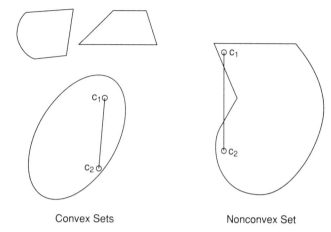

Convex Sets   Nonconvex Set

$$\|\mathbf{x}_0\| = \|\alpha\mathbf{x}_1 + (1 - \alpha)\mathbf{x}_2\| \leq \alpha\|\mathbf{x}_1\| + (1 - \alpha)\|\mathbf{x}_2\| \leq [\alpha + (1 - \alpha)]\max\{\|\mathbf{x}_1\|, \|\mathbf{x}_2\|\}$$

$$= \max\{\|\mathbf{x}_1\|, \|\mathbf{x}_2\|\} \leq \tau$$

Because $\|\mathbf{x}_0\| \leq \tau$, it follows that $\mathbf{x}_0$ belongs to B_τ.

B_τ contains its boundary set $\{\mathbf{x} \in E^N\colon \|\mathbf{x}\|_2 = \tau\}$ and is thus a *closed* ball (a ball that contains all of its boundary points), but Proposition 4a also holds for the *open* ball $B_\tau{}^\circ = \{\mathbf{x} \in E^N\colon \|\mathbf{x}\|_2 < \tau\}$. Now let $y = f(\mathbf{x})$ be a real-valued function defined on a convex subset $C \subset E^N$. We say that $f(-)$ is a *convex function* on C if and only if for every pair of vectors $\mathbf{x}_1$ and $\mathbf{x}_2$ in C and every α, $0 \leq \alpha \leq 1$, it satisfies

$$f(\alpha\mathbf{x}_1 + (1 - \alpha)\mathbf{x}_2) \leq \alpha f(\mathbf{x}_1) + (1 - \alpha)f(\mathbf{x}_2) \tag{4a.3}$$

When the inequality is a strict inequality, then we say that $f(-)$ is *strictly* convex. Convex functions have certain properties, among which are the following: (i) Any *level set* of the form $L_\beta = \{\mathbf{x}\colon \mathbf{x} \in C \text{ and } f(\mathbf{x}) \leq \beta\}$ is convex; (ii) if $f(-)$ has a local minimum, then it is a global minimum and the set of all such minima is a convex set; (iii) when $f(-)$ is strictly convex, then there is a unique minimum $\mathbf{x}_{\min}$ for $f(-)$; and (iv) $f(-)$ is lower semicontinuous.

A real-valued function $F(v) = F(v_1,..., v_M)$ is *quasi-convex* on any convex subset C of E^N whenever

$$F(\alpha\mathbf{v}_1 + (1 - \alpha)\mathbf{v}_2) \leq \max\{F(\mathbf{v}_1), F(\mathbf{v}_2)\} \tag{4a.4}$$

for any $\mathbf{v}_1$, $\mathbf{v}2 \in E^N$ and any $\alpha \geq 0$ such that $0 \leq \alpha \leq 1$. $F(\mathbf{v})$ is *strictly* quasi-convex whenever the "$\leq$" is replaced by "$<$" in Equation (4a.4). The geometric interpretation is that the level sets of $F(\mathbf{v})$ of the form

$$L_\beta = \{\mathbf{v} \in E^N\colon F(\mathbf{v}) \leq \beta\} \tag{4a.5}$$

are all convex. Thus $\alpha\mathbf{v}_1 + (1 - \alpha)\mathbf{v}_2$ is in L_β whenever $\mathbf{v}_1$ and $\mathbf{v}_2$ are. $F(\mathbf{v})$ is *uniformly quasi-convex* on a convex domain C whenever for any given $\epsilon > 0$, there exists $\delta(\epsilon) > 0$ such that for any $\mathbf{v}_1, \mathbf{v}_2 \in C$ with $\|\mathbf{v}_1 - \mathbf{v}_2\| \geq \epsilon$, it is true that

$$F(\tfrac{1}{2}\mathbf{v}_1 + \tfrac{1}{2}\mathbf{v}_2) \leq \max\{F(\mathbf{v}_1), F(\mathbf{v}_2)\} - \delta(\epsilon) \tag{4a.6}$$

Figure 4a.2 shows an example of convex, nonconvex, and quasi-convex functions. The quasi-convex function is shown with a level set L_α. When $F(-)$ is uniformly quasi-convex, then $F(\mathbf{v})$ is strictly quasi-convex and does not approach a flat (horizontal) surface on any line between any two vectors $\mathbf{v}_1$ and $\mathbf{v}_2$ (Looney, 1973).

4a.2. Minimization of Quasi-Convex Functions

When $F(\mathbf{v})$ is continuous and strictly quasi-convex on a closed and bounded convex set C of E^M, then $F(\mathbf{v})$ assumes a *unique* local minimum on C. C is finite-dimensional, so that closed and bounded sets are compact (in finite-dimensional space, closed and bounded sets are compact because of completeness of the real numbers). Because F is continuous, it assumes its minimum value on C and is uniformly quasi-convex when C is compact (Looney, 1977). Therefore F has a unique minimum on C at some point $\mathbf{v}^*$. If the local minimum were not unique, then there would be two vectors $\mathbf{v}_1$ and $\mathbf{v}_2$ that were both minima; and letting $\|\mathbf{v}_1 - \mathbf{v}_2\| = \epsilon$, this would violate Equation (4a.6).

A *minimizing sequence* in a convex set C for an error function $E(\mathbf{v})$ is any sequence $\{\mathbf{v}^{(i)}\}$ in $C \subset E^N$ such that

$$\lim_{(i \to \infty)} E(\mathbf{v}^{(i)}) = \min_{\mathbf{v} \in C} E(\mathbf{v}) \tag{4a.7}$$

It is known that gradient methods are guaranteed to converge on convex compact sets to a global minimum for uniformly quasi-convex functions (Looney, 1977). In such cases, gradients generate minimizing sequences.

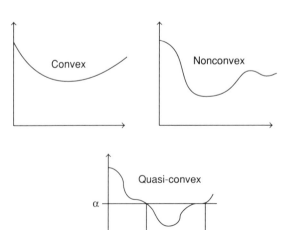

Figure 4a.2. Convex, nonconvex, and quasi-convex functions.

Proposition 4a.2. The composition of a nonzero linear function followed by a (strictly) quasi-convex function is (strictly) quasi-convex.

Proof: Let f be the linear function and g be the second function that is (strictly) quasi-convex. Then

$$g(f(\tfrac{1}{2}\mathbf{v}_1 + \tfrac{1}{2}\mathbf{v}_2)) = g(\tfrac{1}{2}f(\mathbf{v}_1) + \tfrac{1}{2}f(\mathbf{v}_2)) \leq \max\{g(f(\mathbf{v}_1)),g(f(\mathbf{v}_2))\} \qquad (4a.8)$$

This shows that $g(f(-))$ is (strictly) quasi-convex.

Proposition 4a.3: Let a neural network have a single neurode, a single exemplar input $\mathbf{y}^{(1)} = (y_1^{(1)},..., y_M^{(1)})$, weights $\mathbf{u} = (u_1,..., u_M)$, and output value $z = g(s)$ as shown in Figure 4a.3, where $g(-)$ is a sigmoid. Then the composition output function $z(\mathbf{u}) = g(s(\mathbf{u}))$ is uniformly quasi-convex on any closed bounded convex region C of E^M and assumes its unique minimum on C.

Proof: Let $g(s)$ be the sigmoid function, which is continuously differentiable and strictly monotonic increasing on s. Then $g(s)$ is strictly quasi-convex. The composition mapping

$$\mathbf{u} \rightarrow s = \textstyle\sum_{(m=1, M)} y_m u_m = f(\mathbf{u}) \rightarrow g(f(\mathbf{u})) = \mathbf{z} \qquad (4a.9)$$

is quasi-convex by Proposition 4a.2. Because it is also continuous and thus uniformly continuous on any closed bounded convex set C or $[a,b]^N$, it is uniformly quasi-convex and assumes its unique minimum.

Proposition 4a.4: Let a single neurode have nonnegative sigmoid as activation function, and let there be $Q \geq 2$ exemplar pairs for training. Then the total SSE $E(\mathbf{v}) = (t^{(1)} - z^{(1)})^2 + \cdots + (t^{(Q)} - z^{(Q)})^2$ is uniformly quasi-convex on closed bounded convex sets C if and only if there is a single weight vector $\mathbf{v}_{\min}$ that is the unique local minimum for

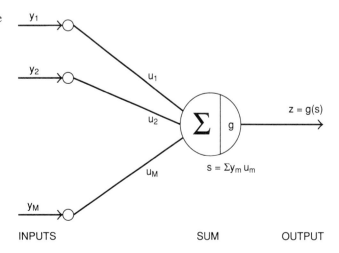

Figure 4a.3. A single neurode neural network.

INPUTS   SUM   OUTPUT

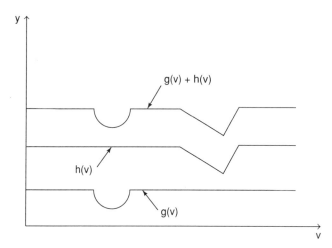

Figure 4a.4. The sum of two quasi-convex functions with different minima.

each and every one of the Q partial sum-squared error (PSSE) functions $E^{(1)}$,..., $E^{(K)}$, where each PSSE is determined by a single qth exemplar.

Proof: We first assume that there is not a unique minimum for each PSSE $E^{(q)}$. Suppose that $E^{(1)}(\mathbf{v})$ and $E^{(2)}(\mathbf{v})$ are the partial SSE functions for exemplars $q = 1$ and $q = 2$, respectively, with training outputs t_1 and t_2, where $t_1 \neq t_2$. Let $\mathbf{v}_1$ and $\mathbf{v}_2$ ($\mathbf{v}_1 \neq \mathbf{v}_2$) be the minimizing weight points for $E^{(1)}(\mathbf{v})$ and $E^{(2)}(\mathbf{v})$, respectively. Now consider the total sum-squared errors $E(\mathbf{v}) = E^{(1)}(\mathbf{v}) + \mathrm{E}^{(2)}(\mathbf{v})$, and restrict $E(-)$ to a single dimension along the line segment through $\mathbf{v}_1$ and $\mathbf{v}_2$, denoted by $\mathbf{u}$. Then $F(-)$, restricted to $\mathbf{u}$, is continuous and has two local minima: (i) The first is where $\mathbf{u} = \mathbf{v}_1$, and (ii) the second is where $\mathbf{u} = \mathbf{v}_2$. Therefore $F(\mathbf{v})$ is not strictly quasi-convex, even though each of $E^{(1)}(\mathbf{v})$ and $E^{(2)}(\mathbf{v})$ is strictly quasi-convex (see Figure 4a.4). Therefore, if there is *not* a unique single local minimum common to all PSEE functions, then the total SSE $F(\mathbf{v})$ is *not* strictly quasi-convex. By contrapositive logic, strict quasi-convexity of the total SSE implies a unique single local minimum for all SSE functions.

On the other hand, let $\mathbf{v}_{\min}$ be the unique single local minimum that is common to each of the Q partial SSE functions. Each PSSE is strictly increasing in any direction from $\mathbf{v}_{\min}$. Therefore, the sum of these SSE functions is strictly increasing in any direction from $\mathbf{v}_{\min}$, is therefore strictly quasi-convex, is therefore uniformly quasi-convex on compact weight domains C, and thus assumes its unique minimum $\mathbf{v}_{\min}$ there. This completes the proof.

When there are two or more neurodes in the middle layer, the outputs are summed and the sum of the individual SSE functions over all Q exemplars is no longer a strictly quasi-convex function, unless it just happens that all individual SSEs share the same unique minimum. Figure 4a.4 shows the case where two quasi-convex functions of a single dimension, each having a different unique local minimum, are summed. The result is a function with two local minima. In view of this, we cannot expect the total SSE function of a FANN with more than a single neurode, nor more than a single exemplar, to have an error function with a single local minimum. Such a case would be an extremely rare event.

Appendix 4b

Vector Calculus and Intuitive Chain Rules

4b.1. Functions on Euclidean Vector Spaces

Preliminaries

We recall that the N-dimensional Euclidean space E^N is: (i) the set of N-tuples $E^N = \{\mathbf{x} = (x_1,..., x_N): x_n$ is real, $1 \leq n \leq N\}$; and (ii) the Euclidean *norm* (distance measure) as defined on all *N-tuples* in E^N via

$$\|\mathbf{x}\| = [x_1{}^2 + \cdots + x_N{}^2]^{1/2} \tag{4b.1}$$

$$\|\mathbf{x}^{(1)} - \mathbf{x}^{(2)}\| = [(x_1{}^{(1)} - x_1{}^{(2)})^2 + \cdots + (x_N{}^{(1)} - x_N{}^{(2)})^2]^{1/2} \tag{4b.2}$$

The N-tuples are called N-dimensional *vectors*, and they obey the following rules of a *vector space*:

(i) $\mathbf{x} + \mathbf{y} \in E^N$ whenever $\mathbf{x}, \mathbf{y} \in E^N$ ($\mathbf{x} + \mathbf{y} = (x_1 + y_1,..., x_N + y_N)$)

(ii) $\mathbf{x} + \mathbf{y} = \mathbf{y} + \mathbf{x}$ for any $\mathbf{x}, \mathbf{y} \in E^N$

(iii) $\mathbf{0} \in E^N$, where $\mathbf{0} = (0_1,..., 0_N)$, and satisfies $\mathbf{0} + \mathbf{x} = \mathbf{x}$ for any $\mathbf{x} \in E^N$

(iv) for any $\mathbf{x} \in E^N$ there exists $-\mathbf{x} \in E^N$ such that $\mathbf{x} + -\mathbf{x} = \mathbf{0}$

(v) $\alpha\mathbf{x} \in E^N$ for any real number α and any $\mathbf{x} \in E^N$ ($\alpha\mathbf{x} = (\alpha x_1,..., \alpha x_N)$)

(vi) $\alpha(\mathbf{x} + \mathbf{y}) = \alpha\mathbf{x} + \alpha\mathbf{y}$ for any real α and any $\mathbf{x}, \mathbf{y} \in E^N$

(vii) $(\alpha\beta)\mathbf{x} = \alpha(\beta\mathbf{x})$ for any real α, β, and any $\mathbf{x} \in E^N$

(viii) $(\alpha + \beta)\mathbf{x} = \alpha\mathbf{x} + \beta\mathbf{x}$ for any real α and β, and any $\mathbf{x} \in E^N$

(ix) $1\mathbf{x} = \mathbf{x}$ for any $\mathbf{x} \in E^N$

(x) $\|\mathbf{x}\| \geq 0$ for any $\mathbf{x} \in E^N$

(xi) $\|\alpha\mathbf{x}\| = |\alpha| \|\mathbf{x}\|$ for any real α and any $\mathbf{x} \in E^N$

(xii) $\|\mathbf{x} + \mathbf{z}\| \leq \|\mathbf{x} + \mathbf{y}\| + \|\mathbf{y} + \mathbf{z}\|$, for any $\mathbf{x}$, $\mathbf{y}$ and $\mathbf{z} \in E^N$ (triangle inequality)

(xiii) the *dot* (*inner*) product defined by $\mathbf{x} \circ \mathbf{y} = \sum_{(n=1, N)} x_n y_n$, satisfies

$$\mathbf{x} \circ \mathbf{x} = \|\mathbf{x}\|^2 \tag{4b.3}$$

$$|\mathbf{x} \circ \mathbf{y}| \leq \|\mathbf{x}\|^{1/2} \|\mathbf{y}\|^{1/2} \qquad \text{(Cauchy–Schwarz inequality)} \tag{4b.4}$$

$$(\alpha\mathbf{x}) \circ \mathbf{y} = \alpha(\mathbf{x} \circ \mathbf{y}) \tag{4b.5}$$

$$\mathbf{x} \circ \mathbf{y} = \mathbf{y} \circ \mathbf{x} \tag{4b.6}$$

A subset $S \subset E^N$ is a *vector subspace* if and only if S is a vector space in and of itself. Hyperplanes that pass through $\mathbf{0}$ are vector subspaces. So is any *projection* space $E^M \subset E^N$ ($M \leq N$) obtained by the mapping $(x_1,..., x_M, x_{M+1},..., x_N) \rightarrow (x_1,..., x_M)$ of E^N onto E^M. An M-dimensional projection may also map any M components of $(x_1,..., x_M, x_{M+1},..., x_N)$ into M-tuples as long as the order is not changed.

A set of vectors $\{\mathbf{x}_j: 1 \leq j \leq J\}$ is said to be *linearly independent* whenever no one of the vectors, say $\mathbf{x}_i$, can be represented as a *linear combination* $\mathbf{x}_i = \sum_{(j \neq i)} \alpha_j \mathbf{x}_j$ of the remaining ones. N linearly independent vectors *span* E^N in that any vector in E^N can be expressed as a linear combination of them. Any linearly independent set of vectors B that spans E^N is said to be a *basis* for E^N, because in that case, any vector in E^N can be expressed as a unique linear combination of the vectors in B. The *canonical* basis for E^N is $\{e_1,..., e_N\}$, where $e_1 = (1,0,..., 0)$, ..., $e_N = (0,..., 0,1)$.

Orthogonality

Two vectors are said to be *orthogonal* if and only they intersect at right angles. In this case, the projection of either one of them on the other one has zero length. Because the dot product is one way of projecting one line onto an other one, we use it in working with orthogonality. Let $\mathbf{x}$ and $\mathbf{y}$ be two vectors in E^N, and suppose that $\theta_{xy} \leq \pi/2$ is the angle of intersection. Then the projection of $\mathbf{x}$ onto $\mathbf{y}$ is given by

$$\mathbf{x} \circ \mathbf{y} = \mathbf{x}^t \mathbf{y} = \Sigma_{(n=1, N)} x_n y_n \tag{4b.7}$$

$$\mathbf{x} \circ \mathbf{y} = \|\mathbf{x}\| \|\mathbf{y}\| \cos(\theta_{xy}) \tag{4b.8}$$

where the superscript t designates the *transpose* of the column vector $\mathbf{x}$ into a row vector so that regular matrix multiplication yields the dot product of two vectors. If $\mathbf{x} \circ \mathbf{y} = 0$, but $\|\mathbf{x}\| \|\mathbf{y}\| > 0$, then $\cos(\Theta_{xy}) = 0$, so that the angle between the lines along $\mathbf{x}$ and $\mathbf{y}$ is $\Theta_{xy} = 90°$. This means that $\mathbf{x} \perp \mathbf{y}$, that is, $\mathbf{x}$ and $\mathbf{y}$ are orthogonal.

Let $f(-)$ and $g(-)$ be functions on E^N with gradient vectors ∇f and ∇g. If $(\nabla f) \circ (\nabla g) = 0$ at some point $\mathbf{x}$, then the gradients (i.e., the directions of steepest ascent) of $f(-)$ and $g(-)$

at **x** are orthogonal. Two vectors **x** and **y** are said to be *canonically conjugate* whenever **x∘y** = 0, that is, **x**'**y** = 0. We can also write this more generally as **x**'*I***y** = 0, where *I* is the $N \times N$ identity matrix (*I***y** = **y**). More generally, if **x**'*H***y** = 0 for some symmetric $N \times N$ matrix *H*, then we say that **x** and **y** are *H-conjugate*.

> **Proposition 4b.1:** If a set of *N* vectors B = {**x**$_n$: *n* = 1,..., *N*} are all pairwise *H*-conjugate for a symmetric (nonzero) matrix *H*, then the vectors in B are linearly independent and span E^N, and are therefore a basis for E^N.

Real-Valued Functions on E^N

A real-valued function *f*(–) on E^N maps vectors into real values **x** → *f*(**x**) = *r*. It is continuous at **x**$^{(0)}$ if and only if, for every sequence {**x**$^{(r)}$} such that **x**$^{(r)}$ → **x**$^{(0)}$ it is true that *f*(**x**$^{(r)}$) → *f*(**x**$^{(0)}$). The *gradient* ∇*f*(**x**) of *f*(–) at **x** is defined as the vector whose components are the rates of change of *f*(**x**) with respect to the *N* components, that is, the gradient is

$$\nabla f(\mathbf{x}) = (\partial f(\mathbf{x})/\partial x_1,..., \partial f(\mathbf{x})/\partial x_N)$$

where each partial derivative is defined to be the limit

$$\partial f(\mathbf{x})/\partial x_n = \lim \delta x_n \to 0 \, [f(\mathbf{x} + \delta x_n) - f(\mathbf{x})]/\delta x_n$$

The *N*-dimensional truncated Taylor series for continuously differentiable functions *f*(–) is

$$f(\mathbf{x} + \Delta\mathbf{x}) = f(\mathbf{x}) + (\Delta\mathbf{x})^t \nabla f(\mathbf{x}) + (1/2)(\Delta\mathbf{x})^t H(\mathbf{x})(\Delta\mathbf{x}) + e(\mathbf{x},\Delta\mathbf{x})\|\mathbf{x}\|_2^2 \qquad (4b.9)$$

where *e*(**x**, Δ**x**) → 0 as Δ**x** → 0. The superscript *t* signifies the transpose, so the dot product is implied. Here, *H*(**x**) is the Hessian matrix of mixed second partial derivatives $\partial^2 f(\mathbf{x})/\partial x_i \partial x_j$ given by

$$H(\mathbf{x}) = \begin{pmatrix} \partial^2 f(\mathbf{x})/\partial x_1^2 & ... & \partial^2 f(\mathbf{x})/\partial x_1 \partial x_N \\ \vdots & & \vdots \\ \partial^2 f(\mathbf{x})/\partial x_N \partial x_1 & ... & \partial^2 f(\mathbf{x})/\partial x_N^2 \end{pmatrix} \qquad (4b.10)$$

To minimize *f*(–) we may use the first two terms of Taylor's series on the right hand side of Equation (4b.9) to obtain the *linearization*

$$f(\mathbf{x} + \Delta\mathbf{x}) = f(\mathbf{x}) + (\Delta\mathbf{x})^t \nabla f(\mathbf{x}) \qquad (4b.11)$$

We can express this using Δ**x** = **x**$^{(r+1)}$ − **x**$^{(r)}$ and **x** = **x**$^{(r+1)}$ to obtain

$$f(\mathbf{x}^{(r+1)}) = f(\mathbf{x}^{(r)}) + (\mathbf{x}^{(r+1)} - \mathbf{x}^{(r)})^t \nabla f(\mathbf{x}) \qquad (4b.12)$$

Assuming that the current point is $\mathbf{x}^{(r)}$ and that $\mathbf{x}^{(r+1)}$ is the nearby local minimum of $f(-)$ where the gradient is zero (the necessary condition $\nabla f(\mathbf{x}^{(r+1)}) = \mathbf{0}$ is satisfied), we can apply the gradient operator ∇ to both sides of Equation (4b.12) to obtain

$$\nabla f(\mathbf{x}^{(r+1)}) = \mathbf{0} = \nabla f(\mathbf{x}^{(r)}) + H(\mathbf{x})(\mathbf{x}^{(r+1)} - \mathbf{x}^{(r)}) \qquad (4b.13a)$$

$$\mathbf{0} = \nabla f(\mathbf{x}^{(r)}) + H(\mathbf{x})(\mathbf{x}^{(r+1)} - \mathbf{x}^{(r)}) \qquad (4b.13b)$$

Upon premultiplying each side of Equation (4b.13b) by the inverse of the symmetric Hessian matrix (which is positive definite in a region of the local minimum) and solving for $\mathbf{x}^{(r+1)}$, the result is

$$\mathbf{x}^{(r+1)} = \mathbf{x}^{(r+1)} - H(\mathbf{x})^{-1}\nabla f(\mathbf{x}^{(r)}) \qquad (4b.14)$$

This is the *second-order* (*quadratic*) form of Newton's method, and it takes care of the step size as well as the direction. Unfortunately, the Hessian matrix of second mixed partial derivatives and its inverse are computationally expensive unless $f(-)$ is, say, a quadratic polynomial function, in which case H is a positive definite constant matrix. When $f(-)$ is convex this second-order method converges quickly. Quadratic functions are either convex or concave, in which case $-f(-)$ is convex.

The Conjugate Gradient Method

Conjugate gradient methods were introduced by Hestenes and Stiefel, (1962) for quadratic functions used in solving linear equations. It was extended by Fletcher and Reeves (1964). Both Himmelblau (1972) and Mital (1976) are good references for general conjugate gradient methods, and Fletcher (1980) is a practical one. The algorithm below moves from a current point $\mathbf{x}^{(0)}$ through N steps in N directions that are H-conjugate in the case when H is fixed and positive definite, that is, the function is a second-order polynomial in N dimensions (i.e., a quadratic function). The N directions are linearly independent vectors that span E^N, and thus they form a basis. We assume that an initial point $\mathbf{x}^{(0)}$ has already been selected, I total iterations have been specified, and the count has been set to zero (the count is the number of iterations, where a single iteration consists of running N steps in H-conjugate directions). Chapter 5 derives three types of conjugate gradient algorithms for training MLPs. The following algorithm assumes that the number of iterations I and dimension N are given.

Step 1: $\mathbf{y}^{(0)} \leftarrow -\nabla f(\mathbf{x}^{(0)}); \mathbf{s}^{(0)} \leftarrow -\mathbf{y}^{(0)};$ /Initial direction $\mathbf{y}^{(0)}$ is steepest descent/
           $H^{(0)} \leftarrow H(\mathbf{x}^{(0)}); r \leftarrow 0;$ /Initialize Hessian matrix/

Step 2: $\alpha^{(r)} \leftarrow -[(\mathbf{s}^{(r)})^t(\mathbf{y}^{(r)})]/[(\mathbf{y}^{(r)})^t H^{(r)}(\mathbf{y}^{(r)})];$ /At nth iteration/
           $\mathbf{x}^{(r+1)} \leftarrow \mathbf{x}^{(r)} + \alpha^{(r)}(\mathbf{y}^{(r)});$

Step 3: $\mathbf{s}^{(r+1)} \leftarrow \nabla f(\mathbf{x}^{(r+1)});$
           $H^{(r+1)} \leftarrow H(\mathbf{x}^{(r+1)});$ /Compute new Hessian/
           $\beta^{(r+1)} \leftarrow [(\mathbf{s}^{(r+1)})^t H^{(r+1)}(\mathbf{y}^{(r)})]/$

$$\times [(\mathbf{y}^{(r)})^t \mathbf{H}^{(r+1)}(\mathbf{y}^{(r)})];$$
$$\mathbf{y}^{(r+1)} \leftarrow -\mathbf{s}^{(r+1)} + \beta^{(r+1)}(\mathbf{y}^{(r)}); \qquad \text{/Compute new conjugate direction/}$$

Step 4: $r \leftarrow r + 1;$
if $(r < N)$ then goto Step 2;   /If N conjugate steps done/
else count $\leftarrow$ count $+ 1;$ /then update number of iterations/
if (count $> I$) then stop;
else $\mathbf{x}^{(0)} \leftarrow \mathbf{x}^{(r)};$ /Initialize for N new steps/
goto Step 1;

4b.2. Intuitive Chain Rules

Let $s = s(x)$ be continuously differentiable for all x. When graphed in the plane, small intervals of x about any point x_0 are mapped into intervals about $s_0 = s(x_0)$. The rate at which the intervals $[x_0 - \epsilon, x_0 + \epsilon]$ are contracted/dilated about s_0 is $r = ds(x_0)/dx$, which is the slope of $s(x)$ at x_0. Now let $v = v(s)$ be a function of s. It dilates or contracts an interval about s_0 into an interval about $v_0 = v(s_0)$ at a rate about s_0 that is $dv(s_0)/ds$. The functional composition $v = v(s(x))$ is now a function of x, and contracts/dilates an interval about x_0 by two stages: The first has rate $ds(x_0)/dx$, and the second has rate $dv(s_0)/ds$. Therefore, the rate dv/dx is the product $(dv/ds)(ds/dx)$ at any point x_0, which is the fundamental chain rule

$$dv/dx = (dv/ds)(ds/dx) \qquad (4b.15)$$

When $v = v(r,s) = v(r(x), s(x))$, each of $r(x)$ and $s(x)$ is scaled about x_0 by $dr(x_0)/dx$ and $ds(x_0)/dx$, respectively. Then $v = v(r(x), s(x))$ is scaled about x_0 by each of r and s, and each of these is the product of two rates. Thus v is has scaling rates $dv(r(x_0))/dx = (\partial v(r_0)/\partial r)(dr(x_0)/dx)$ and $dv(s(x_0))/dx = (\partial v(s_0)/\partial s)(ds(x_0)/dx)$, each according to Equation (4b.15). Thus, at any point x, the total scaling is

$$dv/dx = (\partial v(r)/\partial r)(dr(x)/dx) + (\partial v(s)/\partial s)(ds(x)/dx) \qquad (4b.16)$$

Functions of the form $v = v(r(x, y), s(x, y))$ have rates of contraction/dilation with respect to each of x and y, as shown above. Therefore the two respective rates of scaling along the respective directions x and y are shown by Equation (4b.16) to be

$$\partial v/\partial x = (\partial v/\partial r)(\partial r/\partial x) + (\partial v/\partial s)(\partial s/\partial x) \qquad (4b.17)$$

$$\partial v/\partial y = (\partial v/\partial r)(\partial r/\partial y) + (\partial v/\partial s)(\partial s/\partial y) \qquad (4b.18)$$

References

Fletcher, R. (1980), *Practical Methods of Optimization*, vol. I: *Unconstrained Optimization*, Wiley, New York.

Fletcher, R., and Reeves, C. M. (1964), Function minimization by conjugate gradients, *Comput. J.*, vol. 7, 149–154.

Hestenes, M. R., and Stiefel, E. L. (1962), Method of conjugate gradients for solving linear systems, *J. Res. Natl. Bur. Stand.*, vol. 49, no. 6, 409–436.

Himmelblau, D. M. (1972), *Applied Nonlinear Programming*, McGraw-Hill, New York.

Looney, C. G. (1973), Locally quasi-convex programming, *SIAM J. Appl. Math.*, vol. 28, no. 4, 881–884.

Looney, C. G. (1977), Convergence of minimizing sequences, *J. Math. Anal. Appl.*, vol. 61, no. 3, 835.

Mital, K. V. (1976), *Optimization Methods*, Wiley Eastern Ltd., New Delhi (Wiley, New York).

Part III

Advanced Fundamentals of Neural Networks

Chapter 5

Acceleration and Stabilization of Supervised Gradient Training of MLPs

This chapter provides algorithmic improvements that stabilize and accelerate the convergence of supervised training of multiple layered perceptrons with gradient descent methods.

5.1. Types of Speedups for Gradient Algorithms

Backpropagation (BP) was first used by Rumelhart et al. (1986) to train multiple-layered perceptrons (MLPs), which are a type of feedforward artificial neural networks (FANNs). BP is by far the most widely used algorithm for training MLPs for pattern recognition and other purposes. Many researchers nowadays modify the original formulation, however, to attempt to overcome slow convergence and instability. For completeness, we mention that Werbos (1974) used this method for nonlinear regression, which is described also in Werbos (1994). It was later discovered that Robbins and Monro (1951) had previously employed a similar method called *stochastic approximation*.

The training of MLPs is NP-complete (Judd, 1987), and thus we must use heuristic rules to reach a state of satisfactory learning. For an MLP with a single hidden layer, the learning time is $O(W^3)$, where $W = NM + MJ$ is the number of weights (Hinton, 1989). It is extremely desirable to speed up the convergence of BP on MLPs because it is a slow and unreliable process (Hoehfeld and Fahlman, 1992).

The material in this chapter is directed at training MLPs but may apply to the gradient training of other FANNs where learning rates η are used. The four major tasks for establishing stability and increasing the rate of convergence are (i) the *adjustment of an initial weight point* to a region of the weight space where the total sum-squared error (TSSE) E is low so that an efficient descent can start, (ii) the *stabilization of erratic weight adjustments* on each iteration, (iii) the use of *more efficient gradient descent* steps to accelerate convergence, and (iv) the *engineering of an appropriate architecture* so as to avoid overdetermination. We address the first three of these here. Chapter 9 covers neural engineering that includes architectural design.

5.2. Selection of Initial Weights

The Criticality of the Initial Weight Set

It is known that two different initial weight sets can lead to drastically different convergence behaviors (Li et al., 1993). Early studies concluded that the initial weight set should have small values (less than 0.5 in magnitude) and that they must not be approximately equal or too large lest they fail to converge. Fahlman's empirical study (Fahlman, 1988) showed that it does not make any difference whether the initial weights are limited to 0.5 or 1.0 or 2.0 in magnitude on the datasets upon which he tested. Our own experience is that the initial weights need not have magnitudes smaller than 0.5, but it is safer to select them small to avoid saturation (see Section 5.3). Initialization of weights is discussed in Fahlman (1988), Zurada (1992, p. 209), Russo (1991), and (Nguyen and Widrow (1990).

Russo (1991) provides the an empirical rule for drawing random initial weights that are unlikely to cause premature saturation (where the proximity of sigmoid derivatives to zero cause the weight increments to be essentially zero): Draw each initial weight $u_{mj}^{(i)}$ from the uniform distribution so that

$$-2.4/M \leq u_{mj}^{(i)} \leq 2.4/M$$

where M is the number of lines coming into the neurode where the weight resides.

Li et al. (1993) argue that if the initial weight point could be started from zero (all weights are zero), then the iterative steps would move along a broad shallow area with a large step size that causes quicker convergence. While BP does not converge from the zero weight point in the weight space, the perceptron does. Therefore, Li et al. partition the MLP into perceptrons, train from zero, and arrive at an initial weight set for BP training. Their reported results on the datasets used are good, although the technique adds extra complexity to the training algorithm. Some researchers (Riedmiller and Braun, 1993) claim that some methods in the literature for selecting a good initial weight set did not improve convergence. We note that the results also depend on (i) the dataset used (i.e., the size and quality of the exemplar sample), (ii) the architecture of the FANN, (iii) the step gain and its adaptive strategy, (iv) the momentum coefficient (see Section 5.3), (v) the floating point word size, (vi) the initial weight set, and (vii) the activation functions (unipolar or bipolar, sigmoids, logarithms, arctangents, etc.).

The Nguyen–Widrow Hidden Weight Initialization Procedure

The Nguyen–Widrow weight initialization process distributes the initial weights at the hidden neurodes so that it is more likely that each input exemplar will cause a hidden neurode to learn efficiently (Nguyen and Widrow, 1990). Let N be the number of input lines and M be the number of hidden nodes. They put

$$\beta = 0.7(M^{1/N}) \tag{5.1a}$$

and then draw the initial weights $\{w_{nm}^{(i)}\}$ randomly between, -1 and 1. Next, they obtain an initial weight point upon modifying each initially drawn weight $w_{nm}^{(i)}$ via

$$w_{nm}^{(0)} \leftarrow (\beta/\|\mathbf{w}^{(i)}\|)w_{nm}^{(i)} \tag{5.1b}$$

where $\mathbf{w}^{(i)} = (w_{11}^{(i)},...,w_{NM}^{(i)})$. The weight set $\{w_{nm}^{(0)}\}$ is then taken to be the starting weight set for the hidden neurodes in gradient descent. This helps to prevent premature saturation at the hidden nodes, which would retard convergence. Russo's method can be used on the weights at the neurodes in the output layer. We caution that the behavior can vary significantly, depending upon the data.

A Nguyen–Widrow–Russo Algorithm for Selection of Initial Weights

---

Step 1. /Draw entire weight set randomly/
    $w \leftarrow 0.0$;   /Summing variable for $\|\mathbf{w}\|$/
    $\beta \leftarrow (0.7)\exp((\ln(M)/N)$;   /Nguyen–Widrow parameter/
    for $m = 1$ to M do
        for $j = 1$ to J do
            draw u_{mj} randomly in $[-1,1]$;   /Output layer weights/
            $u_{mj} \leftarrow (2.4/M)u_{mj}$;   /Russo's method/
        for $n = 1$ to N do
            draw w_{nm} randomly in $[-1,1]$; /Hidden layer weights/
            $w \leftarrow w + w_{nm}^{2}$;   /Sum squares of hidden weights/
    $w = \sqrt{w}$; $\beta \leftarrow \beta/w$;
    for $m = 1$ to M do
        for $n = 1$ to N do $w_{nm} \leftarrow \beta w_{nm}$;   /The Nguyen–Widrow method/

Examples 5.1.   **Comparing Weight Initializations**

Consider the XOR exemplar input data $\{(0.1,0.1), (0.1,0.9), (0.9,0.1), (0.9,0.9)\}$. Let $N = 2$ (inputs), $M = 4$ (the number of neurodes in the hidden layer) and suppose initial weights drawn at the first hidden neurode are $(w_{11}^{(i)}, w_{21}^{(i)}) = (0.94, 0.98)$. When $(x_1, x_2) = (0.9, 0.9)$ enters the first hidden neurode, the sum is

$$r_1 = (0.94)(0.9) + (0.98)(0.9) = 1.728$$

Letting $b_1 = 1.0$ and $\alpha_1 = 2.0$, we obtain

$$y_1 = h(r_1) = h(1.728) = 1/[1.0 + \exp(-2.0*(1.728) + 1.0)] = 0.9210$$

$$h'(r_1) = y_1(1 - y_1) = 0.9210(1 - 0.9210) = 0.0727$$

With a small step gain η and small derivative $h'(r_1)$ appearing in $\partial E/\partial w_{11}$ and $\partial E/\partial w_{21}$, the increments

$$\Delta w_{11} = -\eta \partial E/\partial w_{11}, \qquad \Delta w_{21} = -\eta \partial E/\partial w_{21}$$

would be very small in magnitude. With another small derivative $g'(s_j) = z_j(1 - z_j)$, however, the weight increments would be reduced even more. For example, let $\eta = 0.1$, $h'(r_1) = 0.01$ and $g'(s_j) = 0.01$. Then the weight increments at the neurode would be

$$\Delta w_{nm} = -\eta \partial E/\partial w_{nm} = (0.1)(0.01)(0.01)\sum_j(t_j - z_j)u_{mj}x_n = 0.00001cu_{mj}x_n$$

where u_{mj} and x_n are less than unity in magnitude and c is a small scalar value. For $\Delta w_{nm} = 0.00001$, it would take 10,000 adjustments to sum up to 0.1.

Another saturation trap exists when the weights are allowed to exceed 1 in magnitude. For example, let the weights be $(w_{11}, w_{21}) = (2.0, 2.0)$ and $(x_1, x_2) = (0.9, 0.9)$. Then $y_1 = h(r_1) = 1/[1 + \exp(-2 \times 3.6 + 1)] = 0.99925$. Therefore

$$h'(r_1) = y_1(1 - y_1) = (0.99925)(1.0 - 0.99925) = 0.00075$$

If we also had

$$g'(s_j) = 0.00075, \quad \eta = 0.1$$

then the product would be

$$\eta h'(r_1)g'(s_j) = 0.00000005425$$

so that 20,000 adjustments of this size would add only 0.001085 to a weight, or 200,000 updates would add 0.01085. A random initial weight set may lead to weight paths outside of $[-1,1]$.

Obtaining Starting Weights via Individual Weight Search

We also suggest other methods for adjusting an initial weight set to obtain a good starting weight set from which gradient methods can perform reasonably well. These are more computationally intensive, but are often worth the extra initial cost to reduce the overall cost. Use the following procedure: (i) Select an initial weight set; and (ii) adjust a single weight at a time or all weights at a time via search. The first three methods are *univariate searches* that keep all weights fixed except a single one at a time that is to be adjusted. The first method randomly draws a sample for a single weight of size six between -1 and 1 (uniformly) and evaluates the sum-squared error (SSE) E at each one. The sample value with the lowest SSE is kept and the others are discarded. After each weight has been adjusted this way, the overall process is repeated once. This works well for small networks.

The second method takes the five values $\{-0.866, -0.433, 0.0, 0.433, 0.866\}$ across the range of a single weight v_{ps} (which may represent u_{mj} or w_{nm}) from -1 to 1 and the TSSE is found at each weight value. This method fits a quartic (fourth degree) polynomial function $E = p_4(v_{ps})$ of a single weight v_{ps} to five points and then performs a quick search of the polynomial by evaluating $p_4(-1.0), p_4(-0.8),..., p_4(1.0)$. The argument value with the lowest polynomial value is taken to be the new weight. Slices of the TSSE function E appear to be essentially quartic or quadratic in form (see Figures 4.7 through 4.11), which is an empirical reason to use quartic polynomials (which can assume quadratic form also).

In each of the univariate methods, each weight $w_{11},..., w_{NM}, u_{11},..., u_{MJ}$ is adjusted singly in turn. This usually gets all of the weights in a better position, but because the random initial weights may be far from a good solution, the procedure is repeated once to yield a *starting* weight point $\mathbf{v}^{(0)}$. It is not necessary to obtain a fine preliminary approximation here. Gradient methods are very quick from anywhere inside the well of attraction of a deep minimum where the function is essentially quadratic, provided that the step sizes are appropriate. This also works well for small networks.

A third method starts at the initial weight point $\mathbf{v}^{(i)} = (w_{11}^{(i)},..., w_{NM}^{(i)}, u_{11}^{(i)},..., u_{MJ}^{(i)})$ and draws a random direction $\mathbf{d}$ in the weight space. It selects five points on the line segment from $\mathbf{v}^{(i)}$ to $\mathbf{v}^{(i)} + \mathbf{d}$. The TSSE is computed at these five points, a quartic polynomial is passed through the points in this slice of E, and the minimum is found as the new weight point. This process is repeated a few iterations, but uses many fewer evaluations of E than do the univariate searches. The univariate searches, however, lower the TSSE more and are in orthogonal directions along the weight axes and thus should be used only for relatively small MLPs. Section 6.4 provides the quartic line search in random directions.

The Univariate Random Search Algorithm to Adjust Initial Weights

---

Step 1. /Draw entire weight set randomly/
        for $m = 1$ to M do
                for $j = 1$ to J do draw u_{mj} randomly in $[-0.5, 0.5]$;
                for $n = 1$ to N do draw w_{nm} randomly in $[-0.5, 0.5]$;

Step 2. /Do twice the overall process of adjusting each single weight 6 times/

$E_{old} \leftarrow E(\mathbf{w}, \mathbf{u})$;	/Evaluate the SSE E/
for $r = 1$ to 2 do	/Do overall process twice/
for $m = 1$ to M do	/For each $m \leq M$/
for $j = 1$ to J do	/adjust each u_{mj} for all j/
for $i = 1$ to 6 do	/Sample size $\equiv 6$/
$u_{hold} \leftarrow u_{mj}$;	/Hold current weight/

$$u_{mj} \leftarrow \text{random}(-1,1); \qquad \text{/Draw appropriate value/}$$
$$E_{\text{new}} \leftarrow E(u_{mj}); \qquad \text{/Evaluate new SSE/}$$
$$\text{if } E_{\text{new}} < E_{\text{old}} \text{ then } E_{\text{old}} \leftarrow E_{\text{new}}; \text{ else } u_{mj} \leftarrow u_{\text{hold}};$$
$$\text{for } n = 1 \text{ to } N \text{ do} \qquad \text{/Adjust each } w_{nm}/$$
$$\quad \text{for } i = 1 \text{ to } 6 \text{ do} \qquad \text{/sample size} \equiv 6/$$
$$\quad\quad w_{\text{hold}} \leftarrow w_{nm}; \qquad \text{/Hold current weight/}$$
$$\quad\quad w_{nm} \leftarrow \text{random } (-1,1); \qquad \text{/Draw appropriate value/}$$
$$\quad\quad E_{\text{new}} \leftarrow E(w_{nm}); \qquad \text{/Evaluate new SSE/}$$
$$\quad\quad \text{if } E_{\text{new}} < E_{\text{old}} \text{ then } E_{\text{old}} \leftarrow E_{\text{new}}; \text{ else } w_{nm} \leftarrow w_{\text{hold}}$$

The observed *advantages* of univariate initial weight adjustments to obtain a good starting weight point are as follows: (i) It is much more likely that convergence will occur; and (ii) when the second stage of gradient convergence occurs, it is to a deeper minimum and is much quicker. The starting weight point derived via this procedure appears to fall into a well of attraction of deep minima, rather than of a shallow one. The result is that convergence from the starting weight point occurs. The *disadvantage* is that for a large number $W = (NM + MJ)$ of weights, this adds an extra computational burden because the SSE function E must be computed multiple times for each weight adjustment.

In practice, we use the quartic univariate approximation because it adjusts all weights at one time. For small FANNs, the random univariate search can find a good starting weight point with a small amount of computation. Once a quartic search has located a point with lowered SSE, then computationally cheaper quadratic search can be done on a finer grid in the direction of steepest descent. The algorithm for quartic search is given in detail in Chapter 6.

Example 5.2.   Univariate Quadratic Search

Suppose that an N–M–J MLP is to be trained on an exemplar dataset $\{(\mathbf{x}^{(q)}, \mathbf{t}^{(k(q))})\}$. First we draw a set of weights via the uniform distribution on $[-\frac{1}{2},\frac{1}{2}]$. Now we want to adjust these initial weights by quadratic search. We take the first weight w_{11} and substitute $w_{11} = -0.6667$ and compute the TSSE function $E_1 = E(w_{11})$. Next we substitute $w_{11} = 0.0$ and compute the TSSE value E_2. Then we take the third value $w_{11} = 0.6667$ from the weight interval and compute the TSSE value E_3. Letting $y_1 = E_1$, $y_2 = E_3$ and $y_3 = E_3$ and putting $x_1 = -0.667$, $x_2 = 0.0$, $x_3 = 0.667$, we now have the three points $\{(x_i, y_i): i = 1,2,3\}$.

It is a quick task to compute the polynomial $y = p_2(x) = ax^2 + bx + c$ by substituting in the values to obtain

$$y_1 = ax_1^2 + bx_1 + c$$
$$y_2 = ax_2^2 + bx_2 + c$$
$$y_3 = ax_3^2 + bx_3 + c$$

and solving for the unknowns a, b, and c (see Section 6.3). Figure 5.1 presents the situation along a weight dimension denoted by v.

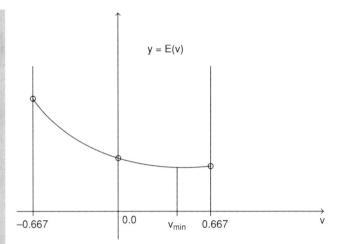

Figure 5.1. Quadratic search for a weight.

Next, we repeat the above process with weight w_{21}, and so on, until all weights $w_{11},...,$ w_{NM}, $u_{11},...,$ u_{MJ} have been adjusted. For small-sized networks, this is feasible, but for larger ones, we could use quartic search in the direction of steepest descent.

5.3. Stabilizing and Accelerating Gradient Descent

Avoiding Saturation of the Sigmoid Derivatives

A weight point may enter a region of the weight space (the *saturation region*) where a sigmoid has slope near zero (Lee et al., 1991). If the sign of the output value from a neurode is different from the target value at that node, then the saturation of that node causes the weight increment to be essentially zero while the error is relatively large. It may take an extremely large number of iterations to escape from such a region, or escape may never be achieved. The effects of saturation can happen prematurely, or at any time. Figure 5.2 shows

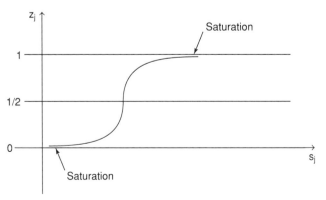

Figure 5.2. The Saturation regions of a unipolar sigmoid.

saturation regions for a unipolar sigmoid. Figure 5.3 displays the saturations of a bipolar sigmoid.

The sigmoids are strictly increasing and so their derivatives are always positive and form a bell-shaped curve. They approach zero very rapidly away from the center of the sigmoid. Fahlman adds the value $\Delta = 0.1$ to every sigmoid derivative, whether or not it is smaller than that (Fahlman, 1988). We have tried this on several data sets and it improved convergence significantly. In fact, there are times when convergence does not occur from an initial weight point without it. A modification of this technique tests sigmoid derivatives against a lower bound by

$$\text{if } (g'(s) < 0.1) \text{ then } g'(s) = 0.1 \tag{5.2a}$$

$$\text{if } (h'(r) < 0.1) \text{ then } h'(r) = 0.1 \tag{5.2b}$$

When one or more sigmoid derivatives are essentially zero, it makes the weight increments essentially zero so that certain weights may change only imperceptibly on each update—that is, beyond the number of digits of precision in use. Examples of respective weight increments and sigmoid activation functions are

$$\Delta u_{mj}^{(r+1)} = \eta[(t_j - z_j)g'(s_j)]y_m, \qquad g'(s_j) = z_j(1 - z_j) \quad \text{(unipolar)}$$

(see Equations (4.15) and (4.21a,b), as well as Equations (4.27a,b) and (4.28a,b)). When $z \approx 0$ or $z \approx 1$, then $g'(s_j) \approx 0$. Similarly, when $y \approx 0$ or $y \approx 1$, $h'(r) \approx 0$ at the hidden neurodes for $y_m = h(r_m)$. For bipolar sigmoids, the derivatives are $G'(s_j) = (1 + z_j)(1 - z_j)/2$ and $H'(r_m) = (1 + y_m)(1 - y_m)/2$. These are saturated when $z_j \approx \pm 1$ or $y_m \approx \pm 1$, respectively.

Vitela and Reifman (1994) analyzed necessary conditions for premature saturation. They found that saturation can start very early in the steepest descent process due to the initial

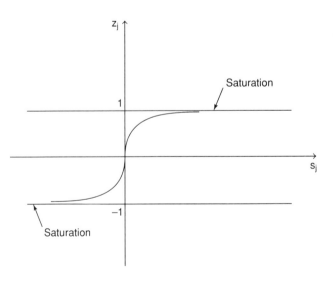

Figure 5.3. Saturation of bipolar sigmoids.

weights being in a region of skewed error surface $E(\mathbf{v}^{(r)})$. If the sign changes on two consecutive iterations of a component of $E(\mathbf{v}^{(r)})$ at the jth output neurode, then the projection $\mu \Delta v^{(r-1)}$ onto $\nabla E(\mathbf{v}^{(r)})$ may not be in the direction of the negative gradient. When the projected value is larger than the corresponding magnitude $-\eta \nabla E(\mathbf{v}^{(r)})$, the first-order effect is to increase, not decrease, the error.

The experiments of Vitela and Reifman (1994) used 20–10–3 networks. Of these, three neurodes saturated during training, but two of them saturated on the third training cycle (epoch). Their resulting method puts the momentum coefficient $\mu = 0$ on the first few cycles, but then it changes to $\mu = 0.9$ for high smoothing (see the next subsection for momentum).

Saturation-Resistant Activation Functions

Unipolar sigmoids have derivatives of the form $\theta(1 - \theta)$, while bipolar sigmoids have derivatives of the form $(1 + \theta)(1 - \theta)/2$, where θ represents y_m or z_j. In the respective cases of $\theta \approx 0$ or $\theta \approx 1$ or of $\theta \approx \pm 1$, the derivatives are approximately zero. Other activations that resist saturation have been tried. One used by Hecht-Nielsen (1990) is graphed in Figure 5.4 with a bipolar sigmoid. It is the *bipolar logarithmic* activation function defined by

$$g(s) = \log(1 - s), \quad s < 0 \tag{5.3a}$$

$$g(s) = \log(1 + s), \quad s \geq 0 \tag{5.3b}$$

The logarithm is to the base 10. The derivatives are

$$g'(s) = 1/(1 - s), \quad s < 0 \tag{5.3c}$$

$$g'(s) = 1/(1 + s), \quad s \geq 0 \tag{5.3d}$$

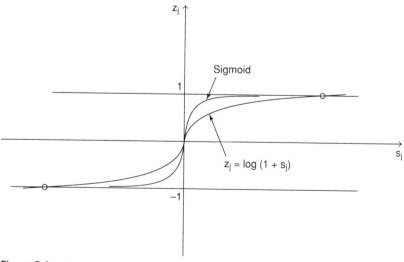

Figure 5.4. Logarithm versus sigmoid.

The sum $s = a_1\Phi_1 + \cdots + a_M\Phi_M$ at a neurode with M incoming values $\{\Phi_m\}$ and M weights $\{a_m\}$ may assume a value between $-M$ and M because each term is between -1 and 1 (approximately). When $s \approx \pm M$, say, $s \approx M$, then $g'(s) = 1/(1 + M)$ approaches $1/M$ for large M. This can be quite small for a large number M of inputs to the neurode.

Thus, the effects of saturation are possible here, but not as likely (especially for small networks) so the logarithmic activations can speed up convergence (for example, see Fausett (1994)). The value of $\log(1 + M)$, however, can be greater than 1. For examples, consider $\log(1 + 100) = 2.004321$ and $\log(1 + 1000) = 3.000434$. The activation outputs are supposed to be squashed down into $[0,1]$ (or $[-1,1]$). Otherwise, the numbers can become too large and result in overflow errors in the computer. We avoid logarithmic activation functions for neurodes that have a number of inputs larger than 10 ($1/(1 + 10) < 0.1$).

Fausett (1994, p. 314) gives an example where XOR data are trained by standard BP using (i) bipolar sigmoid activations and (ii) bipolar logarithmic activations. The same initial weights were used on each training run. The network architectures were both N–M–J = 2–4–1 with the desired outputs being 0.1 for 0 and 0.9 for 1. The bipolar sigmoidal network required 387 epochs (1548 complete weight updates), while the bipolar logarithm required only 144 epochs (576 complete weight updates). When the data were modified to -0.8 for 0 and 0.8 for 1, the sigmoid required 265 epochs (1056 complete weight updates) and the logarithm required 77 epochs (308 complete weight updates). This is impressive, but $\log(1 + 4) = 0.69897$, which is well below 1.0 (four weighted inputs are being summed for a total of up to 1.0 each). A possibly fruitful method is to use $\log_M(1 + s)$, where M is the number of incoming lines. We anticipate that $1 + s < M$ would virtually always occur, so that $\log_M(1 + s) < 1$ would always hold.

An alternative bipolar activation function that is simple but effective was proposed by (Syu and Tsao, 1994) to prevent saturation. It is

$$g(s) = as/(1 + |s|) \tag{5.4a}$$

which approaches the asymptotes $g(s) = \pm a$ ($a > 0$) as the sum s approaches $\pm\infty$. We can adapt this to the unipolar form via

$$g(s) = (a/2)(s - b)/[1 + |(s - b)|] + a/2 \tag{5.4b}$$

We have translated the origin to b, scaled it down to the range $\pm(a/2)$ and translated it up on the vertical axis by a/2 so the new range is 0 to a. The derivative of the bipolar form is

$$g'(s) = a/(1 + |s|)^2 \tag{5.4c}$$

This goes to zero more slowly than do the sigmoid derivatives. Equation (5.4c) can be substituted into Equations (4.21a) and (4.21b) or in (4.28a) and (4.28b) appropriately for the bipolar sigmoid derivatives $h'(r)$ and $g'(s)$.

Smoothing the Direction of Descent with Momentum

To overcome wide swings in the direction $-\nabla E^{(q)}(\mathbf{v})$ of steepest descent on consecutive steps, Rumelhart smoothed the direction of descent with an extra first-order (velocity) term which he called *momentum* (Rumelhart et al., 1986). The weight update formulation with momentum becomes

$$\mathbf{v}^{(r+1)} = \mathbf{v}^{(r)} - \eta\nabla E(\mathbf{v}^{(r)}) + \mu[\mathbf{v}^{(r)} - \mathbf{v}^{(r-1)}] \tag{5.5a}$$

$$v_{ps}^{(r+1)} = v_{ps}^{(r)} - \eta(\partial E(v_{ps}^{(r)})/\partial v_{ps}) + \mu\Delta v_{ps}^{(r-1)} \tag{5.5b}$$

where $v_{ps}^{(r)} = w_{nm}^{(r)}$ or $u_{mj}^{(r)}$ is a component of the weight vector on the rth weight update (iteration) and μ is the *momentum parameter* (or *momentum coefficient*). This smoothing of the direction helps to prevent oscillations, provided that reasonable values for μ can be determined. This adds the effect of a frictional resistance that depends on velocity (the rate of change in the weights), which smooths the weight increments.

Figure 5.5 shows the path of gradient descent steps on the contour lines of a curving narrow canyon topography of the error surface of E. The smoothed path is much quicker in terms of computational time and number of steps. It is helpful in case the data are noisy or when there are multiple patterns in the classes. Some use values for μ as low as 0.05 while others use values as high as 0.9. MLPs behave differently when training on different datasets (and with different scales of architecture), so it is difficult to make universal claims.

A study by Perantonis and Karras (1995) studied the effects of momentum. They found that without a momentum term there was oscillatory descent and that the momentum term substantially reduced the number of steps required. They used Lagrange multipliers to develop an update formula with two extra parameters that must be given by the user. This technique yielded improvements of 41% to 53% for good values of these parameters. The learning was faster than BP with momentum, QP (quickpropagation), and the delta-bar-delta methods on a variety of problems. At worst, it was comparable to QP.

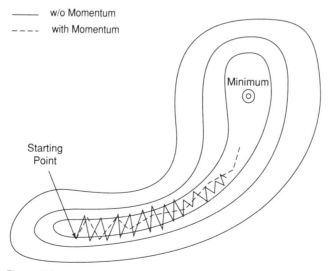

Figure 5.5.   Steepest descent with and without momentum.

Momentum Revisited: The Methods of Watrous, Eaton–Olivier, and Yu

According to Fahlman (1988), very little, if any, improvement is achieved by momentum terms, while Riedmiller and Braun (1993) claim that although it may help in some cases, it can actually hinder the convergence in others. On the other hand, with a good selection of the parameters, the convergence speed can be increased significantly, according to Zurada (1992, p. 213). This shows the sensitivity of the value of μ to the data. When the data are noisy, so as to make the $\partial E/\partial v_{ps}$ jumpy, then the smoothing with the momentum term is very desirable. The noisier the data, the larger the momentum coefficient μ should be ($0 \leq \mu < 1$). It also appears that the more nonsimilar exemplars there are in each class, then the more smoothing that will be required and the larger μ should be. Some researchers use values as low as 0.1, while others use values as high as 0.9.

We note that Fahlman did many tests on the N–M–N datasets (see Appendix 11a) such as the 10–5–10 and 20–10–20 data. His data were "clean" (deterministic) rather than noisy. Fahlman (1988) mentions the strategy of Plaut et al. (1986) that first sets μ to a small value and then increases it over the iterations.

Watrous considers the difference equation (Watrous, 1987, p. 624)

$$(\Delta v)^{(r+1)} - \mu(\Delta v)^{(r)} = -\eta \partial E/\partial v \tag{5.6a}$$

and shows that the momentum μ applies an approximate gain of $\eta/(1 - \mu)$ to the step after the filter settles over many iterations ($0 \leq \mu < 1$). Equation (5.6a) is a recursive input/output system that acts as a low-pass filter whose gain and cutoff are both controlled by μ (Eaton and Olivier, 1992). Equation (5.6a) follows when we write

$$\mathbf{v}^{(r+1)} - \mathbf{v}^{(r)} - \mu[\mathbf{v}^{(r)} - \mathbf{v}^{(r-1)}] = -\eta \nabla E(\mathbf{v}^{(r)}) \tag{5.6b}$$

The z-transform of this transfer function is

$$H(z) = \eta z^{-1}/(1 - \mu z^{-1}) = \eta/(z - \mu) \tag{5.7a}$$

The effective cutoff is between $|z| = 1$ and $|z| = 2$. Note that $z = \exp(jw)$, so that $w = 0$ means that $z = \exp(0) = 1$. Thus the low frequency (direct current, or constant) is

$$H(1) = G = \eta/(1 - \mu) \tag{5.7b}$$

Eaton and Olivier use the gain $G = \eta/(1 - \mu)$ derived from Equation (5.6b) by the z-transforms of the left and right sides

$$1 - z^{-1} - \mu z^{-1} + \mu z^{-2}, \quad -\eta z^{-1} \tag{5.7c}$$

so that

$$H(z) = \eta z/[(z^2 - (1 + \mu)z + \mu] = \eta z/[(z - 1)(z - \mu)] = \{\eta/(z - 1)\}\{z/(z - \mu)\} \tag{5.7d}$$

This represents two filters cascaded where the first one has gain η and the second has gain $1/(1 - \mu)$. Thus they use a gain of $G = \eta[1/(1 - \mu)] = \eta/(1 - \mu)$.

Eaton and Olivier (1992) also use the heuristic rule

$$\eta = 1.5/\sqrt{(K_1^2 + \cdots + K_P^2)} \tag{5.7e}$$

where K_p is the number of exemplars of the pth class (pattern type) and $\sqrt{(K_1^2 + \cdots + K_P^2)}$ is an approximation to the average gradient length. They state that a gain of about $G = 3.5$ works well in practice on many datasets. It is possible to choose the momentum parameter

$$\mu = 1 - \eta/3.5 \tag{5.7f}$$

to suboptimize the training, upon solving Equations (5.7e) and (5.7b). They train in the batch mode. They found that a large momentum coefficient, say, $\mu = 0.9$, speeds up convergence when there is a large number of pattern types. When there are few pattern types, then a lower value may provide more rapid training. With a larger value of μ, the sensitivity of the training to variations in $-\eta \nabla E(\mathbf{v})$ is lowered. The optimal value of μ is experimental, but depends on η.

Figure 5.6 shows two runs on the Digit12 data given in Appendix 11a at the end of Chapter 11. In the first run shown in part (a), the momentum is set at $\mu = 0.1$. In the second run, it is set at $\mu = 0.4$. There were 10 patterns and one exemplar feature vector for each pattern. The differences in the root mean square error (RMSE) on the vertical axis versus iteration number on the horizontal axis is due solely to the change in the value of μ. On the first run, there were no misses—that is, incorrect recognition of the exemplar vectors on which it trained. On the second run, there were four misses out of 10 vectors. We have seen similar oscillations caused by a setting as low as $\mu = 0.16$. We observe here that the larger momentum helped on the early iterations but caused havoc on the later ones.

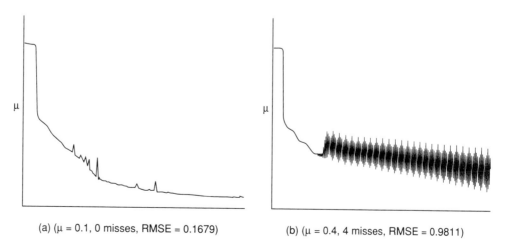

(a) ($\mu = 0.1$, 0 misses, RMSE = 0.1679)   (b) ($\mu = 0.4$, 4 misses, RMSE = 0.9811)

Figure 5.6.   RMSE versus iteration number for fullpropagation runs on the Digit12 dataset. (random seed = 333 for draw of initial weights).

The *adaptive momentum* method of Yu et al. (1993) uses a changing momentum term that tends to orthogonalize the directions of search, and thus forms a *conjugate directions* methodology (see Section 5.9). Orthogonality of consecutive gradient directions requires that

$$(\nabla E(\mathbf{v}^{(r)}))^t(\nabla E(\mathbf{v}^{(r-1)})) = 0 \tag{5.8}$$

where the superscript t denotes the transpose of the gradient column vector (so the resulting row-by-column vector multiplication is the *dot product*). Yu et al. derive a momentum term $\mu^{(r)}$ via Gram–Schmidt orthogonalization such that

$$\mathbf{v}^{(r+1)} = \mathbf{v}^{(r)} - \eta(\nabla E(\mathbf{u}^{(r)})) + \mu^{(r)}(\mathbf{v}^{(r)} - \mathbf{v}^{(r-1)}) \tag{5.9a}$$

$$\mu^{(r)} = [\nabla E(\mathbf{u}^{(r)}))^t(\nabla E(\mathbf{v}^{(r-1)})]/[\nabla E(\mathbf{v}^{(r-1)}))^t(\nabla E(\mathbf{v}^{(r-1)})] \tag{5.9b}$$

where $\nabla E(\mathbf{u}^{(r)})$ is the gradient found from the gradient equations (see Equations (4.21a,b)) and $\nabla E(\mathbf{v}^{(r)})$ and $\nabla E(\mathbf{v}^{(r-1)})$ are the gradients computed on the current and previous iterations using the adaptive momentum method of Equations (5.9). If BP with momentum uses $O(W)$ computations per iteration, then this takes $O(cW)$ computations per iteration, where $0 < c < 3$ and W is the number of weights.

Yu et al. (1993) found that while the convergence of the adaptive momentum back-propagation was slower on the initial iterations, it performed much better on the later iterations and yielded a significantly lower SSE.

Optimal Use of Steepest Descent: Techniques of Dahl and Hush–Salas

Once a direction of steepest descent is computed from the negative gradient, BP takes a single small step in that direction. Some researchers have argued that this is underutilization of costly computation. The Hush–Salas technique of *gradient reuse* employs a computed gradient repeatedly until the SSE decreases only negligibly (Hush and Salas, 1988) or increases.

Another technique to accelerate training is *line search* (Dahl, 1987). Let $\mathbf{v}$ be the current weight vector, and let $\mathbf{u}$ be the direction of steepest descent of the SSE function E from $\mathbf{v}$. Line search seeks to find α^* to minimize $E(\mathbf{v} + \alpha\mathbf{u})$. A parabola (quadratic) is fitted to three points along $\mathbf{v} + \alpha\mathbf{u}$, and the minimum of E is approximated by the minimum of the parabola. This works when the weight points have entered the well of a minimum, where quadratic approximation is appropriate. See Chapter 6 for a detailed description of minimizing with polynomials along a one-dimensional slice of E. This is equivalent to the QP (quickprop) algorithm of Fahlman (1988) which is discussed in Section 5.4. Quartic line search (see Chapter 6) is more powerful on earlier iterations before a deep well is reached.

Adaptive Step Gains: Jacob's Delta-Bar-Delta Method

The second problem of gradient training is that an optimal or suboptimal step gain is not known. One technique is to iteratively adjust the step gain $\eta = \eta^{(r)}$ (*learning rate*) on each rth epoch. An extension of this is to use different step gains $\eta_{nm}^{(r)}$ and $\eta_{mj}^{(r)}$ for each weight

$w_{nm}^{(r)}$ and $u_{mj}^{(r)}$, respectively. Each of these individual learning rates is updated when the associated weight is updated.

The *delta-bar-delta* technique was originated by Jacobs (1988) for backpropagation. Similar approaches were done before and after this method, respectively, by Saridis (1970) and Riedmiller and Braun (1993). The delta-bar-delta technique uses

$$w_{nm}^{(r+1)} = w_{nm}^{(r)} - \eta_{nm}^{(r+1)}[\partial E(\mathbf{w}^{(r)}, \mathbf{u}^{(r)})/\partial w_{nm}] \tag{5.10a}$$

$$u_{mj}^{(r+1)} = u_{mj}^{(r)} - \eta_{mj}^{(r+1)}[\partial E(\mathbf{w}^{(r)}, \mathbf{u}^{(r)})/\partial u_{mj}] \tag{5.10b}$$

where the superscript on the PSSE $E^{(q)}$ is suppressed for convenience. The iteration number first goes from $r = 1$ to $r = Q$ and then keeps going with $r = Q + 1,...,$ until $r = IQ$ is reached (I is the total number of epochs desired). The basic idea is that if a slope $\partial E/\partial v_{ps}$ (v_{ps} is either w_{nm} or u_{mj}) has the same sign on two consecutive updates, then the process has not reached the minimum. In this case, the step gain is increased. When the slopes on two consecutive updates have differing signs, then the step is too big and the minimum is somewhere in between, so the step gain η is decreased.

The delta-bar-delta rules for updating the step gains are listed below for given β, δ, and θ.

(i) Take the convex combination of the current partial derivative of E with respect to the weight and the previous delta-bar for that weight via

$$^-\Delta_{nm}^{(r)} = \beta[^-\Delta_{nm}^{(r-1)}] + (1 - \beta)[\partial E(\mathbf{w}^{(r)}, \mathbf{u}^{(r)})/\partial w_{nm}] \qquad (0 < \beta < 1)$$

$$^-\Delta_{mj}^{(r)} = \beta[^-\Delta_{mj}^{(r-1)}] + (1 - \beta)[\partial E(\mathbf{w}^{(r)}, \mathbf{u}^{(r)})/\partial u_{mj}] \qquad (0 < \beta < 1)$$

(ii) Update the step gains via

$$\eta_{nm}^{(r+1)} = \eta_{nm}^{(r)} + \delta, \qquad \text{if } [^-\Delta_{nm}^{(r-1)}][\partial E(\mathbf{w}^{(r)}, \mathbf{u}^{(r)})/\partial w_{nm}] > 0$$

$$\eta_{mj}^{(r+1)} = \eta_{mj}^{(r)} + \delta, \qquad \text{if } [^-\Delta_{mj}^{(r-1)}][\partial E(\mathbf{w}^{(r)}, \mathbf{u}^{(r)})/\partial u_{mj}] > 0$$

$$\eta_{nm}^{(r+1)} = \theta\eta_{nm}^{(r)}, \qquad \text{if } [^-\Delta_{nm}^{(r-1)}][\partial E(\mathbf{w}^{(r)}, \mathbf{u}^{(r)})/\partial w_{nm}] < 0$$

$$\eta_{mj}^{(r+1)} = \theta\eta_{mj}^{(r)}, \qquad \text{if } [^-\Delta_{mj}^{(r-1)}][\partial E(\mathbf{w}^{(r)}, \mathbf{u}^{(r)})/\partial u_{mj}] < 0$$

$$\eta_{nm}^{(r+1)} = \eta_{nm}^{(r)}, \qquad \text{if } [^-\Delta_{nm}^{(r-1)}][\partial E(\mathbf{w}^{(r)}, \mathbf{u}^{(r)})/\partial w_{nm}] = 0$$

$$\eta_{mj}^{(r+1)} = \eta_{mj}^{(r)}, \qquad \text{if } [^-\Delta_{mj}^{(r-1)}][\partial E(\mathbf{w}^{(r)}, \mathbf{u}^{(r)})/\partial u_{mj}] = 0$$

The *advantage* of such weight adjustments is that each weight has its own adjustable step gain to help speed up convergence. A *disadvantage* is that for a large number of weights the process consumes nonnegligible extra memory and time. *In practice*, the factor θ and the additive increment δ must be specified by the user (they satisfy $\delta > 0$ to increase the step size and $0 < \theta < 1$ to decrease the step size). Reasonable values to start with are $\delta = 0.04$ and $\theta = 0.72$. The convex coefficient β must also be specified. One may initially take $\beta = 0.3$ to start the process and then move toward $\beta = 0.7$ after a selected number of epochs.

Adaptive Step Gain and the Parlos–Fernandez–Atiya–Muthusami–Tsai Technique

The above subsection discussed and provided the delta-bar-delta technique for adjusting the step gains. A large amount of research has been done on adaptive step gains (learning rates), and Section 5.10 covers special methods for determining η that provide up to an order faster convergence. Other approaches have been done. Here we include one by Parlos et al. (1994) which they implemented in the epochal batch mode of BP.

The usual gradient weight update for any weight v_{ps} is $\Delta v_{ps} = -\eta(\partial E/\partial v_{ps})$. Parlos et al. discuss three options on η with which they have experimented. These are

$$\eta^{(r)} = \eta_0/\|\nabla E\|$$

$$\eta^{(r)} = \eta_0 E(\mathbf{v}^{(r-1)})/\|\nabla E\|^2$$

$$\eta^{(r)} = \eta_0 \tanh(E(\mathbf{v}^{(r-1)})/E_0)/\|\nabla E\|^2$$

The second and third formulations are functions of the previous SSE value E, and E_0 is a standardizing (early) value of the SSE.

Parlos et al. argue that as E decreases to a minimum, the gradient components $\partial E/\partial v_{ps}$ approach zero, so that $-\eta(\partial E/\partial v_{ps})$ may become so near zero as to stymie the movement toward the local minimum with unduly small steps. This accounts for the extremely slow convergence of BP in the vicinity of a local minimum. Parlos et al. implemented a modified update formulation that keeps the gradient at unit magnitude via

$$\Delta v_{ps} = [-\eta E(\partial E/\partial v_{ps})]/\|\partial E/\partial v_{ps}\|^2 \tag{5.11}$$

The results presented by Parlos et al. show outstanding results on analog data compared to both BP and QP (quickprop, to be discussed in the next section), but was no better on digital data. They were an order faster than BP and from 2.5 to 6 times faster than QP on the data tested. They used 1–15–1 and 1–30–1 networks on sinusoidal data from $y = \sin(x)$ from -2π to 2π and also used 2–10–1 and 2–20–1 networks on $z = f(x, y) = 0.05 + 0.1x_2\cos(y + 3.0) + 0.5xy \exp[-(y^2 - 1.0)]$. Networks with many inputs behave differently on different datasets. Parlos et al. warn that the behavior can become jumpy as the minimum is approached.

Second-Order Gradient Methods

It is generally agreed that the fastest general-purpose gradient methods for nonlinear unconstrained optimization are those of the quasi-Newton type (Gill et al., 1981). While these work well on convex functions, which include quadratics, they do require more computation and storage. They also have the local minimum problem, but are sometimes worth the extra cost because they reduce the overall volume of computation (Watrous, 1987). They compute the

Hessian matrix **H** of second mixed partial derivatives at every step (or every pth step and reuse the Hessian p times). For large neural networks with $W = NM + MJ$ weights, this requires W^2 computations of derivatives and memory locations each time **H** is recomputed.

The next fastest methods are conjugate gradient directions (Barnard and Casasent, 1989), which are discussed in Section 5.9. For modern applicable references, see Watrous (1987) and Shanno (1990). Conjugate gradient directions use $O(W)$ (the *order* of W, where $W = NM + MJ$) memory word locations and computed values as opposed to $O(W^2)$ for quasi-Newton methods. They are up to 10 times faster than BP, but also have the pitfall of local minima, as do all gradient methods (so it is important to find a good starting weight point and to avoid premature saturation). None of the second-order methods requires a step gain nor a momentum term. For further discussion of second-order gradient methods, see Fletcher (1980).

Full second order methods increase the rate of convergence from first order (linear) to second order (quadratic). Let $\mathbf{v}^*$ be the minimum. By definition, if $\left\|\mathbf{v}^{(r+1)} - \mathbf{v}^*\right\| \le \beta\left\|\mathbf{v}^{(r)} - \mathbf{v}^*\right\|^c$ for some power c and constant β, then we say the convergence is *of order c*. Second order gradient methods ($c = 2$) automatically include the step size, which is unknown in the linear case ($c = 1$).

The Newton formulation

$$\mathbf{v}^{(r+1)} = \mathbf{v}^{(r)} - \mathbf{H}^{-1}(\mathbf{v}^{(r)})\nabla E(\mathbf{v}^{(r)}) \tag{5.12}$$

has the step gain built in because it moves to the minimum of the quadratic form in a neighborhood of a local minimum (see Equation (4b.14) in Appendix 4). It can be derived from the second-order approximation of the SSE function E via the Taylor series expansion

$$E(\mathbf{v}^{(r+1)}) = E(\mathbf{v}^{(r)}) + (\nabla E(\mathbf{v}^{(r)}))^t(\mathbf{v}^{(r+1)} - \mathbf{v}^{(r)})$$
$$+ \tfrac{1}{2}(\mathbf{v}^{(r+1)} - \mathbf{v}^{(r)})^t\mathbf{H}(\mathbf{v}^{(r)})(\mathbf{v}^{(r+1)} - \mathbf{v}^{(r)}) + \epsilon \tag{5.13}$$

where the superscript t denotes the transpose, ϵ is the remainder of the infinite series, and $\mathbf{H}(\mathbf{v}^{(r)})$ is the *Hessian* matrix of second-order mixed partial derivatives evaluated at the current weight vector $\mathbf{v}^{(r)}$, defined by

$$\mathbf{H}(\mathbf{v}^{(r)}) = [(\partial^2 E(v_{ps}^{(r)})/\partial v_{ps}\partial v_{qt})] \tag{5.14a}$$

Upon dropping the third-order (and higher) error term ϵ in Equation (5.13) and letting $\mathbf{v}^{(r+1)}$ denote the minimum desired, the gradient of each side of Equation (5.13) (see Section 4b.1 of Appendix 4b and Equations (4b.9) to (4b.14)) yields

$$\nabla E(\mathbf{v}^{(r+1)}) = 0 = \nabla E(\mathbf{v}^{(r)}) + \mathbf{H}(\mathbf{v}^{(r)})(\mathbf{v}^{(r+1)} - \mathbf{v}^{(r)}) + \text{(third-order term)} \tag{5.14b}$$

(Fletcher, 1980; Gill et al., 1981; Mital, 1976). We premultiply both sides of Equation (5.14b) by $\mathbf{H}^{-1}(\mathbf{v}^{(r)})$ and solve for the minimum $\mathbf{v}^{(r+1)}$ to obtain Newton's formulation given by Equation (5.12), which provides both a direction and a stepsize for moving to reach the quadratically approximated minimum.

A strong *advantage* of second-order methods is that while $E(\mathbf{v})$ is not actually quadratic, and thus $\mathbf{v}^{(r+1)}$ is not the actual minimum, once in the well of a local minimum where E is essentially quadratic, continued iterations approach a local minimum extremely rapidly via near-second order convergence. The inverse Hessian matrix yields a step size as well as direction and is much more accurate than the linear process.

A *disadvantage* of the full second-order Newton method is that $\mathbf{H}^{-1}(-)$ must be computed on each iteration or every pth iteration and stored in memory, while that matrix may be quite large. An $(NM + MJ)^2$ matrix must be computed and inverted each time.

In practice, we may update $\mathbf{H}^{-1}(-)$ on, say, every fifth iteration to save computation, although this *Hessian-inverse-reuse* lowers the convergence rate somewhat. *Quasi-Newton* methods were first used for training MLPs by Parker (1982) and discussed by Watrous (1987). They are more practical, computationally. They start at an initial point $\mathbf{v}^{(0)}$ with the initial matrix $\mathbf{G}^{-1} = \mathbf{I}$ (the identity matrix) as a rough approximation for $\mathbf{H}^{-1}$. Over the iterations, $\mathbf{G}^{-1} \rightarrow \mathbf{H}^{-1}$ and $\mathbf{v}^{(r)} \rightarrow \mathbf{v}^*$ (local minimum) as $r \rightarrow \infty$. The quasi-Newton methods are computationally less costly than Newton's method and go from linear convergence on the first iteration to near quadratic on the later ones. The approximate Hessian inverse matrix need not be updated on every iteration.

The Techniques of Cater and of Stornetta-Huberman

It is often fruitful to use a very large step gain (Cater, 1987) on the early iterations to step out of the wells of local minima. The weight point $\mathbf{v}$ that provides the lowest SSE value $E(\mathbf{v})$ up to the current time is saved in memory. After a reasonable amount of time, a small step gain should be used that starts from the weight point that yielded the lowest SSE. Cater's Heuristic Learning Algorithm (HLA) increases the step gain when the SSE E is large and the increments Δv are small. It also decreases the step gain by 50% if the SSE increases by more that 1%. In other words, the step gain is made very large (up to 10.0), but decreases greatly when it begins to fail.

A very important technique noted by many researchers, but pointed out early by Stornetta and Huberman (1987), is the use of the bipolar sigmoid activation function

$$G(s) = [1 - \exp(-\alpha s)]/[1 + \exp(-\alpha s)] = 2g(s) - 1 \qquad (5.15)$$

in place of the unipolar sigmoid

$$g(s) = 1/[1 + \exp(-\alpha s + b)] \qquad (5.16)$$

This puts zero as the center of the asymmetry of s, which eliminates the biases b as a source of error. It also eliminates the need to train on the biases. It reduced the training time by 30% to 50% on the data used by Stornetta and Huberman (1987) and significantly lowered the variance of the number of iterations required.

According to Haykin (1994), asymmetric activation functions appear to yield faster training than other kinds. According the Hornik–Stinchcombe–White theorem (see Chapter 3), almost any kind of a nonconstant, nondecreasing activation function could be used. When unipolar sigmoids are used, the output data must be between 0 and 1, but bipolar sigmoids allow targets between -1 and 1. When the data are positive, the training with bipolar sigmoids is not as good and takes longer to converge. But when positive and negative values are used for high and low, the convergence is faster and the results are better. The use of bipolar data from the alphabet $\{-1,1\}$, where -0.8 is substituted for -1 and 0.8 for 1 (to avoid saturation), speeds up the training (Fausett, 1994).

5.4. Fahlman's Quickpropagation: A Lineal Second-Order Algorithm

Scott Fahlman's 1988 technical report at Carnegie Mellon University described a continuing study of the convergence properties of backpropagation methods (Fahlman, 1988). It was supported by the National Science Foundation and the Defense Advanced Research Projects Agency and has been disseminated internationally via email. In recent years, a method described in that technical report, known as *quickpropagation* (QP or *quickprop*), has become popular among researchers who use FANN applications. Appendix 5a provides instructions on how to obtain *quickprop* and Fahlman's 1988 report via email.

Fahlman used the *N–M–N* encoding problem (see the 10–5–10 dataset in Appendix 11a) to test the effects of the parameters η (step gain), μ (momentum factor), and the range $[-b, b]$ for the weights. He trained on a single class at a time in the BP mode of Rumelhart. The training time was taken to be the number of epochs completed before the FANN accurately output the correct identifier vectors of 0s and 1s for the exemplar feature vectors used for training. Thresholds of 0.4 and 0.6 were used: If the output z satisfied $z \le 0.4$, then z was set to 0; if $z \ge 0.6$, then z was set to 1; and if $0.4 < z < 0.6$, then there was no decision and the network continued to train. He ran each test multiple times (25 to 100 for most) from different starting weight points, and he recorded the average number of epochs until all input exemplars were correctly output. He used backpropagation weight adjustments. We note that this dataset is not noisy, so a momentum term is not necessary and likely could slow convergence (see Sections 4.2 and 5.3).

Fahlman found that the momentum term was not necessary on his datasets. It slowed down the learning during the earlier epochs, while it speeded it up slightly in the later ones. Others have also found the momentum term to be of little help (Riedmiller and Braun, 1993) on certain data. It may be used according to some strategy, however, such as that of Eaton and Olivier (1992) or Plaut et al. (1986). Fahlman also found that convergence was *improved significantly* by adding 0.1 to the derivatives $h'(r)$ and $g'(s)$ of the sigmoids, which prevents the effects of saturation. This caused the average number of epochs required for learning the 10–5–10 encoding problem (see Chapter 11) to decrease from 129 to 75. Thus the weight increments of Equations (4.17) and (4.20) should contain

$$(h'(r) + 0.1), \qquad (g'(s) + 0.1)$$

as replacements for $h'(r)$ and $g'(s)$.

The most significant advance in QP (quickprop) is that it uses a *lineally* second-order process that is more efficient than the purely linearized method of Equations (5.5). The error function $E(v_{ps}^{(r)})$ of a single weight along the $v_{ps}^{(r)}$ axis is fit by a parabola in an efficient formulation given below. This well-known approach in computational mathematics works well on the average, although not on all individual iterations. There is an implicit assumption of independence between weights (this is actually violated as a change in one weight changes the requirements on the others; that is, there is a moving target effect). The gradients $\{\partial E^{(q)}(v_{ps}^{(r-1)})/\partial v_{ps}\}$ of the previous update are saved, as well as the previous weight increments $\{\Delta v_{ps}^{(r-1)}\}$. Recall that v_{ps} designates either u_{mj} or w_{nm}.

Letting the total slope be

$$S^{(r+1)} = \sum_{(q=1,\ Q)} \partial E^{(q)}(v_{ps}^{(r)})/\partial v_{ps}$$

the process starts with the first update weight increment

$$\Delta v_{ps}^{(1)} \leftarrow \eta S^{(1)}$$

The new slopes are computed via

$$S_{mj}^{(r+1)} \leftarrow -\sum_{(q=1,\ Q)} (t_j^{(q)} - z_j^{(q)})[z_j^{(q)}(1 - z_j^{(q)}) + 0.1]y_m^{(q)}; \qquad \text{(for } u_{mj})$$

$$S_{nm}^{(r+1)} \leftarrow -\sum_{(q=1,\ Q)}\sum_{(j=1,\ J)}(t_j^{(q)} - z_j^{(q)})[z_j^{(q)}(1 - z_j^{(q)})$$
$$+ 0.1]u_{mj}[y_m^{(q)}(1 - y_m^{(q)}) + 0.1]x_n^{(q)}; \qquad \text{(for } w_{nm})$$

Each weight is updated via

$$v_{ps}^{(r+1)} \leftarrow v_{ps}^{(r)} + \{S_{ps}^{(r)}/[S_{ps}^{(r-1)} - S_{ps}^{(r)}]\}\Delta v_{ps}^{(r-1)} = v_{ps}^{(r)} + \Delta v_{ps}^{(r)};$$

Fahlman's formula is

$$\Delta v_{ps}^{(r)} = \{[\partial E^{(q)}(v_{ps}^{(r)})/\partial v_{ps}]/[(\partial E^{(q)}(v_{ps}^{(r-1)})/\partial v_{ps})$$
$$- (\partial E^{(q)}(v_{ps}^{(r)})/\partial v_{ps})]\}$$
$$\cdot \Delta v_{ps}^{(r-1)} - \eta(\partial E^{(q)}(v_{ps}^{(r)}))/\partial v_{ps} \qquad (5.17)$$

when training on a single qth exemplar with partial SSE function $E^{(q)}$. Fahlman used the partial SSEs in the epochal batch mode of BP (update averaged increments are added to the weights at the end of each epoch). This lowered the average number of epochs to about 22 on Fahlman's 10–5–10 test (220 evaluations of E) and roughly halved the standard deviation (the root mean-squared error from the average).

The usual incremental term $-\eta(\partial E^{(q)}(v_{ps}^{(r)}))/\partial v_{ps}$ on the right in Equation (5.17) is added on only when two consecutive partial derivatives for a particular weight have the same sign. A *maximum growth factor* μ_g is also used so that the current weight increment cannot exceed μ_g times the previous weight increment. Because quickprop is a rather *greedy* algorithm in that it takes risks for increased gain in an average sense (but may incur penalties as well), the maximum growth factor smooths it.

The *advantage* of QP is that it often increases the learning speed dramatically over BP. A *disadvantage* is that it fails to converge at times. *In practice*, the Fahlman strategy should be used with QP. It is as follows: (i) Train for a certain number of iterations; and (ii) if convergence is not occurring, then start over from another initial weight set.

Appendix 5 contains instructions for obtaining, via *e mail*, the material on quickprop and the program (in C) from a computer file at Carnegie Mellon University. Appendix 5 also covers the famous algorithm (Fahlman and Lebiere, 1990) called *cascade correlation*, which starts with a simple network that contains only input branching nodes and output neurodes, but is expanded incrementally during training by adding multiple hidden layers of single neurodes, one at a time, until the network is sufficiently powerful for the learning task at hand. For further information on cascade correlation, see Hoehfeld and Fahlman (1992), and Fahlman and Lebiere (1990). The algorithm reduces the moving target effect and uses QP to train a single hidden neurode at a time when it is adjoined to the network as a layer.

5.5. Riedmiller–Braun Resilient Propagation

Resilient Propagation

It is known that the step gain must be adjusted during the training iterations to achieve convergence, and such adaptive step gain techniques have been proposed—for example, the delta-bar-delta method (Jacobs, 1988) given in Section 5.3. Here we present the method of Riedmiller and Braun (1993), called *rprop* (or RP) for *resilient propagation*. It appears to be effective at adapting the weight increments as the iterations proceed. Recall that on the update of each weight v_{ps}, BP adds an increment according to

$$v_{ps}^{(r+1)} = v_{ps}^{(r)} + \Delta v_{ps}^{(r+1)} \tag{5.18}$$

where $\Delta v_{ps}^{(r+1)} = -\eta(\partial E(v_{ps}^{(r)})/\partial v_{ps})$.

Riedmiller and Braun take a similar, but different, approach to that of Jacobs (1988) to prevent the blurring of the weight updating process by inaccurate gradient errors and inappropriate step gains. Each *weight adapter* $\delta_{ps}^{(r)}$ is initially set to $\delta_{ps}^{(0)} = 0.5$. During the training process, it is updated via

$$\delta_{ps}^{(r+1)} = \eta^+(\delta_{ps}^{(r)}), \qquad \text{if } [\partial E(v_{ps}^{(r+1)})/\partial v_{ps}][\partial E(v_{ps}^{(r)})/\partial v_{ps}] > 0 \tag{5.19}$$

$$\delta_{ps}^{(r+1)} = \eta^-(\delta_{ps}^{(r)}), \qquad \text{if } [\partial E(v_{ps}^{(r+1)})/\partial v_{ps}][\partial E(v_{ps}^{(r)})/\partial v_{ps}] < 0 \tag{5.20}$$

$$\delta_{ps}^{(r+1)} = \delta_{ps}^{(r)}, \qquad\quad \text{otherwise} \tag{5.21}$$

where $0 < \eta^- < 1 < \eta^+$. The explanation is as follows: (i) When the partial derivative sign does not change from the rth to the $(r + 1)$st iterations, as in Equation (5.19), the weight adapter is increased; (ii) when the derivative sign changes per Equation (5.20), the weight adapter is decreased (the local minimum was overstepped); and (iii) if the rth or $(r + 1)$st partial derivative is zero, then there is no change (the local minimum of this weight has been reached for the given values of the other weights).

While the weight adapters are always nonnegative, the weight increment signs are determined via

$$\Delta v_{ps}^{(r+1)} = -\delta_{ps}^{(r+1)}, \qquad \text{if } \partial E(v_{ps}^{(r+1)})/\partial v_{ps} > 0 \tag{5.22}$$

$$\Delta v_{ps}^{(r+1)} = \delta_{ps}^{(r+1)}, \qquad \text{if } \partial E(v_{ps}^{(r+1)})/\partial v_{ps} < 0 \tag{5.23}$$

$$\Delta v_{ps}^{(r+1)} = 0, \qquad \text{if } \partial E(v_{ps}^{(r+1)})/\partial v_{ps} = 0 \tag{5.24}$$

This is for the case given in Equation (5.19). However, if $[\partial E(v_{ps}^{(r+1)})/\partial v_{ps}][\partial E(v_{ps}^{(r)})/\partial v_{ps}] < 0$—that is, a sign change occurred in the partial derivative (the case of Equation (5.20))—then the updating increment went past the minimum point, so the sign must change per

$$\Delta v_{ps}^{(r+1)} = -\text{sgn}(\Delta v_{ps}^{(r)})\delta_{ps}^{(r+1)} \tag{5.25}$$

where $\text{sgn}(x) = -1$ if $x < 0$, or $\text{sgn}(x) = 1$ if $x \geq 0$ (the *sign* function). In this case, Riedmiller and Braun prevented the sign from oscillating on successive iterations by putting

$$\partial E(v_{pq}^{(r+1)})/\partial v_{pq} = 0 \tag{5.26}$$

for that particular weight. Once the weight increments $\Delta v_{ps}^{(r+1)}$ are computed, the weights are updated via

$$v_{ps}^{(r+1)} = v_{ps}^{(r)} + \Delta v_{ps}^{(r+1)} \tag{5.27}$$

Riedmiller and Braun use δ_{max} and δ_{min} to keep the weight adapters from growing too large or becoming too small. Nominal values are $\delta_{max} = 1.0$ and $\delta_{min} = 10^{-6}$. They use this technique in the BP mode in which they iterate on a single exemplar training pair at a time until all exemplar pairs have been exercised (one epoch). The epochs are repeated as many times as required.

The FRP Hybrid Algorithm

We combine RP (rprop) with fullpropagation, which is steepest descent of the TSSE function E over all exemplar training pairs simultaneously to minimize $E = E^{(1)} + \cdots + E^{(Q)}$ on each adjustment of the weights, rather than on each partial SSE $E^{(q)}$ sequentially (see Section 5.7). We call the resulting algorithm *FRP (full resilient propagation)*. The FRP algorithm follows, in which sgn(—) is the sign function defined above.

Inputs: {the number N of input nodes; the number M of middle neurodes; the number J of output neurodes; the number Q of exemplar vectors; the exemplar feature vectors $\{\mathbf{x}^{(q)}\}$ and their paired identifier vectors $\{\mathbf{t}^{(k(q))}\}$; number of iterations I; and parameters $\delta_{nm}^{(0)}$, $\delta_{mj}^{(0)}$, η^+, η^-, δ_{max}, and δ_{min}}

Outputs: {the weights $\mathbf{w} = (w_{11}, w_{21},..., w_{NM})$ and $\mathbf{u} = (u_{11}, u_{21},..., u_{MJ})$; and total SSE E}

Step 1. /Input N, M, J, Q, and exemplar input vectors and corresponding output training vectors/
read network file;   /Data are stored in file/

Step 2. /Set initial parameters/
$\delta_{nm}^{(0)} \leftarrow 0.5$; $\delta_{mj}^{(0)} \leftarrow 0.5$;
$\eta^+ \leftarrow 1.2$; $\eta^- \leftarrow 0.6$; $\delta_{max} \leftarrow 2.0$; $\delta_{min} \leftarrow 10^{-5}$
$\alpha_1 \leftarrow 2.4$; $\alpha_2 \leftarrow 2.4$;   /Provide parameters for bipolar/
                                                     /sigmoids/

$\eta \leftarrow 1.0$;
$E_{old} \leftarrow 999999.9$; r $\leftarrow 0$;   /Initialize SSE, iteration number/
Get I;   /Input no. iterations from keyboard/
$\delta \leftarrow 0.1$;   /Increment for changes to α_1, α_2/

Step 3. /Generate initial weights randomly between 0 and 1/
for $m = 1$ to M do
    for $n = 1$ to N do $w_{nm} \leftarrow$ Random( );   /Draw uniform random number -1/
                                                     /to 1/

    for $j = 1$ to J do $u_{mj} \leftarrow$ Random( );   /Draw uniform random number -1/
                                                     /to 1/

  $E_{new} \leftarrow$ **Update_NN( )**;   /Computes neurodal outputs, new/
                                                     /SSE/

$\partial E(u_{mj}^{(r)})/\partial u_{mj} \leftarrow 1$; $\partial E(w_{nm}^{(r)})/\partial w_{nm} \leftarrow 1.0$;

Step 4. /Update all weights at the output layer first, then middle layer/
for $m = 1$ to M do   /For each jth output neurode/
                                                     /weight/
    for $j = 1$ to J do   /compute partial derivatives/
      $\partial E(u_{mj}^{(r+1)})/\partial u_{mj} \leftarrow \sum_{(q=1,\, Q)} [t_j^{(k(q))} - z_j^{(q)}][z_j^{(q)}(1 - z_j^{(q)})]y_m^{(q)}]$;
      if $[\partial E(u_{mj}^{(r+1)})/\partial u_{mj}][\partial E(u_{mj}^{(r)})/\partial u_{mj}] > 0$ then
        $\delta_{mj}^{(r+1)} \leftarrow \min\{\eta^+ \delta_{mj}^{(r)}, \delta_{max}\}$;   /Derivative sign unchanged/
        $\Delta u_{mj}^{(r+1)} \leftarrow -\text{sign}[\partial E(u_{mj}^{(r+1)})/\partial u_{mj}](\delta_{mj}^{(r+1)})$;
        $u_{mj}^{(r+1)} \leftarrow u_{mj}^{(r)} + \Delta u_{mj}^{(r+1)}$;
      else
        if $[\partial E(u_{mj}^{(r+1)})/\partial u_{mj}][\partial E(u_{mj}^{(r)})/\partial u_{mj}] = 0$ then
          $u_{mj}^{(r+1)} \leftarrow u_{mj}^{(r)}$; $\delta_{mj}^{(r+1)} \leftarrow \delta_{mj}^{(r)}$; /One derivative is 0/
        if $[\partial E(u_{mj}^{(r+1)})/\partial u_{mj}][\partial E(u_{mj}^{(r)})/\partial u_{mj}] < 0$ then
          $\delta_{mj}^{(r+1)} \leftarrow \max\{\eta^- \delta_{mj}^{(r)}, \delta_{min}\}$;   /Derivative sign changed/
          $\Delta u_{mj}^{(r+1)} \leftarrow \text{sign}[\partial E(u_{mj}^{(r+1)})/\partial u_{mj}](\delta_{mj}^{(r+1)})$;
          $u_{mj}^{(r+1)} \leftarrow u_{mj}^{(r)} + \Delta u_{mj}^{(r+1)}$;
          $\partial E(u_{mj}^{(r+1)})/\partial u_{mj} \leftarrow 0$;   /Avoid oscillatory sign change/
      $\partial E(u_{mj}^{(r)})/\partial u_{mj} \leftarrow \partial E(u_{mj}^{(r+1)})/\partial u_{mj}$;   /Update old partial derivatives/
    for $n = 1$ to N do   /For each mth middle neurode/
                                                     /weight/
                                                     /compute partial derivatives/
      $\partial E(w_{nm}^{(r+1)})/\partial w_{nm} \leftarrow \sum_{(q=1,\, Q)}\{\sum_{(j=1,\, J)} [t_j^{(k(q))} - z_j^{(q)})z_j^{(q)}(1 - z_j^{(q)}) \cdot u_{mj}\}y_m^{(q)}$
        $(1 - y_m^{(q)})x_n^{(q)}$;
      if $[\partial E(w_{nm}^{(r+1)})/\partial w_{nm}][\partial E(w_{nm}^{(r)})/\partial w_{nm}] > 0$ then
        $\delta_{nm}^{(r+1)} \leftarrow \min\{\eta^+ \delta_{nm}^{(r)}, \delta_{max}\}$;

$$\Delta w_{nm}^{(r+1)} \leftarrow - \text{sign}[\partial E(w_{nm}^{(r+1)})/\partial w_{nm}](\delta_{nm}^{(r+1)});$$
$$w_{nm}^{(r+1)} \leftarrow w_{nm}^{(r)} + \Delta w_{nm}^{(r+1)};$$

else

  if $[\partial E(w_{nm}^{(r+1)})/\partial w_{nm}][\partial E(w_{nm}^{(r)})/\partial w_{nm}] = 0$, then
    $w_{nm}^{(r+1)} \leftarrow w_{nm}^{(r)};\ \delta_{nm}^{(r+1)} \leftarrow \delta_{nm}^{(r)};$
  if $[\partial E(w_{nm}^{(r+1)})/\partial w_{nm}][\partial E(w_{nm}^{(r)})/\partial w_{nm}] < 0$, then
    $\delta_{nm}^{(r+1)} \leftarrow \max\{\eta^{-}\delta_{nm}^{(r)},\ \delta_{\min}\};$
    $\Delta w_{nm}^{(r+1)} \leftarrow \text{sign}[\partial E(w_{nm}^{(r+1)})/\partial w_{nm}](\delta_{nm}^{(r+1)});$
    $w_{nm}^{(r+1)} \leftarrow w_{nm}^{(r)} + \Delta w_{nm}^{(r+1)};$
    $\partial E(w_{nm}^{(r+1)})/\partial w_{nm} \leftarrow 0;$ /Avoid oscillation on sign change/
$\partial E(w_{nm}^{(r)})/\partial w_{nm} \leftarrow \partial E(w_{nm}^{(r+1)})/\partial w_{nm};$ /Update old partial derivative/

Step 5. /Check stopping criterion on number of iterations I/
  $E_{\text{new}} \leftarrow$ **Update_NN**( );   /Call procedure to update FANN/
                                                 /outputs/
  if $r > I$ then stop;   /Either stop or/
  else $E_{\text{old}} \leftarrow E_{\text{new}};\ r \leftarrow r + 1$; goto Step 4*;   /update parameters/

Procedure Update_NN( );   /Update neurode outputs and SSE E_{new}/
  SSE $\leftarrow 0$;   /Initialize sum-squared error to zero/
  for $q = 1$ to Q do   /Do on all Q exemplars/
    for $m = 1$ to M do   /For each middle neurode/
      $r_m^{(q)} \leftarrow 0$;   /initialize each mth middle neurode sum/
      for $n = 1$ to N do   /For each input component sum the/
        $r_m^{(q)} \leftarrow r_m^{(q)} + w_{nm}x_n^{(q)};$ /weighted inputs to mth neurode/
      $y_m^{(q)} \leftarrow h(r_m^{(q)});$ /Put through sigmoid, activate neurode/
    for $j = 1$ to J do   /For each output neurode/
      $s_j^{(q)} \leftarrow 0$;   /initialize each output neurode output/
      for $m = 1$ to M do   /For values from middle neurodes/
        $s_j^{(q)} \leftarrow s_j^{(q)} + u_{mj}r_m^{(q)};$ /Sum weighted inputs to jth neurode/
      $z_j^{(q)} \leftarrow g(s_j^{(q)});$ /Put sum through sigmoid for output/
    for $j = 1$ to J do   /Sum SSE over all j and q/
      SSE $\leftarrow$ SSE $+ (t_j^{(q(k))} - z_j^{(q)})^2;$ /Sum errors: all J neurodes, K classes/
  $E_{\text{new}} \leftarrow$ SSE;   /Save new SSE value/

The *advantages* of FRP are as follows: (i) The step gain is adjusted up or down for each weight during the iterations to adapt the direction of steepest descent to be more accurate and provide more efficient convergence without momentum terms, and (ii) the training is on all exemplars simultaneously for greater efficiency.

The *disadvantages* are as follows: (i) A shallow local minimum may trap the process (all gradient methods have this problem and it is necessary to make multiple runs from different initial weight sets and select the best resulting weights); (ii) it takes a significant number of iterations for the weight increments to adjust to the proper level, during which the SSE decreases very little; and (iii) the process does not always converge. *In practice*, however, once the weights have adjusted to the proper level, the TSSE decreases very rapidly.

5.6. Sigmoid Parameters, Weight Drift, and Specialization

Adjustment of the Exponential Rates

The exponentials of the sigmoid functions contain a decay rate constant α. In the unipolar sigmoids, where the bias b is included, they take the form

$$\exp(-\alpha s + b) \tag{5.28}$$

In the bipolar sigmoids, without bias, they are

$$\exp(-\alpha s) \tag{5.29}$$

The constant α is positive and its value affects the shape of the sigmoid: (i) As α increases, the sigmoid approaches a hard threshold (step) function, but it is everywhere smooth (continuously differentiable); and (ii) for small values of α the sigmoid approximates a linear function on its domain of interest. This parameter has some effect on the learning because it determines where the saturation regions begin, with larger values of α yielding a larger saturation region (due to a steeper curve that approaches its asymptotes closer to the point of asymmetry). We use a different sigmoid at each layer of neurodes, so there are two different parameters, α_1 (at the single hidden layer) and α_2 at the output layer. These parameters may be the same, or different for more flexibility. For multiple hidden layers there are more α's.

Automatic adjustment of the decay rate was addressed in Shea and Looney (1992). Both α_1 and α_2 were adjusted for the hidden and output layers, respectively. The α's were started small to avoid premature saturation and then adjusted, say, every fifth iteration only on the early iterations, to be larger. This helps the learning and convergence. The continued adjustment causes a moving target for the SSE function $E_{\alpha_1,\alpha_2}(\mathbf{v})$ so that the weights can not converge. For this reason, the α's should be adjusted during the early iterations, but not on every iteration, and should become fixed by halfway through the training so the final weights can be trained on them. With an initial increment of $\delta = 0.04$ and initial value of $\alpha = 1.4$ (empirically determined to be good over a wide range of data sets), we adjust α via the steps given below.

A Rate Adjustment Algorithm

Step 0.   set I; $r \leftarrow 0$;   /Repeat I times, set zeroeth iteration/

Step 1. $\alpha_h \leftarrow \alpha$;   /Hold (save) alpha value/

Step 2. $\alpha \leftarrow \alpha_h + \delta$;   /Increment α/

Step 3. $E_{\text{new}} \leftarrow$ **Update_NN( )**;   /Get new error/

Step 4. if $E_{\text{new}} > E_{\text{old}}$ then   /If error increases/
$\qquad \alpha \leftarrow \alpha_h; \ \delta \leftarrow -0.9\delta;$ /change sign, reduce size/
$\qquad$ else $E_{\text{old}} \leftarrow E_{\text{new}};$ /else keep new value/
$\qquad\qquad \delta \leftarrow 1.04\delta;$ /and increase size of increment/

Step 5. $r \leftarrow r + 1;$
$\qquad$ if $r > I$, then stop;
$\qquad$ else goto Step 1;

An alternative method computes values of the SSE, $y_1 = E(\alpha - \delta)$, $y_2 = E(\alpha)$, and $y_3 = E(\alpha + \delta)$. A quadratic polynomial can then be passed through these three points. The minimum of the polynomial then becomes the new α. Another method is that of Zurada, which is given below.

The Techniques of Zurada and Yamada

Zurada's paper (Zurada, 1993) also adapted α. His method was to treat each α as an additional weight and to compute the derivative $\partial E / \partial \alpha$ on each iteration. At a single hidden layer, he used

$$\Delta\alpha_m = \eta_1 h'(r_m) r_m \sum\nolimits_{(j=1,\,J)} (t_j - z_j) g'(s_j) \tag{5.30a}$$

as the α-increment for a single exemplar q. For the output layer, Zurada used the α-increment

$$\Delta\alpha_j = \eta_2 (t_j - z_j) g'(s_j) s_j \tag{5.30b}$$

We derive α_j at the jth output neurode and α_m at the mth hidden layer via

$$\partial E / \partial \alpha_j = (\partial E / \partial z_j)(\partial z_j / \partial \alpha_j) = [(-2)(t_j - z_j)][g'(s_j)s_j] = -2(t_j - z_j)z_j(1 - z_j)s_j \tag{5.31a}$$

$$\partial E / \partial \alpha_m = \sum\nolimits_{(j=1,\,J)} (\partial E / \partial z_j)(\partial z_j / \partial s_j)(\partial s_j / \partial y_m)(\partial y_m / \partial \alpha_m)$$

$$= [-2\sum\nolimits_{(j=1,\,J)} (t_j - z_j)g'(s_j)u_{mj}][h'(r_m)r_m$$

$$= [-2\sum\nolimits_{(j=1,\,J)} (t_j - z_j)z_j(1 - z_j)u_{mj}][(y_m(1 - y_m)r_m] \tag{5.31b}$$

We can now state the update formulas as

$$\alpha_j{}^{(r+1)} = \alpha_j{}^{(r)} + 2\eta(t_j - z_j)z_j(1 - z_j)s_j \tag{5.32a}$$

$$\alpha_m{}^{(r+1)} = \alpha_m{}^{(r)} + \eta[2\sum\nolimits_{(j=1,\,J)} (t_j - z_j)z_j(1 - z_j)u_{mj}][(y_m(1 - y_m)r_m] \tag{5.32b}$$

Yamada et al. (1989) noted that in training a rather large multiple layered perceptron, when all values put out by one layer of neurodes are nearly zero (or else nearly 1), the learning was suspended in a *standstill* state. The problem is that the weights for the layer of neurodes have moved to the saturation region of the sigmoids. For example, when

$$|t_j - z_j| > \delta \quad \text{and} \quad \sum |y_m z_j (1 - z_j)| < \epsilon \qquad (5.33)$$

for all $j = 1,..., J$, then standstill has occurred. Yamada et al. reduce the decay rate α by one-half whenever standstill occurs, and the shape of the sigmoids is changed to alleviate saturation. They report that such a strategy speeded up the training as much as threefold. Their training data used well more than 100 features. We caution, however, that this reduction of α by one-half cannot be repeated unless the original α were large. Small α makes the neurodes more linear-like, so that the nonlinear separation ability becomes diminished as α decreases below 1.

Adjusting the Biases

The biases b_1 and b_2 may also be adjusted for near-optimal values when the sigmoids $h(r)$ and $g(s)$ at the hidden and output layers, respectively, are unipolar. Usually, we use $\{w_{0m}, u_{0j}\}$ as the bias weights for $b_1 = w_{0m}$ and $b_2 = u_{0j}$ and adjust them similarly to the other weights via $\Delta b_i = -\eta(\partial E/\partial b_i)$. This may also be done by adding or subtracting a delta δ. It is usual to train the biases as extra weights (Fausett, 1994).

We derive bias updates at the respective output and hidden neurodes for a single qth exemplar by

$$\partial E/\partial b_2 = (\partial E/\partial z_j)(\partial z_j/\partial b_2) = -2\sum_{(j=1,\, J)}(t_j - z_j)z_j(1 - z_j)(-1)$$
$$= 2\sum_{(j=1,\, J)}(t_j - z_j)z_j(1 - z_j) \qquad (5.34a)$$

$$\partial E/\partial b_1 = (\partial E/\partial z_j)(\partial z_j/\partial s_j)(\partial s_j/\partial y_m)(\partial y_m/\partial b_2)$$
$$= 2\sum_{(j=1,\, J)}(t_j - z_j)z_j(1 - z_j)\Sigma_{(m=1,\, M)}u_{mj}[(y_m(1 - y_m)] \qquad (5.34b)$$

Weight Drift and Specialization

The network may become overtrained to achieve a small total SSE value E but have poor generalization capability. The best training does not necessarily yield the weight set with the lowest total SSE. Rumelhart et al. (1986) and others have noticed that the weights that yield the lowest SSE are sometimes not as robust as those that yield a greater SSE. Overtraining appears to sometimes cause *weight drift*, where some weights change substantially under training while other weights change to compensate for them. The phenomenon of *specialized* learning achieves a small total SSE and fits each training exemplar closely by "memorization" of each errored datum, but does not correctly recognize some novel input vectors. Specialization is further described in Section 9.3.

One cause of *weight drift* appears to be training a network that is *underdetermined*; that is, there are too few data points for the number of weights (coefficients). In such situations, there exists an infinite number of solution weight points, so the weights are not constrained to move toward any single solution. An analogous case is the fitting of a high-degree polynomial to a few data points. Consider fitting a fifth-degree polynomial to three data points, or solving three linear equations in five unknowns. In this latter case, any two unknowns could be set to any particular values and they would determine a solution for the other three. But different values for these two unknowns determine different solutions for the three others. In MLPs with too many weight coefficients for the (training) data points, a subset of the weights can be given arbitrary values, which then fixes the remaining ones. The weights with arbitrary values can drift under training. The moving target effect is exaggerated as the arbitrary values move, and, in fact, in underdetermined systems, every weight acts as an arbitrary coefficient when it is changed.

In cases where a set of weights correctly maps the exemplars, as well as novel (nonexemplar) input vectors near the exemplars, into the correct identifiers, then we say that the learning is *generalized*. If the weights map the exemplars correctly, but not some novel feature vectors that are close to them, then we say the learning is *specialized*. Rumelhart et al. (1986) noted that a decrease in the error over the training data does not mean a decrease over novel, or nontraining, data and may lead to a lower generalization ability. In other words, too much training may cause specialization, where the feature vectors with noise included are "memorized" precisely with a loss of generalizing capability. For further discussion, see Schmidt et al. (1993). Example 5.3 explains specialization further. A network is *overdetermined* by too many data points (more than the number of weights), but a least sum-squared error solution exists that smooths (generalizes) the data.

Weight drift can be especially severe if a desired output component value is put to the exact high or low values $t_j = 0$ or $t_j = 1$ for unipolar sigmoid activation functions, or at $t_j = -1$ or $t_j = 1$ for bipolar activation functions. This is because, for example, $g'(s) = z_j(1 - z_j)$ cannot be driven to 0 or 1 (Haykin, 1994) unless the weight coefficients are driven to $\pm\infty$.

Example 5.3.   Specialization versus Generalized Learning of XOR Logic

Figure 5.7a shows an example of overlearning of XOR logic by BP on the unit square determined by $0 \leq x \leq 1$, $0 \leq y \leq 1$. Figure 5.7b shows a generalized form of learning (by the *cubronn* algorithm described in Chapter 6). While both examples have learned to classify correctly the exemplar input vectors (0,0), (0,1), (1,0), and (1,1), the more generalized learning will more accurately classify novel (x, y) pairs. The most general learning possible would produce four equal symmetrical quarters of the unit square as output. In the training, 0.1 is used for 0 and 0.9 is used for 1 (or even better, 0.2 and 0.8 could be used for 0 and 1, respectively). The SSE was actually lower in the more specialized MLP whose results are shown in Figure 5.7a.

5.7. The Fullpropagation Algorithm

Thrashing and Batching: An Invitation to the Dance

The backpropagation algorithm adjusts all of the weights on each iteration to decrease a single PSSE $E^{(q)}$ for any fixed q ($1 \leq q \leq Q$) by using the weight increments $\Delta\mathbf{v} = -\eta\nabla E^{(q)}(\mathbf{v})$. It then does another iteration to decrease $E^{(q+1)}$, and so on, until Q iterations for the Q partial SSEs have been done (one iteration for each qth exemplar pair). This completes one epoch. Epochs are repeated until a stopping criterion is met. The weight adjustments to decrease $E^{(q)}$, however, may actually increase $E^{(p)}$ for $p \neq q$. Thus an epoch of training can be self-opposing in that it partially undoes what it has already done. Such a repeated process of doing and undoing is called *thrashing*. Thrashing is computationally inefficient and slow.

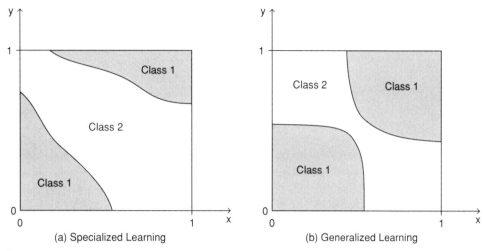

Figure 5.7. Learning of XOR logic.

In the *batch* technique, all weight increments are computed for an exemplar pair to reduce its PSSE function $E^{(q)}$, in turn (sequentially), but the increments are not added onto the current weights at the time they are computed. Instead, all increments from the iterations are summed and added to the weights at the end of the epoch. A batch does not necessarily need to be over an entire epoch, but averaged increments may be added after training exemplar-wise over a portion of an epoch. Batching does not alleviate thrashing, which also occurs in the summing of the weight increments for each weight.

Batching is *not* the same as training on all exemplars simultaneously, via $\mathbf{v}^{(r+1)} = \mathbf{v}^{(r)} - \eta \nabla E(\mathbf{v})$ rather than via $\Delta \mathbf{v}^{(r+1)} = -\eta \nabla E^{(q)}(\mathbf{v}^{(r)})$, for $q = 1,..., Q$ and then updating $\mathbf{v}^{(r+1)}$. A single update of the weights in the direction $-\nabla E(\mathbf{v})$ is a single step in the direction of steepest descent of the total SSE function $E = E^{(1)} + \cdots + E^{(Q)}$. It actually updates the weights for each of $E^{(1)},..., E^{(Q)}$ in that single step rather than updating the weights Q times in the sequence of directions of steepest descent of each of the partials $\nabla E^{(1)}, \nabla E^{(2)},..., \nabla E^{(Q)}$. We call the mode of full error backpropagation the *fullpropagation* (FP) algorithm. When more exemplars are being used simultaneously, it also reduces the effect of errors in single exemplars on the direction of steepest descent.

We are aware that batching prevents the beneficial effects of successive over-relaxation and can be less efficient than BP. On the other hand, our studies show that FP (fullpropagation) is significantly faster than BP (see Chapter 11). Pao (1989) also suggests that training be done over the total SSE function.

Some Bells and Whistles

The improvements that we want to exploit here are as follows: (i) training on all exemplars simultaneously (hence the name *fullpropagation, fprop*, or FP) to reduce the total SSE function E on each weight update; (ii) adjusting a single step gain for the total SSE E, rather than multiple ones for the partial SSEs $E^{(q)}$ or one for each weight (we could adapt η using the energy projection method covered in Section 5.10); (iii) adjustment of the sigmoid parameters α_1 and α_2, respectively, for the middle layer and output layer sigmoids on every fifth iteration, up to about halfway through the training, starting at $\alpha_1 = \alpha_2 = 1.82$; (iv) bounding each sigmoid derivative from below by 0.1 (recall these derivatives are always positive; (v) either using the bipolar sigmoids so the biases b_1 and b_2 are eliminated as sources of error, or putting $b_1 = N/2.0$ and $b_2 = M/2.0$ and updating them as weights; and (vi) using a momentum of $\mu = 0.1$ on the early iterations and then setting μ to zero. Adjusting the step gains up or down as E goes down or up is the *en route* method. It works well for full propagation.

Empirical studies showed good results when a constant value is used for μ and changed once during the training: Start with $\mu = 0.1$, but change to $\mu = 0.0$ after 2/5 of the expected number of iterations have been completed. The results may also be quite good when no momentum term is used, but not always. Our empirical studies show that the step gain $\eta > 0$ can also be successfully adjusted by the *en route* method as follows: (i) When the SSE decreases on an iteration, increase η slightly; and (ii) when the SSE E increases on an iteration, then decrease η slightly. The empirically determined values for such increasing and decreasing are given in the algorithm below (Looney, 1996b, p. 25). The FP1 algorithm discussed incorporates some bells and whistles.

The FP1 Algorithm

Inputs: {the number N of input nodes; the number M of middle neurodes; the number J of output neurodes; the number Q of exemplar vectors; the exemplar feature vectors $\{\mathbf{x}^{(q)}\}$ and their paired identifier vectors $\{\mathbf{t}^{(k(q))}\}$; number of iterations I; and increment δ for updating α_1, α_2}

Outputs: {the weights $\mathbf{w} = (w_{11}, w_{21},..., w_{NM})$ and $\mathbf{u} = (u_{11}, u_{21},..., u_{MJ})$}

Step 1.   /Input N, M, J, Q, and exemplar input vectors and corresponding output training vectors/
read network file;   /Data are stored in file/

Step 2.   /Set initial parameters/
$\alpha_1 \leftarrow 1.82$; $\alpha_2 \leftarrow 1.82$;   /Provide preliminary parameters/
$\eta_1 \leftarrow 0.6$; $\eta_2 \leftarrow 1.0$; $\mu \leftarrow 0.1$;   /Set step gain, momentum parameters/
$r \leftarrow 0$;   /Initialize SSE, iteration number/
input I;   /Input no. iterations from keyboard/
$\delta\alpha_1 \leftarrow 0.04$; $\delta\alpha_2 \leftarrow 0.04$;   /Increments for changes to α_1, α_2/
$[b_1 \leftarrow N/2.0$; $b_2 \leftarrow M/2.0;]$ [/Biases, if unipolar sigmoids are used/]

Step 3.   /Generate initial weights randomly between -1 and 1 (bipolar sigmoids)/
$W \leftarrow 0$;   /Weight summing variable/
for $m = 1$ to M do

for $n = 1$ to N do
  $w_{nm}^{(0)} \leftarrow$ random( ); /Draw uniform random no., -1.0 to/
  /1.0/

  $W \leftarrow W + w_{nm}^{(0)}$; /Sum weights at hidden neurodes/
for $j = 1$ to J do
  $u_{mj}^{(0)} \leftarrow$ random; /Draw uniform random no. -1 to 1/
  $u_{mj}^{(0)} \leftarrow (2.4/M)u_{mj}^{(0)}$; /Russo adjustment of initial weights/
  $\beta \leftarrow 0.7(\exp(\ln(M)/N)/W$; /Compute Nguyen–Widrow factor/
for $m = 1$ to M do
  for $n = 1$ to N do
    $w_{nm}^{(0)} \leftarrow \beta w_{nm}^{(0)}$; /Nguyen–Widrow adjustment/
  $E_{\text{old}} \leftarrow$ **Update_NN( )**; /Compute new SSE, MLP outputs/

Step 4. /Adjust all weights via Newton's linear approximation method/
  for $m = 1$ to M do /Update MJ u_{mj}'s/
    for $j = 1$ to J do
      $dgds \leftarrow \alpha_2(1 + z_j^{(q)})(1 - z_j^{(q)})/2$; /Compute bipolar sigmoid derivative/
      $[dgds \leftarrow \alpha_2 z_j^{(q)}(1 - z_j^{(q)})]$ [/Unipolar sigmoid, if used instead/]
      if $(dgds < 0.1)$ then $dgds \leftarrow 0.1$; /Bound it below by 0.1/
      $\Delta u_{mj}^{(r+1)} \leftarrow \eta_2 \sum_{(q=1, Q)}[(t_j^{(q)}$ /Compute wt. increment/
        $- z_j^{(q)})[dgds]y_m^{(q)}]$;
      $u_{mj}^{(r+1)} \leftarrow u_{mj}^{(r)} + \Delta u_{mj}^{(r+1)}$ /Update weight with increment/
        $+ \mu \Delta u_{mj}^{(r)}$;
    $E_{\text{new}} \leftarrow$ **Update_NN( )**; /Compute new SSE, neurode outputs/
    call **Step_Gain_Adjust**(η_2); /Adjust step gain η_2 appropriately/
    for $m = 1$ to M do /Update NM w_{nm}'s/
      for $n = 1$ to N do /For all hidden neurodes and Q/
        /exemplars/

        $dhdr \leftarrow \alpha_1(1 + y_m^{(q)})(1 - y_m^{(q)})/2$; /Compute bipolar sigmoid derivative/
        $[dhdr \leftarrow \alpha_1 y_m^{(q)}(1 - y_m^{(q)})$;] [/If unipolar sigmoid/]
        if $(dhdr < 0.1)$ then $dhdr \leftarrow 0.1$; /Bound it below by 0.1/
        $\Delta w_{nm}^{(r+1)} \leftarrow \eta_1 \sum_{(q=1, Q)}\{\sum_{(j=1, J)}(t_j^{(q)} - z_j^{(q)})[dhdr]u_{mj}[dgds]x_n^{(k)}\}$;
        $w_{nm}^{(r+1)} \leftarrow w_{nm}^{(r)} + \Delta w_{nm}^{(r+1)}$ /Update weight with increment/
          $+ \mu \Delta w_{nm}^{(r)}$;
      $E_{\text{new}} \leftarrow$ **Update_NN( )**; /Compute new SSE, neurode outputs/
      call **Step_Gain_Adjust**(η_1); /Adjust step gain η_1 appropriately/

Step 5. /Update the decay rate parameter α in the sigmoids/
  if $(\text{remainder}(r/5) = 0)$ AND /If correct iteration, adjust α's/
    $(r < I/2)$ then
  $\alpha_h \leftarrow \alpha_1$; $\alpha_1 \leftarrow \alpha_1 + \delta\alpha$; /Hold α_1 and increment new α_1/
  $E_{\text{new}} \leftarrow$ **Update_NN( )**; /Get new SSE value/
  if $(E_{\text{new}} < E_{\text{old}})$ then /If new SSE decreases/
    $E_{\text{old}} \leftarrow E_{\text{new}}$; /then update old SSE value/
    $\delta\alpha \leftarrow 1.1\delta\alpha$; /Increase delta size/
  else $\alpha_1 \leftarrow \alpha_h - \delta\alpha$; /else increment in negative direction/

$E_{\text{new}} \leftarrow$ **Update_NN( )**; /If SSE decreases/
if $(E_{\text{new}} < E_{\text{old}})$ then /If SSE decreases/
$\quad E_{\text{old}} \leftarrow E_{\text{new}}$; /then update old SSE value/
$\quad \delta\alpha \leftarrow 1.1\delta\alpha$; /Increase delta size/
else $\alpha_1 \leftarrow \alpha_h$; /If not, then put old α_1 back in place/
$\quad\quad \delta\alpha \leftarrow 0.9\delta\alpha$ /and reduce increment size/
$\alpha_h \leftarrow \alpha_2$; $\alpha_2 \leftarrow \alpha_2 + \delta\alpha$; /Do same process for α_2/
$E_{\text{new}} \leftarrow$ **Update_NN( )**;
if $(E_{\text{new}} < E_{\text{old}})$ then /If SSE decreases/
$\quad E_{\text{old}} \leftarrow E_{\text{new}}$; /then update old SSE value/
$\quad \delta\alpha \leftarrow 1.1\delta\alpha$; /Increase delta size/
else $\alpha_2 \leftarrow \alpha_h - \delta\alpha$; /else increment in negative direction/
$\quad E_{\text{new}} \leftarrow$ **Update_NN( )**;
$\quad$ if $(E_{\text{new}} < E_{\text{old}})$ then /If SSE decreases/
$\quad\quad E_{\text{old}} \leftarrow E_{\text{new}}$; /then update old SSE/
$\quad\quad \delta\alpha \leftarrow 1.1\delta\alpha$; /Increase delta size/
$\quad$ else $\alpha_2 \leftarrow \alpha_h$; /If not, then put back old α_2/
$\quad\quad \delta\alpha \leftarrow 0.9\delta\alpha$; /and reduce delta size/

Step 6. /Check criterion and stop, else adjust step gain η and momentum coefficient μ/
/and continue/
if $r \geq I$ then stop; /Either stop, or/
else
$\quad r \leftarrow r + 1$; /Increment iteration number/
$\quad$ if $(r = I/2)$ then $\mu \leftarrow 0.0$; /Adjust μ to zero halfway through/
$\quad$ goto Step 4; /Repeat until termination/

Procedure Step_Gain_Adjust(η): /Adjust step gain en route/
$\quad$ if $E_{\text{new}} < E_{\text{old}}$ then $\eta \leftarrow 1.024\eta$; /Increase on success/
$\quad$ else $\eta \leftarrow 0.92\eta$; /Decrease on failure/
$\quad E_{\text{old}} \leftarrow E_{\text{new}}$;

Procedure Update_NN( ); /Update FANN and SSE/
$\quad$ for $q = 1$ to Q do /Do output process on all Q exemplars/
$\quad\quad$ for $m = 1$ to M do /For each middle neurode/
$\quad\quad\quad r_m^{(q)} \leftarrow 0$; /initialize each mth hidden neurode sum/
$\quad\quad\quad$ for $n = 1$ to N do /For each input component, sum the/
$\quad\quad\quad\quad r_m^{(q)} \leftarrow r_m^{(q)} + w_{nm}x_n^{(q)}$; /weighted inputs to mth neurode/
$\quad\quad\quad y_m^{(q)} \leftarrow h(r_m^{(q)})$; /Activate at hidden layer sigmoid/
$\quad\quad$ for $j = 1$ to J do /For each output neurode/
$\quad\quad\quad s_j^{(q)} \leftarrow 0$; /initialize each output neurode/

$$
\begin{aligned}
&\text{for } m = 1 \text{ to } M \text{ do} && \text{/For each hidden neurode component/} \\
&\quad s_j^{(q)} \leftarrow s_j^{(q)} + u_{mj} r_m^{(q)}; && \text{/sum weighted inputs to } j\text{th neurode/} \\
&\quad z_j^{(q)} \leftarrow g(s_j^{(q)}); && \text{/Activate at output layer sigmoid/} \\
&\text{SSE} \leftarrow 0; && \text{/Initialize SSE to zero/} \\
&\text{for } j = 1 \text{ to } J \text{ do} && \text{/Sum SSE over all } j \text{ and } q/ \\
&\quad \text{SSE} \leftarrow \text{SSE} + (t_j^{(k(q))} - z_j^{(q)})^2; && \text{/SSE: all } j \text{ and } q/ \\
&\text{return SSE;} && \text{/Save new SSE in global variable/}
\end{aligned}
$$

The *advantages of FP1* are as follows: (i) It trains on all exemplars simultaneously so that on a single iteration, the adjustment to the weights is an adjustment over all of the Q exemplar training pairs to reduce all Q partial SSEs $E^{(q)}$ at once without the Q different adjustments to them via BP (see Section 5.3); (ii) it adjusts the step gains η_1 and η_2 and the total SSE function $E(\mathbf{w}, \mathbf{u})$ on each iteration; (iii) it adjusts the momentum term according to an empirical rule; (iv) it adds the constant 0.1 to each sigmoid derivative that is less than 0.1, to bound it away from zero; (v) it adjusts the decay rates α_i on certain early iterations to improve the learning; and (vi) it may use bipolar sigmoids to eliminate bias errors and adjustments and to improve convergence. Its *disadvantages* are the same as those for all gradient methods in that it may enter the well of a shallow local minimum, and so training may need to be done several times to choose the weight point that passes validation and verification tests (see Chapter 9).

In practice, we use this algorithm with starting weights obtained by adjusting the randomly drawn initial weights to a weight region of low lying SSE values. Then a single training run of a few dozen iterations is often sufficient because the algorithm converges quickly.

5.8. Full Cubic Propagation: A Lineal Third-Order Algorithm

The Cubic Line Search Method

We call this algorithm *FCP* because it uses a full propagation with cubic approximation along a slice of E in the direction of steepest descent. Let $\mathbf{v}^{(r)}$ be the current weight vector

$$
\mathbf{v}^{(r)} = (w_{11}, \dots, w_{NM}, u_{11}, \dots, u_{MJ}) \tag{5.35}
$$

and let $\mathbf{v}^{(*)} = \mathbf{v}^{(r)} + \Delta\mathbf{v}$ be the weight vector determined by the gradient via the FP algorithm, where $\Delta\mathbf{v} = -\eta \partial E(\mathbf{v}^{(r)})/\partial\mathbf{v}$ has been normalized to have unit length. We obtain the two additional weight points

$$
\mathbf{v}^{(1/3)} = \mathbf{v}^{(r)} + (1/3)(\mathbf{v}^{(*)} - \mathbf{v}^{(r)}) = \mathbf{v}^{(r)} + (1/3)\Delta\mathbf{v} \tag{5.36}
$$

$$
\mathbf{v}^{(2/3)} = \mathbf{v}^{(r)} + (2/3)(\mathbf{v}^{(*)} - \mathbf{v}^{(r)}) = \mathbf{v}^{(r)} + (2/3)\Delta\mathbf{v} \tag{5.37}
$$

These four weight vectors $\mathbf{v}^{(r)}$, $\mathbf{v}^{(1/3)}$, $\mathbf{v}^{(2/3)}$, $\mathbf{v}^{(*)}$ all fall on a line segment in the direction of steepest descent from $\mathbf{v}^{(r)}$ toward $\mathbf{v}^{(*)}$. We now take this line in the weight space to be the *x*-axis, so that we consider a function $y = E(x)$ in the *xy*-plane (a planar slice of the graph of E). A cubic polynomial can be fit to the four distinct points by solving a 4×4 matrix equation. The following method, however, is computationally more efficient and more accurate.

Let us put $x_0 = 0$, $x_1 = 1/3$, $x_2 = 2/3$, and $x_3 = 1$ as points on the normalized line segment from $\mathbf{v}^{(r)}$ to $\mathbf{v}^{(*)}$, and $y_0 = E(\mathbf{v}^{(r)})$, $y_1 = E(\mathbf{v}^{(1/3)})$, $y_2 = E(\mathbf{v}^{(2/3)})$, and $y_3 = E(\mathbf{v}^{(*)})$. The four points $\{(x_i, y_i): i = 0,..., 3\}$ determine a cubic polynomial $y = ax^3 + bx^2 + cx + d$ in the plane. Given these four points, we can solve for the minimum value of the cubic polynomial that passes through them by means of derivatives of the polynomial. Substituting in the values 0, 1/3, 2/3, and 1 for x in $y = ax^3 + bx^2 + cx + d$ yields

$$x = 0.0 \qquad\qquad y_0 = d,$$

$$x = 0.333333 \qquad\qquad y_1 = (1/27)a + (1/9)b + (1/3)c + d$$

$$x = 0.666667 \qquad\qquad y_2 = (8/27)a + (4/9)b + (2/3)c + d$$

$$x = 1.0 \qquad\qquad y_3 = a + b + c + d$$

To solve these equations for a, b, and c we first eliminate c and d from two equations via

$$
\begin{array}{ll}
-2(y_3 - y_0) & = -2a - 2b - 2c \\
3(y_3 - y_1) & = (26/9)a + (8/3)b + 2c \\
\hline
y_3 - 3y_1 + 2y_0 = (8/9)a + (2/3)b & \text{(adding the above equations)}
\end{array}
\qquad (5.38)
$$

Similarly

$$
\begin{array}{ll}
(y_3 - y_0) & = a + b + c \\
-3(y_3 - y_2) & = (-19/9)a - (5/3)b - c \\
\hline
-2y_3 + 3y_2 - y_0 = (-10/9)a - (2/3)b & \text{(adding the above equations)}
\end{array}
\qquad (5.39)
$$

Upon adding Equations (5.38) and (5.39), we solve for a and backsubstitute to obtain

$$a = (9/2)[y_3 - 3y_2 + 3y_1 - y_0] \qquad (5.40a)$$

$$b = (3/2)[y_3 - 3y_1 + 2y_0 - (8/9)a] \qquad (5.40b)$$

$$c = [y_3 - y_0 - a - b] \qquad (5.40c)$$

To minimize the cubic polynomial that fits the four points, we put

$$dy/dx = 3ax^2 + 2bx + c = 0 = Ax^2 + Bx + C$$

where $A = 3a$, $B = 2b$, and $C = c$. We now check the discriminant for $B^2 - 4AC \geq 0$. If true, then we obtain two roots via the quadratic formula

$$z^{(1)} = [-B + (B^2 - 4AC)^{1/2}]/(2A) \tag{5.41a}$$

$$z^{(2)} = [-B - (B^2 - 4AC)^{1/2}]/(2A) \tag{5.41b}$$

We now test these by substituting them into the second derivative, which must satisfy

$$d^2y/dx^2 = 2Ax + B > 0 \tag{5.42}$$

One of $(2Az^{(1)} + B)$ or $(2Az^{(2)} + B)$ is positive for a minimum to exist. If so, then we take that value, say $z^{(1)}$, and use it to determine the new minimizing weight set via

$$\mathbf{v}^{(r+1)} = \mathbf{v}^{(r)} + z^{(1)}\Delta\mathbf{v} \tag{5.43}$$

where $\Delta\mathbf{v}$ is the unit vector previously computed. The step is the positive, or negative, proportion $\mathbf{z}^{(1)}$ of the distance from $\mathbf{v}^{(r)}$ to $\mathbf{v}^{(r+1)}$. If the roots are complex, then we step to the new weight point that has the lowest SSE y over x_0, x_1, x_2, x_3.

The FCP1 Algorithm

The inputs and the first three steps are the same as for the *FP1* (fullpropagation) algorithm given previously. However, Step 4 is modified to become Steps 4* and 5* given below. Note that $\mathbf{v} = (\mathbf{w}, \mathbf{u})$ is the total weight vector. We use bipolar sigmoids.

Step 4*. /Update weight sets and get four points for cubic approximation/
  $\mathbf{v}^{(hold)} \leftarrow \mathbf{v}^{(r)}$;   /Save current weight point $\mathbf{v} = (\mathbf{w}, \mathbf{u})$/
  $y[0] \leftarrow E_{new}$;   /Get SSE at point $\mathbf{v}^{(r)}$/
  for $m = 1$ to M do   /Update output and middle weights/
    for $j = 1$ to J do   /Compute output partial derivatives/
      $\partial E(u_{mj}^{(r)})/\partial u_{mj} \leftarrow -\sum_{(q=1, Q)} [t_j^{(q)} - z_j^{(q)}][\alpha_2(1 + z_j^{(q)})(1 - z_j^{(q)})/2]y_m^{(q)}$;
      $u_{mj}^{(*)} \leftarrow u_{mj}^{(hold)} + \eta\partial E(u_{mj}^{(r)})$ /Update output weights to $\mathbf{v}^{(*)}$/
       /∂u_{mj};
    for $n = 1$ to N do   /Compute middle partial derivatives/
      $\partial E(w_{nm}^{(r)})/\partial w_{nm} \leftarrow$
       $-\sum_{(q=1, Q)}\{\sum_{(j=1, J)} [t_j^{(q)} - z_j^{(q)}][\alpha_2(1 + z_j^{(q)})$
       $(1 - z_j^{(q)})/2]u_{mj}[\alpha_1(1 + y_m^{(q)}) \cdot (1 - y_m^{(q)})/2]x_n^{(q)}$;
      $w_{nm}^{(*)} \leftarrow w_{nm}^{(hold)} +$ /Update middle weights to $\mathbf{v}^{(*)}$/
       $\eta\partial E(w_{nm}^{(r)})/\partial w_{nm}$;

            /$\mathbf{v}^{(*)}$ contains $\{w_{nm}^{(*)}, u_{mj}^{(*)}\}$/
  $y[3] \leftarrow$ **Update_NN( )**;   /Get SSE at point $\mathbf{v}^{(*)}$/
  $\mathbf{v}^{(r)} \leftarrow \mathbf{v}^{(hold)} + (1/3)(\mathbf{v}^{(*)} - \mathbf{v}^{(hold)})$; /Put weight point $\mathbf{v}^{(1/3)}$ in $\mathbf{v}^{(r)}$/
  $y[1] \leftarrow$ **Update_NN( )**;   /Get SSE at point $\mathbf{v}^{(1/3)}$/
  $\mathbf{v}^{(r)} \leftarrow \mathbf{v}^{(hold)} + (2/3)(\mathbf{v}^{(1)} - \mathbf{v}^{(hold)})$; /Put weight point $\mathbf{v}^{(2/3)}$ in $\mathbf{v}^{(r)}$/
  $y[2] \leftarrow$ **Update_NN( )**;   /Get SSE at point $\mathbf{v}^{(2/3)}$/
  $a \leftarrow 4.5(y[3] - 3y[2] + 3y[1]$ /From 4 SSE function values/
    $- y[0])$;

$b \leftarrow 1.5(y[3] - 3.0y[1] + 2.0y[0]$ /compute coefficients a, b/
  $- 0.88889a)$;
$c \leftarrow (y[3] - y[0] - a - b)$;   /and c for cubic polynomial/
$A \leftarrow 3a$; $B \leftarrow 2b$; $C \leftarrow c$;   /Coefficients for quadratic derivative/
if $(B^2 \geq 4.0AC)$, then   /Test root of $y' = Ax^2 + Bx + C$/
  $z[1] \leftarrow (-B + (B^2 - 4.0AC)^{1/2})$ /Compute first root of y'/
        $/(2.0A)$;
  $z[2] \leftarrow (-B - (B^2 - 4.0AC)^{1/2})$ /Compute second root of y'/
        $/(2.0A)$;
  $z \leftarrow 0.0$;   /Zero out minimum/
  if $(2.0Az[1] + B > 0.0)$ /If first root is minimum, use it/
        then $z \leftarrow z[1]$;
  if $(2.0Az[2] + B > 0.0)$ /If second root is minimum, use it/
        then $z \leftarrow z[2]$;
  if $z \neq 0.0$ then   /If minimum exists, then update weights/
     for $m = 1$ to M do
        for $j = 1$ to J do   /Update output weights at cubic/
                                    /minimum/
          $u_{mj}^{(r+1)} \leftarrow u_{mj}^{(hold)} + z(u_{mj}^{(*)} - u_{mj}^{(hold)})$;
        for $n = 1$ to N do   /Update middle weights at cubic/
                                    /minimum/
          $w_{nm}^{(r+1)} \leftarrow w_{nm}^{(hold)} + z(w_{nm}^{(*)} - w_{nm}^{(hold)})$;
  else $z = 0.0$;   /Else no real root/
  if $(z = 0.0)$ then $\beta = $ **Minim**( );   /β is step to minimum point y_i/
        $\mathbf{v}^{(r+1)} \leftarrow \mathbf{v}^{(hold)} + \beta(\mathbf{v}^{(*)} - \mathbf{v}^{(hold)})$;

Step 5*. /Check stopping criterion on number of iterations/
  $E_{new} \leftarrow$ **Update_NN**( );   /Update FANN outputs, get current SSE/
  if $r \geq I$ then stop   /Either stop, or/
  else $E_{old} \leftarrow E_{new}$; $r \leftarrow r + 1$;   /Update iteration no. and continue/
     goto Step 5*;

The procedure **Update_NN**( ) is the same as in the previous algorithm and is not duplicated here. It updates all of the neurode outputs with the current weight set and computes the new SSE. The procedure **Minim**( ) finds the value β from 0, 1/3, 2/3, or 1 such that $y_{i\text{-}max}$ is the minimum of the four known SSE values ($y[0]$, $y[1]$, $y[2]$, and $y[3]$).

The *advantage* of this method is that instead of just taking a step when the step size is not known, a step is taken in the direction of steepest descent to the minimum value along that directional slice (up to the accuracy of the cubic approximation of the slice of E).

The *disadvantages* are as follows: (i) Three extra functional evaluations of E are computed on each iteration, and (ii) a local minimum may be found instead of a global one. *In practice*, we use a preliminary stage of adjusting the initial weights to obtain a good starting weight point in a region where E assumes low values.

5.9. The Johansson–Dowla–Goodman Conjugate Gradient Training of MLPs

The Hestenes–Stiefel, Polak–Ribierère, and Fletcher–Reeves Methods

These were invented by Hestenes and Stiefel (1962) for linear systems and adapted by Fletcher and Reeves (1964) for nonlinear functional minimization. The conjugate gradient method for minimizing a quadratic function was described in Appendix 4b and is derived in general below. Johansson et al. (1992) adapt the conjugate gradient methods of Hestenes and Stiefel (1952), Polak and Ribière (1969), Fletcher and Reeves (1964), and Shanno (1990) to train MLPs with rather impressive results. The training was an order faster than that done by BP with a momentum term (thus it is faster than quickprop). See Gill et al. (1981) and Fletcher (1980) for further discussion of the conjugate gradient methods. We do not include the Shanno variation here because of its computational complexity and the fact that it does not always converge, although it is numerically the most powerful when it does.

Two P-dimensional vectors $\mathbf{u}^{(r+1)}$ and $\mathbf{u}^{(r)}$ are said to be *H-conjugate* whenever

$$[\mathbf{u}^{(r+1)}]^t \mathbf{H} \mathbf{u}^{(r)} = 0 \tag{5.44}$$

where $\mathbf{H}$ is a P-by-P matrix that is symmetric and positive definite (as would be the case if $\mathbf{H}$ were the Hessian matrix of second mixed partial derivatives of a convex function F). A set of direction vectors $\{\mathbf{u}^{(r)}\}$ is an *H-conjugate set* of directions whenever each pair of non-identical vectors are H-conjugate. We may successively generate a set of H-conjugate directions for a quadratic function $F(\mathbf{v})$ from an initial point $\mathbf{v}^{(0)}$ via

$$\mathbf{u}^{(0)} = -\nabla F(\mathbf{v}^{(0)})$$
$$\mathbf{u}^{(r+1)} = -\nabla F(\mathbf{v}^{(r+1)}) + \beta^{(r)} \mathbf{u}^{(r)} \tag{5.45}$$

for $r = 0,...,\ P - 1$. To require that Equation (5.44) is satisfied, we substitute $\mathbf{u}^{(r+1)}$ in Equation (5.45) into Equation (5.44) to obtain

$$[-\nabla F(\mathbf{v}^{(r+1)}) + \beta^{(r)} \mathbf{u}^{(r)}]^t \mathbf{H} \mathbf{u}^{(r)} = 0 \tag{5.46}$$

which yields the scalar value

$$\beta^{(r)} = [\nabla F(\mathbf{v}^{(r+1)})]^t \mathbf{H} \mathbf{u}^{(r)} / [\mathbf{u}^{(r)}]^t \mathbf{H} \mathbf{u}^{(r)} \tag{5.47}$$

that makes $\mathbf{u}^{(r+1)}$ orthogonal to $\mathbf{u}^{(r)}$ in Equation (5.45).

The basic idea here is to move from the current weight point $\mathbf{v}^{(r)}$ in the conjugate direction $\mathbf{u}^{(r)}$ to obtain a new updated weight point $\mathbf{v}^{(r+1)}$. Thus we take

$$\mathbf{v}^{(r+1)} = \mathbf{v}^{(r)} + \eta^{(r)} \mathbf{u}^{(r)} \tag{5.48}$$

Now we want to choose $\eta^{(r)}$ so that it minimizes the SSE function E along the conjugate direction from $\mathbf{v}^{(r)}$—that is, minimizes $E(\mathbf{v}^{(r)} + \eta^{(r)} \mathbf{u}^{(r)})$ so that

$$dE(\mathbf{v}^{(r)} + \eta \mathbf{u}^{(r)})/d\eta = 0 = (\nabla E(\mathbf{v}^{(r)} + \eta \mathbf{u}^{(r)}))^t \mathbf{u}^{(r)} \tag{5.49}$$

which is known as the *directional derivative*. An important observation is that Equation (5.47) contains the matrix $\mathbf{H}$, which we do not have. Further, our SSE function E is not convex nor quadratic, in general, so if we computed the Hessian, it may not be positive definite. We need to eliminate $\mathbf{H}$.

From the Taylor series approximation of the gradient

$$\nabla E(\mathbf{v}^{(r+1)}) = \nabla E(\mathbf{v}^{(r)}) + \mathbf{H}(\mathbf{v}^{(r+1)} - \mathbf{v}^{(r)}) \tag{5.50}$$

we obtain

$$\begin{aligned}
\nabla E(\mathbf{v}^{(r+1)}) - \nabla E(\mathbf{v}^{(r)}) &= \mathbf{H}(\mathbf{v}^{(r+1)} - \mathbf{v}^{(r)}) \tag{5.51}\\
&= \mathbf{H}((\mathbf{v}^{(r)} + \eta^{(r)}\mathbf{u}^{(r)}) - \mathbf{v}^{(r)}) = \eta^{(r)}\mathbf{H}\mathbf{u}^{(r)} \tag{5.52}
\end{aligned}$$

which comes from $\mathbf{v}^{(r+1)} \approx \mathbf{v}^{(r)} + \eta^{(r)}\mathbf{u}^{(r)}$. Thus $\mathbf{H}$ can be eliminated in Equation (5.47) by using

$$\eta^{(r)}\mathbf{H}\mathbf{u}^{(r)} = \nabla E(\mathbf{v}^{(r+1)}) - \nabla E(\mathbf{v}^{(r)}) \tag{5.53}$$

from Equation (5.52) consecutively in the numerator and denominator to obtain the result

$$\begin{aligned}
\beta^{(r)} &= [\nabla E(\mathbf{v}^{(r+1)})]^t \eta^{(r)}[\nabla E(\mathbf{v}^{(r+1)}) - \nabla E(\mathbf{v}^{(r)})]/[\mathbf{u}^{(r)}]^t \mathbf{H}\mathbf{u}^{(r)}\\
&= [\nabla E(\mathbf{v}^{(r+1)})]^t[\nabla E(\mathbf{v}^{(r+1)}) - \nabla E(\mathbf{v}^{(r)})]/[\mathbf{u}^{(r)}]^t[\nabla E(\mathbf{v}^{(r+1)}) - \nabla E(\mathbf{v}^{(r)})] \tag{5.54}
\end{aligned}$$

This is the *Hestenes–Stiefel* formula for the conjugate gradient algorithm. It depends upon finding $\eta^{(r)}$ via a line search to minimize $E(\mathbf{v}^{(r)} + \eta^{(r)}\mathbf{u}^{(r)})$ so $\mathbf{H}$ can be eliminated. By different substitutions for $\mathbf{H}$, the *Polak–Ribière* and the *Fletcher–Reeves* formulations are derived. We list these below and note that Shanno (1990) has shown that the second two can be unstable when the line searches are inexact, for which reason we prefer the Hestenes–Stiefel formulation.

The **Hestenes–Stiefel** formulation is

$$\beta^{(r)} = [\nabla E(\mathbf{v}^{(r+1)})]^t[\nabla E(\mathbf{v}^{(r+1)}) - \nabla E(\mathbf{v}^{(r)})]/[\mathbf{u}^{(r)}]^t[\nabla E(\mathbf{v}^{(r+1)}) - \nabla E(\mathbf{v}^{(r)})] \tag{5.55}$$

The **Polak–Ribière** formulation is

$$\beta^{(r)} = [\nabla E(\mathbf{v}^{(r+1)})]^t[\nabla E(\mathbf{v}^{(r+1)}) - \nabla E(\mathbf{v}^{(r)})]/[\nabla E(\mathbf{v}^{(r+1)})]^t[\nabla E(\mathbf{v}^{(r)})] \tag{5.56}$$

while the **Fletcher–Reeves** formulation is

$$\beta^{(r)} = [\nabla E(\mathbf{v}^{(r+1)})]^t[\nabla E(\mathbf{v}^{(r+1)})]/[\nabla E(\mathbf{v}^{(r)})]^t[\nabla E(\mathbf{v}^{(r)})] \tag{5.57}$$

Other variations exist, such as the Shanno conjugate gradient method (Johansson et al., 1992). When the function $E(-)$ is quadratic with Hessian matrix $\mathbf{H}$ (constant) that is strictly positive definite, then a unique minimum exists, and because the $\{\mathbf{u}^{(r)}\}$ are orthogonal and therefore form a basis for the vector space domain, the solution is reached in exactly P steps, where P is the dimension of the vector space domain. Every P iterations, the process is started over from a new "zero point" gradient at the current weight point. Because $E(\mathbf{v})$ is not quadratic, nor even convex (see Appendix 4a), the convergence may take multiple sets of P steps in conjugate directions. However, once the weight point is inside a well of a minimum, the SSE function E approximates a quadratic function and the convergence is very quick.

The Johansson–Dowla–Goodman Conjugate Gradient MLP Training Algorithms

The inputs are the same as for the *fprop* algorithm. The outputs are the weights $\mathbf{v}$ that minimize the SSE function E. The dimension of $\mathbf{v}$ is P and the number of iterations I is an integral multiple sP of P.

Step 1. Select weights $\mathbf{v}^{(0)}$ randomly from   /Initialize/
-1 to 1; $r \leftarrow 0$;

Step 2. $\mathbf{u}^{(0)} \leftarrow -\nabla E(\mathbf{v}^{(0)})$; normalize $\mathbf{u}^{(0)}$;   /Initialize for P conjugate directions/

Step 3. Search from $\mathbf{v}^{(r)}$ along $\mathbf{v}^{(r+1)} = \mathbf{v}^{(r)} + \eta^{(r)}\mathbf{u}^{(r)}$ to find $\eta^{(r*)}$ that minimizes $E(\mathbf{v})$;
$\mathbf{v}^{(r+1)} \leftarrow \mathbf{v}^{(r)} + \eta^{(r*)}\mathbf{u}^{(r)}$;   /update weights/

Step 4. if $(r \geq I)$ then stop;

Step 5. if $(r + 1$ modulo $P = 0)$ then   /Start new updates from current point/
$\mathbf{u}^{(r+1)} \leftarrow -\nabla E(\mathbf{v}^{(r+1)})$;

else $\beta^{(r+1)} \leftarrow \text{Beta}(\ )$;   /Beta computes either Hestenes–Stiefel/
$\mathbf{u}^{(r+1)} \leftarrow -\nabla E(\mathbf{v}^{(r+1)})$ /or Polak–Ribière or Fletcher–Reeves/
$\qquad + \beta^{(r+1)}\mathbf{u}^{(r)}$;   /$\beta^{(r+1)}$/
normalize $\mathbf{u}^{(r+1)}$;   /Equations (5.55) to (5.57) as updates/

Step 6. $r \leftarrow r + 1$; goto Step 3;   /form of β at $(r + 1)$st iteration/

The *advantages* of conjugate gradient training of FANNs are as follows: (i) Once a point is obtained in the well of attraction of a local minimum, the convergence is extremely quick along orthogonal directions so that it essentially converges to the minimum in a number of steps equal to the dimension P of the weight space; and (ii) the stepsize for updating the weights is built into the algorithm and need not be "guestimated" a priori nor adjusted.

The *disadvantages* are as follows: (i) A line search must be made on each iteration for the $\eta^{(r)}$ that minimizes $E(\mathbf{v}^{(r+1)}) = E(\mathbf{v}^{(r)} + \eta^{(r)}\mathbf{u}^{(r)})$ (but it involves only a single dimension along a directional slice and is very quick as a quadratic approximation); and (ii) the local minimum trap exists, as it does with all gradient methods. *In practice*, we find a good starting weight point in the well of a deep minimum where E is approximately quadratic. Then a conjugate gradient method converges quickly to that minimum.

5.10. The Kung–Diamantaras–Mao–Taur Projection Techniques

The Energy Projection Technique

This mission here is to estimate a suboptimal step gain $\eta^{(r)}$ on each iteration to be used in a gradient descent method. These techniques appear in Kung et al. (1991). The SSE function $E = E(\mathbf{w}, \mathbf{u})$ is scalar-valued and is often called the *energy function* defined by

$$E = \sum_{(q=1,\,Q)} E^{(q)} = \sum_{(q=1,\,Q)} \|\mathbf{t}^{(q)} - \mathbf{z}^{(q)}\|^2 = \sum_{(q=1,\,Q)} \sum_{(j=1,\,J)} (t_j^{(q)} - z_j^{(q)})^2 \qquad (5.58)$$

Let $E(\mathbf{v}^{(r)})$ be the energy (error) function on the rth iteration, where $\mathbf{v}^{(r)} = (\mathbf{w}^{(r)}, \mathbf{u}^{(r)})$ is the combined weight point for all layers of neurodes on the rth iteration.

Based on the assumption that the step gain η on the next step will take us to the desired point where the error (energy) will be zero, we put $0 = E(\mathbf{v}^{(r+1)})$ and expand $E(\mathbf{v}^{(r+1)})$ as a function of the weights in a linear Taylor series. Thus we obtain

$$0 = E(\mathbf{v}^{(r+1)}) = E(\mathbf{v}^{(r)}) + (\nabla E(\mathbf{v}^{(r)}))^t \Delta \mathbf{v}^{(r)} \qquad (5.59)$$

where $\Delta \mathbf{v}^{(r)} = \mathbf{v}^{(r+1)} - \mathbf{v}^{(r)}$. Upon substituting $\Delta \mathbf{v}^{(r)} = -\eta \nabla E(\mathbf{v}^{(r)})$ into Equation (5.59), the result is

$$0 = E(\mathbf{v}^{(r)}) - \eta (\nabla E(\mathbf{v}^{(r)}))^t \nabla E(\mathbf{v}^{(r)}) = E(\mathbf{v}^{(r)}) - \eta \|\nabla E(\mathbf{v}^{(r)})\|^2 \qquad (5.60)$$

This yields, upon setting the right-hand side to zero and solving for η, the formulation

$$\eta^{(r+1)} = \eta = E(\mathbf{v}^{(r)}) / \|\nabla E(\mathbf{v}^{(r)})\|^2 \qquad (5.61)$$

Equation (5.61) is the *energy projection* estimate for the step gain $\eta^{(r+1)}$.

As pointed out by Kung et al., the assumption that $E(\mathbf{v}^{(r+1)}) = 0$ cannot actually be true because the current direction of local steepest descent almost never points in the true direction of the local minimum in whose well of attraction the current weight point lies. Thus any algorithm that implements this projective estimate will be a *greedy algorithm* in that it races ahead under high risk that sometimes yields great rewards, but at other times may provide penalties. Therefore, we use a heuristic rule of Kung et al. and put $\lambda = 1/\sqrt{J}$, where J is the number of neurodes in the output layer, so that

$$\eta^{(r+1)} = (1/\sqrt{J}) E(\mathbf{v}^{(r)}) / \|\partial E(\mathbf{v}^{(r)})\|^2 \qquad (5.62)$$

For small J, we suggest $\lambda = 1/\sqrt{J+1}$. See Kung and Hwang (1988) for a related paper.

Parlos et al. (1994) used this same method and reported that it speeded up BP by about one order on the data for a real-valued function (single output). They also reported that the SSE was very jumpy (contains spikes). We have also observed such spikes, as has (Nachtsheim, 1995), who devised a technique to avoid the spikes as follows: if the update error E_{new} is not less than the old error E_{old}, then multiply the step gain η by a number less than unity, say 0.92, and repeat this until either $E_{new} < E_{old}$ or a certain number of attempts have been made.

The Least-Squares Projection Technique

In this technique (Kung et al., 1991), the output of the jth neurode in the output layer is denoted as a function of the weights $\mathbf{v}$. The function is designated as $z_j(\mathbf{v})$. The idea is to minimize the qth partial SSE error function

$$E^{(q)} = \sum_{(j=1,\,J)}(t_j^{(q)} - z_j^{(q)}(\mathbf{v}^{(r+1)}))^2 \tag{5.63}$$

Using the linear Taylor series expansion of $z_j(\mathbf{v}^{(r+1)})$, we obtain (suppressing the q for now)

$$z_j(\mathbf{v}^{(r+1)}) = z_j(\mathbf{v}^{(r)}) + (\nabla z_j(\mathbf{v}^{(r)}))^t \Delta \mathbf{v}^{(r)} \tag{5.64}$$

Again, we substitute $\Delta \mathbf{v}^{(r)} = -\eta \nabla E(\mathbf{v}^{(r)})$, so that Equation (5.64) becomes

$$z_j(\mathbf{v}^{(r+1)}) = z_j(\mathbf{v}^{(r)}) - \eta(\nabla z_j(\mathbf{v}^{(r)}))^t \nabla E(\mathbf{v}^{(r)}) \tag{5.65}$$

We denote the right-hand factor of the rightmost term in Equation (5.65) by

$$c_j^{(q)} = (\nabla z_j(\mathbf{v}^{(r)}))^t \nabla E(\mathbf{v}^{(r)}) \tag{5.66}$$

This causes Equation (5.65) to be

$$z_j(\mathbf{v}^{(r+1)}) = z_j(\mathbf{v}^{(r)}) - \eta c_j^{(q)} \tag{5.67}$$

which can now be substituted back into Equation (5.63) to yield

$$E^{(q)} = \sum_{(j=1,\,J)}(t_j^{(q)} - z_j(\mathbf{v}^{(r)}) + \eta c_j^{(q)})^2 \tag{5.68}$$

Upon setting the derivative of $E^{(q)}$ to zero and summing up the parts, we solve for

$$\eta^{(r+1)} = \eta = [\sum_{(j=1,\,J)}(t_j^{(q)} - z_j(\mathbf{v}^{(r)}))c_j^{(q)}] / [\sum_{(j=1,\,J)}(c_j^{(q)})^2 \tag{5.69}$$

The *advantages* of projection methods are as follows: (i) They determine a suboptimal (approximately optimal) step gain that moves suboptimally on each update, and (ii) this causes them to be much faster than BP (claims of an order faster, which means roughly 10 times as fast, are common).

The *disadvantages* are as follows: (i) The energy projection technique is greedy, but it can be tamed to some extent by λ as described above in the subsection on energy projection; and (ii) the least-square projection technique is very computationally complex (it learns in fewer epochs, but often this is not enough to make up for the extra computation when compared with conjugate gradients, even when $\eta^{(r+1)}$ is backpropagated).

The conjugate gradient methods also contain projection methods for estimating the adaptive step gain $\eta^{(r)}$ as can be seen by the algorithms in Section 5.9. We will not repeat them here. Conjugate gradient algorithms are, however, less greedy and almost as good on the average, judging from the results provided by Kung et al. (1991).

5.11. Some Important Comparative Studies

Barnard and Holm (1994) used MLPs for the classification of minerals. In Task 1, they used a 3–5–3 network with $K = 3$ classes and $Q = 96$ exemplars. For Task 2, they used a 15–9–9 MLP with $K = 3$ classes and $Q = 1635$ exemplars (526 were used as test samples). Ten different initial weight sets were generated and run using the three algorithms: (i) conjugate gradient batch mode; (ii) the leapfrog optimization of Snyman (1988); and (iii) an adaptive parameter form of BP (Silva and Almeida, 1990). The first two algorithms beat adaptive BP substantially, trained faster on the earlier iterations, and had a higher recognition success rate. The conjugate gradient algorithm was the best.

Other researchers (de Groot and Würtz, 1994) used MLPs to estimate sunspot numbers. They used 106 annual values from the year 1750 A.D. forward. On this data, $\eta = 0.2$ worked best with $\mu = 0$. All runs were for 10 seconds of CPU time on a CRAY YM-P. BP was the worst of the methods tried. The polytope method of minimization was second best at reducing the error. The conjugate gradient method was the best, followed by a quasi-Newton method. The Levenberg–Marquardt method, which is a full second-order (quasi-Newton) method is known to be more powerful. We note here, though, that the results depend somewhat on the data, and that all gradient methods have the local minimum trap property.

Exercises

5.1. Write a complete (detailed) algorithm for QP (*quickprop*). Make a detailed flowchart also.

5.2. Write a complete algorithm and draw a flowchart for the RP(*rprop*) algorithm.

5.3. Write out a complete algorithm that uses fullpropagation and an adaptive momentum as derived by Yu et al. What are the expected advantages and disadvantages of such an algorithm?

5.4. Explain why the Riedmiller–Braun algorithm can be improved via some type of adaptive momentum term, or else explain why such a term is not likely to improve convergence.

5.5. Write out an algorithm for the quasi-Newton method (you will need to search a library database to obtain a description of the quasi-Newton method).

5.6. Write a complete detailed algorithm for training an MLP via the Hestenes–Stiefel method of conjugate directions.

5.7. Study Figure 5.1 and then devise a way to jump out of a shallow local minimum.

5.8. Write a computer program that implements the *rprop* (Riedmiller–Braun) algorithm. Train it on the Digit12 dataset given in Appendix 11.

5.9. Modify the program from Exercise 5.8 to implement the *frprop* algorithm. Train it on the Digit12 dataset of Appendix 11, and compare the results with those of the **rprop** algorithm.

5.10. Write out the complete algorithm that uses the fullpropagation scheme, the adaptive momentum of Yu et al. to stabilize the direction, and cubic minimization along the directions and that includes the adjustments of the decay rates α_1 and α_2.

5.11. Repeat Exercise 5.10, but use the Eaton–Olivier momentum strategy in place of Yu's technique.

5.12. Develop a computer program that implements the algorithm of either Exercise 5.10 or 5.11 (give reasons for your selection). Train it on the Digit12 dataset of Appendix 11. Compare the results with those from any other runs, such as the *rprop* and *frprop* algorithms above.

5.13. Draw two concentric circles in the plane, with radii that are not too close in size. Now pick several points around the circumference of the outer circle to use as exemplars for the outer circle. Repeat this for the inner circle to obtain exemplar points for it. Use one of the more stable, quicker converging algorithms to train an MLP on these two exemplar sets. Can the MLP learn the two concentric circles? If so, pick a few points at random on each circle and test the network's ability to generalize by recognizing their class (circle) correctly. If the MLP cannot learn these two classes, then add two neurodes in a second hidden layer and then train that network.

5.14. Analyze the following situation by means of an MLP with two inputs, two hidden neurodes, and a single output neurode: Let a weight change (drift) to become arbitrarily large in magnitude. Can this happen? Examine the terms in the sums that feed into the sigmoid activations and compute the sigmoidal output values.

5.15. Make a flow chart and write an algorithm that searches along each single weight axis at a time via cubic approximation. The search should be on the interval $[-1, 1]$.

5.16. Analyze the algorithm of Exercise 5.15 above as to the possibility of drifting of the weights.

5.17. Write an algorithm that does the following iterations: Randomly draw p sample weight points, evaluate the SSE at each, use three or four (or more) of the lowest of these values to determine a direction, and search along that direction via cubic approximation over four equally spaced weight points. The process is to be repeated until the SSE stops decreasing nonnegligibly. What are the advantages and disadvantages of this algorithm? Can it learn appropriately?

5.18. What are the advantages and disadvantages of an algorithm that (i) draws an initial set of weights randomly, (ii) does a univariate search of the weight space (from -2 to 2) along each weight with a quartic polynomial approximation and repeats this process once, and (iii) then uses a conjugate gradient method to quickly converge down to the minimum in whose well the previously obtained starting weight point dwells?

5.19. Write out the complete algorithm for the method given in Exercise 5.18.

5.20. Write a complete algorithm for an MLP with a single hidden layer of neurodes that has an extra set of connecting lines from each input node to each neurode in the output layer. The weights on these new lines at the output layer will have different weight increments in the training. Determine these weight increments (denoted by Δv_{nj}).

5.21. In Exercise 5.20, what purpose do the extra connecting lines and their weights serve? We know that the hidden weights partition the feature space and the output weights join the convex regions to form classes, but how do these extra weights fit into the scheme?

5.22. Consider slickpropagation from Section 4.9. What are the advantages at the output layer? What range of values are permissible for the target (output) components? Discuss saturation at the output layer.

5.23. Develop a fast method that uses slickpropagation (see Section 4.9) at the output layer and trains there via steepest descent, but uses unipolar sigmoids at a single hidden layer where it trains via quartic approximation in random directions. Discuss the advantages, disadvantages, and practical aspects. Why would we want to use steepest descent at the output nodes but avoid it at the hidden nodes?

References

Barnard, E., and Holm, J. E. W. (1994), A comparative study of optimization techniques for backpropagation, *Neurocomputing* vol. 6, 19–34.

Barnard, E., and Casasent, D. (1989), Image processing for image understanding with neural networks, *Proc. IEEE/INNS Int. Joint Conf. Neural Networks*, Washington D.C., vol. 1, 111–115.

Cater, J. P. (1987), Successfully using peak learning rates of 10 (and greater) in backpropagation networks with the heuristic learning rule, *Proc. First IEEE Int. Conf. Neural Networks*, San Diego, vol. 2, 645–651.

Dahl, E. D. (1987), Accelerated learning using the generalized delta rule, *Proc. First IEEE Int. Conf. Neural Networks*, San Diego, vol. 2, 523–530.

de Groot, C., and Würtz, D. (1994), Plain backpropagation and advanced optimization techniques: a comparative study, *Neurocomputing* **6**, 153–161.

Eaton, H. A. C., and Olivier, T. L. (1992), Learning coefficient dependence on training set size, *Neural Networks*, vol. 5, 283–288.

Fahlman, S. E., and Lebiere, C. (1990), *The Cascade-Correlation Learning Architecture*, Technical Report CMU-CS-90-100, Carnegie Mellon University.

Fahlman, S. E. (1988), *An Empirical Study of Learning Speed in Backpropagation*, Technical Report CMU-CS-88-162, Carnegie Mellon University.

Fausett, L. (1994), *Fundamentals of Neural Networks*, Prentice-Hall, Englewood Cliffs, NJ.

Fletcher, R. (1980), *Practical Methods of Optimization, vol. 1: Unconstrained Optimization,* Wiley, New York.

Fletcher, R., and Reeves, C. M. (1964), Function minimization by conjugate gradients, *Comput. J.* vol. 7, 149–154.

Gill, P. E., Murray, W., and Wright, M. H. (1981), *Practical Optimization*, Academic Press, London.

Haykin, S. (1994), *Neural Networks*, Macmillan, New York.

Hecht-Nielsen, R. (1990), *Neurocomputing*, Addison-Wesley, Reading, Mass.

Hestenes, M. R., and Stiefel, E. L. (1962), Methods of conjugate gradients for solving linear systems, *J. Res. Natl. Bur. Stand.*, vol. 49, no. 6, 409–436.

Hinton, G. E. (1989), Connectionist learning procedures, *Artif. Intell.*, vol. 40, 185–134.

Hoehfeld, M., and Fahlman, S. E. (1992), Learning with limited numerical precision using cascade correlation algorithm, *IEEE Trans. Neural Networks*, vol. 3, no. 4, 602–611.

Hush, D. R., and Salas, J. M. (1988), Improving the learning rate of backpropagation with the gradient reuse algorithm, *Proc. IEEE Int. Conf. Neural Networks*, San Diego, vol. 1, 441–447.

Jacobs, R. A. (1988), Increased rates of convergence through learning rate adaptation, *Neural Networks*, vol. 1, no. 4, 295–307.

Johansson, E. M., Dowla, F. U., and Goodman, D. M. (1992), Backpropagation learning for multilayer feed-forward neural networks using the conjugate gradient method, *Int. J. Neural Systems*, vol. 2, no. 4, 291–301.

Judd, S. (1987), Learning in networks is hard, *Proc. First IEEE Int. Conf. Neural Networks*, San Diego, vol. 2, 685–692.

Kosko, B. (1992), *Neural Networks and Fuzzy Systems*, Prentice-Hall, Englewood Cliffs, NJ.

Kung, S. Y., and Hwang, J. N. (1988), An algebraic projection analysis for optimal hidden units size and learning rate in backpropagation, *Proc. IEEE Int. Conf. Neural Networks*, San Diego, vol. 1, pp. 363–370.

Kung, S. Y., Diamantaras, K., Mao, W. D., and Taur, J. S. (1991), Generalized perceptron networks with nonlinear discriminant functions, in *Neural Networks Theory and Applications*, edited by R. J. Mammone and Y. Y. Zeevi, Academic Press, Harcourt Brace-Jovanovich, Boston, pp. 245–279.

Lee, Y., Oh, S.-H., and Kim, M. (1991), The effect of initial weights on premature saturation in back-propagation learning, *Proc. 1991 Int. Joint Conf. Neural Networks*, Seattle, vol 1, 765–770.

Li, G., Alnuweiri, H., and Wu, W. (1993), Acceleration of backpropagation through initial weight pre-training with delta rule, *Proc. 1993 IEEE Int. Conf. Neural Networks*, San Francisco, vol. 1, 580–585.

Looney, C. G. (1996a), Advances in feedforward neural networks: demystifying knowledge acquiring black boxes, *IEEE Trans. Knowl. Data Eng.*, vol. 8, no. 2, 211–228.

Looney, C. G. (1996b), Stabilization and speedup of convergence in training feedforward neural networks, *Neurocomputing 10*, 7–31.

Mital, K. V. (1976), *Optimization Methods*, Halstead Press, Wiley Eastern Ltd., New Delhi.

Nachtsheim, P. R. (1995), A first order adaptive learning rate algorithm for backpropagation networks, *Proc. 1995 IEEE Int. Conf. on Neural Networks*, vol. 1, 257–262.

Nguyen, D., and Widrow, B. (1990), Improving the learning speed of two-layer neural networks by choosing initial values of the adaptive weights, *Proc. 1990 IEEE Int. Joint Conf. Neural Networks*, San Diego, vol. 3, pp. 21–26.

Pao, Y. H. (1989), *Adaptive Pattern Recognition and Neural Networks*, Addison-Wesley, Reading, MA.

Parker, D. B. (1982), *Learning Logic*, Invention Report S81-64, File 1, Office of Technology Licensing, Stanford University, Stanford, CA.

Parlos, A. G., Fernandez, B., Atiya, A. F., Muthusami, J., and Tsai, W. K. (1994), An accelerated learning algorithm for multilayer perceptron networks, *IEEE Trans. Neural Networks*, vol. 5, no. 3, 493–497.

Perantonis, S. J. and Karras, D. A. (1995), An efficient constrained learning algorithm with momentum acceleration, *Neural Networks*, vol. 8, no. 2, 237–249.

Plaut, D. C., Nowlan, S. J., and Hinton, G. E. (1986), *Experiments on Learning by Backpropagation*, Technical Report CMU-CS-86-126, Carnegie Mellon University, Pittsburgh.

Polak, E., and Ribière, G. (1969), Note sur la convergence de methods de directions conjures, *Revue Français Information Recherche Operationnelle*, vol. 16, 35–43.

Riedmiller, M., and Braun, H. (1993), A direct adaptive method for faster backpropagation learning: the *RPROP* algorithm, *Proc. 1993 IEEE Int. Conf. Neural Networks*, San Francisco, vol. 1, 586–591.

Robbins, H., and Monro, S. (1951), A stochastic approximation method, *Ann. Math. Stat.*, vol. 22, 400–407.

Rumelhart, D. E., Hinton, G. E., and Williams, R. J. (1986), Learning internal representations by error propagation, in *Parallel Distributed Processing: Explorations in the Microstructure of Cognition*, edited by D. E. Rumelhart and J. L. McClelland, MIT Press, Cambridge, MA, pp. 318–362.

Russo, A. P. (1991), Neural networks for sonar signal processing, Tutorial No. 8, *IEEE Conf. on Neural Networks for Ocean Engineering*, Washington, D.C.

Saridis, G. N. (1970), Learning applied to successive approximation algorithms, *Science and Cybernetics*, vol. 6, 97–103.

Schmidt, W., Raudys, S., Kraaijveld, M., Skurikhina, M., and Duin, R. (1993), Initializations, Back-Propagation and Generalization of Feed-Forward Classifiers, *Proc. 1993 IEEE Int. Conf. Neural Networks*, vol. 1, 598–604.

Shanno, D. F. (1990), Recent advances in numerical techniques for large-scale optimization, in *Neural Networks for Control*, MIT Press, Cambridge, MA.

Shea, Y. L., and Looney, C. G. (1992), Two-stage random optimization of neural networks with sensitivity based pruning of weights, *Proc. 1992 Golden West Int. Conf. Intell. Syst.*, University of Nevada, Reno, 18–23.

Silva, F. M., and Almeida, L. B. (1990), Acceleration techniques for the backpropagation algorithm, *Neural Networks—EURASIP Workshop 1990*, edited by L. B. Almeida and C. J. Wellekens, Springer-Verlag, Berlin, pp. 110–119,

Snyman, J. A. (1988), A convergent dynamic method for large minimization problems, *Comput. Math.*, vol. 16, no. 9, 737–745.

Stornetta, W. S., and Huberman, B. A. (1987), An improved three-layer backpropagation algorithm, *Proc. First IEEE Int'l Conf. Neural Networks*, San Diego, vol. 2, 645–651.

Syu, M. J., and Tsao, G. T. (1994), A saturation-type transfer function for backpropagation network modelling of biosystems, *Proc. 1994 IEEE Int. Conf. Neural Networks*, vol. 5, 3265–3270.

Vitela, J. E., and Reifman, J. (1994), The causes for premature saturation with backpropagation training, *Proc. 1994 IEEE Int. Conf. Neural Networks*, vol. 3, 1449–1453.

Watrous, R. L. (1987), Learning algorithms for connectionist networks: applied gradient methods of nonlinear optimization, *Proc. First IEEE Int. Conf. Neural Networks*, San Diego, vol. 2, 619–627.

Werbos, P. J. (1974), *Beyond Regression: New Tools for Prediction and Analysis in the Behavioral Sciences*, Ph.D. thesis, Harvard University.

Werbos, P. J. (1994), *The Roots of Backpropagation*, Wiley, New York.

Yamada, K., Kami, H., and Tsukomo, J. (1989), Handwritten numerical recognition by multilayered neural network with improved learning algorithm, *IEEE Joint Int. Conf. Neural Networks*, vol. 2, 259–266.

Yu, X., Loh, N., and Miller, W. (1993), A new acceleration technique for the backpropagation algorithm, *Proc. 1993 IEEE Int'l Conf. Neural Networks*, vol. 3, San Francisco, 1157–1161.

Zurada, M. (1992), Artificial Neural Systems, West Publishing, St. Paul, MN.

Zurada, M. (1993), Lambda learning rule for feedforward neural networks, *Proc. IEEE Int. Conf. Neural Networks*, vol. 3, 1808–1811.

Appendix 5a

How to Get Quickprop and Fahlman's Report

The interested reader may obtain the report in a compressed postscript formatted file via e mail from Carnegie Mellon University, as well as the source C program for either DOS or UNIX (translated from Common Lisp by Terry Regier [regier@cogsci.berkeley.edu] at the University of California, Berkeley). To obtain the files, you must be logged onto a UNIX-based system with Internet e mail services, and type the underline parts given below.

```
unix > ftp ftp.cs.cmu.edu
Name: anonymous
Password: <your user id>              /Your local password will do/
ftp > cd /afs/cs/project/connect/tr   /Tech. report subdirectory/
ftp > binary                          /Files are compressed/
ftp > get filename.ps.Z               /Download files this way/
ftp > quit                            /Exit from ftp/
unix > uncompress filename.ps.Z       /File must be unzipped/
unix > lpr -Pprintername filename.ps  /However you print postscript file/
```

The *filename* part of *filename*.ps.Z may be one of those listed below.

```
qp-tr              (technical report on quickpropagation)
quickprop.dos.c    (source code for DOS: text—do not use "binary" in ftp for this)
quickprop.unix.c   (source code for UNIX: text—do not use "binary" in ftp for this)
```

Note: As we prepare to go to press, we have heard that this file may no longer be available. However, other use files may be useful and available (e.g., the technical report cited in the next section).

Appendix 5b

The Fahlman–Lebiere Cascade
Correlation Method

The *cascade-correlation* algorithm (Fahlman and Lebiere, 1990) starts with only the N input branching nodes and the J output neurodes, so that there is no middle layer at first, as shown in Figure 5b.1. The weights at the output neurodes are trained over all K classes in the single layer perceptron mode. A single hidden neurode at a time is adjoined to the network and trained. The first is connected to each input node by lines from them to the inputs of the new middle neurode. Generally, the outputs of any other hidden neurodes that have been adjoined previously are also connected as inputs to the new middle neurode.

Figures 5b.2 and 5.b3 clarify the process of enlargening the structure. A second hidden neurode is not yet connected to the output neurodes by its output. The input weights to the new neurode are trained over all Q exemplar pair instances via a gradient method until the output of the new middle neurode correlates maximally with the residual error over all of the output neurodes. This is done by gradient steepest ascent on the correlation sum given

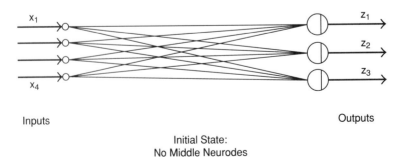

Inputs

Outputs

Initial State:
No Middle Neurodes

Figure 5b.1.   The beginning cascade correlation network.

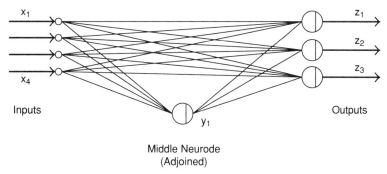

Figure 5b.2. The cascade correlation network with middle neurode adjoined.

below. At this point, those input weights to the newly added hidden neurode are saved, another set of initial weights is selected, and training is performed again over the input weights to the new hidden neurode to maximize the correlation of its output with the network outputs. After several such training sessions with different initial input weights on the new hidden neurode, the weight set that yields the maximum correlation with the network output error is selected, and these weights are never changed again.

After a new hidden neurode has been added and its input weights from both the input branching nodes and all previously adjoined hidden neurodes have been trained to maximize the correlation of its output with the network's residual output error over all outputs and all classes, then the training of the weights at the network *output neurodes* are trained to minimize the output sum-squared error (SSE). During this weight training at the output neurodes, only the simpler backpropagation for the output weights is done (no further training is done on the hidden neurode weights). After the output weights have been trained, the SSE E is computed. The process stops when the SSE is sufficiently small, else it adds another hidden neurode and trains its weights.

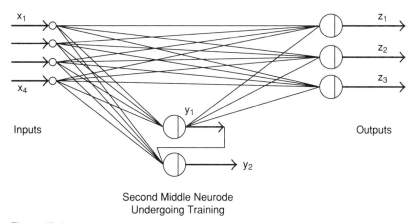

Figure 5b.3. The network with a second middle neurode connected for training.

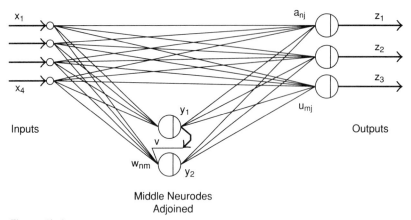

Middle Neurodes
Adjoined

Figure 5b.4. The cascade correlation network with second neuron adjoined.

Figure 5b.1 displays the starting network, while Figure 5b.2 displays the network after a single middle neurode has been adjoined. Figure 5b.3 shows the network after a second middle neurode has been adjoined, but before it has been connected to the output neurodes as shown in Figure 5b.4. Let y_m be the output of the mth hidden neurode that was just adjoined, and let α_{ym} be the average value of the outputs y_m over all Q exemplar pairs. The correlation to be maximized by training a new middle neurode is

$$C = \Sigma_{(j=1,\,J)}|\Sigma_{(q=1,\,Q)}\,(y_m^{(q)} - \alpha_{ym})(E_j^{(q)} - \alpha_{Ej})| \qquad (5b.1)$$

where $E_j^{(q)} = (z_j^{(q)} - t_j^{(q)})$ is the error at the jth output neurode for the qth exemplar pair, and α_{Ej} is the average error at node j over all Q exemplar pair instances.

To maximize C, we iterate at the $(r + 1)$st iteration on the weights for steepest ascent via

$$w_{nm}^{(r+1)} = w_{nm}^{(r)} + \eta(\partial C(w_{nm}^{(r)})/\partial w_{nm}) \qquad (5b.2)$$

$$v_{qm}^{(r+1)} = v_{qm}^{(r)} + \eta(\partial C(v_{qm}^{(r)})/\partial v_{qm}) \qquad (5b.3)$$

where $w_{nm}^{(r)}$ is the weight on the line from the nth input to the new mth middle neurode, and $v_{qm}^{(r)}$ is the weight from the qth middle neurode to the new mth middle neurode. According to Fahlman and Lebiere (1990), the weight increments are computed to be

$$\eta(\partial C(w_{nm}^{(r)})/\partial w_{nm}) = \eta\Sigma_{(j=1,\,J)}\Sigma_{(q=1,\,Q)}\sigma_j(E_j^{(q)} - \alpha_E)f'(s^{(q)})x_n^{(q)} \qquad (5b.4)$$

where $f(-)$ is the sigmoid, $s^{(q)}$ is the sum of the weighted values coming into the middle neurode, σ_j is the sign of the correlation between y_m and z_j and $x_n^{(q)}$ is the input from the nth input node for the qth exemplar pair instance. During the training of the output weights $\{u_{mj}\}$ and $\{a_{nj}\}$, where the u_{mj} are on lines from the hidden neurodes and the a_{nj} are on lines from N input nodes, BP for the output weights is used.

The *advantages* of this method are as follows: (i) The network training at first involves a single layer at the output neurodes to account for the linear relations; (ii) the training at a hidden neurode involves only a single neurode at a time with its set of weights to add nonlinear relations; and (iii) the total number of hidden neurodes is determined by the size of the SSE at the output neurodes (over all Q exemplars) and need be no greater than is necessary for the SSE to stop decreasing nonnegligibly. The training is done in stages where the early stages are very quick because of the small size of the hidden layer. These networks are powerful and perform very well on difficult highly nonlinear problems (Fahlman and Lebiere, 1990) such as the dual spirals problem and n-bit parity problems.

The *disadvantage* is that the addition of a many middle neurodes in single neurode layers causes the operational mode to become progressively slower (the length of the pipeline, which is the longest sequential path through the network, becomes longer). The length of the network should be kept as small as possible.

Reference

Fahlman, S. E., and Lebiere, C. (1990), *The Cascade-Correlation Learning Architecture*, Technical Report CMU-CS-90-100, Carnegie Mellon University.

Chapter 6

Supervised Training via Strategic Search

This chapter exposes some strategic search methodologies and derives stable training algorithms for feedforward artificial neural networks.

6.1. Optimization by Strategic Search

Introduction

Although Hopfield's paper (Hopfield, 1982) rekindled general interest in neural networks, it was the backpropagation (BP) algorithm by Rumelhart et al. (1986) that made real world applications possible immediately. By the early 1990s there was much dismay because of the problems in trying to use BP on complex data. Some of the many modifications brought some successes, but the use of BP is yet problematic for most people who would like to use multiple-layered perceptrons (MLPs). On the other hand, fuzzy rule-based systems have gained favor in recent years. Other "neural" network schemes are as complicated as the more flexible, powerful, and explanatory rule-based systems they would replace (Looney, 1993).

Most *failures* of MLPs, which are the most common type of FANN (feedforward artificial neural networks), spring from *faults* in gradient training, the data and in the architecture. There is nothing unstable in a FANN that has been well trained and which passed proper testing on data that are separable into reasonable classes in a linear or nonlinear manner.

Because many slices of the TSSE function $E(\mathbf{v})$ of the weights $\mathbf{v} = (w_{11},..., w_{NM}, u_{11},..., u_{MJ})$ are not convex, nor even quasi-convex (see Appendix 4), gradient methods do not necessarily converge to a global minimum on a weight space $[-1,1]^{NM+MJ}$. In the 1960s, researchers were forced to look at nongradient methods to solve large-scale complex nonlinear optimization problems and they proposed many techniques. The slices of E appear to be of quartic or quadratic forms on the weight space $[-b, b]^{NM+MJ}$. This knowledge can be used in nongradient schemes to search for solutions. It is known (see Section 9.3 on neural engineering) that for certain situations the training of MLPs can be very complex and time-consuming unless we use a second hidden layer of neurodes. For two (or more) hidden layers, the BP algorithm loses its computational simplicity. For such MLPs the strategic search algorithms can be competitive in speed, so that their other advantages make them desirable. With the powerful computers available today, search is a viable method to solve many problems, including the training of MLPs.

A High-Level General Process

We describe *optimization via strategic search* to minimize $E(\mathbf{v})$ via a high-level algorithm.

Step 1. For $r = 0$, choose an initial weight vector $\mathbf{v}^{(r)}$ in the permissible domain of $E(\mathbf{v})$.

Step 2. Select a set of weight vectors $\{\mathbf{u}\}$ using information about $\mathbf{v}^{(r)}$ and $E(\mathbf{v}^{(r)})$.

Step 3. Search on $\mathbf{v}^{(r)}$ and $\{\mathbf{u}\}$ to obtain $\mathbf{v}^{(r+1)}$ that lowers the *cost function* $E(\mathbf{v})$

Step 4. If r is sufficiently large, or if $E(\mathbf{v})$ is sufficiently low, then stop;
else increment r and goto Step 2 above.

The function $E(\mathbf{v})$ must be evaluated at each trial $\mathbf{v}^{(r)}$ to ascertain whether or not it decreases and perhaps to also determine by how much it decreases. In *line search* methods, the $(r + 1)$st iterative weight vector is found by use of a *direction* vector $\mathbf{u}$ to be

$$\mathbf{v}^{(r+1)} = \mathbf{v}^{(r)} + \eta^{(r)}\mathbf{u}^{(r)} \tag{6.1}$$

For *evolutionary* methods (Goldberg, 1989), pairs of weight vectors from an rth set $\{\mathbf{u}\}$ are combined genetically to reproduce an offspring weight set $\{\mathbf{v}^{(r+1)}\}$ whose members are more fit to the extent that they lower the value of the cost function $E(\mathbf{v})$. *Genetic algorithms* (*evolutionary search*) select from a population of "solution" vectors to combine in a way so as to form a progressively more fit population of approximate solutions.

Other strategies may use *purely random* selection of $\mathbf{v}$; selection of *random directions* $\mathbf{u}$ along which a search is made; *univariate search* (along a single weight axis, say v_{ps} of $\mathbf{v}$, in turn, while keeping all other weights fixed); and other types of search. Excluding purely random search, we call this *pattern search*, where some pattern is used to select directions and/or points. Methods that move in a direction of descent (or ascent) of the cost function are also known as *hill-climbing* methods. Purely random search is very inefficient, but, when guided by a pattern strategy, it becomes competitive in many cases.

Random search techniques were first proposed by Anderson (1953). Optimization via search was suggested by Hooke and Jeeves (1961) early in the development of computational optimization. Random optimization appears to have been used first by Favreau and Franks (1959). Optimization by search was later used by researchers such as Fletcher and Reeves (1964), Fletcher (1965), Matyas (1965), and Powell (1970) to minimize large-scale nonlinear complex functions such as those that modeled chemical and industrial plants. For classic works on nonlinear optimization that cover both gradient and search methods, see Cooper and Steinberg (1970), Fletcher (1970, 1980), Gill et al. (1981), Himmelblau (1972), Lootsma (1972), Mital (1976), and Whittle (1971). More recently, Dahl (1987) proposed a type of line search in the direction of steepest descent for training MLPs. A parabola (quadratic polynomial) was used along the line in the direction of the negative gradient from the current weight point (see Section 5.8 for cubic line search in the direction of steepest descent).

6.2. Random Optimization Algorithms

Random Optimization

In *random optimization*, the weight vectors are picked in some random fashion. For example, a direction $\mathbf{u}$ may be randomly chosen and searches made along the directions to lower the error function E—that is, to move downhill from the current weight point $\mathbf{v}^{(r)}$. In a *purely random* search, a vector $\mathbf{v}^{(r+1)}$ may be picked at random and kept if it decreases the cost function, or else it is discarded. Figure 6.1 shows a search path determined by some strategy. While no search is guaranteed to find the global minimum in a given number of iterations (as do conjugate gradient methods for quadratic functions, described in Appendix 4 and Chapter 5), random search is guaranteed to find a global minimum with *probability 1* (the probability of finding the global minimum gets arbitrarily close to 1 as the sample size gets arbitrarily large).

Matyas (1965) used a method of random optimization. Starting at an initial vector $\mathbf{v}^{(0)}$, he selected the direction $\mathbf{u}$ at random and then searched along the directional line $\mathbf{w} = \mathbf{v} + \eta\mathbf{u}$. Modified versions of Matyas' random optimization appeared much later (Baba et al., 1977; Solis and Wets, 1981). The first usage of random optimization for training neural networks appeared in (Baba, 1989). It used a version of the Solis-Wets technique. Baba reports

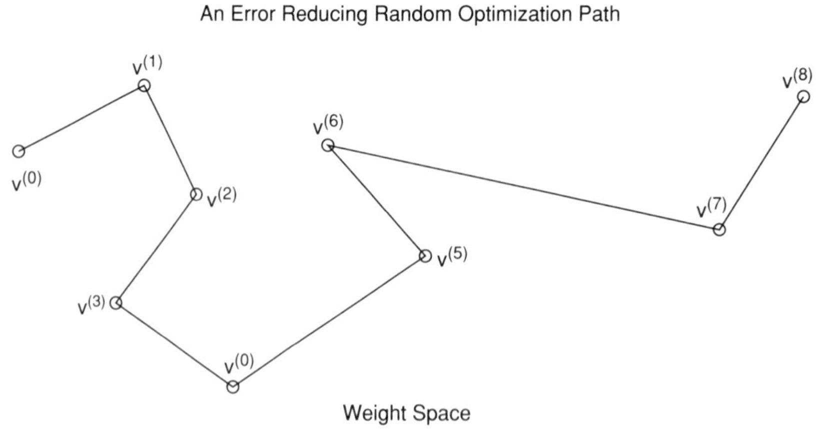

An Error Reducing Random Optimization Path

Weight Space

Figure 6.1.   A search process for training neural networks.

that it converged satisfactorily, and usually outperformed BP. It was shown in (Baba et al., 1977) that random optimization converges with probability 1, while it is well known that BP does not guarantee any type of convergence.

In Shea and Looney (1992) and Looney (1993), neural networks were trained via a strategy that consisted of two stages: (i) a *global stage*, where purely random selection of a weight point on each iteration provides the **v** that replaces the current weight vector only if it reduces the TSSE function $E(\mathbf{v})$; and (ii) a *local stage* of univariate search where a sample of values for each single weight v_{ps}, in turn, is selected at random, and the value that yields the least total sum-squared error (TSSE) replaces that weight value if it reduces the current TSSE.

We present two earlier algorithms for random optimization of the function E, and then a modification. The first one is that of Matyas (1965). The second one, by Solis and Wets (1981), modifies the first one by perturbing the direction of search by changing the center of the Gaussian distributions from which the weights were drawn. The third is that of Looney (1993). Random optimization requires the selecting of random values according to a probability distribution. Baba, and also Solis and Wets, used Gaussian distributions.

The Matyas Algorithm

Inputs: {number N of input nodes, number M of hidden neurodes, number J of output neurodes, and number Q of exemplar feature vectors; exemplar pairs of training vectors $\{(\mathbf{x}^{(q)}, \mathbf{t}^{(k(q))})\}$; and number I of iterations}

Outputs: {the vector set **v** of trained weights}

Step 1. /Initialize iteration number and randomly select a weight point (vector)/
$r \leftarrow 0$; randomly select initial weight set $\mathbf{v}^{(0)}$;

Step 2. /Save (hold) current weight set, choose random direction (unit vector **u**)/
$\mathbf{v}_{hold} \leftarrow \mathbf{v}^{(r)}$;
repeat
    generate Gaussian random direction $\mathbf{u}^{(r)}$ /$\mathbf{u}^{(r)}$ has unit length/
until $\mathbf{v}^{(new)} = \mathbf{v}^{(r)} + \mathbf{u}^{(r)}$ is in the domain $[-b, b]$ of E;

Step 3. /If new weight point reduces E, use it, else get back old weight vector/
if $E(\mathbf{v}^{(new)}) < E(\mathbf{v}^{(r)})$, then $\mathbf{v}^{(r+1)} \leftarrow \mathbf{v}^{(new)}$; else $\mathbf{v}^{(r+1)} \leftarrow \mathbf{v}_{hold}$;

Step 4. /Stop if all iterations are done/
if $r \geq I$, then stop
else $r \leftarrow r + 1$; goto Step 2;

The Solis–Wets Algorithm

The inputs and outputs here are the same as in the Matyas algorithm above. The parametric values 0.4, 0.2, and 0.5 in Step 3 were empirically determined (and thus depend on the data).

Step 1. /Initialize/

$r \leftarrow 0$;   /Set initial iteration no./

$\mathbf{b}^{(0)} \leftarrow \boldsymbol{\theta}$;   /Initial distribution center is zero vector/

select weight set $\mathbf{v}^{(0)}$ centered on $\mathbf{b}^{(0)}$ from Gaussian distribution;

Step 2. /Hold current weight set, generate direction randomly/

$\mathbf{v}_{\text{hold}} \leftarrow \mathbf{v}^{(r)}$;

repeat

　　generate Gaussian (centered on $\mathbf{b}^{(r)}$) random direction $\mathbf{u}^{(r)}$

until $\mathbf{v}^{(\text{new})} = \mathbf{v}^{(r)} + \mathbf{u}^{(r)}$ is in domain of E;

Step 3. /Test whether or not new vector reduces E/

if $E(\mathbf{v}^{(\text{new})}) < E(\mathbf{v}^{(r)})$, then   /If new vector reduces E,/

　　$\mathbf{v}^{(r+1)} \leftarrow \mathbf{v}^{(\text{new})}$;   /then update to good one/

　　$\mathbf{b}^{(r+1)} \leftarrow 0.4(\mathbf{u}^{(r)}) + 0.2\mathbf{b}^{(r)}$;   /Update perturbing vector/

else   /Else use opposite direction/

　　if $E(\mathbf{v}^{(r)} - \mathbf{u}^{(r)}) < E(\mathbf{v}^{(r)})$, then

　　　　$\mathbf{v}^{(r+1)} \leftarrow \mathbf{v}^{(r)} - \mathbf{u}^{(r)}$;   /If good, use it for updating/

　　　　$\mathbf{b}^{(r+1)} \leftarrow \mathbf{u}^{(r)} - 0.4\mathbf{b}^{(r)}$;

　　else $\mathbf{v}^{(r)} \leftarrow \mathbf{v}_{\text{hold}}$;   /Else return to previous vector/

　　　　$\mathbf{b}^{(r+1)} \leftarrow 0.5\mathbf{b}^{(r)}$;   /and change distribution center/

Step 4. /If I iterations done, then stop, else repeat/

if $r \geq I$, then stop;

else $r \leftarrow r + 1$; goto Step 2;

The Solis–Wets algorithm moves the Gaussian distribution to the center $\mathbf{b}^{(r)}$ that moves toward the solution weight set. Figure 6.2 shows the level curves for the movable Gaussian distribution. Upon applying both of the above algorithms to the training of neural networks, Baba (1989) compared the results to those of BP. He used various sizes of variance for the distributions from which the random drawings of directions were made. He found the Solis–Wets algorithm to be the quickest on the average. He also found that both of the random optimization algorithms usually performed better than BP. Although he tried various step gains for BP, he found that it often required an excessive amount of time and that the (constant) step gain value was critical to convergence. The coefficients for updating the center $\mathbf{b}^{(r+1)}$ of the probability distribution from which to draw the weights were determined empirically on the datasets used.

The *advantages* of the above algorithms are as follows: (i) When there is no a priori information available from which to choose a search direction, they perform minimization (and thus training of MLPs); (ii) when E is a complex function with a large number of weight variables and local minima, so that BP may exhibit convergence problems by oscillating or converging to a shallow minimum, they will converge eventually to the global minimum; and (iii) the learning is generalized without weight drift, gradients, or chaotic influence.

The *disadvantages* are as follows: (i) These algorithms are usually slower than *FP*, *RP*, *QP*, and *SP* algorithms (see Chapter 5 for *fullprop*, *resilientprop*, and *quickprop*, and Chapter

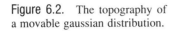

Figure 6.2. The topography of a movable gaussian distribution.

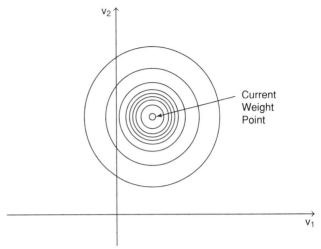

4 for *slickprop*), and as the error becomes smaller, the convergence becomes even slower (property of most minimization algorithms); and (ii) the Gaussian distributions cause the values to be drawn mostly from a region near the current weight region of search, although the optimal weight point may be located away from this region (such conservatism could limit the process, but could also speed it up in the well of a local minimum).

In practice, we draw each weight from the uniform distribution over the entire weight range $[-b, b]$. We usually select b to be 1 and use $[-b, b]$ for the weight interval. Without a priori knowledge of where the global minimum resides, it is preferable to use uniform distributions. We also use bipolar sigmoid activations with all random based methods.

In the algorithm given below (Looney, 1993), Step 3 draws a single random weight at a time and checks to see whether or not it lowers the TSSE. A small sample of size 6 is used for each weight and checked sequentially so that the one that yields the lowest TSSE is retained. When all weights have been so adjusted to make one iteration, the entire process is repeated again until I iterations are completed. As in FP (*fullprop*), all exemplars are used in the training on each weight adjustment. N is the number of input features, M is the number of neurodes in the hidden layer, J is the number of neurodes in the output layer, and Q is the number of exemplar pair instances to be used for training.

The Univariate Randomly Optimized Neural Network Algorithm

Inputs: $\{N, M, J, Q$; exemplar training pairs $\{(\mathbf{x}^{(q)}, \mathbf{t}^{(k(q))})\}$; sample size I_S; number of outer iterations I; and $b \equiv$ bound of weight range$\}$

Outputs: $\{$trained weights $(\mathbf{w}, \mathbf{u})\}$

Step 1. /Input size I_S of sample to use and number I of overall iterations/
  $I_S \leftarrow 6$; input I;   /Set sample size, no. iterations/
  $i \leftarrow 0$; b $\leftarrow 1.0$;   /Set iteration no., weight range $[-b, b]$/

Step 2. /Draw uniform random initial weights between -0.5 and 0.5, compute initial error/
  for $m = 1$ to M do
      for $n = 1$ to N do   /Draw middle initial weights w_{nm}/
          $w_{nm} \leftarrow$ random$(0,1) - 0.5$;
      for $j = 1$ to J do   /Draw output initial weights u_{mj}/
      $u_{mj} \leftarrow$ random$(0,1) - 0.5$;
  $E_{\text{hold}} \leftarrow$ **Update_NN**( );   /Update network, get TSSE/

Step 3. /Each global iteration draws I_S values randomly for each weight, tests E/
  for $m = 1$ to M do   /Use each mth neurode as pivot/
      for $n = 1$ to N do   /Minimize on middle weights/
          for $i = 1$ to I_S do   /Sample each w_{nm} I_S times/
              $w_{\text{hold}} \leftarrow w_{nm}$;   /Hold current weight and draw new one/
              $w_{nm} \leftarrow (2b)$random$(0, 1) - b$; $E \leftarrow$ **Update_NN**( );
              if $E < E_{\text{hold}}$, then $E_{\text{hold}} \leftarrow E$;   /Keep new TSSE if lower/
              else $w_{nm} \leftarrow w_{\text{hold}}$;   /else get old weight back/
      for $j = 1$ to J do   /Minimize output weights/
          for $i = 1$ to I_S do   /Draw each weight u_{mj} I_S times/
              $u_{\text{hold}} \leftarrow u_{mj}$;   /Hold current weight/
              $u_{mj} \leftarrow (2b)$random$(0, 1) - b$; $E \leftarrow$ **Update_NN**( );
              if $E < E_{\text{hold}}$, then $E_{\text{hold}} \leftarrow E$;   /Keep new TSSE if lower/
              else $u_{mj} \leftarrow u_{\text{hold}}$;   /else get old weight/

Step 4. /If all iterations are done, then stop, else repeat/
  if $i \geq I$, then stop;
  else $i \leftarrow i + 1$;
      $E \leftarrow E_{\text{hold}}$; goto Step 3;

The *advantages* of this algorithm that we call *uronn* (*univariate randomly optimized NN*) are as follows: (i) Large-scale feedforward standard neural networks can be trained independently of parametric settings for which no information is available; (ii) the initial rate of convergence is reasonably good with a small sample size ($I_S = 6$ may be used); (iii) the learning is very generalized (see Section 5.6 for an example of specialized and generalized learning); and (iv) it easily moves out of the well of shallow local minima to deeper local or global minima.

The *disadvantages* are as follows: (i) The convergence rate is slow, and slows appreciably as the iterations increase; and (ii) there is the extra computational load of, say, $I_S = 6$ evaluations of E for every single weight adjusted. The TSSE can not be reduced much beyond a certain point, and certainly not as much as by the QP (*quickprop*), FP, RP (*rprop*) or SP (*slickprop*) algorithms, which means that overtraining is difficult. In practice, I_S should start small (about 5) and be increased (to about 12) on later iterations.

6.3. A Cubic Random Optimization Algorithm

The Method of Cubic Approximation

This algorithm, called *cubronn* (*cubic ronn*), is quite different from the *uronn* algorithm. After we choose a random direction, we take four points along the line from the current weight vector in the selected direction and pass a cubic polynomial through them. We then find the minimum of the cubic polynomial and move to that weight point as the updated weight vector. A cubic is more flexible than a quadratic, but can represent quadratic data as well.

When the current weight point is $\mathbf{v}^{(r)}$, we randomly select a normalized weight direction $\mathbf{u}$ and put $\mathbf{v}^{(1)} = \mathbf{v}^{(r)} + \mathbf{u}$. Figure 6.3 shows the scheme. We use four weight vectors $\mathbf{v}^{(r)}$, $\mathbf{v}^{(1/3)}$, $\mathbf{v}^{(2/3)}$, and $\mathbf{v}^{(1)}$ that all fall on a line segment from the first to the last weight point in the direction from $\mathbf{v}^{(r)}$ toward $\mathbf{v}^{(1)}$. We obtain the two additional weight points between these weight points via

$$\mathbf{v}^{(1/3)} = \mathbf{v}^{(r)} + (1/3)(\mathbf{v}^{(1)} - \mathbf{v}^{(r)}) = \mathbf{v}^{(r)} + (1/3)\mathbf{u} \tag{6.2}$$

$$\mathbf{v}^{(2/3)} = \mathbf{v}^{(r)} + (2/3)(\mathbf{v}^{(1)} - \mathbf{v}^{(r)}) = \mathbf{v}^{(r)} + (2/3)\mathbf{u} \tag{6.3}$$

The TSSE function E can be restricted to this one-dimensional line, taken to be the x-axis, so that $y = E(x)$ is in the xy-plane. This is a slice of $E(\mathbf{v})$ along the line from $\mathbf{v}^{(r)}$ through $\mathbf{v}^{(1)}$. We now put $x_0 = 0$, $x_1 = 1/3$, $x_2 = 2/3$, and $x_3 = 1$ as points on the normalized line segment from $\mathbf{v}^{(r)}$ to $\mathbf{v}^{(1)}$, and $y_0 = E(\mathbf{v}^{(r)})$, $y_1 = E(\mathbf{v}^{(1/3)})$, $y_2 = E(\mathbf{v}^{(2/3)})$, and $y_3 = E(\mathbf{v}^{(1)})$. The four points $\{(x_i, y_i): i = 0,..., 3\}$ determine a cubic polynomial $y = ax^3 + bx^2 + cx + d$

Figure 6.3.   Selecting four weights on a line.

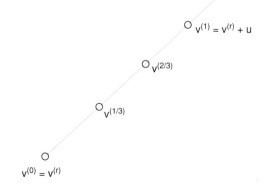

in the plane. Given the four points, we can solve for the minimum value of the cubic polynomial that passes through these points. The Vandermonde equation is

$$\begin{bmatrix} x_0^3 & x_0^2 & x_0 & 1 \\ x_1^3 & x_1^2 & x_1 & 1 \\ x_2^3 & x_2^2 & x_2 & 1 \\ x_3^3 & x_3^2 & x_3 & 1 \end{bmatrix} \begin{bmatrix} a \\ b \\ c \\ d \end{bmatrix} = \begin{bmatrix} y_0 \\ y_1 \\ y_2 \\ y_3 \end{bmatrix}$$

which can be solved for a, b, c, and d. We solve by a more efficient and accurate method below.

Upon substituting in the four values 0, 1/3, 2/3, and 1 for x, we obtain the four functional values

$$y_0 = d, \qquad\qquad\qquad y_1 = (1/27)a + (1/9)b + (1/3)c + d$$

$$y_2 = (8/27)a + (4/9)b + (2/3)c + d, \qquad y_3 = a + b + c + d$$

To solve these for a and b, we first eliminate c and d from pairs of equations via

$$2(y_3 - y_0) \qquad = 2a + 2b + 2c$$

$$\underline{-3(y_3 - y_1) \qquad = (-26/9)a - (8/3)b - 2c}$$

$$-y_3 + 3y_1 - 2y_0 = (-8/9)a - (2/3)b \qquad \text{(add the above two equations)} \quad (6.4)$$

$$(y_3 - y_0) \qquad\quad = a + b + c$$

$$-3(y_3 - y_2) \qquad = (-19/9)a - (5/3)b - c$$

$$\rule{7cm}{0.4pt}$$

$$-2y_3 + 3y_2 - y_0 = (-10/9)a - (2/3)b \qquad \text{(add the above two equations)} \quad (6.5)$$

Upon subtracting Equation (6.5) from Equation (6.4), we obtain

$$y_3 - 3y_2 + 3y_1 - y_0 = (2/9)a \qquad\qquad\qquad (6.6)$$

from which we solve for a, then backsubstitute into Equation (6.4) to obtain

$$a = (9/2)[y_3 - 3y_2 + 3y_1 - y_0] \qquad\qquad (6.7a)$$

$$b = (3/2)[y_3 - 3y_1 + 2y_0 - (8/9)a] \qquad\qquad (6.7b)$$

$$c = [y_3 - y_0 - a - b] \qquad\qquad (6.7c)$$

To minimize the cubic polynomial that fits the four points, we put

$$dy/dx = 3ax^2 + 2bx + c = 0 = Ax^2 + Bx + C$$

where $A = 3a$, $B = 2b$, and $C = c$. Next, the quadratic formula yields the two roots

$$z^{(1)} = [-B + (B^2 - 4AC)^{1/2}]/(2A) \qquad (6.8a)$$

$$z^{(2)} = [-B - (B^2 - 4AC)^{1/2}]/(2A) \qquad (6.8b)$$

The second derivative test must satisfy

$$d^2y/dx^2 = 2Az^{(i)} + B > 0 \qquad (6.9)$$

One of $[2Az^{(1)} + B]$ or $[2Az^{(2)} + B]$ must be positive for a minimum to exist. We take that value, say $z^{(1)}$, which is the proportion of the way between 0 and 1 where the minimum is located and use it to determine the new minimizing weight set via

$$\mathbf{v}^{(r+1)} = \mathbf{v}^{(r)} + z^{(1)}\mathbf{u} \qquad (6.10)$$

where $\mathbf{u}$ is the weight direction vector previously selected. The step size is the positive or negative proportion, $z^{(1)}$, of the distance from $\mathbf{v}^{(r)}$ to $\mathbf{v}^{(r+1)}$.

The Cubronn Algorithm

The current weight vector $\mathbf{v}^{(r)}$ is being held in $\mathbf{v}_{hold}$, and $\mathbf{u}$ is the direction with $\mathbf{v}^{(1)} = \mathbf{v}^{(r)} + \mathbf{u}$. We use weight vectors $\mathbf{v}^{(r)}$, $\mathbf{v}^{(1/3)}$, $\mathbf{v}^{(2/3)}$, and $\mathbf{v}^{(1)}$ along the line from $\mathbf{v}^{(r)}$ to $\mathbf{v}^{(1)}$. The procedure **Update_NN( )** updates all neurodal outputs and computes the TSSE as before.

Inputs: $\{N, M, J,$ and Q; exemplar feature vectors $\mathbf{x}^{(q)}$; output identifier vectors $\mathbf{t}^{(k)}$; the number of iterations I; and ϵ $(\epsilon > 0)\}$

Outputs: {the vector of trained weights $\mathbf{v}$}

Step 1. /Initialize parameters/
$\epsilon \leftarrow 0.002$;   /Input value for root test/
$r \leftarrow 0$;   /Initialize iteration no./
select uniform random weight set $\mathbf{v}^{(0)}$;   /Uniform: $-1 < v_p < 1$/
$E_{hold} \leftarrow$ **Update_NN( )**;   /Evaluate and hold TSSE/

Step 2. /Save (hold) current weight set, choose random direction (unit vector $\mathbf{u}$)/
$\mathbf{v}_{hold} \leftarrow \mathbf{v}^{(r)}$;
get random weight vector $\mathbf{w}^{(r)}$;   /Uniform $[-b, b]$/
$\mathbf{u} \leftarrow \mathbf{w}^{(r)} - \mathbf{v}_{hold}$;   /Subtract to get direction/
$\|\mathbf{u}\| \leftarrow (\sum_p u_p^2)^{1/2}$;   /Find length/
$\mathbf{u} \leftarrow \mathbf{u}/\|\mathbf{u}\|$; /Normalize/

Step 3. /Get function values along unit direction $\mathbf{u}$, compute coefficients/
$y[0] \leftarrow E_{hold}$;   /Get TSSE as y value for $\mathbf{v}^{(r)}$/
$\mathbf{v}^{(r)} \leftarrow \mathbf{v}_{hold} + (1/3)\mathbf{u}$;   /Get next weight point $\mathbf{v}(1/3)$/

$y[1] \leftarrow$ **Update_NN( )**;   /Get TSSE as y value for $\mathbf{v}(1/3)$/
$\mathbf{v}^{(r)} \leftarrow \mathbf{v}_{\text{hold}} + (2/3)\mathbf{u}$;   /Get next weight point $\mathbf{v}^{(2/3)}$/
$y[2] \leftarrow$ **Update_NN( )**;   /Get TSSE as y value for $\mathbf{v}^{(2/3)}$/
$\mathbf{v}^{(r)} \leftarrow \mathbf{v}_{\text{hold}} + \mathbf{u}$;   /Get next weight point $\mathbf{v}^{(1)}$/
$y[3] \leftarrow$ **Update_NN( )**;   /Get TSSE as y value for $\mathbf{v}^{(1)}$/
$a \leftarrow 4.5(y[3] - 3y[2] + 3y[1] - y[0])$;   /Equation (6.7a)/
$b \leftarrow 1.5(y[3] - 3y[1] + 2y[0] - 0.88889a)$; /Equation (6.7b)/
$c \leftarrow (y[3] - y[0] - a - b)$;   /Equation (6.7c)/
$A \leftarrow 3a; B \leftarrow 2b; C \leftarrow c$;   /Convert to standard coefficients/

Step 4. /Find roots of derivative, and test to see which one is minimum, then use it/
if $B^2 > 4AC$, then
$\quad z[1] \leftarrow (-B + (B^2 - 4AC)^{1/2})/(2A)$;   /Compute first possible minimum/
$\quad z[2] \leftarrow (-B - (B^2 - 4AC)^{1/2})/(2A)$;   /Compute second possible minimum/
$\quad$ if $(2Az[1] + B > 0.0)$, then $z \leftarrow z[1]$;   /If first root is minimum, use it/
$\quad$ if $(2Az[2] + B > 0.0)$, then $z \leftarrow z[2]$;   /If second root is minimum, use it/
else $z \leftarrow 0.2$;   /else move slightly/
for $m = 1$ to M do   /Update weights/
$\quad$ for $j = 1$ to J do   /at output neurodes/
$\quad\quad u_{mj}^{(r+1)} \leftarrow u_{mj}^{(\text{hold})} + z(u_{mj}^{(1)} - u_{mj}^{(\text{hold})})$;
$\quad$ for $n = 1$ to N do   /and at hidden neurodes/
$\quad\quad w_{nm}^{(r+1)} \leftarrow w_{nm}^{(\text{hold})} + z(w_{nm}^{(1)} - w_{nm}^{(\text{hold})})$;

Step 5. /Evaluate TSSE function at new weight set, check for decrease/
$E_{\text{new}} \leftarrow$ **Update_NN( )**;   /Evaluate E at new vector/
if $E_{\text{new}} < E_{\text{hold}}$, then $E_{\text{hold}} \leftarrow E_{\text{new}}$;   /Update error value/
else $\mathbf{v}^{(r+1)} \leftarrow \mathbf{v}_{\text{hold}} + \boldsymbol{\epsilon}$;   /Else get old weights back and perturb/

Step 6. /If I iterations are done, then stop, else repeat/
if $r \geq I$, then stop
else $r \leftarrow r + 1$; goto Step 2;

The *advantages* of *cubronn* are as follows: (i) The convergence is faster than *quadratic line search* because a cubic polynomial is a better fit to the TSSE function E along a line than is a quadratic or linear function; (ii) it is faster than other random optimization algorithms; (iii) the weights do not drift nor does it overtrain as do gradient methods and the learning tends to be more generalized; (iv) there is no saturation; (v) there are no parameters that have nonoptimal values; and (vi) it does not get stuck in a local minimum. During the first segment of iterations it is about as fast as BP but then slows somewhat.

Its *disadvantage* is that it is slower than gradient algorithms and requires four functional evaluations for each updating of the weights.

In practice, we use the modification given below.

$$x_0: \quad \mathbf{v}^{(r)} - \mathbf{u} \equiv \mathbf{v}^{(-1)}, \qquad x_1: \quad \mathbf{v}^{(r)} - (1/3)\mathbf{u} \equiv \mathbf{v}^{(-1/3)}$$

$$x_2: \quad \mathbf{v}^{(r)} + (1/3)\mathbf{u} \equiv \mathbf{v}^{(1/3)}, \qquad x_3: \quad \mathbf{v}^{(r)} + \mathbf{u} \equiv \mathbf{v}^{(1)}$$

$$y_0 = E(\mathbf{v}^{(-1)}), \qquad y_1 = E(\mathbf{v}^{(-1/3)}), \qquad y_2 = E(\mathbf{v}^{(1/3)}), \qquad y_3 = E(\mathbf{v}^{(1)})$$

This spreads the points out on both sides of $\mathbf{v}^{(r)}$ in the directions of $-\mathbf{u}$ and $\mathbf{u}$ across the weight (solution) space. *Cubronn* is similar to FCPI (full cubic propagation) except that it performed cubic line search in the direction of steepest descent (see Section 5.8), which is not as fast on some data.

6.4. Quartic Random Optimization

The Method of Quartic Approximation

This algorithm is called *quartronn* (*quartic ronn*) because it approximates slices of E with quartic polynomials. Figure 6.4 shows five points in a plane and the quartic polynomial that passes through them. Our strategy is to take the current weight point $\mathbf{v}^{(r)}$ as the center, choose a random weight $\mathbf{v}^{(*)}$, compute a direction vector $\mathbf{u} = \mathbf{v}^{(*)} - \mathbf{v}^{(r)}$, normalize $\mathbf{u}$, and then select two points on each side of $\mathbf{v}^{(r)}$ along the line through $\mathbf{v}^{(r)}$ in the direction of $\mathbf{u}$. The five points are equally spaced and determine a quartic polynomial through the associated planar points:

$$
\begin{aligned}
x_0: \quad & \mathbf{v}^{(r)} - 2\mathbf{u} \equiv \mathbf{v}^{(-2)} & y_0 = E(\mathbf{v}^{(-2)}) \\
x_1: \quad & \mathbf{v}^{(r)} - \mathbf{u} \equiv \mathbf{v}^{(-1)} & y_1 = E(\mathbf{v}^{(-1)}) \\
x_2: \quad & \mathbf{v}^{(r)} \equiv \mathbf{v}^{(0)} & y_2 = E(\mathbf{v}^{(0)}) \\
x_3: \quad & \mathbf{v}^{(r)} + \mathbf{u} \equiv \mathbf{v}^{(1)} & y_3 = E(\mathbf{v}^{(1)}) \\
x_4: \quad & \mathbf{v}^{(r)} + 2\mathbf{u} \equiv \mathbf{v}^{(2)} & y_4 = E(\mathbf{v}^{(2)})
\end{aligned}
\qquad (6.11)
$$

Figure 6.4. Quartic approximation of slices of E.

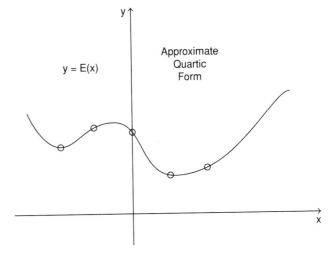

The quartic polynomial through the five points $\{(x_i, y_i)\}_{0 \le i \le 4}$ is

$$y = ax^4 + bx^3 + cx^2 + dx + e \tag{6.12}$$

The matrix equation for solving for a, b, c, d, and e is given below.

$$
\begin{bmatrix}
x_0^4 & x_0^3 & x_0^2 & x_0 & 1 \\
x_1^4 & x_1^3 & x_1^2 & x_1 & 1 \\
x_2^4 & x_2^3 & x_2^2 & x_2 & 1 \\
x_3^4 & x_3^3 & x_3^2 & x_3 & 1 \\
x_4^4 & x_4^3 & x_4^2 & x_4 & 1
\end{bmatrix}
\begin{bmatrix}
a \\ b \\ c \\ d \\ e
\end{bmatrix}
=
\begin{bmatrix}
y_0 \\ y_1 \\ y_2 \\ y_3 \\ y_4
\end{bmatrix}
$$

It is more convenient and numerically accurate to use the same type of equivalent method that we used for the cubic fittings of polynomials to data points. For the values $x = -2, -1, 0, 1,$ and 2, this becomes

$$
\begin{aligned}
y_0 = y(-2) &= 16\,a - 8\;b + 4\,c - 2\,d + e \\
y_1 = y(-1) &= \quad a - \quad b + \quad c - \quad d + e \\
y_2 = y(0) &= \qquad\qquad\qquad\qquad\qquad e \\
y_3 = y(1) &= \quad a + \quad b + \quad c + \quad d + e \\
y_4 = y(2) &= 16\;a + 8\;b + 4\,c + 2\,d + e
\end{aligned}
\tag{6.13}
$$

To solve these for the coefficients, we eliminate e by changing variables per

$$
\begin{aligned}
u_0 = (y_0 - y_2) &= 16a - 8b + 4c - 2d, & u_1 = (y_1 - y_2) &= \quad a - \quad b + \quad c - \quad d \\
u_2 = (y_3 - y_2) &= \quad a + \quad b + \quad c + \quad d, & u_3 = (y_4 - y_2) &= 16a + 8b + 4c + 2d
\end{aligned}
\tag{6.14}
$$

Now we eliminate, in turn, b and d and then a and c via

$$
\begin{aligned}
v_0 = u_0 + u_3 &= 32a + 8c, & v_1 = u_1 + u_2 &= 2a + 2c \\
v_2 = u_0 - u_3 &= -16b - 4d, & v_3 = u_1 - u_2 &= -2b - 2d
\end{aligned}
\tag{6.15}
$$

Combining Equations (6.15) appropriately, we obtain

$$v_0 - 4v_1 = 24a, \qquad v_2 - 2v_3 = -12b \tag{6.16a,b}$$

From Equations (6.16a), (6.16b), and (6.15), we solve for

$$a = (v_0 - 4v_1)/24 \tag{6.17a}$$

$$b = -(v_2 - 2v_3)/12 \tag{6.17b}$$

$$c = (v_1 - 2a)/2 \tag{6.17c}$$

$$d = -(v_3 + 2b)/2 \tag{6.17d}$$

Now that the coefficients a, b, c, and d are known, we set the derivative of the quartic equal to zero:

$$dy/dx = 4ax^3 + 3bx^2 + 2cx + d = 0 \tag{6.18}$$

For $a > 0$, Equation (6.12) has two local minima (and one local maximum), at least one of which is a global minimum for a slice. Equation (6.18) is equivalent to

$$Ax^3 + Bx^2 + Cx + D = 0$$

where $A = 4a$, $B = 3b$, $C = 2c$, and $D = d$. Dividing through by A, we obtain

$$f(x) = x^3 + (B/A)x^2 + (C/A)x + (D/A) = 0 \tag{6.19}$$

To solve Equation 6-19 for a root, we may use fixed point iteration. Putting

$$g(x) = x - f(x)$$

so that at a root z of $f(x)$, we obtain $g(z) = z - f(z) = z - 0 = z$, so that z is a fixed point of the function $g(x)$. To speed up the evaluation of $f(x)$, we use the nesting

$$f(x) = (D/A) + x(C/A + x(B/A + x)) \tag{6.20}$$

To speed up the fixed point convergence, we may use Newton's convergent formulation

$$g(x) = x - [f(x)/f'(x)] \tag{6.21}$$

which becomes

$$g(x) = x - \{[D/A + x(C/A + x(B/A + x))] / [C/A + x(2B/A + 3x)]\} \tag{6.22}$$

We know that there are three roots of the derivative polynomial. If two of them are not complex conjugates of each other, then there are three real roots of the derivative polynomial. The local maximum root is in between the other two (minimum) roots (see Figure 6.4), which are local minima roots on the outside. Thus we expect the local maximum root to be closer to the current weight point represented by x_2 and expect the two local minima roots to be outside of that. Instead of computing roots, we search along the line. We start our search for the local minima of $y = ax^4 + bx^3 + cx^2 + dx + e$ away from the current weight point and evaluate y at, say, 20 values of x between -2.0 and 2.0 to find an approximate minimum along the line segment from $\mathbf{v}^{(r)} - 2\mathbf{u}$ to $\mathbf{v}^{(r)} + 2\mathbf{u}$. That is the way we minimize the quartic polynomials in the algorithm.

The Quartron Algorithm

The inputs to *quartron* are the same as for the *cubronn* algorithm given above. All steps are the same except for the third and fourth ones, which we show here also as modified Steps 3* and 4*. Recall that the current weight vector $\mathbf{v}^{(r)}$ is being held in $\mathbf{v}_{\text{hold}}$, and $\mathbf{u}$ is a normalized direction with $\mathbf{v}^{(1)} = \mathbf{v}^{(r)} + \mathbf{u}$. We use weight vectors $\mathbf{v}^{(-2)}$, $\mathbf{v}^{(-1)}$, $\mathbf{v}^{(0)}$, $\mathbf{v}^{(1)}$, and $\mathbf{v}^{(2)}$ along the line from $\mathbf{v}^{(r)}$ through $\mathbf{v}^{(1)}$. The procedure **Update_NN( )** updates all neurodal outputs and computes the TSSE E as before.

Step 3*. /Get functional values along unit direction u, compute coefficients/

$y[2] \leftarrow E_{\text{hold}}$;   /Get $y_2 = E(\mathbf{v}^{(r)})$ at $x_2 = 0$/
$\mathbf{v}^{(r)} \leftarrow \mathbf{v}_{\text{hold}} - 2\mathbf{u}$;   /Get x_0 value for $\mathbf{v}^{(-2)}$/
$y[0] \leftarrow$ **Update_NN( )**;   /Get y_0 as $E(\mathbf{v}^{(-2)})$/
$\mathbf{v}^{(r)} \leftarrow \mathbf{v}_{\text{hold}} - \mathbf{u}$;   /Get x_1 value for $\mathbf{v}^{(-1)}$/
$y[1] \leftarrow$ **Update_NN( )**;   /Get y_1 as $E(\mathbf{v}^{(-1)})$/
$\mathbf{v}^{(r)} \leftarrow \mathbf{v}_{\text{hold}} + \mathbf{u}$;   /Get x_3 value for $\mathbf{v}^{(1)}$/
$y[3] \leftarrow$ **Update_NN( )**;   /Get y_3 as $E(\mathbf{v}^{(1)})$/
$\mathbf{v}^{(r)} \leftarrow \mathbf{v}_{\text{hold}} + 2\mathbf{u}$;   /Get x_4 value for $\mathbf{v}^{(2)}$/
$y[4] \leftarrow$ **Update_NN( )**;   /Get y_4 as $E(\mathbf{v}^{(2)})$/
$u_0 = (y_0 - y_2)$; $u_1 = (y_1 - y_2)$; $u_2 = (y_3 - y_2)$; $u_3 = (y_4 - y_2)$;
$v_0 = u_0 + u_3$; $v_1 = u_1 + u_2$; $v_2 = u_0 - u_3$; $v_3 = u_1 - u_2$;
$a \leftarrow (v_0 - 4v_1)/24$; $b \leftarrow (2v_3 - v_2)/12$;   /Solve for coefficients/
$c \leftarrow (v_1 - 2a)/2$; $d \leftarrow -(v_3 + 2b)/2$;

Step 4*. /Search from $-b$ to b to find minimum for $y = ax^4 + bx^3 + cx^2 + dx + e$/

$x \leftarrow b$; $y_{\text{min}} \leftarrow 99999.9$; $x_{\text{min}} \leftarrow 99.9$;
while $x \geq -b$ do
    $y \leftarrow x(d + x(c + x(b + xa)))$;   /We don't need to add e/
    if $y \leq y_{\text{min}}$, then $y_{\text{min}} \leftarrow y$; $x_{\text{min}} \leftarrow x$;   /Check for minimum, record/
    $x \leftarrow x - \delta$;
for $m = 1$ to M do   /Update all weights/
    for $j = 1$ to J do
        $u_{mj}^{(r+1)} \leftarrow u_{mj}^{\text{(hold)}} + x_{\text{min}}(u_{mj}^{(1)} - u_{mj}^{\text{(hold)}})$;
    for $n = 1$ to N do
        $w_{nm}^{(r+1)} \leftarrow w_{nm}^{\text{(hold)}} + x_{\text{min}}(w_{nm}^{(1)} - w_{nm}^{\text{(hold)}})$;

The *advantages* of *quartron* are those of *cubronn*, but *quartron* learns more rapidly on the early iterations because many slices are approximately quartic in form. It is faster than other random optimization algorithms for training MLPs and moves in a few iterations to a region of a global minimum, where quadratic search or gradient descent could then be used to converge quickly on the near-quadratic portion of the TSSE function.

Its *disadvantage* is that it may become slow on the later part of the training, where the quartic approximation is not fine enough for a close fit. *In practice*, we use *quartron* to find a region of the weight space $[-b, b]^{NM+MJ}$ where the TSSE function E assumes low values and then switch to FP for quick descent to the minimum thereabouts. The search along the quartic polynomial is quick, but could perhaps be speeded up slightly with *golden section search* (Cooper and Steinberg, 1970).

6.5. The Baba–Mogami–Kohzaki–Shiraishi–Yoshida Hybrid Search Algorithm

A newer method of random optimization (Baba et al., 1994) uses the Solis–Wets random optimization algorithm in conjunction with BP to overcome some drawbacks of each. The Solis–Wets algorithm sometimes takes a long time to converge, while BP is not guaranteed to converge even to a local minimum. This hybrid algorithm converges to a global minimum with probability 1.

Baba et al. start with either the BP algorithm or a conjugate gradient algorithm and train until the criterion

$$\left| E_{\text{old}} - E(v^{(r)}) \right| < \epsilon$$

is satisfied. If this difference is sufficiently small, say, less than ϵ_1, or $r \geq I$ (number of epochs or iterations desired), then the process stops. Otherwise, the Solis–Wets algorithm is then used to iterate until

$$\left| E_{\text{old}} - E(v^{(r)}) \right| > cE(v^{(r)})$$

This indicates that the current weight point has jumped to the well of lower minimum. Then they resume with BP, and so forth, until convergence is achieved at a global minimum.

In simulations on an MLP with the architecture of $N–L–M–J = 8–8–8–1$, Baba et al. trained the MLP successfully to make a particular prediction. With 8 inputs at 10 A.M. that correlate with the density of the pollutant SO_2, the network was able to accurately predict the level of SO_2 in the air in downtown Tokyo at 12 noon. Their success opens the door to modifications for yet better performance. For example, FP could be used for a few iterations, followed by the Solis–Wets algorithm to jump out of the well of the current minimum, until a global minimum is found.

In comparisons of learning, "plain vanilla" backpropagation had a best time of 302.64 seconds of CPU time and reduced the error to 0.4999, while the Solis–Wets algorithm took an average of 60 seconds to achieve an error less than 10^{-4} (the best time was 4.04 seconds and the worst was 230 seconds). In contrast to these, the hybrid algorithm took an average of 5.12 seconds of CPU time to reduce the error to less than 10^{-4} (the best time was 1.63 seconds and the worst was 21.0 seconds). In a second set of tests on octane ratings of gasoline, the resulting differences were not so dramatic but were substantial.

6.6. Evolutionary Search: Genetic Algorithms

The Genetic Concept

The economist Malthus noted that the reproductive potential of the various species would cause exponential growth in their populations should all members reproduce successfully

(Malthus, 1826). Charles Darwin noticed a principle that the fittest survive. In his 1859 work, *On the Origin of Species*, he stated, "I have called this principle, by which each slight variation, if useful, is preserved, by the term of Natural Selection." Wright (1932) introduced the concept of an adaptive topography that describes the fitness of organisms, which undergoes time-varying transformations that correspond to environmental variation. Individuals are mapped onto the adaptive topography, where peaks correspond to optimized genetic structures (maximum fitness). Fraser (1957) was the first one to use computer simulation of genetics. Bremermann (1962) posited the idea of optimization via evolution and recombination. Fogel et al. (1966) considered the problem of predicting time series based on input–output data and optimally controlling an unknown process with respect to an arbitrary payoff function through simulated evolution.

According to Fogel (1994), evolution is a parallel process and the development of more powerful parallel computers will make possible the solution of complex problems in many areas. We recommend Atmar (1994) for an enlightening discussion of computational evolution.

John Holland's book (Holland, 1975) established a firm theoretical framework with his canonical genetic algorithm that abstracted Darwinian evolution. An *evolutionary system* consists of (i) a *population* of individuals (represented by their chromosomes), (ii) a set of *codewords*, or *chromosomes* that are string encodings of features where each chromosome represents an individual of the population, (iii) *genes* in an alphabet of characters (*alleles*) from which combinations are taken to form the chromosomic strings, (iv) the basic operators defined by Goldberg (1989), which are *reproduction*, *crossover*, and *mutation*, and (v) a *fitness measure* that directs the evolutionary process by permitting the fittest to reproduce with greater likelihood.

Reproduction operates by selecting a set of parents from the fittest chromosomes, as judged by the fitness measure: The parents are chosen with probability of selection being proportional to fitness. Crossover maps two parental, or *progenitor*, chromosomes to two offspring, or *progeny*, chromosomes. A *strategy*, usually entailing some degree of randomness, defines the crossover operator. Crossover involves the selection of points, or gene positions in the chromosome, where the progenitor chromosomes are to be broken and pieces exchanged between the progenitor chromosomes to form new progeny chromosomes. A very small probability of mutation is built into the strategy.

Mutation is performed when the mutation operator selects one or more alleles in the chromosome to be replaced with another allele from the alphabet. The progenitors are eliminated after reproduction, which leaves a new population that represents the current *emerged state* of "solutions" of the evolutionary process. Figure 6.5 shows the process for two progenitors generating two progeny chromosomes under a one-point crossover strategy and a single gene mutation where the alphabet is {0,1}. The progenitors are chromosomes a and b, which have been selected by reproduction. We randomly pick a crossover point (the fourth gene in Figure 6.5, which means that the chromosomes break between the fourth and fifth genes). The third gene bit is selected for mutation, and that gene's allele is replaced by a different one.

In genetic terminology, the chromosomal forms are called *genotypes*. They determine the actual population that are called *phenotypes*. It is the genotypes that determine evolutionary processes. Holland used bits as his alphabet, so the chromosomes were strings of 0s and 1s. His reason for using mutation is to ensure against the loss of diversity that could lead

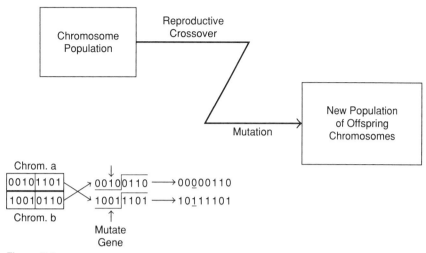

Figure 6.5.   The process of generating new populations.

to a dead end that is not a good solution. The three operators of selection (reproduction), crossover, and mutation drive the evolutionary process, while the fitness measure guides, or navigates, it in a direction from which the emerged states unfold over time. The fitness measure affects the selection of the fit progenitors from the emerged population to produce a new population. A higher relative fitness of a chromosome, as judged by the fitness measure, increases the likelihood that it reproduces (Louis, 1993). This guides the process to a more fit population, while mutation prevents it from reaching a dead end with a lack of sufficient diversity.

Crossover causes genotypical chromosomes to be cut and spliced. The cut substrings define regions of the search space called schema. Formally, a *schema* is a template that identifies a subset of strings with similarities at certain positions. For example, in the set of all binary strings of length 6, the schema 1**0*1 describes the subset of all strings where the first, fourth, and sixth positions are fixed as shown, while the second, third, and fifth (denoted by *) are free to vary over the alphabet {0,1}. The order of a schema is the number of fixed positions in the template and in this example it is 3. The *fitness of a schema* is the average of the fitness of all of the strings matching the schema. The *defining length* of a schema is the difference in positions from the first to last fixed positions. Letting $m(h, r)$ be the expected number of schema h at the rth generation (iteration), $f(h)$ be the fitness of schema h, and $f_A(r)$ be the average fitness of the population at the rth generation, Holland's Fundamental Theorem of GAs (Goldberg, 1989, p. 33), also known as the *Schema Theorem*, states

$$m(h, r + 1) \geq [m(h, r)f(h)/f_A(r)]\{1 - P_c\delta(h)/(L - 1) - O(h)P_m\} \qquad (6.23)$$

where P_c and P_m are the probabilities, respectively, of crossover and mutation, the genotype length is L, $\delta(h)$ is the defining length, and $O(h)$ is the order of schema h. P_c is generally greater than 0.5 (usually 0.66), while $P_m \approx 0.001$ is usual. The Building Block Hypothesis (Goldberg, 1989) states:

> A genetic algorithm seeks near-optimal performance through the juxtaposition of short, low-order, high performance schemata, i.e., building blocks.

Optimizing Functions with Genetic Algorithms

Genetic algorithms are viable processes for optimizing large-scale nonlinear functions such as the total sum-squared error (TSSE) of a neural network, when the TSSE function $E(-)$ to be optimized is used as the fitness measure. Greater optimality of $E(\mathbf{v})$ (smaller values) implies greater fitness of the argument $\mathbf{v}$. Let $E(\mathbf{v}) \geq 0$ be a function of $\mathbf{v} = (v_1,...,v_P)$, and suppose the problem is to minimize $E(-)$. We form a chromosome via the concatenation $\mathbf{c} = v_1 v_2...v_P$, and (following tradition) substitute in the bits for each randomly initialized value v_p. Given a population $\{\mathbf{c}^{(s)}\}$ of such chromosomes (codewords), we could define the fitness measure to be $f(\mathbf{c}^{(s)}) \equiv 1/[E(\mathbf{v}^{(s)}) + 1]$, but we just take lower functional values to mean higher fitness instead. Thus a relatively higher fitness of $\mathbf{c}^{(s)}$ means that its associated vector $\mathbf{v}^{(s)}$ has a lower functional value $E(\mathbf{v}^{(s)})$.

To start the optimization process, we randomly choose a population $\{\mathbf{v}^{(1)},..., \mathbf{v}^{(S)}\}$ and evaluate the fitness of the associated chromosomes $\{\mathbf{c}^{(1)},..., \mathbf{c}^{(S)}\}$ via $E(\mathbf{v}^{(s)})$. Then we draw a pair of progenitors from the more fit parents by assigning higher probabilities to their random selection. Next, we execute crossover and mutation. We repeat this until a completely new population of the same size replaces the previous one. These steps are iterated until we have progeny that are sufficiently fit—that is, that yield approximate minima for the cost function $E(-)$. For reports of MLP training with genetic algorithms, see Kitano (1990), Montana and Davis (1989), and Sudeep et al. (1995).

Example 6.1.   Goldberg's Example: Optimization via a Genetic Algorithm

The example presented in Tables 6.1 and 6.2 is due to Goldberg (1989). Let $f(x) = x^2$ be a cost function to be maximized over the domain of integers $0 \leq x \leq 31$. These take binary values 00000 to 11111. Table 6.1 shows the initial population. Now we draw four uniform(0,1) random numbers (between 0 and 1) and select 2 pairs of parents according to the probability range the drawn number falls into. The percentages shown in Table 6.1 are com-

Table 6.1.
An Example of Optimization with GAs

String Number	Initial Population	x Value	$f(x)$	%	Probability Range
1	01101	13	169	14	0–0.14
2	11000	24	576	49	0.14–0.63
3	01000	8	64	6	0.63–0.69
4	10011	19	361	31	0.69–1.00

Table 6.2.
The Results after a Generation

(Random) Mate Number	Mate Pool after Selection	Random Crossover Position	New Population	x Value	f(x)
(1) 2	0110 ∣ 1	4	01100	12	144
(2) 1	1100 ∣ 0	4	11001	25	625
(2) 4	11 ∣ 000	2	11011	27	729
(4) 2	10 ∣ 011	2	10000	16	256

puted by dividing each $f(x)$ value by the sum of all of the $f(x)$ values. Table 6.2 shows the results. String number 2 was selected twice because of its high fitness, while string 3 was not chosen because it was least fit.

The High-Level Genetic Algorithm

Formally, the higher-level algorithm can be stated as given below, where $P^{(r)}$ is the population of chromosomes at generation number r (Louis, 1993).

Step 1. $r \leftarrow 0$;
            initialize $P^{(0)}$;   /Select first progenitor chromosomes/

Step 2. evaluate $P^{(0)}$;   /Apply fitness measure to each/

Step 3. while (termination condition not true) do
             select $P^{(r+1)}$ from $P^{(r)}$;   /Select fit parental subset/
             recombine $P^{(r+1)}$;   /Crossover and mutate/
             evaluate $P^{(r+1)}$;   /Apply fitness measure/
             $r \leftarrow r + 1$;

A Genetic Algorithm for Training MLPs

In the lower-level algorithm given below, we use real-valued strings as chromosomes to circumvent the need to convert them back and forth from binary to real numbers. For a discussion of this, see Wright (1991). Note that the fitness measure uses real values, while crossover and mutation traditionally use binary string representations.

Inputs: {sample size Q; exemplar input feature vectors $\mathbf{x}^{(q)}$ and exemplar output vectors $\mathbf{t}^{(k)}$; the MLP parameters N, M, J; size S of population; and number of iterations I}

Outputs: {the vector of solution weights $\mathbf{v}$}

Step 1. /Initialize iteration no., draw initial weight vector population randomly/
$r \leftarrow 0$;
for $\ell = 1$ to S do randomly draw $\mathbf{v}^{(\ell)}$; /S is an even integer/

Step 2. /Evaluate each member of weight vector population/
for $s = 1$ to S do
$\quad$ Fit[s] ← **Update_NN**($\mathbf{v}^{(s)}$); $\qquad$ /Use TSSE as fitness/

Step 3. /Reproduce new population with crossover and mutation/
$s \leftarrow 0$;
repeat
$\quad \{\mathbf{w}^{(s)}\} \leftarrow$ **Reproduce**( ); $\qquad$ /Select fit pair of parent weight vectors/
$\quad \{\mathbf{w}^{(s)}\} \leftarrow$ **Crossover**( ); $\qquad$ /Pick random position and do crossovers/
$\quad \{\mathbf{w}^{(s)}\} \leftarrow$ **Mutate**( ); $\qquad$ /Mutate both new chromosomes at random/

$\quad s \leftarrow s + 2$;
until ($s \geq S$);
for $s = 1$ to S do $\mathbf{v}^{(s)} \leftarrow \mathbf{w}^{(s)}$; $\qquad$ /Replace population/

Step 4. /Evaluate fitness/
for $s = 1$ to S do Fit[s] ← **Update_NN**($\mathbf{v}^{(s)}$); /Use TSSE as fitness/

Step 5. /Test stopping criterion/
$r \leftarrow r + 1$;
if $r \leq I$, then goto Step 3; $\qquad$ /Iterate again, or else/
else **Get_solution**( ); $\qquad$ /Get best solution from population/
$\quad$ stop;

The procedure **Reproduce**( ) randomly selects one of the pairs of progenitor weight vectors according to fitness, so, lower TSSE values for the MLP are more likely. It sets up the indices of the two weights selected, which are then used by **Crossover**( ) to produce two new chromosomes (weight vectors), and **Mutate**( ) to mutate a position that is picked at random with probability P_m. In a weight vector, each component value (weight) is a chromosome to be combined with other chromosomes of the same component (the stratified subpopulation strategy). **Update_NN**( ) updates the MLP and returns the TSSE, which is the fitness measure (a lower value designates higher fitness). The procedure **Get_solution**( ) picks the fittest of the current population.

Note that there are constraints that the weight vector components must be between $-b$ and b for the bipolar case, so we use a number of bits that are sufficient for the resolution desired. For example, 8 bits would allow 256 values from 00000000 to 11111111. Thus there would be 128 values for $-b$ to 0 and 128 values for 0 to b. Letting 00000000 represent $-b$, then 00000001 would represent $-b + (b)/128$, 00000010 would represent $-b + (2b)/128$, and binary i would represent $-b + (ib)/128$ for $0 \leq i \leq 255$. Thus $i = 128$ would represent $-b + 128b/128 = 0$, and $i = 255$ would represent $-b + 255b/128 = 0.9921875b$, which is $b/128$ short of 1.0. Once the number of bits is selected, the progeny chromosomes will never go out of bounds for this problem. Higher resolution requires more bits in representing the real numbers (see Wright, 1991).

The *advantages* of GAs in training FANNs by search are as follows: (i) They can find a global minimum without getting stuck in a local minimum (McInerney and Dhawan, 1993); (ii) they require no MLP training parameters such as step gain or momentum coefficient or gradients to be determined; and (iii) the search strategy is independent of the MLP problem (Gonzalez-Seco, 1992). They are simple to implement, but have tremendous power to improve the training. The *disadvantage* is that they often require substantial computation. Typically, the minimization graph of the TSSE function E versus time has the form of a decaying exponential. This decreasing form is typical of strategic search methods where the decrease is rapid at first but then slows down progressively.

In practice, GAs are more suitable for preliminary adjustment of the initial weights (Sudeep et al., 1995). We may also use GAs to find the optimal network architecture for a given dataset (Whitley and Hanson, 1989; Harp et al., 1989). Another use is to obtain a good starting point for a fast descending gradient method such as FP. GA training of MLPs was done by Sudeep et al. (1995) for this purpose. Each weight was represented by 17 bits, with the 17th bit being used as a sign bit. This provided binary values from $-65,536$ to $65,535$. The length of the chromosomes was $L = 17 \times (NM + MJ)$. Single-point crossover was used with $P_c = 0.66$ for small networks. For larger ones, the initial probability of crossover was 0.66, but was increased to 0.99 to exploit the region at the endgame situation. The individuals (chromosomic strings) in the consecutive old and new populations were ranked by fitness (lowness of the TSSE). The fittest were copied to a modified new population, which is a method known as *CHC elitism* (Eshelman, 1991). When the difference in the population became sufficiently small, the 10 best solutions were taken as starting points for FP. These results showed that by using GAs or quartic preliminary search, the results of FP yielded a higher accuracy in optical character recognition.

Exercises

6.1. Assume that for any given normalized direction **u**, an algorithm finds the exact minimum of $E(-)$ along the line determined by that direction from the current weight point **v** to **v** + **u**. Must the algorithm converge to a local minimum if we pick directions at random? What if we use the gradient to obtain the local direction of steepest descent? Are any other conditions required on $E(-)$?

6.2. Write an algorithm and computer program (*uronn*) for univariate random optimization that uses bipolar sigmoids as activation functions. Train the MLP on the Digit12 data in Appendix 11.

6.3. Repeat the above problem for *qronn* (quadratic random optimization). Train it on the Digit12 dataset from Appendix 11. Compare the results of the training with those from Exercise 6.2 above.

6.4. Analyze how the training with random optimization can be accelerated by adapting the probability distributions from the which the weights are drawn. Is there any kind of optimality involved with these distributions?

6.5. Write a random optimization algorithm that chooses multiple unit direction vectors $\{\mathbf{u}^{(p)}\}$ and then selects a direction based on the error values in $\{E(\mathbf{v} + \mathbf{u}^{(p)})\}$. When this direction has been selected, then minimize E in that direction in some fashion (quadratic or cubic). What are the tradeoffs.

6.6. Develop a way to estimate a weight set based on a sample of several weight sets obtained on iterations that lowered the TSSE. The estimated weight set can be a convex combination of the sample weight sets, or other extension of a weighted average. The coefficients are greater for a weight set with lower SSE. Discuss the advantages and disadvantages.

6.7. Write a computer program that uses random optimization during the early iterations, and then switches to FP with adaptive step gain. Note that if the weights are to be handed off from one to another algorithm, then both must use the same sigmoid activations and must also use the same alpha values, and so on. Train it on the Digit12 and Parity3 datasets from Appendix 11.

6.8. Print the digits 0, 1,..., 9 neatly in a box of 8×8 (grid) cells of equal size. Divide the box of 64 cells into 16 square *sections* of 4 cells each and use the proportion of black to total cells in each section as features (feature values will be 0, 0.25, 0.5, 0.75, and 1.0). Assuming black (0) text on white (1) background, make up a set of exemplars for the digits, and train an MLP using random optimization to recognize the digits. Test the learning on the exemplars and a set of new samples. Note: Use 0.1 and 0.9, respectively, for 0 and 1.

6.9. Discuss the following technique for the *uronn* algorithm: after initial iterations with small I_S values, check to see what each weight contributes to the decrease in the TSSE over the sample, and then hold constant (do not train) those weights that contribute an insignificant amount. Instead, train the important weights with larger samples. Would the reduction in processing be worth the extra computation to determine the contributions?

6.10. Repeat Exercise 6.9 above, but instead of not changing the weights that contribute negligibly to the TSSE, change those weights with very large steps to move them to a region where the descent will be more pronounced. Discuss the tradeoffs between this and the previously given strategy in the above exercise.

6.11. Write a computer program to implement the *cubronn* algorithm. Train it on the Digit12 data from Appendix 11. Compare the results with those of Exercise 6.2 and 6.3 above.

6.12. Write an algorithm that uses *uronn* for 200 iterations to obtain a good initial weight set and then uses the Riedmiller–Braun algorithm to converge quickly.

6.13. Write a computer program for training an MLP using a genetic algorithm. Train it on the Digit12 dataset of Appendix 11. This dataset is an easy one to train on, so the GA should do fairly well if it is to be competitive with *cubronn*. Compare the results with those of Exercises 6.2, 6.3, and 6.11 above.

6.14. Write an algorithm to train a feedforward MLP by a genetic algorithm that selects the directions to search from a fixed initial weight set, rather than selecting the weights.

Then use an efficient technique to find the minimum in that direction through the weight space. The fitness measure is the TSSE. The search could be done by cubic or quartic approximation of the TSSE function on the directions selected by the GA.

6.15. Write out a complete computer program for the *quartron* algorithm. Make a flow chart for it and check the steps. Run it on the Digit12 dataset in Appendix 11.

6.16. Discuss the following process: (i) Use *quartron* to train on a set of exemplar pairs, (ii) eliminate all weights near zero by setting them at zero, and (iii) further train the MLP with the eliminated weights kept at zero (do not update weights that are zero). Experiment with this technique. Does it decrease the errors? Is the learning valid?

6.17. Design an algorithm that uses the high speed power of steepest descent on the weights at the output layer, where the computations are simple and quick, but uses a line search in random directions on the weights at the hidden layer. Describe its advantages and disadvantages.

6.18. Repeat Exercise 6.17 to modify the *slickprop* algorithm (see Section 4.9). Does this eliminate saturation (see Section 5.3)?

References

Anderson, R. L. (1953), Recent advances in finding the best operating conditions, *J. Am. Stat. Assoc.*, vol. 48, 147–169.

Atmar, W. (1994), Notes on the simulation of evolution, *IEEE Trans. Neural Networks*, vol. 6, no. 1, 130–147.

Baba, N. (1989), A new approach for finding the global minimum of error function of neural networks, *Neural Networks*, vol. 2, no. 5, 367–373.

Baba, N., Shoman, T., and Sawaragi, Y. (1977), A modified convergence theorem for a random optimization method, *Inf. Sci.*, vol. 13, 159–166.

Baba, N. Mogami, Y., Kohzaki, M., Shiraishi, Y., and Yoshida, Y. (1994), A hybrid algorithm for finding the global minimum of error function of neural networks and its applications, *Neural Networks*, vol. 7, no. 8, 1253–1265.

Bremermann, H. J. (1962), Optimization through evolution and recombination, in *Self-Organizing Systems*, edited by M. C. Yovits, G. T. Jacobi, and G. D. Goldstine, Spartan Books, Washington, D.C., pp. 93–106.

Cooper, L., and Steinberg, D. (1970), *Introduction to Methods of Optimization*, Saunders, Philadelphia.

Dahl, E. D. (1987), Accelerated learning using the generalized delta rule, *Proc. First IEEE Int. Conf. Neural Networks*, San Diego, vol. 2, 523–530.

Eshelman, L. J. (1991), The CHC adaptive search algorithm: how to have search when engaging in nontraditional genetic recombination, in *Foundations of Genetic Algorithms I*, edited by G. J. E. Rawlins, Morgan Kaufmann, San Mateo, CA.

Favreau, R. R., and Franks, R. G. E. (1959), Random Optimization by Analog Techniques, *Proceedings of the 2nd International Conference for Analog Computation*, Strasbourg, France, Presses Academiques Europeenes, Brussels, pp. 437–443.

Fletcher, R. (1965), Functional minimization without evaluating derivatives—a review, *Comput. J.*, vol. 8, no. 1, 33–41.

Fletcher, R. (1970), A new approach to variable metric algorithms, *Comput. J.*, vol. 13, no. 3, 317–322.

Fletcher, R. (1980), *Practical Methods of Optimization, vol. 1: Unconstrained Optimization*, Wiley, New York.

Fletcher, R., and Reeves, C. M. (1964), Function minimization by conjugate gradients, *Comput. J.*, vol. 7, 149–154.

Fogel, D. B. (1994), An introduction to simulated evolutionary optimization, *IEEE Trans. Neural Networks*, vol. 5, no. 1, 3–14.

Fogel, L. J., Owens, A. J., and Walsh, M. J. (1966), *Artificial Intelligence through Simulated Evolution*, Wiley, New York.

Fraser, A. S. (1957), Simulation of genetic systems by automatic digital computers, I. Introduction, *Australian J. Biol. Sci.*, vol. 10, 484–491.

Gill, P. E., Murray, W., and Wright, M. H. (1981), *Practical Optimization*, Academic Press, London.

Goldberg, D. E. (1989), *Genetic Algorithms in Search, Optimization, and Machine Learning*, Addison-Wesley, Reading, MA.

Gonzalez-Seco, J. (1992), A genetic algorithm as the learning procedure for neural networks, *Proc. IEEE/INNS Int'l Conf. Neural Networks*, vol. 1, 835–840.

Harp, S. A, Samad, T., and Guha, A. (1989), Towards the genetic synthesis of neural networks, *Third International Conference on Genetic Algorithms*, Morgan Kaufmann, San Mateo, CA.

Himmelblau, D. M. (1972), *Applied Nonlinear Programming*, McGraw-Hill, New York.

Holland, J. H. (1975), *Adaptation in Natural and Artificial Systems*, University of Michigan Press, Ann Arbor, MI.

Hooke, R., and Jeeves, T. A. (1961), Direct search solutions of numerical and statistical problems, *J. ACM*, vol. 8, 212.

Hopfield, J. J. (1982), Neural networks and physical systems with emergent collective computational abilities, *Proc. Natl. Acad. Sci.*, vol. 79, 2554–2558.

Kitano, H. (1990), Empirical study on the speed of convergence of neural networks training using genetic algorithms, *Proc. AAAI-90*.

Kosko, B. (1992), *Neural Networks and Fuzzy Systems*, Prentice-Hall, Englewood Cliffs.

Looney, C (1993), Neural networks as expert systems, *J. Expert Syst. Appl.*, vol. 6, no. 2, 129–136.

Looney, C. (1996), Stabilization and speed up of convergence in training feedforward neural networks, *Neurocomputing* vol. 10, 7–31.

Lootsma, F. A., editor (1972), *Numerical Methods for Non-linear Optimization*, Academic Press, New York.

Louis, S., *Genetic Algorithms as A Computational Tool for Design*, Ph.D. Dissertation, Indiana University, Aug. 1993.

Malthus, T. R. (1826), *An Essay on the Principle of Population, as it Affects the Future Improvement of the Society*, 6th edition, Murray, London.

Matyas, J. (1965), Random optimization (English translation), *Autom. Remote Control* vol. 26, 246–253.

McInerney, M., and Dhawan, A. (1993), Use of genetic algorithms with backpropagation in training of feedforward neural networks, *Proc. IEEE Int. Conf. Neural Networks*, vol. 1, 203–208.

Mital, K. V. (1976), *Optimization Methods*, Wiley Eastern Ltd., New Delhi (Wiley, New York).

Montana, D. J., and Davis, Lawrence (1989), Training feedforward neural networks using genetic algorithms, *Proc. 11th Joint Int. Conf. Artif. Intell.*, 762–767.

Powell, M. J. D. (1970), A survey of numerical methods for unconstrained optimization, *SIAM Rev.*, vol. 12, 79.

Rumelhart, D. E., Hinton, G. E., and Williams, R. J. (1986), Learning internal representations by error backpropagation, in *Parallel and Distributed Processing: Explorations in the Microstructure of Cognition*, edited by D. E. Rumelhart and J. L. McClelland, MIT Press, Cambridge, MA, pp. 318–362.

Shea, Y., and Looney, C. (1992), Random optimization of neural networks with sensitivity based pruning of weights, *Proc. 1992 Golden West Int. Conf. on Intell. Syst.*, Reno, 18–23.

Solis, F., and Wets, J. (1981), Minimization by random search techniques, *Math. Oper. Res.* 6, 19–30.

Sudeep, S., Looney, C., and Louis, S. (1995), Computational experiments in training feedforward neural networks, *Fourth Golden West Int. Conf. Intell. Syst.*, San Francisco, ISCA.

Whitley, D., and Hanson, T. (1989), Optimizing neural networks using faster, more accurate genetic search, *Third International Conference on Genetic Algorithms*, Morgan Kaufmann, San Mateo, CA.

Whittle, P. (1971), *Optimization under Constraints*, Wiley, Chichester.

Wright, S. (1932), The roles of mutation, inbreeding, crossbreeding, and selection in evolution, *Proc. 6th Int. Congr. Genetics*, Ithaca, NY, vol. 1, 356–366.

Wright, Alden (1991), Genetic algorithms for real parameter optimization, appeared in *Foundations of Genetic Algorithms*, edited by G. J. E. Rawlins, Morgan Kaufmann, San Mateo, CA, pp. 205–218.

Chapter 7

Advances in Network Algorithms for Classification and Recognition

This chapter reviews some important applicable research on other paradigms for classification and recognition.

7.1. Unsupervised Competitive Learning Networks

A General Competitive Learning Algorithm

The training of a recognition system requires a sample of Q exemplar feature vectors $\{\mathbf{x}^{(q)}: q = 1,..., Q\}$ from K classes, where each such vector $\mathbf{x}^{(q)} = (x_1^{(q)},..., x_N^{(q)})$ has N standardized features (components) in [0,1]. A classification network must partition these feature vectors into K clusters that represent the K classes. A neurode may be used for each cluster in a *competitive learning* (CL) network that employs a single layer of $M = K$ neurodes (one for each class). Each neurode contains a *center vector* $\mathbf{v}^{(m)} = (v_1^{(m)},..., v_N^{(m)})$ that represents the mth neurode. A scaling function I_m specifies a sign and magnitude. The center weight vector for each neurode is also called the *neurodal center vector* because it serves as the center of a cluster represented by that neurode.

The general high-level *competitive learning algorithm* given below uses a *learn-only-if-it-wins* principle to change a neurode on each update (Chung and Lee, 1994). Figure 7.1 presents the network and shows the situation where $\mathbf{v}^{(1)}$ is the winner and gets adjusted. In the

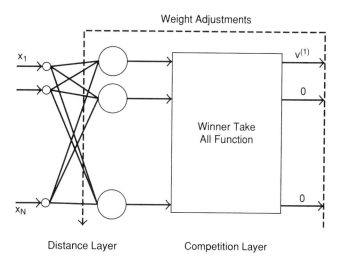

Figure 7.1. A competitive learning network.

following general algorithm, η is the *learning rate* (step gain), I_m is a scaler, and each neurodal center vector $\mathbf{v}^{(m)}$ is to be adjusted toward the exemplar.

Step 1. /Initialize the system: $K =$ number of competing neurodes, $Q =$ no. input vectors/
input K; input Q;   /K is give number of classes/
$M \leftarrow K$;   /M is no. of neurodes in single layer/
for $m = 1$ to M do   /Randomly select centers/
    draw $\mathbf{v}^{(m)}$ randomly in $[0,1]^N$;   /$v_n^{(m)}$ is uniformly distributed in
                                                         $[0,1]$/

Step 2. /Compute distances between feature vectors and center vectors, update neurodes/
for $q = 1$ to Q do   /Present qth exemplar to network/
    for $m = 1$ to M do   /Compute distance to each neurode/
        $D_{qm} \leftarrow \|\mathbf{x}^{(q)} - \mathbf{v}^{(m)}\|^2$;   /$m$th neurode has center vector $\mathbf{v}^{(m)}$/
    find m^* so D_{qm^*} is minimum distance;   /Minimum distance winner take all/
    for $m = 1$ to M do   /Update neurode centers/
        $\mathbf{v}^{(m)} \leftarrow \mathbf{v}^{(m)} + \eta I_m[\mathbf{x}^{(q)} - \mathbf{v}^{(m)}]$;   /$I_{m^*} = 1$; $I_m = 0$, $m \neq m^*$ may be
                                                         used/

Step 3. /Stop or repeat another learning epoch again/
if stopping criterion is met then stop; else go to Step 2;

A Gradient Unsupervised Competitive Learning Algorithm

The next algorithm is also described in Chung and Lee (1994). This algorithm employs the competitive learning algorithm above and is called the *unsupervised competitive learning* (UCL) algorithm because it self-organizes (performs clustering). In addition to each neurodal center vector $\mathbf{v}^{(m)}$, it also uses a binary *neurodal coefficient* w_{qm} for each mth neurode and each qth feature vector. This coefficient weights the distances used in the competitive learning (CL) algorithm. Let $F(W,V)$ be the error function to be minimized, where $W = \{w_{qm}: 1 \leq m \leq M, 1 \leq q \leq Q\}$ is the set of neurodal coefficients and $V = \{\mathbf{v}^{(m)}: 1 \leq m \leq M\}$ is a set of neurodal center vectors. F is defined by

$$F(W,V) = \sum_{(q=1,\,Q)}\sum_{(m=1,\,M)} w_{qm} D_{qm} \tag{7.1}$$

The constraints on W are

$$\sum_{(m=1,\,M)} w_{qm} = 1, \qquad w_{qm} \in \{0,1\} \tag{7.2}$$

for each q $(q = 1,\dots, Q)$ and also for each q

$$w_{qm*} = 1, \qquad \text{if } D_{qm*} = \min\{D_{qm}: 1 \leq m \leq M\}$$

$$w_{qm} = 0, \qquad \text{otherwise} \tag{7.3}$$

The UCL algorithm is similar to the CL algorithm, except for the updating, so Step 2 becomes the new Step 2* given below. The difference is that this algorithm uses the gradient of $F(W,V)$ in a steepest descent adjustment of the centers $\{\mathbf{v}^{(m)}\}$.

Step 2*. /Winning neurode learns to exclusion of all other neurodes/
 for $q = 1$ to Q do   /Present each $\mathbf{x}^{(q)}$ to network/
  for $m = 1$ to M do   /Compute distance to each neurode/
   $D_{qm} \leftarrow \|\mathbf{x}^{(q)} - \mathbf{v}^{(m)}\|^2$;
  find minimum distance D_{qm*};   /Competition by min. distance/
  for $m = 1$ to M do
   if $m = m^*$, then   /Use Equation (7.4) below to update/
    $\mathbf{v}^{(m)} \leftarrow \mathbf{v}^{(m)} - \eta[\nabla F(W,V)]$;   /winning neurode via steepest descent/
                                                 /Others remain static/

The winning neurode update can also be written in the simplified form

$$\mathbf{v}^{(m*)} = \mathbf{v}^{(m*)} - \eta[\nabla F(W,V)] = \mathbf{v}^{(m*)} + \eta w_{qm*}[\mathbf{x}^{(q)} - \mathbf{v}^{(m*)}]$$

so that

$$\mathbf{v}^{(m*)} = \mathbf{v}^{(m*)} + \eta[\mathbf{x}^{(q)} - \mathbf{v}^{(m*)}] \tag{7.4}$$

A Frequency-Sensitive Technique to Prevent Underutilization

The UCL problem of *underutilization of neurodes* was mentioned by Grossberg (1976) and Ahalt et al. (1990). In some cases, a subset of well-located neurodes does all of the learning, which may mean that there are too many neurodes. A modification to the UCL algorithm called *frequency-sensitive* competitive learning (FSCL) addresses this problem. In order to give the other neurodes a chance to learn and thus be utilized along with the winner, the winning distance is penalized by too many successes. This gives other neurodes a chance to become cluster centers. The distance functions are modified (Krishnamurthy et al., 1990) by defining a new "distance" via

$$d_{qm} = D_{qm}n_m \tag{7.5}$$

where n_m is the number of times neurode m won in the previous learning competitions. The more neurode m wins, the less likely it is to win again according to this regimen. This new distance function forces the neurodes to learn an approximately equal number of times and is one implementation of Grossberg's *conscience principle* (Grossberg, 1976).

7.2. Two Self-Organizing Algorithms for Clustering

The Pal–Bezdek–Tsao Generalized Clustering Algorithm

It is well known that the learning vector quantization (LVQ) method discussed in Section 3.12 depends heavily on initialization. Although convergence occurs, it is sometimes meaningless as far as determining valid clusters when an initial center is outside of the convex hull of the input data (Pal et al., 1993). This is partly due to the fact that the method updates only the winning neurode for every input vector. Pal et al. develop a method called *generalized learning vector quantization* (GLVQ) to overcome such shortcomings. The process is like the UCL algorithm given above, but with a different function $F(W,V)$ whose gradient is used for updating the neurodes. GLVQ updates multiple neurodes rather than just the winner, which is like Kohonen's self organizing feature maps in this respect.

The basic idea here is to use a weighting of the various neurodal centers $\{\mathbf{v}^{(m)}\}$ to update all of them rather than just the winner. Consider the UCL algorithm described above. This time, for each presented exemplar vector $\mathbf{x}^{(q)}$, we let V denote the set of neurodal centers and define

$$F^{(q)}(W,V) = \sum_{(m=1,\,M)} w_{qm} \|\mathbf{x}^{(q)} - \mathbf{v}^{(m)}\|^2 \tag{7.6a}$$

$$w_{qm*} = 1, \quad \text{if } m = m* \tag{7.6b}$$

$$w_{qm} = 1/[\sum_{(p=1,\,M)} \|\mathbf{x}^{(q)} - \mathbf{v}^{(p)}\|^2], \quad \text{if } m \neq m* \tag{7.6c}$$

We adjust the $\{\mathbf{v}^{(m)}: m = 1,..., M\}$ by taking steps in the direction of the negative gradient $-\nabla F(W,V)$ to minimize the error functional $F(W,V)$ over the sequence of exemplar inputs $\{\mathbf{x}^{(q)}: q = 1,..., Q\}$. In other words, we want to minimize the total error function

$$F(W,V) = \sum_{(q=1,\,Q)} F^{(q)}(W,V) = \sum_{(q=1,\,Q)} \sum_{(m=1,\,M)} w_{qm} \|\mathbf{x}^{(q)} - \mathbf{v}^{(m)}\|^2 \tag{7.7}$$

The gradient is found by Pal et al. (1993), under the assumption of certain reasonable conditions. The algorithm is like the UCL. We substitute the following updates (based on the presentation of each $\mathbf{x}^{(q)}$)

$$\mathbf{v}^{(m*)} = \mathbf{v}^{(m*)} + \eta[\mathbf{x}^{(q)} - \mathbf{v}^{(m*)}]\{D_q^2 - D_q + \|\mathbf{x}^{(q)} - \mathbf{v}^{(m*)}\|^2\}/D_q^2 \qquad (7.8)$$

for the winning neurode $m*$ (for fixed q), where

$$D_q = \sum_{(m=1,\,M)}\|\mathbf{x}^{(q)} - \mathbf{v}^{(m)}\|^2$$

For the nonwinning neurodes, the update is

$$\mathbf{v}^{(m)} = \mathbf{v}^{(m)} + \eta[\mathbf{x}^{(q)} - \mathbf{v}^{(m)}]\{\|\mathbf{x}^{(q)} - \mathbf{v}^{(m)}\|^2\}/D_q^2 \qquad (7.9)$$

The *advantages* of this algorithm are as follows: (i) Either all nodes are updated or none are updated on each iteration (for each presented exemplar vector $\mathbf{x}^{(q)}$); (ii) when there is a perfect match, no neurode is updated; (iii) the updating of each neurode $\mathbf{v}^{(m)}$ is proportional to the inverse of its distance to the presented datum $\mathbf{x}^{(q)}$; (iv) the process attempts to minimize a well-defined objective function; and (v) the process learns when the initial vectors are outside of the convex hull of the exemplar inputs. Further, the learning appears to be insensitive to the initial choice of center vectors in that the final cluster centers are essentially the same (up to three digits of precision). This is unlike LVQ, where different initializations can lead to quite different solutions (Pal et al., 1993). *In practice*, they use a decreasing learning rate (step gain) η such that $\eta \rightarrow 0$ (slowly, as guaranteed by $\sum \eta \rightarrow \infty$).

The Bi–Bi–Mao Stochastically Competitive Learning Algorithm with Annealing

This *stochastically competitive learning* (SCL) algorithm prevents the settling of the process into a local minimum by incorporating an *annealing* process. The basic idea of the stochastic competition is to update the neurodal center vectors $\mathbf{v}^{(m)}$ via a competition according to a probability distribution for each presented input $\mathbf{x}^{(q)}$ and neurode $\mathbf{v}^{(m)}$, defined by

$$P_m(\mathbf{x}^{(q)}) = \exp[-\|\mathbf{x}^{(q)} - \mathbf{v}^{(m)}\|^2/T]/[\sum_{(k=1,\,M)}\exp[-\|\mathbf{x}^{(q)} - \mathbf{v}^{(k)}\|^2/T] \qquad (7.10)$$

T is a constant called the *temperature*. The *state* of the network $\{\mathbf{v}^{(1)},...,\mathbf{v}^{(M)}\}$, which is also called the *codebook V*, is to be updated in the Kohonen self-organizing manner via

$$\mathbf{v}^{(m*)} = \mathbf{v}^{(m*)} + \eta^{(m*)}[\mathbf{x}^{(q)} - \mathbf{v}^{(m*)}] \qquad (7.11a)$$

for the winning neurode $m*$, but for all other neurodes, the static update is

$$\mathbf{v}^{(m)} = \mathbf{v}^{(m)}, \ m \neq m* \qquad (7.11b)$$

There is a separate learning rate $\eta^{(m)}$ for each mth neurode.

When T is large, the state moves are "blind" so that the vector quantizer *melts*—that is, pulls away from any local minimum. As T decreases, the spread of the distribution decreases and the probability values increase, so the system moves with more confidence, probabilistically. At $T = 0$, it uses the Euclidean distance criterion to determine the winner. In other words, the neurode $\mathbf{v}^{(m*)}$ with the greatest probability value is the winner when $T > 0$, but in the limit it coincides with the minimum Euclidean distance criterion used by Kohonen. A fast *cooling strategy* for decreasing T rapidly over the epochs yields quicker learning, but the learning is not as satisfactory. On the other hand, a slow cooling strategy yields an excellent solution, but takes too much computing time. The cooling strategy used in Bi et al. (1994) is a tradeoff between $T = c/\log(1 + L)$, where c is a constant and L is the epoch number, and $T = (T_0)(\rho^L)$, where T_0 is a constant and $0 < \rho < 1$. The first cools too slowly, while the latter cools too quickly. Bi et al. use

$$T = c/L \qquad (7.12)$$

The learning rate, which is different for each of the M neurodes, is defined by

$$\eta^{(m)} = 1/[A + n_m] \qquad (7.13)$$

where A is a constant and n_m is the number of times $\mathbf{v}^{(m)}$ has been updated. From Equations (7.11) and (7.13), the $(n_{m*} + 1)^{\text{st}}$ update is the convex combination

$$\mathbf{v}^{(m*)}(n_{m*} + 1) = [1 - n_{m*}\eta^{(m*)}]\mathbf{v}^{(m)}(n_{m*}) + [n_{m*}\eta^{(m*)}]\mathbf{x}^{(q)}(n_{m*}) \qquad (7.14a)$$

After r_1 updates have been done at the mth neurode, its center is

$$\mathbf{v}^{(m)} = [A/(A + r_1)]\mathbf{v}^{(0)} + \sum_{(r=1, r_1)}[\mathbf{x}^{(q)}(r)/(A + r_1)] \qquad (7.14b)$$

When $A = 0$, $\mathbf{v}^{(m)}$ becomes the sample mean of the presented exemplar vectors and the convergence has rate $1/n_m$, but forgets its previous training. Bi et al. use small A, where $A > 0$. The algorithm is given below.

Step 1. /Initialize/
input ϵ;   /$\epsilon > 0$ is very small/
for $m = 1$ to M do
  initialize $n_m \leftarrow 0$;   /Number of updates of $\mathbf{v}^{(m)}$/
  draw $\mathbf{v}^{(m)}$ randomly in $[0,1]^N$;   /Draw centers, $0 \leq v_n^{(m)} \leq 1$/

Step 2. /Present each exemplar, compute all probabilities, find winner/
for $q = 1$ to Q do   /present $\mathbf{x}^{(q)}$ to the network/
  for $m = 1$ to M do
    compute $P_m(\mathbf{x}^{(q)})$;   /Equation (7.10), exponential function/
  find $m*$ for maximum value $P_{m*}(\mathbf{x}^{(q)})$;
  for $m = 1$ to M do
    update $\mathbf{v}^{(m)}$;   /Use Equations (7.11a,b) for update/

Step 3. /If process has annealed, then stop, else continue it/
if $T > \epsilon$, then
  update T;   /Use Equation (7.12)/

go to Step 1;
else stop;

Bi et al. used $c = 20$, $c = 10$, and $c = 5$ in Equation (7.12), with the latter one providing the best results on the data used. They used $A = 0$, $A = 1$, and $A = 5$, but $A = 1$ was most satisfactory. They also used an adaptive strategy, where they made a copy of the codebook $V = \{\mathbf{v}^{(1)},..., \mathbf{v}^{(M)}\}$, reinitialized $\{n_m\}_{m=1, M}$, and trained further on novel data. If the new codebook were not close to the previous one, it was replaced. The *advantage* of this method over LVQ is that the learning is better. The *disadvantage* is the same as for all annealing methods: The computation takes a long time.

7.3. The McKenzie–Alder Unsupervised (Dog–Rabbit) Training Algorithm

Desirable Clustering Properties

The unsupervised learning problem is equivalent to that of finding clusters in sample data. The K-means algorithm does this, but it depends upon the initial ordering (the set of final clusters is different for different initial centers), and it requires K to be given. For incorrect K it finds the given number K of cluster centers so that one center may be found for two or more classes or two or more centers may be found for a single class. Note that clusters based on assignment by minimum distance to the centers are linearly separable, but lots of small clusters can represent linearly separable subclasses that can be adjoined to form nonconvex classes. Such adjoining requires another layer of output neurodes and the extra training of their weights.

The clustering strategy of McKenzie and Alder (1994) moves a neurodal center vector toward the currently presented input datum (exemplar vector) under a dynamic potential while using (i) a degree of *lateral inhibition* to move one neurode significantly more toward the presented datum and (ii) a policy of *habituation* so that when the neurode enters a region of clustered data, it stabilizes by not moving away. The main ideas are that when an input vector $\mathbf{x}^{(q)}$ is presented to the network, the neurode $\mathbf{v}^{(m*)}$ closest to $\mathbf{x}^{(q)}$ moves toward it, but the other neurodes move only a slight amount toward it. The winning neurodal center ("dog") will not move away later by chasing other exemplar vectors ("rabbits") that are farther away. McKenzie and Alder relate this to the dogs and rabbits game, where a rabbit (a presented input vector) pops up out of a hole. The nearest dog (neurodal center) barks and runs toward the rabbit, but the other dogs (neurodes) do not move much because they know the barking dog is closer. The more rabbits (data) a particular dog (neurode) chases, the more fatigued it becomes so that it doesn't run as far. Thus at the end of the game, each dog is resting in the midst of a group (cluster) of rabbits. The barking dog models lateral inhibition and the fatigue principle represents habituation.

The dynamic by which neurodes move is a function of the distance $D_{qm} = \left\| \mathbf{x}^{(q)} - \mathbf{v}^{(m)} \right\|$ between the rabbit $\mathbf{x}^{(q)}$ and the dog $\mathbf{v}^{(m)}$. This function, $d = d(D_{qm})$, provides the learning rate (step gain), which must (i) be nonnegative, (ii) be zero at $D_{qm} = 0$, (iii) reach its maximum value of 1 when $D_{qm} = 1$, (iv) have a large positive slope near zero, and (v) go to zero quickly as $D_{qm} \to \infty$. Figure 7.2 presents the form of the required function that can be represented by

Figure 7.2. The learning rate function.

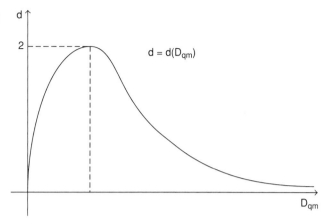

$$d(D_{qm}) = 2D_{qm}/(1 + D_{qm})^p \tag{7.15}$$

where $p > 1$. This leads to the updating

$$\mathbf{v}^{(m)} = \mathbf{v}^{(m)} + d(D_{qm})[\mathbf{x}^{(q)} - \mathbf{v}^{(m)}] \tag{7.16}$$

of each neurode $\mathbf{v}^{(m)}$.

Habituation is the principle whereby a neurode $\mathbf{v}^{(m)}$ that approaches a cluster center remains in the vicinity. The fatigue parameter introduced by McKenzie and Alder (1994) is the exponent p in $d(D_{qm})$ in Equation (7.15) above, which is replaced by f_m at the mth neurode. The new learning rate function becomes

$$d(D_{qm}) = 2D_{qm}/(1 + D_{qm})^{f_m} \tag{7.17}$$

where $f_m \geq 1$. When f_m increases, the denominator increases so that $d(D_{qm})$ decreases (the dog becomes more fatigued). Lateral inhibition of the losers requires that all close losers be inhibited by a function $\alpha(D_{qm})$ defined by

$$\alpha(D_{qm}) = D_{qm}/(A + D_{qm}) \tag{7.18}$$

The inhibition parameter is A, where $A > 0$. For large distance D_{qm}, $\alpha(D_{qm})$ is closer to 1, which is the limit as the distance increases without bound. Thus the movement is not inhibited for neurodes that are far away from the presented exemplar. For small distance, $\alpha(D_{qm})$ is smaller and goes to zero as the distance goes to zero, so that loser neurodes close to the presented exemplar are strongly inhibited from moving toward it.

Figure 7.3 shows a simple self-organizing (clustering) network of the Kohonen type where the winning (highest) output y_{m*} identifies the cluster to which the input feature vector belongs. Extra processing to account for habituation and lateral inhibition is not shown in the network, but is done in the dog-rabbit algorithm. To contrast with supervised learning, Figure 7.4 shows the learning vector quantization networks where the outputs are checked

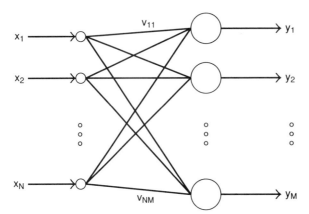

Figure 7.3. A Kohonen-type clustering network.

against targets to determine whether or not they are correct (which determines the updating as described in Section 3.12). Such LVQ networks can learn only with supervised training.

The Dog–Rabbit Algorithm

The updating of the winning neurode center [Equation (7.16)] permits the following algorithm, modified by the fatigue factor of Equation (7.17) for the winning neurode. For the other neurodes, however, the laterally inhibiting function of Equation (7.18) is used in addition to the fatigue factors.

Step 1. Input K; $M \leftarrow K$;   /K is number of clusters/
          input δ;   /Fatigue distance threshold/
          for $m = 1$ to M do
              randomly initialize $\mathbf{v}^{(m)}$ in $[0,1]^N$;   /Uniform distribution on $[0,1]$/

Step 2. For $q = 1$ to Q do   /Present each $\mathbf{x}^{(q)}$/
              for $m = 1$ to M do   /For each presentation,/
                  compute D_{qm};   /get distances to neurodes and/
              find index m^* for minimum D_{qm^*};   /find minimum distance/
              for $m = 1$ to M do   /Update centers based on $\mathbf{x}^{(q)}$/
                  if $m = m^*$ then   /Update winner and losers/
                      $\mathbf{v}^{(m)} = \mathbf{v}^{(m)} + [(2D_{qm})/(1 + D_{qm})^{fm}][\mathbf{x}^{(q)} - \mathbf{v}^{(m)}]$;   (7.19)
                  else   /Use $\alpha(-)$ of Equation (7.18) on losers/
                      $\mathbf{v}^{(m)} = \mathbf{v}^{(m)} + \alpha(D_{qm})[(2D_{qm})/(1 + D_{qm})^{fm}][\mathbf{x}^{(q)} - \mathbf{v}^{(m)}]$;   (7.20)
              if $D_{qm^*} < \delta$, then increase f_{m^*};   /Increase fatigue of winner/

Step 3. If stopping criterion met, then stop;
          else go to Step 2;

The *advantages* of the dog–rabbit algorithm are as follows: (i) It is essentially independent of the initial neurodal centers $\{\mathbf{v}^{(m)}\}$; (ii) it centers the M neurodes on M valid clusters

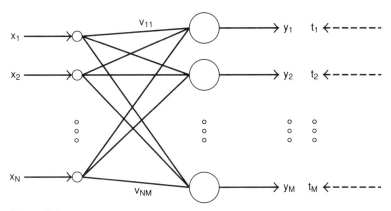

Figure 7.4. Trainable clustering networks: the learning vector quantization network.

even when there are $K > M$ clusters in the data; (iii) for $M > K$ it finds K valid centers (neurodes) and moves the $M - K$ extra neurodes to center points near the center of gravity of the input data; and (iv) it centers neurodes correctly on overlapping data clusters. After training, all centers that do not win over the presentations of all input exemplars can be pruned, so that a correct number K of centers is attained. The *disadvantage* is that each epoch takes approximately $2NM$ calculations for N feature components in the input data and M neurodes, while the k-means algorithm requires only NM. The dog–rabbit algorithm, however, converges in about half the iterations of the k-means algorithm, so that this is not truly a disadvantage. *In practice*, we can start with $f_m = 1$ and increase it by 1 when required in Step 2. To find a value for A, some experimentation is required because McKenzie and Alder (1994) provide no values for A in their study. We suggest a value from 1 to 2.

7.4. Fuzzy Logic Basics

Fuzzy Truths and Fuzzy Sets

A short introduction provides sufficient background (Kruse et al., 1994) for fuzzy systems. In binary logic, a *proposition P* is a statement that must be true or false. It has a truth value of 0 (false) or 1 (true). A two-way electrical switch is either off (0) or on (1). Considering a switch as a two-valued variable S, either no electrons flow ($S = 0$) or they flow at the full rate ($S = 1$) induced by a potential (voltage) energy.

Now consider a valve (faucet) on a water pipe that can be fully off (0), fully on (1), or any proportion f of the way in between ($0 \leq f \leq 1$). This is an analog switch, rather than a binary switch. When the valve is fully open (1), the water molecules can flow according to the full potential (pressure), but if it is open some proportion f, where $f < 1$, then the water flows to an extent (proportion) f of the full flow. In the case of the binary switch, the proposition $P \equiv$ "the switch is on" is either true (1) or false (0), as is the complementary proposition NOT $P \equiv$ "the switch is off (not on)." In the case of the analog (continuous) switch, P is either true (1), false (0), or some proportional truth f in between ($0 \leq f \leq 1$). The *fuzzy truth* (analog truth) f implies the extent, or level, to which a proposition is true. If we pick our propositions carefully, their fuzzy truths can give us continuous quantitative information that can be used to make decisions.

A proposition P may be true or false in binary logic, but in fuzzy logic it may have a fuzzy truth $f = |P|$, $0 \leq |P| \leq 1$ and $|P|$ denotes the fuzzy truth value of P. Propositions are used in reasoning via rules to make decisions. But the question arises as to how do we ascertain the fuzzy truth of a proposition.

A bounded interval on a real axis, which represents a dimension such as temperature T, may be assigned *linguistic variables* such as LOW, MEDIUM, HIGH, and VERY HIGH. It is all relative, but in some context for a certain situation, each of these linguistic variables has a degree of truth for any input temperature value such as $T = 100°C$. The linguistic variables have no hard delimiters between them. Consider MEDIUM and HIGH, so $T = 100°$ has truth extents of MEDIUM and extents of HIGH. The description of a dimension by linguistic variables such as MEDIUM and HIGH allows us to use propositions such as

$$P \equiv \text{``}(T = T_0) \text{ is MEDIUM,''} \quad Q \equiv \text{``}(T = T_0) \text{ is HIGH''}$$

For example, we could have $|P| = 0.5$ and $|Q| = 0.76$, which tells use that "$(T = T_0)$ is HIGH" is more true than is "$(T = T_0)$ is MEDIUM."

If T_0 is at the center of the *region of response* for MEDIUM—that is, where the fuzzy truth is high for P—then P is true to the fullest extent so its fuzzy truth should be $|P| = 1$. If T_0 is near the left or right edge of the MEDIUM response region, then $T = T_0$ is not so MEDIUM so that $|P|$ is closer to zero than unity.

We use *fuzzy set membership functions* (Zadeh, 1965) to assign fuzzy truths to propositions involving linguistic variables. The bounded interval of interest for a variable T is called the *universal set U*. Each fuzzy set is defined on its universal set by a membership function. Regular *crisp* (nonfuzzy) set membership functions $\phi_X(x)$ for a subset X of U take on only the two values on the universal set U ($\phi_X(x)$ is called the *characteristic function* for X), which are

$$\phi_X(x) = 1, \quad \text{if } x \in X$$

$$\phi_X(x) = 0, \quad \text{if } x \notin X \ (x \in U - X)$$

A fuzzy set membership function, however, has a range of values between 0 and 1. Let $\mu_{\text{MED}}(t)$ give the extent to which a temperature value $T = t$ is in the MEDIUM region of response ($0 \leq \mu_{\text{MED}}(t) \leq 1$). This is the fuzzy set membership function for MEDIUM. Figure 7.5 presents a fuzzy set membership function for the linguistic variable MEDIUM for T. The process of obtaining fuzzy truths for a value $T = t$ is called the *fuzzification* of t. Any value t of temperature is *fuzzified* by putting t through the mapping $t \rightarrow \mu_{\text{MED}}(t)$. Because there are no hard boundaries between the regions that the linguistic variables (such as MEDIUM) represent, the fuzzification of t involves putting it through a fuzzy set membership function for each of the linguistic variables on U via

$$t \rightarrow \mu_{\text{LOW}}(t), \quad t \rightarrow \mu_{\text{MED}}(t), \quad t \rightarrow \mu_{\text{MED\_HI}}(t), \quad t \rightarrow \mu_{\text{HI}}(t)$$

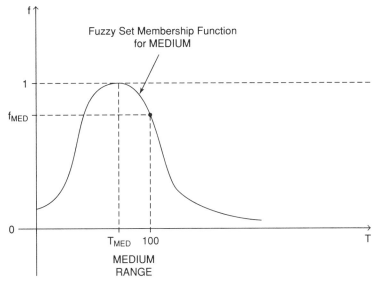

Figure 7.5. A fuzzy set membership function for T = MEDIUM.

The usual case is that only one or two of these will be sufficiently high so as to be useful for a single given value t.

The bell-shaped (Gaussian) fuzzy set membership function shown in Figure 7.5 is a convenient form defined by

$$f(T) = \exp[-(T - T_{\text{MED}})^2/2\sigma_{\text{MED}}^2]$$

that depends upon the two parameters T_{MED} and σ_{MED}. There is a central point at $T = T_{\text{MED}}$ such that the fuzzy truth is 1.0. Moving away from this point on either side, the fuzzy truth (extent) that T is MEDIUM becomes slightly less until a region is reached where it falls off rapidly (values of T become not very MEDIUM). Figure 7.5 presents a Gaussian fuzzy set membership function for the proposition $P \equiv$ "$T = 100$ is MEDIUM." While trapezoidal and triangular membership functions are in widespread use, Gaussian functions are easier to store and manipulate as two parameters T and σ. Triangular membership functions decrease too rapidly as the variable moves away from the maximum and the trapezoidal membership functions do not decrease in the immediate vicinity of the central maximum. Gaussians, however, behave remarkably well.

Consider now the dimension s of the speed of a vehicle. The total practical range U is the universe of discourse as far as speed values are concerned for a given context; that is, $U = [0, s_{\text{max}}]$ for some upper bound s_{max}. We may use, for example, the propositions $P \equiv$ "the speed is LOW," $Q \equiv$ "the speed is MEDIUM," $R \equiv$ "the speed is MEDIUM HIGH," and $S \equiv$ "the speed is VERY HIGH." The fuzzy truth of Q is, then, the extent to which a given value $s = s_0$ is in the range MEDIUM. If s_0 is at the central point of the MEDIUM region of response of U, then $|Q| = 1$. If not, then $|Q| = f$ such that $0 < f < 1$.

Figure 7.6 shows Gaussian fuzzy set membership functions for each of the linguistic variables LOW, MEDIUM, MEDIUM HIGH, and VERY HIGH for the speed dimension. When, for example, s takes the central value μ_{MED} that gives the maximum fuzzy value for MEDIUM, then s is the most MEDIUM that it can be. As the value for s moves away from the maximum slightly, s is still MEDIUM with a high fuzzy truth. As the value moves away farther, it becomes less MEDIUM and becomes more something else, such as LOW or MEDIUM HIGH. We could set the intersections of the fuzzy set membership functions at the fuzzy value of $f = 0.5$ so that any speed s would have a fuzzy truth of at least 0.5 for one linguistic variable.

Suppose that a measurement yields $s = s_0$ as shown in Figure 7.6. Then "the speed is MEDIUM" has a fuzzy truth of f_1, while "the speed is MEDIUM HIGH" has a fuzzy truth of f_2. Both of these propositions are true in that s_0 belongs to the fuzzy sets for both linguistic variables MEDIUM and MEDIUM HIGH to a nonnegligible extent. The combination of these two propositions models the speed situation precisely (s_0 is fairly strongly MEDIUM and is also MEDIUM HIGH to a much lesser extent, with $f_1 > f_2$).

If additional linguistic variables are used on U, then the resolution becomes higher. Because we use Gaussian fuzzy set membership functions, they are never zero, but we ignore fuzzy set membership values that have fuzzy values less than $\epsilon > 0$ (e.g., $\epsilon = 0.2$ is useful).

Approximate Reasoning with Fuzzy Logic

It is remarkable that so little formal logic is required to implement successful fuzzy reasoning. In real-world applications, propositions may be *atomic* statements such as, "the temperature is HIGH." They cannot be decomposed into simpler propositions. *Compound* propositions are composed of finitely many atomic (simple) ones combined together by ANDing ($\wedge$), ORing ($\vee$), and NOTing ($\sim$). If P, Q, and R are propositions, then so are, for example,

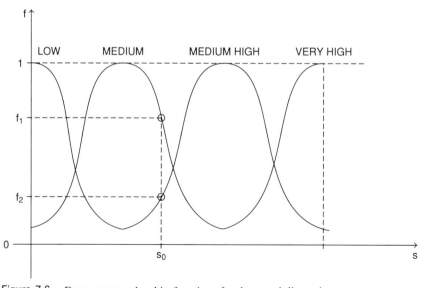

Figure 7.6. Fuzzy set membership functions for the speed dimension.

$$P \vee Q, P \wedge Q, P \vee Q \vee R, P \vee Q \wedge (\sim R)$$

and so on, where $\vee$ denotes OR, $\wedge$ designates AND, and $\sim R$ signifies NOT R. These combinations come from natural language, such as, "Condition P holds or Condition Q holds and Condition R does not hold." Table 7.1 provides some basic fuzzy combinational logic. The last definition is not unique.

Given a situation and a pertinent set of atomic propositions, a *propositional algebra* is a set of: (i) atomic propositions, (ii) all finite combinations of ANDed atomic propositions, (iii) all finite combinations of ORed atomic propositions, (iv) all NOTed atomic propositions, (v) and all combinations of finitely many of the above propositions combined with AND, OR, and NOT. Any implication R $\rightarrow$ S, where R and S are any propositions, is called a *rule*.

The binary law of *modus ponens* states

$$\text{IF } (P \wedge (P \rightarrow Q)) \text{ THEN } Q \tag{7.21}$$

which means: "if P is true and if the rule $(P \rightarrow Q)$ is true, then Q is true." We say that P *enables* $(P \rightarrow Q)$ or *fires* the rule to *activate* Q. But Q may already be true due to some other implication (logical cause), in which case it remains true.

The last combinational formulation of Table 7.1 is one of several forms (Bouchon-Meunier, 1991). *Fuzzy propositional logic* is propositional algebra under fuzzy combinational operations. It has a set of axioms and laws that can be proved from them, just as in regular propositional logic. Many laws of propositional logic do not extend to fuzzy logic, but some important ones do.

Fuzzy modus ponens is the fuzzy version of the main logic law for reasoning by rules. In fuzzy logic, the situation is, well, somewhat fuzzy. Let P have fuzzy truth $|P|$ and suppose the rule $(P \rightarrow Q)$ has fuzzy truth $|P \rightarrow Q|$, both of which are positive (greater than zero). Then

$$(P \wedge (P \rightarrow Q)) \rightarrow Q \tag{7.22}$$

is the fuzzy modus ponens, where we must yet ascertain the fuzzy truth of Q. As above for binary logic, the fuzzy truth of P enables the rule $(P \rightarrow Q)$ to fire and thus activate Q with a fuzzy truth. The fuzzy truth transferred to Q by $P \wedge (P \rightarrow Q)$ is

$$|Q| = |P| \text{ MIN } |P \rightarrow Q| \tag{7.23}$$

Table 7.1.
Fuzzy Combinational Logic Truth Values

AND	$\lvert P \wedge Q \rvert = \lvert P \rvert \text{ MIN } \lvert Q \rvert$
OR	$\lvert P \vee Q \rvert = \lvert P \rvert \text{ MAX } \lvert Q \rvert$
NOT	$\lvert \sim P \rvert = 1 - \lvert P \rvert$
IMPLIES	$\lvert P \rightarrow Q \rvert = 1$, if $\lvert Q \rvert \geq \lvert P \rvert$, else $\lvert P \rightarrow Q \rvert = 1 - (\lvert P \rvert - \lvert Q \rvert)$

If either of P or $(P \rightarrow Q)$ is not true to some extent, then Q is not true to that extent (it takes both P and $(P \rightarrow Q)$ to make it true. Thus NOT Q is not true to the maximum extent of NOT P or NOT $(P \rightarrow Q)$. In the usual situation, the rule has fuzzy truth $|P \rightarrow Q| = 1$, but this need not be the case.

If Q already has a fuzzy truth before the firing, denoted by $|Q|^-$, and $|Q|^- \geq (|P| \text{ MIN } |P \rightarrow Q|)$, then the new fuzzy value $|Q|^+$ remains the same, that is, $|Q|^+ = |Q|^-$. But if $(|P| \text{ MIN } |P \rightarrow Q|) > |Q|^-$, then firing of the rule activates Q with the greater fuzzy truth so that $|Q|^+ = |P| \text{ MIN } |P \rightarrow Q|$. In general form, then, the new truth of Q is expressed by

$$|Q|^+ = |Q|^- \text{ MAX } (|P| \text{ MIN } |P \rightarrow Q|) \tag{7.24}$$

When $|P \rightarrow Q| = 1$ (a common case), then $|Q|^+ = |Q|^- \text{ MAX } |P|$. This is explained in Looney (1988a, 1988b, and 1994).

It is proved in Wang and Mendel (1992) that fuzzy systems with Gaussian fuzzy set membership functions are universal approximators on compact sets. That means that for normalized features, the feature vectors in the hypercube $[0,1]^N$ can be mapped to any output identifier vectors as closely as desired, provided that there are sufficiently many fuzzy sets and fuzzy rules—that is, that the resolution of the system is high enough.

Example 7.1.   Defuzzification and Approximate Reasoning

Consider Figure 7.6 again. Let $P_M \equiv$ "the speed is MEDIUM," and $P_{MH} \equiv$ "the speed is MEDIUM HIGH." Further, assume the rules

$$P_M \wedge P_{MH} \rightarrow Q, \qquad P_M \rightarrow R$$

where $Q \equiv$ "no change in accelerator" and $R \equiv$ "increase accelerator by delta." Assuming that $|Q|^-$ and $|R|^-$ have been reset to zero and that the rules have fuzzy truths of unity (a common situation), then the updates are

$$|Q|^+ = |P_M| \text{ MIN } |P_{MH}|$$
$$|R|^+ = |P_M|$$

Now there are two different fuzzy consequents, Q and R, with two different fuzzy truths for the output variable that designates accelerator change ("no change in accelerator" and "increase accelerator by delta"). When both are true to nonnegligible extents (fuzzy truths), then both need to be taken into account in the decision as to what to do about the accelerator. In this case we take a fuzzy weighted average of the weights $f_1 = |Q|$ and $f_2 = |R|$, using the proportional weights

$$\alpha_1 = f_1/(f_1 + f_2), \qquad \alpha_2 = f_2/(f_1 + f_2) \tag{7.25}$$

These nonnegative weights add up to unity, and so their use constitutes a convex combination.

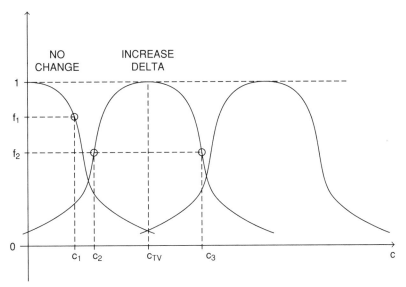

Figure 7.7. Defuzzification of accelerator change.

Figure 7.7 shows the weighted average value for accelerator change c. The value c_{TV}, called the *true value* of the linguistic variable INCREASE_DELTA ("increase accelerator by delta"), is used as the representative value because f_2 intersects that fuzzy set membership function in two points on either side of it at c_2 and c_3, while c_{TV} is the center of the region of response. The fuzzy set membership function for the other linguistic variable, NO_CHANGE, intersects f_1 at c_1. The convex combination, or weighted average output value of c_1 and c_{TV}, using α_1, $\alpha_2 \geq 0$ and $\alpha_1 + \alpha_2 = 1$, is

$$c_{out} = \alpha_1 c_1 + \alpha_2 c_{TV} = [f_1 c_1 + f_2 c_{TV}]/(f_1 + f_2) \tag{7.26}$$

The actual reasoned accelerator change is the value c_{out}. The use of two or more fuzzy values to obtain a resulting value c_{out}, for example, is called *defuzzification*. It provides a more accurate output value than would the use of only a single one such as the value with maximum fuzzy truth, which in this case would be c_1 because f_1 is the maximum of the two fuzzy values.

Working with Fuzzy Rules

From Figure 7.8, we see that the value $T = 100°$ on the T-axis yields fuzzy truths greater than the threshold ϵ for both MEDIUM and HIGH. In other words, $T = 100°$ is a value that belongs to the fuzzy set MEDIUM to the extent f_{MED} and also belongs to the fuzzy set HIGH to the extent f_{HI}. To be able to reason approximately using fuzzy rules with linguistic variables for T, we need two kinds of fuzzy logic: (i) *fuzzy combinational logic* that allows multiple conditions to be put together with AND, OR, and NOT, according to natural language used in human reasoning and (ii) *fuzzy propositional laws* that allow reasoning to be done through implications and substitutions.

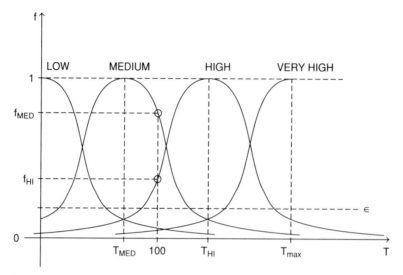

Figure 7.8. Fuzzy set membership truths for $T = 100°$.

The fuzzy combinational logic of Table 7.1 provides the MIN and MAX rules that correspond to AND and OR, respectively. For example, the rule

IF [(T is MEDIUM (f_{MED})) **AND** (T is HIGH (f_{HI})], **THEN** [C is DECREASED (f_{DECR})]

relates a linguistic variable DECREASED for a dimension c (the control knob) with conditions on T, to the *antecedent* (left-hand side) of this rule, which is

$$P \equiv (T \text{ is MEDIUM } (f_{MED})) \textbf{ AND } (T \text{ is HIGH } (f_{HI})$$

The *consequent* (right-hand side) is

$$Q \equiv (c \text{ is DECREASED } (f_{DECR}))$$

The fuzzy truth of P is $f_P = \min\{f_{MED}, f_{HI}\} = f_{MED} \text{ MIN } f_{HI}$.
In the fuzzy OR case, the fuzzy truth of

$$A = B \ (f_B) \textbf{ OR } C \ (f_C)$$

where $f_B = |B|$ and $f_C = |C|$, is $|A| = f_A = \max\{f_B, f_C\}$. The fuzzy truth of **NOT** A (f_A) is $1 - f_A$. The fuzzy truth of the *consequent* (right-hand side) of a rule depends upon the laws of fuzzy propositional logic.

We do not need to use fuzzy rules of the form $(P \textbf{ OR } Q) \rightarrow R$. This is because we may use each part as a separate rule as

$$P \rightarrow R$$

$$Q \rightarrow R$$

and the system is equivalent as long as we can never reduce the fuzzy value of R by an implication (Looney, 1988a). Both rules would be checked according to a schedule and fired if enabled (inclusive OR). We also never use rules of the form: $A \rightarrow (B$ **OR** $C)$. Such rules are not specific (which of B or C or both B and C is true due to the rule being fired?).

It is not necessary to use rules of the form $A \rightarrow (B$ **AND** $C)$, because such a rule can be replaced by the two rules

$$A \rightarrow B$$

$$A \rightarrow C$$

Each of these would be checked also, according to the schedule, to either fire or not fire, so that all right-hand sides (consequents) are activated via fuzzy modus ponens. When two or more rules imply fuzzy truths of the same consequent R, then it is more effective to use defuzzification to obtain |R|.

Some Different Fuzzy Set Membership Functions

Many types of mathematical weightings are nowadays called *fuzzy* and can be used in the fuzzy logic described above. A fuzzy set membership function that fits our intuition or has some explanatory rationale is most useful, but it is also useful to use numbers from 0 to 1 that arise in various weighting schemes. Such weightings can be used as fuzzy truth values and thereby enter into fuzzy reasoning.

For example, consider a gray scale $M \times N$ image of MN pixels (picture elements, or dots in a rectangular array) such that each pixel has gray levels from 0 to 255. This represents 256 shades of gray, or light intensities, where 0 is black (no light intensity) and 255 represents white (full light intensity). The image is the set of pixel values $\{f(m, n): m = 1,..., M$ and $n = 1,..., N\}$. Each pixel value satisfies $0 \leq f(m, n) \leq 255$. We may use the universe U of values 0 to 255 and define the linguistic variable BRIGHT to have fuzzy value 1 at a gray level of 255. Further, for any gray level g, we fuzzify it with respect to the linguistic variable BRIGHT via $\mu_B(g) = g/255$, $0 \leq g \leq 255$.

It is possible to cluster the pixels into groups according to their membership n BRIGHT. First, we find the fuzzy value for each pixel $f(m, n)$ in the image. The pixels that are "close" in fuzzy extent of BRIGHT are lumped together just as in a distance lumping. Next, we find the typical gray level (defuzzification) in each cluster, convert all pixels in each cluster to the typical gray level, and write the results to another image file. This coarser discretization of the gray levels of the image can be useful in segmentation of the image for recognition of blobs contained in the image.

Other types of fuzzification may be purely mathematical. The distance between a given vector $\mathbf{x}$ and each of a population of vectors $\{\mathbf{v}^{(m)}: m = 1,..., M\}$ can be used to determine fuzzy values, just as the gray scale closeness was in the above paragraph. A standardization of the distances yields fuzzy weights via

$$D = \{\sum_{(m=1, M)} \|\mathbf{x} - \mathbf{v}^{(m)}\|^2\}^{1/2}$$

$$D_m = \|\mathbf{x} - \mathbf{v}^{(m)}\| / D$$

$$D_1 + \cdots + D_M = 1$$

Many others are possible, as we shall see in the following sections.

7.5. Unsupervised Fuzzy Competitive Learning Networks

An Unsupervised Fuzzy Competitive Learning Algorithm

The *unsupervised fuzzy competitive learning* (UFCL) algorithm is similar to the unsupervised competitive learning (UCL) given above (Chung and Lee, 1994). The difference is that fuzzy competition and learning are implemented. Instead of only the single winning neurode (minimum distance) being adjusted, each neurode is adjusted to some fuzzy extent. Figure 7.9 presents a UFCL network.

Let $D_{qm} = \|\mathbf{x}^{(q)} - \mathbf{v}^{(m)}\|$ be the distance between the qth input exemplar vector and the mth center vector. The functional

$$F(W,V) = \sum_{(q=1, Q)}\sum_{(m=1, M)} (w_{qm})^p D_{qm} \tag{7.27}$$

is to be minimized subject to the constraints on the fuzzy membership values w_{qm}

$$\sum_{(m=1, M)} w_{qm} = 1, \quad \text{for every fixed } q$$

$$w_{qm} \in [0,1], \quad \text{for all } q \text{ and } m$$

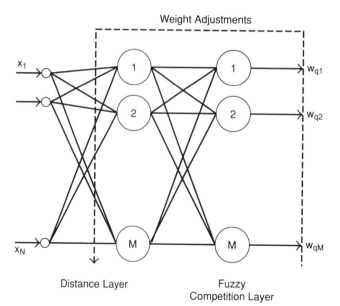

Figure 7.9. The UFCL network.

Distance Layer

Fuzzy Competition Layer

where $W = \{w_{qm}: 1 \leq q \leq Q, 1 \leq m \leq M\}$. The steepest descent adjustment with Lagrangian constraints leads to the update formulation

$$\mathbf{v}^{(m)} = \mathbf{v}^{(m)} - \eta[\nabla F(U,V)] = \mathbf{v}^{(m)} + \eta(w_{qm})^p[\mathbf{x}^{(q)} - \mathbf{v}^{(m)}] \qquad (7.28a)$$

where w_{qm} is the weighting for the qth exemplar and mth center vectors defined as a weighting of distance reciprocals

$$w_{qm} = [1/D_{qm}]^{1/(p-1)}/\sum_{(m=1, M)}[1/D_{qm}]^{1/(p-1)} \qquad (7.28b)$$

The UFCL Algorithm

Step 1. /Initialize the system/
  input K; input Q; $M \leftarrow K$;   /one for each class/
  randomly draw all $\mathbf{v}^{(m)}$ in [0,1];   /initialize neurodes/

Step 2. /Compute distances between feature vectors and weights/
  for $q = 1$ to Q do   /For each exemplar $\mathbf{x}^{(q)}$/
    Denom(q) $\leftarrow$ 0;
    for $m = 1$ to M do   /and neurode $\mathbf{v}^{(m)}$/
      $D_{qm} \leftarrow \|\mathbf{x}^{(q)} - \mathbf{v}^{(m)}\|^2$ /compute distances between them/
      Denom(q) $\leftarrow$ Denom(q) + (1/D_{qm});   /Used in computing w_{qm} below/
    Denom(q) $\leftarrow$ [Denom(q)]$^{1/(p-1)}$;   /Start with $p = 2.2$/

Step 3. /Compute fuzzy weightings w_{qm}/
  for $q = 1$ to Q do   /Present each exemplar $\mathbf{x}^{(q)}$/
    for $m = 1$ to M do
      $w_{qm} \leftarrow [1/D_{qm}]^{1/(p-1)}$/Denom(q);   /Standard inverse weighting/

Step 4. /Update every neurodal center vector—no exclusion/
  for $m = 1$ to M do
    $\mathbf{v}^{(m)} \leftarrow \mathbf{v}^{(m)} + \eta(w_{qm})^p[\mathbf{x}^{(q)} - \mathbf{v}^{(m)}]$;   /$\eta$ is the learning rate/

Step 5. /Repeat Steps 2 through 5 until stopping criterion is satisfied/
  if stopping criterion is met then stop;
  else goto Step 2;

The *advantages* of such fuzzy c-means classifiers (Selim and Kamel, 1992) are that the clusters may touch or overlap, the far away neurodes have a chance to move to the exemplar regions, an objective function is minimized, and closeness criteria are used in the dynamic for the learning process. The *disadvantages* are that the volume of computation can be large and the separation is linear.

In practice, the value $p = 2.2$ is used to start the process and is then reduced over time toward 1. Chung and Lee (1994) put the learning rate η at 0.01, 0.1, or 0.5 and obtained better results with the latter two values. The derivation of the w_{qm} can be found in Bezdek (1981), which develops the fuzzy c-means algorithm for fuzzy pattern recognition. Such derivation uses Lagrange multipliers. Chung and Lee used the monotonic learning rate function of the iteration number r defined by

$$\eta(r) = \eta(0)(1.0 - r/maxtrain) \tag{7.29}$$

where *maxtrain* is the maximum number of training updates allowed. Thus the learning rate is 0 at $r = maxtrain$. Chung and Lee set $maxtrain = 30Q$, so that each of the Q input exemplar feature vectors $\mathbf{x}^{(q)}$ is used 30 times in the training (i.e., 30 epochs). During the operational mode, the neurode with the maximal fuzzy membership value w_{qm*} determines the $m*$ neurode as the winner (representing Class $m*$).

The Park–Dagher Gradient-Based Fuzzy C-Means Algorithm

This algorithm is called the *gradient-based fuzzy c-means* (GBFCM) algorithm by its inventors (Park and Dagher, 1994). It combines the characteristics of (i) single exemplar presentation at a time to the network and (ii) gradient descent (Kohonen, 1986) with the continuous values of membership grades of the *fuzzy c-means* (FCM) algorithm of (Bezdek, 1981). Kohonen's gradient descent uses

$$\mathbf{v}^{(m)} \leftarrow \mathbf{v}^{(m)} - \eta \nabla E(\mathbf{v}^{(m)})$$

where on the qth presentation of $\mathbf{x}^{(q)}$ the error gradient is

$$\nabla E(\mathbf{v}^{(r)}) = (\partial[x_1^{(q)} - v_1^{(m)}]^2/\partial v_1,..., \partial[x_N^{(q)} - v_N^{(m)}]^2/\partial v_N)$$

and so the update becomes

$$\mathbf{v}^{(m)} \leftarrow \mathbf{v}^{(m)} + \eta[\mathbf{x}^{(q)} - \mathbf{v}^{(m)}] \tag{7.30}$$

For the FCM algorithm, Bezdek used

$$F(W,V) = \sum_{(q=1, Q)}\sum_{(m=1, M)} (w_{qm})^p D_{qm}^2 \tag{7.31}$$

where w_{qm} is the membership value $\mathbf{x}^{(q)}$ in the mth cluster, p is a weighting exponent, $D_{qm} = \|\mathbf{x}^{(q)} - \mathbf{v}^{(m)}\|$, M is the number of neurodes in a single layer (one for each cluster, or class), and there are Q exemplar feature vectors $\{\mathbf{x}^{(q)}\}$ of N features each.

Bezdek minimized $F(W,V)$ with

$$w_{qm} = [\sum_{(k=1, M)}(D_{qm}/D_{qk})^{2/(p-1)}]^{-1} \tag{7.32}$$

$$\mathbf{v}^{(m)} = \sum_{(q=1, Q)}\alpha_{qm}\mathbf{x}^{(q)} \tag{7.33}$$

where the α_{qm} are the convex weightings that sum to unity, defined by

$$\alpha_{qm} = (w_{qm})^p/\sum_{(j=1, Q)}(w_{jm})^p \tag{7.34}$$

Equations (7.32) and (7.33) are computed iteratively until the approximate solutions $\{\mathbf{v}^{(m)}\}$ approach a fixed solution.

Park and Dagher use the qth partial function

$$F^{(q)}(W,V) = w_{q1}[\mathbf{x}^{(q)} - \mathbf{v}^{(1)}]^2 + \cdots + w_{qM}[\mathbf{x}^{(q)} - \mathbf{v}^{(M)}]^2 \tag{7.35}$$

subject to the constraint

$$w_{q1} + \cdots + w_{qM} = 1 \tag{7.36}$$

that corresponds to presenting a single exemplar $\mathbf{x}^{(q)}$ to the network at a time. Thus

$$-\eta\nabla F^{(q)}(W,V) = \eta(2w_{q1}(\mathbf{x}^{(q)} - \mathbf{v}^{(1)}),..., 2w_{qM}(\mathbf{x}^{(q)} - \mathbf{v}^{(M)})) \tag{7.37}$$

so that

$$\mathbf{v}^{(m)} = \mathbf{v}^{(m)} + \eta(w_{qm})^2[\mathbf{x}^{(q)} - \mathbf{v}^{(m)}] \tag{7.38}$$

Upon setting

$$\partial F^{(q)}/\partial w_{qm} = 0 \tag{7.39}$$

for each q and m, the solutions found for the membership grades are

$$w_{qm} = 1/\sum_{(k=1, M)}(D_{qm}/D_{qk})^2 \tag{7.40}$$

This completes the Park–Dagher algorithm, which is provided below.

Step 1. Input K, p, ϵ, η; $M \leftarrow K$; error $\leftarrow 0$; $r \leftarrow 0$;
for $m = 1$ to M do
    initialize $\mathbf{v}^{(m)}(0)$ randomly in $[0,1]^N$;

Step 2. $e(r) \leftarrow 0$;
for $q = 1$ to Q do
    for $m = 1$ to M do $D_{qm} \leftarrow \|\mathbf{x}^{(q)} - \mathbf{v}^{(m)}(r)\|$;
    for $m = 1$ to M do $w_{qm} \leftarrow 1/\sum_{(k=1, M)}(D_{qm}/D_{qk})^2$;
    for $m = 1$ to M do
        $\mathbf{v}^{(m)}(r + 1) \leftarrow \mathbf{v}^{(m)}(r) + \eta(w_{qm})^2[\mathbf{x}^{(q)} - \mathbf{v}^{(m)}(r)]$;
    $e(r + 1) \leftarrow e(r) + \|\mathbf{v}^{(m)}(r + 1) - \mathbf{v}^{(m)}(r)\|$;

Step 3. error $\leftarrow e(r)$;
dif $\leftarrow |e(r + 1) - e(r)|$;
if dif < 0.0001, then $\eta \leftarrow (15/16)\eta$;

Step 4.   if error $> \epsilon$ then

$r \leftarrow r + 1$; go to Step 2;

else stop;

An Unsupervised Fuzzy Frequency-Sensitive Competitive Learning Algorithm

The *unsupervised fuzzy frequency-sensitive competitive learning* (UFFSCL) algorithm is essentially the same as the UFCL given above, except that the competition is modulated to make it fairer. Because the UFCL algorithm disposed of the problem of underutilized neurodes, this algorithm may seem to be unnecessary. The simulation runs of Chung and Lee (1994), however, show that it is sometimes more powerful. The distance functions are modified via

$$d_{qm} = D_{qm}\mu_m(r - 1) \tag{7.41}$$

where $\mu_m(r - 1)$ is the accumulated membership winnings for the mth neurode

$$\mu_m(r - 1) = \sum_{(n=1,r-1)}(w_{nm})^p$$

over the previous $r - 1$ competitions. A neurode that has won many times has larger distances and thus is less likely to win again.

An *advantage* of the frequency-sensitive type of algorithm is that it implements the conscience principle of Grossberg (1976) and the conscience method of DeSieno (1988). This overcomes the problem where neurodes with center vectors that are far from any input feature vectors never get a chance to learn (Chung and Lee, 1994), which wastes the network resources.

A Fuzzy Learning Vector Quantization Algorithm

Kohonen's *learning vector quantization* (LVQ) method (Kohonen, 1986) is extended to a fuzzy version in Chung and Lee (1994). Kohonen's version is a *supervised* competitive learning paradigm. Each competing neurode must be labeled beforehand as representing a specific class. Starting with the CL algorithm given in Section 7.1, the LVQ method is different in that the scaling function $I_k(r)$ is defined by either rewarding or punishing a neurode via

$$I_m(r) = 1, \qquad \text{if Class}(\mathbf{v}^{(m)}) = \text{Class}(\mathbf{x}^{(q)}) \tag{7.42a}$$

$$I_m(r) = -1, \qquad \text{if Class}(\mathbf{v}^{(m)}) \neq \text{Class}(\mathbf{x}^{(q)}) \tag{7.42b}$$

The target value t_{qm} for the output of each mth neurode for exemplar input $\mathbf{x}^{(q)}$ must be given to the algorithm. The idea here is to minimize the error of classification. Figure 7.10 displays the *fuzzy learning vector quantization* (FLVQ).

While Kohonen did not minimize a functional, (Chung and Lee, 1994) use

$$F(W,V) = \sum_{(q=1,\, Q)}\sum_{(m=1,\, M)} [(t_{qm})^p - (w_{qm})^p]D_{qm} \tag{7.43a}$$

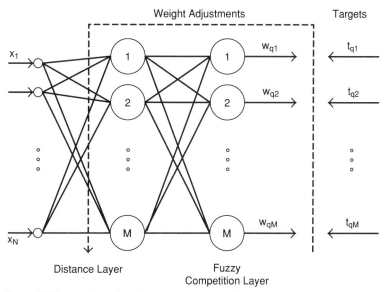

Figure 7.10. A fuzzy learning vector quantization network.

constrained for each fixed q by

$$\sum_{(m=1, M)} w_{qm} = 1$$

where $w_{qm} \in [0,1]$ for all q and m.

Chung and Lee state that without the constraint, $F(W,V)$ would assume the trivial minimal solution that assigns 1 to membership. Without the parameter p, the application of Lagrange multipliers to the w_{qm} produces zeros. The Lagrangian derivation (see Section 10.3, Equations (10.10) through (10.13) yields

$$w_{qm} \leftarrow [1/D_{qm}]^{1/(p-1)} / [\sum_{(n=1, M)}(1/D_{qm})]^{1/(p-1)} \qquad (7.43b)$$

Using the steepest descent with the gradient method

$$\mathbf{v}^{(m)} \leftarrow \mathbf{v}^{(m)} - \eta[\nabla F(W,V)]$$

the update algorithm becomes

$$\mathbf{v}^{(m)} \leftarrow \mathbf{v}^{(m)} + \eta[(t_{qm})^p - (w_{qm})^p][\mathbf{x}^{(q)} - \mathbf{v}^{(m)}] \qquad (7.44)$$

The *advantages* of the FLVQ method are that it knows what class each neurode represents at the start and can force the output toward the output target, the errors between the target and actual outputs are decreased by minimizing the objective function, and the errors are used to determine the fuzzy extents of the weight adjustments. The *disadvantage* is related directly to this, because the algorithm does not perform unsupervised (self-organizing) learning. In computer runs, the FLVQ usually comes out as well or better than the unsupervised algorithms.

7.6. Advances in Functional Link Nets

A Fuzzy Functional Link Net

Huang (1994) applied the fuzzy multiple-layered perceptron (MLP) approach of Keller and Hunt (1985) to the functional link net of Pao (1989) to obtain a useful algorithm for recognition. The Keller–Hunt rule reduces the influence of uncertainties on the linear discrimination boundary, as the algorithm will show. Huang applied the *fuzzy functional link net* (FFLN) to the recognition of valid and invalid seismic traces.

There were four features $\{x_1,..., x_4\}$, but with the addition of six tensor terms of the form $x_i x_j$, a total of 10 features $\{x_1,..., x_{10}\}$ were used. The FFLN consisted of $N = 10$ input components and a single neurode at the single neurodal layer. For comparison, Huang trained an MLP on the same data, so it used $N = 10$ inputs, $M = 5$ hidden neurodes, and $J = 1$ output neurode. Figure 7.11 displays both the 10–1 FFLN and the 10–5–1 MLP.

Huang's FFLN algorithm follows below.

Step 1. /Initialize the weights and threshold, input parameters/
for $n = 1$ to N do
$\quad w_n^{(0)} \leftarrow \text{random}(0,1) - 0.5;$ /$-0.5 < w_n < 0.5$/
$w_{N+1} \leftarrow \text{random}(0,1);$ /Input bias $b = w_{N+1}$/
input $Q;$ /Number of training exemplars used/
input $\eta;$ input $p;$ input $I;$ $r \leftarrow 0;$ /I is number of iterations desired/

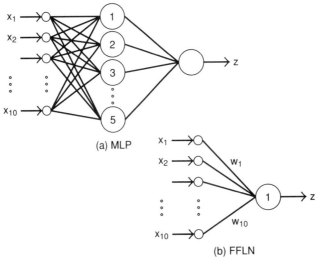

(a) MLP

(b) FFLN

Figure 7.11. The FFLN and MLP networks for seismic trace recognition.

Step 2. /Calculate fuzzy membership values and update weights/
      for $q = 1$ to Q do
            $n_1 \leftarrow$ no. nearest neighbors of $\mathbf{x}^{(q)}$ in Class 1;
            $n_2 \leftarrow Q - n_1$;   /Number of nearest neighbors of $\mathbf{x}^{(q)}$ in/
                                                                      /Class 2/

            if $\mathbf{x}^{(q)}$ is in Class 1, then
                  $f_1^{(r)} \leftarrow 0.51 + (n_1/Q)0.49$;   /Fuzzy membership values for Class 1/
                  $f_2^{(r)} \leftarrow (n_2/Q)0.49$;   /Fuzzy membership values for Class 2/
            else
                  $f_1^{(r)} \leftarrow (n_1/Q)0.49$;   /Fuzzy membership values if Class 2/
                  $f_2^{(r)} \leftarrow 0.51 + (n_2/Q)0.49$;   /Update network output $z^{(q)}$/
            $z^{(q)} \leftarrow h(\Sigma_{(n=1, N+1)} w_n^{(r)} x_n^{(q)})$;   /$w_{N+1}$ is bias b, $x_{N+1}^{(q)} = 1$, all q/
            for $n = 1$ to $N + 1$ do   /Update weights using membership/
                                                               /values/

$$w_n^{(r+1)} \leftarrow w_n^{(r)} + \eta |f_1^{(r)} - f_2^{(r)}|^p \quad \text{/and error between target } t \text{ and } z/$$
$$\times [t^{(q)} - z^{(q)}] x_{n(q)};$$

Step 3. /Check stopping criterion at end of each epoch/
      if $r \geq I$, then stop;
      else $r \leftarrow r + 1$; go to Step 2;

Huang used a total of 32 exemplars $\{\mathbf{x}^{(q)}: q = 1,..., 32\}$ in all, but he trained on 12 of these, of which 6 were valid traces and 6 were invalid ($K = 12$). All 32 exemplars were used for testing. The backpropagation algorithm was used on the MLP network. Both the MLPs and the FFLNs were able to learn sufficiently well that they recognized all 32 exemplars with 100% success. The difference, however, was in training time. The FFLN learned in 4 seconds of computing time, while the MLP required 300 seconds. Huang did not report what values were used for p and η. He reported that the target values were $t^{(k)} = 1$ for Class 1 and $t^{(k)} = -1$ for Class 2 (invalid seismic traces). In the operational (recognition) mode, the computed output is either positive (Class 1) or negative (Class 2), which could be extended to more than two classes.

The Pao–Park–Sobajic Random Vector FLN

Higher-order generalized MLPs were considered by Giles and Maxwell (1987), but were expanded on by Pao et al. (1994) to develop a model called the *random vector functional link net* (RVFLN). This approach had been considered in various forms by Pao in previous work. The basic idea is to move the hidden layer of an *N–M–J* MLP network to a supplemental input layer. This causes a simplification in the network architecture, which then has $N + M$ inputs, of which M are enhanced inputs that are actually the outputs of the M "hidden" neurodes, each of which receives the N inputs as shown in Figure 7.12. While this causes a rather large number of inputs, Pao et al. argue that a large fraction of the enhanced inputs can be pruned. The scheme shown in the figure has the hidden neurodes remaining in an offset hidden position to allow the N original inputs to feed directly (linearly) to the output layer of neurodes.

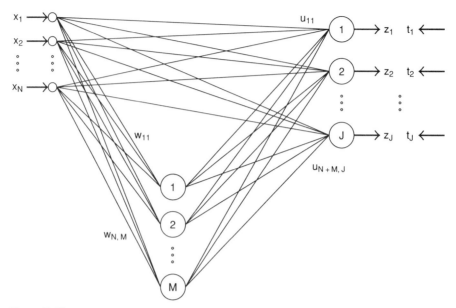

Figure 7.12. The RVFLN model.

The training method of Pao et al. differs significantly from the backpropagation or full-propagation type of steepest descent. The training is greatly simplified and is much quicker than in the usual MLPs. The weights $\{w_{nm}\}$ are not adjusted in any way, but are selected at random under the following constraint: The output of each mth "hidden" neurode, $y_m = h(r_m + b) = h(w_{1m}x_1 + ... + w_{Nm}x_N + b_m)$, where b_m is the bias, is not saturated most of the time. One way to help ensure that the constraint is met is to choose the w_{nm} to be small and to be combinations of positive and negative values.

After the weights $\{w_{nm}\}$ have been randomly drawn in an appropriate manner, the RVFLN is ready for training, which consists of adjusting the weights $u_{11},..., u_{N+M, J}$ to minimize the mean-squared error (MSE)

$$E = [1/(N + M)]\Sigma_{(q=1, Q)}\Sigma_{(j=1, J)}(t_j^{(q)} - z_j^{(q)})^2 \tag{7.45}$$

where $t_j^{(q)}$ is the target output value at the jth output neurode when exemplar $\mathbf{x}^{(q)}$ is input. We take a different approach here to adjusting the weights, but adjust only the $\{u_{pj}\}$ ($p = 1,..., N + M$) as does Pao.

Differentiating E with respect to u_{nj} ($1 \leq n \leq N$), for which there are no hidden layers to pass through, we obtain

$$\partial E/\partial u_{nj} = (\partial E/\partial z_j)(\partial z_j/\partial v_{nj}) = [1/N]\Sigma_{(q=1, Q)}\Sigma_{(s=1, J)}(\partial/\partial u_{nj})(t_s^{(q)} - \Sigma_{(n=1, N)}u_{ns}x_n^{(q)})^2$$

$$= [-2/N]\Sigma_{(q=1, Q)}(t_j^{(q)} - z_j^{(q)})x_n^{(q)} \tag{7.46}$$

Note that this is the fullpropagation mode where all Q exemplars are presented to the network simultaneously. Thus the update on these weights is

$$u_{nj}^{(r+1)} \leftarrow u_{nj}^{(r)} + [2\eta/N]\sum_{(q=1, Q)}(t_j^{(q)} - z_j^{(q)})x_n^{(q)} \tag{7.47}$$

for $n = 1,..., N$ and $j = 1,..., J$.

The weights $u_{N+1, j},..., u_{N+M, j}$ on the fan-in lines from the hidden neurodes to the jth neurode in the output layer are the same as the weights on these lines in a standard N–M–J MLP, so we can use Equation (4.21a) for backpropagation and sum over the Q exemplars. We must, however, replace the derivative of the sigmoid $z_j = g(s_j)$, which is $z_j(1 - z_j)$, with the constant $1/M$ to obtain

$$u_{pj}^{(r+1)} \leftarrow u_{pj}^{(r)} + [2\eta/M]\sum_{(q=1, Q)}(t_j^{(q)} - z_j^{(q)})y_p^{(q)} \tag{7.48}$$

for $u_{N+1, j},..., u_{N+M, j}$ $(p = N + 1,..., N + M)$.

The algorithm for training the RVFLN is analogous to the fullpropagation algorithm for N–M–J MLPs except that Equations (7.47) and (7.48) are used for the updating of the weights. Other than $\{u_{pj}\}$, no other weights are updated. Pao et al. (1994) have indicated that they have a proof that the RVFLN can approximate any vector mapping to any accuracy desired, provided sufficiently many enhanced inputs (hidden neurodes) are used. An outline of that proof appears in Igelnik and Pao (1993).

Pao et al. compared the learning of the RVFLN with an MLP and backpropagation for learning a function. They both learned the function from data points given. The tradeoff was that the RVFLN required a much larger set of weights, but learned very well on 12,065 iterations, while the MLP required 1,161,496 iterations. When the MLP training was stopped at 200,000 iterations, the MLP did not interpolate correctly between the data points. On a second set of noisy data, the MLP overspecialized, while the RVFLN did not.

The FLN is an example of a more general architecture where the connections are not strictly from one layer to a succeeding layer. The cascade correlation network given in Appendix 5 is another example. Another one is described in Smid (1994), where a layered MLP is wired with extra connections. In this case, Smid connects some of the hidden neurodes to other hidden neurodes, so there are intralayer connections. For example, to learn XOR logic with a two layered network, he uses a 2–2–1 MLP as the initial structure and then connects the first hidden neurode to the second one. Thus there is only a single extra connection in this small structure. Smid found that this provides extra learning power, reduces the number of neurodes required to learn a dataset, and enhances the approximation of functions.

7.7. Radial Basis Function Networks

How They Work: Training and Operation

RBF networks were introduced in Chapter 3. They are becoming popular because of their quick training, conceptual clarity, and elegance. They originated as potential functions in Bashkirov et al. (1964), Aizerman et al. (1964), and Sprecht (1968). The were brought to widespread attention by Moody and Darken (1989) and by Broomhead and Lowe (1988). The basic idea is that the feature space $[0,1]^N$ is covered with M overlapping circular hyperball regions. For each such region there is a continuous radial basis function that assumes its maximum value at the center of the region, but which takes values near zero outside of it. Each of the M regions has a center vector $\mathbf{v}^{(m)}$ that represents a neurode. Figure 7.13 presents such a region, its center, and the radial basis function for that region in two-dimensional feature space. Such functions are called *radial* basis functions because the vectors $\mathbf{x}$ of equal distance to the *center* $\mathbf{v}^{(m)}$ have equal functional values.

The RBFs used predominantly by researchers have the Gaussian form

$$f_m(\mathbf{x}^{(q)}; \mathbf{v}^{(m)}) = \exp[-\|\mathbf{x}^{(q)} - \mathbf{v}^{(m)}\|^2 / 2\sigma_m^2] \tag{7.49}$$

Gaussian functions have the shape shown in Figure 7.13. The idea here is to center each RBF on a small cluster that represents a subclass. A set of M clusters with centers $\{\mathbf{v}^{(m)}\}$ are covered by M RFBs with the appropriate *spread parameters* σ_m^2 such that a larger σ_m means that the RBF is spread out more to cover a larger cluster. The neurodes represented by the M centers $\{\mathbf{v}^{(m)}\}$ make up the hidden layer of an N–M–J feedforward artificial neural network as shown in Figure 7.14. The output layer contains summing perceptrons with weights $\{u_{mj}\}$ that must be trained just as in an MLP.

During operation with a trained network, an input feature vector $\mathbf{x}$ is presented to the network. It is processed at each mth hidden neurode to produce an output

$$y_m = f_m(\mathbf{x}; \mathbf{v}^{(m)}) \tag{7.50}$$

Any input vector $\mathbf{x}$ is closest to one of the M neurodal centers $\mathbf{v}^{(m*)}$, so the output y_{m*} of the corresponding hidden neurode is greater than any other y_m, $m \neq m*$.

The vector $\mathbf{y} = (y_1, ..., y_M)$ that is output from the hidden layer of neurodes is processed by each neurode in the output layer in a manner similar to that of an MLP output neurode.

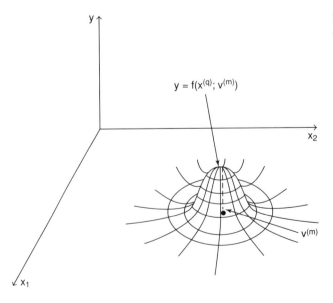

Figure 7.13. A cluster center and its RBF.

$y = f(x^{(q)}; v^{(m)})$

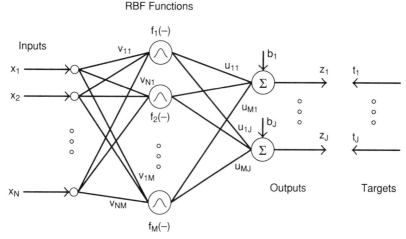

Figure 7.14. An RBF network.

While a sigmoid activation could be used at the output neurodes, it is more efficient here to use the averaging squashing function

$$z_j = (1/S)\sum_{(m=1, M)} u_{mj} y_m, \qquad S = y_1 + \cdots + y_M \qquad (7.51)$$

or

$$z_j = (1/M)\sum_{(m=1, M)} u_{mj} y_m \qquad (7.52)$$

The output vector $\mathbf{z}$ from the output layer is then tested against each of the K target vectors $\mathbf{t}^{(1)},..., \mathbf{t}^{(K)}$ that identify the K classes. These values may be large rather than constrained from 0 to 1 and so many users do not use the factor $1/S$ in Equation (7.51). We use $1/M$ in place of $1/S$ very successfully. The $\mathbf{t}^{k*}$ to which $\mathbf{z} = (z_1,..., z_J)$ is closest represents the class k^* to which $\mathbf{x}$ belongs. Thus $\mathbf{x}$ is recognized.

Why RBF Networks Work

It is now obvious how and why RBF networks work. The RBFs determine to which small cluster (subclass) an input vector $\mathbf{x}$ belongs because the RBF for that region has the greatest value. The output layer of neurodes ORs (adjoins) certain of these regions in the feature space by putting out a particular identifier $\mathbf{t}^{(k)}$ when $\mathbf{x}$ belongs to one or more of the small clusters that constitute the kth class. A class is the union of such convex subclasses in the feature space and so classes can be nonconvex (and only nonlinearly separable).

There is another more elegant explanation. Each RBF is a *fuzzy set membership function* on the feature space. Any given feature vector $\mathbf{x}$ belongs to one or more of the regions of response of the fuzzy sets and is fuzzified by each of the radial basis functions. The linguistic variables have the form REGION-M. The regions of response are the locations of subclusters. A combination of fuzzy membership strengths, $\mathbf{y} = (y_1,..., y_M)$, put out from the hidden layer determines the position of **x** in the feature space. The output layer of neurodes maps this combination, as well as certain other combinations, into a particular output vector that identifies **x** as belonging to the class that is the union of certain subclusters. The output vector **z** is a coded consequent of the implicit fuzzy rules. The weights at the output neurons must be trained to perform the appropriate joins (unions), that is, to activate fuzzy rules to make the correct mappings.

The Full Training Algorithm for RBFNs

When the number Q of exemplar input vectors for training is not too large, *quick training* (QT) with $M = Q$ hidden neurodes works efficiently. We put $\mathbf{v}^{(m)} \leftarrow \mathbf{x}^{(m)}$ for $m = 1,..., Q$, put $\sigma = 0.1$ or $\sigma = 0.05$ and use $\sigma_m = \sigma$ for $m = 1,..., M$. The initial weights $\{u_{mj}\}$ at the output neurodes are selected uniformly, randomly between -0.5 and 0.5. Let $\{\mathbf{x}^{(q)}: q = 1,..., Q\}$ and $\{\mathbf{t}^{(k(q))}: q = 1,..., Q\}$ be the respective exemplar input vectors and associated target output vectors, where $\mathbf{x}^{(q)}$ is to be mapped by the network to $\mathbf{t}^{(k(q))}$ ($k = 1,..., K$) for K classes. We then compute $y_m = f_m(\mathbf{x}; \mathbf{v}^{(m)})$ for $1 \leq m, q \leq M = Q$ one time only.

Iterating via *steepest descent* adjusts only the output weights $\{u_{mj}\}$ in QT to minimize the *total sum-squared error* (TSSE) E over all Q exemplars, which is defined via

$$E = \sum_{(q=1, Q)} \sum_{(j=1, J)} (t_j^{(q)} - z_j^{(q)})^2$$

The computational formula for steepest descent, where η is the *learning rate*, is

$$u_{mj} \leftarrow u_{mj} - \eta(\partial E/\partial u_{mj}) = u_{mj} + (2\eta/M)\sum_{(q=1, Q)}[\sum_{(j=1, J)}(t_j^{(k(q))} - z_j^{(q)})]y_m^{(q)} \quad (7.53)$$

When Q is too large, we select M to be smaller than Q, draw M center vectors $\{\mathbf{v}^{(m)}\}$ at random from the sample $\{\mathbf{x}^{(q)}: q = 1,..., Q\}$ and adjust these centers via steepest descent along with the output weights $\{u_{mj}\}$. This is the *full training* (FT) algorithm for RBFNs. Each initial weight u_{mj} is selected at random as was done in the QT algorithm. The spread parameters σ_m^2 may also be adjusted via steepest descent. The FT algorithm modifies QT (see Section 3.11) by including (for all n and m)

$$v_n^{(m)} \leftarrow v_n^{(m)} + [2\eta_2/(M\sigma^2)]\sum_{(q=1, Q)}\{\sum_{(j=1, J)}(t_j^{(k(q))} - z_j^{(q)})u_{mj}\}y_m^{(q)}(x_n^{(q)} - v_n^{(m)}) \quad (7.54)$$

$$\sigma_m^2 \leftarrow \sigma_m^2 + (2\eta_3/M)\sum_{(q=1, Q)}\{\sum_{(j=1, J)}(t_j^{(k(q))} - z_j^{(q)})$$
$$\times \sum_{(m=1, M)}[u_{mj}y_m^{(q)}\|\mathbf{x}^{(q)} - \mathbf{v}^{(m)}\|^2/(2\sigma_m^4)]\} \quad (7.55)$$

Step 1. /Use the given Q input exemplar vectors $\{\mathbf{x}^{(q)}\}$ as centers of hidden neurodes/
         input Q; Input M;   /M hidden neurodes, $M < Q$/
         for m = 1 to M do   /Assign neurode center components/
            for n = 1 to N do   /by random numbers from 0 to 1/
               $v_n^{(m)} \leftarrow$ random(0,1);

input I; i ← 1;   /I is no. of iterations wanted/
E ← 99999.9; ϵ ← 0.001;   /Assign initial TSSE E, ϵ for stopping/
η_1 ← 1.6; η_2 ← 1.0; η_3 ← 1.0;   /Input initial learning rate, or use 2.6/

Step 2. /Initialize the weights at the neurodes in the output layer/
    for m = 1 to M do
        for j = 1 to J do
            u_{mj} ← random(0,1) − 0.5;   /Uniform random numbers in $[-0.5, 0.5]$/

Step 3. /Use a single small spread parameter/
    σ ← 0.05;   /use σ for each σ_m (may use a smaller/
                                         /value/

Step 4. /Compute $y_m^{(q)} = f_m(\mathbf{x}^{(q)}; \mathbf{v}^{(m)})$, $m = 1, ..., M$ for each input exemplar feature vector $\mathbf{x}^{(q)}$/
    for q = 1 to Q do   /For each $\mathbf{x}^{(q)}$ and $\mathbf{v}^{(m)}$ vectors/
        for m = 1 to M do   /compute output $y_m^{(q)}$ at mth hidden/
                                      /neurode/
            if $q = m$ then $y_m^{(q)}$ ← 1;   /For $\mathbf{x}^{(q)} = \mathbf{v}^{(m)}$, $y_m^{(q)} = \exp(0) = 1$/
            else $y_m^{(q)}$ ← exp([neg$\|\mathbf{x}^{(q)}$ /else compute values for $y_m^{(q)} < 1$/
                   − $\mathbf{v}^{(m)}\|^2/(2\sigma^2))$;

Step 5. /Call **Update**(k) procedure to update network and adjust η_k/
    Update(0);   /Update network, but do not adjust any η_i/

Step 6. /Adjust weights $\{u_{mj}\}$ in the neurodes of the output layer according to steepest/
    /descent/
    for m = 1 to M do   /For each weight u_{mj}/
        for j = 1 to J do   /use steepest descent update/
            u_{mj} ← u_{mj} + $(2\eta_1/M)\sum_{(q=1,\,Q)}(t_j^{(k(q))} - z_j^{(q)})y_m^{(q)}$;
    Update(1);   /Update network and adjust η_1/
    for m = 1 to M do
        for n = 1 to N do
            $v_n^{(m)}$ ← $v_n^{(m)}$ + $[2\eta_2/(M\sigma^2)]\sum_{(q=1,\,Q)}\{\sum_{(j=1,\,J)}$
                × $(t_j^{(k(q))} - z_j^{(q)})u_{mj}\}y_m^{(q)}(x_n^{(q)} - v_n^{(m)})$
    Update(2);
    for m = 1 to M do
        σ_m^2 ← σ_m^2 + $(2\eta_3/M)\sum_{(q=1,\,Q)}\{\sum_{(j=1,\,J)}(t_j^{(k(q))} - z_j^{(q)})$
            × $\sum_{(m=1,\,M)}[u_{mj}y_m^{(q)}\|\mathbf{x}^{(q)} - \mathbf{v}^{(m)}\|^2/(2\sigma_m^4)]\}$
    Update(3);

Step 7. /Stop or repeat training of $\{u_{mj}\}$/
    if $(i \geq I)$ or $(E < \epsilon)$ then stop;
    else $i \leftarrow i + 1$; go to Step 4;   /Go to Step 4 to compute new y_m's that/
                                        /change/

/Procedure Update(k) to update outputs $z_j^{(q)}$, compute TSSE, adjust learning rate η_r/
    $r \leftarrow k$;   /assign $k = 1$ to r here/
    $E_{new} \leftarrow 0$;   /Start new error sum at 0/
    for $q = 1$ to Q do   /For each exemplar vector $\mathbf{x}^{(q)}$/
        for $j = 1$ to J do   /and each output node/
            $z_j^{(q)} \leftarrow (1/M)\sum_{(m=1,\,M)}u_{mj}y_m^{(q)}$; /update outputs of output layer/
            $E_{new} \leftarrow E_{new} + (t_j^{(k(q))} - z_j^{(q)})^2$; /Sum up new TSSE/
    if $E_{new} < E$ then $\eta_r \leftarrow \eta_r*1.04$; /If lower error, make η_1 slightly larger/
    else $\eta_r \leftarrow \eta_r*0.92$;   /Otherwise, make smaller learning rate/
    $E \leftarrow E_{new}$;   /Update current TSSE value for E/

The Quick and Full Training Algorithms for RBF-RVFLNs

It is logical to use the *random vector functional link network* (RVFLN) of Pao et al (1994) with the RBFs as activations, as is shown in Figure 7.12, as contemplated by Pao. We modify the FT algorithm for RBF activations. The RBF-RVFLN output layer contains the weights $\{u_{mj}\}$ on the M lines from the hidden neurodes as does the RBFN, but it also contains the additional weights $\{w_{nj}\}$ on the N direct lines from the input nodes. These are selected initially in the same way as the $\{u_{mj}\}$.

In the updating of the network outputs in Step 5, the computation of $\{z_j^{(q)}\}$ becomes

$$z_j^{(q)} \leftarrow \{(1/M)\sum_{(m=1,\,M)}u_{mj}y_m^{(q)} + (1/N)\sum_{(n=1,\,N)}w_{nj}x_n^{(q)}\})^2 \qquad (7.56)$$

The new total sum-squared error (TSSE) function E is defined via

$$\begin{aligned} E &= \sum_{(q=1,\,Q)}\sum_{(j=1,\,J)}(t_j^{(q)} - z_j^{(q)})^2 \\ &= \sum_{(q=1,\,Q)}\sum_{(j=1,\,J)}(t_j^{(q)} - \{(1/M)\sum_{(m=1,\,M)}u_{mj}y_m^{(q)} + (1/N)\sum_{(n=1,\,N)}w_{nj}x_n^{(q)}\})^2 \quad (7.57) \end{aligned}$$

In Step 6, we add the steepest descent update of the weights $\{w_{nj}\}$ via

$$w_{nj} \leftarrow w_{nj} + [2\eta_2/N]\sum_{(q=1,\,Q)}(t_j^{(k(q))} - z_j^{(q)})x_n^{(q)}; \qquad (7.58)$$

The appropriately modified Step 6 of the RBFN FT algorithm provides the FT algorithm for the RBF-RVFLN. The learning rate η_2 for updating $\{w_{nj}\}$ should be updated in the same manner as was η_1 by calling the **Update**(k) procedure of the RBFN FT algorithm with $k = 2$. To obtain the FT algorithm for RBF-RVFLNs, we employ Equations (7.56), (7.57) and (7.58) and call procedure **Update**(k) to update the network outputs and TSSE and adjust the learning rates η_r. The new Step 6 is given below for the RBF-RVFLN FT (for the RBF-RVFLN QT, omit the updates of the $v_n^{(m)}$ and σ_m^2 (below the dashed line). Note that we update σ^2 every fifth iteration only.

Step 6. /Adjust $\{u_{mj}\}$, $\{w_{nj}\}$, $\{v_n^{(m)}\}$ and $\{\sigma_m^2\}$ via steepest descent/

    for $j = 1$ to J do   /Adjust each u_{mj}/

        for $m = 1$ to M do   /use steepest descent update/

            $u_{mj} \leftarrow u_{mj} + [2\eta_1/M]\Sigma_{(q=1,\,Q)}(t_j^{(k(q))} - z_j^{(q)})y_m^{(q)};$

    Update(1);   /Update network, TSSE, adjust η_1/;

    for $j = 1$ to J do

        for $n = 1$ to N do   /Adjust each w_{nj}/

            $w_{nj} \leftarrow w_{nj} + [2\eta_2/N]\Sigma_{(q=1,\,Q)}(t_j^{(k(q))} - z_j^{(q)})x_n^{(q)};$

    Update(2);   /Update network, TSSE, adjust η_2/

    for $n = 1$ to N do

        for $m = 1$ to M do

            $v_n^{(m)} \leftarrow v_n^{(m)} + [2\eta_3/(M\sigma^2)]\Sigma_{(q=1,\,Q)}\{\Sigma_{(j=1,\,J)}(t_j^{(k(q))} - z_j^{(q)})u_{mj}\}$

                    $\times\ y_m^{(q)}(x_n^{(q)} - v_n^{(m)})$

    Update(3);   /Update network, TSEE, adjust η_3/

    if (i % 5 = 0)   /Every fifth iteration, update σ_m's/

        for $m = 1$ to M do

            $\sigma_m^2 \leftarrow \sigma_m^2 +$

                    $(2\eta_4/M)\Sigma_{(q=1,\,Q)}\{\Sigma_{(j=1,\,J)}(t_j^{(k(q))} - z_j^{(q)}) -$ $_{(m=1,\,M)}$

                    $\times\ [u_{mj}y_m^{(q)}\|\mathbf{x}^{(q)} - \mathbf{v}^{(m)}\|^2/(2\sigma_m^4)]\}$

    Update(4);   /Update network, TSEE, adjust η_4/

Example 7.2.   **An Illustrative Example of Adjoined Clusters**

The simple nonlinear XOR data provides a remarkably clear example of the power of radial basis function networks (RBFNs). The exemplars are

$$\mathbf{x}^{(1)} = (0,0), \qquad \mathbf{x}^{(2)} = (0,1), \qquad \mathbf{x}^{(3)} = (1,0), \qquad \mathbf{x}^{(4)} = (1,1)$$

Because there are $K = 4$ subclasses in these $Q = 4$ exemplars, we use $M = 4$ clusters (one for each subclass). One way to proceed is to use $\mathbf{v}^{(m)} = \mathbf{x}^{(m)}$, $m = 1,...,4$, as the cluster centers for subclasses.

Figure 7.15 presents the contour curves for the case where we use the exemplars given above as neurode centers. In contrast to this, Figure 7.16 presents the case where we use (0.3,0.3), (0.3,0.7), (0.7,0.3), and (0.7,0.7) as centers. As the spread parameter is changed from small to larger, the contour curves spread farther apart.

RBF Networks for Applications

Some researchers think that RBF networks, which originated from potential functions, are extremely good for recognition, but that they are not as good as MLPs for the approximation of functions because the number of RBFs and their associated hidden neurodes and

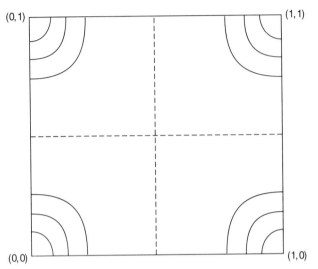

Figure 7.15. RBF Contours for XOR logic, first set of centers.

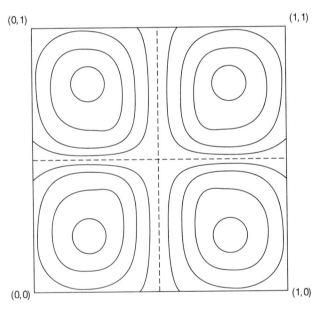

Figure 7.16. RBF contours for XOR logic, second set of centers.

weights becomes too large for very small errors. An enlightening paper by Mak et al. (1994) compares RBF networks with MLPs for speaker recognition. Each was trained to recognize one of 10 speakers based on training with features from spoken names of the digits 0,..., 9. They used 546 exemplar feature vectors for each of the training and test sets, where each set contained data for the utterances of the 10 digits by a different speaker. The training and test data were recorded 30 minutes apart. The inputs were the 12th-order cepstrum coefficients of the audio signals that were filtered to pass between 50 Hz and 3500 Hz.

Table 7.2.
Comparison of MLP and RBF Performance

	MLP	RBF Network
Number of hidden nodes:	20	100
Identification accuracy:	90.2%	90.0%
Training time:	214 min	36 min
Memory storage per processor:	109 Kbytes	386 Kbytes
Recognition time/pattern:	15 msec	21 msec

[Maximum accuracy: MLP—90.2%, RBFN—98.7% (300 hidden neurodes)]

Mak et al. performed experiments with 50, 100, 200, and 300 hidden neurode centers. Both MLP and RBF networks were implemented on six T800 transputers with 2 Mbytes of memory for each and with no interprocessor communications required (concurrent but independent computation). Various combinations of training on from one to ten digits at a time were tried. The numbers of hidden neurodes in the MLP training were 10, 20, and 40.

The best performance for the MLP was achieved by the network with 20 hidden neurodes with 90.2% identification accuracy, while the best performance for the RBF network used 300 hidden neurodes and had an identification accuracy of 98.7%. Table 7.2 provides a summary for the MLP with 20 hidden neurodes compared with an RBF network with 100 hidden neurodes that had similar accuracy of 90.0%.

Mak et al. reported that the MLP training process sometimes became stuck in a local minimum and that much computation time was wasted before they realized this and started the process over. Such wasted time is not reflected in Table 7.2.

The *advantages* of the RBF network over the MLP are as follows: (i) They do not get stuck in local minima (there aren't any); (ii) the training time is much shorter; (iii) the weight values do not have to be restrained for training to take place (if the training is not restrained for MLPs, the weights will drift and saturation will take place); (iv) the momentum coefficient and the learning rate must be estimated without a priori knowledge; and (v) exemplars that are far from decision boundaries have little influence in RBF networks, while in MLPs, they have more influence on the training. The *disadvantages* of the RBF networks compared to the MLPs are as follows: (i) More memory is required because of the large number of hidden neurodes required; (ii) some RBF networks require a second algorithm to be programmed to perform clustering to find the centers for the hidden neurodes; (iii) the speed of operation is slightly slower than for MLPs; (iv) the centers and spread parameters σ^2 are not optimal in any sense; and (iv) there is so far no good way to implement the hidden neurodes in hardware.

In practice, we put each exemplar as a center and put σ^2 small, say $\sigma^2 = 0.1$, for quick training. Some researchers do not solve for the weights at the neurodes of the output layer by means of steepest descent. This is a linear problem when no nonlinear activation functions are used. Therefore, the weights satisfy

$$z^{(q)} = b + \sum_{(m=1,\,M)} u_m f_{mq}(\mathbf{x}^{(q)};\, v^{(m)}) = \sum_{(m=1,\,M+1)} u_m f_{mq} \tag{7.59}$$

where f_{mq} denotes the value $f_{mq}(\mathbf{x}^{(q)}; \mathbf{v}^{(m)})$ and $f_{M+1,q}$ is the constant function that maps $u_{M+1} = 1$ into the bias b. For each fixed $z^{(q)}$ output at the output layer neurode, we have the matrix equation $F\mathbf{u} = \mathbf{z}$, where $F = \{f_{mq}\}$, $\mathbf{u} = (u_1,..., u_M)$ and $\mathbf{z} = (z^{(1)},..., z^{(Q)})$. But we really want that $z^{(q)} = t^{(q)}$ for each input exemplar $\mathbf{x}^{(q)}$, so we use $t^{(q)}$ in place of $z^{(q)}$ to obtain

$$F\mathbf{u} = \mathbf{t} \tag{7.60}$$

Because this represents the system

$$f_{11}u_1 + f_{21}u_2 + \cdots + f_{M1}u_M + f_{M+1,1}u_{M+1} = t^{(1)}$$
$$\vdots \qquad\qquad \vdots$$
$$f_{1q}u_1 + f_{2q}u_2 + \cdots + f_{Mq}u_M + f_{M+1,q}u_{M+1} = t^{(q)}$$
$$\vdots \qquad\qquad \vdots$$
$$f_{1Q}u_1 + f_{2Q}u_2 + \cdots + f_{MQ}u_M + f_{M+1,Q}u_{M+1} = t^{(Q)} \tag{7.61}$$

we can see that the system is overdetermined, that is, there are Q equations in M unknowns (assuming that $Q > M$). In the case when $M = Q$ and there is a hidden neurode center for each exemplar, this equation is solvable for the weights $u_1,..., u_M$ at the output neurode (the system is exactly determined). In the overdetermined case, we can use the generalized inverse by taking

$$F^t F\mathbf{u} = F^t \mathbf{t} \tag{7.62}$$

The matrix $F^t F$ is a square $Q \times Q$ matrix that is almost always nonsingular. The inverse of $F^t F$ is $(F^t F)^{-1} = F^{-1}(F^t)^{-1}$. Upon putting $F^* = (F^t F)^{-1} F^t$ and premultiplying Equation (7.60) by it, we see that

$$F^*(F^t F\mathbf{u}) = F^*(F^t \mathbf{t}) \tag{7.63}$$

yields

$$(F^t F)^{-1} F^t (F\mathbf{u}) = F^{-1}(F^t)^{-1}(F^t F\mathbf{u}) = F^{-1}((F^t)^{-1} F^t) F\mathbf{u} = F^{-1} F\mathbf{u} = \mathbf{u} \tag{7.64}$$

on the left-hand side of Equation (7.63) and on the right-hand side it yields

$$F^*(\mathbf{t}) = (F^t F)^{-1} F^t \mathbf{t}$$

Summing up, the system is solvable for the weights $\mathbf{u}$ by

$$\mathbf{u} = (F^t F)^{-1} F^t \mathbf{t} \tag{7.65}$$

According to Mak et al. (1994), the use of larger ranges on the inputs and target outputs makes it likelier that the matrix $(F^t F)^{-1} F^t$ will not be ill-conditioned (an ill-conditioned matrix has two or more rows that are almost dependent). When they used 300 hidden neurodes, they could not solve the system for $Q = 546$ exemplars. But they were able to solve the system for 200 hidden neurodes.

Example 7.3.   Some Comparisons

Tables 7.3, 7.4, 7.5 and 7.6 show the Blood10 Dataset from Appendix 11, but with different numbers of outputs in the unipolar or bipolar target vectors. There are $N = 8$ inputs and $Q = 7$ exemplars. Tables 7.7 through 7.11 show the results of training on this data. The backpropagation MLP runs use *epochs*, where an epoch consists of $Q = 7$ separate adjustments of the entire weight set. One iteration for RBFNs or RVFLNs adjusts the entire weight set once. Thus an MLP epoch is more computationally expensive than is an RBFN or RBF-RVFLN iteration. All RBFN and RBF-RVFLN runs use the QT algorithm and are extremely fast.

Table 7.3.
Dataset 1 (Single Output Component)

Inputs								Outputs
0.2890	0.0550	0.4840	0.3850	0.5450	0.5750	0.3410	0.9950	0.1000
0.0310	0.4840	0.2200	0.1230	0.3000	0.3800	0.0890	0.2100	0.2000
0.1260	0.3910	0.3540	0.2750	0.4420	0.5150	0.1750	0.3950	0.3000
0.0600	0.4140	0.2400	0.1620	0.3040	0.3680	0.1100	0.2700	0.4000
0.0950	0.3650	0.3600	0.2340	0.4800	0.5400	0.1650	0.1900	0.5000
0.0630	0.2220	0.3320	0.2100	0.4600	0.5360	0.1550	0.3200	0.6000
0.1890	0.2470	0.4150	0.3120	0.5100	0.5620	0.2750	0.3200	0.7000

Table 7.4.
Dataset 2 (Three Output Components)

Inputs								Outputs		
0.2890	0.0550	0.4840	0.3850	0.5450	0.5750	0.3410	0.9950	0.100	0.100	0.100
0.0310	0.4840	0.2200	0.1230	0.3000	0.3800	0.0890	0.2100	0.200	0.500	0.900
0.1260	0.3910	0.3540	0.2750	0.4420	0.5150	0.1750	0.3950	0.300	0.900	0.500
0.0600	0.4140	0.2400	0.1620	0.3040	0.3680	0.1100	0.2700	0.400	0.100	0.500
0.0950	0.3650	0.3600	0.2340	0.4800	0.5430	0.1650	0.1900	0.500	0.900	0.300
0.0630	0.2220	0.3320	0.2100	0.4600	0.5360	0.1550	0.3200	0.900	0.500	0.200
0.1890	0.2470	0.4150	0.3120	0.5100	0.5620	0.2750	0.3200	0.900	0.900	0.900

Table 7.5.
Dataset 3 (Single Bipolar Output)

Inputs								Outputs
0.28900	0.05500	0.48400	0.38500	0.54500	0.57500	0.34100	0.99500	−0.9000
0.03100	0.48400	0.22000	0.12300	0.30000	0.38000	0.08900	0.21000	−0.6000
0.12600	0.39100	0.35400	0.27500	0.44200	0.51500	0.17500	0.39500	−0.3000
0.60000	0.41400	0.24000	0.16200	0.30400	0.36800	0.11000	0.27000	0.0000
0.09500	0.36500	0.36000	0.23400	0.48000	0.54300	0.16500	0.19000	0.3000
0.06300	0.22200	0.33200	0.21000	0.46000	0.53600	0.15500	0.32000	0.6000
0.18900	0.24700	0.41500	0.31200	0.51000	0.56200	0.27500	0.32000	0.9000

Table 7.6.

Dataset 4 (Three Bioplar Outputs)

Inputs								Outputs		
0.2890	0.0550	0.4840	0.3850	0.5450	0.5750	0.3410	0.9950	−1.0	−1.0	−1.0
0.0310	0.4840	0.2200	0.1230	0.3000	0.3800	0.0890	0.2100	−1.0	0.0	0.0
0.1260	0.3910	0.3540	0.2750	0.4420	0.5150	0.1750	0.3950	−1.0	1.0	1.0
0.0600	0.4140	0.2400	0.1620	0.3040	0.3680	0.1100	0.2700	0.0	0.0	−1.0
0.0950	0.3650	0.3600	0.2340	0.4800	0.5430	0.1650	0.1900	0.0	−1.0	0.0
0.0630	0.2220	0.3320	0.2100	0.4600	0.5360	0.1550	0.3200	1.0	−1.0	1.0
0.1890	0.2470	0.4150	0.3120	0.5100	0.5620	0.2750	0.3200	1.0	1.0	−1.0

Table 7.7.

Results of Training an MLP Network on Datasets 1 and 2

Run	Q	N	M	J	No. Epochs	RSS Error	Accuracy	Dataset
1	7	8	8	1	1000	0.124	71.5%	1
2	7	8	8	1	1500	0.089	85.7%	1
3	7	8	10	1	1000	0.257	42.8%	1
4	7	8	12	1	1500	0.222	57.1%	1
5	7	8	12	1	1000	0.040	100%	1
6	7	8	12	1	1500	0.024	100%	1
7	7	8	10	3	1000	0.263	100%	2
8	7	8	10	3	1500	0.184	100%	2
9	7	8	12	3	800	0.489	100%	2
10	7	8	12	3	600	0.580	100%	2
11	7	8	12	3	500	0.621	85.7%	2

Table 7.8.

Results of Training an RBF Network on Datasets 1 and 2

Run	Q	N	M	J	No. Iterations	RSS Error	Accuracy	Dataset	σ
1	7	8	7	1	100	0.00510	100.0%	1	0.10
2	7	8	7	1	60	0.16951	57.1%	1	0.10
3	7	8	7	1	60	0.16951	57.1%	1	0.05
4	7	8	7	1	50	0.28319	14.3%	1	0.10
5	7	8	7	3	100	0.00500	100.0%	2	0.10
6	7	8	7	3	60	0.29538	100.0%	2	0.10
7	7	8	7	3	50	0.53578	100.0%	2	0.10
8	7	8	7	3	30	1.29835	42.8%	2	0.10

Table 7.9.

Results of Training an RBFN on Dataset 3 (Single Bipolar Output)

Run	Q	N	M	J	No. Iterations	RSS Error	Accuracy	Dataset	σ
1	7	8	7	1	100	0.00271	100.0%	3	0.10
2	7	8	7	1	60	0.16016	100.0%	3	0.10
3	7	8	7	1	50	0.17936	71.4%	3	0.10
4	7	8	7	1	30	0.70322	42.8%	3	0.10
5	7	8	7	1	30	0.70322	42.8%	3	0.05

Table 7.10.
Results of Training an RBFN on Dataset 4 (3 Bioplar Outputs)

Run	Q	N	M	J	No. Iterations	RSS Error	Accuracy	Dataset	σ
1	7	8	7	3	200	0.00006	100.0%	4	0.10
2	7	8	7	3	100	0.00670	100.0%	4	0.10
3	7	8	7	3	60	0.39555	100.0%	4	0.10
4	7	8	7	3	30	1.73865	100.0%	4	0.10
5	7	8	7	3	20	2.40931	42.8%	4	0.10

Table 7.11.
Results of Training an RBF-RVFLN on Datasets 1, 2, 3, and 4

Run	Q	N	M	J	No. Iterations	RSS Error	Accuracy	Dataset	σ
1	7	8	7	1	60	0.0054	100.0%	1*	0.10
2	7	8	7	1	50	0.0139	100.0%	1*	0.10
3	7	8	7	1	30	0.0482	100.0%	1*	0.10
4	7	8	7	1	20	0.0996	85.7%	1*	0.10
5	7	8	7	3	50	0.0704	100.0%	2***	0.10
6	7	8	7	3	30	0.2855	100.0%	2**	0.10
7	7	8	7	3	20	0.4707	100.0%	2**	0.10
8	7	8	7	3	15	0.5938	100.0%	2**	0.10
9	7	8	7	3	10	0.9232	100.0%	2**	0.10
10	7	8	7	3	50	0.0498	100.0%	3†	0.10
11	7	8	7	3	30	0.1702	100.0%	3†	0.10
12	7	8	7	3	20	0.3224	57.1%	3†	0.10
13	7	8	7	3	15	0.4648	42.8%	3†	0.10
14	7	8	7	3	30	0.3618	100.0%	4‡	0.10
15	7	8	7	3	20	0.6511	100.0%	4‡	0.10
16	7	8	7	3	15	0.9092	100.0%	4‡	0.10
17	7	8	7	3	10	1.6777	85.7%	4‡	0.10

* single unipolar output   ** three unipolar outputs   † single bipolar output   ‡ three bipolar outputs

It is clear from the tables that RBFNs are more powerful than MLPs, but the RBF-RVFLNs are the most powerful. Their speed and accuracy are incredible. We also made runs on larger datasets, such as a subset of the Wisconsin Breast Cancer data (N = 83 inputs, Q = 99 exemplars, and J = 1 output) and the results were similar.

7.8. Supernets

Section 7.6 described the random vector functional link net (RVFLN) of Pao, which has the extra connectivity of the FLN (see Chapter 3) along with any functions put into the offset hidden neurodes. Also, Smid (1994) showed that the addition of connections between the hidden neurodes adds extra learning power. We could start with the RVFLN of Pao et al., use the Gaussian radial basis functions in the hidden neurodes, and add extra connectivity between the hidden neurodes. This new architecture, shown in Figure 7.17, is what we call *supernet* (SN).

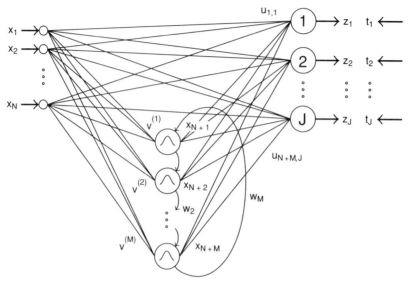

Figure 7.17. A supernet.

We leave it as an exercise to determine the update equations. However, we note that the updates for $\{u_{nj}: n = 1,..., N\}$ are simple and that the updates for the weights $\{u_{pj}: p = N + 1,..., N + M\}$ are the same as for the RBFNs. The interconnectivity weights $\{w_m: m = 1,..., M\}$ at the hidden layer are the most tedious to derive and present a new problem (see Exercise 7.16).

Exercises

7.1. Why is underutilization considered to be a fault? Describe its effects.

7.2. Does either of the UCL or the GLVQ have the underutilization problem? Explain.

7.3. Why is lateral inhibition desired? Which of the algorithms use it. Describe how they implement it.

7.4. Does the SCL have the underutilization property? Does it have any lateral inhibition?

7.5. Which of the algorithms in this chapter are self-organizing? Of those that are, describe any parameters that must be given by the user.

7.6. Does the dog–rabbit algorithm have frequency sensitivity? If so, what is it called? Describe how it works. Why is frequency sensitivity desirable?

7.7. Write a program that implements the dog–rabbit algorithm. Run the program on some datasets (see the appendix to Chapter 11).

7.8. Modify the program in Exercise 7.7 so that when starting with a large number of dogs (neurode centers), those that are not needed are pruned.

7.9. Write a set of fuzzy rules that operate on exemplar input feature vectors and make a decision as to the class to which it belongs. Describe the entire system that uses Gaussian fuzzy set membership functions. There should be defuzzified output linguistic variables for each class, and the class that has the strongest implication is the winner.

7.10. Develop the FFLN (fuzzy functional link net) into a full blown recognition algorithm for any number K of classes.

7.11. Write a program that implements a functional link net algorithm.

7.12. Write an algorithm that uses the dog–rabbit algorithm to do the clustering, then computes the spread parameters, and then does the usual RBF neural network algorithm.

7.13. If Q is the number of input exemplars to be used for training, then use $M = Q$ as the number of hidden neurodes for a RBF network. Write an algorithm that solves for the weights $u_1,..., u_M$ by solving the linear system of Equation (7.58).

7.14. Write a program that implements the algorithm of either Exercise 7.12 or 7.13 above. Test it on the Digit12 dataset in Appendix 12a.

7.15. Write an algorithm that combines functional link nets with radial basis function networks.

7.16. Determine the update equations for all weights (steepest descent) of the *supernet* (SN) architecture given in Section 7.8.

7.17. Chapter 4 describes a simplified form of MLP network architecture and algorithm called *slickprop*. Develop an architecture where the inputs also go directly to the outputs and hidden neurodes are connected to each other (call it *superslickprop*).

7.18. How would you proceed to train an RBF-RVFLN on a dataset with a large number Q of examplars and a small number K of classes?

References

Ahalt, S. C., Krishnamurthy, A. K., Chen, P., and Melton, D. E. (1990), Competitive learning algorithms for vector quantization, *Neural Networks* vol. 3, 277–290.

Aizerman, M. A., Braverman, E. M., and Rozonoer, L. I. (1964), Theoretical foundations of the potential function method in pattern recognition learning, *Automation and Remote Control* vol. 25, 821–837.

Bashkirov, O. A., Braverman, E. M., and Muchnik, I. B. (1964), Potential function algorithms for pattern recognition learning machines, *Automation and Remote Control*, vol. 25, 629–631.

Bezdek, J. C. (1981), *Pattern Recognition with Fuzzy Objective Function Algorithms*, Plenum Press, New York.

Bi, H., Bi, G., and Mao, Y. (1994), Stochastically competitive learning algorithm for vector quantizer design, *IEEE 1994 Int. Conf. Neural Networks*, vol. 2, 622–626.

Bouchon-Meunier, B. (1991), Inferences with inaccuracy and uncertainty in expert systems, in *Fuzzy Expert Systems*, edited by A. Kandel, CRC Press, Boca Raton, FL, pp. 43–54.

Broomhead, D. S., and Lowe, D. (1988), Multivariable functional interpolation and adaptive networks, *Complex Systems* vol. 2, 321–355.

Chung, F. L., and Lee, T. (1994), Fuzzy competitive learning, *Neural Networks*, vol. 7(3), 539–551.

DeSieno, D. (1988), Adding a conscience to competitive learning, *Proc. IEEE 1988 Int. Conf. Neural Networks*, 1117–1124.

Giles, C. L., and Maxwell, T. (1987), Learning invariance and generalization in high-order neural networks, *Applied Optics* vol. 26, 4972–4978.

Grossberg, S. (1976), Adaptive pattern classification and universal recoding: 1. Parallel development and coding of neural feature detectors, *Biological Cybernetics*, vol. 23, 121–134.

Huang, K. Y. (1994), Fuzzy functional-link net for seismic trace, *Proc. IEEE 1994 Int. Conf. Neural Networks*, vol. 3, 1650–1653.

Igelnik, B., and Pao, Y. H. (1993), Additional perspectives on feedforward neural-nets and the functional link, *Proc. 1993 Int. Joint Conf. Neural Networks*, 2284–2287.

Keller, J. M., and Hunt, D. J. (1985), Incorporating fuzzy membership functions into the perceptron algorithm, *IEEE Trans. Pattern Anal. Mach. Intell.*, vol. 7, no. 6, 693–699.

Kohonen, T. (1986), *Learning Vector Quantization for Pattern Recognition*, Technical Report TKK-F-A601, Helsinki University of Technology.

Krishnamurthy, A. K., Ahalt, S. C., Melton, D. E., and Chen, P. (1990), Neural networks for vector quantization of speech and images, *IEEE J. on Selected Areas in Communications*, vol. 8, 1449–1457.

Kruse, R., Gebhart, J., and Klawonn, F. (1994), *Foundations of Fuzzy Systems*, Wiley, Chichester, UK.

Looney, C. G. (1988a), Fuzzy Petri nets for rule based decisionmaking, *IEEE Trans. Systems, Man Cybernetics*, vol. 18, no. 1, 178–183.

Looney, C. G. (1988b), Expert control design with fuzzy rule matrices, *Int. J. Expert Systems*, vol. 1, no. 2, 159–168.

Looney, C. G. (1994), Fuzzy Petri nets and applications, in *Fuzzy Reasoning in Information, Decision and Control Systems*, edited by S. G. Tzafestas and A. N. Venetsanopoulis, Kluwer Academic Publishers, pp. 511–527.

Mak, M. W., Allen, W. G., and Sexton, G. G. (1994), Speaker identification using multilayer perceptrons and radial basis function networks, *Neurocomputing*, vol. 6, 99–117.

McKenzie, P., and Alder, M. (1994), Unsupervised learning: the dog rabbit strategy, *IEEE 1994 Int. Conf. Neural Networks*, vol. 2, 616–621.

Moody, J. E., and Darken, C. J. (1989), Fast learning in networks of locally-tuned processing units, *Neural Comput.*, vol. 1, 281–294.

Pal, N. R., Bezdek, J. C., and Tsao, E. C. K. (1993), Generalized clustering networks and Kohonen's self-organizing scheme, *IEEE Trans. Neural Networks*, vol. 4, no. 4, 549–557.

Pao, Y. H., Park, G. H., and Sobajic, D. J. (1994), Learning and generalization characteristics of the random vector functional link net, *Neurocomputing*, vol. 6, 163–180.

Pao, Y. H. (1989), *Adaptive Pattern Recognition and Neural Networks*, Addison-Wesley, Reading, MA.

Park, D. C., and Dagher, I. (1994), Gradient based fuzzy c-means (GBFCM) Algorithm, *Proceedings IEEE 1994 Int. Conf. Neural Networks*, 1626–1631.

Selim, S. Z., and Kamel, M. S. (1992), On the mathematical and numerical properties of the fuzzy c-means algorithm, *Fuzzy Sets and Systems*, vol. 49, 181–191.

Smid, J. (1994), Layered neural networks with horizontal connections can reduce the number of units, *Proc. 1994 IEEE Int. Conf. Neural Networks*, vol. 3, 1346–1350.

Sprecht, D. F. (1968), *A Practical Technique for Estimating General Regression Surfaces*, Report LMSC-6-79-68-6, Lockheed Missile and Space Co., Inc., Palo Alto, CA.

Wang, L. X., and Mendel, J. M. (1992), Backpropagation fuzzy systems as nonlinear dynamic system identifiers, *Proc. 1992 IEEE Int. Conf. Fuzzy Systems*, 1409–1418.

Zadeh, L. A. (1965), Fuzzy sets, *Information and Control*, vol. 8, 338–353.

Chapter 8

Recurrent Neural Networks

This chapter exposes the inner workings of recurrent neural networks.

8.1. The Hopfield Network Architecture

The Amari–Hopfield Discrete Model

The Amari–Hopfield model was introduced in Chapter 3. Because of its theoretically proved convergence properties, we consider here the Hopfield architecture, which is displayed in Figure 8.1 below. At time $t = 0$, an input feature vector $\mathbf{x} = (x_1,..., x_N)$ is presented to the network's single layer of neurodes, one component value per neurode. This *initial* input vector is also the initial output vector $\mathbf{y}^{(0)} = (y_1^{(0)},..., y_N^{(0)}) = (x_1,..., x_N) = \mathbf{x}$. Each input component may be either 1 or -1. Each initial output is fed back to a branching node, where it fans out to each of the neurodes except itself, as shown in the figure. These feedback fan-out lines lead into the neurodes and are excited or inhibited by the weights $\{w_{ij}\}$, where w_{ij} designates the weight on the line from output neurode i to input neurode j ($w_{jj} = 0$ for each j). At any jth neurode, the incoming $N - 1$ weighted values are summed and put through a threshold activation function $f(-)$ to yield an updated output on the $(r + 1)$st iteration via

$$y_j^{(r+1)} = f(\textstyle\sum_{(i=1,\,N)}[w_{ij}y_i^{(r)}] - \tau_j) \tag{8.1}$$

where the thresholds τ_j are taken to be zero, in which case the threshold activation becomes the sign function

$$f(s) = \text{sgn}(s) = 1, \quad s > 0; \qquad f(s) = \text{sgn}(s) = -1, \quad s < 0 \tag{8.2}$$

The activated value is $y_j^{(r+1)} = y_j^{(r)}$ when $s = 0$ (i.e., no change).

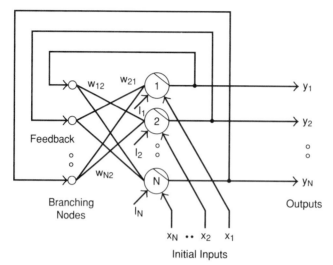

Figure 8.1. The Hopfield network architecture.

In his original paper, Hopfield used the values of 0 and 1 for the outputs (Hopfield, 1982). However, the values of 1 and -1 are now in common usage (Lippmann, 1987; or Zurada, 1992) for convenience in using the zero threshold. In summary, the initial input vector $\mathbf{x} = (x_1,..., x_N)$ consists of component values of 1 and -1, the weight entries on the main diagonal of the weight matrix $W = \{w_{ij}\}$ are $w_{jj} = 0$ ($j = 1,..., N$), and the activated outputs $y_j^{(r+1)}$ also take values of 1 or -1.

Random Serial and Fully Parallel Operation Modes

For *parallel synchronous* action, the updating of all outputs concurrently yields the updated vector output as the vector of thresholded sums

$$\mathbf{y}^{(r+1)} = \mathbf{f}(W\mathbf{y}^{(r)} - \boldsymbol{\tau}) \tag{8.3}$$

at the output of the N neurodes, where $\mathbf{f}(-) = (f_1(-),..., f_N(-))$ and $f_i(-) = f(-)$ for $i = 1,..., N$. To overcome the convergence failure of the Amari recurrent model, the Hopfield network was specified to fire *asynchronously* in the following manner: (i) On each update, only a single randomly selected neurode would fire (be activated), so that a single updated output $y_j^{(r+1)}$ would be generated; (ii) a random input I_j would be added to its sum in the updating (the asynchronicity and random term represent delay, noise, and jitter that are certainly present in biological systems); and (iii) the new updated output would be held and used to update each future asynchronous firing of any neurode. This mode is called *random serial* operation because there is no parallel updating of two or more neurodes simultaneously. Nowadays, researchers also use a parallel firing model, where two or more, possibly all, neurodes may fire simultaneously. The complete Hopfield recurrent neural network (HRNN) model, with random inputs $\{I_j\}$, fires in random serial fashion at the jth neurode to update the single jth output $y_j^{(r+1)}$ via

$$y_j^{(r+1)} = f(\sum_{(i=1,\,N)}[w_{ij}y_i^{(r)}] - \tau_j + I_j) \tag{8.4}$$

Considering $\mathbf{y}^{(r)} = (y_1^{(r)},..., y_N^{(r)})$ as the current *state* of an HRNN, we see that only a single state component changes on each firing. The question now is, Do the changing state vectors converge to an identifier for the given input feature vector? In the next section, we show that the HRNN does indeed converge under certain conditions. In a later section, we provide an algorithm. Section 8.3 describes the computation of the weights.

When the system is operating in the *fully parallel* mode, we write

$$\mathbf{y}^{(r+1)} = F(\mathbf{y}^{(r)}) \tag{8.5}$$

to represent Equation (8.4). However, the most interest is in asynchronicity (see below). Hopfield noted in his original paper (Hopfield, 1982) that synchronous computations of a conventional computer do not model biological systems, where asynchrony exists due to delays of nerve signal propagation (and we note that there are multiple paths of differing lengths, different signal levels, etc.). He implied that asynchronous computations can have useful properties in a collective sense where some stable state emerges, and that these are quite different from those of synchronous machines. The intellectual elegance and potential of these models attracted a large following in the 1980s.

The use of Hopfield networks for recognition is straightforward. Weights are computed by a simple and quick correlational formula without iterated training. Then a sample feature vector to be recognized is input and the network iterates on it until the output vector (state) becomes fixed (i.e., does not change further), in which case we say that the network has *converged* to a decision state. The fixed output vector is the identifier for the class to which the initial input feature vector belongs. Convergence has been proved only for the weight matrix $W = \{w_{ij}\}$ being symmetric or antisymmetric, as discussed in the next section. Researchers are still experimenting with variations of Hopfield's model to achieve more efficiency and effectiveness. Paik and Katsaggelos (1992) have proposed a modified HRNN for image restoration. Kosko's bidirectional associative mapping (BAM) is another extended model (Kosko, 1987), which is described in Section 8.8.

8.2. Hopfield Networks as Finite Automata

States, Attractors, and Cycles

We consider the state transitions here for the average case, where the random value of each noise I_j assumes its average value of zero. The *state* of a Hopfield network with N neurodes at any time $t = r$ is $\mathbf{y}^{(r)} = (y_1^{(r)},..., y_N^{(r)})$, where each state component can take one of the two values 1 or -1. There are 2^N possible different states of the network in the binary hypercube $\{-1,1\}^N$. Starting from the initial state $\mathbf{y}^{(0)}$, the state changes every time a neurode fires (its output is activated by $f(-)$), so the system moves through a trajectory of states over time. When only a single neurode is allowed to fire at a time, in random serial mode, the state changes in a single component at a time.

In full parallel operational mode, all neurodes change simultaneously, and the updating is described by

$$\mathbf{y}^{(r+1)} = F(\mathbf{y}^{(r)}) = F^2(\mathbf{y}^{(r-1)}) = \cdots = F^{r+1}(\mathbf{y}^{(0)}) \tag{8.6}$$

where $F(\mathbf{y}^{(r)})$ is defined by Equation (8.3) to be

$$F(\mathbf{y}^{(r)}) = \mathbf{f}(W\mathbf{y}^{(r)} - \boldsymbol{\tau}) = (f(\textstyle\sum_{(i=1,\,N)}[w_{i1}y_i^{(r)}] - \tau_1), \,...,\, f(\textstyle\sum_{(i=1,\,N)}[w_{iN}y_i^{(r)}] - \tau_N)) \tag{8.7}$$

In the asynchronous modes where one neurode is updated simultaneously, we use A_j to denote the updating function when $y_j^{(r)}$ is the single component to be updated. Then

$$\begin{aligned}
A_j(\mathbf{y}^{(r)}) &= (y_1^{(r)},...,\, f(\textstyle\sum_{(i=1,\,N)}[w_{ij}y_i^{(r)}] - \tau_j), \,...,\, y_N^{(r)}) \\
&= (y_1^{(r)},...,\, y_j^{(r+1)},...,\, y_N^{(r)}) = (y_1^{(r+1)},...,\, y_j^{(r+1)},...,\, y_N^{(r+1)})
\end{aligned} \tag{8.8}$$

In Figure 8.2, we denote the states by $S_0,...,\, S_Q$. A state S_q is called *stable* whenever $A_j(S_q) = S_q$ for all j and $F(S_q) = S_q$, where A_j is the asynchronous, and F is the synchronous, *transition* process. A set of states, possibly a single one, from which there is no escape once reached, is called an *attractor*. A sequence of distinct states $\{S_{j1},...,\, S_{jk}\}$ is called a *cycle of length k* if continuing iterations of state transitions cause this sequence to be repeated. There are paths (trajectories) in the figure going from S_0 to S_7, but once the path reaches state S_7, it can never escape. Thus S_7 is stable—that is, is a singleton attractor. A transition from one state to another is determined by the randomly selected jth neurode to fire and the noise I_j, so the transitions are *stochastic*.

Finite Automata

A *finite automaton* (or *finite-state machine*) is a system (as displayed in Figure 8.3) that accepts a string of symbols from an alphabet as inputs, puts out symbols from an alphabet as outputs, and contains a memory for N symbols, collectively called the *state*, such that (i) the

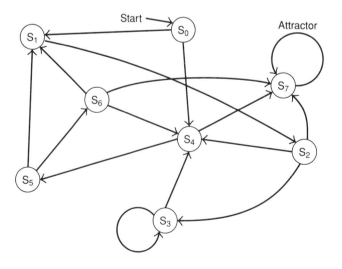

Figure 8.2. A state transition diagram.

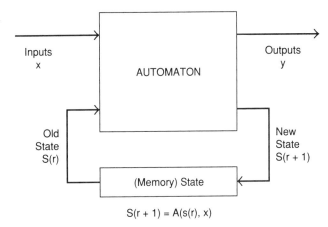

Figure 8.3. A finite-state machine.

$$S(r + 1) = A(s(r), x)$$

next state is a function of the current state and the current input symbol and (ii) the output symbol is also a function of the current state and current input symbol. A system that satisfies the above criteria, except that it does not have any inputs, is called a *finite-state generator* (it generates a sequence of outputs as a function of the current state). A system that accepts inputs but does not generate any outputs is called a *finite-state recognizer*. When a sequence of inputs leads to a stable state (an identifier), we say that the system has *recognized* the input sequence pattern (the input feature string). An automaton can be used as either a finite-state generator or a finite-state recognizer. In fact, it convenient to use it as a finite-state recognizer to put out a special character when recognition is made, but put out a different character at all other times.

Because the order of the firings is random, a Hopfield network is a *stochastic* finite-state recognizer. The initial input vector $\mathbf{y}^{(0)} = \mathbf{x}$ is the input and initial state, and it causes a nondeterministic process to ensue due to the firing of the neurodes in random order. If a stable state is reached, the Hopfield network has *recognized* the initial input feature vector, and the stable state is the identifier for it.

8.3. Computing The Weights

A Simple Learning Rule: The Computational Formula

The weights for an HRNN and a set of exemplars $\{\mathbf{x}^{(q)}\}$ are computed (Lippmann, 1987) by

$$w_{ij} = \mathrm{sgn}(\textstyle\sum_{(q=1, Q)} x_i^{(q)} x_j^{(q)}), \quad \text{for } i \neq j; \qquad w_{ii} = 0, \quad \text{for } i = j \tag{8.9}$$

where $\mathbf{x}^{(q)}$ is the feature vector for the kth class. Section 8.7 provides background on why this rule is used. Note that the values for the weights are 1 or -1, except for the entries on the main diagonal, which are all zero because lines do not exist for them. Hopfield showed that stable states existed when W is symmetrical. Other states may also exist, as well as cycles of states. Empirical studies show that some feature vectors converge to cyclic attractors (which repeat ad infinitum without escape) or wander chaotically through the *state space* (the set of all possible states). Hopfield's proof of convergence, provided in the next section, establishes convergence to stable states but requires symmetry of the weight matrix W.

Example 8.1. An Example of Weight Computation and State Updating

Let a Hopfield network have $N = 3$ neurodes. The *state space* is $S = \{(1,1,1),(1,1,-1),...,(-1,-1,-1)\}$, where $|S| = 2^3 = 8$ is the size of the state space. First, we put $w_{ii} = 0$ for $i = 1,...,3$. Let there be two identifier state vectors (also called *memory* vectors): $\mathbf{x}^{(1)} = (-1,-1,1)$ and $\mathbf{x}^{(2)} = (1,1,-1)$. Next, we compute the remaining weights from Equation (8.9): $w_{12} = w_{21}$ are found from $(-1)(-1) + (1)(1) = 2 > 0$, so the weight value is 1; $w_{13} = w_{31}$ are found from $(-1)(1) + (1)(-1) = -2 < 0$, so the weight value is -1; and $w_{23} = w_{32}$ are found from $(-1)(1) + (1)(-1) = -2 < 0$, which yields a weight value of -1. Thus the rows of W are

$$
\begin{aligned}
&\text{Row 1:} \quad 0, \quad 1, \quad -1 \\
&\text{Row 2:} \quad 1, \quad 0, \quad -1 \\
&\text{Row 3:} \quad -1, \quad -1, \quad 0
\end{aligned}
$$

Let the initial input be $\mathbf{x} = (-1, -1, -1)$. Then the initial state of the system is $\mathbf{y}^{(0)} = (-1,-1,-1) = \mathbf{x}$. Suppose that the second neurode is the first to fire and that the random disturbances are zero. The state component $y_2^{(1)}$ at the second neurode is obtained by multiplying the second row times $\mathbf{y}^{(0)}$ per

$$
y_2^{(1)} = \text{sgn}(\textstyle\sum_{(i=1,\,3)} w_{2i} y_2^{(0)}) = \text{sgn}((w_{21} y_1^{(0)}) + (w_{22} y_2^{(0)}) + (w_{23} y_3^{(0)}))
$$

$$
= \text{sgn}((1)(-1) + (0)(-1) + (-1)(-1)) = \text{sgn}(0) = y_2^{(0)} \to -1 \text{ (no change)}
$$

The scheme is

Neurode j	W			$\mathbf{y}^{(r)}$		$\mathbf{y}^{(r+1)}$
1	0	1	−1	−1		−1 (does not fire)
2	1	0	−1	−1	$\to \text{sign}(-1 + 0 + 1) \to$	−1 (fires with no change)
3	−1	−1	0	−1		−1 (does not fire)

Because the first and third components of $\mathbf{y}^{(r)}$ do not fire on this first transition and so do not change, the transition to the new state $(-1,-1,-1) \to (-1,-1,-1)$ doesn't change the state.

If the third neurode fires next, then in a similar fashion, the new third component of the state is determined by $\text{sgn}((-1)(-1) + (-1)(-1) + (0)(-1)) = \text{sgn}(2) = 1$. This causes the following transition to be made: $(-1,-1,-1) \to (-1,-1,1)$. Let the first neurode be the next one to fire. Then the first component of the new state is determined by $\text{sgn}((0)(-1) + (1)(-1) + (-1)(1)) = \text{sgn}(-2) = -1$, which implies the transition $(-1,-1,1) \to (-1,-1,1)$. If the second neurode then fires again, there is no change in the state as before.

If the third neurode fires, then the state remains the same, so a stable attractor has been reached. It sometimes happens that an input will make a sequence of transitions that take it to a stable state that is not one of the identifier states, in which case we say that the system converges to a *spurious* stable state. Noise can lead to spurious states.

8.4. Theorems of Hopfield and Bruck: An Analysis of Convergence

The Transition Paths and Hopfield's Theorem

A finite automaton has a finite number of states. For a binary alphabet such as $\{-1,1\}$, the state space consists of all of the corners of the N-dimensional hypercube. Given an initial state to start from, it may: (i) remain in the initial state forever; (ii) make a finite number of transitions and then remain in a *final* state forever; (iii) move through a repetitive path of states, known as a *cycle*, forever; (iv) move through a sequence of cycles (a supercycle) forever; or (v) wander aimlessly, without any order of repeating cycles. From among this universe of possibilities, Hopfield's result brings order for certain conditions.

> *Hopfield's Theorem.* Let an HRNN with N neurodes operate in the random serial mode (single neurodes fire in random order). When the $N \times N$ weight matrix W is symmetric with nonnegative main diagonal, the input noise is zero, and the thresholds are zero, then the network always converges to a stable state, and there are no cycles in the state space transitions.

> *Proof:* [*Part 1—Show that the energy increments converge to zero*] The energy function for a state is the quadratic function defined via

$$E \equiv \tfrac{1}{2}\mathbf{y}^t W \mathbf{y} - \boldsymbol{\tau}^t \mathbf{y} + \mathbf{I}^t \mathbf{y} \tag{8.10}$$

The gradient of this is

$$\nabla E = (\partial E/\partial y_1,..., \partial E/\partial y_N) = \tfrac{1}{2}(W^t + W)\mathbf{y} - \boldsymbol{\tau} + \mathbf{I} = W\mathbf{y} - \boldsymbol{\tau} + \mathbf{I} \tag{8.11a}$$

The last part follows because $W^t = W$ for symmetric matrices. Because noise is zero and the thresholds are zero, this becomes

$$\nabla E = (\partial E/\partial y_1,..., \partial E/\partial y_N) = \tfrac{1}{2}(W^t + W)\mathbf{y} = W\mathbf{y} \tag{8.11b}$$

The updating without noise and with zero threshold is

$$y_j^{(r+1)} = \text{sgn}(\textstyle\sum_{(i=1,N)}[w_{ij}y_i^{(r)}]) \tag{8.11c}$$

The energy increment from one iteration to another becomes

$$\Delta E = (\nabla E)^t \Delta \mathbf{y} = (0,..., 0, \Delta y_j, 0,..., 0) \tag{8.12}$$

for some j because only the single jth neurode fires on this iteration. The change in $\mathbf{y}$ is

$$\Delta y_j = y_j^{(r+1)} - y_j^{(r)}; \qquad \Delta y_i = 0 \quad \text{for all } i \neq j \tag{8.13}$$

Therefore, the energy difference on the iteration due to only the jth neurode (Equations (8-11b) and (8-12)) is

$$\Delta E = (\textstyle\sum_{(i=1,N)} w_{ij} y_i^{(r)}) \Delta y_j \tag{8.14}$$

The update rule for $y_j^{(r+1)}$ that shows its sign dependence upon the sign of the sum is given by Equation (8-11c). All sign combinations for $\mathbf{y}^{(r+1)}$, $\mathbf{y}^{(r)}$, and ΔE are shown in Table 8.1. The asterisks in the table indicate conditions that are not allowed, i.e., that would violate Equation (8.11c) because $\mathbf{y}^{(r+1)}$ must have the same sign as $\sum_{(i=1,N)} w_{ij} y_i^{(r)}$. This leaves only the first two, and last two, rows as being valid. In the case of the first and last rows in the table, the increments are zero. But in the second and seventh rows, the increment is positive. Thus all valid cases have either a zero or positive energy increment. Because the energy is bounded from above and can only increase or stay the same, the energy converges to a constant. This means that the energy increments converge to zero. This proves the first part.

[*Part 2—Show that the state converges*] Although the energy is always nonnegative, is bounded from above, and is monotonically nondecreasing, so the energy increment must converge to zero, we have not yet showed that there cannot be two or more states (a nonsingleton attractor) with equal energy. Now we note that (i) if $\Delta y_j = 0$, then $\Delta E = 0$ (the state remains the same); and (ii) if ($\Delta y_j \neq 0$ AND $\Delta E = 0$), then some single y_j changed precisely from -1 to 1 or 1 to -1, which contradicts the hypothesis that $\Delta E = 0$ because Equation (8.14) and $\Delta y_j \neq 0$ make the product in Equation (8.14) nonzero (note that if the sum in Equation (8.14) were zero, then it would contradict the assumption that the sign changed according to Equation (8.11c)). Therefore, as the energy increment converges to zero, the ability of the system to change states is diminished to null. Thus the system converges to a single state.

Table 8.1.
Sign Combinations in the Energy Increment

$\sum_{(i=1,N)}[w_{ij}y_i^{(r)}])$	$y_j^{(r+1)}$	$y_j^{(r)}$	$\Delta y_j = y_j^{(r+1)} - y_j^{(r)}$	$\Delta E = \left(\sum_{(i=1,N)} w_{ij}y_i\right)\Delta y_j$
+	+	+	0	0
+	+	−	+	+
+	−	+	*	*
+	−	−	*	*
−	+	+	*	*
−	+	−	*	*
−	−	+	−	+
−	−	−	0	0

It is noteworthy that this convergence holds without noise, or in the average sense with a noise average of zero. If the noise power is sufficiently large at some point before convergence has occurred, however, it may force the state to jump into the field of potential (pull) of another attractor or attractor set and thus converge to an incorrect stable state or final set. Hopfield noted that errors increased as the number of classes increased for a given number N of neurodes and that the number of classes that can be safely recalled is no more than 15% of the number of neurodes. Considering other research such as Hopfield (1983), McEliece et al. (1987), Venktesh and Psaltis (1989), and Dembo (1989), we feel that 10% is a safer level for the standard HRNN.

Bruck's Theorems

The following theorems were proved in Bruck (1990) via graph theoretic methods. They add significantly to the theory of convergence of Hopfield networks.

Bruck's Theorem. If it is true that a symmetric weight matrix W with zero main diagonals implies that the network converges in random serial mode to a stable state, then the following also hold:

(i) If W is symmetric with nonnegative main diagonal, then the network always converges to a stable state.

(ii) If the network is working in full parallel mode and W is a symmetric weight matrix (no conditions on the main diagonal), then the network always converges either to a stable state or to an attractor that is cyclic of length 2.

(iii) If the network is working in full parallel mode and W is an antisymmetric weight matrix with zero main diagonal, then the network always converges to an attractor that is a cycle of length 4.

Bruck's Counterexample Theorems. (1) For $N \geq 2$ and an even integer, there exists a Hopfield network with antisymmetric W and N neurodes whose random serial mode of operation has a cycle of length 2^N. (2) For $N > 0$, there exists a Hopfield network with $3N$ nodes whose fully parallel mode of operation has a cycle of length 2^N.

8.5. An Algorithm for Hopfield Networks

The Hopfield Network Algorithm

This algorithm (Lippmann, 1987) is easy to implement in a computer program. Although no iterative training is required, testing must be done to ensure that each exemplar feature vector used converges to a unique identifier vector for a class. In that case, the network and exemplars are suitable for use, with one proviso (see the paragraph after the algorithm listing).

Inputs: {the number N of neurodes to be used; the number K of classes; the feature exemplar vector $\mathbf{x}^{(k)}$ for each class k; the maximum number I of iterations allowed}

Outputs: {an identifier $\mathbf{y}^{(k)}$ for each of the K classes}

Step 1. /Input data/
input N; input K; input $\{\mathbf{x}^{(k)}\}$;

Step 2. /Assign weight connections to the N neurodes via exemplar correlation/
    for $i = 1$ to N do   /Loop over each node/
      for $j = i$ to N do   /Loop over half of nodes/
        $w_{ij} \leftarrow 0$;
        if $i < j$, then   /Matrix is symmetric/
          for $k = 1$ to K do   /Sum up products, that is, get the/
            $w_{ij} \leftarrow w_{ij} + x_i^{(k)} x_j^{(k)}$;   /correlation of $x_i^{(k)}$, $x_j^{(k)}$ over all K classes/
          $w_{ij} \leftarrow \text{sgn}(w_{ij})$;   /and use the sign/
          $w_{ji} \leftarrow w_{ij}$;   /Symmetry yields other weights/

Step 3. /Input sample feature vector $\mathbf{x}$ to network/
    input $\mathbf{x}$; $r \leftarrow 0$;   /Set iteration count to zero/
    for $i = 1$ to N do $y_i^{(r)} \leftarrow x_i$;   /Input feature vector as initial vector/

Step 4. /Iterate until process converges to stable state or until I iterations are exceeded/
    count $\leftarrow 1$;   /Count 1 to N updates in cycle/
    repeat
      $j \leftarrow \text{Random\_Select}(N)$;   /Select neurode not fired (this cycle) to/
                                     /fire/

      $r \leftarrow r + 1$; sum $\leftarrow 0$;
      for $i = 1$ to N do
        sum $\leftarrow$ sum $+ w_{ij} y_i^{(r)}$;   /Sum up weighted feedback inputs at jth/
                                     /node/
      $I_j \leftarrow \text{Ran\_Noise}(\ )$;   /Select random noise to add on/
      if sum $\neq 0$ then   /Activate jth output if nonzero sum/
        $y_j^{(r)} \leftarrow \text{sgn(sum} + I_j)$;
      else $y_j^{(r)} \leftarrow y_j^{(r-1)}$;   /or else there is no change/
      count $\leftarrow$ count $+ 1$;   /Increment firing count in this cycle/
      stop $\leftarrow$ true;   /To stop or not to stop?/
      if count $\geq N$, then   /If end of update firing cycle of N nodes/
        for $i = 1$ to N do   /then test for any state change/
          if $y_i^{(r)} \neq y_i^{(r-1)}$,   /Don't stop if any change/
            then stop $\leftarrow$ false;
        count $\leftarrow 1$;   /Reset count for next cycle of node/
                                    /firings/
    until (stop = true) OR $(r > I)$;

Step 5. /Choose either to input another sample feature vector for recognition, or stop/
input select;   /Choose to operate again or quit/
if select = true, then goto Step 3; else stop;

A cycle consists of N random serial updates to the N neurodes (exactly one time each). The procedure Ran_Select(N) randomly selects one of the nodes 1, 2,..., N that has not yet been selected in this cycle. The procedure Ran_Noise( ) selects the value for the noise I_j to be added onto the sum at the update of the jth neurode. The variable count keeps track of the number of updates during a single cycle.

The *advantages* of this algorithm are as follows: (i) It iterates on the initially given feature vector until it outputs an *exact* class identifier, and (ii) there is no iterative training required. The *disadvantages* are as follows: (i) The number of classes (final states) should be less than 15% (Hopfield, 1982) or 10% for robustness (Wasserman, 1993) of the number of neurodes (the number of features) according to empirical laws, which severely limits the number of classes (to $N/10$) for a given number N of features; (ii) the recognition in the operational mode requires sequential iterations; and (iii) an exemplar feature vector may converge to an incorrect class identifier if it shares many feature values with another exemplar feature vector for another class and contains noise. *In practice*, Hopfield recurrent neural networks (HRNNs) are appropriate for tasks where there is a large number of features relative to the number of classes. When the $0.1N$ bound is exceeded, the *déjà vu* effect occurs, where the network recalls states that it was never taught (Wasserman, 1993). Work by (McEliece et al., 1987) sets the proportion of states (classes) to features as $K < N/(2 \log_2 N)$. For $N = 16$, this would allow a single class to be recognizable robustly. For $N = 256$ features, this would allow at most $K = 16$ classes, which is less than the number of lowercase letters in the English alphabet.

8.6. Increasing the Capacity of Hopfield Networks

Capacity

Hopfield put the number of stable patterns for the HRNN at $0.15N$ (for N neurodes) in his original paper (Hopfield, 1982). Since then, many others have obtained results that show better performance capability. A state vector $\mathbf{y}^{(r)}$ is said to be *stable* whenever both

$$\mathbf{y}^{(r+1)} = A_j(\mathbf{y}^{(r)}) = \mathbf{y}^{(r)} \tag{8.15}$$

for any asynchronous firing of any jth neuron, where the firing operation is denoted by A_j, and

$$\mathbf{y}^{(r+1)} = F(\mathbf{y}^{(r)}) = \mathbf{y}^{(r)} \tag{8.16}$$

for any parallel firing, denoted by $F(-)$.

An *associative memory* is a process or device that memorizes an association (Anderson, 1968) between an input pattern and an output pattern. The output one may be similar to the input pattern (*autoassociative*), in which case the process of association can eliminate noise on the input. In other systems it may be very different (*heteroassociative*).

The *Hamming distance* $|\mathbf{u} - \mathbf{v}|_H$ between two vectors $\mathbf{u} = (u_1,..., u_N)$ and $\mathbf{v} = (v_1,..., v_N)$ is the number of components in which they differ; for example, $|(1,1,-1,1) - (1,-1,1,1)|_H = 2$ because the two vectors differ in exactly two positions. See Zurada (1992, p. 344) for a discussion of capacity for associative memory systems. Given a stable state $\mathbf{y}$, the *radius of attraction* $\rho(\mathbf{y})$ for $\mathbf{y}$ is a fraction such that every input vector $\mathbf{x}$ within the distance $\rho(\mathbf{y})N$

from $\mathbf{y}$ converges to $\mathbf{y}$ when input to the HRNN. While associative memories must have every input converge to a stable state, this is not necessary for the finite-state recognizers in which we are interested. Recall that in the above algorithm, the weights actually store information about the input feature vectors to be used (their correlation). If any pair of these stored feature vectors are too close, noise on one input vector may cause it to fall within the pull of the other vector. Otherwise, the HRNN performs error correction to map the input into the stable state that identifies it.

The *capacity* of an HRNN is the number c of stable states it has. Obviously, c depends on the weight matrix, which we take to be symmetric with zeros on the diagonal. It was shown by McEliece et al. (1987) that

$$N/[(4)\ln(N)] < c < N/[(2)\ln(N)] \tag{8.17}$$

For 100 neurodes, this yields c that satisfies $5 < c < 10$. The study by McEliece et al. also showed that other spurious vectors existed with small basins of attraction, so that inputs would converge to one of these terminal states if they were in its vicinity. While this appears to doom Hopfield networks to a dismal and hardly useful performance, other researchers have shown that the performance can be made better.

Successive Overrelaxation

The method of *successive overrelaxation* (SOR) was used by Oh and Kothari (1991) to enlarge the capacity of recursive NNs. Chen and Cheung (1993) used this method and obtained a lower bound. A vector $\mathbf{y} = (y_1,..., y_N)$ is a *stable state* if

$$\sum_{(j=1, N)} (w_{ij}y_j - \tau_i)y_i > 0 \qquad (i = 1,..., N) \tag{8.18}$$

from the definition of a stable state in Equations (8.15) and (8.16) above. Let us be given the K training vectors $\{\mathbf{y}^{(1)},..., \mathbf{y}^{(K)}\}$. The weights are adapted by the SOR technique according to

$$\Delta w_{ij} = -[(1 + \delta)/N][S_i^{(k)} - \epsilon y_i^{(k)}]y_j^{(k)}, \qquad \text{if } S_i^{(k)}y_i^{(k)} < \epsilon \tag{8.19}$$

$$\Delta \tau_i = [(1 + \delta)/N][S_i^{(k)} - \epsilon y_i^{(k)}], \qquad \text{if } S_i^{(k)}y_i^{(k)} < \epsilon \tag{8.20}$$

where $S_i^{(k)}$ is the sum

$$S_i^{(k)} = \sum_{(j=1, N)} (w_{ij}y_j^{(k)} - \tau_i) \tag{8.21}$$

and δ is an overrelaxation factor strictly between 0 and 1. The normalizing constant ϵ must be positive. The Hopfield conditions hold here; that is, the weight matrix is symmetric ($w_{ij} = w_{ji}$) and $w_{ii} = 0$.

Chen and Cheung ran simulations using SOR and found stable vectors. After running on small values of N, they extrapolated to large N and concluded a lower bound for the proportion of stable states to be

$$p = (\sqrt{3})^{N-1}$$

when the SOR weight adaptation is used. They also showed that the capacity approaches the asymptote of $\alpha 2^{n-1}$ as $n \to \infty$, where $0 < \alpha < 1$. These appear to be the best results on HRNNs.

8.7. Hopfield Networks as Content Addressable Memory

Content Addressable Memory

A *content addressable memory* is a memory whose address is its contents, or rather a portion of its contents. The basic idea is that the entire contents of a memory buffer area can be recalled by a substring of its contents. The use of a Hopfield network is natural for this purpose because the network associates the initial input $\mathbf{x} = \mathbf{y}^{(0)}$ with a final state $\mathbf{y}^{(f)}$, where $\mathbf{x}$ represents the same string (codeword) as does $\mathbf{y}^{(f)}$, except that $\mathbf{x}$ is corrupted by noise. Because both input and output represent the same codeword, a Hopfield is often called an *autoassociative memory network*.

Thus Hopfield networks are used as CAMs, which feed a noise corrupted codeword $\mathbf{x} = \mathbf{y}^{(0)}$ back through the network a number of times until a final state $\mathbf{y}^{(f)}$ of the same dimension is reached that is the correct contents. In pattern recognition, the noise corrupted features are fed back in a loop until the output is a stable state that represents the uncorrupted features of the pattern, which can then be used as the unique identifier for a class. According to Aiyer et al. (1990), HRNNs can produce useful results, but they suffer from spurious stable points and invalid solutions for the traveling salesman problem.

The Aiyer–Niranjan–Fallside Analysis

Hopfield extended the use of Liapunov functions by (Amari, 1977) from McCulloch–Pitts neurons to two-valued asynchronous neurons in Hopfield (1982). A dynamic system

$$\nabla \mathbf{v} = F(\mathbf{v}, t)$$

is stable whenever there exists a *Liapunov function* $\ell(\mathbf{v})$ that decreases along the trajectories where $d\ell/dt \leq 0$. Such monotonicity of $\ell(\mathbf{v})$ of a Liapunov function is a sufficient (but not necessary) condition for the system to be asymptotically stable. Aiyer et al. (1990) analyze the CAM properties of the discrete and continuous cases of HRNNs. We consider only the discrete case here.

The HRNN processing can be divided into two parts: (i) $\mathbf{v}^{(r+1)} = W\mathbf{y}^{(r)} + \mathbf{I}_j$; and (ii) $\mathbf{y}^{(r+1)} = \text{sgn}(\mathbf{v}^{(r+1)})$, where $\mathbf{I}_j$ contains all zeros except the jth component, which is the value I_j. Hopfield's Liapunov function is

$$E = -\tfrac{1}{2}\mathbf{v}'W\mathbf{v} - \mathbf{I}_j'\mathbf{v} \tag{8.22}$$

Figure 8.4 shows the contours of constant E. For simplicity, Aiyer et al. (1990) omit the noise term $\mathbf{I}_j'\mathbf{v}$. The Liapunov function E is bounded and decreasing, so it converges. In a system with finitely many states (2^N for the N-dimensional states), if the state does not change

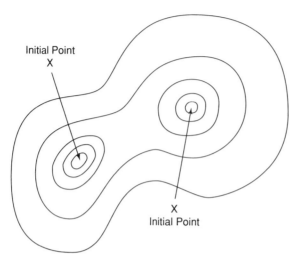

Figure 8.4.   Energy function contours.

Initial Point
X

X
Initial Point

for each neurodal change of its state component (i.e., it does not change further), then a stable state is reached after a finite number of transitions. This is a point (state) of content addressable memory for which the input $\mathbf{x}$ provides an address by partial content.

The weight matrix W is symmetric, so it can be completely characterized by its eigenvalues $\{\lambda_i\}_N$ and orthogonal eigenvectors $\mathbf{e}^{(1)},..., \mathbf{e}^{(N)}$. A state vector $\mathbf{v}$ can be projected onto its space of nondegenerate eigenvectors via

$$\mathbf{v} = \sum_i \lambda_i \mathbf{e}^{(i)} \tag{8.23a}$$

According to Aiyer et al. (1990)

$$W = \sum_i \lambda_i \mathbf{e}^{(i)} (\mathbf{e}^{(i)})^t \qquad \text{(outer products)} \tag{8.23b}$$

and it follows that

$$E = -\tfrac{1}{2}\sum_i \lambda_i \|\mathbf{e}^i\|^2 = -\tfrac{1}{2}\sum_i \lambda_i c_i^2 \tag{8.24a}$$

$$\mathbf{v}^{(r+1)} = W\mathbf{y}^{(r)} = \sum_i \lambda_i \mathbf{e}^i \tag{8.24b}$$

As stated by Aiyer et al. (1990), we can now observe how to minimize E. The HRNN must move $\mathbf{v}$ so as to (i) reduce to zero length all $\mathbf{v}^{(i)} = \lambda_i \mathbf{e}^i$, where $\lambda_i < 0$; and (ii) increase the length of all $\mathbf{v}^{(i)}$, where $\lambda_i > 0$. Because $\mathbf{v}$ and $\mathbf{v}^{(i)}$ belong to the finite-dimensional hypercube, E cannot decrease indefinitely but is minimized when $\mathbf{v} = c_{max}\mathbf{e}^{(max)}$, where $\mathbf{e}^{(max)}$ is the eigenvector for the largest positive eigenvalue $\lambda_{max} > 0$. The eigenvalues of W are critical: If there is a single positive eigenvalue that is multiply degenerate, then E is minimized when $\mathbf{v}$ belongs to the corresponding subspace (the entire subspace is a final, or stable, set of states).

A Simple Learning Rule

The weight matrix W must be selected as follows: (i) The original vectors to be stored as CAM words (states) must be stable points (states) of the network determined by W; and (ii) these stable states should have a *radius of convergence* with respect to the Hamming distance, so that any partial contents—that is, noise corrupted initial state vector—must converge to the contents (the final state, which is the identifier vector). Aiyer et al. show that this means that (a) the null subspace of the state space determined by the complement of the subspace spanned by the eigenvectors must be orthogonal to each of the *memory vectors* (the state vectors that are to be the CAM and thus the final states) $\{\mathbf{y}^{(q)}\}_Q$, (b) the eigenvectors of W must span (at least) the subspace spanned by the memory vectors, and (c) the weight matrix W must have a single positive degenerate eigenvalue corresponding to the memory vector subspace so that $\lambda_i = \lambda > 0$ for $i = 1,..., N$.

Conditions (a), (b), and (c) are met by the simple *learning rule*

$$W_M = \sum_{q=1, Q} \mathbf{y}^{(q)}(\mathbf{y}^{(q)})^t \qquad \text{(outer products)} \qquad (8.25)$$

This is known as the *outer product rule* or is sometimes called the *correlation rule*. On the other hand, there is the argument that if the number of neurodes N is much greater than the number of memory vectors ($N \geq 10Q$), and if the memory vectors are chosen randomly, then the probability is high that the memory vectors are almost orthogonal to each other.

The Venkatesh–Psaltis–Dembo Learning Rule

Another learning rule that has been investigated by Dembo (1989) and by Venkatesh and Psaltis (1989) consists of the following: (i) Choose the memory vectors $\{\mathbf{y}^{(q)}\}_Q$ to be linearly independent; (ii) put $A = \{\mathbf{y}^{(1)},..., \mathbf{y}^{(Q)}\}$ as a matrix of memory vectors; and (iii) take $W = A(A^tA)^{-1}A^t$. The result is that each memory vector $\mathbf{y}$ is a fixed point—that is, a stable state. This rule is substantially more computationally complex than the previous rule.

The memory vectors $\{\mathbf{y}^{(1)},..., \mathbf{y}^{(Q)}\}$ are the CAMs. When a corrupted input vector is presented to the system, that vector is projected onto the space S_M spanned by the memory vectors. All hypercube corners that are in or near the corners contained in S_M but that are not memory vectors are spurious stable states that may become an attractor for any corrupted input memory vector. By setting the main diagonal elements of W to zero, we introduce a negative eigenvalue for the subspace orthogonal to S_M. The HRNN projects an input vector into S_M and then moves that vector to the nearest hypercube corner, which is either a memory vector or a spurious state vector. In this latter case, there is an error in CAM recall—that is, an error in recognition. Aiyer et al. (1990) state that several researchers have found, for different reasons, that the relative number of spurious states decreases as the dimensionality N of the states increases. For N large enough, there are few spurious stable states within a certain Hamming distance of any memory vectors, so that it becomes essentially valid to consider each memory vector as having a radius of convergence.

8.8. Extended Hopfield Networks: Kosko's Bidirectional Associative Memory

In the HRNN, the inputs are multiplied by weights to produce states that are then fed back to the inputs. This model extends to Kosko's *bidirectional associative memory* (Kosko, 1987), also known as BAM, which is a heteroassociative memory. Each input feature vector $\mathbf{x}$ is associated with an output vector $\mathbf{y}$. Let $\mathbf{x} = (x_1,..., x_N)$ have N components, and let $\mathbf{y} = (y_1,..., y_M)$ have M components. A weight matrix W is used to convert $\mathbf{x}$ to $\mathbf{y}$:

$$\mathbf{x} \xrightarrow{W} \mathbf{y} \tag{8.26}$$

This processing is done at the N neurodes at the first layer and feeds the output $\mathbf{y}$ as inputs to the second layer of M neurodes, where the transpose weight matrix W^t is used per

$$\mathbf{y} \xrightarrow{W^t} \mathbf{x} \tag{8.27}$$

Figure 8.5 shows the arrangement that is a two-way associative memory. The weight matrix W and W^t are computed before the iterations start. The algorithm is given below. We assume that there are Q pairs of vectors to be associated, which are $\mathbf{x}^{(1)},..., \mathbf{x}^{(Q)}$ and $\mathbf{y}^{(1)},..., \mathbf{y}^{(Q)}$, where $\mathbf{x}^{(q)}$ is N-dimensional and $\mathbf{y}^{(q)}$ is M-dimensional. We associate $\mathbf{x}^{(q)}$ with $\mathbf{y}^{(q)}$ for each q, $q = 1,..., Q$. The component values of the associated vectors are bipolar—that is, 1 and -1. The threshold function $f(-)$ is the sign function in this case ($f(a) = 1$ if $a \geq 0$, else $f(a) = -1$).

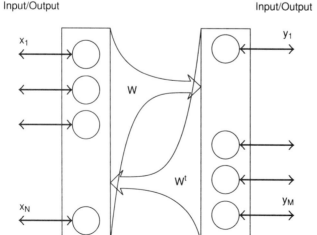

Input/Output   Input/Output   **Figure 8.5.**   Kosko's BAM network.

x_1

W

W^t

x_N

y_1

y_M

Step 1. /Compute the weight matrix W for use as W and W^t/

        for $n = 1$ to N do   /For each first layer neurode/

            for $m = 1$ to M do   /For each second layer neurode/

                $w_{nm} \leftarrow \sum_{(q=1, Q)} \sum_{(p=1, Q)} x_n^{(q)} y_m^{(p)};$ /$W = \{w_{nm}\}$ is sum of outer/

                                                                       /products/

Step 2. /Transform and use the sign function as threshold/

        $r \leftarrow 0;$

        repeat

            for $m = 1$ to M do   /Update $\mathbf{y}(r + 1)$/

                $y_m(r + 1) \leftarrow f(\sum_{(n=1, N)} w_{nm} x_n(r));$

            for $n = 1$ to N do   /Update $\mathbf{x}(r + 1)$/

                $x_n(r + 1) \leftarrow f(\sum_{(m=1, M)} w_{nm}^t y_m(r + 1));$ /w_{nm}^t is in W^t/

            $r \leftarrow r + 1;$ /Update iteration number/

        until $(\mathbf{y}(r + 1) = \mathbf{y}(r))$ or $(r > I);$

Notice that $W \leftarrow \mathbf{x}^{(1)}(\mathbf{y}^{(1)})^t + \cdots + \mathbf{x}^{(Q)}(\mathbf{y}^{(Q)})^t$ in Step 1, that is, W is the sum of the Q $N \times M$ matrices that are generated by the outer products of associated vectors. The input and output vectors are updated consecutively until the output vector does not change. Note that once the network is trained, the user can either present the input vector $\mathbf{x}$ to the network to obtain the associated output vector $\mathbf{y}$ or present the output vector $\mathbf{y}$ to the network to find the associated vector $\mathbf{x}$.

The *advantages* are as follows: (i) The BAM network can be used two ways as explained above; and (ii) it can recognize more classes than the HRNN in that the number of classes cannot exceed the minimum of the number of neurodes in any of the two layers. It is possible to increase the number of classes even further (Haines and Hecht-Nielsen, 1988). A known *disadvantage* is that the associations must be one-to-one.

Exercises

8.1. Write a computer program that implements the HRNN algorithm for any input size N up to $N = 10,000$.

8.2. Set up an HRNN with 20 neurodes to be used as a recognizer for the 3-bit parity problem with inputs x_1, x_2, x_3, where, for example 1, 0, 1 would be in the class of even parity, and 1, 1, 1 would be in the class of odd parity. Use the extra neurodes to help in the convergence, although they do not necessarily have any meaning to the inputs of the problem. Use the computer program from Exercise 8.1 above to run and check the performance.

8.3. Modify the algorithm given in the text so that it runs in fully parallel mode.

8.4. Modify the computer program from Exercise 8.1 so that it runs in the fully parallel mode. Does this help or hinder the performance?

8.5. Make an 8×8 square grid and make the numeral "4" of black and white grid squares to use as a *memory vector* (identifier). Use the value -1 for black and 1 for white. Use the program from Exercise 8.1 above with $N = 640$ neurodes for CAM identification of a corrupted version of that memory vector. The memory vector is to be corrupted using the following scheme: Generate a uniform random number between 0 and 1 for each of the 64 grid squares; and if the number is less than 0.25, change the pixel value (from 1 to -1 or from -1 to 1). Feed this new corrupted feature vector into the network and record the outputs of the first, third, fifth and final iterations on an 8×8 square grid. Does it converge?

8.6. Use the following rule for updating a single jth neurode in random serial fashion: If sum $= 0$, then if $y_j = -1$, sgn(sum) $= 1$ else no change. How does this affect the algorithm? How does it affect the convergence in the energy argument?

8.7. Show that Parts (i) and (ii) of Bruck's theorem are equivalent.

8.8. Devise a scheme to use Hopfield networks in a fully parallel mode. [*Hint*: Put in a sequence detector so that a path cycle can be detected and used for an identifier.]

8.9. Modify the HRNN so that *analog* values for $\mathbf{x}$ and $\mathbf{y}^{(r)}$ can be used on *discrete* time feedbacks. Use a bipolar sigmoid activation function. The values must be between -1 and 1. What can be said about the convergence of energy? What can be said about the convergence of the states?

8.10. In the convergence argument of Hopfield's theorem, the weight matrix W was symmetric. Why did the argument need for W to be symmetric? If W is antisymmetric, how does that affect the proof and what is the result?

8.11. What effect does it have if we take the negative of the weights given in the algorithm for the Hopfield network? How does it affect convergence and can there still be convergence to stable states?

8.12. Does the choice of diagonal weights have any important effect on the energy argument that proves Hopfield's theorem?

8.13. Make a copy of the program developed in Exercise 8.4 above that runs in fully parallel mode. Now run it on the 3-bit parity problem (see Exercise 8.2). What are the results? What purpose do the extra neurodes serve?

8.14. Consider a large Hopfield network where the input feature vector is decomposed into subvectors that represent sensor sets for various variables from the external world. Consider using smaller HRNNs for each subvector and then feeding these results into the large HRNN as a codeword. What would be the effect of missing subvectors on the decision? What if all missing values were set randomly, or at some constant value such as 1?

8.15. Write a program that implements the technique of successive overrelaxation to adapt the weights for a HRNN. Run it on the 3-bit parity problem with the same number of nodes as in Exercise 8.2. Compare the results for accuracy.

8.16. Consider the lower bound of Chen and Cheung for the case when the weights have been adapted via the SOR technique. Find a formula for the increase in stable states that are gained by adding a single node. Is this believable?

8.17. Show that if **y** is a stable state, then it satisfies inequality (8.18).

8.18. Devise a HRNN that has two layers of neurodes where the second layer feeds its states back to the first layer in fully parallel mode. What benefits, if any, would such a HRNN provide? What if bipolar sigmoids were used? What about trainability?

8.19. Write a computer program that implements the BAM network. Run it on a set of 16-bit codewords and try to compress them into 8 bits so that they can be recovered in the opposite direction for decoding.

References

Aiyer, S. V. B., Niranjan, M., and Fallside, F. (1990), A theoretical investigation into the performance of the Hopfield model, *IEEE Trans. Neural Networks*, vol. 1, no. 2, 204–215.

Amari, S. (1977), Neural theory of association and concept formation, *Biological Cybernetics*, vol. 26, 175–185.

Anderson, J. A. (1968), A memory storage model utilizing spatial correlation functions, *Kybernetics*, vol. 5, 113–119.

Bruck, J. (1990), On the convergence properties of the Hopfield model, *Proc. IEEE*, vol. 78, no. 10, 1579–1585.

Chen, C. J., and Cheung, J. Y. (1993), Recursive neural networks with high capacity, *Proc. 1993 IEEE Int. Conf. Neural Networks*, 462–465.

Dembo, A. (1989), On the capacity of associative memories with linear thresholding functions, *IEEE Trans. Inf. Theory*, vol. 35, no. 4, 709–720.

Haines, K., and Hecht-Nielsen, R. (1988), A BAM with increased information storage capacity, *Proc. 1988 IEEE Int. Conf. Neural Networks*, vol. 1, 181–190.

Hopfield, J. J. (1982), Neural networks and physical systems with emergent collective computational abilities, *Proc. Natl. Acad. Sci. USA*, vol. 79, 2554–2558.

Hopfield, J. J. (1983), Unlearning has a stabilizing effect in collective memories, *Nature*, vol. 304, p. 158.

Kosko, B. (1987), Bi-directional associative memories, *IEEE Trans. Syst. Man Cybern.*, vol. 18, no. 1, 49–60.

Kosko, B. (1989), Unsupervised learning in noise, *Proc. 1989 IEEE Joint Int. Conf. Neural Networks*, vol. 1, 7–17.

Kosko, B. (1992), *Neural Networks and Fuzzy Systems*, Prentice-Hall, Englewood Cliffs, NJ.

Lippmann, R. P. (1987), An Introduction to Computing with Neural Nets, *IEEE ASSP Mag.*, 4–22, also reprinted in *Neural Networks: Theoretical Foundations and Analysis*, edited by C. Lau (1992), IEEE Press, New York, pp. 5–23.

McEliece, R. J., Posner, E. C., Rodemich, E. R., and Venkatesh, S. S. (1987), The capacity of the Hopfield associative memory, *IEEE Trans. Inf. Theory*, vol. 33, no. 4, 461–482.

Oh, H. and Kothari, S. C. (1991), A new learning approach to enhance the storage capacity of the Hopfield model, *Proc. 1991 Int. Joint Conf. Neural Networks*, Singapore.

Paik, J. K., and Katsaggelos, A. K. (1992), Image restoration using a modified type Hopfield network, *IEEE Trans. Image Processing*, vol. 1, no. 1, 49–63.

Venkatesh, S. S., and Psaltis, D. (1989), Linear and logarithmic capacities in associative neural networks, *IEEE Trans. Inf. Theory*, vol. 35, no. 3, 558–568.

Wasserman, P. D. (1993), *Advanced Methods in Neural Computing*, Van Nostrand Reinhold, New York.

Zurada, J. M. (1992), *Artificial Neural Systems*, West Publishing, St. Paul, MN.

Part IV

Neural, Feature, and Data Engineering

Chapter 9

Neural Engineering and Testing of FANNs

This chapter analyzes architectural requirements, establishes neural engineering principles and discusses the validation of the training and verification of the feedforward artificial neural network model.

9.1. Sizing Up the Network Architecture

How Many Neurodes and Weights?

Feedforward artificial neural networks (FANNs) include multiple-layered perceptrons (MLPs), functional link nets (FLNs), and radial basis function networks (RBFNs). We first consider the architecture of an MLP with a single hidden layer, as shown in Figure 9.1. Section 9.4 discusses the case of two hidden layers and we discuss FLNs and RBFNs in appropriate places. Let N be the number of input branching nodes, M be the number of hidden neurodes, J be the number of output neurodes, Q be the number of exemplar vectors for training, and K be the number of classes that satisfy $K \leq Q$. The network architecture is determined by the numbers N, M, and J. M and J depend on K, and M also depends on Q. The value of N is determined by the given feature space that represents the objects of a population, so we assume here that N is given. Chapter 10 discusses the selection of N and the features, as well as the engineering of the data.

The data determines N, Q, and K. To establish the architecture from N, Q and K, we must choose the number M of neurodes to be used in the single hidden layer and the number J of neurodes in the output layer. Before we can select M and start the training, though, we need to select disjoint subsets of exemplar pairs of sizes Q_T for training, Q_{Val} for validation of the training, and Q_{Ver} for verification of the model (see Section 9.8), where $Q_T + Q_{Val} + Q_{Ver} = Q$. Section 9.8 covers testing of the training.

Section 9.2 shows that the number M of middle neurodes is related to the number of lin-

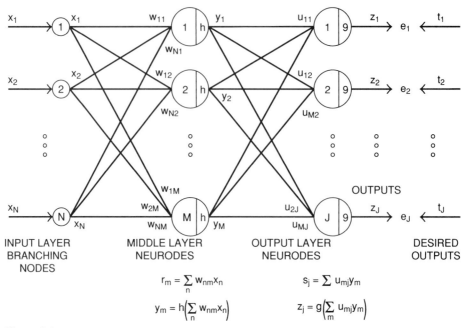

$$r_m = \sum_n w_{nm}x_n \qquad\qquad s_j = \sum_m u_{mj}y_m$$

$$y_m = h\left(\sum_n w_{nm}x_n\right) \qquad\qquad z_j = g\left(\sum_m u_{mj}y_m\right)$$

Figure 9.1.   An MLP with a single hidden layer.

early separable subclasses among the classes. While Huang and Huang (1991) and Kung and Hwang (1988) discuss the number M of hidden neurodes required and Mehrotra et al. (1991) analyze the number Q of samples needed, there is a relationship between Q and M that determines whether or not a unique global sum-squared error solution exists. For RBFNs, the number of hidden neurodes is the number of clusters that serve as linearly separable subclasses to be joined into classes by the output layer. Thus M is related to the number of classes K and even more to the number κ of linearly separable subclasses. For FLNs, there is the additional question of how many auxiliary inputs to use that are functions of the N features. But no process can separate subpopulations unless they are represented by feature vectors that are linearly or nonlinearly separable classes. Thus feature engineering and data engineering are also very important.

MLPs as Parameterized Black Box Mappings

The MLP shown in Figure 9.1 maps input feature vectors $\mathbf{x}^{(q)}$ into their target class identifiers $\mathbf{t}^{(k(q))}$ when in the *operational mode*, where a fixed weight set is employed as coefficients. In the *training mode*, however, the pairs $\{(\mathbf{x}^{(q)}, \mathbf{t}^{(k(q))}): q = 1,..., Q\}$ are parameters and the weights are the variables that vary through the weight space in search of a weight point that minimizes the sum-squared error function E.

The solution weight vector $(\mathbf{w}^*, \mathbf{u}^*)$ minimizes the total sum-squared error (TSSE) E at the J outputs over all Q exemplar pairs. Recall that the TSSE E is defined by

$$E = E(\mathbf{w}, \mathbf{u}) = \sum_{(q=1, Q)} \sum_{(j=1, J)} (z_j^{(q)} - t_j^{(k(q))})^2 \qquad\qquad (9.1)$$

where $z_j^{(q)}$ is the jth output component for input feature vector $\mathbf{x}^{(q)}$ and $t_j^{(k(q))}$ is the jth component of the target identifier vector for class k. The desired output for the qth exemplar input is the kth class identifier $\mathbf{t}^{(k)} = \mathbf{t}^{(k(q))}$, where $k = k(q)$ is the known class of the qth exemplar input vector.

The process of search on the TSSE function seeks to find a weight vector $\mathbf{v} = (\mathbf{w}, \mathbf{u}) = (w_{11},..., w_{NM}, u_{11},..., u_{MJ})$ such that the given set of parameters $\{\mathbf{x}^{(q)}\}_{q=1, Q} = \{(x_1^{(q)},..., x_N^{(q)})\}_{q=1, Q}$ and $\{\mathbf{t}^{(q)}\}_{q=1, Q} = \{(t_1^{(q)},..., t_J^{(q)})\}_{q=1, Q}$ yields a minimum value of E over the weight space. Thus we consider the parameterized mapping

$$(\mathbf{w}, \mathbf{u}) \rightarrow E(\mathbf{w}, \mathbf{u}) = \sum_{(q=1, Q)} \sum_{(j=1, J)} (t_j^{(k(q))} - g(\sum_{(m=1, M)} y_m^{(q)} u_{mj}))^2 \qquad (9.2)$$

where (see Equation (9.1))

$$z_j^{(q)} = g(\sum_{(m=1, M)} y_m^{(q)} u_{mj}) = g(s_j^{(q)}) \qquad (9.3)$$

Figure 9.2 presents a block diagram of the training function $(\mathbf{w}, \mathbf{u}) \rightarrow E(\mathbf{w}, \mathbf{u}; \{(\mathbf{x}^{(q)}, \mathbf{t}^{(q)})\})$, where $\{(\mathbf{x}^{(q)}, \mathbf{t}^{(q)})\}$ represents the set of all exemplar input/output pairs that enter the mapping as parameters. Thus the training mode function is different from the operational mode function where the weights are the parameters.

9.2. Architectural Analysis: How MLPs Work

The Purpose of Architectural Analysis and Design

The goal of analyzing and designing a FANN architecture is simply to satisfy the following: (i) The network must be trained to separate a sample of Q input feature vectors of N components into K classes in a nonlinear fashion, and (ii) the number of neurodes M in a single middle layer (or the numbers L and M of respective neurodes in two hidden layers), as well as the number J of output neurons, should be minimally sufficient so as to separate the K classes in a generalized manner and not introduce extraneous error. Associated with the ques-

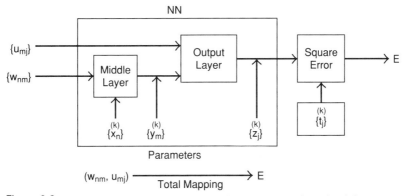

Figure 9.2. A neural network as a parameterized error mapping of weights.

tion of how many hidden neurodes to use is the question of what sample size Q should be used to train the FANN well so that the learning is generalized, rather than specialized. We use the analyses of Bose and Garga (1992, 1993), Makhoul et al. (1989), and Lapedes (1988) below.

Individual Neurodes as Linear Discriminators

It is well known (Minsky and Papert, 1988) that a single neurode discriminates between two half-spaces in the feature vector space. A neurode with weight vector $\mathbf{w}$ performs a scalar (dot) product with an input feature vector $\mathbf{x}$ to obtain the real-valued sum $s = \mathbf{w}^t\mathbf{x}$. A fixed binary decision function $f(-)$ then maps the sum via $s \rightarrow f(s)$ into 0 (left half-space) or 1 (right half-space), depending upon which of the following equations is satisfied

$$s = w_1x_1 + \cdots + w_Nx_N < \tau \tag{9.4}$$

$$s = w_1x_1 + \cdots + w_Nx_N > \tau \tag{9.5}$$

where τ is the threshold. Figure 9.3 shows the resulting half-spaces of planar feature space. The locus of points where $s = \tau$ is the hyperplane itself (the boundary).

The activation function $f(-)$ need not be a step function with discrete outputs, but is taken to be a continuously differentiable approximation to it. It can neither be constant nor decrease by the Hornik–Stinchcombe–Hornik theorem given in Section 3.9. A unipolar or bipolar sigmoid is such an activation function. It squashes the sum s into a value in either $[0,1]$ (unipolar case) or $[-1,1]$ (bipolar case) in a way that tends to push s toward a low or high value to determine the decision halfspace. Thus a neurode performs linear discrimination on the space of feature vectors.

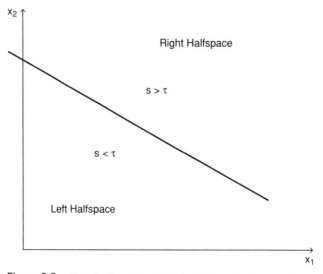

Figure 9.3.   Two half-spaces determined by a single neurode in two-dimensional feature space.

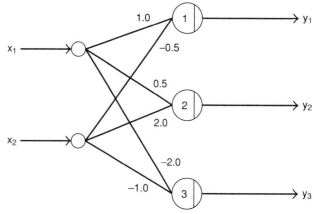

Figure 9.4. A 2–3 single-layer feedforward network.

A Single Layer of Neurodes as Multilinear Discriminators

Let the input layer feed the feature components to a single layer of M neurodes, which we take to be the output layer here by default (there are no other layers of neurodes). Each neurode partitions the feature space into two half-spaces, so the feature space is partitioned by a layer of M neurodes into the intersection of $2M$ half-spaces, which has an upper bound of 2^M and a lower bound of $M + 1$ convex regions in the parallel hyperplane case. We cannot expect these bounds to be actually attained in practice.

Figure 9.4 shows a 2–3 network of a single layer of neurodes ($N = 2$ inputs and $M = 3$ neurodes). Figure 9.5 displays a resulting partition of the N-dimensional feature space by the

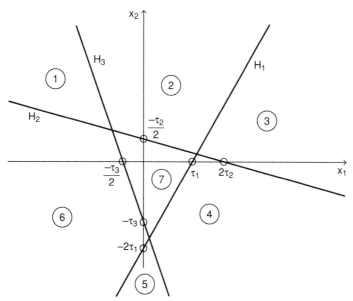

Figure 9.5. A partitioning of the feature space.

three corresponding hyperplanes. The output combination of high and low values for the components of (y_1, y_2, y_3), shown in Figure 9.4, determine to which convex region (an intersection of half-spaces) an input feature vector belongs. The ANDing of any high/low combination of y_1, y_2, and y_3 determines the particular convex region. Such decisionmaking on membership constitutes recognition via linear discrimination.

Example 9.1.   A Single Layer of Perceptrons

Let a 2–3 network have the weight set (see Figure 9.4)

Neurode 1: $w_{11} = 1.0$, $w_{21} = -0.5$
Neurode 2: $w_{12} = 0.5$, $w_{22} = 2.0$
Neurode 3: $w_{13} = -2.0$, $w_{23} = -1.0$

The 3×2 weight matrix maps a 2×1 feature vector $\mathbf{x} = (x_1, x_2)$ into a 3×1 vector of sums by

$$\begin{pmatrix} w_{11} & w_{21} \\ w_{12} & w_{22} \\ w_{13} & w_{23} \end{pmatrix} \begin{pmatrix} x_1 \\ x_2 \end{pmatrix} = \begin{pmatrix} s_1 \\ s_2 \\ s_3 \end{pmatrix}$$

Upon subtracting the threshold values, the resulting equations for the hyperplanes are

$$s_1 - \tau_1 = w_{11}x_1 + w_{21}x_2 - \tau_1 = 1.0x_1 - 0.5x_2 - \tau_1 = 0$$

$$s_2 - \tau_2 = w_{12}x_1 + w_{22}x_2 - \tau_2 = 0.5x_1 + 2.0x_2 - \tau_2 = 0$$

$$s_3 - \tau_3 = w_{13}x_1 + w_{23}x_2 - \tau_3 = -2.0x_1 - 1.0x_2 - \tau_3 = 0 \tag{9.6}$$

A feature vector $\mathbf{x}$ is mapped into one of $2^3 - 1 = 7$ convex regions determined by the intersections of the six half-spaces determined by the three neurodal hyperplanes as is shown in Figure 9.5. For example, all vectors in Region 2 satisfy: left half-space H_1^-, right half-space H_2^+, and right half-space H_3^+.

Nonlinearly Separable Classes as Linearly Separable Subclasses

Consider two classes that are nonlinearly separable only. Figure 9.6 presents such a situation where the classes are decomposed into subclasses that are linearly separable. This can always be done. If necessary, each singleton feature vector can be taken to be a subclass, and because these are discrete points in feature space, each pair of them can be separated by a hyperplane if need be. We can further take the subclasses to be disjoint convex hulls (so the subclasses are pairwise linearly separable). For the definition of convex hull, see Appendix 4. Each pair of these linearly separable subclasses, then, can be separated by a hyperplane determined by a single neurode, which is the purpose of a single layer of neurodes.

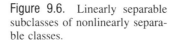

Figure 9.6. Linearly separable subclasses of nonlinearly separable classes.

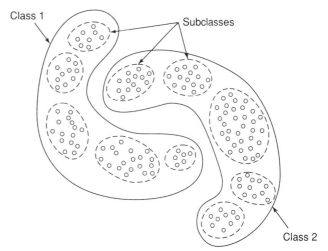

For a population of K subpopulations represented by K classes of the feature space, let the K classes contain, respectively, $\kappa_1,..., \kappa_K$ linearly separable subclasses. Then there are $\kappa = \kappa_1 + \cdots + \kappa_K$ pairwise separable subclasses to be separated pairwise by a maximum of $C(\kappa, 2) = \kappa(\kappa - 1)/2$ (κ items taken two at a time) hyperplanes or a minimum of $\kappa - 1$ parallel hyperplanes. On the other hand, we have seen that κ neurodes determine κ hyperplanes that can separate up to 2^κ regions. Thus $M = \kappa(\kappa - 1)/2$ neurodes are too many, which could separate from $\kappa(\kappa - 1)/2 + 1$ up to $2^{\kappa(\kappa-1)/2}$ regions. Under proper training, up to a maximum of κ subclasses can be separated by M neurons, where $\kappa = 2^M$; that is, $M = \log_2(\kappa)$.

We may thus take from $M = \log_2(\kappa)$ up to $\kappa - 1$ neurodes to separate the κ subclasses. Too many neurodes can lead, however, to overfitting by too many weights, as explained in Section 9.3, to specialization (instead of generalizable learning) and to extraneous noise. On the other hand, too few neurodes can lead to infinitely many solutions, weight drift, and inaccurate overgeneralization.

For κ linearly separable classes, $M = \kappa - 1$ parallel hyperplanes can separate them while as few as $M = \log_2(\kappa)$ can separate them upon proper orientation of the hyperplanes by the training. Upon averaging these values with no a priori knowledge for the κ linearly separable subclasses, we obtain $[(\frac{1}{2})(\kappa - 1) + (\frac{1}{2})\log_2(\kappa)] + 1$, which is approximately $\kappa/2$ when κ is not too small ($\lfloor x \rfloor$ is the greatest integer less than or equal to x). For example, when $\kappa = 256$, $\kappa/2 = 128$ while $\frac{1}{2}(\kappa - 1) + \frac{1}{2}\log_2(256) + 1 \approx 132$.

After selecting the number M of neurodes to separate the κ linearly separable subclasses, there remains the task of adjoining the convex subclasses within a particular class into a single nonconvex class. The class may be nonconvex. This lumping together of subclasses requires a second layer of neurodes to provide a *join* (*union*, or *ORing*) function as described in the next subsection.

Grouping Subclasses into Classes with A Second Layer of Neurodes

Consider the outputs (y_1, y_2, y_3) from the three neurodes of Example 9.1 (see Figure 9.4). If the activations were $(y_1, y_2, y_3) = $ (high, high, low), then this would indicate that the input

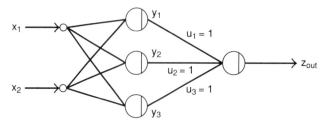

Figure 9.7. Adjoining an output layer.

feature were on the high side of H_1, the high side of H_2, and the low side of H_3, where H_i is one of the three hyperplanes of Figure 9.4, $i = 1, 2, 3$. This determines a particular *meet* (*intersection*, or *ANDing*) function that determines a particular convex region. Each such combination for (y_1, y_2, y_3) determines one of the convex intersections of the halfspaces determined by the hyperplanes (see Figure 9.5).

Now let a new second neurodal layer of a single neurode be connected in an output layer on the right, as presented in Figure 9.7. Let the activated vector (y_1, y_2, y_3) from the previous layer of $M = 3$ neurodes be fed as inputs into the new neurode. This neurode can discriminate its inputs by mapping them into a high or low output value z_{out}. The linear combination at this single neurode in the output layer is $s = s(y_1, y_2, y_3) = u_1 y_1 + u_2 y_2 + u_3 y_3$. We want to activate an output $z_{out} = T(s)$ of a threshold function T from that single output neurode as an identifier for a region that is the union of certain convex regions determined by their convex combinations of high and low values in (y_1, y_2, y_3).

Let us choose weights at the single neurode in the output layer. We put, for example, $u_1 = 1$, $u_2 = 1$, and $u_3 = -1$ and take the threshold $\tau = 0.5$. Whenever a sum s satisfies

$$ s = u_1 y_1 + u_2 y_2 + u_3 y_3 < \tau $$

z_{out} is set to 0, or else it is set to 1. Table 9.1 presents the results. It shows that the convex regions represented by the third, fifth, seventh, and eighth combinations are joined by the output layer neurode into a class defined by $z_{out} = 1$, while the first, second, fourth, and sixth combinations yield $z_{out} = 0$. A different set of weights $\{u_1, u_2, u_3\}$ would have resulted in

Table 9.1.
The Activation of Sums at the Output Neurode

Combination	(y_1, y_2, y_3)	$s = u_1 y_1 + u_2 y_2 + u_3 y_3$ (u_1, u_2, u_3)	s		Threshold	$z_{out} = T(s)$
1	0 0 0	1 1 -1	0	<	0.5	0
2	0 0 1	1 1 -1	-1	<	0.5	0
3	0 1 0	1 1 -1	1	>	0.5	1
4	0 1 1	1 1 -1	0	<	0.5	0
5	1 0 0	1 1 -1	1	>	0.5	1
6	1 0 1	1 1 -1	0	<	0.5	0
7	1 1 0	1 1 -1	2	>	0.5	1
8	1 1 1	1 1 -1	1	>	0.5	1

joins of different convex regions into nonconvex classes. See Example 9.2 for the complete input-output mapping for complemented XOR logic.

With J output neurodes, each has its own weight set that can be adjusted. Thus each of the J neurodes will join a different group of convex regions. Let $J = K$. When the resulting output vector $\mathbf{z} = (z_1,..., z_J)$ contains a single high value in the jth position, then the input feature vector $\mathbf{x} = (x_1,..., x_N)$ belongs to the appropriate joined region for class $k = j$. This gives rise to a *standard* MLP with a single hidden layer and an output layer of neurodes. The learning is more robust when this scheme ($J = K$) is used, but the output layer is larger so that the training takes more time.

Training with the minimum $M = \log_2(\kappa)$ neurodes, where κ is the total number of linearly separable subclasses would usually suffice as an initial estimate (we may increase M as needed during training). Without a priori knowledge of κ, which is the usual case, we may use a moderate initial estimate of $\kappa = 2K$ subclasses, so that $M = \lfloor\log_2(2K)\rfloor + 1 = \lfloor\log_2(K) + 1\rfloor + 1$ gives an initial estimate for the number of hidden neurodes M needed in a single hidden layer. For highly nonlinear data, we may use $\kappa = cK$, where $2 \le c \le 4$, and so forth.

According to Bose and Garga (1992, 1993), the case where the convex classes are not disjoint requires a third layer of neurodes (two hidden layers). While this case may be a property of MLPs, we assume that for the purposes of pattern recognition, the population of objects of interest falls into *disjoint* classes that are (nonlinearly) separable.

Example 9.2.   The 2–2–1 MLP for Complemented XOR Logic

The exemplar inputs for complemented XOR logic (2-bit odd parity) consist of the corner vectors of the unit square in the plane. These are $\{(0,0), (0,1), (1,0), (1,1)\}$. The first and last of these belong to one class (an even number of high values) while the two middle ones belong to another class (an odd number of high values). It can be seen from Figure 9.8 that

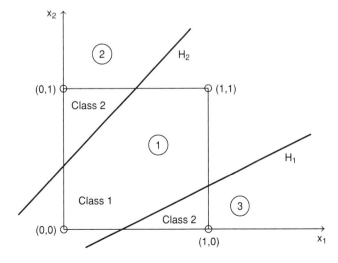

Figure 9.8. Partitioning XOR feature space with two neurodes.

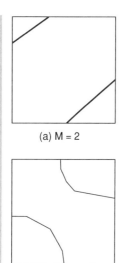

(a) M = 2

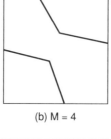

(b) M = 4

(c) M = 8

(d) M = 12

Figure 9.9.   XOR results versus M middle neurodes.

two hyperplanes separate these four feature vectors into three regions, of which Region 1 represents Class 1. Class 2 requires two regions, Regions 2 and 3 (region numbers are shown as circled numbers in the figure). The two hyperplanes require that we use two neurodes in the hidden layer. A single output neurode indicates the class: the value 1 indicates Class 1, while 0 indicates Class 2 (Regions 2 and 3).

There are $Q = 4$ exemplars to be mapped into $K = 2$ classes. The two classes are not linearly separable, but could also be partitioned into two subclasses each for a total of four subclasses that are linearly separable; that is, each exemplar input is a linearly separable subclass. Actually, this is conservative and it can be seen from Figure 9.8 that we only need $\kappa = 3$ linearly separable subclasses and $M = \kappa - 1 = 2$ separating hyperplanes. Otherwise $M = \log_2 (4) = 2$ hyperplanes.

Figure 9.9 shows the results of using different values for the number M of middle neurodes. The unit square in the $x_1 x_2$-plane is partitioned into two classes, of which a central region with two corner regions represents one class and the remaining two corners (subclasses) represent the other class.

How RBFNs and FLNs Work

Radial basis functions cover the N-dimensional feature space with small σ-hyperballs (N-dimensional balls) on which they are centered, and these balls are small clusters that represent subclasses. In Figure 9.6, we could replace the hyperellipses shown with σ-hyperballs, so the radial basis (Gaussian) functions "cover" the feature space and decompose it into convex regions. In a similar fashion to the MLP networks, the output layer of neurodes ORs (joins, or takes the union of) the clusters (subclasses) into classes. These classes may be nonconvex and thus the separation is nonlinear. As was shown in Section 7.7, when the number M of hidden neurodes satisfies $M = Q$, where Q is the number of training exemplars, then an exact solution exists.

We note in passing that hyperellipses may be obtained (as in Figure 9.6) by means of the extended Gaussian function

$$f(\mathbf{x};\mathbf{v}^{(m)}) = \exp[-(\mathbf{x} - \mathbf{v}^{(m)})^t C(\mathbf{x} - \mathbf{v}^{(m)})/2\sigma_m^2]$$

where C is a symmetric (covariance) matrix. Such basis functions are not radial, but may be oriented and elongated via adjustment of the entries in C. This would take considerable computation in training, but could be useful where high accuracy is needed during operation. An application would be for the precise modeling of a highly nonlinear system.

FLNs have the N feature inputs and so use hyperplanes to partition the feature space into convex intersections of half-spaces. Additionally, the functions $f_1(x_1,..., x_N),..., f_H(x_1,..., x_N)$ of the N input features provide for H more inputs. The loci of these functions are hypercurves in feature space and further decompose it further into convex and nonconvex regions. Under proper training, the weights are adjusted so that the final partitions contain the classes. Note that there is no layer that ORs (joins) regions into regions of more complex shapes, which must be done by the functions $f_1(x_1,..., x_N),..., f_H(x_1,..., x_N)$. It is worth investigating the appending of an extra layer to FLNs to achieve greater power with fewer functions.

9.3. Generalized versus Specialized Fitting

Specialization

The purpose of training an MLP is to obtain an approximation to a function that maps Q exemplar feature vector inputs $\{\mathbf{x}^{(q)}\}_{1 \le q \le Q}$ into K associated output target identifier vectors $\{\mathbf{t}^{(k(q))}\}_{1 \le q \le Q}$ in a generalized (smoothed) fashion. The purpose here is to design an appropriate architectural structure that is in some sense an optimal tradeoff of the needs and constraints that govern the intended use of the MLP.

Although the network is a multidimensional function, its purpose is the same as for the analogous situation of a polynomial $y = P_M(x)$ of degree M that maps inputs x into outputs y that generalize Q exemplar data points (Wasserman, 1993). In the case of $M = Q - 1$, the polynomial with $M + 1$ appropriate coefficients passes exactly through each of the Q data points and so the Q polynomial "memorizes" each of the points, even though these individual points may contain errors. In the case of an MLP system for pattern recognition, the feature components are random variables whose assumed values contain random errors. The training of a large number of weights "memorizes" the errors of the particular data used along with the desirable information, a property known as *specialization*.

Figure 9.10 shows the situation for the polynomial mapping. Analogously, an MLP with few neurodes smooths (generalizes) the interpolation as does a polynomial of low degree, because both have fewer coefficients than data points. An MLP with too many neurodes memorizes each exemplar pair (noise and all) rather than a general form in the same way as a polynomial of high degree memorizes each data point. When $M << Q$ (M is much less than Q), the polynomial $y = P_M(x)$ expresses a very generalized form for the Q errored data points. Once the coefficients (weights) of the polynomial of low degree are found, the generalized form $y = P_M(x)$ maps any x into a *smoothed* (generalized) y value.

Overfitting an MLP that has a single hidden layer of M neurodes occurs when the number $NM + MJ$ of weights is greater than the number Q of sample points (Reed, 1993). As described above, it is actually the unknown number κ of linearly separable subclasses to which we should compare the number of weights, rather than Q. There may be multiple exemplars for each of the κ subclasses or K classes among the sample. The system is underdetermined when there are fewer exemplars (data points) than weights (coefficients) to constrain the system. Consider passing a polynomial of degree 9 (with 10 coefficients) through three data points. The three data points determine three equations, each with 10 unknown weights. There are infinitely many solutions so the error function changes when any weight changes and then a different set of solutions exists, which causes weight drift. While the TSSE may decrease and the MLP may learn the training exemplars very well, it may fail to recognize correctly new feature vectors on which it did not train (*novel* feature vectors). For this reason, testing of the training is necessary (see Section 9.8) to avoid specialization.

Wieland and Leighton, (1987) considered training to be curve fitting that smooths to generalize with nonlinear interpolation. According to them, fewer neurodes means smoother interpolation and thus greater generalization, while more neurodes with their extra weights learn more exemplar instances (errors and all) and thus specialize more. Kruschke (1989) found that MLPs generalize better when succeeding layers of neurodes are smaller than the preceding ones. According to Makhoul et al. (1989), the first hidden layer partitions the sample of feature vectors into a number of cells. Succeeding layers of neurodes group the cells into decision classes. This is verified by Bose and Garga (1993) as discussed in Section 9.2.

The conclusion of Hagiwara (1993) is that smaller networks have the advantages that they (i) generalize better, (ii) learn more quickly, (iii) operate more quickly with less complexity and require less memory, and (iv) are simpler to interpret in terms of rules. A result of de Villiers and Barnard (1992) is that two hidden layers are always sufficient. An earlier reference in this regard is Lepedes (1988).

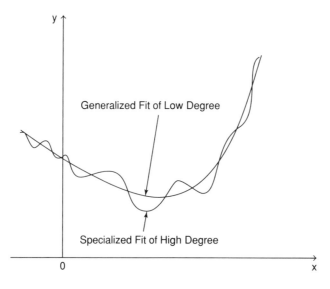

Figure 9.10. Generalized and specialized polynomial approximations.

Generalized Fit of Low Degree

Specialized Fit of High Degree

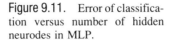

Figure 9.11. Error of classification versus number of hidden neurodes in MLP.

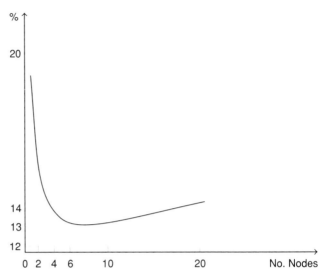

An interesting study (Tarassenko and Roberts, 1994) computed the classification error of a two-layered MLP as a function of the number of hidden neurodes. Figure 9.11 is a graph (reconstructed from the data) that shows the smoothed general tendency. The horizontal axis is the number of neurodes in the single hidden layer and the vertical axis is the percentage of errors. Each network was run 500 iterations through a training database of 4500 patterns. This study compared classification errors of the nearest neighborhood method (26.75%), k-nearest neighbors (19.95%), and an MLP (12.59%). The data were electroencephalogram (EEG) values on human subjects at the single frequency of 128 Hz (cycles per second). The goal was to classify the signal data into three classes: wakefulness, dream sleep, and deep sleep.

Adding Noise for Better Generalization

Several researchers have added noise to the feature values of the exemplars in a sample $\{\mathbf{x}^{(q)}\}_{q=1, Q}$. For example, Holmström and Koistinen (1992) report that they added noise to a sample of feature vectors $\{\mathbf{x}^{(1)},..., \mathbf{x}^{(Q)}\}$ to expand it to the larger set $\{\mathbf{x}^{(1)},..., \mathbf{x}^{(Q)}, \mathbf{x}^{(Q+1)},..., \mathbf{x}^{(P)}\}$. When the number Q of exemplars is less than the number of weights, the system is *underdetermined* (more unknowns than equations, which is overfitting). In this case there are infinitely many solutions, weight drift, and other problems. By adjoining a sufficiently large number of exemplars that are generated by adding noise to the original ones, the system becomes *overdetermined*, so that a least-squares solution exists. The simulation results of Holmström and Koistinen showed that the generalization ability of the network was improved. Their analysis showed the asymptotic consistency of the method.

Holmström and Koistinen draw the additive noise from Parzen–Rosenblatt estimates of the joint density of the input vectors. While this is a difficult approximation, it provides a suboptimal distribution. Gaussian distributions may also be used, based on a priori distributions or sample statistics from the original sample $\{\mathbf{x}^{(q)}\}$. They tested the function $y =$

0.4 sin(x) + 0.5 with an N–M–J = 1–13–1 MLP on Q = 400 samples with additive noise. The result was a smoother and more generalized mapping.

Similar results on generalization were reported in Parisi and Pedone (1992). Many other researchers use the technique. For practical reasons, a network is usually trained first on the original data or on a "good" subset of prototypes that is essentially noise free. After the network has learned this data fairly well, then it is trained on the combination of original and noisy data.

9.4. Networks with Multiple Hidden Layers

The Effects of Two Hidden Layers

In cases where some of the K classes are nonlinearly separable, there is a total number $\kappa >$ K of subclasses that are linearly separable. Section 9.2 shows that a class can always be decomposed into subclusters that are linearly separable in the pairwise sense, even if certain of the feature vectors must be singleton subclasses. When κ is quite large, we may use a single hidden layer of $M = \lceil \log_2(\kappa) \rceil + 1$ initial neurodes to separate them (see Section 9.2). If the output layer of neurodes can lump these κ subclasses into their K proper classes, then the network is appropriate, else we adjoin hidden neurodes and train further. With a very large number of hidden neurodes, the training is more difficult because of the large number of local minima for which directions of local steepest descent are very different from the actual directions of the minima. In this case, it takes a large volume of computation to find a good starting weight set, or else many training runs may be required to obtain satisfactory learning. To simplify matters, some researchers (Mehrotra et al., 1991) use a second hidden layer of neurodes between the first hidden layer and the output layer.

It is known empirically that the use of two hidden layers of neurodes sometimes accelerates learning, but also may slow or prevent it. For example, Johansson et al. (1992) ran training studies on 3-, 4-, and 5-bit parity. On the 3-bit parity, a single hidden layer learned with significantly fewer evaluations of the TSSE function E than did the MLPs with two hidden layers. On the more difficult 4-bit and 5-bit parity problems, however, two hidden layers usually (but not always) learned with significantly fewer functional evaluations than did an MLP with a single hidden layer. Johansson et al. observed this behavior for four types of conjugate gradient training techniques that were an order of magnitude faster than BP with momentum.

The reasoning for a second hidden layer is this: (i) The first hidden layer can be smaller to cluster some groups of subclasses, and (ii) the second smaller hidden layer separates each of these groups further into smaller linearly separable subclasses. The output layer of neurodes then joins the smaller subclasses together into classes. For example, if there were $K =$ 50 classes that were separable only nonlinearly, but with four subclasses of each class that were linearly separable, then we could use as many as $M = \kappa = 200$ neurodes in the hidden layer. On the other hand, we may choose to try $M_1 = 20$ neurodes in the first hidden layer and $M_2 = 10$ neurodes in the second hidden layer. This reduces the total number of hidden neurodes from 200 to 30, because $200 = 20 \times 10$ separations can be made. A second hidden layer reduces the total number of weights dramatically. The output layer must join (OR) the subclasses, as before.

We note that MLPs with two hidden layers are sometimes more difficult to train and that they perform worse in many situations. The report of de Villiers and Barnard (1992) states that while the optimally trained MLPs of one and two hidden layers perform no differently statistically (there is no significant difference between them on the average), the networks with a single hidden layer perform better on recognition. Other findings were that networks with two hidden layers are often more difficult to train and are affected more by the choice of an initial weight set and the architecture. Their study used eight MLPs with 40 neurons and ten MLPs with 60 neurons, and all were trained from randomly drawn initial weights. The arguments of de Villiers and Bernard (1992) and Baum and Haussler (1989) refute the findings of Chester (1990) that MLPs with a single hidden layer were inferior because they could not instantiate certain functions (Baum and Haussler showed that those functions could, in fact, be implemented with a single hidden layer that had an appropriate architecture). For very large MLPs, however, a second hidden layer reduces the number of weights greatly. The training may be more difficult, so computing a good starting weight set is justified (see Section 5.2).

Using Two Hidden Layers

Figure 9.12 presents an MLP with two hidden layers. To keep the right half of the MLP similar to the ones studied in previous chapters and Section 9.1, we use N inputs, L neurodes in the first hidden layer, M neurodes in the second hidden layer, and J output neurodes. We designate the weights at the first hidden layer by $\{v_{nl}\}$, at the second hidden layer by $\{w_{lm}\}$ and at the output layer by $\{u_{mj}\}$. An input vector $\mathbf{x} = (x_1,..., x_N)$ is combined with the weight vector $\mathbf{v}_l$ at each lth neurode in the first hidden layer to produce the sum

$$p_l = \mathbf{x}^t \mathbf{v}_l = \sum_{(n=1,\,N)} x_n v_{nl}, \qquad a_l = f(p_l) \tag{9.7}$$

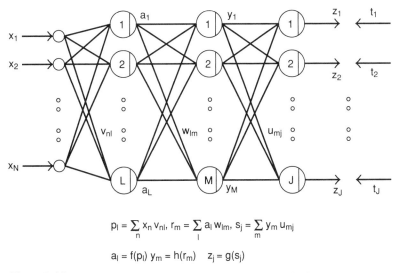

$$p_l = \sum_n x_n v_{nl}, \quad r_m = \sum_l a_l w_{lm}, \quad s_j = \sum_m y_m u_{mj}$$

$$a_l = f(p_l) \quad y_m = h(r_m) \quad z_j = g(s_j)$$

Figure 9.12.   A feedforward neural network with two hidden layers.

The sigmoid $f(-)$ activates the output $a_l = f(p_l)$ from the lth neurode of the first hidden layer.

At the second hidden layer, the inputs are the outputs $\mathbf{a} = (a_1,..., a_L)$ from the first hidden layer. These are then multiplied at each mth neurode by that neurode's weight vector, summed, and put through the sigmoid $h(-)$. Thus we have

$$r_m = \mathbf{a}^t\mathbf{w}_m = \Sigma_{(l=1, L)}a_l w_{lm}, \qquad y_m = h(r_m) \tag{9.8}$$

Next, the activated outputs $y_m = h(r_m)$ of the neurodes at the second hidden layer are fed to the neurodes at the output layer. For the jth output neurode, the incoming $\{y_m\}$ are combined with the weight vectors $\{\mathbf{u}_j\}$ to obtain

$$s_j = \mathbf{y}^t\mathbf{u}_j = \Sigma_{(m=1, M)}y_m u_{mj}, \qquad z_j = g(s_j) \tag{9.9}$$

The weighted sums s_j are put through the sigmoid activation function $g(-)$ to activate the network output vector $\mathbf{z}$, where $z_j = g(s_j)$.

The training of MLPs with two hidden layers is more complicated for gradient methods, but the algorithms for strategic search remain essentially the same as for one, two, or more hidden layers, where a search is done for the weights of each layer in turn, over all exemplars simultaneously, to complete an update of the training. In either case, the extra layer of neurodes actually reduces the total number of weights. In fact, the total weight reduction with two hidden layers implies fewer weights to search in the univariate random search or the univariate cubic or quartic random search. For BP (*backprop*), FP (*fprop*), QP (*quickprop*), RP (*rprop*), or SP (*slickprop*), the weight updates are more complex for the first (leftmost) hidden layer than for the second hidden layer and are more complex for the second hidden layer than for the output layer (see Section 4.6). The gradient updates for the weights at the second hidden and output layers are the same as in the MLPs with a single hidden layer, while those at the first hidden layer are different. Search methods are simpler for multiple layers of hidden neurodes.

A Hybrid Algorithm for Training with Two Hidden Layers

The high-level algorithm given here starts from a randomly drawn weight point and then makes preliminary adjustments via a quartic univariate search on each single weight to obtain a coarse minimum from which to start. Because the number of weights is reduced, there are fewer searches. A cubic search follows in the randomly chosen directions (normalized to unit length) on the weights at the hidden layers. Then it adjusts the weights in the output layer via gradient descent, which is extremely quick on these weights.

Inputs: {the number N of input feature components, the number L of neurodes in the first hidden layer, then number M of neurodes in the second hidden layer, the number J of output neurodes in the output layer, the number Q of exemplar pairs in the training sample and the sample $\{(\mathbf{x}^{(q)}, \mathbf{t}^{(q(k))})\}$ of pairs}

Outputs: {the weights $\mathbf{v} = (v_{11},..., v_{NL})$, $\mathbf{w} = (w_{11},..., w_{LM})$, and $\mathbf{u} = (u_{11},..., u_{MJ})$}

Step 1. /Input data and parameters to MLP/
  read N, L, M, J, Q;   /Read from MLP file/
  read exemplar pairs $\mathbf{x}^{(q)}$, $\mathbf{t}^{(q(k))}$;   /Read from MLP file/
  $I_{\text{prelim}} \leftarrow 2$; $r \leftarrow 0$;   /Number of preliminary/
                                       /iterations/

  $I \leftarrow$ Keyboard;   /Number training iterations/

Step 2. /Draw initial weights/
  for $l = 1$ to L do
    for $n = 1$ to N do $v_{nl} = \text{random}(0,1) - 0.5$;   /Draw random weights from/
                                       /-0.5 to 0.5/

    for $m = 1$ to M do $w_{lm} = \text{random}(0,1) - 0.5$; /Draw random weights from/
                                       /-0.5 to 0.5/

  for $j = 1$ to J do
    for $m = 1$ to M do   /Draw random weights from/
      $u_{mj} = \text{random}(0,1) - 0.5$;   /$-0.5$ to 0.5/

Step 3. /Adjust each weight via quartic approximation/
  for $l = 1$ to L do
    for $n = 1$ to N do $v_{nl} = \textbf{Quartic}(n, l, 1)$;   /Do univariate quartic/
                                       /minimizations/

    for $m = 1$ to M do $w_{lm} = \textbf{Quartic}(l, m, 2)$; /to update hidden layer's/
                                       /weights/

  for $j = 1$ to J do
    for $m = 1$ to M do $u_{mj} = \textbf{Quartic}(m, j, 3)$; /Similarly for output layer/
  $r = r + 1$;
  if $r < I_{\text{prelim}}$ then goto Step 3;   /Do I_{init} quartic univariate/
                                       /searches/

Step 4. /Use cubic search in random directions on 2 hidden layers, FP on output layer/
  for $r = 1$ to I do   /On rth iteration, get a random/
                                       /direction/

    Random_Direction(v,1); **Cubic(v,1)**;   /and use cubic search for/
                                       /weights v_{nl}/

    Update_NN( );   /Compute all new neurodal/
                                       /outputs/

    Random_Direction(w,2); **Cubic(w,1)**;   /Repeat for weights w_{lm} and u_{mj}/
    Update_NN( );
    for $j = 1$ to J do
      for $m = 1$ to M do   /Full steepest descent/
        $u_{mj} \leftarrow u_{mj} + \eta \sum_{(q=1, Q)} (t_j^{(q)} - z_j^{(q)})$ /$h(s)$ is appropriate sigmoid/
            $\times\, h'(s) y_m^{(q)}$;
    Update_NN( );

Quartic( ) makes a univariate quartic search on any given weight while keeping all other weights fixed. By quartic univariate search, we mean that five points along a weight direction are selected and a fourth-degree polynomial is fit to the TSSE values at the points. Then the quartic polynomial is approximately minimized.

The procedure **Random_Direction( )** finds a random normalized direction as was done in the search algorithms of Chapter 6. The parameters 1, 2, and 3 indicate the layer. **Cubic( )** performs a minimization of E on a particular set of weights (either **v**, **w**, or **u**) as indicated by the parameters 1, 2, or 3 via search in a given normalized random direction. The distance from the start of the unit direction to the minimum is used to select the approximately minimized new weight point. **Update_NN( )** updates the MLP with the new weights by putting all exemplars through to compute the total TSSE E.

Example 9.3.   XOR Logic and Blood10 Classification with Two Hidden Layers

Figure 9.13 shows a 2–1–1–1 MLP with two hidden layers of a single neurode each. The $N = 2$ input components are given for XOR logic. The number of outputs is given as $J = 1$. The first hidden layer of a single neurode should theoretically partition the feature space into two half-planes, while the second hidden layer neurode partitions those further. The output neurode performs the ORing to combine any separate convex regions. Figure 9.14 shows the results of training. This 2–1–1–1 MLP failed to learn on several attempts. The 2–2–1–1 network shown in Figure 9.15 learned successfully, however.

In another study, our 8–4–3–1 and 8–4–2–1 MLPs both succeeded in learning the difficult Blood10 data (Looney, 1996b) in Table 9.2 for which there are $Q = 7$ exemplar feature vectors of 8 features each that represent $K = 7$ blood disease conditions. The single output neurode is what makes the learning so difficult (see Example 7.3, where the training on different numbers of output neurodes is compared). On the Digit12 data from Appendix 11, a 12–5–4–2 network failed, while a 12–6–3–2 network succeeded. A 12–12–2 MLP with a single hidden layer succeeded in learning with about 25% less computation and had a lower TSSE value. Our runs showed that the networks with two hidden layers seem more susceptible to the network architecture and to falling into local minima. We trained several times with univariate random search and then trained several times on a second set of runs with cubic line search in random directions. The univariate random search gave better results than random search.

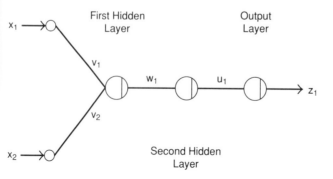

First Hidden Layer   Output Layer

Figure 9.13. A 2–1–1–1 MLP for XOR logic.

Second Hidden Layer

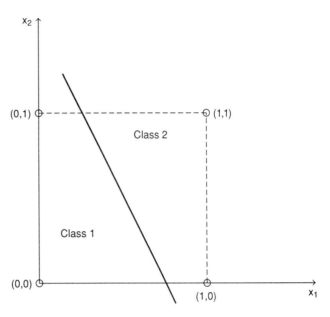

Figure 9.14. Results of XOR logic on 2–1–1–1 MLP.

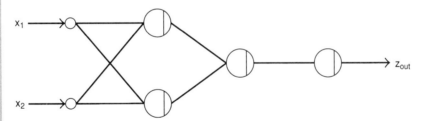

Figure 9.15. A 2–2–1–1 FANN for XOR logic.

Table 9.2.
Blood Data for Seven Patients

Vector Number	Feature Vector (in Thousandths)	Known State and Output Value	
1	(289, 55, 484, 385, 545, 575, 341, 995)	Normal	0.1
2	(32, 484, 220, 123, 300, 380, 89, 210)	Hepatitis B	0.2
3	(126, 391, 354, 275, 442, 515, 175, 395)	HIV Early	0.3
4	(60, 414, 240, 162, 304, 368, 110, 270)	HIV Late	0.4
5	(95, 365, 360, 234, 480, 543, 165, 190)	IUP	0.5
6	(63, 222, 332, 210, 460, 536, 155, 320)	Leukemia	0.6
7	(189, 247, 415, 312, 510, 562, 275, 320)	Malnutrition	0.7

These examples indicate that even when two hidden layers are used, there must be sufficiently many neurodes in the first hidden layer to partition the feature space into sufficiently many convex regions. More research is needed in this area to analyze the workings of two or more hidden layers.

9.5. General Principles for Neural Engineering

Some Design Principles

A fundamental principle of nature and physics is that activity takes place in a manner that minimizes energy. A design principle is that simplicity is beneficial and desirable. These can be stated in a principle for the design of neural networks.

> **Principle 9.1.** To obtain optimal generalized learning, an MLP structure should have the minimal number of neurodes necessary to map the Q exemplar input instances for K classes into the associated K target identifiers (outputs) and should satisfy the validation and verification tests (see Section 9.8 for testing).

Kung and Hwang (1988) found that the number M of neurodes in a single middle layer should be equal to the number of distinct training patterns K. Their argument used an algebraic projection analysis. On the other hand, Masahiko concluded (1989) that K input patterns required $K - 1$ neurodes in a single hidden layer to separate feature vectors with binary values. Gutierrez et al. (1989) made a conservative estimate of the number M of neurodes needed in a single hidden layer where the inputs were binary. They stated that the hidden neurodes appeared to partition the input (feature) space into regions (verified by the analysis of Section 9.2). McCormack and Doherty (1993) noted that the initial architecture has a strong influence on the learning (separating) ability of a MLP. They also noted that the architecture depends on the data to be learned.

Hayashi (1993) postulated a principle that $M = c \sqrt{(NJ)}$ is suitable for a single hidden layer, where N is the number of input features, J is the number of output components, and c is a constant. He also computed the covariance of the $M \times Q$ y-values put out by the M hidden neurodes (over the Q exemplars). He used the rank of this covariance matrix as the number M of hidden neurodes to use. The covariance based estimate appears to be more justifiable and less dependent upon the dataset used.

Our analysis takes a different path. Let Q exemplar pairs represent K classes ($Q \geq K$). When $Q > K$, then more than one exemplar of $\{\mathbf{x}^{(q)}\}_{q=1, Q}$ belong to at least one class. Multiple exemplars for a class allow the possibility of only nonlinear separability for that class. Suppose now that these K classes can be further partitioned into a minimum of κ subclasses that are linearly separable, where it must be true that $K \leq \kappa \leq Q$. The task is to separate the κ subclasses with hyperplanes, as discussed in Section 9.2.

The feature space is the bounded hypercube $[0,1]^N$ in the unipolar case (or $[-1,1]^N$ in the bipolar case), so a neurodal hyperplane separates it into two distinct regions after training. In the *minimal* case, each consecutive new hyperplane almost doubles the number of regions already existing before it is added. Using a conservative factor of 3/2, the number of neurodes needed in a single hidden layer to separate κ subclasses is $M = \lceil \log_2(\kappa) \rceil$.

Thus the a priori expected number of regions after $r + 1$ hyperplanes is $\kappa = 2(3/2)^r$. Letting $M = r$ neurodes for a single hidden layer, we find M from

$$\log_2(\kappa) = \log_2(2[3/2]^M) = \log_2(2) + M\{\log_2(3) - \log_2(2)\}$$

to be

$$M = \{\log_2(\kappa) - 1\}/\{\log_2(3) - \log_2(2)\} = \{\log_2(\kappa) - 1\}/\{1.58496 - 1.0\}$$

$$= \{\log_2(\kappa) - 1\}/0.58496 = 1.7095\{\log_2(\kappa) - 1\} \tag{9.10}$$

In the *maximal* case, only one new region will be added (parallel hyperplanes). In this case, the first hyperplane yields two regions while every succeeding hyperplane yields one more, so that M neurodes would yield $M + 1$ regions, which implies that $M = \kappa - 1$ neurodes are required in a single hidden layer.

> ***Principle 9.2.*** Let the number of feature components be N, the number of exemplar pair instances be Q, the number of classes be K, and the number of components in the target (output) identifiers be J. Now assume that the K classes contain a total of κ linearly separable subclasses. Then the maximum number M of hidden neurodes required in an MLP with a single hidden layer is $\kappa - 1$ (parallel hyperplane case). On the other hand, the minimum number of neurodes required in a single hidden layer is $M = \lceil \log_2(\kappa) \rceil$. Without a priori knowledge of κ, we initially select the expected value $M = 1.7095 \{\log_2(\kappa) - 1\}$ from Equation (9.10), assuming that there is an average of two linearly separable subclasses in each of the K classes that must be separated. Thus we obtain $M_{ave} = \lceil 1.7095 \log_2(2K) \rceil$, which is a reasonable estimate.

The strategy of starting small and adding more neurodes to the hidden layer if necessary is efficient because it adjoins rather than prune neurodes (see Section 9.6 for adjoining and pruning neurodes and weights). Thus we could start with $M_0 = 1.7095 \log_2(K)$.

> ***Principle 9.3.*** When K is large, two hidden layers of neurodes may be used to reduce the total number of neurodes and weights required for nonlinear separation so as to avoid overfitting and specialization. When two hidden layers are used, then $L = \lceil \sqrt{(2K)} \rceil + p$ neurodes for the first hidden layer and $M = \lceil \sqrt{(2K)} \rceil - p$ neurodes for the second hidden layer are good numbers, where p depends on K. The principle of Kruschke (Kruschke, 1989) requires that $L > M$, which is supported by our examples given above. The parameter p should satisfy $2 \le p \le \lceil \sqrt{(2K)}/2 \rceil$.

Let $K = 100$, so that $\sqrt{(2K)} \approx 14$. For $p = 6$, we obtain $L = 20$ and $M = 8$. For $p = 5$, we have $L = 19$ and $M = 9$. When $p = 4$, then $L = 18$ and $M = 10$. On our limited data tests, it appears safe to choose p so that L is slightly less than twice the size of M (thus the case of $p = 4$ would be better in this case). We note that the number of total hidden weights remains constant for $2 \le p \le \lceil \sqrt{(2K)}/2 \rceil$.

Principle 9.4. For small K, the preferable number J of neurodes in the output layer is $J = K$. When K is larger (say, $K \geq 16$), the number $J = [\log_2(K)] + 1$ should be used (where $[x]$ is the greatest integer less than or equal to x). Too few components in the target output vectors can cause failure to train, less accuracy, and less generalization (see Section 9.7).

Earlier work (Baum and Haussler, 1989) suggested that the total number of weights needed is proportional to the number Q of training pairs of exemplars and targets and that the constant of proportion is about 0.1. For 700 such training pairs this would limit the number of weights to 70, to be divided up among the middle and output layers. This could present a problem for larger values of N and K or small values of Q. The crucial numbers are the number of unique (up to noise) exemplars and the number of hidden weights, which should be approximately equal (there may be more exemplars than weights).

Example 9.4. A Hypothetical Design Case

Suppose that we are to use an MLP to recognize a set of 100 different symbols for which $N = 60$ features have been determined. Let there be $Q = 240$ exemplars. Suppose that we suspect, in lieu of a priori knowledge, that some of the classes can be separated only nonlinearly. Using the estimate $\kappa = 2K = 200$ for the number of linearly separable subclasses, we could take either of

$$M_0 = [1.7 \log_2(100)] + 1 = 11, \qquad M_{ave} = [1.7 \log_2(200)] + 1 = 12$$

for the number of neurodes in a single hidden layer of a standard MLP. We added the value 1 to each to account for truncation error.

Note that there are $NM_0 = 60 \times 11 = 660$ weights at the single hidden layer even with this small number of hidden neurodes. Because $Q = 240$ is much less than the 660 weights, the system is very much overfitted (underdetermined) with many more coefficients than data points. We need more data. We could generate noise and add it to the 240 exemplar feature vectors, but this provides no new unique exemplars.

For the output layer, we could use the upper bound $J = 100$, where a single high value activated by the jth neurode would identify the jth class. This is rather large, so we could use the lower bound of

$$J = [\log_2(K)] + 1 = 7 \qquad (2^7 = 128 > 100 > 2^6 = 64)$$

Our most optimistic design provides for $M = 11$ hidden neurodes and $J = 7$ output neurodes, which is a fairly small MLP (60–11–7). The most pessimistic case would require $M = 99$ hidden neurodes (single hidden layer) and 100 output neurodes (60–99–100). Upon using $J = 7$ output neurodes, and averaging the maximum and minimum numbers of hidden neurodes to obtain $M = (11 + 99)/2 = 55$, as determined above, our network would be 60–55–7.

Two Studies Verifying a Design Process

In a study on building an architecture while training, Ash (1989) started an MLP with a small number of hidden neurodes, trained it via BP, and consecutively added one neurode at a time and trained further with BP. This process of growing the network while training was successful on all data tested. It required only 5 hidden nodes for 5-bit parity (it is difficult to train on 5-bit parity starting with 5 hidden neurodes).

In another study, Setiono and Hui (1993) use Ash's method, but with the BFGS quasi-Newton optimization algorithm for training the MLP. The Wisconsin Breast Cancer Data of 699 patterns (458 benign and 241 malignant) were used. Two-thirds of the data were used on the training and one-third were used to test the generalization capability of the trained network. After training and testing, the network achieved a 98% correct rate.

9.6. Adjoining and Pruning Hidden Neurodes

Adjoining versus Pruning Hidden Neurodes in MLPs

We have seen that a feedforward neural network learns in a more generalized fashion when there are not too many neurodes in the hidden layers. However, if there are not enough hidden neurodes, then the MLP will not learn to separate all of the classes. If we know the number κ of linearly separable subclasses, which we almost never do in practice, then we could use $\lfloor \log_2(\kappa) \rfloor + 1$ hidden neurodes in a single hidden layer to start. If κ were large, then we could use two hidden layers and divide κ into two factors, κ_1 and κ_2, such that κ_1 and κ_2 ($\kappa \leq \kappa_1 \kappa_2$) are the sizes of the first and second hidden layers, respectively, and $\kappa_1 > \kappa_2$ in accordance with Kruschke's principle (Kruschke, 1989) given in the previous section.

There are three ways to proceed in the usual situation of nonlinear classes when we do not know how many linearly separable subclasses there are: (i) Use a high initial estimate of near $K - 1$ neurodes in a single hidden layer to separate K classes on the assumption that they require a near maximum number of hyperplanes for separation, and then prune neurodes and weights while training until the MLP learns to separate all K classes successfully (when K is not large); (ii) start small with $M = \lfloor \log_2(K) \rfloor + 1$ and adjoin neurodes to the hidden layer and train until the MLP learns properly; or (iii) start with two hidden layers of neurodes of sizes L and M, where $L > M$ (say $L = \sqrt{(2K)} + p$ and $M = \sqrt{(2K)} - p$, where L is the number of neurodes in the first hidden layer, then add neurodes to the first hidden layer as needed, and then prune and train further as the last iterative process.

There are opposing notions on how to proceed. Some researchers feel that smaller MLPs are easier to train, and the likelihood of success is greater on fewer training runs. If the MLP does not learn to separate all of the classes on the first architectural configuration, it will learn to separate some of them. With each added hidden neurode, it will learn to separate more classes. If we start with two small hidden layers with $L > M$, then we add neurodes to increase L if necessary. On the other hand, some other researchers (Reed, 1993) feel that a larger MLP is easier to train during the initial stages because it is less sensitive to changes in single weights. These researchers start with an oversized architecture, train, and then prune neurodes. It requires more computation to prune, and the procedure is more complex. The reported results in both cases have been very good.

If we can choose to start small and add neurodes as needed, then why should we ever need to prune? The answer is that by adding neurodes to an MLP that is already partially trained we make it easier to train further by modeling more nonlinear interactions. During this process, however, the additional neurodes and further training may force the MLP to become too specialized and also generate too much extraneous noise. Even with an appropriate number of neurodes and a well-trained MLP, the network may yet benefit (Seitsma and Dow, 1988) from a reduction in neurodes that (i) reduces the operational size, (ii) reduces extraneous error, and (iii) improves the rate of successful recognition by generalizing the learning further. As a rule, it is a good procedure to do whatever pruning can be done at the end of any training runs to smooth the learning and reduce errors.

Sietsma and Dow (1988) report the following situation. A sufficiently large MLP was trained and then pruned and retrained, iteratively, until its size was considerably less and its learning was quite general. Upon starting with a small untrained MLP of the final reduced size, they found that it would not train. This would seem to answer the correct way to proceed, but the Setioni–Hui study related below indicates that neurodes can be adjoined to the minimal architecture to make it trainable. Thus a good strategy is to start small, add neurodes as needed and train, and then prune and train to generalize.

The Setioni–Hui Algorithm for Growing an MLP

Setioni and Hui (1993) start with a small MLP architecture. They use two neurodes in a single hidden layer, train the MLP, and then add a single neurode in the single middle layer. They repeat this *incremental approach* of adding and training until the MLP has learned satisfactorily. Their training uses a quasi-Newton algorithm. The result is that their network learns n-bit parity for various values for n and the learning uses less than n neurodes in the hidden layer. The higher-level algorithm follows.

Step 1.   Initialize weights of single hidden layer of 2 neurodes.

Step 2.   Train on current weights.

Step 3.   If all exemplar vectors are correctly recognized then go to testing phase;
else add neurode to middle layer; draw small initial weights for it; goto Step 2.

Note that this algorithm makes a *training run*. To *validate* the training after a run, we should put novel input feature vectors through the system and check the TSSE, as described in Section 9.8. The *advantage* of the Setioni–Hui method is that the network is grown from a small one that accounts mainly for linear interactions, and it adjoins neurodes to account for nonlinear interactions until the network passes the training check on the exemplar input feature vectors. *In practice*, we may start with $\lfloor \log_2(K) \rfloor + 1$ hidden neurodes instead of 2 and then prune at the end.

A High-Level Brute Force Neurode Pruning Algorithm

A simple brute force algorithm for pruning weights is given by Reed (1993) for illustrative purposes to demonstrate a pruning process. We assume that the MLP has more than a sufficient number of neurodes, has been trained and checked on the training exemplar inputs, and has successfully recognized them. We have modified the algorithm here to eliminate an unnecessary hidden neurode rather than just weights in the case that every weight used by that neurode is unimportant. By elimination we mean that all weights of the neurode are zeroed out, which effectively eliminates it from affecting the operational mode.

Step 1. Train MLP; compute total TSSE value E;

Step 2. For $m = 1$ to M do   /Do at each mth middle neurode/
    $P_\mathrm{m} \leftarrow$ FALSE;   /Elimination flags are false/
    for $n = 1$ to N do   /Zero all weights at mth neurode/
        $w\mathrm{hold}_{nm} \leftarrow w_{nm}$; $w_{nm} \leftarrow 0$;   /Hold old values for restoring/
    compute E_new;   /Error with zeroed out neurode/
    if $E_\mathrm{new} > E + \epsilon$, then   /If error increases too much, then/
        for $n = 1$ to N do $w_{nm} \leftarrow w\mathrm{hold}_{nm}$;   /restore all weights at mth node, else/

    else $P_m \leftarrow$ TRUE;   /pruning flag is set at TRUE/

Step 3. For $m = 1$ to M do
    if $P_m \equiv$ TRUE, then   /If mth neurode is negligible, then/
        for $j = 1$ to J do   /zero (prune) weights on its output/
            $u_{mj} \leftarrow 0$;

An *advantage* of this method is that it finds the direct effect of removing a neurode. The main *disadvantage* of this method is that it is computationally expensive when the number of weights is large. A number of passes is usually required. On subsequent training, any weights that are zero are not updated. After training, the neurodes can be reindexed to omit any zeroed neurodes. *In practice*, we use a modification given at the end of this section.

The Optimal Brain Damage Weight Reduction Algorithm

Other methods attempt to assess the sensitivity of the MLP to the weights at a hidden unit in a more efficient manner. Many methods exist in the literature, including *skeletonization* by Mozer and Smolensky (1989) and other methods by Karnin (1990), Le Cun et al. (1990), Chauvin (1989), and Weigend et al. (1991). Interestingly, Whitley and Bogart (1990) prune neurodes by means of genetic algorithms, which can design and train at the same time. It appears that all of these are somewhat computationally expensive.

For example, Le Cun et al. (1990) use an approach they call *optimal brain damage*, where the *saliency* of a weight v_{nm} is defined as

$$\sigma_{nm} = [\delta E(v_{nm})](v_{nm})^2 \tag{9.11}$$

The factor $\delta E(v_{nm})$ is the second partial derivative of E with respect to the weight v_{nm}, which can be calculated using the updated weights and neurodal outputs.

Step 1. Repeat
        train MLP; check for learning of exemplars;
     until all exemplars are learned;

Step 2. for $m = 1$ to M do   /Do at each mth middle neurode/
        for n $= 1$ to N do
            $\sigma_{nm} \leftarrow$ Compute_Saliency
            if $\sigma_{nm} < \epsilon$, then
                $w_{nm} \leftarrow 0;$
                for $j = 1$ to J do
                    $u_{mj} \leftarrow 0;$ /Zero out lines from eliminated weights/

Step 3. If (Stop_Criterion) then stop;
        else goto Step 1;

The *advantages* here are as follows: (i) The saliency is computationally cheap to compute from the terms and factors already computed for backpropagation; and (ii) individual weights, rather than neurodes, are eliminated to provide more flexibility. Note that the elimination of weights at the hidden neurodes does not reduce the overall size of the network unless all weights of a neurode are zeroed out.

Mozer and Smolensky (1989) use the *relevancy* defined to be the difference in the TSSE E with and without a particular hidden neurode, and is thus closer to the brute force method. Hinton (1989) used the *weight decay* method that added a penalty term to E. The penalty term is the sum of the squares of the weights, so the weights will be penalized in the optimization training for being larger. Thus the new cost function to be minimized becomes (with constant c)

$$F = E(w) + c\sum_{(n=1, N)}\sum_{(m=1, M)} w_{nm}^{2} \tag{9.12}$$

This adds a substantial computational burden, also. A similar method called *weight elimination* was used by Weigend et al. (1990b).

Sietsma and Dow (1988) employ user interactive heuristics to identify neurodes that do not contribute to the solution, which is as follows: (i) If a neurode has constant output over all patterns, then it does not contribute to anything except bias; and (ii) if two neurodes have highly correlated outputs over all patterns, then they are redundant so that one can be removed. They also used the method on MLPs with multiple hidden layers. They successfully reduced many networks to quite small ones, which, when taken as starting architectures, were unable to learn (Sietsma and Dow, 1988).

A Simple Efficient Weight Elimination Algorithm

A simple heuristic method used by some early researchers was to train first and then eliminate any weights with small magnitudes. Although this works sometimes, there are situations where the network mapping is sensitive to small weights. There is simplicity to this method and also to the brute force method. We combine them here to eliminate the main weaknesses of both. The idea is to (i) train a sufficiently large MLP, (ii) select and order the set of weights whose magnitudes are closest to zero, (iii) eliminate each one in turn in order of the smallest ones first and determine the change in the TSSE, and (iv) restore any of these that affect the TSSE E in a nonnegligible way.

Step 1. Train MLP; compute total TSSE value E;

Step 2. Order all hidden weights v with $|v| < \delta$ into List;   /Make ordered list/

Step 3. Repeat   /Fetch from List/
    get next_weight from List;   /and save in/
    $v$hold $\leftarrow$ next_weight;   /variable vhold/
    next_weight $\leftarrow 0$;   /If TSSE error degrades/
    compute E_{new};   /nonnegligibly, then/
    if $E_{\text{new}} > E + \epsilon$, then next_weight $\leftarrow v$hold;   /restore, else leave zeroed out/
  until end of List;

Step 4. If (Stop_Criterion), then stop
    else goto Step 1;

The *advantage* of this approach is a considerable reduction in computation because only candidates whose magnitudes are small are selected. The continued training does not update weights whose values are zero. *In practice*, we start with a small hidden layer, adjoin hidden neurodes as needed while training, and then prune the final network (followed by a final segment of training, of course). We should, of course, train the network further after we eliminate a weight and then obtain the new TSSE, in which case all old weights must be saved.

Castellano et al. (1993) examine the performance of three pruning algorithms. They tested the Pelillo–Fanelli algorithm (Pelillo and Fanelli, 1993), the Burkitt algorithm (Burkitt, 1991), and the one discussed above by Sietsma and Dow (1988). Their results indicated that the Seitsma–Dow method was not sufficiently robust, but the Burkitt and Pelillo–Fanelli algorithms worked quite well in the sense that the networks were reduced while maintaining satisfactory performance. The Burkitt algorithm puts in an extra linear layer for each hidden layer of neurodes and occasionally has convergence problems. These methods are also rather computationally expensive.

9.7. Effects of the Output Layer

Tests on MLPs and RBFNs

The number of output neurodes of a neural network affects the ability of the network to learn as well as recognize accurately. We train both MLP and RBF networks on Dataset 1 (shown in Table 9.3), which has only a single unipolar (nonnegative) output component. Next, we train them both on Dataset 2 (shown in Table 9.4), which has the same input vectors but has three output (unipolar) components. Both of these datasets have $N = 8$ input features and $Q = 7$ exemplar feature vectors.

Table 9.3.
Dataset 1 (Single Output)

Inputs								Outputs
0.28900	0.05500	0.48400	0.38500	0.54500	0.57500	0.34100	0.99500	0.1000
0.03100	0.48400	0.22000	0.12300	0.30000	0.38000	0.08900	0.21000	0.2000
0.12600	0.39100	0.35400	0.27500	0.44200	0.51500	0.17500	0.39500	0.3000
0.06000	0.41400	0.24000	0.16200	0.30400	0.36800	0.11000	0.27000	0.4000
0.09500	0.36500	0.36000	0.23400	0.48000	0.54300	0.16500	0.19000	0.5000
0.06300	0.22200	0.33200	0.21000	0.46000	0.53600	0.15500	0.32000	0.6000
0.18900	0.24700	0.41500	0.31200	0.51000	0.56200	0.27500	0.32000	0.7000

This dataset is taken from Looney (1996) and represents features from measurements of mechanical properties of blood from patients with different diseases. The seven input vectors represent normal, hepatitis B, HIV early, HIV late, IUP (pregnancy), leukemia, and malnutrition. This small real-world dataset is taken from a larger dataset with more features but allows a simpler exposition of the principles involved.

In the following backpropagation runs on MLPs, an epoch makes Q separate adjustments of the entire weight set, once for each exemplar training input vector. One iteration of the *quick training* algorithm for RBFNs or FLNs adjusts the entire weight set once only. Thus the MLP runs with backpropagation training are more computationally expensive than is shown by the number of epochs and iterations.

Table 9.5 shows the results of training an MLP network on Datasets 1 and 2 with Q exemplar input vectors and the N–M–J architecture shown. The number of epochs, root-mean-square (RMS) error, accuracy in recognizing the input exemplar vectors used for training, and the dataset number are also given. All runs used the same random number sequence to generate the initial weights. The extra output components in Dataset 2 make the difference shown, which is significant even on small datasets.

Table 9.6 shows the results of training an RBFN on the two datasets shown in Tables 9.4 and 9.5. The accuracy is significantly better on the dataset with three outputs rather than a single one. While the three output components of Dataset 2 triple the size of the RMS error (in the average sense) over the single output of Dataset 1, this did not happen here. The averaged errors (divided by 3) would actually be smaller here for the multiple outputs.

Table 9.4.
Dataset 2 (3 Outputs)

Inputs								Outputs		
0.2890	0.0550	0.4840	0.3850	0.5450	0.5750	0.3410	0.9950	0.100	0.100	0.100
0.0310	0.4840	0.2200	0.1230	0.3000	0.3800	0.0890	0.2100	0.200	0.500	0.900
0.1260	0.3910	0.3540	0.2750	0.4420	0.5150	0.1750	0.3950	0.300	0.900	0.500
0.0600	0.4140	0.2400	0.1620	0.3040	0.3680	0.1100	0.2700	0.400	0.100	0.500
0.0950	0.3650	0.3600	0.2340	0.4800	0.5430	0.1650	0.1900	0.500	0.900	0.300
0.0630	0.2220	0.3320	0.2100	0.4600	0.5360	0.1550	0.3200	0.900	0.500	0.200
0.1890	0.2470	0.4150	0.3120	0.5100	0.5620	0.2750	0.3200	0.900	0.900	0.900

Table 9.5.
Results of Training an MLP Network on Datasets 1 and 2

Run	Q	N	M	J	No. Iterations	RMS Error	Accuracy (%)	Dataset
1	7	8	8	1	1000	0.124	71.5	1
2	7	8	8	1	1500	0.089	85.7	1
3	7	8	10	1	1000	0.257	42.8	1
4	7	8	10	1	1500	0.222	57.1	1
5	7	8	12	1	1000	0.040	100	1
6	7	8	12	1	1500	0.024	100	1
7	7	8	10	3	1000	0.263	100	2
8	7	8	10	3	1500	0.184	100	2
9	7	8	12	3	800	0.489	100	2
10	7	8	12	3	600	0.580	100	2
11	7	8	12	3	500	0.621	85.7	2

Table 9.6.
Results of Training an RBF Network on Datasets 1 and 2

Run	Q	N	M	J	No. Iterations	RMS Error	Accuracy (%)	Dataset	σ
1	7	8	7	1	100	0.00510	100.0	1	0.10
2	7	8	7	1	60	0.16951	57.1	1	0.10
3	7	8	7	1	60	0.16951	57.1	1	0.05
4	7	8	7	1	50	0.28319	14.3	1	0.10
5	7	8	7	3	100	0.00500	100.0	2	0.10
6	7	8	7	3	60	0.29538	100.0	2	0.10
7	7	8	7	3	50	0.53578	100.0	2	0.10
8	7	8	7	3	30	1.29835	42.8	2	0.10

Example 7.3 in Section 7.7 shows the results of training an RBF-RVFLN on this data and on bipolar output data. The results are similar.

9.8. Testing of the Training and Architecture for MLPs

Types of Training Situations

Rather different situations arise in the use of MLPs for classification and recognition. *Type 1* data is where the prototypical feature vectors for patterns are known and are available. The exemplar feature vectors may not be as numerous as we desire, but they tend to be clean (low noise) or exact representative archetypes. In this case, the sample can be enlarged and the learning generalized if new exemplar feature vectors are generated by adding Gaussian noise (random errors) of moderate level to copies of the original exemplar feature vectors (see Section 9.3). The error values to be added can be drawn from Gaussian distributions with zero means and small standard deviations. For example, $\sigma = 0.25$ yields a moderate level of noise power ($\sigma^2 = 0.04$ watts/ohm). The original feature vectors should be reasonably good prototypes, but they may contain low noise already. The component values of the new feature values with generated noise should not be allowed to be too close to zero or unity (or -1 or 1 in the bipolar data case). The selection of the target identifier vectors to be used in the training is covered in Section 4.7. An example is a set of prototypical printed characters in a certain font, from which a set of features is selected and a target vector is determined for each prototype (see the Digit 12 dataset in Appendix 11).

Type 2 data is where there is a voluminous set of data in the form of records, in which case Q is large. The records contain fields and each field contains a datum. In the usual case, there may be missing data and considerable noise throughout the data. The feature vectors for the classes are not known, and the data must be examined and each feature chosen carefully to be either the raw data or else functions of one or more data fields (see Chapter 10). Suppose, for example, that a large set of medical records contains historical data for patients with a certain type of cancer. Let the goal here be to train an MLP to provide prognoses for new cancer patients. Each record may contain several fields for values such as age, sex, health condition, smoker/nonsmoker, stage of the disease, and so on. We desire to classify the data into two classes: (i) those who are alive 5 years after treatment began and (ii) those who are not alive 5 years after treatment began. There may be a large amount of noisy and missing data. The learning requires careful and generalized training with validation and verification testing being a crucial stage.

Preprocessing Datasets

For *Type 2* data, we sometimes need to extract the feature data, examine it, and perhaps throw out records that are missing certain values. Sometimes the average value of a field over all records is used to fill in a missing datum. Then we can obtain exemplar feature vectors for which we know the class—for example, the 5-year alive or dead status. The extracted data must be preprocessed to provide feature values in the proper range. It is not enough to normalize the data to the range [0,1], which would cause some values to have insignificant effects relative to others. An example is: $x_n^{(1)} = 0.00012$ and $x_n^{(2)} = 1327.0$. The minimum value of an nth feature (over all Q records) must be mapped to, say, 0.1, while the maximum value can be mapped to, say, 0.9. A linear mapping P_n is used for each fixed component n ($1 \leq n \leq N$) so that

$$P_n : [x_{n(\min)}, x_{n(\max)}] \rightarrow [0.1, 0.9] \qquad \text{(linearly)}$$

The linear mapping is the transformation $y = P_n(x)$ defined via

$$y = P_n(x) = [0.8(x - x_{n(\min)})]/[x_{n(\max)} - x_{n\min}] + 0.1 \qquad (9.13a)$$

It can be seen that $P_n(x_{n(\min)}) = 0.1$ and $P_n(x_{n(\max)}) = 0.9$. In case there are negative values in the data, so that $x_{n(\min)}$ is negative, the same process applies, but the mapping must transform the data into the bipolar interval $[-0.9, 0.9]$ (the output activation functions are bipolar); that is,

$$y = P_n(x) = [1.8(x - x_{n(\min)})]/[x_{n(\max)} - x_{n\min}] - 0.9 \qquad (9.13b)$$

The Processes of Training and Validation

Weigend et al. (1990a) conceptualized the oversized MLP, where the number of weights are of the order of the number Q of training pairs. Weigend et al. trained on a disjoint subset of the exemplars and used a "cross-validation" subset of exemplars. They trained on the training set and then checked the TSSE E_{val} on the validation set. They repeated this and stopped the training when the cross-validation measure E_{val} stopped improving (first started to increase) because continued training resulted in overtraining on the training data subset of exemplars, which resulted in a loss of generalization ability on the cross-validation set.

The process of ensuring general learning in an MLP consists of (i) *training*, (ii) *validating*, and (iii) *verification*. This requires three disjoint sets of exemplar pairs: (a) a *training set* (the largest), (b) a *validation set*, and (c) a *verification set*. Validation should be done after each segment of training over several iterations to determine when the TSSE E_{val} on the validation set of exemplar pairs stops decreasing. E_{val} begins to decrease as the training gets underway, but then stops decreasing or even begins increasing as the training becomes more specialized on the training exemplar pairs. The validation dataset is small compared to the training set. In the verification phase, a set of exemplar pairs whose size is roughly half that of the training set is used to verify that the trained MLP is indeed a correct pattern recognition system for the data to be used—that is, to verify the model.

Poh's Implementation of the Weigend–Rumelhart–Huberman Methodology

The straightforward procedure used by Poh (1991) on a given number Q of original training exemplar pairs is as follows: (i) Randomly select $Q_T = (0.65)Q$ of the pairs to be used for training, (ii) take 10% of the exemplar pairs to be used for cross-validation ($Q_{val} = 0.1Q$), and (iii) take the remaining 25% of the original pairs to be used for verification testing of the MLP model. These randomly selected sets for training, validation, and verification must be disjoint. After a number of iterations of training, the cross-validation is performed as follows: (a) Use the 10% exemplar–identifier pairs and feed only them through the MLP to obtain the total TSSE, denoted E_{val}; and (b) repeat this loop of training and cross-validation until the E_{val} first starts to increase. Continued training reduces the TSSE E_T on the training subset by specializing on the training data, but such specialization increases the TSSE E_{val} of the exemplars on which no training is done. After validation, the MLP is ready for verification testing.

The remaining Q_{ver} exemplar pairs (reserved for verification testing) are now put through the MLP and the total TSSE, denoted E_{ver}, is computed and divided by the number of exemplar–identifier pairs used for testing; that is, we use the mean-square error, MSE_{ver}. If this value is less than twice the MSE_T on the *last* training iteration, then the training is acceptable. Figure 9.16 presents the process of training, validating, and testing the model (verification). The validation and verification together constitute the *acceptance testing* of a trained neural network.

9.9. Putting Things Together—A Strategy for Training MLPs

An Overview

In view of the findings of researchers discussed in the previous sections, we make the following suggestions that form a strategy for neural engineering of a feedforward MLP. We

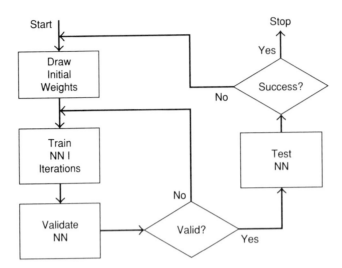

Figure 9.16. The High-level algorithm for training, validating, and verification.

assume here that the exemplar pairs $\{(\mathbf{x}^{(q)}, \mathbf{t}^{(q)}): q = 1,..., Q\}$ are given, so that the number N of features is determined and that the number J of output identifier components is given from the $\mathbf{t}^{(q)}$ ($J = K$ for small K or else $J = \lfloor \log_2(K) \rfloor + 1$). Other information follows from the exemplar pairs, such as the number Q of exemplar pairs and the number K of classes. Let $M = \lfloor \log_2(K) \rfloor + 1$. The exemplar feature vectors at hand should be divided into three sets: (i) a larger training set consisting of about 60% of the exemplars selected at random, (ii) a smaller set of about 15% of the exemplars selected at random for validation, and (iii) the remaining 25% of the exemplar pairs to be used for verification of the MLP architecture (see Section 9.8). The strategy is given below.

1. Make sure target components $t_j^{(q)}$ are: (i) not too close to either 0 or 1 (unipolar sigmoid activation functions) or to -1 or 1 (bipolar sigmoid activation functions). Our experience shows better results with unipolar sigmoids with $b_1 = M/2$, $b_2 = N/2$, $\alpha_1 = \alpha_2 = 2.2$, but the latter two parameters may be adjusted upward during the training.

2. For a number of classes $K < 50$, use a single hidden layer. If the patterns are intertwined nonlinearly with a greater number of classes, then two hidden layers may be useful.

3. Randomly select $Q_T = 0.6Q$ exemplar pairs on which to train, $Q_{val} = 0.15Q$ exemplar pairs on which to do cross-validation testing, and set the remaining $Q_{ver} = 0.25Q$ exemplar pairs aside for verification testing. If Q is small, generate new noisy exemplars from the originals to increase the size of Q.

4. For a single hidden layer, put the number of hidden neurodes to $M = \lfloor \log_2(2K) \rfloor + 1$. If $Q < M$, then generate extra exemplars using the original ones and adding Gaussian noise to components. If two hidden layers are used, then start with the number $L = \lfloor \sqrt{(2K)} \rfloor + p$ in the first one and $M = \lceil \sqrt{(2K)} \rceil - p$ in the second one ($2 \leq p < \lfloor \sqrt{(2K)} \rfloor$), so that $L > 2M$.

5. Draw initial weights uniformly randomly in $[-0.5, 0.5]$ and then use an initial weight adjustment procedure that adjusts the initial weight set into a good starting weight set in a region where the TSSE values E are low. For a large number of weights, avoid univariate search on each weight (use cubic or quartic search in random directions).

6. Iteratively add a single neurode to the (first) hidden layer and train further until the learning is valid.

7. Verify the MLP as a correct pattern recognition system; if it fails, go to Step 5.

8. Put all weights of small magnitude into an ordered list. Zero out these weights one at a time while checking to determine whether or not the TSSE is affected nonnegligibly; if so, assign the weight its previous value, or else leave it set at zero (i.e., leave it pruned).

9. Train further with the Q_T exemplar feature vectors used for training using a validation test with the Q_{val} exemplar pairs.

10. Make a final verification test. If this test is passed, then stop, else go to step 4.

Example 9.5.   Engineering the Training of an MLP on Stock Market Data

The StockMarket40 dataset is shown in Appendix 11. It consists of 40 pairs of input/output exemplars. An input feature vector consists of 12 features that are financial market indicators. Each output identifier consists of a single component that is an investment indicator. Each pair of input/output exemplars represents a particular week, so 52 pairs make up a year of activity (only 40 weeks of data are shown). The idea here is to train on about 5 years of data at a time to predict the next months activity, given the current 4 weeks of activity. The datasets we have included are merely for illustration. The data show that some input components, and also the single output component, take on negative as well as positive values. Therefore, we select bipolar sigmoids in the first design step.

The data shown (Appendix 11) come from larger datasets that cover many years. An examination of the data shows that each datum value is between -0.9 and 0.9. The raw data were rather spread out, with some values being around 1300 while others were about -0.111. It should be clear that just normalizing such data components is unsatisfactory, because the magnitude of $-0.111/1300 \approx 0$ is insignificant compared to $1300/1300 = 1$ and would have little or no influence on the training. The value -0.111 may well be important and should be learned. To resolve this problem, we condition the data by translating and contracting via a linear mapping $[x_n^{(min)}, x_n^{(max)}] \rightarrow [-0.9, 0.9]$ on each nth component datum via

$$x_n^{(q)} \leftarrow 1.8(x_n^{(q)} - x_n^{(min)})/(x_n^{(max)} - x_n^{(min)}) - 0.9$$

where $x_n^{(q)}$ is the nth component of $\mathbf{x}^{(q)}$ being transformed into a value in $[-0.9, 0.9]$, $x_n^{(max)}$ is the maximum over all $q = 1,..., Q$ of the nth components, $x_n^{(min)}$ is the minimum over all $q = 1,..., Q$ of the nth components, and $1.8 = (0.9 - (-0.9))$. Thus our transformation satisfies the following: (i) $x_n^{(min)}$ maps to -0.9, (ii) $x_n^{(max)}$ maps to 0.9, and (iii) every other value maps to a value proportionately between -0.9 and 0.9.

In the strategy of investment to be followed here, when the neural network looks at this week's data and predicts an output based on previous learning, that output is either positive or negative. If it is positive, we withdraw our money from cash certificates (if it is currently there) and put it into stocks, where it will remain for the next 4 weeks. If the output is negative, our money is withdrawn from stocks (if it is there) and put into cash certificates. Thus we have only two classes of feature vectors, of which one indicates stocks and the other indicates cash certificates. In this case we could put $M = 2$ as the number of hidden neurodes in a single layer.

We used an MLP with two hidden layers with an architecture of $N–L–M–J = 12–12–8–1$, which provided even more power. If we were considering an FLN, we would use $H = N = 12$ and take $x_1 x_2,..., x_{11} x_{12}, x_{12} x_1$ as extra inputs. We expect that this 24–1 network may have sufficient separating power. For an RBF network, we would choose $M = Q$ to obtain a hidden neurode for each exemplar. The network would then have an $N–M–J = 12–40–1$ architecture for the StockMarket40 dataset. For small σ^2 value, say 0.1, this should learn quickly.

In an actual project (Austin et al., 1997), we used a very large number of exemplars: 52 weeks per year for 5 years, or $Q = 260$. In that case, we decided to build in more learning power with $M = 16$ to account for the possibility of several linearly separable subclasses. The strategy, run over 12 years of data from the 1980s and 1990s, showed a net return of 26% and even predicted the "Black Monday" crash in the later 1980s. For the case of using a moving window of 5 years of data for training, we may not want to use *quick training* on an RBFN because it would require $M = 260$ neurodes. Nevertheless, an RBFN would be a powerful tool, and power is more important than the speed of the operational mode when money is at risk.

Exercises

9.1. Consider the case of a single neurode in a single hidden layer as the initial MLP architecture. We are to train and add one extra hidden layer of a single neurode at a time and train further, until the training is validated and the MLP is verified. Determine the advantages and disadvantages of this method over starting with a substantial number of hidden neurodes.

9.2. Construct a simple example using the XOR data to implement the strategy of growing a hidden layer (see Exercise 9.1 above).

9.3. Consider the training situation where a threshold activation is used at each neurode of an MLP instead of a sigmoid. What affect would this have on a strategic search algorithm for training?

9.4. Use a computer program to train an MLP on the Digit12 dataset of Appendix 11. Make several training runs from the beginning with $N = K = 10$ (given) and $M = 10$ and $J = 1$. Repeat this with $M = 12$. Then use $M = 10$ and $J = 4$. Compare and explain any differences.

9.5. Design an MLP and provide full justification of all decisions, where the task is to recognize symbols from an alphabet of 200 symbols with 100 components in each feature vector.

9.6. Find (invent) a data set that is simpler but analogous to that given in Figure 9.6. Assuming $\kappa = 4K$ is the number of linearly separable subclasses, use a single hidden layer of neurodes with $M = \log_4[4K]$ and train via an algorithm given in Chapter 6 or 7. Now use $M = 2$ hidden neurodes and train again, adding a new hidden neurode at a time until the training is good. Compare the results?

9.7. Explain what effect the number J of output neurodes has on the training of an MLP. Discuss the tradeoffs of adding more or less output neurodes.

9.8. Suppose that we choose an MLP architecture such that there is a single hidden layer. What can we say about the weights at any output layer neurode influencing the output at another output neurode? In view of this, do more output neurodes provide for greater or less separability? Justify your answer.

9.9. The tasks of two layers of neurodes are analyzed in Section 9.2. Each layer has a function. If two hidden layers are to be used, what is the function of the neurodes in the second hidden layer? Use a simple example and demonstrate the effect.

9.10. In Example 9.1, shade in the part of Figure 9.5 that represents the combinations of (y_1, y_2, y_3) when a single output neurode is adjoined to the network of Figure 9.4 that makes z_{out} high when its weights are $u_1 = 1$, $u_2 = 1$, and $u_3 = -1$ and $\tau = 0.5$ (τ is the threshold that activates z_{out} from the single output neurode).

9.11. Derive the backpropagation algorithm in full for a feedforward MLP with two hidden layers of neurodes. Use the unipolar sigmoid.

9.12. Repeat the derivation of Exercise 9.11 above, except use the bipolar sigmoid.

9.13. Derive the *cubronn* algorithm for the case of two hidden layers (see Section 6.3).

9.14. Suppose that a large number S ($S > 5,000$) of medical records are available in a database, each with a fixed number N of data fields. A computer program is to read large samples of size Q and transform the N field values for each record into a number x such that $0 < x < 1$. The class is known for each sample record. An MLP program is to train on this noisy data with some missing components in a small proportion of the records. There are $K = 4$ classes. Devise a strategy for selecting the datasets for training and testing where the MLP must be exceptionally well trained so as to be usable for future patients.

9.15. Provide a definition for a *well-trained* feedforward neural network.

9.16. In Exercise 9.14, suppose that there is missing data in many records. How could the records be salvaged and made usable. Consider the case where most records have a single missing datum, but some have two, and so on.

9.17. Use your own ingenuity to devise a method for testing the learning of an MLP when the learning must be exceptionally good and a great volume of computation can be allowed for the training.

9.18. In a situation where a large amount of data is available for training a FANN that must perform very accurately, what kind of FANN would you choose? Justify your answer. What are the tradeoffs, if any?

References

Ash, T. (1989), Dynamic node creation, *Connect. Sci.*, vol. 1, no. 4, 365–375.

Austin, M., Looney, C., and Zhuo, J. (1996), Security market timing using neural network models, *New Rev. Appl. Expert Syst.* (in press).

Baum, E. B., and Haussler, D. (1989), What size net gives valid generalization? *Neural Comput.*, vol. 1, p. 151–160.

Bose, N. K., and Garga, A. K. (1992), Neural network design using Voronoi diagrams: preliminaries, *1992 Int. Joint IEEE/INNS Conf. Neural Networks*, Baltimore, vol. 3, 127–132.

Bose, N. K., and Garga, A. K. (1993), Neural network design using Voronoi diagrams, *IEEE Trans. Neural Networks*, vol. 4, no. 5, 778–787.

Burkitt, A. N. (1991), Optimization of the architecture of feedforward neural networks with hidden layers by unit elimination, *Complex Syst.*, vol. 5, 371–380.

Castellano, G., Fanelli, A. M., and Pelillo, M. (1993), An empirical comparison of node pruning methods for layerd feed-forward neural networks, *Proc. 1993 Int. Joint Conf. Neural Networks*, Nagoya, vol. 1, 321–330.

Chauvin, Y. (1989), A back-propagation algorithm with optimal use of hidden units, in *Advances in Neural Information Processing*, vol. 1, edited by D. S. Touretzky, Denver, NIPS, pp. 519–526.

Chester, D. (1990), Why two hidden layers are better than one, *Proc. 1990 IEEE Joint Int. Conf. Neural Networks*, Washington, D.C., vol. 1, 265–268.

de Villiers, J., and Barnard, E. (1992), Backpropagation neural nets with one and two hidden layers, *IEEE Trans. Neural Networks*, vol. 4, no. 1, 136–141.

Gutierrez, M., Wang, J., and Grondin, R. (1989), Estimating hidden unit number for two-layer perceptrons, *Proc. IEEE/INNS Int. Joint Conf. Neural Networks*, Washington D.C., vol. 1, 677–681.

Hagiwara, M. (1993), Removal of hidden units and weights for backpropagation networks, *Proc. 1993 Int. Joint Conf. Neural Networks*, Nagoya, vol. 1, 351–354.

Hayashi, M. (1993), A fast algorithm for the hidden units in a multilayer perceptron, *Proc. IEEE 1993 Int. Joint Conf. Neural Networks*, Nagoya, vol. 1, 339–342.

Hinton, G. E. (1989), Connectionist learning procedures, *Artif. Intell.*, vol. 40, 185–234.

Holmström, L., and Koistinen, P. (1992), Using additive noise in backpropagation training, *IEEE Trans. Neural Networks*, vol. 3, no. 1, 24–38.

Huang, S. C., and Huang, Y. F. (1991), Bounds on the number of hidden neurons in multilayer perceptrons, *IEEE Trans. Neural Networks*, vol. 2, no. 1, 47–55.

Johansson, E. M., Dowla, F. U., and Goodman, D. M. (1992), Backpropagation learning for multilayer feedforward neural networks using the conjugate gradient method, *Int. J. Neural Systems*, vol. 2, no. 4, 291–301.

Karnin, E. D. (1990), A simple procedure for pruning back-propagation trained neural networks, *IEEE Trans. Neural Networks*, vol. 1, no. 2, 239–242.

Kruschke, J. K. (1989), Improving generalization in backpropagation networks with distributed bottlenecks, *Proc. IEEE/INNS Int. Joint Conf. Neural Networks*, Washington, D.C., vol 1, 443–447.

Kung, S. Y., and Hwang, J. N. (1988), An algebraic projection analysis for optimal hidden units size and learning rate in backpropagation learning, *Proc. IEEE Int. Conf. Neural Networks*, San Diego, vol. 1, 363–370.

Lapedes, A. (1988), How neural networks work, *NIPS* (Neural Info. Proc. Sys.), American Institute of Physics, 442–456.

Le Cun, Y., Denker, J. S., and Solla, S. A. (1990), Optimal brain damage, in *Advances in Neural Information Processing* 2, edited by D. S. Touretzky, Denver, NIPS pp. 598–605.

Looney, C. (1996a), Neural Data Engineering, Technical Report 96-6-1 CS Dept., University of Nevada, Reno.

Looney, C. (1996b), Stabilization and speedup of convergence in training feedforward neural networks, *Neurocomputing* 10, 7–31.

Makhoul, J., El-Jaroudi, A., and Schwartz, R. (1989), Formation of disconnected decision regions with a single hidden layer, *Proc. IEEE/INNS Int. Joint Conf. Neural Networks*, Washington, D.C., vol. 1, 455–460.

Masahiko, Arai, (1989), Mapping abilities of three-layer neural networks, *Proc. IEEE/INNS Int. Joint Conf. Neural Networks*, Washington D.C., vol. 1, 419–423.

McCormack, C., and Doherty, J. (1993), Neural network super architectures, *Proc. 1993 Int. Joint Conf. Networks*, Nagoya, vol. 1, 301–304.

Mehrotra, K. G., Mohan, C. K., and Ranka, S. (1991), Bounds on the number of samples needed for neural learning, *IEEE Trans. Neural Networks*, vol. 2, no. 6, 548–558.

Minsky, M. L., and Papert, S. A. (1988), *Perceptrons*, MIT Press, Cambridge, MA.

Mozer, M. C., and Smolensky, P. (1989), Skeletonization: a technique for trimming the fat from a network via relevance assessment, in *Advances in Neural Information Processing* 1, edited by D. S. Touretzky, Denver, NIPS, pp. 107–115.

Pao, Y. H., Park, G. H., and Sobajic, D. J. (1994), Learning and generalization characteristics of the random vector functional link net, *Neurocomputing* vol. 6, 1994, 163–180.

Parisi, D., and Pedone, R. (1992), How noise helps generalization in feedforward neural networks, in *Fifth Italian Workshop on Neural Networks*, WIRN VIETRI-92, Vietri sul Mare, Italia, World Scientific, pp. 133–139.

Pelillo, M., and Fanelli, A. M. (1993), A method of pruning layered feed-forward neural networks, *Proc. IWANN'93*, Sitges, Barcelona, Springer-Verlag, Berlin.

Poh, H. L. (1991), *A Neural Network Approach for Marketing Strategies Research and Decision Support*, Ph.D. Thesis, Stanford University.

Reed, Russell (1993), Pruning algorithms—a survey, *IEEE Trans. Neural Networks*, vol. 4, no. 5, 740–747.

Setioni, R., and Hui, L. C. K. (1993), Some *n*-bit parity problems are solvable by feedforward networks with less than *n* hidden units, *Proc. 1993 Int. Joint Conf. Neural Networks*, Nagoya, vol. 1, 305–308.

Setioni, R., and Hui, L. C. K. (1995), Use of a quasi-Newton method in a feedforward neural network construction algorithm, *IEEE Trans. Neural Networks*, vol. 6, no. 1, 273–277.

Sietsma, J., and Dow, R. J. F. (1988), Neural net pruning—Why and How? *Proc. IEEE Int. Conf. Neural Networks*, San Diego, vol. 1, 325–333.

Tarassenko, L., and Roberts, S. (1994), Supervised and unsupervised learning in radial basis function classifiers, *IEE Proc. Vis. Image Signal Processing*, vol. 141, no. 4, 210–216.

Wasserman, P. (1993), *Advanced Methods in Neural Computing*, Van Nostrand Reinhold, New York.

Weigend, A. S., Huberman, B. A., and Rumelhart, D. E. (1990a), *Predicting the Future: A Connectionist Approach*, Stanford PDP Research Group Report 90-01.

Weigend, A. S., Rumelhart, D. E., and Huberman, B. A. (1990b), Backpropagation, weight elimination, and time series prediction, *Proc. 1990 Connectionist Models Summer School*, 65–80.

Weigend, A. S., Rumelhart, D. E., and Huberman, B. A. (1991), Generalization by weight-elimination applied to currency exchange rate prediction, *Proc. Int. Joint Conf. Neural Networks*, Seattle, vol. 1, 837–841.

Whitley, D., and Bogart, C. (1990), The evolution of connectivity: pruning neural networks using genetic algorithms, *Proc. Int. Joint Conf. Neural Networks*, Washington D.C., vol 1, 134–138.

Wieland, A., and Leighton, R. (1987), Geometric analysis of neural network capabilities, *Proc. First IEEE Int. Conf. Neural Networks*, San Diego, vol. 3, 385–392.

Chapter 10

Feature and Data Engineering

The goal of this chapter is to make accessible some useful art and science of designing and implementing features.

10.1. The Role of Features

The Goals of Feature Extraction

The objects in a population possess many attributes that can be sensed or measured, many of which may be used to distinguish between one or more different subpopulations. For example, color distinguishes between red raspberries and blackberries but does not distinguish between lemons and grapefruit, although size, shape, texture, and scent do. A *pattern* $(p_1,..., p_A)$ is a vector template of attributes for members of a population of objects. A pattern *instance* is associated with each individual object. Pattern vectors may contain information that is redundant or superfluous, in which case we want to select a subset to reduce extraneous noise. The number of attributes could be large, in which case a reduction should be made by mapping the larger number of attributes into a smaller number of *features*.

The *goals* for mapping the *pattern space* (or *observation space*) into a reduced *feature space* are to (i) retain as much of the original information as possible, (ii) remove as much as possible of the redundant and irrelevant information that could cause extraneous noise and degrade the classification performance (Devijver, 1982), and (iii) render the measurement data to variables that are more suitable for decision making (Nadler and Smith, 1993). The first of these goals is to select a set of features that contains essentially all of the information of the patterns that is necessary for classifying the subpopulations, but in a more efficient form. Certain features distinguish between two or more classes, while other features distinguish between yet other classes. Multiple sets of features may be used (Watanabe and Pakvasa, 1973), or a hierarchy of them, but it is convenient to use a single set of features of a fixed dimension N.

The second goal involves the elimination of redundancy to reduce both the complexity and the error rate. It is known that more independent features provide greater discrimination power, but more features that are correlated can actually increase the error rate. The third goal is met by transforming the pattern space into more suitable features that have more meaning to humans, such as phonemes from speech signals or strokes for optical character recognition, or features that represent a function of multiple pattern components that combines or summarizes their decision power.

Figure 10.1 shows an abstracted reduction process where an array of pattern attribute values are converted to a feature vector. Data may accumulate rapidly, for example, in a speech recognition system, so the samples must be reduced to significantly fewer features. Phonemes are one kind of audio features. Strokes, edges, shape parameters, and so on, are features reduced from images that may contain an extremely large number of attributes.

The Need for Reduction

The number of *pixels* (picture elements) in a particular 1024×768 SVGA video image is 786,432. Each 8-bit pixel may be one of 256 shades of gray (or colors). On the new *true color* graphics systems, the image could be 1280×1024 and the colors could number as high as 2^{24} (16 million 24-bit pixel values). Many important attributes of an image, such as angles between edges, or blobs of a particular shade, do not depend upon the size, location, or orientation, but may be dilated, contracted, rotated, or translated. They may number only a few dozen, or even less. Texture features usually number about a half-dozen. Therefore, we rarely use pixels as features, except on small portions of an image. For speech recognition, the data are usually sampled at about 10,000 samples per second (10 Ksps), where a sample may be a byte (8 bits for a resolution of 256 distinct values) or larger. The volume of "atomic" data becomes overwhelmingly large.

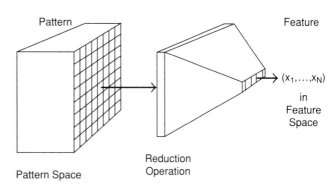

Figure 10.1. Reduction of patterns to feature vectors.

Pattern

Feature

$(x_1,...,x_N)$ in Feature Space

Pattern Space

Reduction Operation

10.2. Feature Design and Extraction

Independence of Features

Some attributes in pattern space may be independent, while those that depend significantly on other attributes are correlated with other attributes in that their magnitudes go high or low together on the average and may go positive together or positive against negative on the average (the latter case is negative correlation). The feature selection process should eliminate features that are essentially redundant (strongly correlated). Any extracted feature set that satisfies the first two of the goals given above (i.e., contains all necessary information but is not redundant) is called an *optimal* feature set (Therrien, 1989). Near-optimal feature sets are desirable in practice.

There exist probabilistic methods (see Therrien, 1989, Chapter 5); Bow, 1984, Chapter 6; or Kittler, 1977), for extracting features, but they require a priori distributions and are more computationally complex, and so they suffer the same faults as Bayesian methods of pattern recognition (although they usually work well in a linear environment). In practice, feature extraction is similar to clustering into classes and is a de facto *preclustering* process. We must already have pattern vectors that we know a priori are from different classes or else we must select them some way. For further discussion, see Bow (1984) and Therrien (1989). If there are A attributes and we wish to select a set of N features ($N < A$), then the number of different combinations is $C(A, N) = A!/[(A - N)!N!]$, which may be an astronomically large number. Exhaustive search is the only way to find a true optimal feature set, but this is not practical in most situations.

Features are not just a selected subset of attributes. They are often in the "eye of the beholder," such as a picture of George Washington on a one-dollar bill. The usual case of features that are perceived by humans cannot be made up of a simple set of attributes combined in some way. It may be an extremely unlikely combination of attributes. Thus there is the element of creative and heuristic combinations of attributes that form features that humans perceive well.

Observability

A variable v is *observable* if we can (i) sense or measure a value for v directly, (ii) compute a value indirectly for v as a function of other variables that can be obtained directly, (iii) estimate a value for it based on other directly obtained variables with which it is correlated, or (iv) compute or estimate a value for it based on values that were obtained by any finite combination of the previous three methods.

A variable is said to be *controllable* if we can (i) change its value directly or (ii) cause its value to change indirectly by changing, directly or indirectly, other variables upon which it depends either functionally or stochastically (correlationally). Figure 10.2 shows the situation where the worlds of observable and controllable variables meet. We are primarily concerned with observable variables, and especially with a subset of them that are essentially independent.

Types of Features

Features can be classified (Tou and Gonzalez, 1974) into three groups: (i) physical sensory, (ii) structural, and (iii) mathematical. While humans smell fragrance, see color, and

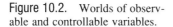

Figure 10.2. Worlds of observable and controllable variables.

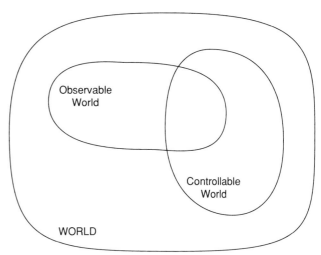

perceive shape, angles, edges, lines, and curves, machines are generally not equipped to perform such feature extractions efficiently. Physical sensory devices may be used by machines such as video cameras in image processing systems, or some systems can detect the presence of explosives via certain airborne chemicals that are transduced by sensors into a signal. Structural features are relationships of physical sensory features, such as (a) the relative locations of certain lines, edges, curves, and blobs or (b) the direction and width-to-height ratio of grains of a texture. A mathematical feature is obtained by mapping pattern measurements (observations) $p_1,..., p_A$ via a function $x = f(p_1,..., p_A)$ of measurements such that the value of x in the range of $f(-)$ has the power to distinguish two or more different classes.

A High-Level Feature Selection Algorithm

We should start with a large set of attributes to ensure a powerful set of independent features for the discrimination of classes. First, preprocessing is usually necessary on the observation data to perform operations such as scaling, normalization, smoothing, and other estimation and "cleaning" of the data (Bezdek and Pal, 1992). After that, some important attributes that distinguish between members of two or more classes may be used directly as features, while others may be mapped into features such as ratios, logarithms of products, sums or powers, and so on. The *selection* of features requires some experience with the population at hand, so that knowledge of how humans perceive the objects and the differences of the subpopulations is available. Figure 10.3 shows a flow chart for a scheme for reducing the many attributes to a smaller set of features that contain essentially all of the data in the attributes. We list below a high-level feature selection algorithm based on Figure 10.3 that yields a suboptimal constructive (iterative) solution to the problem of selecting features.

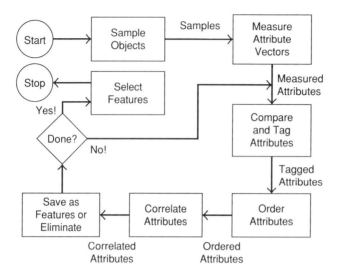

Figure 10.3. A high-level feature selection algorithm.

Step 1. Select a sample of objects in an unbiased manner from the population.

Step 2. Measure all of the attributes of the sample objects that are feasible.

Step 3. Repeat the following steps until no further significant features can be determined.
   (i) Select and tag attributes whose values vary the most over the sample of objects.
   (ii) Order tagged attributes from most important to least important in distinguishing objects.
   (iii) Correlate each tagged attribute pair over the population; and if correlation coefficients are relatively large in magnitude, eliminate the attribute of lower ranking to obtain independent attributes.

Step 4. Stop.

The first part of Step 3 above involves, for each fixed ath attribute p_a, finding the range $[p_a^{(min)}, p_a^{(max)}]$ of all values $p_a^{(q)}$ over the sample of Q patterns, where $p_a^{(min)}$ and $p_a^{(max)}$ are the respective minimum and maximum of these values. The attributes with the greatest ranges are likely to be the most important, but most of the attribute values of the objects should be spread out over the range. If the range is large and the distribution covers well that range, then that attribute is tagged as a candidate.

The correlation in Step 3 above may be done by letting $p_a^{(q)}$ be the value for the ath attribute of the qth sample pattern and finding the *correlation* of attributes a and b over the sample population by

$$c_{ab} = (1/Q)\sum_{(q=1, Q)} (p_a^{(q)} - \mu_a)(p_b^{(q)} - \mu_b) \tag{10.1}$$

where μ_a is the expected value of the ath attribute over the sample population of size Q. The standardized dimensionless *correlation coefficient* is

$$\rho_{ab} = c_{ab}/\sqrt{(c_{aa}c_{bb})} \qquad (10.2)$$

The correlation coefficients can be compared because of standardization.

In Step 3 of the above algorithm, the 2-D display (Bezdek and Pal, 1992) is useful. From the A-dimensional attribute data, we take two dimensions x_i and x_j at a time and display the values as points in the plane to see beforehand what can be done rather than measuring what was done after doing it (Tukey, 1977). This can also be done with prospective features, as shown in Figure 10.4, which shows the cases (a) of correlated data that do not separate classes and (b) that does. According to Bezdek and Pal (1992), it is a method for looking at data to see what the data seems to say, as opposed to confirming or contradicting afterward what we hypothesized may be true. For example, if we fix attribute a and view the graphs of attributes (or features) a and b, for all $b \neq a$, then we can determine whether or not the ath attribute should be used as a feature or as an argument of a function that determines a feature.

> *Feature Design Principle 10.1.* Any selected feature (i) must discriminate clearly between two or more classes of objects, (ii) must not be correlated with another feature to any moderately strong extent, and (iii) should have meaning for humans.

For a mathematical–statistical theory of feature extraction, see Kittler (1986). In practice, however, these methods are difficult to implement without a priori assumptions, such as Gaussian distributions for which the sample statistics can be computed. Correlational analysis (which is covered next) is sometimes practical, provided that the sample is large enough. For nonlinearly separable classes, statistical methods per se are inadequate.

Correlation of Features

Step 3 of the above algorithm may reveal that some of the features are correlated to a significant extent. It is useful to determine which ones depend strongly on which other ones, pairwise, and eliminate the one that is *lower* in order of importance. To do this, we must

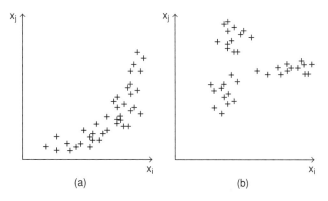

Figure 10.4. Displaying two attributes of feature candidates at a time with (a) correlated and (b) uncorrelated.

have a measure of dependency. The usual measure of dependence is the correlation coefficient defined above in Equation (10.2).

Let the feature vectors have dimension N and let the components of the feature vectors $\mathbf{x} = (x_1,..., x_N)$ be ordered according to the ranked feature importance. The importance of a feature may be assigned by the total magnitude of its range (greatest values minus the least values), its variance, or by its ability to separate the feature vectors as determined by observing 2-dimensional graphs. Recall that a feature vector is actually a vector of random variables $\mathbf{X} = (X_1,..., X_N)$. Any random variable component may have a multimodal distribution caused by two or more subclasses that are separable. Suppose that $\{\mathbf{x}^{(1)},..., \mathbf{x}^{(Q)}\}$ is a sample of feature vectors that are sufficiently numerous and different so as to be from all of the different classes. The sample correlation of two features is defined in the same way as for attributes, where $\mathbf{E}$ is the expected value operator, by

$$c_{ij} = \text{Cor}(X_i, X_j) = (1/Q)\sum_{(q=1, Q)}\mathbf{E}[(x_i^{(q)} - \mu_i)(x_j^{(q)} - \mu_j)] \tag{10.3}$$

The *correlation coefficient* of Equation (10.2), which is

$$\rho_{ij} \equiv c_{ij}/\sqrt{(c_{ii}c_{jj})} \tag{10.4a}$$

satisfies the Cauchy–Schwartz inequality

$$-1 \leq \rho_{ij} \leq 1 \tag{10.4b}$$

Greater independence of X_i and X_j means that ρ_{ij} is closer to zero ($c_{ij} \approx 0$).

We assume henceforth that the features are standardized so that the range of each is [0,1]. The correlation coefficient of any feature X_i with itself is $\rho_{ii} = 1$ as can be easily seen from Equation (10.4a). However, for two different features X_i and X_j that are essentially independent, their correlation is close to zero because the product terms in Equation (10.3) tend to be negative as often as positive and of similar magnitudes of products that cancel out on the average. A larger sample size Q yields a more accurate measure, and yields more power to differentiate the classes, as does a larger number of features, provided the features are essentially independent. For two dependent features X_i and X_j, the products over the classes tend to (i) go together in sign more often so that ρ_{ij} is closer to 1 or (ii) oppose each other in sign more often, in which case ρ_{ij} is closer to -1. Therefore, if any two features are highly correlated, say, $|\rho_{ij}| > 0.707$, then more than half of the mean-squared variation of one feature is accounted for by the other ($0.707^2 = 0.5$). We should rank the correlation coefficients ρ_{ij} by magnitude; and for the ones that are significantly high, eliminate the feature x_i or x_j of least importance.

10.3. Feature Weighting

The Concept of Weighting Features by Importance

Given an ordering of features, $f_1 > \cdots > f_N$, where ">" denotes "is more important than," we may weight the features by such importance. The most important feature f_1 would be weighted with the largest weight v_1, and so on, until f_N is weighted with the smallest weight v_N. Then the weighted feature values $f_1v_1,..., f_Nv_N$ replace the feature values both in the classification training mode and in the operational recognition mode. This prevents features of lesser importance from overriding more important features in the decisionmaking. The weighting should reflect that different features have different importances in the decisionmaking.

The Tou–Gonzalez Method of Weighting Features

A method that appeared in Tou and Gonzalez (1974) uses Lagrange multipliers to determine the weightings v_j that minimize the total average distances between vectors in a cluster. Suppose there are N components for each feature vector, that is, $\mathbf{x} = (x_1,..., x_N)$. The squared distance between any vector $\mathbf{x}^{(q)}$ and any other vector $\mathbf{x}^{(r)}$ in the same cluster is

$$D^2(\mathbf{x}^{(q)}, \mathbf{x}^{(r)}) = \Sigma_{(n=1, N)}(x_n^{(q)} - x_n^{(r)})^2 = \left\| \mathbf{x}^{(q)} - \mathbf{x}^{(r)} \right\|^2 \tag{10.5}$$

For a cluster that contains R vectors $\{\mathbf{x}^{(1)},..., \mathbf{x}^{(R)}\}$, the *mean-squared distance* from fixed $\mathbf{x}^{(1)}$ to all other $R - 1$ vectors within that cluster is

$$(1/(R - 1))\Sigma_{(r=2, R)}D^2(\mathbf{x}^{(1)}, \mathbf{x}^{(r)}) = (1/(R - 1))\Sigma_{(r=2, R)}\left\| \mathbf{x}^{(1)} - \mathbf{x}^{(r)} \right\|^2$$
$$= (1/(R - 1))\Sigma_{(r=2, R)} \Sigma_{(n=1, N)}(x_n^{(1)} - x_n^{(r)})^2 \tag{10.6}$$

The *intraset distance* D_I over this same cluster is obtained by letting $\mathbf{x}^{(q)}$ vary over all R vectors in the cluster—that is, taking the average of all of the mean-squared distances from each $\mathbf{x}^{(q)}$ $(i = 1,..., R)$ so that

$$D_I^2 = (1/R)\Sigma_{(q=1, R)}[1/(R - 1)]\Sigma_{(r \neq q)}D^2(\mathbf{x}^{(q)}, \mathbf{x}^{(r)})$$
$$= (1/R)\Sigma_{(q=1, R)}[1/(R - 1)]\Sigma_{(r \neq q)}\Sigma_{(n=1, N)}(x_n^{(q)} - x_n^{(r)})^2$$
$$= [1/(R(R - 1))]\Sigma_{(q=1, R)}\Sigma_{(r \neq q)}\Sigma_{(n=1, N)}(x_n^{(q)} - x_n^{(r)})^2 \tag{10.7}$$

Upon rearranging and expanding the squares and substituting well-known statistical definitions for the mean and variance, we can now give the intraset distance of Equation (10.7) as

$$D_I^2 = [2R/R(R - 1)]\Sigma_{(n=1, N)}\Sigma_{(r=1, R)}(x_n^{(r)} - \mu_n^{(r)})^2$$
$$= [2R/(R - 1)]\Sigma_{(n=1, N)}(1/R)\Sigma_{(r=1, R)}(x_n^{(r)} - \mu_n^{(r)})^2$$
$$= 2\Sigma_{(n=1, N)}\sigma_n^2 \tag{10.8}$$

where σ_n^2 is the *biased variance* and the unbiased variance is $\sigma_n^2 = [R/(R - 1)]\sigma_n^2$. Using the unbiased variance now, we obtain

$$D_I^2 = 2\Sigma_{(n=1, N)}\sigma_n^2 \tag{10.9}$$

We minimize D_I^2 with the *weighted* components $v_n\sigma_n$ in place of σ_n in Equation (10.9), subject to the constraint that $v_1 + \cdots + v_N = 1$, so we use the cost function

$$F \equiv 2\sum_{(n=1,\,N)}(v_n\sigma_n)^2 - \rho(\sum_{(n=1,\,N)}v_n - 1) \tag{10.10}$$

where ρ is the Lagrange multiplier. Setting each jth partial derivative $\partial F/\partial v_j$ to zero yields the result

$$2(2v_j\sigma_j^2) - \rho = 0$$

so that

$$v_j = \rho/4\sigma_j^2 \tag{10.11}$$

Setting $\partial F/\partial\rho = 0$ and solving yields the constraint

$$v_1 + \cdots + v_N = 1 \tag{10.12}$$

Upon substituting Equation (10.11) into Equation (10.12), we factor out ρ and solve for ρ to obtain

$$\rho = 4/\sum_{(n=1,\,N)}\sigma_n^{-2} \tag{10.13}$$

Upon putting this back into Equation (10.11), we obtain

$$v_j = [\sigma_j^2\sum_{(n=1,\,N)}\sigma_n^{-2}]^{-1} \tag{10.14}$$

Because the summation part is the same for each jth component of the feature vectors, $j = 1,..., N$, it is a constant, so we see that each weight v_j is proportional to $1/\sigma_j^2$. The weights $v_j = 1/\sigma_j^2$ may therefore be used upon setting the constant of proportion to unity. This yields

$$v_j = 1/\sigma_j^2, \qquad n = 1,..., N \tag{10.15a}$$

In practice, we would take the constant $c = 1/\sigma_1^2 + \cdots + 1/\sigma_N^2$ and use

$$v_j = 1/c\sigma_j^2, \qquad n = 1,..., N \tag{10.15b}$$

It is clear that $v_1 + \cdots + v_N = 1$ in this latter case.

Some Other Weighting Techniques

If the mean square error (variance) is known for each feature (component) over the population, or it can be estimated over the sample $\{x^{(q)}\}$, then one way of assigning weights (ignoring any previous ranking of the features as to importance) is

$$v_n = 1/\sigma_n^2, \qquad n = 1,..., N \tag{10.16}$$

This result coincides with the maximal likelihood estimate used in Kalman filtering. It states that if the mean-squared error of a feature is larger, so that feature is more likely to have larger errors, then that feature is to be weighted lower, that is, larger σ_j^2 has smaller weighting $1/\sigma_j^2$. This could violate a previous ordering of the features by importance based on some other criterion, but it reflects the statistical importance of the features. It can be modified by taking a weighted average of the $v_n = 1/\sigma_n^2$ with the other weighting that reflects another importance ordering.

For features that satisfy $x_1 > \cdots > x_N$, the simplest weighting method is to assign weights that reflect the importance ordering by taking the inverse of the indices, which yields

$$v_n = 1/n \tag{10.17}$$

This works for a small number of features, but for a large number, the weightings of the features of lesser importance could be too small. In such cases, we may take the weights to be

$$v_n = 1/\ln(n + 1) \tag{10.18}$$

or

$$v_n = 1/\log(n + 1) \tag{10.19}$$

For example, a feature ranked 100th in the ordering would have weightings of $1/n = 0.01$, $1/\ln(n + 1) = 0.217$, or $1/\log(n + 1) = 0.499$, depending upon whether we use Equation (10.17), (10.18), or (10.19), respectively. The most important feature would have respective weights of $1/1 = 1$, $1/\ln(1 + 1) = 1.443$, or $1/\log(1 + 1) = 3.32$. The weightings of Equations (10.17) through (10.19) do not sum to unity, but do if each is divided by the constant c, where, respectively,

$$c = 1 + 1/2 + \cdots + 1/N, \qquad c = 1/\ln(2) + \cdots + 1/\ln(N + 1)$$

or

$$c = 1/\log(2) + \cdots + 1/\log(N + 1)$$

If the covariance matrix $[\sigma_{ij}]$ for the features is known (it can be computed over the sample of feature vectors as

$$\sigma_{ij} = (1/Q)\sum_{(q=1, Q)} (x_i^{(q)} - \mu_i)(x_j^{(q)} - \mu_j) \tag{10.20}$$

then we can compute the Mahalanobis distance (see Section 0.10) between vectors $\mathbf{x}^{(p)}$ and $\mathbf{x}^{(q)}$, which is defined by

$$d_M(\mathbf{x}^{(p)}, \mathbf{x}^{(q)}) = (\mathbf{x}^{(p)} - \mathbf{x}^{(q)})^t C^{-1}(\mathbf{x}^{(p)} - \mathbf{x}^{(q)}) \tag{10.21}$$

where C is the covariance matrix. The inverse covariance matrix C^{-1} weights the component differences according to their independence from each other and the smallness of their mean-squared error. This distance assigns sample feature vectors to clusters, via minimal distance $d_M(\mathbf{x}^{(q)}, \mathbf{z}^{(k)})$ to the cluster center $\mathbf{z}^{(k)}$, based on dependence. When C is a diagonal matrix, then the diagonal differences only are squared and summed via the dot product, so the distance is the Euclidean distance.

Let δ_n be the Mahalanobis distance of the nth feature only. Then the Mahalanobis distance based on all N features is

$$d_M = \sum_{(n=1,\,N)} \delta_n \tag{10.22}$$

Assuming that the decreasing importance of the features can be modeled by

$$\delta_n = \epsilon \delta_{n-1} \tag{10.23}$$

for some ϵ such that $0 < \epsilon < 1$, then

$$d_M{}^2 = \sum_{(n=1,\,N)} \epsilon^2 \delta_1{}^2 = \delta_1{}^2 [(1 - \epsilon^{2N})/(1 - \epsilon^2)] \tag{10.24}$$

We can use this to find N for the minimal number of features upon computing $d_M{}^2$ for both N and $N + 1$ and taking the difference. If such a difference is negligible, then N is large enough.

10.4. Real-World Features

Example 10.1.   Features for Digit Recognition

In a real-world situation, we must find a way to select the features and then either order them by importance or apply some method that will assign an importance weight—for example, $v_n = 1/\sigma_n{}^2$. To see what must be done in a typical case, we take an example from optical character recognition of digits from scanned images. Consider the digit "7" shown in Figure 10.5. Suppose that we put a box around each digit and contract or dilate the box to some standard size in terms of *pixels* (picture elements, or dots on the screen of a video monitor).

There are many ways to select features, but first we need to *register* each digit with respect to location by, say, left justification and top justification in a box of a standard size. For simplicity, we assume here that we have a 16 × 14 (rows by columns) matrix of pixels. To humans, the lines and their relationships define the digit. The lines, in turn, are composed of dark pixels on a background of light pixels (or vice versa). The relationships of the light and dark pixels, then, determine the character. Our simple approach uses the relationships along rows and columns. Our features are not *rotation invariant*; that is, they change when the digit is rotated to any nonnegligible extent.

We number the rows from top to bottom as 0, 1, ..., 15 and the columns from left to right as 0, 1, ..., 13. To reduce the redundant information, we do not use all rows and columns. Instead, we use rows 1, 4, 7, 8, 11, and 14 and columns 1, 4, 6, 7, 9, 12. Along each row, going from left to right, we count the number of times a change occurs from black to white or white to black between adjacent pixels. Similarly, we count the number of changes along columns. These counts are the prefeatures, of which there are 6 for rows and 6 for columns, for a total of 12 counts. They do not depend upon the thickness of the lines and so are line

Figure 10.5. Optical character for digit 7.

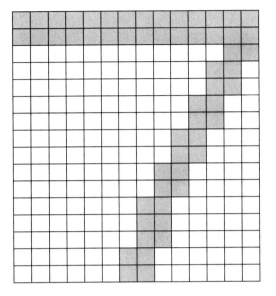

width invariant. To convert the counts into standardized features, we divide each one by 7, which is the maximum number of changes that could occur (actually, less changes than that always occur). Thus each feature vector has 12 components, which are standardized row counts and standardized column counts. Table 10.1 presents the table of prefeature counts for the digits 0–9, and Table 10.2 displays the standardized feature values.

We have reduced the pattern attributes from 224 pixels to a meager set of 12 features that intrinsically capture the relationships along the rows and columns. We could also use the number of changes along diagonal lines to capture more relationships, of which some may be redundant while others may be independent of the ones we already have. We use only the 12 row and column features for illustrative purposes. In a real-world application, we would set all zeros in the input feature data of Table 10.2 to 0.1 for training an MLP with unipolar sigmoids, but would not change them for training RBFNs or FLNs.

Table 10.1.
The Prefeature Counts Before Standardization

Digit	Count of Changes
0	(4, 3, 3, 2, 2, 4; 2, 3, 2, 2, 3, 2)
1	(2, 2, 2, 2, 2, 2; 0, 0, 0, 0, 1, 0)
2	(2, 1, 1, 2, 2, 1; 1, 3, 4, 4, 4, 3)
3	(0, 2, 2, 2, 2, 2; 0, 3, 3, 4, 7, 4)
4	(4, 4, 3, 0, 2, 2; 0, 3, 2, 2, 0, 2)
5	(2, 2, 4, 1, 1, 2; 2, 4, 4, 4, 4, 3)
6	(2, 2, 2, 3, 2, 2; 2, 5, 4, 4, 4, 4)
7	(0, 2, 2, 2, 2, 2; 0, 1, 2, 3, 3, 1)
8	(1, 3, 1, 1, 3, 3; 0, 7, 4, 4, 4, 4)
9	(4, 4, 3, 6, 2, 2; 0, 4, 3, 4, 5, 1)

Table 10.2.
Standardized Feature Vectors and Identifiers for Digits 0–9

Digit	Feature Vector Values as Count Proportions												Outputs	
	1	2	3	4	5	6	7	8	9	10	11	12	1	2
0	(0.500,	0.375,	0.375,	0.250,	0.250,	0.500;	0.250,	0.375,	0.250,	0.250,	0.375,	0.250)	(0.1,	0.1)
1	(0.250,	0.250,	0.250,	0.250,	0.250,	0.250;	0.000,	0.000,	0.000,	0.000,	0.125,	0.000)	(0.2,	0.5)
2	(0.250,	0.125,	0.125,	0.250,	0.250,	0.125;	0.125,	0.375,	0.500,	0.500,	0.500,	0.375)	(0.3,	0.1)
3	(0.000,	0.250,	0.250,	0.250,	0.250,	0.250;	0.000,	0.375,	0.375,	0.500,	0.875,	0.500)	(0.4,	0.5)
4	(0.500,	0.500,	0.375,	0.000,	0.250,	0.250;	0.000,	0.375,	0.250,	0.250,	0.000,	0.250)	(0.5,	0.1)
5	(0.250,	0.250,	0.500,	0.125,	0.125,	0.250;	0.250,	0.500,	0.500,	0.500,	0.500,	0.375)	(0.5,	0.9)
6	(0.250,	0.250,	0.250,	0.375,	0.250,	0.250;	0.250,	0.625,	0.500,	0.500,	0.500,	0.500)	(0.6,	0.5)
7	(0.000,	0.250,	0.250,	0.250,	0.250,	0.250;	0.000,	0.125,	0.250,	0.375,	0.375,	0.125)	(0.7,	0.9)
8	(0.125,	0.375,	0.125,	0.125,	0.375,	0.375;	0.000,	0.875,	0.500	0.500,	0.500,	0.500)	(0.8,	0.5)
9	(0.500,	0.500,	0.375,	0.750,	0.250,	0.250;	0.000,	0.500,	0.375,	0.500,	0.625,	0.125)	(0.9,	0.9)

There are multiple ways to order features by importance. We demonstrate here by finding the range of variation for each feature. For example, Table 10.2 shows that the first feature varies from 0.0 to 0.5 (look at the column under feature 1), while the second feature varies from 0.125 to 0.5. Thus we judge the first feature to be more important than the second one. The eleventh feature varies from 0.0 to 0.875 and is therefore more important than either the first or the second. It separates "3" (0.875) from "4" (0.000) and "0" (0.375), but does not separate "2" from "5" nor "6" or "8" for which the eleventh feature value is 0.500. But, for example, "2" and "8" are separated by feature number 8 with respective values of 0.375 and 0.875. Continuing, we can order the features from the most important to the least important by the width of their range of values over the sample.

Once the features are ordered so that x_1 is the most important, x_2 is the next most important,..., and x_{12} is the least important, we can assign weights $v_1,..., v_{12}$ to them that reflect their importance. Because there are only 12 features here, we could use $v_n = 1/\ln(n + 1)$. This yields the weights

$$v_1 = 1/\ln(2) = 1.442695, \qquad v_2 = 1/\ln(3) = 0.9102392$$

$$v_3 = 1/\ln(4) = 0.7213475, \qquad v_4 = 1/\ln(5) = 0.6213349$$

$$v_5 = 1/\ln(6) = 0.5581106, \qquad v_6 = 1/\ln(7) = 0.5138983$$

$$v_7 = 1/\ln(8) = 0.4808983, \qquad v_8 = 1/\ln(9) = 0.4551196$$

$$v_9 = 1/\ln(10) = 0.4342944, \qquad v_{10} = 1/\ln(11) = 0.4170323$$

$$v_{11} = 1/\ln(12) = 0.4024296, \qquad v_{12} = 1/\ln(13) = 0.3898712$$

In order to standardize these weights to fall between 0 and 1, we divide each of these numbers by the largest weight $v_1 = 1.442695$ to obtain

$$v_1 = 1.0, \quad v_2 = 0.6309297,..., \quad v_{12} = 0.2702381$$

Upon dividing each by the sum $c = v_1 + \cdots + v_{12}$, it would lower the weight values.

The correlations of the original features to see which are dependent on others, based on the sample, are computed via

$$c_{ij} = (1/10)\sum_{(q=1,10)}(x_i^{(q)} - \mu_i)(x_j^{(q)} - \mu_j) \tag{10.25a}$$

for features i and j, $1 \leq i,j \leq 12$. The computational formula is

$$c_{ij} = [(1/10)\sum_{(q=1,10)}[x_i^{(q)}x_j^{(q)}] - [\mu_i\mu_j] \tag{10.25b}$$

From Table 10.2 and the use of $\mu_i = (x_i^{(1)} + \cdots + x_i^{(10)})/10$, we obtain

$$\mu_1 = 0.2625, \qquad \mu_2 = 0.3125, \qquad \mu_1^2 = 0.0689062, \qquad \mu_2^2 = 0.0976562$$

$$c_{11}^2 = 0.1015625 - 0.0689062 = 0.0326563,$$

$$c_{22}^2 = 0.1109375 - 0.0976562 = 0.0132813$$

$$c_{12}^2 = 0.0953125 - 0.0820312 = 0.0132812$$

$$\begin{aligned}
r_{12} &= [c_{12}^2/c_{11}c_{22}]^{1/2} \\
&= \{0.0132812/[(0.0326563)(0.0132813)]^{1/2}\}^{1/2} \\
&= \{0.0132812/[0.0004337]^{1/2}\}^{1/2} = \{0.0132812/0.0208259\}^{1/2} \\
&= 0.6377251^{1/2} = 0.7985769
\end{aligned}$$

We see from this last result that the first and second features are quite strongly correlated. This means that we should keep the one that has the highest importance weighting and drop the other one. Performing this process on the given features would likely eliminate other features as well. It is desirable to start with a sufficiently large set of features so we can eliminate the most correlated ones to arrive at a final set of essentially independent features without redundancy but with enough separating power. In such a situation, there is the need to estimate the number of final features required to separate ten patterns. If each feature discriminated between only two patterns, then we would need a larger number of features. However, certain strong features will discriminate between more than a single pair of patterns. It is crucial that all patterns be separated by two or more independent features to increase robustness.

Example 10.2. Texture Features

Many real-world problems are difficult at best, but can be solved only if a creative set of features can be designed and extracted. Consider the case where aerial photographs of terrain are to be processed to recognize regions of crops of certain types, woods, and so on. Each type of region has a particular *texture*, which is a complex property that consists of variations of shades of gray that form repeating similar patterns. A block of pixels of a constant gray shade has no texture, while a block with a uniform distribution of small subblocks of a shade of gray on a background of a different gray shade appears to have a texture. Fine textures have higher rates of variation and coarse textures have lower rates of variation of the gray shades across the spatial dimensions. Textures may have a direction because of lower rates of change in one direction than others, in which case there may be a granular appearance. The absolute gray levels do not determine the texture because the image may be darkened or lightened with the texture remaining. It is the differences, or variations, along with the distribution of differences that form a pattern—that is, make the texture.

Texture in an image is examined by means of a rectangular block of pixels. We assume that the block consists of an $N \times N$ array of contiguous pixels. The size of the block is important because a coarse texture needs a larger block than does a finer one to adequately sample the texture. One or more full patterns should be contained in the block. More patterns provide a better sample, but if the block is too large, it may contain portions of other textures, which degrades the texture of interest. Multiple blocks of the same pattern allow stochastic learning of a texture. Textures have noise and other variations due to the driving forces that create the texture patterns; for example, variations of soil minerals can cause the leaves of a certain plant to vary in size and color.

The requirement here is to extract features of texture from an $N \times N$ block of pixels. A single feature is not sufficient to identify a particular texture. Multiple features should be extracted so as to provide more recognition power—that is, greater likelihood that the correct texture is recognized. Measures of the gray level content and variation include the mean gray level, variance, and histogram of the block. While different textures may have different gray level means, variances and histograms, however, it is also possible that they may have the same ones. Consider the two 5×5 blocks of pixels shown in Figure 10.6. Each contains

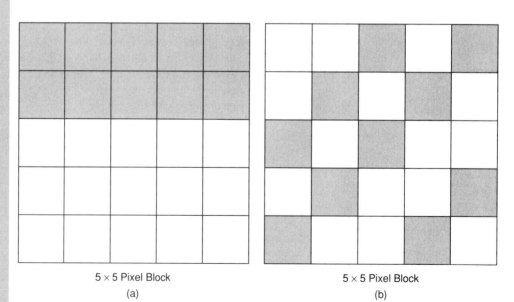

5 × 5 Pixel Block   5 × 5 Pixel Block
(a)   (b)

Figure 10.6. Two blocks with equal means, variances, and histograms with (a) Contiguous Shades of Gray and (b) Noncontiguous Shades of Gray.

two shades of gray and the same number of dark (10) and white subblocks (15). The only differences are the positions that determine the variations of the gray levels, which we denote by 0 and 1. Thus the histograms of the blocks are both

$$h(0) = 10/25 = 2/5, \qquad h(1) = 15/25 = 3/5$$

The mean gray level of each block is

$$\mu = (0)(2/5) + (1)(3/5) = 3/5$$

Similarly, the variance of each is the sum of the squared differences between the pixel values and the mean gray level, which is

$$\sigma^2 = (2/5)(0 - 3/5)^2 + (3/5)(1 - 3/5)^2$$
$$= (2/5)(9/25) + (3/5)(4/25) = (18 + 12)/125 = 6/25$$

Thus the mean, variance (mean-squared error), and histogram would not differentiate between the textures of these two blocks.

The spatial rate of variation of the gray levels gives rise to frequencies of the gray level signal in both the horizontal and vertical directions. The power spectrum of the first block (Figure 10.6(a)) that is obtained by the two-dimensional Fourier transform would show no power at frequencies across the horizontal directions because there are no changes in the gray level. In the vertical direction there is a step function that jumps from light to dark. Arbitrarily high frequencies are required to square a jump in the spatial-time domain, but the power at these higher frequencies goes to zero as the frequency increases. The power spectrum of the other block in Figure 10.6 would be quite different.

We now propose two features for texture. The first is a standardized variance. Let $\{p_{ij}\}$ be a 5×5 block of pixel values ($1 \leq i, j \leq 5$). First we find the mean gray level

$$\mu = (1/25)\Sigma_{ij}p_{ij}$$

We next find the *standardized block variance*

$$\sigma_s^2 = \Sigma_{ij}(p_{ij} - \mu)^2/\mu^2$$

It is clear from the above discussion that this will be the same for both blocks in Figure 10.6 because μ is the same and their differences ($p_{ij} - \mu$) are the same, although distributed differently. This feature measures the *total variation* of the block, but not the local variation between the pixels and their contiguous neighbors. The next feature does that.

Each pixel in a block has eight contiguous neighbors, if we allow the neighbors to fall outside of the block. The difference between the gray levels of the *ij*th pixel and each of its 8 neighbors provides a discrete derivative $d_{ij}(r)$ with respect to the *r*th neighbor in gray scale. Thus there are 8 derivative values (differences) at each pixel in the directions shown by

Figure 10.7. We square these at each pixel, sum them, and then divide by 8 to obtain the *pixel variation*

$$v_{ij}^2 = (1/8)\sum_{(r=1,8)} d_{ij}^2(r)$$

as a measure of variation at that pixel. Similarly, we obtain such a measure at each of the other 24 pixels in the 5×5 block. We then average all of these pixel variations to obtain the *block mean pixel variation* μ_b and compute the *block pixel variation* feature

$$v_b^2 = (1/\mu_p^2)\sum_{ij} v_{ij}^2$$

If a pixel is at the boundary of an image, then it will not have 8 contiguous neighbors. In this case, we use the number of contiguous neighbors it has and divide by that number (from 3 to 7) instead of 8.

It is clear that both of the defined texture features, the standardized block variance σ_s^2, and the block pixel variation v_b^2 are rotation-invariant. In fact, the former is invariant under any redistribution. The second is invariant under rotation because the gradients of each pixel remain fixed, but it changes under any other type of redistribution.

Some properties of texture are as follows: (i) coarseness or fineness; (ii) orientation, or direction of grains or line segments; (iii) proportion of light tones to dark tones; (iv) frequencies of tonal changes in both horizontal and vertical (or other) directions; (v) mean values of gray tones; (vi) variance (mean-squared error) of gray tones; (vii) entropy of tonal information; and (vii) correlation of individual blocks of pixels with blocks of same size that are offset in the vertical, horizontal, or diagonal directions. There are others, to be sure. To recognize a texture, features of texture must be extracted to form exemplar feature vectors. This is done by a measure of texture.

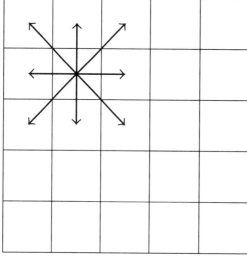

Figure 10.7.   The pixel variation directional derivatives.

5 × 5 Pixel Block

The classic paper (Haralick et al., 1973) specifies 14 different texture features, although it would be unusual to use more than about four of these on a single application (usually, the first four). Some of these features were used by Weszka et al. (1976) to recognize types of terrain from aerial photographs. In that study, the frequency domain features did not perform as well as statistical spatial domain features.

10.5. The Belue–Bauer Method of Selecting Features

The Relevancy Method

Suppose that a rather large set of N features has been selected and a sample of size Q feature vectors has been obtained for training a feedforward artificial neural network for recognition operation. If there are too many features, extraneous noise can cause errors in the recognition. The task here is to reduce the number of input features to improve the learning of the multiple-layered perceptron (MLP). The previous methods of correlational analysis could be used to eliminate the ones dependent on other features, but for large N there are $O(N^2)$ pairs of features to correlate. In addition to the methods listed above, a trained network could be retrained with various subsets of the inputs to determine which inputs work best, but this exhaustive enumeration is not always practical.

A method due to Belue and Bauer (1995) uses the MLP itself in the selection of those features that make a significant contribution to the capability of the network to discriminate between classes over the sample. First, they train the MLP on the full set of N features on the Q exemplars in the sample $\{\mathbf{x}^{(q)}\}$. Then they use the training to determine the relative significance of the input features and eliminate the ones that have low significance. The tool used is a *relevancy metric*, proposed in a dissertation (Tarr, 1991). The simple relevance metric is defined on the nth input component x_n by

$$\lambda_n = \sum_{(m=1,\,M)} w_{nm}^2 \qquad (10.26)$$

where w_{nm} is the weight on the line from the nth input node to the mth hidden neurode of an MLP with a single hidden neurode.

This metric is a great simplification over the one introduced in Ruck et al. (1990), but it captures the importance of feature x_n according to the training of the MLP over the entire sample of exemplars. The trained hidden weights are the most important in determining which input features are significant. The idea here is that the sensitivity of the network output to each input feature is determined and the input features are ranked in order $x_{n(1)},...,x_{n(N)}$. The features on the low end of the ordering may be eliminated, provided that their relevancies are sufficiently low compared with those of the important features. A high-level algorithm is given below, where the number of iterations I is set to 30 and r is initially set at 1.

Step 1. Randomly initialize the weights, randomly select the training and test sets of exemplar vectors and train the network appropriately on the training exemplars so as to pass validation and verification.

Step 2. Compute all feature relevancy metrics $\lambda_n^{(r)}$, $n = 1,..., N$, on rth iteration.

Step 3. If the above steps have been done less than I times, then put $r \leftarrow r + 1$ and go to Step 1, else for each $n = 1,..., N$ average the computed relevancy metric values over all I iterations via
$$\lambda_n = (1/I)[\lambda_n^{(1)} + \cdots + \lambda_n^{(I)}]$$

Step 4. Order the features by highest to lowest relevancy metric values
$$x_{n(1)},..., x_{n(N)}$$
and eliminate those features with relatively low λ_n.

Step 5. Retrain the network with the selected features.

Example 10.3. Elimination of Irrelevant Features

One of the tests run by Belue and Bauer (1995) consisted of the XOR data, but supplemented with extra features x_3, x_4, x_5, and x_6 for which uniform random sample values were drawn between 0 and 1. A noise injection variable x_7 was also adjoined. Table 10.3 presents the results of their study. Belue and Bauer used the injected noise to determine the features that were noise. They used a Gaussian distribution about the relevancy mean of the injected noise. All features whose relevancies fell within a 90% interval around the noise relevancy mean were rejected as representing noise. This method rejected features x_3, x_4, x_5, and x_6 (x_7 was known noise against which the features were tested). Thus the usual XOR logic variables x_1 and x_2 were retained as being useful in this case. A similar result followed for the four-class problem (Belue and Bauer, 1995).

Table 10.3.
Results of the Belue–Bauer Study for XOR Logic

Feature Number n	Mean for λ_n	Standard Deviation
1	1184.23	138.42
2	1186.83	144.11
3[a]	56.76	30.86
4[a]	67.83	28.95
5[a]	58.21	48.57
6[a]	72.17	48.66
7[a]	69.73	25.81

[a]Not important (within $\pm \sigma$ of $\mu = 69.73$).

10.6. Data Engineering

The Kwon–Feroz–Cheng Histogram Equalization of Feature Values

Once a set of features is found that has sufficient separating power, is not redundant to any significant extent, and is possibly weighted, it is still possible to process it further so that better learning can be achieved more quickly. Kwon et al. (1994) do such processing to yield better generalization and faster convergence and to prevent premature saturation. The basic idea is to spread out the feature values more uniformly over the desired ranges.

First, the input data $\{x_n^{(q)}: q = 1,..., Q, n = 1,..., N\}$ or training are standardized to, say, 0 to 1 (or -1 to 1 for bipolar data). Then the range is *discretized* (*quantized*), or broken into a set of D evenly spaced discrete points $\{p_1,..., p_D\}$. Each feature value $x_n^{(q)}$ is assigned to the nearest discrete value in its range. For example, we may use $p_1 = -0.9$, $p_2 = -0.8,...,$ $p_D = 0.9$ in place of $[-1,1]$.

The *histogram* of the input data $\{x_n^{(q)}: q = 1,..., Q, n = 1,..., N\}$ is the discrete function defined on the indices d via

$$h(d) = N_d/(NQ), \qquad d = 1,..., D \qquad (10.27)$$

where N_d is the number of values $x_n^{(q)}$ that were discretized to d and N is the number of features (components) in each of the Q exemplar input feature vectors. Figure 10.8 presents a histogram as a bar graph with constant value across each subinterval between discretized points. All histogram values $h(d)$ sum up to unity; that is,

$$\sum_{(d=1, D)} h(d) = 1 \qquad (10.28)$$

because $N_1 + \cdots + N_d + \cdots + N_D = NQ$. Thus the histogram is a discrete frequency distribution (probability mass function) for the discretized sample.

The *equalization* of the histogram $\{h(d)\}_{d=1, D}$ is a transformation that redistributes the feature values in a way that spreads them out more uniformly, or equitably, over the discrete range of feature values. This is a process that is also used in digital image processing to equalize and increase the dynamic range of gray levels of image pixels (picture elements, or dots). Figure 10.9 shows an equalized histogram. See Gonzales and Woods (1992) for the derivation of the equalization mapping. Note that for a continuous distribution the equalized histogram would be the uniform distribution, but for discrete distributions it is only an ap-

Figure 10.8. A histogram of discrete feature values.

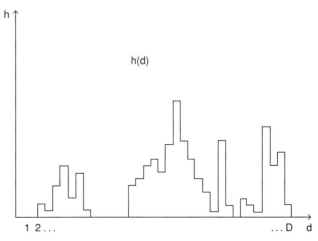

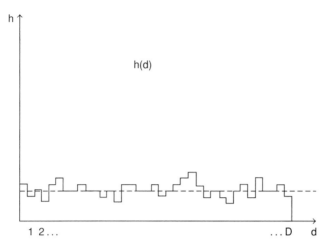

Figure 10.9. An equalized histogram of discrete feature values.

proximation to it. The approximation is better for larger samples and can be poor for small ones.

The equalization and scaling transformation of Kwon et al. (1994) is a mapping that takes any value $x_n^{(q)}$ into a new one $s_n^{(q)}$ via

$$s_n^{(q)} = T(x_n^{(q)}) = |s_{\max} - s_{\min}| \sum_{j=1, d} h(j) + s_{\min} \qquad (10.29)$$

where $s_{\min}$ and $s_{\max}$ are the respective minimum and maximum of the new range over which the new discrete feature values are to be equalized. Actually, Kwon et al. developed the following transformation, where $x_{\min}$ and $x_{\max}$ are the respective minimum and maximum values of the original discrete range for feature values, $\alpha > 0$ and $\beta > 0$ $(\alpha + \beta = 1)$:

$$s = T(x) = \{\alpha[(x - x_{\min})/(x_{\max} - x_{\min})] + \beta|s_{\max} - s_{\min}|\sum_{j=1, d} h(j)\} + s_{\min} \qquad (10.30)$$

For $n = 1,..., N$ and $q = 1,..., Q$, each feature value $x_n^{(q)}$ is mapped into one of the discrete points $p_n^{(q)}$ and then transformed via

$$s_n^{(q)} = T(p_n^{(q)}) \qquad (10.31)$$

and the new discrete transformed feature vectors $\{s^{(q)}\}$ are used for training. Kwon et al. used $s_{\min} = -0.8$ and $s_{\max} = 0.8$ for MLP networks. This prevents premature saturation and increases the training speed, while yielding better generalized learning.

Engineering Well-Distributed Input Data

Suppose that a set of Q pairs $\{(\mathbf{x}^{(q)}, \mathbf{t}^{(k(q))}): q = 1,..., Q\}$ of input feature vectors and their associated output target vectors are given. The first data modification is to standardize each set of nth feature (component) values $\{x_n^{(q)}: q = 1,..., Q\}$ separately, $n = 1,..., N$. Now let n be fixed. We may use the linear transformation L_n on the nth component range $[x_{\min(n)}, x_{\max(n)}]$

to map each datum $x_n^{(q)}$ into the range $[0,1]$ for RBF networks. For MLPs, we map each $x_n^{(q)}$ into the range $[\epsilon, 1 - \epsilon]$, because MLPs do not train properly on 0s and 1s as inputs. The linear transformation L_n for RBFNs or FLNs on each set $\{x_n^{(q)}: q = 1,..., Q\}$, is defined on each $x_n^{(q)}$ via

$$x \to s = L_n(x) = (x - x_{\min(n)})/(x_{\max(n)} - x_{\min(n)}) \tag{10.32}$$

Then $L_n(x_{\min(n)}) = 0$ and $L_n(x_{\max(n)}) = 1$. For MLPs, the transformation becomes

$$x \to s = L_n(x) = (1 - 2\epsilon)(x - x_{\min(n)})/(x_{\max(n)} - x_{\min(n)}) + \epsilon \tag{10.33}$$

so that $L_n(x_{\min(n)}) = \epsilon$ and $L_n(x_{\max(n)}) = 1 - \epsilon$. A good value for ϵ is 0.2 (or 0.15).

In case that there are small values disproportionately close together and the large values are spread out (for fixed n), the logarithmic transformation $G_n: [x_{\min(n)}, x_{\max(n)}] \to [0, 1]$ is suitable, where

$$x \to s = G_n(x) = \ln((x - x_{\min(n)})/(x_{\max(n)} - x_{\min(n)}) + 1)/\ln(2) \tag{10.34}$$

Again, we see that $G_n(x_{\min(n)}) = 0$ and $G_n(x_{\max(n)}) = 1$. This spreads out the small values and pushes the larger values closer together. The situation for MLPs is analogous to the linear case above.

For large values close together and small values farther apart, the exponential transformation

$$x \to s = X_n(x) = (1 - \exp[-(x - x_{\min(n)})/(x_{\max(n)} - x_{\min(n)})])/(1 - \exp[-1]) \tag{10.35}$$

spreads out the large values and pushes the small values closer together. We can verify that $X_n(x_{\min(n)}) = 0$ and $X_n(x_{\max(n)}) = 1$. Again, we use ϵ and $1 - \epsilon$ for MLPs.

We usually scale the data first with the linear transformation L_n, for each component $n = 1,..., N$. When the standardized values have disproportionate spacings that are neither increasing nor decreasing monotonically across the interval, then we need a transformation that is nonmonotonically nonlinear and that approximately equalizes the number of component values in each subinterval of equal length. For a fixed n, the Q component values $\{x_n^{(q)}: q = 1,..., Q\}$ are scaled to fall into $[0,1]$. We partition $[0,1]$ into P subintervals $\{I_1,..., I_P\}$ of equal length and assign to the function $h(p)$ the proportion of values in the pth interval. This yields a histogram, which is a mapping on the interval index p into $[0,1]$, defined by

$$h(p) = N_p/Q \tag{10.36a}$$

where N_p is the number of $x_n^{(q)}$ values that belong to the pth interval I_p. To approximately equalize the number of values in each subinterval, a histogram equalization transformation H_n is used on all nth component values. This is the same type of transformation as is used in image processing (Gonzales and Woods, 1992), but is different from that used by Kwon et al. (1994) in that they equalized all exemplar vector components over all samples together in a single histogram (see the previous subsection). The approximation is much better for a

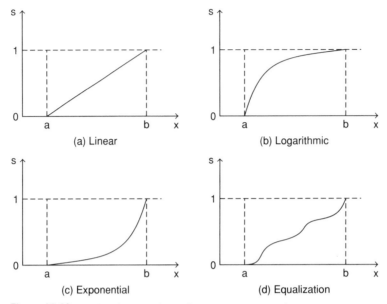

Figure 10.10.   Pointwise transformations on component data.

relatively large number of input vectors (large Q). The histogram equalization transformation is

$$x \rightarrow s = H_n(x) = (1/Q)\Sigma \; \{N_k\colon k \le p \text{ and } x \in I_p\} = \Sigma_{(r=1,\, p;\, x \in Ip)} h(r) \quad (10.36b)$$

Thus any value x between 0 and 1 is remapped into the sum of histogram values for all subintervals up to and including the one in which x lies. The results are also between 0 and 1 because

$$N_1/Q + \cdots + N_P/Q = 1$$

Kwon et al. report that such histogram equalization resulted in a significant improvement in the learning ability of the network. Figure 10.10 shows linear, logarithmic, and exponential transformations and a possible histogram equalization.

Example 10.4.   Histogram Equalization

Our approach to histogram equalization is to fix each nth input component and equalize the set $\{x_n^{(q)}\colon q = 1,\dots, Q\}$ of all nth component values over the sample of size Q (see Looney, 1996). This provides flexibility. First, we map the values for each fixed component into an interval such as $[0,1]$ (or $[\epsilon, 1 - \epsilon]$ for MLPs, which do not train properly on 0s and 1s). Then we apply histogram equalization on that component. This is done for $n = 1,\dots, N$, and so requires N different mappings of component data sets.

Table 10.4.
Dataset A (Three Unipolar Outputs)

Inputs								Outputs		
0.2890	0.0550	0.4840	0.3850	0.5450	0.5750	0.3410	0.9950	0.100	0.100	0.100
0.0310	0.4840	0.2200	0.1230	0.3000	0.3800	0.0890	0.2100	0.200	0.500	0.900
0.1260	0.3910	0.3540	0.2750	0.4420	0.5150	0.1750	0.3950	0.300	0.900	0.500
0.0600	0.4140	0.2400	0.1620	0.3040	0.3680	0.1100	0.2700	0.400	0.100	0.500
0.0950	0.3650	0.3600	0.2340	0.4800	0.5430	0.1650	0.1900	0.500	0.900	0.300
0.0630	0.2220	0.3320	0.2100	0.4600	0.5360	0.1550	0.3200	0.900	0.500	0.200
0.1890	0.2470	0.4150	0.3120	0.5100	0.5620	0.2750	0.3200	0.900	0.900	0.900

Consider the data in Table 10.4 that has seven exemplar vectors as inputs, each with eight components that represent laser-measured mechanical properties of red blood cells from blood samples of people with particular diseases. The seven exemplar vectors represent, respectively, normal, hepatitis B, HIV early, HIV late, IUP (pregnancy), leukemia, and malnutrition. These eight features were selected from a set of 12 features and present a rigorous test of learning for a neural network. We selected the output vector codewords to provide good separation (see Example 7.3).

We used three types of FANNs to train on this data: multiple-layered perceptrons (MLPs), radial basis function networks (RBFNs), and random vector functional link networks (RBF-RVFLNs). These are described in Chapter 7. All runs used the same sequence of random numbers to generate the initial weight sets. Figure 10.11 shows the three network structures. Here, we use only the RBF-RVFLN.

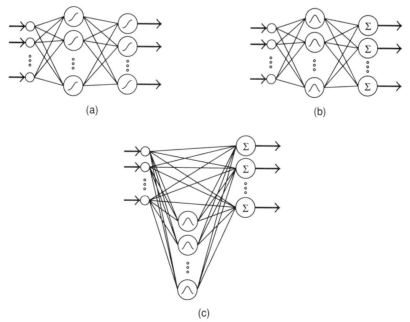

Figure 10.11.   MLP, RBFN, and FLN structures (a), (b), and (c) respectively.

Table 10.5.
Results of Training an RBF-RVFLN on Dataset A

Run	Q	N	M	J	Number of Iterations	RMS Error	Accuracy (%)	σ
1	7	8	7	3	50	0.2309	100.0	0.10
2	7	8	7	3	30	0.4778	100.0	0.10
3	7	8	7	3	20	0.7363	100.0	0.10
4	7	8	7	3	15	0.9058	100.0	0.10
5	7	8	7	3	10	1.2478	85.7	0.10

Table 10.6.
Results of Training an RBF-RVFLN on Equalized Dataset A

Run	Q	N	M	J	Number of Iterations	RMS Error	Accuracy (%)	σ
1*	7	8	7	3	20	0.3780	100.0	0.10
2*	7	8	7	3	15	0.5865	100.0	0.10
3*	7	8	7	3	10	1.0266	100.0	0.10

[a]Histogram equalized data.

Table 10.5 presents the results of training the powerful radial basis function random vector functional link network (RBF-RVFLN) described in Chapter 7 on the same dataset (Dataset A). The results are rather incredible but true. There is obviously no need to process the input data, and on such a small dataset we would expect no advantage for equalization. However, we do equalize the data for sake of illustration. Table 10.6 displays the results of training the RBF-RVFLN on the histogram equalized data from Dataset A. Run 3 of Table 10.6 indicates improved results with a smaller error and higher accuracy.

Fuzzy Equalization of Input Data

A transformation called the *fuzzy histogram equalization* was done by Schneider and Craig (1992) to equalize image histograms. To use such a mapping, we need to find a typical, or central, value of the set of component values $\{x_n^{(q)}: q = 1,..., Q\}$. The expected value, the *fuzzy expected value* (Kandel, 1981), or the *weighted fuzzy expected value* (Schneider and Craig, 1992) would suffice. The *clustering fuzzy expected value*, conceptualized by Vassiliadis et al. (1994), was used by Henson-Mack et al. (1996) for fuzzy histogram equalization of medical images so that edge detection could produce lines that were better connected.

The weighted fuzzy expected value μ_n is generally a better typical value than the fuzzy expected value or expected value, so we use it here. The basic idea is that the values closer to μ_n are weighted more than ones farther away, so that the outliers and near outliers have less effect. The measure of closeness used in the weighted fuzzy average is the fuzzy set membership function

$$D(x_n^{(q)}, \boldsymbol{\mu}_n) = \exp(-\beta|x_n^{(q)} - \boldsymbol{\mu}_n|) \qquad (q = 1,..., Q) \qquad (10.37)$$

The mean value p_{ave} of the histogram arguments $1,..., p,..., P$ is found by averaging their standardized values $1/P,..., p/P,..., P/P = 1$. Thus the function on $x_n^{(q)}$ to be averaged is

$$f(x_n^{(q)}) = p/P, \qquad p = 1,..., P, \qquad x_n^{(q)} \in I_p \qquad (10.38)$$

The average is to be weighted by the histogram "probability" values $h(p) = h(p(x_n^{(q)}))$ (where $x_n^{(q)} \in I_p$) and also by the closeness of each $x_n^{(q)}$ to the weighted fuzzy average $\boldsymbol{\mu}_n$ as determined by the closeness measure of Equation (10.37). A crisp average would be

$$p_{ave} = \sum_{(q=1, Q)} f(x_n^{(q)}) h(p(x_n^{(q)})) \qquad (10.39)$$

The *weighted fuzzy expected value* (WFEV) of Schneider and Craig (1992) is defined recursively via

$$\boldsymbol{\mu}_n = \{\sum_{(q=1, Q)} [\exp(-\beta|x_n^{(q)} - \boldsymbol{\mu}_n|) h(p)^\lambda] f(x_n^{(q)})\} / \{\sum_{(q=1, Q)} \exp(-\beta|x_n^{(q)} - \boldsymbol{\mu}_n|) h(p)^\lambda\} \qquad (10.40)$$

They use $\lambda = 2$. Because both sides of Equation (10.40) contain the variable $\boldsymbol{\mu}_n$, Picard iteration on the initial value $\boldsymbol{\mu}_n^{(0)} = p_{ave}$ yields an approximate solution via

$$\boldsymbol{\mu}_n^{(k+1)} = F(\boldsymbol{\mu}_n^{(k)}) \qquad (10.41)$$

where $F(-)$ is the expression on the right-hand side of Equation (10.41).

Thus the WFEV is

$$\boldsymbol{\mu}_n = \sum_{(q=1, Q)} \alpha_q f(x_n^{(q)}) \qquad (10.42)$$

where

$$\alpha_q = [\exp(-\beta|x_n^{(q)} - \boldsymbol{\mu}_n|) h(p(x_n^{(q)}))^\lambda] / \sum_{(r=1, Q)} \exp(-\beta|x_n^{(r)} - \boldsymbol{\mu}_n|) h(p(x_n^{(r)}))^\lambda \qquad (10.43)$$

The fuzzy equalization transformation $x \rightarrow s = W(x)$ depends upon the closeness of any nth component value $x_n^{(q)}$ to the weighted fuzzy expected value $\boldsymbol{\mu}_n$, per

$$s_n^{(q)} = W(x_n^{(q)}) = \max \{0, \boldsymbol{\mu}_n - (\boldsymbol{\mu}_n^2 - (x_n^{(q)})^2)^{1/2}\}, \qquad \text{if } x_n^{(q)} \leq \boldsymbol{\mu}_n \qquad (10.44)$$

$$s_n^{(q)} = W(x_n^{(q)}) = \min \{1, \boldsymbol{\mu}_n + ((x_n^{(q)})^2 - \boldsymbol{\mu}_n^2)^{1/2}\}, \qquad \text{if } x_n^{(q)} \geq \boldsymbol{\mu}_n \qquad (10.45)$$

The maximum and minimum values ensure that the $s_n^{(q)}$ never go outside of $[0,1]$.

A Modified Fuzzy Equalization

We modify the closeness measure of Equation (10.37) to become the Gaussian fuzzy set membership function that goes to zero more slowly as $x_n^{(q)}$ gets farther from the weighted fuzzy expected value μ_n and goes to unity more rapidly as $x_n^{(q)}$ gets closer to the WFEV. We also do not square the probabilities $h(p)$ so as to let them be larger to have more influence in determining μ_n and on the histogram equalization. A "standard deviation" value such as $\sigma = 1/2$ in the Gaussian function sets a width parameter on the bell-shaped curve. Thus we use

$$G(x_n^{(q)};\ \mu_n) = \exp(-(x_n^{(q)} - \mu_n)^2/2\sigma^2) = \exp(-2(x_n^{(q)} - \mu_n)^2) \qquad (10.46)$$

The fuzzy weights become

$$\alpha_q = G(x_n^{(q)};\ \mu_n)h(p(x_n^{(q)}))/\textstyle\sum_{(r=1,\ Q)}G(x_n^{(r)};\ \mu_n)h(p(x_n^{(r)})), \qquad q = 1,...,Q \qquad (10.47)$$

where $p(x_n^{(q)})$ denotes the index p of the interval I_p in which $x_n^{(q)}$ lies. Note that the values α_q sum to unity so that the weighted sum is a convex combination of the values $f(x_n^{(q)}) = p(x_n^{(q)})/P = p/P$ (for $x_n^{(q)} \in I_p$) and so they never fall outside of the interval 0 to 1. Our iteration to find μ_n becomes

$$\mu_n^{(k+1)} = F(\mu_n^{(k)}) = \textstyle\sum_{(q=1,\ Q)}\alpha_q f(x_n^{(q)}) \qquad (10.48)$$

The WFEV μ_n converges rapidly and changes only negligibly after a few iterations (about 5).

After the WFEV μ_n is found, then we transform all nth input components $x_n^{(q)}$ via the equalization process given in Equations (10.44) and (10.45) to obtain the remapped value $s_n^{(q)} = W_n(x_n^{(q)})$.

We trained an RBF-RVFLN on the parity 5 dataset with $N = 5$ inputs, $J = 1$ (single bipolar output), and $Q = 32$ different input vectors. The output was set at -0.9 for an even number of high values and set at 0.9 for an odd number. There is only a single exemplar vector for each of the 32 combinations possible and no noise. This is a stringent test to find a difference in the effects of the two types of histogram equalization, but it has more data than the previous test.

Table 10.7 shows the results of training on data remapped by the histogram equalization method and by the modified weighted fuzzy histogram equalization technique. While the root-mean-squared errors (RMSEs) between datasets cannot be compared because a larger number of output components yields larger errors (E is not standardized), we can compare errors on runs with the same architecture and same datasets. Thus the observation that the training on the modified weighted fuzzy histogram equalized (WFHE) data had smaller errors across all runs than did the training on regular histogram equalized data has important meaning. On Run 1, which is more like an actual training run, the error on the modified WFHE data was 0.000023 versus 0.000168 for the histogram equalized data. On Run 4, the modified WFHE data yielded more accurate learning on 20 iterations. It appears that for larger datasets, the modified WFHE tool can ensure smaller errors, quicker training, and more robust learning.

Table 10.7.
Training an RBF-RVFLN on Equalized and Modified WFHE Parity 5 Data

Run	Iterations	RMS Error	Accuracy (%)
1[a]	100	0.000168	100.0
2[a]	40	1.2487	100.0
3[a]	30	2.1580	100.0
4[a]	20	3.8084	88.8
1[b]	100	0.000023	100.0
2[b]	40	0.8975	100.0
3[b]	30	1.7039	100.0
4[b]	20	2.7996	100.0

[a]Parity 5 histogram equalization data.
[b]Parity 5 modified weighted fuzzy histogram equalization data.

Exercises

10.1. Choose a set of five characters (Roman, Arabic, Hebrew, Chinese, Cyrillic, or Japanese). Study them and pick out some differences between them. Design these differences into features and order them by importance. Justify your ordering. Compute the correlation coefficients between the features.

10.2. Fill in the steps to derive Equation (10.8) from Equation (10.7).

10.3. Derive Equation (10.9) from Equation (10.8).

10.4. Suppose that you want to automate the detection of microscope images for the presence of a type of cancer cell. The normal cells are smaller, darker, and longer, while the cancerous cells will be larger, more rounded, and lighter and will have whitish spots in the middle. However, the cells will be dense and overlapping in the image. Describe how you would select features to recognize the cancerous cells.

10.5. A complex speech recognition system is to use 200 features that are to be weighted. Design a weighting system that does not weight the most important feature too high or weight the least important feature too low. The range of weights must be [0,1].

10.6. Aerial photographs are the sources for images from which it is desired to recognize motor trucks. The terrain is hilly with large rocks, bushes, and sparse trees. Develop a method to isolate blobs in the images that may be trucks, design features to be extracted from the blobs, and provide a flow chart of the process. Assume the images are in 256 shades of gray (no color).

10.7. Design a set of features for optical character recognition that are invariant under rotation of the character (that are not affected by rotations).

10.8. Video cameras are to be mounted on the front and rear of an automobile. A computerized system is to monitor the front and rear situation to recognize any situation that could become dangerous. Describe such a system with a functional block diagram and a flow chart of the data flow and decisionmaking. Describe the dangerous situations and the features that must be extracted from the images to determine distance and relative velocity with respect to objects in the front and rear.

10.9. In Example 10.1 we computed some correlations between features. This gave us the relative independence of the features, but not the importance of them. Find the range of each feature—that is, the difference between the greatest and least values. Next compute the average difference between feature components over the set of all pairs of feature vectors in the sample. Use these values in some way to establish the importance of the features in separating two or more digits.

10.10. A population of patterns is known to contain 17 different classes. Suppose that it has been decided that for the sake of robustness, we are to select three features that separate each pair of classes. Find upper and lower bounds on the total number of features. What can be said about the expected value on the number of features? What can be said in the general case of P different classes of patterns and the total number of features for separation of each pair of classes by at least r features?

10.11. Select a set of features for handwritten digits 0,..., 9. Look at those given in Appendix 11 for the Digit12 dataset. Select a pair of digits, say 3 and 7, and compare their values two at a time. Which feature pairs are the strongest in discriminating between the digits?

10.12. Develop two new features for textures. Are they rotation invariant?

10.13. Write a computer program to (i) draw a set of 100 values from the triangular probability density function

$$p(x) = 4x, \qquad 0 \le x \le \tfrac{1}{2}$$
$$p(x) = 4 - 4x, \qquad \tfrac{1}{2} \le x \le 1$$

(ii) make a histogram of those 100 values and plot its graph, and (iii) equalize the histogram and plot its graph.

10.14. Make up a set of data for 5-bit parity. The exemplar input vectors have five components, each of which is to be -1 or 1. There are 32 such different combinations. The single output target component takes on either -1 or 1, where -1 represents even parity and 1 represents odd parity. Now generate an additional 64 input exemplars by

for $i = 1$ to 2 do
  for $q = 1$ to 32 to
    select a number r randomly from 1 to 5
    add to the rth component of qth exemplar a random number from
      uniform($-0.3,0.3$) distribution

Now equalize the histogram for each of the five input components of the 96 exemplar input vectors and train an RBFN or RBF-RVFLN. Train on the unequalized dataset and compare.

References

Belue, L. M., and Bauer, K. W. (1995), Determining input features for multilayer perceptrons, *Neurocomputing* vol. 7, 111–121.

Bezdek, J., and Pal, S. (1992), Fuzzy models for pattern recognition, in *Fuzzy Models for Pattern Recognition*, edited by J. Bezdek and S. Pal, IEEE Press, New York, pp. 1–27.

Bow, S. (1984), *Pattern Recognition*, Marcel Dekker, New York.

Devijver, P. (1982), Statistical Pattern Recognition, appeared in *Applications of Pattern Recognition*, edited by K. S. Fu, CRC Press, Boca Raton, FL, pp. 15–36.

Gonzales, R. C., and Woods, R. E. (1992), *Digital Image Processing*, Addison-Wesley, Reading, MA.

Haralick, R. M., Shanmugam, K., and Dinstein, I. (1973), Textural features for image classification, *IEEE Trans. Syst. Man Cybern.*, vol. 3, no. 6, 610–621.

Henson-Mack, K. P., Looney, C., and H. C. Chen (1996), Fuzzy processing of medical images, in *Proceedings of the ISCA 11th International Conference on Computers and Their Applications*, San Francisco, pp. 243–246.

Kandel, A. (1981), Fuzzy expectation and energy states in fuzzy media, *Fuzzy Sets and Systems*, 145–160.

Kittler, J. (1977), A review of feature extraction methods based on probabilistic separability measures, *Proceedings of the SITEL-ULG Conference on Pattern Recognition*, Société Belge des Ingenieurs des Telecommunications et d'Electronique, Orphain, B. S. I., Belgium, pp. 227–232.

Kittler, J. (1986), Feature selection and extraction, in *Handbook of Pattern Recognition and Image Processing*, edited by T. Y. Young, and K.S. Fu, Academic Press, San Diego, pp. 60–83.

Kwon, T. M., Feroz, E. H., and Cheng, H. (1994), Preprocessing of training set for backpropagation algorithm: histogram equalization, *Proc. IEEE 1994 Int. Conf. Neural Networks*, vol. 1, 425–430.

Looney, C., Neural data engineering, Proc. ISCA Int. Conf. on Computers and Their Applications, Phoenix (forthcoming).

Nadler, M., and Smith, E. (1993), *Pattern Recognition Engineering*, Wiley-Interscience, New York.

Ruck, D. W., Rogers, S. K., and Kabrisky, M. (1990), Feature selection using a multilayer perceptron, *Neural Network Comput.* vol. 20, 40–48.

Schneider, M., and Craig, M. (1992), On the use of fuzzy sets in histogram equalization, *Fuzzy Sets Syst.*, vol. 45, 271–278.

Tarr, G. (1991), *Multi-layered Feedforward Neural Networks for Image Segmentation*, Ph.D. dissertation, Air Force Institute of Technology, Wright-Patterson AFB, OH.

Therrien, C. W. (1989), *Decision, Estimation and Classification*, Wiley, New York.

Tou, J. T., and Gonzalez, R. C. (1974), *Pattern Recognition Principles*, Addison-Wesley, Reading, MA.

Tukey, J. (1977), *Exploratory Data Analysis*, Reading, MA.

Vassiliadis, S., Triantafyllos, G. and Pechanek, G. (1994), A method for computing the most typical fuzzy expected value, *IEEE Int. Conf. Fuzzy Syst.*, 2040–2045.

Wasserman, P. D. (1993), *Advanced Methods in Neural Computing*, Van Nostrand Reinhold, New York.

Watanabe, S., and Pakvasa, N. (1973), Subspace method in pattern recognition, in *Proceedings of the First International Conference on Pattern Recognition*, Washington, D.C., pp. 25–32.

Weszka, J. S., Dyer, C. R., and Rosenfeld, A. (1976), A comparative study of texture measures for terrain classification, *IEEE Trans. Syst., Man Cybern.*, vol. 6, no. 4, 269–283.

Part V

Testing and Applications

Chapter 11

Some Comparative Studies of Feedforward Artificial Neural Networks

The goal here is to assess the relative performance of learning algorithms for feedforward artificial neural networks that are well suited to pattern recognition.

11.1. A Hierarchy of Artificial Neural Networks

Thus far we have discussed several algorithms for the training of feedforward artificial neural networks (FANNs) that include multiple-layered perceptrons (MLPs), functional link networks (FLNs) and radial basis function networks (RBFNs). Other types of artificial neural networks that we have considered are the Amari–Hopfield recurrent neural networks (RNNs) and the self-organizing maps (SOMs) of Kohonen, Kosko (BAMs), and others. We have made passing mention of Sprecht's (1968) probabilistic neural networks (PNNs) and Grossberg's adaptive resonance theory networks (ARTNs). Table 11.1 categorizes these different types of artificial neural networks.

Figure 11.1 presents three different types of FANNs: (i) part (a), which is a two-layered MLP with a single hidden layer; (ii) part (b), which is an FLN (see Chapters 3 and 7) that passes the inputs directly to the output layer, but also combines them via a separate hidden layer to generate additional input components as functions of the original inputs; and (iii) part (c), which is a radial basis function network.

These Category 1 networks all have weights that are adjusted by steepest descent dur-

Table 11.1.
A Hierarchy of Artificial Neural Networks

Category	Type	Name of Network Type
1	Feedforward (FANNs)	MLPs (multiple-layered perceptrons)
		FLNs (functional link networks)
		RBFNs (radial basis function networks)
		LVQNs (learning vector quantization networks)
2	Recurrent (RNNs)	Amari networks (parallel)
		Hopfield networks (random serial)
3	Self-organizing maps (SOMs)	Kohonen's SOFMs (self-organizing feature maps)
		Sprecht's probabilistic networks
		Bezdek's fuzzy c-means networks
		Hybrid learning vector quantization networks
		Grossberg's ART networks (adaptive resonance theory)
		SOLVQNs (self-organizing LVQNs)

ing supervised training. They also have other parameters that may or may not be adjusted during the training. Such supervised training requires a set of Q exemplar input vectors $\{\mathbf{x}^{(q)}\}$ and a set of K output identifiers $\{\mathbf{t}^{(k)}\}$ that are paired as $\{(\mathbf{x}^{(q)}, \mathbf{t}^{(k(q))})\}$ so that $\mathbf{x}^{(q)} \to \mathbf{t}^{(k(q))}$ for $q = 1,..., Q$. The identifier vectors can be designed according to Section 4.7.

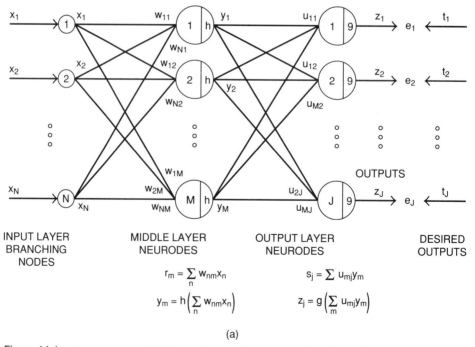

$$r_m = \sum_n w_{nm}x_n \qquad\qquad s_j = \sum_m u_{mj}y_m$$

$$y_m = h\left(\sum_n w_{nm}x_n\right) \qquad\qquad z_j = g\left(\sum_m u_{mj}y_m\right)$$

(a)

Figure 11.1.   Feedforward artificial neural networks; (a) A multiple-layered perceptron network;

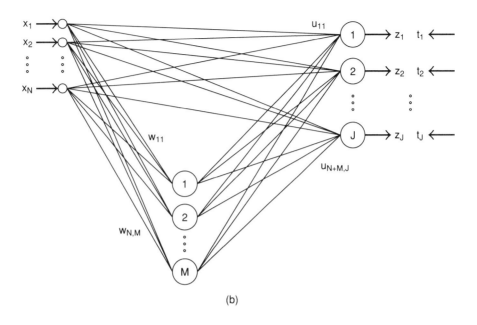

(b)

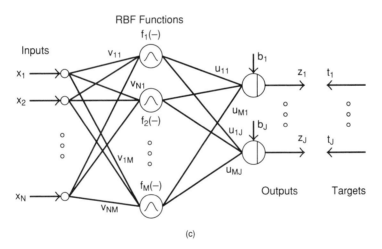

(c)

Figure 11.1. continued.   (b) A functional link network; (c) A radial basis function network.

The networks in Category 2 may be trained to some extent to adjust the field of attraction for the different classes, but are not yet sufficiently reliable or efficient. Category 3 networks are self-organizing and perform linearly separable clustering of data without supervision. For our purposes, the Category 1 networks are the most powerful, versatile, and reliable nonlinear classifier-recognizers.

The evaluation of the performance of neural network classifiers (Musavi et al., 1994) should consider (i) time efficiency, (ii) memory size, (iii) complexity, and (iv) generalization ability. Further, the errors are usually used, but these cannot provide adequate information about the network performance on novel inputs. Still, errors are related to learning and generalization, which are the interests here.

11.2. A Preliminary Discussion of FANN Algorithms

Training Methodologies: Gradient Descent and Strategic Search

The training of FANNs, whether MLPs, FLNs, or RBFNs, involves the adjustment of weights by either (i) gradient descent or (ii) strategic search. For RBFNs, the centers $\{w^{(m)}\}$ and spread parameters $\{\sigma_m\}$ at each hidden neurode may also be adjusted during training, but we consider here the output layer weights. The gradient algorithms include *backpropagation* (BP), which trains by adjusting all of the weights on a single step to decrease a qth partial sum-squared error $E^{(q)}$ for a single qth exemplar pair $(\mathbf{x}^{(q)}, \mathbf{t}^{(k(q))})$ at a time. Q such steps complete one epoch. On the other hand, *fullpropagation* (FP) descends on the total sum-squared error (TSSE)

$$E = E^{(1)} + \cdots + E^{(Q)}$$

on each update of the weights. BP can be done in the *batch mode* where the weight increments are averaged over a subset of exemplar pairs and then the averaged increments are added to the weights. This does not alleviate thrashing, where decreasing $E^{(q)}$ increases $E^{(p)}$ for one or more p, $p \neq q$. Averaging is a thrashing process.

Other gradient approaches apply various speedups to BP. These include (a) Fahlman's *quickpropagation* (QP), which speeds up BP by using a lineally second-order search along the linearly approximated direction of steepest descent, and (b) the Riedmiller–Braun *resilient propagation* (RP), which adjusts a different step gain for each weight. Both of these are given in Chapter 5. Both of them train, however, on a single qth exemplar pair at a time by adjusting all weights to decrease only a single partial sum-squared error $E^{(q)}$ (BP or BP batch mode). Still, the results of both QP (Fahlman, 1988) and RP (Riedmiller and Braun, 1993) are better than BP as was shown by comparisons on the 10–5–10 and other data. RP was reported to be slightly faster than QP on the datasets tested, which include the 10–5–10 dataset.

The energy projection method of Kung et al. (1991), which is equivalent to the method of (Parlos et al., 1994), applies a speedup to BP by computing an approximate optimal step gain η on each weight adjustment. According to Parlos et al. (1994), BP with their step gain formulation is up to an order faster than BP on the limited data on which it was tested, which makes it faster than *quickprop* or *rprop* on the tested data. Parlos et al. report also that the error jumps while training. It is doubtful that such superior speed can hold over datasets in general without special tuning for each dataset. Other powerful methods for gradient descent are the *conjugate gradient* training algorithms (Johansson et al, 1992) and the *quasi-Newton* algorithms (Gill et al., 1981) that are more computationally complex but are sometimes worth it in convergence speed.

Theoretically, once the weight points have reached the well of a local minimum, the TSSE function E is approximately quadratic so that the conjugate gradient method can complete the convergence with a fixed number of steps ($NM + MJ$ steps for an N–M–J architecture), which eliminates a major problem of BP. There remains the problem of finding the well of a deep (global or near global) minimum. All gradient methods have the local minimum problem, and so a starting weight set in the region of a deep minimum should be found in a first stage of strategic search.

The strategic search methods include (i) *purely random optimization* (brute force), (ii) *univariate line search*, (iii) other *line searches* in selected directions (random or steepest descent), (iv) *genetic algorithms*, and (v) other types of *pattern directed search*. The first method is not really a strategic search in that it uses a complete lack of strategy, while the others use a strategy for greater efficiency. Any taxonomy is somewhat arbitrary, though. Gradient methods could be considered as a type of strategic search, but we classify them as strategic search only when a search is made along the direction of steepest descent.

Most of the discussion in the following subsections pertains to MLPs, but extends to the weights in the output neurodes of FLNs, RBFNs and RBF-RVFLNs.

Gradient Descent versus Strategic Search

It is theoretically more optimal to descend on the surface of an error function E by stepping in the direction of steepest descent. But with such first-order descent, it is never known how large the step size should be. Further, the local direction of steepest descent changes from step to step and may be very different from the actual direction to the minimum in whose well of attraction the current weight point dwells. Highly nonlinear functions have (a) slopes that twist and turn and (b) multiple local minima that may be shallow. Adjusting the step gain properly is the most critical problem in all steepest descent methods. On a long slope with low rate of descent, or near a local minimum, the gradient may be approximately zero so that a small step size requires a very large number of steps. When a shallow minimum is reached (approximately), the process is usually trapped there and cannot escape.

Section 4.8 (Figures 4.7 to 4.11) presents some slices of the TSSE function E that tend to be somewhat quadratic or quartic in the region of interest around the origin of the weight space. Therefore, we expect better results in polynomial search when quartics are used early, although quadratics may be used efficiently once the well of attraction of a deep or global minimum has been entered. Gradient descent may also be used at that point. But how do we know when that point is reached? Preliminary quartic univariate search usually finds a weight region where a global minimum resides after two complete iterations (see Chapter 6). For an N–M–J MLP, this is $(NM + MJ) = M(N + J)$ weight searches per iteration over a weight space such as $[-2,2]^{NM+MJ}$. A second iteration of univariate search finds a better coarse approximate to a global minimum due to the moving target effect. The quartic iterations are somewhat costly because each single weight adjustment requires five functional evaluations of E.

Purely random optimization draws a weight point (set) at random and then checks the TSSE to determine whether or not the new weight point is more optimal than the current one. It is a slow but sure method that eventually finds an optimal solution with probability 1. Univariate search (Looney, 1993) computes a single weight value at a time while the other weights are held fixed. The learning is generalized in the sense that there is no weight drift because the values are picked from the allowable range. In cases where it is extremely important to obtain a generalized well-trained weight set, this is always an alternative.

Strategic search can be made in the direction of local steepest descent where a polynomial is fitted to a number of points and then minimized in some fashion (Looney, 1996b). It can also be done by choosing the direction at random and then performing polynomial search in the chosen direction. While it appears that descent in random directions would be much slower than in directions of steepest descent, it may not be so because the latter are approximations to the directions of local steepest descent, which are not the actual directions to minima.

11.3. Fullpropagation versus Backpropagation

Preliminary Discussion

The well-known characteristics of BP are (i) slow convergence after the first few epochs, (ii) inefficiency, (iii) instability, and (iv) convergence to a shallow local minimum. Chapter 5 discusses the problems, some of which are due to thrashing and others are due to the nature of gradient methods. While many of the papers referred to in this text have compared their modified BP algorithms to BP, in fairness it should be said that most algorithms can be tuned to a certain dataset to outperform BP dramatically on that particular dataset. Any comparisons should be done over several datasets selected in advance, and no tuning should be allowed for those particular datasets.

On the other hand, FP (Looney, 1996a) computes the weight increments by steepest descent of the TSSE $E = E^{(1)} + \cdots + E^{(Q)}$ rather than sequentially on partial SSEs $E^{(q)}$. While it overcomes the "built-in" thrashing of BP and is more efficient, it also has failures due to the faults of gradient methods. The fullpropagation algorithm developed in Chapter 5 uses the efficient *en route* method of adapting the single step gain to accelerate the convergence. This cannot be done properly in BP because the training is done sequentially on each of the single partial SSE functions $E^{(1)},..., E^{(Q)}$ over the epochal cycle and the step gain is dependent on the current error function $E^{(q)}$. If a distinct step gain (learning rate) $\eta^{(q)}$ were kept for each qth partial SSE, then by the time the epochal cycle is traversed and $E^{(q)}$ accessed again the function would be different and need a different value for $\eta^{(q)}$. We have tried this approach, but it slowed down the process instead of accelerating it.

A Study to Compare Total Sum-Squared Error and Speed

Table 11.2 shows the results on the standard data set 10–5–10 that was used by Fahlman (1988) and Riedmiller and Braun (1993) and others. These data are given in Appendix 11 as the Ten5ten dataset. The input feature vectors are the 10 vectors of 10-tuples ($N = 10$), where each vector has zeros in all components except for the unit value in a single unique component. The output training vectors are identical to the inputs ($J = 10$). Five neurodes are used in the single hidden layer to cause a bottleneck ($M = 5$). According to standard practice, we used 0.1 for 0 and 0.9 for 1 in the runs. Both BP and FP used unipolar sigmoids in a single hidden layer and an output layer of neurodes, the same sequence of random numbers for generating initial weight sets and the same biases of $b_1 = (N + 1)/2$ and $b_2 = (M + 1)/2$, and initial exponential rates of $\alpha_1 = \alpha_2 = 2.4$ in the sigmoids at the respective hidden

Table 11.2.
BP and FP Runs on the 10–5–10 Dataset

300 BP Epochs						300 FP Iterations			
BP-1		BP-2		BP-3		FP-1		FP-2	
RSSE	Misses	RSSE	Misses	RSSE	Misses	RSSE	Misses	RSSE	Misses
0.08277	0	0.08075	0	0.06716	0	0.06128	0	0.06049	0
0.08251	0	0.07853	0	0.07070	0	0.06194	0	0.07085	0
0.08323	0	0.07653	0	0.07034	0	0.06158	0	0.06282	0
0.08632	0	0.07778	0	0.06954	0	0.06619	0	0.07303	0
0.07771	0	0.08250	0	0.06834	0	0.06713	0	0.06915	0
0.07990	0	0.07747	0	0.06676	0	0.06232	0	0.06920	0
0.07962	0	0.07681	0	0.06582	0	0.06195	0	0.07498	0
0.08108	0	0.08536	0	0.06945	0	0.06860	0	0.07586	0
0.08227	0	0.08111	0	0.07097	0	0.06964	0	0.07035	0
0.08355	0	0.08616	0	0.06503	0	0.07247	0	0.07314	0

Running Times for 300 Epochs/Iterations on 486DX2 80MHz PC
BP-2: 20.7 sec   FP-2: 8.1 sec
3000 complete weight adjustments   300 complete weight adjustments

and output layers. None of the runs adjusted the biases. All exponential rate adjustments were done only on every tenth iteration or epoch for the first half of the run.

The three backpropagation runs are: BP-1, with no preliminary adjustment of the initial weights and no adjustments of exponential rates α_1 and α_2; BP-2, with two preliminary iterations of cubic adjustment of all initial weights via univariate cubic approximation on one weight at a time and no adjustments of the exponential rates; and BP-3, with two preliminary iterations of cubic weight adjustment and also adjustment of exponential rates during training. The two fullpropagation runs are: FP-1, with no preliminary adjustment of the initial weights nor adjustments of the rates α_1 and α_2; and FP-2, with one preliminary quartic weight adjustment iteration and with no adjustments of α_1 and α_2. Both BP and FP adjusted the step gain *en route* (η is increased slightly if E decreases or else it is decreased slightly).

The *RSSE* in Table 11.2 is the *root sum-squared error* ($\sqrt{E}$), which is larger than the TSSE. The *Misses* column gives the number of exemplar (training) vectors that were incorrectly recognized. We used 300 epochs for BP ($300 \times 10 = 3000$ complete weight adjustments) and 300 iterations for FP (300 complete weight adjustments). Often, but not always, 100 epochs or iterations were sufficient for successful training.

To compare the relative computing time given at the bottom of Table 11.2, we timed the BP-2 and FP-2 runs on 2000 epochs and 2000 iterations, respectively, and rounded to seconds. FP-2 required only 39% (54 sec) as much time as BP-2 (138 sec). On multiplying by 300/2000, the times for 300 epochs of BP-2 and 300 iterations for FP-2 were, respectively, 20.7 and 8.1 sec. Results on the Parity3, Parity5, and Digit12 datasets (see Appendix 11) showed similar proportional differences. FP does not run Q times faster than BP because of extra overhead in summing each weight increment over the Q partial increments.

We postulate the empirical law that FP takes about 40% of the computational time of BP to run $1/Q$ as many total weight adjustments. But FP usually learns better in 40% of the computing time of BP (compare the RSSE for BP-2 to the RSSE for FP-2 in Table 11.2). We note that these programs were compiled in Borland Turbo C++. When compiled with Semantec's Zortech C++ compiler (32-bit instructions running in protected mode under extended DOS with DPMI) and optimized for speed on the 80486, the iterations were 28% faster than for Turbo C++.

A Study to Compare Error Values in Recognition

The comparison of the relative performance of BP and FP that we describe next is due to Iychettira (1994), a graduate student in Electrical Engineering who worked with the author on a project that covered optical character recognition of the digits 0 through 9. He used $N = 15$ features that included parameters for describing the curvature of lines so that the features were invariant to thickness and positions of lines and to rotations of characters. The architecture used $N–M–J = 15–16–2$ and $Q = 12$ exemplars that included two exemplars each for two of the digits. It is noteworthy that the network did not learn properly when a single output neurode was used ($J = 1$), nor did it recognize all digits when only $N = 9$ features were used. When M was increased to more than 16, the learning was slowed but was no better, so the architecture was appropriate. The network learning was tested with 39 novel feature vectors that used different thicknesses of lines and different positions of digits in a box.

To compare the learning efficiency of BP and FP, Iychettira first trained the network via BP, and then trained it with FP by starting over with the same set of initial weights. Each training process was run for 1000 BP epochs or 1000 FP iterations over all 12 exemplar feature vectors, and the errors of recognition were recorded for each of the digits. The rounded RSSEs of recognition of each exemplar training vector after the 1000 epochs (12,000 adjustments of each weight) or 1000 iterations (1000 adjustments of each weight) are shown in Table 11.3. Other runs gave similar results. BP initially decreased faster than FP on some runs, but then oscillated and had more trouble converging. FP was noticeably faster overall on all runs, although no timing was done. All of the novel digit feature vectors were recognized correctly after both kinds of training.

Because FP results are as good or better than those of BP and take less than half the computing time in training, we prefer FP to BP unless the dataset is too large to fit into computer memory. But even so, a partial FP is desirable. If Q exemplar feature vectors are to be used in training and $Q = 100,000$, then a *partial FP* could be done by training on the sequence of, for example, 10 sets of 10,000 exemplars each. Such a dataset would overwhelm the epochal process of BP. But for small datasets, BP is a usable method, although the step gain adjustment is not efficient and BP takes more computing time.

Table 11.3.
Errors of Exemplar Recognition after 1000 Epochs/Iterations of BP/FP

Error	Digit									
	0	1	2	3	4	5	6	7	8	9
BP error	0.10	0.12	0.08	0.12	0.01	0.06	0.06	0.10	0.04	0.06
FP error	0.02	0.04	0.06	0.03	0.04	0.06	0.03	0.12	0.03	0.05

11.4. Some Effects and Comparisons of MLP Algorithms

Discussions of the Runs

In the following sections, we use the following algorithms: (i) FQP0, a "plain vanilla" computer program that uses quartic search first followed by fullpropagation that uses a fixed step gain η that can be given by the user; (ii) FQP1, our standard computer program with quartic search followed by fullpropagation that adjusts the step gain *en route* on each iteration by multiplying η by 1.024 if the RSSE has decreased or multiplying η by 0.92 if the RSSE has increased (empirically obtained numbers over runs on various datasets); and (iii) FQPx, the quartic search with fullpropagation program that adjusts the step gain η in a manner similar to that of Kung et al. (1991) and Parlos et al. (1994) by dividing by the gradient norm. Table 11.4 shows the capability of the computer programs for the FQP0, FQP1, and FQPx programs.

FQP0, FQP1, and FQPx may use preliminary adjustments of the initially drawn random weights (user selectable). They also allow the selection of adjusting exponential rates α_1 and α_2 and biases b_1 and b_2 in the unipolar sigmoids at the hidden and output layers, respectively. The user may set the momentum coefficient μ to zero or to some positive number ($\mu = 0.1$ appears to be best for most datasets, but could be too high for some or too low for others). Any adjustment of parameters may cause spikes (jumps) in the graph of the RSSE error over the iterations, as many of the following graphs show. Such spikes are not problematic if they stop before the last iterations, but otherwise the run may end on a spike.

The Effect of Adjustable Step Gain

Figure 11.2 demonstrates the step gain phenomena, where parts (a) and (b) show FQP0 runs with different constant step gains and parts (c) and (d) show FQP1 and FQPx runs, respectively. The horizontal axis is the number of iterations and the vertical axis is the RSSE, which is $\sqrt{E}$. These runs are all done on the Ten5ten dataset given in Appendix 11 and none gave any misses (incorrect recognition) on the exemplar vectors used for training. The maximum RSSE value is 3.0 and the maximum iteration number is 639. A constant step gain $\eta = c$ yields the smoothest graph of RSSE versus iteration number, but does not take advantage of the opportunities to decrease the error more quickly nor to stop oscillations when η is too large.

Table 11.4.
Given and Selectable Properties of FQP0, FQP1, and FQPx

Property	FQP0	FQP1	FQPx
Adjustable step gain η	No	Yes	Yes
Selectable preliminary weight adjustment	Yes	Yes	Yes
Selectable random seed for random weights	Yes	Yes	Yes
Selectable adjustment of rates and biases	Yes[a]	Yes[a]	Yes[a]
Display of RSSE versus iteration graphics	Yes	Yes	Yes

[a]Adjustments of both sigmoidal rates and biases are on or off simultaneously.

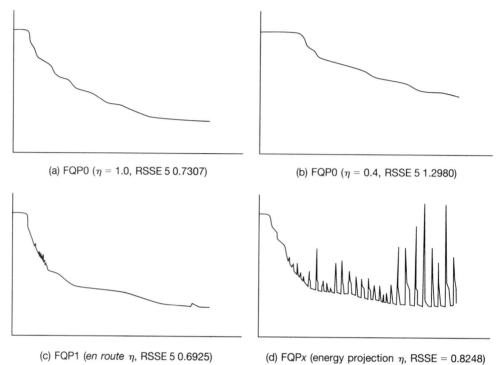

(a) FQP0 (η = 1.0, RSSE 5 0.7307)   (b) FQP0 (η = 0.4, RSSE 5 1.2980)

(c) FQP1 (*en route* η, RSSE 5 0.6925)   (d) FQPx (energy projection η, RSSE = 0.8248)

Figure 11.2.   RSSE versus iterations of training runs on the 10–5–10 dataset (random seed = 531, 630 iterations, μ = 0.1, no bias or rate adjustments, zero misses on each).

The larger step gain constant decreases the error more rapidly as can be seen by comparing Parts (a) and (b). If the step gain is too large, however, the process will oscillate and not converge. We do not know a priori what constant η to use, so adjustments are needed. The adjustable step gains of parts (c) and (d) reduce the error more rapidly, although the energy projection method causes spikes (jumps) at points where the norm of the gradient adjusts. The *en route* step gain is clearly the winner here.

The Effect of Momentum

Chapter 5 describes how a momentum term can smooth the directions of steepest descent to prevent oscillation on the surface of a nonlinear function E that forms a curving canyon. Figures 11.3 through 11.6 depict FQPx training runs with and without momentum terms. The horizontal axis is the number of iterations and the vertical axis is the RSSE value $\sqrt{E}$ (E is the TSSE). The vertical scale is greatly exaggerated with a range of 0 to 3.0. In each of the figures, Parts (a) and (b) (the top graphs) represent training runs without momentum (the momentum coefficient is μ = 0). Part (a) compares with part (c) in that everything is the same (including the initial weights determined by the same random seed) except the momentum coefficient μ. Likewise, part (b) compares with part (d) in that everything is the

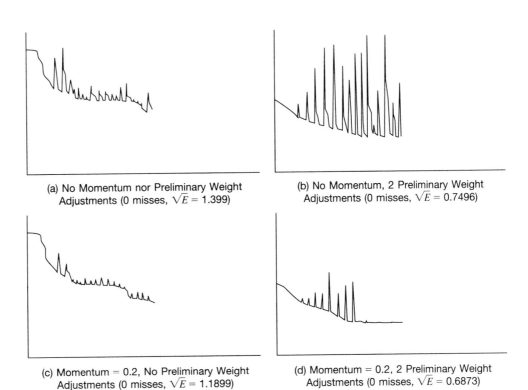

(a) No Momentum nor Preliminary Weight Adjustments (0 misses, $\sqrt{E} = 1.399$)

(b) No Momentum, 2 Preliminary Weight Adjustments (0 misses, $\sqrt{E} = 0.7496$)

(c) Momentum = 0.2, No Preliminary Weight Adjustments (0 misses, $\sqrt{E} = 1.1899$)

(d) Momentum = 0.2, 2 Preliminary Weight Adjustments (0 misses, $\sqrt{E} = 0.6873$)

Figure 11.3. FQPx runs, RSSE versus iterations on the 10–5–10 dataset (random seed = 333, 400 iterations, no bias nor rate adjustments).

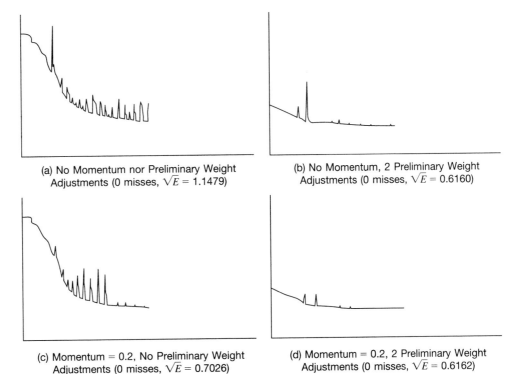

(a) No Momentum nor Preliminary Weight Adjustments (0 misses, $\sqrt{E} = 1.1479$)

(b) No Momentum, 2 Preliminary Weight Adjustments (0 misses, $\sqrt{E} = 0.6160$)

(c) Momentum = 0.2, No Preliminary Weight Adjustments (0 misses, $\sqrt{E} = 0.7026$)

(d) Momentum = 0.2, 2 Preliminary Weight Adjustments (0 misses, $\sqrt{E} = 0.6162$)

Figure 11.4. FQPx runs, RSSE versus iterations on the 10–5–10 dataset (random seed = 111, 400 iterations, no bias nor rate adjustments).

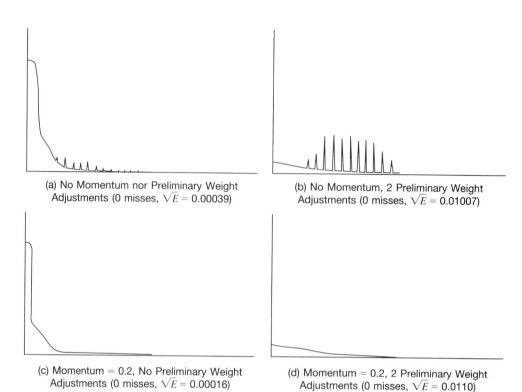

(a) No Momentum nor Preliminary Weight
Adjustments (0 misses, $\sqrt{E} = 0.00039$)

(b) No Momentum, 2 Preliminary Weight
Adjustments (0 misses, $\sqrt{E} = 0.01007$)

(c) Momentum = 0.2, No Preliminary Weight
Adjustments (0 misses, $\sqrt{E} = 0.00016$)

(d) Momentum = 0.2, 2 Preliminary Weight
Adjustments (0 misses, $\sqrt{E} = 0.0110$)

Figure 11.5. FQPx runs, RSSE versus iterations on the Rotate9 dataset (random seed = 111, 400 iterations, no bias nor rate adjustments).

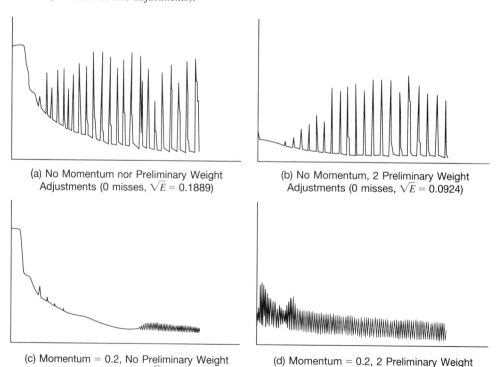

(a) No Momentum nor Preliminary Weight
Adjustments (0 misses, $\sqrt{E} = 0.1889$)

(b) No Momentum, 2 Preliminary Weight
Adjustments (0 misses, $\sqrt{E} = 0.0924$)

(c) Momentum = 0.2, No Preliminary Weight
Adjustments (1 miss, $\sqrt{E} = 0.3062$)

(d) Momentum = 0.2, 2 Preliminary Weight
Adjustments (4 misses, $\sqrt{E} = 0.1645$)

Figure 11.6. FQPx runs, RSSE versus iterations on the Digit12 dataset (random seed = 111, 600 iterations, no bias nor rate adjustments).

same except the momentum coefficient μ. In Figures 11.3 through 11.5, the bottom graphs (parts (c) and (d)) with momentum $\mu = 0.2$ are smoother than the upper ones that have $\mu = 0.0$. The graphs that have preliminary (quartic search) weight adjustments start the descent at a much lower RSSE as a result of these adjustments.

In Figure 11.6, the bottom graphs with $\mu = 0.2$ have spikes of lower amplitude because of the momentum smoothing, but their oscillations have higher frequency. Both runs end on thin spikes. To show that this indicates that the momentum coefficient $\mu = 0.2$ is too high, Figure 11.7 shows graphs of runs where the momentum coefficient has been lowered to $\mu = 0.1$ in parts (a), (b), (c), and (d). Notice that in parts (a) and (b) of Figure 11.7, the frequency of oscillation is again lower but the RSSE is considerably smoothed over the runs shown in Figure 11.6, parts (a) and (b). Our experiences have shown that a value of $\mu = 0.05$ to 0.10 usually helps without causing the higher frequency oscillations. We conclude that the training process can be somewhat sensitive to small changes in the momentum parameter and that a very small momentum coefficient helps, while larger ones can cause high-frequency oscillations of lower amplitude.

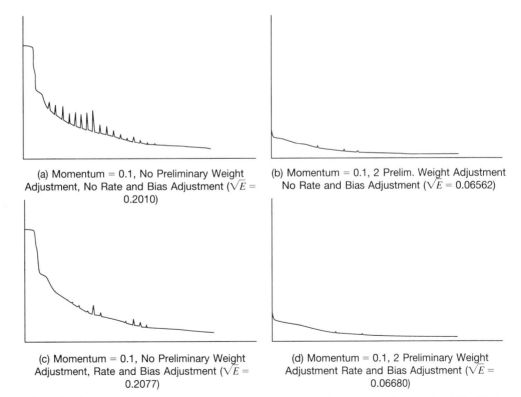

(a) Momentum = 0.1, No Preliminary Weight Adjustment, No Rate and Bias Adjustment ($\sqrt{E} = 0.2010$)

(b) Momentum = 0.1, 2 Prelim. Weight Adjustment No Rate and Bias Adjustment ($\sqrt{E} = 0.06562$)

(c) Momentum = 0.1, No Preliminary Weight Adjustment, Rate and Bias Adjustment ($\sqrt{E} = 0.2077$)

(d) Momentum = 0.1, 2 Preliminary Weight Adjustment Rate and Bias Adjustment ($\sqrt{E} = 0.06680$)

Figure 11.7.   FQPx runs, RSSE versus iterations on the Digit12 dataset (random seed = 111, 600 iterations, 0 misses on each run).

The Effect of Preliminary Adjustment of Initial Weights

In each of the Figures 11.3 through 11.7, comparisons of part (a) with part (b) and of part (c) with part (d) show the effects of preliminary adjustments of the randomly drawn initial weights by univariate quartic search (see Chapter 6). The left-hand graphs in the figures show runs that have no preliminary adjustment of the initial random weights, while the right-hand parts do (everything else is the same). A preliminary weight adjustment iteration searches once on each weight and so adjusts all weights one time each. The right-hand graphs show that the preliminary weight adjustments, made prior to the start of the fullpropagation descent iterations shown in the graphs, provide a much lower RSSE with which gradient descent starts its first iteration. Of course, this extra preliminary computation costs extra computer time but can be a profitable tradeoff. A larger number of quartic univariate preliminary adjustments, say 8 or 10, can also provide a well-trained (generalizing) weight set with no further iterations.

All of the figures except Figure 11.6, where the momentum coefficient μ is too high, show that the lowest errors and smoothest error graphs occur when both very low momentum and preliminary quartic weight adjustments are made, which provide a more reliable training run. The spikes in the later iterations present a danger. Even when the error is mostly low, the run may end on a spike of high amplitude and fail to provide a trained weight set.

Figure 11.8 allows us to examine the spikes a little closer. The runs are the same as in Figure 11.3 except that the training continues for 630 iterations and the momentum coefficient has been set at $\mu = 0.1$ here instead of 0.2. An adjustment of a parameter during training tends to cause a jump in the RSSE function E. It appears from Figure 11.8 that the preliminary weight adjustments in the right-hand graphs cause the spikes to be more pronounced during the most difficult part of the descent. The range on which the pronounced spikes occur is limited when preliminary weight adjustments are made, but persists across all iterations without it. It is as though the preliminary weight adjustments put the position in a low region of a rocky canyon that can be followed downhill to arrive on the valley floor. The spikes are where a slight movement in a direction jumps up the side of the wall of the canyon and further movement jumps back down the wall. Once on the valley floor, the jumps essentially subside, but the floor may not be a convex bowl-shaped region.

The Effect of Adjustment of Exponential Rates and Biases

Figure 11.7 compares the effects of adjusting the exponential rates α_1 and α_2 and the biases b_1 and b_2 in the unipolar sigmoids $1/[1 + \exp(-\alpha_1 r + b_1)]$ and $1/[1 + \exp(-\alpha_2 s + b_2)]$, respectively, at the hidden neurodes and neurodes in the output layer. The runs shown in parts (a) and (b) have no rate or bias adjustments, while those in parts (c) and (d) have rate and bias adjustments on every tenth iteration during the first half of the iterations, so as to not cause large disturbances. Our experience indicates that an excessive amount of rate and bias adjustment is counterproductive. When comparing parts (a) and (c), it is obvious that the rate adjustments help, whereas the difference between parts (b) and (d) is barely discernible on this dataset. In fact, the RSSE is very slightly lower in the top parts without such adjustments. The lowest RSSE does not necessarily yield the weight set for the best generalized learning, however.

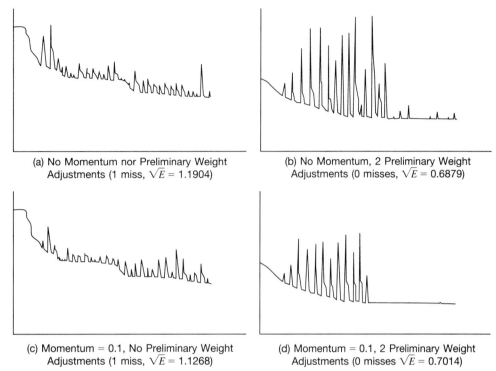

(a) No Momentum nor Preliminary Weight
Adjustments (1 miss, $\sqrt{E} = 1.1904$)

(b) No Momentum, 2 Preliminary Weight
Adjustments (0 misses, $\sqrt{E} = 0.6879$)

(c) Momentum $= 0.1$, No Preliminary Weight
Adjustments (1 miss, $\sqrt{E} = 1.1268$)

(d) Momentum $= 0.1$, 2 Preliminary Weight
Adjustments (0 misses $\sqrt{E} = 0.7014$)

Figure 11.8. FQPx runs, RSSE versus iterations on the 10–5–10 dataset (random seed $= 333$, 630 iterations, no bias nor rate adjustments).

FQP1 versus FQPx

Figure 11.9 shows the results of training on the Digit12 dataset with FQP1, which uses the *en route* method of adjusting the step gain (Looney, 1996b). In parts (a) and (b) there are no adjustments of rate nor biases, but even so, the performance is very good. Parts (c) and (d) show the results of rate and bias adjustments. Upon comparing Figure 11.9 with Figure 11.7, it appears that the FQPx algorithm performed better than the FQP1 algorithm overall. Only validation and verification could determine which of these training runs yields the most generalized weight solution. But FQPx appears to be better when preliminary weight adjustments and momentum are used and the rates and biases in the sigmoids are adjusted. The different datasets also cause somewhat different behavior.

The Effect of Random Seed

A comparison of the parts of Figure 11.3 with their corresponding parts in Figure 11.4 show the effect of random seed or, equivalently, the effect of initial random weights determined by the seed. Everything except the random seed is the same in the corresponding parts of the two figures. The spikes are different as are the rates of descent. The seed in Figure 11.3

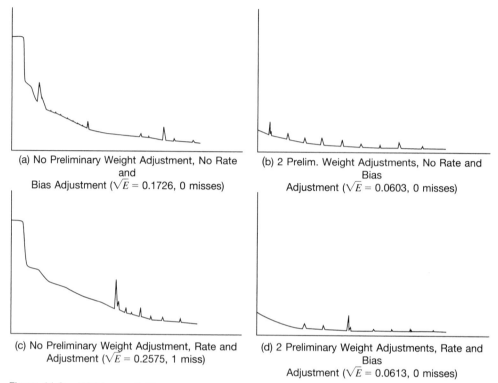

(a) No Preliminary Weight Adjustment, No Rate and Bias Adjustment ($\sqrt{E} = 0.1726$, 0 misses)

(b) 2 Prelim. Weight Adjustments, No Rate and Bias Adjustment ($\sqrt{E} = 0.0603$, 0 misses)

(c) No Preliminary Weight Adjustment, Rate and Adjustment ($\sqrt{E} = 0.2575$, 1 miss)

(d) 2 Preliminary Weight Adjustments, Rate and Bias Adjustment ($\sqrt{E} = 0.0613$, 0 misses)

Figure 11.9.   FQP1 runs, RSSE versus iterations on the Digit12 dataset (random seed = 111, 600 iterations, $\mu = 0.1$).

was 333, which led to a downward path where preliminary weight adjustments caused spikes of large amplitude (a deep curving canyon). There is no guarantee that a good random seed for one dataset will be good for another. Thus we cannot eliminate the stochastic effect ("the luck of the draw"), although preliminary weight adjustment helps to overcome this at a computational cost.

The Effect of the Number of Output Neurodes

Figure 11.10 presents the runs of FQP1 on the two datasets Blood10 and Blood10x that are described in Appendix 11. The Blood10 dataset determines an architecture of $N–M–J = 8–10–1$ with a single output component z_1. On the other hand, the Blood10x dataset uses an architecture of $N–M–J = 8–10–3$, so the combinations of outputs (z_1, z_2, z_3) form the seven identifiers. Parts (a) and (c) of Figure 11.10 show the results of training on Blood10, while parts (b) and (d) show the results of training on the Blood10x dataset. On all runs, the parameters are as follows: $\mu = 0.1$, random seed = 333, rate and biases are adjusted, and preliminary quartic weight adjustments are made. We add that the learning with $J = 3$ is also more robust as our testing has shown. This coincides with the results from Section 9.7 for MLPs, FLNs, and RBFNs (also see section 7.3).

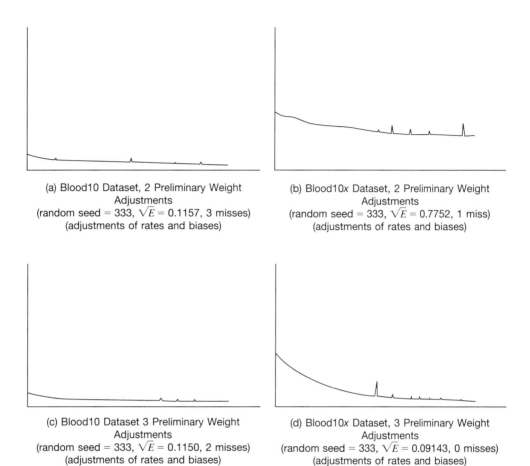

(a) Blood10 Dataset, 2 Preliminary Weight
Adjustments
(random seed = 333, $\sqrt{E}$ = 0.1157, 3 misses)
(adjustments of rates and biases)

(b) Blood10x Dataset, 2 Preliminary Weight
Adjustments
(random seed = 333, $\sqrt{E}$ = 0.7752, 1 miss)
(adjustments of rates and biases)

(c) Blood10 Dataset 3 Preliminary Weight
Adjustments
(random seed = 333, $\sqrt{E}$ = 0.1150, 2 misses)
(adjustments of rates and biases)

(d) Blood10x Dataset, 3 Preliminary Weight
Adjustments
(random seed = 333, $\sqrt{E}$ = 0.09143, 0 misses)
(adjustments of rates and biases)

Figure 11.10. FQP1 training on Blood10 and Blood10x datasets (630 iterations).
(Blood 10: N–M–J = 8–10–1, Blood 10x: N–M–J 5 8–10–3)

When comparing parts (a) and (c) with parts (b) and (d), we see that the value $J = 3$ provides better training than $J = 1$. We also note that the RSSE errors are larger for $J = 3$, which is to be expected because the sum is over more differences ($[z_1 - t_1]^2 + [z_2 - t_2]^2 + [z_3 - t_3]^2$ for Blood10x versus $[z_1 - t_1]^2$ for Blood10). This example shows that better training can be done on the same number of iterations with more output neurodes (up to a point, of course).

Purely Quartic Search versus Gradient Descent

Upon comparing parts (a) with (c) (and (b) with (d)) of Figure 11.10 for runs on Blood10 with two and three preliminary weight adjustments, respectively, as the only difference, we see that there are fewer misses with more preliminary weight adjustments. When we continue these preliminary quartic univariate adjustments without the gradient descent, the result is the univariate quartic search algorithm that we call *uniquart*, or just UQ. Quartic polynomials can also fit cubic, quadratic, and linear data. Figure 11.11 shows the results of UQ runs on the Ten5ten, Digit12, and Blood10x datasets that are given in Appendix 11. In these graphs, we plot the RSSE for each adjusted weight, rather than for one entire iteration over all weights adjustments. For the Ten5ten dataset, there are 100 weights so that six iterations provide 600 individual weight adjustments as shown in part (a).

In part (b), there are 144 weights for the Digit12 dataset for $N–M–J = 10–12–2$, so we show only four complete iterations (576 single weight adjustments) of RSME values. However, we continued for another four iterations in part (c), for a total of eight. In this case the number of misses was reduced to zero. But while UQ decreases the error rapidly at first, our implementation of the algorithm in UQ is too coarse (for the sake of efficiency) to finely adjust the weight set for a final solution. The method used to minimize the quartic polynomial is to search across the weight domain $[-2, 2]$ while evaluating the quartic at a given number of points (say, 20). Part (d) shows the results for five iterations of UQ on the Blood10x dataset ($N–M–J = 8–10–3$). There were two misses on the recognition of the $Q = 7$ exemplar vectors. On five more iterations, the number of misses went to a single one, and after 10 more iterations, there were zero misses. We also tested UQ on the Rotate9 dataset (see

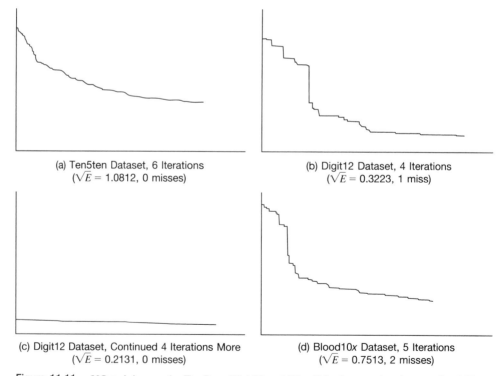

(a) Ten5ten Dataset, 6 Iterations
($\sqrt{E} = 1.0812$, 0 misses)

(b) Digit12 Dataset, 4 Iterations
($\sqrt{E} = 0.3223$, 1 miss)

(c) Digit12 Dataset, Continued 4 Iterations More
($\sqrt{E} = 0.2131$, 0 misses)

(d) Blood10x Dataset, 5 Iterations
($\sqrt{E} = 0.7513$, 2 misses)

Figure 11.11. UQ training on the Ten5ten, Digit12 and Blood10x datasets (random seed = 333; μ, rates, and biases are not applicable).

Appendix 11). After the first five iterations, there was a single miss, but there was none after five more iterations.

We conclude that the quartic univariate adjustments reduce the error very rapidly during the early iterations (the first, second, and third). Their computational cost of further evaluations of E for each quartic approximation on each weight is too high compared to FQP1 and FQPx. We can most advantageously use two or three univariate quartic preliminary iterations so full propagation can start in the well of a deep minimum.

11.5. A Plethora of MLP Algorithms

Tabulating the Algorithms

Tables 11.5a and 11.5b list the gradient algorithms and some comments on their relative capabilities, properties, and basic methodologies for training. There is no single MLP algorithm that is clearly the best for every problem in classification and recognition. A researcher needs a few of the best ones implemented in computer programs. Many of the algorithms would be very good on certain datasets provided that they were tuned by adjustments of the parameters. We seek to eliminate the ones that are less dependable and find the ones that are the best overall.

Table 11.6 lists the strategic search algorithms that use no gradient descent. Instead, these draw random numbers as weight values, draw a random direction and use polynomial line search along the directional line in the weight space, or related schemes.

Table 11.5a.
Some Gradient Algorithms and Properties

Algorithm	Features and Basic Methodology
BP (backpropagation)	Trains on single exemplar at a time, weakest form of linear gradient descent, very slow and unstable.
FP0 (fullpropagation)	Trains on all exemplars at once, full linear gradient descent, no momentum, nonadjusting step gain, faster than BP, unstable.
QP (quickpropagation)	Trains on a single exemplar at a time, lineal second order, can be unstable, faster than BP.
FP1 (fullprop with adjustment)	Trains on all exemplars at once, full linear gradient descent, en route step gain adjustment, uses momentum, faster than BP, can be unstable.
fqprop (full quadratic propagation)	Trains on all exemplars at a time, quadratic search in direction of steepest descent, faster than BP, fairly stable.
RP (resilient propagation)	Trains on one exemplar at a time, adapts step gains for each weight, takes time to adjust all step gains, then converges faster, faster than QP, unstable.
FRP (RP with fullpropagation)	Trains on all exemplars at a time, adaptive step gain for each weight, converges faster on later iterations after adjustment of step gains, fast, can be unstable.
fcprop (full cprop)	Trains on all exemplars at a time, cubic search in direction of steepest descent, stable.
FPx (FP with energy projection)	Trains on all exemplars at a time, uses momentum, adjusts step gain by energy projection, may adjust rates and biases, can be fast and can be unstable.

Table 11.5b.
More Gradient Algorithms and Properties

Algorithm	Features and Basic Methodology
FQP0 (FP with quartic search)	Trains via fullpropagation and momentum but with a fixed step, uses quartic search for preliminary weight adjustment, stability and speed depend on step gain.
FRRP (FRP, random preliminary)	Trains via RP with adjustable step gain for each weight, preliminary adjustment of weights by random draws to get good starting weight set, can be unstable.
fhcprop (fcprop with cubic search)	Trains on all exemplars at once from good starting weights obtained by cubic search, can be unstable, same as fcprop.
FCP1 (FP1 with cubic search)	Trains by FP on all exemplars at once from good starting weights found by cubic univariate cubic search, momentum, *en route* adjustment of step gain, usually stable.
FCQx (FP with cubic search)	Trains on all exemplars at once from starting weights found by cubic search, uses momentum, adjusts step gains by energy projection.
FQP1 (FP with quartic search)	Trains via FP with momentum and *en route* adjustment of step gain, quartic search adjustment of initial weights, adjustment rates and biases, usually fast, stable.
FQPx (quartic FP, preliminary)	Trains on all exemplars at a time, quartic preliminary weight adjustment, momentum, energy projection step gain adjustment, adjusts rates and biases, fast, jumpy.

Table 11.6.
Some Search Algorithms and Properties

Algorithm	Features and Basic Methodology
ronn (random optimum NN)	Trains on all exemplars at once, random search on single weight or on all weights, no weight drift, learning is more general, slow, stable, global minimum.
qronn (ronn with quadric search)	Trains on all exemplars at a time, quadratic search in random directions, generalized learning, slow, stable, global minimum usual.
gensrch (genetic algorithms)	Trains on all exemplars at a time, searches for "fittest" weight set populations using TSSE E as fitness measure, finds global minimum.
cubronn (cubic ronn)	Trains on all exemplars at a time, cubic search in random directions, global minimum usual, generalized learning, stable, fast on earlier iterations.
hcubronn (cubronn with cubic search)	Adjusts initial weights by cubic univariate search, global minimum usual, cubic search in random directions, better performance than cubronn, fast, stable, generalizable.
hcbrnv (inverse hybrid cubic)	Adjusts initial weights, by universal cubic search, then cubic search in random directions, global minimum usual, inverse sigmoids are used in output neurodes, stable, fast for search.
UQ (univariate quartic)	Adjusts each weight with a quartic polynomial fit to five points along dimension of each weight, all weight updates make one iteration, quick descent on early iterations, lots of computing overhead.

Criteria for Comparisons

The testing methodology of Fahlman (1988) established a standard test base for comparison. Fahlman counts the number of epochs until the NN recognizes all of the exemplar input vectors accurately and stops each run at that point. Because the test runs start at different randomly generated initial weight points, he makes multiple runs of each test and averages the number of epochs for the runs of each test. He also computes the standard deviation of the number of runs. But our algorithms do not use epochs of training over the sequence of single exemplar pairs at a time, so we cannot use the number of epochs as a criterion. Instead, we count the total number of adjustments on the entire weight set.

Most of our tests consist of 10 runs on the same dataset for a fixed number of iterations for that dataset. The same random seed is given at the start, so all initial weight set sequences are the same. A test is made for each of the various algorithms listed in the tables. The number of training exemplars that are incorrectly recognized is recorded for each run as misses and the root sum-squared error (RSSE) used here is $\sqrt{E}$, (not $(1/P)\sqrt{E}$ for some P). The total sum-squared error (TSSE) function E has too many zeros to the right of the decimal point, so we use its square root, the RSSE, which is larger. We do not compare all algorithms on all datasets, but instead we use a Latin square approach for the design of experiments. We want to identify the least capable algorithms and eliminate them.

We have ascertained from experience with these datasets the number of iterations to use for tests on each, and we chose the numbers so that not all runs successfully learn all of the training vectors. The idea here is to compare the number of failures and the RSSEs after a fixed number of iterations of training. The two reasons for computing are (i) to obtain numerical solutions and (ii) to gain insight. The latter reason, known as *Hamming's principle*, applies here.

Some Computer Runs and Analysis of Results

Tables 11.7 through 11.12 show the first set of runs to ascertain the least capable algorithms. Each algorithm has two columns that display its runs. The first column records the RSSE $\sqrt{E}$ for each of the 10 runs, while the second column provides the number of misclassifications, or misses, upon completion of the given number of iterations. The runs for the different algorithms all start with the same random seed for drawing random initial weights on the same given dataset. An iteration is a complete updating of the entire weight set one time.

The column pairs of Table 11.7 show that for a given number of iterations, FCP1 had two misses on the run of 1100 iterations, but on further iterations it learned sufficiently well that there were no misses. FCP1 and *cubronn* are the winners on the Parity3 dataset.

Some of the listed algorithms use a preliminary stage to adjust the randomly drawn initial weight set to a good starting weight set in a region of low TSSE error. This is done either by drawing and testing random univariate samples or by univariate cubic or quartic search. Table 11.8 presents the runs of 1100 iterations on the rather linearly separable Rotate9 dataset. FCP1 did well again and two new candidates emerged, which are fhcprop and FRRP. Tables 11.9 and 11.10 show that FCP1 and FRRP did well on the Ten5ten Dataset, but Table 11.10 shows that FRRP did not do well on the difficult Blood10 dataset.

Of the tested algorithms that use gradients (FP0, fcprop, FRP, fhcprop, FRRP, and FCP1), the FCP1 algorithm (preliminary cubic univariate search to obtain a good starting weight set

Table 11.7.
Results on the Parity3 Dataset with 1100 Iterations

qronn		cubronn		FPO		fcprop[a]		FCP1[b]		FRP[c]	
RSSE	Misses	RSSE	Misses	RSSE	Misses	RSSE	Misses	RSSE	Misses	RSSE	Misses
0.534	0	0.016	0	0.621	1	0.321	0	0.001	0	0.622	1
0.239	0	0.569	2	0.244	0	0.724	1	0.002	0	0.244	0
0.275	0	0.047	0	0.233	0	0.714	1	0.011	0	0.233	0
0.580	0	0.186	0	0.622	1	0.726	1	0.011	0	0.622	1
0.856	1	0.070	0	0.246	0	0.032	0	0.002	0	0.246	0
0.707	0	0.034	0	0.248	0	0.727	1	0.696	2	0.248	0
0.454	0	0.194	0	0.622	1	0.745	1	0.002	0	0.622	1
0.381	0	0.094	0	0.622	1	0.317	0	0.007	0	0.622	1
0.921	2	0.100	0	0.298	0	0.723	1	0.004	0	0.298	0
0.562	0	0.202	0	0.622	1	0.306	0	0.000	0	0.622	1
Totals:	3		2		5		6		2		5

[a]Many of these runs with misclassification errors converged to eliminate the error when run for another 1000 iterations. However, some could not be eliminated with 10,000 extra iterations, which indicates that they were in the well of a shallow local minimum.
[b]On the sixth run where RSSE = 0.696, we continued with 1000 extra iterations to obtain an RSSE of 0.024, misses = 0.
[c]The learning appeared to stagnate on the first few hundred iterations, but then began to quickly converge, apparently as the weight increment parameters adjusted to an appropriate level.
Note: qronn is doing two, and cubronn is doing three, extra functional evaluations of E on each iteration (weight update) because they evaluate the TSSE function E at three and four weight points, respectively. Thus they run slower and do more while running the same number of iterations. Also, FCP1 does extra computation on each weight up front and thus consumes more time to find a good starting weight set, especially for large NNs with a large number of weights.

Table 11.8.
Results on the Rotate9 Dataset with 1100 Iterations

cubronn		FPO[a]		fcprop		fhcprop		FCP1		FRP		FRRP	
RSSE	Misses	RSSE	Misses	RSSE	Misses	RSSE	Misses	RSSE	Misses	RSSE	Misses	RSSE	Misses
0.028	0	0.001	0	0.025	0	0.053	0	0.008	0	0.007	0	0.0000	0
0.042	0	0.006	0	0.019	0	0.045	0	0.001	0	0.007	0	0.0000	0
0.045	0	0.002	0	0.027	0	0.011	0	0.000	0	0.007	0	0.0000	0
0.076	1	0.000	0	0.015	0	0.050	0	0.001	0	0.007	0	0.000	0
0.026	0	0.002	0	0.021	0	0.040	0	0.001	0	0.007	0	0.0000	0
0.023	0	0.000	0	0.024	0	0.015	0	0.000	0	0.006	0	0.0000	0
0.045	0	0.003	0	0.007	0	0.003	0	0.006	0	0.007	0	0.0000	0
0.041	0	0.181	4	0.025	0	0.048	0	0.001	0	0.007	0	0.001	0
0.035	0	0.666	8	0.018	0	0.022	0	0.002	0	0.006	0	0.0000	0
0.057	1	0.008	0	0.003	0	0.054	0	0.002	0	0.007	0	0.0000	0
Totals:	2		12		0		0		0		0		0

[a]On the eighth and ninth runs of this test, extra thousands of iterations did not improve the RSSE, which oscillated, giving the appearance of being in the well of a shallow local minima with a step size that is too large. This dataset is easy for an NN to learn, and thus there is a lesson to be learned here in using gradient descent without some method to find a starting point in the well of a deep minimum.
Note: Because cubronn and FPO did not adjust the initial weight set, their convergence was not as good. However, the random selection of a small sample for each weight in fhcprop helped in the convergence that followed. It is also noteworthy that FCP1, FRP, and FRRP were the most effective in reducing the error, although this is not a bona fide measure of performance. It is not clear why fcprop did so well except that these data are easy to learn (it is nearly linearly separable).

Table 11.9.
Results on the Ten5ten Dataset with 1000 Iterations

cubronn		FP0		fcprop		FRRP		fhcprop[a]		FCP1	
RSSE	Misses	RSSE	Misses	RSSE	Misses	RSSE	Misses	RSSE	Misses	RSSE	Misses
1.851	0	0.670	0	0.674	0	0.674	0	1.864	1	0.659	0
1.845	1	0.648	0	0.751	0	0.620	0	1.831	2	0.661	0
1.852	2	0.673	0	0.719	0	0.645	0	1.857	1	0.636	0
1.847	1	0.723	0	0.714	0	0.647	0	1.847	1	0.634	0
1.854	1	0.628	0	0.674	0	0.628	0	1.847	1	0.673	0
1.853	1	0.702	0	0.710	0	0.672	0	1.864	1	0.666	0
1.828	2	0.671	0	0.690	0	0.634	0	1.856	1	0.618	0
1.848	1	0.913	0	0.669	0	0.706	0	1.823	1	0.666	0
1.851	1	0.720	0	0.659	0	0.693	0	1.840	2	0.647	0
1.842	0	0.720	0	0.750	0	0.670	0	1.855	0	0.652	0
Totals:	10		0		0		0		11		0

[a]With 2000 extra iterations, the first run yielded misses = 0.

followed by FP-type steepest descent) did well. Tables 11.11 and 11.12 verify the FCP1 is the best algorithm tested here. We note that according to Riedmiller and Braun (1993), RP was faster than *quickprop*. Therefore we also eliminate *quickprop* (QP), as well as RP, FRP, and FRRP. Table 11.12 summarizes the results of runs on the Parity5 dataset that is somewhat difficult to learn.

Table 11.10.
Results on the Blood10 Dataset with 1500 Iterations

hcubronn		cubronn[a]		FP0[b]		FCP1		FRP		FRRP[c]	
RSSE	Misses	RSSE	Misses	RSSE	Misses	RSSE	Misses	RSSE	Misses	RSSE	Misses
0.036	0	0.186	3	0.046	0	0.036	0	0.548	6	0.098	0
0.051	0	0.101	1	0.031	0	0.071	0	0.548	6	0.096	1
0.045	0	0.095	2	0.038	0	0.025	0	0.548	6	0.063	0
0.034	0	0.102	2	0.040	0	0.045	0	0.548	6	0.123	3
0.034	0	0.024	0	0.041	0	0.039	0	0.548	6	0.025	0
0.022	0	0.052	0	0.152	3	0.022	0	0.548	6	0.041	0
0.085	1	0.034	0	0.158	3	0.042	0	0.548	6	0.075	1
0.080	1	0.061	0	0.185	4	0.027	0	0.548	6	0.034	0
0.081	0	0.076	1	0.143	3	0.049	0	0.548	6	0.046	0
0.059	0	0.129	2	0.076	1	0.049	0	0.548	6	0.083	0
Totals:	2		11		14		0		60		5

[a]On successive segments of 1000 more continuation iterations, the first run went to 2, then 1, then 0 misses with RSSE = 0.131, 0.081, and 0.051, respectively. This corroborates what we had previously seen: cubronn finds a near-global minimum of the TSSE if sufficiently many iterations are allowed, unlike gradient methods that can fail on a particular run.
[b]On the sixth, seventh, eighth, and ninth runs, there was oscillation that sometimes settled down to permit convergence, but other times continued as long as we cared to iterate.
[c]The continuation of 1000 more iterations on the fourth run yielded RSSE = 0.049 and 0 misses, which demonstrates the power of finding a good starting weight set.

Table 11.11.
Results on the Digit12 Dataset with 1100 Iterations

hcubronn		FP0[a]		FCP1		fhcprop[b]		FRP		FRRP	
RSSE	Misses	RSSE	Misses	RSSE	Misses	RSSE	Misses	RSSE	Misses	RSSE	Misses
0.188	0	0.034	0	0.017	0	0.055	0	1.276	4	0.019	0
0.129	0	0.010	0	0.008	0	0.084	0	1.065	2	0.011	0
0.121	0	0.010	0	0.005	0	0.451	3	1.323	8	0.032	0
0.151	0	0.011	0	0.011	0	0.444	3	1.131	4	0.010	0
0.139	0	0.023	0	0.007	0	0.220	0	1.246	9	0.028	0
0.135	0	0.008	0	0.006	0	0.435	2	1.087	4	0.035	0
0.143	0	0.028	0	0.006	0	0.397	2	1.069	3	0.042	0
0.158	0	0.389	3	0.011	0	0.134	0	1.331	8	0.035	0
0.127	0	0.009	0	0.008	0	0.436	3	1.314	8	0.036	0
0.150	0	0.021	0	0.009	0	0.439	2	1.300	8	0.033	0
Totals:	0		3		0		15		58		0

[a]1000 more iterations on eighth run did not converge.
[b]1000 more iterations on third, fourth runs converged.

One conclusion that is clear from the data is that whenever extra computation is used to obtain a good starting weight set by adjusting the randomly drawn initial weight set, the convergence is faster and more stable. The importance of finding a good initial weight set should not be underestimated (Li et al., 1993) because it strongly influences the convergence speed and stability.

The StockMarket20 and StockMarket40 datasets contain a high level of noise (random error) and are extremely difficult to learn. Additionally, the inputs include negative values. We tried two commercial neural network programs, as well as our steepest descent program FPx, but none of these were able to learn these datasets. One of our cubic search programs, cubronn, learned on transformed data for both of these datasets and also on a larger one (StockMarket100). It used bipolar sigmoids. For an application to several years of stock market indicators and an investment strategy, see Chapter 12.

Table 11.12.
Summary of Runs on the Parity5 Dataset

MLP Architecture for Parity5 dataset:

$N = 5$ inputs, $M = 32$, $J = 1$, $Q = 32$ exemplar pairs

Results:

hcubronn and FCP1 learned to successfully recognize all exemplar vectors on 2600 iterations, while FP0, fcprop, fhcprop, FRP, and FRRP were problematic[a]

[a]The latter algorithms required a significant increase in the number of iterations to recognize all exemplar feature vectors. On some runs, 5000 iterations were successful, but not on others.

Analysis and Conclusions for MLPs

We now make other empirically based conclusions concerning the training of MLPs, using all of the results thus far in this chapter and the transitivity of comparisons.

Conclusion 1: Fullpropagation is more efficient than backpropagation on gradient descent.

Conclusion 2: The steepest descent algorithms learn faster and are more stable when a preliminary stage is used to adjust the initial weight set to a quadratic well of low errors.

Conclusion 3: BP, FP0, qronn, cubronn, RP, FRP, fcprop, fhcprop, FPx, and FRRP (see Table 11.10) are all inferior in learning speed to at least one of FCP1 (or one of its quartic analogs, FQP1 or FQPx).

Conclusion 4: Quartic search is best during the early training until a deep well is found, but then quadratic search or steepest descent are faster for descending to the minimum in that well.

Conclusion 5: Steepest descent works well on many datasets, but is problematic on others. On some noisy datasets, it does not train properly.

Conclusion 6: Polynomial search, notably quartic search, learns robustly on some difficult datasets.

Conclusion 7: A repertoire of programs that implement both gradients and nongradient methods is necessary for MLP training needs for classification and recognition. No single algorithm satisfies all needs.

For our purposes, we keep FCP1 and its quartic offspring FQP1 and FQPx for steepest descent.

11.6. Functional Link Network Performance

The Algorithm

Figure 11.1(b) shows a generalized FLN called a *random vector FLN*, or RVFLN (Pao et al., 1994). The hidden (offset) neurodes are used to generate functions of the N input variables to provide more input variables in a higher-dimensional space in which the N-dimensional features are embedded for easy separation of nonlinearly separable classes (see Section 3.10). We use Pao's original product functions (Pao, 1989) here, but not all of them, which would make the network much larger than needed. We generate the extra inputs as products of consecutively indexed pairs of the original features; that is, we use

$$x_{N+1} = x_1 x_2, \quad x_{N+2} = x_2 x_3, \dots, \quad x_{2N-1} = x_{N-1} x_N, \quad x_{2N} = x_N x_1 \qquad (11.1a)$$

The "hidden" neurodes of the RVFLN (see Figure 11.1(b)) are the functions that generate the new inputs. A method to obtain products of independent features is to compute the correlations

$$c_{ij} = x_i^{(1)}x_j^{(1)} + \cdots + x_i^{(q)}x_j^{(q)} + \cdots + + x_i^{(Q)}x_j^{(Q)} \tag{11.1b}$$

over the sample of Q exemplars for each pair i and j of inputs. The pairs that have the lowest correlation are the most independent and their product functions can form a new independent input variable.

Recall that only the weights $\{u_{pj}\}$ are trained in FLNs, where $p = 1,\ldots, 2N$ is this case. To train these weights, we use the fullpropagation algorithm with the *en route* adjustment of the step gain η, where the steepest descent steps on the $(r + 1)$st iteration are

$$u_{pj}^{(r+1)} = u_{pj}^{(r)} + \eta(t_j^{(q)} - z_j^{(q)})[z_j^{(q)}(1 - z_j^{(q)})]x_p^{(q)} \tag{11.2}$$

η is the adjustable step gain (learning rate), and u_{pj} is the weight from the pth input to the jth (output) neurode. In the runs, we add 0.1 to the sigmoid derivatives $[z_j(1 - z_j)]$ to prevent premature saturation. We call this the FFLN1 algorithm because it is the fullpropagation version of the FLN that uses *en route* adjustment of the step gain (increase η if E decreases, else decrease η).

Other similar versions, for larger spaces in which to embed the features, use more alternative input variables. For example, FFLN2 uses the double products that are offset by both one and two indices; that is, we use in addition to the new input variables of Equation (11.1a) the ones defined by

$$x_1 x_3, x_2 x_4, \ldots, x_{N-2} x_N, x_{N-1} x_1, x_N x_2 \tag{11.3}$$

The use of all double products with nonequal indices would require $N(N - 1)$ new components so the total number of inputs would become $N + N(N - 1) = N^2$ inputs. This grows very quickly. For $N = 10$ input features, this would require 100 inputs. For $N = 100$, it would require 10,000, which is not very practical. FFLN1 would require 20 inputs when $N = 10$, and FFLN2 would require 30. Thus our versions save a lot of computing by not using more separating power.

Some FLN Results for Comparison

Figures 11.12 through 11.13 show the results of runs with FFLN1, which used only N products of two inputs for a total of $2N$ inputs. No momentum term nor preliminary weight adjustments were used with these runs. The random seeds and number of iterations are as shown. The results appear to show that FLNs are less dependent on the random seed than are MLP networks. FFLN1 failed to learn the Parity3 dataset from many different random seeds and on continuation runs. It appears that the $2N$ inputs used in FFLN1 are not powerful enough to perform the highly nonlinear separation required for 3-bit parity data, which has eight linearly separable subclasses. On the other hand, it learned well on the 10–5–10 data. We did not, however, use the optimal N products in these runs.

The figures show that FFLN1 has a very sharp drop off of the RSSE on the first few iterations. After that, it still decreases rapidly when compared to MLPs. The speed of training is the most striking thing about running FFLN1. While we did not time the FFLN1 runs, it was clear that they were much more than an order of magnitude faster than gradient training of MLPs with a single hidden layer.

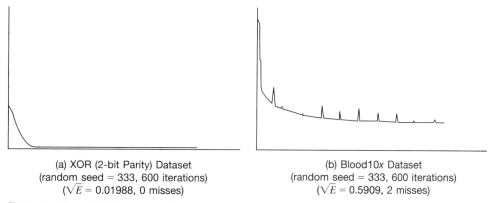

(a) XOR (2-bit Parity) Dataset
(random seed = 333, 600 iterations)
($\sqrt{E}$ = 0.01988, 0 misses)

(b) Blood10x Dataset
(random seed = 333, 600 iterations)
($\sqrt{E}$ = 0.5909, 2 misses)

Figure 11.12.   FFLN1 runs on selected datasets.

We had some difficulty with FFLN2 that uses $3N$ inputs because it did not always start converging. Once it did, it was extremely rapid. Therefore we used one preliminary weight adjustment iteration, which broke it loose. We are not sure yet whether this is an intrinsic property of such networks with $3N$ features made up of N features or a happenstance.

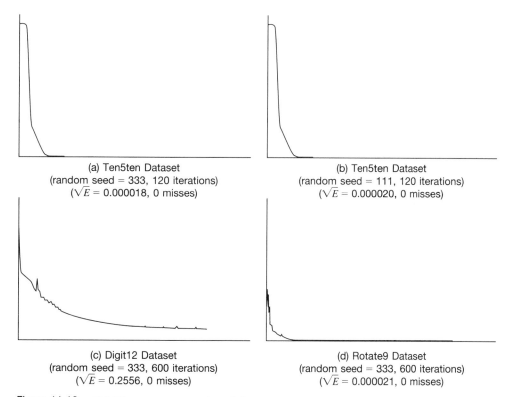

(a) Ten5ten Dataset
(random seed = 333, 120 iterations)
($\sqrt{E}$ = 0.000018, 0 misses)

(b) Ten5ten Dataset
(random seed = 111, 120 iterations)
($\sqrt{E}$ = 0.000020, 0 misses)

(c) Digit12 Dataset
(random seed = 333, 600 iterations)
($\sqrt{E}$ = 0.2556, 0 misses)

(d) Rotate9 Dataset
(random seed = 333, 600 iterations)
($\sqrt{E}$ = 0.000021, 0 misses)

Figure 11.13.   FFLN1 runs on more selected datasets.

The *random vector functional link net* (RVFLN) is discussed in Sections 7.6 and 10.6 (see Figures 7.12 and 10.11(c)). The results presented in Tables 10.5 and 10.6 of Section 10.6 show that the RBF-RVFLN is the most powerful FANN of all. Those results show its relative power and move it to the top of our list.

Analysis and Conclusions for FLNs

The great *advantage* of FLNs is their speed of learning. Thousands of iterations can be done as rapidly as dozens of BP epochs on MLPs. Absent from the FLN training were oscillations and local minima. A *disadvantage* is that on large networks, the total number of inputs to each output neurode can become very large. While this is usually not a severe problem for training, it slows the operational speed, which could be a problem for on-line recognition systems with a large number of features. If few functions are used to keep the number of total inputs low, then convergence may fail on certain datasets. *In practice*, we compute the correlations of Equation (11.1b), or, better yet, we use the RBF-RVFLN.

11.7. The Performance of Radial Basis Function Networks

The RBFN Algorithm Recalled

Recall from Chapters 3 and 7 that RBFNs cover the exemplar feature vectors (or feature space) with response regions of Gaussian functions, each of which is activated if an incoming feature vector is close to its center (see Figure 11.1(c)). For the training, we put $M = Q$ and set the center $\mathbf{w}^{(m)} = (w_1^{(m)},..., w_N^{(m)})$ at the mth hidden neurode equal to an exemplar vector $\mathbf{x}^{(q)}$. Thus $M = Q$. The network outputs are then updated by putting through each exemplar vector $\mathbf{x}^{(q)}$ ($q = 1,..., Q$) via

$$\mathbf{x}^{(q)} \rightarrow \begin{Bmatrix} y_1^{(q)} = \exp(-\|\mathbf{x}^{(q)} - \mathbf{w}^{(1)}\|^2/(2\sigma^2)) \\ \vdots \qquad \qquad \vdots \\ y_M^{(q)} = \exp(-\|\mathbf{x}^{(q)} - \mathbf{w}^{(M)}\|^2/(2\sigma^2)) \end{Bmatrix} \rightarrow \begin{Bmatrix} z_1^{(q)} = (1/M)\sum_m u_{m1}y_m^{(q)} \\ \vdots \qquad \qquad \vdots \\ z_J^{(q)} = (1/M)\sum_m u_{mJ}y_m^{(q)} \end{Bmatrix} \qquad (11.4)$$

The algorithm for testing here is *quick training*, which was described in Section 3.11 and in Section 7.7. FRBFP1 is the full propagation algorithm for RBFNs via *quick training*.

Results and Conclusions for RBFNs

Figures 11.14 and 11.15 present the results of training FRBFP1 on some of the datasets in Appendix 11. The first figure shows the effects of the spread parameter σ^2 and the preliminary weight adjustments. The next figure shows runs on the Digit12 and Blood10x datasets. In the first figure, a comparison of part (a) with (c) and of part (b) with (d) shows that the smaller value for the spread parameter σ^2 facilitates convergence. Upon comparing parts (a) and (b) with (e), and then parts (b) and (d) with (f), we see that $\sigma^2 = 0.04$ ($\sigma = 0.2$) facilitates very rapid convergence of this dataset.

Parts (b) and (c) of Figure 11.15 show that convergence is difficult with σ^2 values that are too large. Part (c) is a continuation of Part (b) for the Digit12 dataset. On the other hand, part (a) of this figure shows how a small value of σ enables extremely rapid convergence. Part (d) shows quick convergence on the Blood10x dataset.

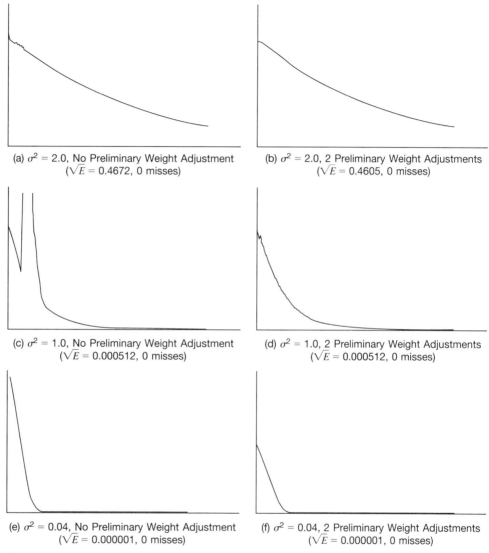

(a) σ^2 = 2.0, No Preliminary Weight Adjustment
($\sqrt{E}$ = 0.4672, 0 misses)

(b) σ^2 = 2.0, 2 Preliminary Weight Adjustments
($\sqrt{E}$ = 0.4605, 0 misses)

(c) σ^2 = 1.0, No Preliminary Weight Adjustment
($\sqrt{E}$ = 0.000512, 0 misses)

(d) σ^2 = 1.0, 2 Preliminary Weight Adjustments
($\sqrt{E}$ = 0.000512, 0 misses)

(e) σ^2 = 0.04, No Preliminary Weight Adjustment
($\sqrt{E}$ = 0.000001, 0 misses)

(f) σ^2 = 0.04, 2 Preliminary Weight Adjustments
($\sqrt{E}$ = 0.000001, 0 misses)

Figure 11.14. FRBFP1 runs on the 10–5–10 dataset (630 iterations, random seed = 333, μ = 0, *en route* adjustment of η).

While Tarassenko and Roberts (1994) found that RBFNs did not perform quite as well as MLPs on the recognition of EEG patterns, their problem appears to be that their dataset was so large that they were forced to draw random input vectors and then adjust them to obtain centers of the hidden neurodes. Rather than adjust the centers via steepest descent, they made adjustments via

$$w_{nm}^{(r+1)} \leftarrow w_{nm}^{(r)} + \eta(x_n^{(q)} - w_{nm}^{(r)}) \qquad (11.5)$$

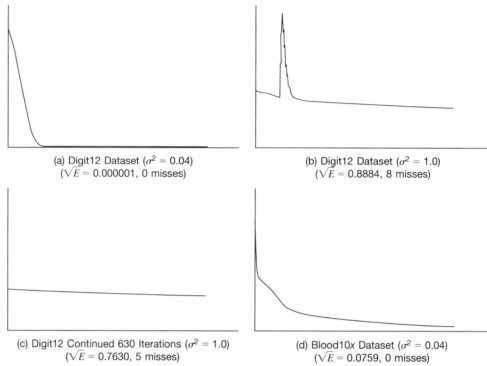

(a) Digit12 Dataset ($\sigma^2 = 0.04$)
($\sqrt{E} = 0.000001$, 0 misses)

(b) Digit12 Dataset ($\sigma^2 = 1.0$)
($\sqrt{E} = 0.8884$, 8 misses)

(c) Digit12 Continued 630 Iterations ($\sigma^2 = 1.0$)
($\sqrt{E} = 0.7630$, 5 misses)

(d) Blood10x Dataset ($\sigma^2 = 0.04$)
($\sqrt{E} = 0.0759$, 0 misses)

Figure 11.15. FRBFP1 runs on other datasets (630 iterations, random seed = 333, $\mu = 0$, *en route* adjustment of η, no preliminary adjustments).

where $\mathbf{x}^{(q)} = (x_1^{(q)},..., x_N^{(q)})$ is the qth exemplar input vector for adjusting the weights (they updated in the epochal mode of BP). Their carefully chosen dataset of 9000 exemplars was broken into a training set of 4500 and a validation set of the same number. In this case, they did not use $M = 4500$ hidden neurodes, which would be impractical. They drew a subsample at random for the different test runs, up to 300 exemplars. These were used as the centers and adjusted by putting the 4500 training exemplars through the network and using Equation (11.5). When an exemplar fails to be correctly recognized, they adjoined it to the set of centers.

In conclusion, RBFNs are ideal for quick robust training when the number Q of exemplars in the dataset is not too large. Otherwise, there are two choices. Either find a suitably smaller subsample that represents all linearly separable subclasses and use them as centers, or else use an MLP.

MLPs versus RBFNs: The Study of Mak, Allen, and Sexton

Mak et al. (1994) compared RBF networks with MLPs for recognition of 10 speaker voices, based on training with features from spoken names of the digits 0,..., 9. They used 546 exemplar feature vectors for each of the training and test sets. Each set contained different data for the utterances of the 10 digits. The training and test data were the twelfth-order cepstrum coefficients of the audio signals that were filtered to pass between 50 Hz and 3500 Hz. The two datasets were recorded 30 minutes apart.

Their experiments used 50, 100, 200, and 300 hidden neurode centers for the RBFNs. Both networks were implemented on six T800 transputers with 2 Mbytes of memory each and with no interprocessor communications required (concurrent but independent computation). Various combinations of training on from one to ten digits at time were tried. The MLPs used in the training had 10, 20, and 40 hidden neurodes.

The RBF network with the best performance used 300 hidden neurodes and had an identification accuracy of 98.7%, while the best performance for the MLP was achieved by the network with 20 hidden neurodes with 90.2% identification accuracy. Table 11.13 provides a summary for the MLP with 20 hidden neurodes compared with an RBF network with 100 hidden neurodes that had a similar accuracy of 90.0%. Mak et al. reported that the MLP training process sometimes became stuck in a local minimum, but a lot of computation time was wasted before they realized this and started the process over. Such wasted time is not reflected in Table 11.13.

The *advantages* of RBFNs over MLPs are as follows: (i) They do not get stuck in local minima (there aren't any); (ii) the training time is much shorter; (iii) the weight values do not have to be restrained for training to take place (if the training is not restrained for MLPs, the weights will drift and saturation will take place); (iv) the momentum coefficient is not needed for RBFNs; and (v) exemplars that are far from decision boundaries have little influence in RBF networks, while in MLPs they influence the training. RBFNs do not saturate during training.

The *disadvantages* of the RBFNs compared to the MLPs are as follows: (i) They can require more memory because of the large number of hidden neurodes sometimes required; (ii) the speed of operation can be slower than for MLPs due to the extra hidden neurodes; (iii) the centers and spread parameters σ^2 are not optimal in any sense; and (iv) there is so far no good way to implement the hidden neurodes in hardware.

In practice, we would always use an RBF-RVFLN in place of an RBFN. However, for large Q, we may prefer an MLP.

Table 11.13.
Comparison of MLP and RBF Performance

Parameter	MLP	RBF Network
Number of hidden nodes	20	100
Identification accuracy	90.2%	90.0%
Training time	214 min	36 min
Memory storage per processor	109 Kbytes	386 Kbytes
Recognition time/pattern	15 msec	21 msec

Maximum accuracy: MLP 90.2%, RBFN 98.7% ($M = 300$)

Exercises

11.1. The Parity5 dataset was used in MLP networks that have 5 input nodes, 32 middle neurodes, and a single output neurode. It was a particularly difficult NN to train with this data. Consider the question of whether or not an NN that has 2 output neurodes would be easier to train. Would fewer hidden neurodes work better? Justify your answers.

11.2. What would be the effect of using $M = 16$ neurodes in the hidden layer for the Parity5 dataset? Make computer runs and compare the results.

11.3. Run a steepest descent algorithm such as FCP1 or FQPx to train an MLP on the Parity5 dataset with $N = 5$ input components, $M = 8$ hidden neurodes, and $J = 2$ output neurodes. Then run again with $M = 32$. What can you conclude?

11.4. Write out an algorithm that uses only loops of univariate quartic approximation. Must it converge? Why?

11.5. Implement a program for hcubronn (hybrid cubic search) that uses a first stage of cubic univariate approximation to obtain a good starting weight point and then goes into a second stage of cubic search in randomly selected directions. Test it on the Blood10, Digit12, and Parity5 datasets.

11.6. Repeat Exercise 11.5 using quartic univariate search followed by quartic search in random directions.

11.7. Substitute the direction of steepest descent in Exercise 11.6, so that quartic search is made in the direction of steepest descent. Compare the results.

11.8. Write an algorithm for training an MLP that randomly draws an initial weight set, draws a random direction, and searches along that direction with quartic search. On all later iterations, generate a direction that is orthogonal to all previous directions and search along it with quartic search. What are its advantages and disadvantages?

11.9. Write a computer program that implements a simple cubic approximation with no preliminary stage of weight adjustment. Use bipolar sigmoids. Train an MLP on the noisy StockMarket20 (or the StockMarket40) dataset. The class identifiers are not the desired outputs in this case. What are they?

11.10. Modify the RBFN training algorithm so that it can learn in a self-organizing (unsupervised training) mode. Select a number J of output neurodes, come up with a set of identifier vectors for classes such that every component is either 0 or 1 and every pair of vectors differ in two or more components. In this case, if there is an error in a single component, it will be obvious (error detection). During the self-organizing mode, assign the first input feature vector as the center for a single hidden neurode and train to output the first identifier. In general, input the $(q + 1)$st feature vector. If it maps to an actual output vector sufficiently close to a used identifier, then classify in that class and adjust the weights appropriately. But if it maps to a new (unused) identifier, then assign it as the center for a new neurode and associate it with that identifier and train accordingly. Note that it must map to either a used or unused identifier, because the actual output vector for it is closest to some identifier.

11.11. Does quartic univariate search use conjugate directions? Justify your answer. What can be said about the efficiency?

11.12. In the random vector functional link network, find N new input features so the total number will be $2N$ by using N functions of combinations of the N original inputs. The problem here is to find N functions of the original input features. Try minimal correlation products.

11.13. Experiment with a random vector FLN algorithm where the "hidden" neurodes are taken to be RBF hidden neurodes, each exemplar input feature vector is assigned as a center (you may use some or all of the exemplars, provided that there are not too many). The RBFs are defined by $f_m(\mathbf{x}; \mathbf{v}) = 1$ if $\|\mathbf{x} - \mathbf{v}\| < \epsilon$, $f_m(\mathbf{x}; \mathbf{v}) = \min\{1, \epsilon/\|\mathbf{x} - \mathbf{v}\|\}$ otherwise. What are the advantages and disadvantages of such a FANN?

11.14. Write a computer program that implements the algorithm of Exercise 11.13. Test it on some datasets. Document the results.

11.15. Radial basis functions cover the feature space with their balls of radius σ_m centered on the centers $\mathbf{v}^{(m)}$, $m = 1,..., M$. How can the radial basis functions be changed to include elliptical shaped regions, or squares or rectangles? Could such regions of the feature space be useful for classification and recognition? Consider the Mahalanobis distance and city block norm of Section 0.10.

11.16. Design an MLP algorithm that is the most efficient at finding a good starting point, and then is the most efficient in descending to the minimum in a well.

11.17. Design an RVFLN architecture and algorithm, giving all of the equations for updating all weights, where each hidden neurode connects to each other hidden neurode. What can be said about trading off size in terms of nodes for connectivity? What properties does the extra connectivity have?

11.18. Discuss a full propagation type algorithm where steepest descent is used at the output neurodes, but quartic search is used at the hidden neurodes.

References

Fahlman, S. E. (1988), *An Empirical Study of Learning Speed in Backpropagation*, Technical Report CMU-CS-88-162, Carnegie Mellon University.

Gill, P. E., Murray, W., and Wright, M. H. (1981), *Practical Optimization*, Academic Press, London.

Iychettira, A. (1994), *Character Recognition Using Feedforward Neural Networks*, Final Project Report CS773c, Fall Semester, University of Nevada.

Johansson, E. M., Dowla, F. U., and Goodman, D. M. (1992), Backpropagation learning for multilayer feedforward neural networks using the conjugate gradient method, *Int. J. Neural Systems*, vol. 2, no. 4, 291–301.

Kung, S. Y., Diamantaras, K., Mao, W. D., and Taur, J. S. (1991), Generalized perceptron networks with nonlinear discriminant functions, in *Neural Networks: Theory and Applications*, edited by R. J. Mammone and Y. Y. Zeevi, Academic Press, Harcourt Brace Jovanovich, Boston, pp. 245–279.

Li, G., Alnuweiri, H., and Wu, W. (1993), Acceleration of backpropagation through initial weight pretraining with delta rule, *Proc. 1993 IEEE Int. Conf. Neural Networks*, San Francisco, vol. 1, 580–585.

Looney, C. (1993), Neural networks as expert systems, *J. Expert Syst. Appl.*, vol. 6, no. 2, 129–136.

Looney, C. (1996a), Advances in neural networks: demystifying knowledge acquiring black boxes, *IEEE Trans. Knowledge Data Eng.*, vol. 8, no. 2, 211–226.

Looney, C. (1996b), Stabilization and speedup of convergence in training feedforward neural networks, *Neurocomputing*, vol. 10, 7–31.

Mak, M. W., Allen, W. G., and Sexton, G. G. (1994), Speaker identification using multilayer perceptrons and radial basis function networks, *Neurocomputing*, vol. 6, 99–117.

Musavi, M. T., Chan, K. H., Hummels, D. M., and Kalanti, K. (1994), On the generalization ability of neural network classifiers, *IEEE Trans. Pattern Anal. Mach. Intelli.*, vol. 16, no. 6, 659–663.

Pao, Y. H. (1989), *Adaptive Pattern Recognition and Neural Networks*, Addison-Wesley, Reading, MA.

Pao, Y. H., Park, G. H., and Sobajic, D. J. (1994), Learning and generalization characteristics of the random vector function link net, *Neurocomputing* vol. 6, 163–180.

Parlos, A. G., Fernandez, B., Atiya, A. F., Muthusami, J., and Tsai, W. K. (1994), An accelerated learning algorithm for multilayer perceptron networks, *IEEE Trans. Neural Networks*, vol. 5, no. 3, 493–497.

Riedmiller, M., and Braun, H. (1993), A direct adaptive method for faster backpropagation learning: the RPROP algorithm, *Proc. 1993 IEEE Int. Conf. Neural Networks*, San Francisco, vol. 1, 586–591.

Sprecht, D. F. (1968), A practical technique for estimating general regression surfaces, Report LMSC-6-79-68-6, Lockheed Missiles and Space Co., Inc., Palo Alto, CA.

Tarassenko, L., and Roberts, S. (1994), Supervised and unsupervised learning in radial basis functions, *IEE Proc. Vis. Image Signal Process.*, vol. 141, no. 4, 210–216.

Appendix 11

Some Datasets for Testing

11a. The Nine Datasets

We use nine small sets of data to test the main algorithms presented in the previous chapters. The first is the 3-bit parity data shown in Table 11b.1 and the second is the 5-bit parity data listed in Table 11b.2. These are highly nonlinear datasets that are difficult to learn. The third is the Rotate9 dataset that consists of nine vectors, where each is a shift left circular rotation of the component values 0.1, 0.2, 0.3,..., 0.9. Table 11c.1 presents these data.

The fourth and fifth datasets, given in Tables 11d.1 and 11d.2, are the Blood10 and Blood10x datasets of features extracted from measurements on blood samples from persons with known conditions and infections. The only difference between the Blood10 and the Blood10x datasets is that the latter is set up with $J = 3$ instead of $J = 1$ (three output neurodes instead of a single one). The sixth is the Digit12 dataset that consists of 16×14 rectangular grids upon which the digits 0, 1, ..., 9 are encoded in black and white pixels (picture elements), which is applicable to the automatic recognition of postal ZIP codes. This dataset is shown in raw counts of changes from black to white and white to black along the selected rows and columns as presented in Table 11e.1 and in usable standardized form in Table 11e.2.

The seventh dataset comes from Fahlman (1988) and is the now a standard N–M–N dataset for testing MLPs. The data are to be used to train a standard FANN, with $N = 10$ input nodes, $M = 5$ middle neurodes, and $J = 10$ output neurodes, to put out the input exemplars. The input exemplars have a nonzero value in only a single component, and that value is 1. The middle-layer bottleneck is a severe test. This data are presented in Table 11f.1, where zeros are put at 0.1 and ones are put at 0.9. The eighth and ninth datasets are the StockMarket20 and StockMarket40 data, which are indicator data from which an investment strategy can be followed by shifting between stocks and money certificates depending upon whether or not the forecast indicator is positive or negative. These are shown in Tables 11g.1 and 11g.2.

11b. Datasets 1 and 2—The Parity3 and Parity5 Feature Vectors

The input vectors for the Parity3 data are the eight combinations of three bits, while the output is a single bit equal to 1 if there is an odd number of high bits or 0 if there is an even number of high bits. Table 11b.1 displays these data. Thus the NN architecture contains $N = 3$ inputs, $M \le 8$ middle neurodes, $J = 1$ output neurode, and $Q = 8$ exemplars (recall the results of Chapter 7, where we may use any approximation to $M = K$ (K is the number of subclasses). In this case, $K = Q$. The Parity5 data are similar. They contain all 32 combinations of five bits, and so have $N = 5$ inputs, $M \le 32$ middle neurodes, $J = 1$ output neurode, and $Q = 32$ exemplars. Table 11b.2 presents these data. Recall that in the actual training of an MLP using gradient descent, the zeros are set to 0.1 and the ones are set to 0.9, whereas the RBFNs can train on 0s and 1s.

11c. Dataset 3—The Rotate9 Feature Vectors

The third dataset consists of the nine shift-left/rotate vectors $\mathbf{x}^{(1)} = (0.1, 0.2, 0.3, 0.4, 0.5, 0.6, 0.7, 0.8, 0.9)$, $\mathbf{x}^{(2)} = (0.2, 0.3, 0.4, 0.5, 0.6, 0.7, 0.8, 0.9, 0.1),..., \mathbf{x}^{(9)} = (0.9, 0.1, 0.2, 0.3, 0.4, 0.5, 0.6, 0.7, 0.8)$. They are presented in Table 11c.1. These are each distinct and should easily form nine different classes during classification training. The training outputs (identifiers) that we use are the values shown on the right in Table 11c.1. It should be noted that if these values were reversed, then each would be the same as the first components of the exemplar feature vectors and so the corresponding weights would be high while all other weights would be low. Under the scheme given, the related component in the exemplar feature vectors jump around uniquely over the nine exemplar input vectors.

Table 11b.1.
Dataset 1: The Parity3 Dataset (3–8–1)

Input Vector Number	Input Vector	Identifier (Output) Value
1	(0,0,0)	0
2	(0,0,1)	1
3	(0,1,0)	1
4	(0,1,1)	0
5	(1,0,0)	1
6	(1,0,1)	0
7	(1,1,0)	0
8	(1,1,1)	1

Note: We use 0.1 in place of 0 and 0.9 in place of 1 in the actual training of an MLP.

Table 11b.2.
Dataset 2: The Parity5 Dataset (5–12–1)

Input Vector Number	Input Vector	Identifier (Output) Value
1	(0,0,0,0,0)	0
2	(0,0,0,0,1)	1
3	(0,0,0,1,0)	1
4	(0,0,0,1,1)	0
5	(0,0,1,0,0)	1
6	(0,0,1,0,1)	0
7	(0,0,1,1,0)	0
8	(0,0,1,1,1)	1
9	(0,1,0,0,0)	1
10	(0,1,0,0,1)	0
11	(0,1,0,1,0)	0
12	(0,1,0,1,1)	1
13	(0,1,1,0,0)	0
14	(0,1,1,0,1)	1
15	(0,1,1,1,0)	1
16	(0,1,1,1,1)	0
17	(1,0,0,0,0)	1
18	(1,0,0,0,1)	0
19	(1,0,0,1,0)	0
20	(1,0,0,1,1)	1
21	(1,0,1,0,0)	0
22	(1,0,1,0,1)	1
23	(1,0,1,1,0)	1
24	(1,0,1,1,1)	0
25	(1,1,0,0,0)	0
26	(1,1,0,0,1)	1
27	(1,1,0,1,0)	1
28	(1,1,0,1,1)	0
29	(1,1,1,0,0)	1
30	(1,1,1,0,1)	0
31	(1,1,1,1,0)	0
32	(1,1,1,1,1)	1

Note: We use 0.1 in place of 0 and 0.9 in place of 1 in the actual training of an MLP.

Table 11c.1.
Dataset 3: The Nine Rotated Vectors (9–9–1)

Class Number	Exemplar Input Vector	Exemplar (Output) Value
1	(0.1, 0.2, 0.3, 0.4, 0.5, 0.6, 0.7, 0.8, 0.9)	0.9
2	(0.2, 0.3, 0.4, 0.5, 0.6, 0.7, 0.8, 0.9, 0.1)	0.8
3	(0.3, 0.4, 0.5, 0.6, 0.7, 0.8, 0.9, 0.1, 0.2)	0.7
4	(0.4, 0.5, 0.6, 0.7, 0.8, 0.9, 0.1, 0.2, 0.3)	0.6
5	(0.5, 0.6, 0.7, 0.8, 0.9, 0.1, 0.2, 0.3, 0.4)	0.5
6	(0.6, 0.7, 0.8, 0.9, 0.1, 0.2, 0.3, 0.4, 0.5)	0.4
7	(0.7, 0.8, 0.9, 0.1, 0.2, 0.3, 0.4, 0.5, 0.6)	0.3
8	(0.8, 0.9, 0.1, 0.2, 0.3, 0.4, 0.5, 0.6, 0.7)	0.2
9	(0.9, 0.1, 0.2, 0.3, 0.4, 0.5, 0.6, 0.7, 0.8)	0.1

Table 11d.1.
Dataset 4: Blood Data for Seven Patients (Blood10, 8–10–1)

Vector Number	Feature Vector (in Thousandths)	Known State	Identifier Value
1	(289, 55, 484, 385, 545, 575, 341, 995)	Normal	0.1
2	(31, 484, 220, 123, 300, 380, 89, 210)	Hepatitis B	0.2
3	(126, 391, 354, 275, 442, 515, 175, 395)	HIV Early	0.3
4	(60, 414, 240, 162, 304, 368, 110, 270)	HIV Late	0.4
5	(95, 365, 360, 234, 480, 543, 165, 190)	IUP	0.5
6	(63, 222, 332, 210, 460, 536, 155, 320)	Leukemia	0.6
7	(189, 247, 415, 312, 510, 562, 275, 320)	Malnutrition	0.7

11d. Datasets 4 and 5—The Blood10 and Blood10x Feature Vectors

The fourth dataset is real-world medical data that are displayed in Table 11d.1. Each of seven blood samples from $Q = 7$ different patients with $K = 7$ different diseases/conditions (classes) was put into an instrumentation system that made certain measurements over time. These measurements were transformed into 12 features that varied according to blood properties caused either by disease that infected the patient or by other conditions. The data presented here are limited to only the first eight of the original 12 features. These eight features are minimally sufficient, but provide a rigorous nonlinear learning test. The values in the feature vectors represent thousandths. The Blood10 name comes from the fact the we use $M = 10$ middle neurodes ($M > K$ here as more partitioning power is needed). Table 11d.2 presents the extended Blood10 data, called the Blood10x data, which has $J = 3$ unipolar output components.

11e. Dataset 6—The Digit12 Feature Vectors

The sixth dataset comes from hand printed digits for machine recognition of ZIP codes. Each digit must be written in a rectangular box printed on an envelope. Prototypes of the digits 0, 1,..., 9 are written on the bottom right of the envelope for the user to imitate. The scanner senses 256 different shades of gray from 0 (black) to 255 (white) for each *pixel* (picture el-

Table 11d.2.
Dataset 5: Blood Data for Seven Patients (Blood10x, 8–10–3)

Vector Number	Feature Vector (in Thousandths)	Known State	Identifier Vector
1	(289, 55, 484, 385, 545, 575, 341, 995)	Normal	(0.100,0.100,0.100)
2	(31, 484, 220, 123, 300, 380, 89, 210)	Hepatitis B	(0.100,0.500,0.900)
3	(126, 391, 354, 275, 442, 515, 175, 395)	HIV Early	(0.100,0.900,0.900)
4	(60, 414, 240, 162, 304, 368, 110, 270)	HIV Late	(0.500,0.100,0.500)
5	(95, 365, 360, 234, 480, 543, 165, 190)	IUP	(0.500,0.900,0.100)
6	(63, 222, 332, 210, 460, 536, 155, 320)	Leukemia	(0.900,0.100,0.900)
7	(189, 247, 415, 312, 510, 562, 275, 320)	Malnutrition	(0.900,0.900,0.900)

ement), which the processor converts to black if a pixel has a gray level below a threshold value of 127, or to white if the pixel has a gray level of 127 or above. Then a single bit represents a pixel with black = 0 and white = 1 in the processed image. The scanned rectangular box is scaled to be 16 rows by 14 columns, for a total of 224 pixels, where each pixel value is 0 or 1 for black or white, respectively. Thus the pattern space for a digit has 224 attributes. We map the attribute/pattern space into a feature space of much lower dimension, as described below.

Figure 11e.1 shows a rectangle of 224 pixels with a neat handwritten digit that is an exemplar for the numeral seven. We start at the top left and number the rows downward from 0 to 15, and then we number the columns from left to right from 0 to 13. We reduce the number of features from the 224 black/white attributes as follows: (i) We use only rows numbered 1, 4, 7, 8, 11, 14 and only columns numbered 1, 4, 6, 7, 9, 12; (ii) starting from the left and moving across the rectangle in each of the six selected rows, we count the number of *changes* from black to white and from white to black to obtain the first six counts $c_1,..., c_6$; and (iii) starting from the top and moving down the selected columns, we count the number of changes in each to obtain six more counts $c_7,..., c_{12}$. For example, the first feature for the digit 7 shown in Figure 11e.1 is the number of changes in row 1 (the second row from the top—that is, row 1), which has value zero changes. Thus the first count for digit 7 is $c_1 = 0$.

Table 11e.1 presents the counts of changes, which are features that reduce the dimension of our patterns from 224 to 12 while retaining much of the information. The reason we count changes rather than the number of black (or white) pixels is that the width of the lines may vary, and we want to avoid performing the computationally intensive task of *skeletonization*––that is, reducing each character to lines of only one pixel in width. If characters are slightly rotated and translated, the features are affected, so the learning must be robust.

Figure 11e.1. A digit in a 16 × 14 pixel box.

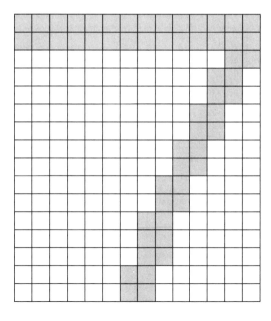

Table 11e.1.
Feature Counts for the Decimal Digits

Digit	Count of Changes	Outputs
0	(4, 3, 3, 2, 2, 4; 2, 3, 2, 2, 3, 2)	(0.1, 0.9)
1	(2, 2, 2, 2, 2, 2; 0, 0, 0, 0, 1, 0)	(0.2, 0.9)
2	(2, 1, 1, 2, 2, 1; 1, 3, 4, 4, 4, 3)	(0.3, 0.9)
3	(0, 2, 2, 2, 2, 2; 0, 3, 3, 4, 7, 4)	(0.4, 0.9)
4	(4, 4, 3, 0, 2, 2; 0, 3, 2, 2, 0, 2)	(0.5, 0.9)
5	(2, 2, 4, 1, 1, 2; 2, 4, 4, 4, 4, 3)	(0.5, 0.1)
6	(2, 2, 2, 3, 2, 2; 2, 5, 4, 4, 4, 4)	(0.6, 0.1)
7	(0, 2, 2, 2, 2, 2; 0, 1, 2, 3, 3, 1)	(0.7, 0.1)
8	(1, 3, 1, 1, 3, 3; 0, 7, 4, 4, 4, 4)	(0.8, 0.1)
9	(4, 4, 3, 6, 2, 2; 0, 4, 3, 4, 5, 1)	(0.9, 0.1)

Table 11e.2.
Dataset 6: The Feature Values for the Decimal Digits (12–12–2)

Digit	Feature Vector Values as Count Proportions	Outputs
0	(0.5, 0.375, 0.375, 0.25, 0.25, 0.5; 0.25, 0.375, 0.25, 0.25, 0.375, 0.25)	(0.1, 0.1)
1	(0.25, 0.25, 0.25, 0.25, 0.25, 0.25; 0.0, 0.0, 0.0, 0.0, 0.125, 0.0)	(0.2, 0.5)
2	(0.25, 0.125, 0.125, 0.25, 0.25, 0.125; 0.125, 0.375, 0.5, 0.5, 0.5, 0.375)	(0.3, 0.1)
3	(0.0, 0.25, 0.25, 0.25, 0.25, 0.25; 0.0, 0.375, 0.375, 0.5, 0.875, 0.5)	(0.4, 0.5)
4	(0.5, 0.5, 0.375, 0.0, 0.25, 0.25; 0.0, 0.375, 0.25, 0.25, 0.0, 0.25)	(0.5, 0.1)
5	(0.25, 0.25, 0.5, 0.125, 0.125, 0.25; 0.25, 0.5, 0.5, 0.5, 0.5, 0.375)	(0.5, 0.9)
6	(0.25, 0.25, 0.25, 0.375, 0.25, 0.25; 0.25, 0.625, 0.5, 0.5, 0.5, 0.5)	(0.6, 0.5)
7	(0.0, 0.25, 0.25, 0.25, 0.25, 0.25; 0.0, 0.125, 0.25, 0.375, 0.375, 0.125)	(0.7, 0.9)
8	(0.125, 0.375, 0.125, 0.125, 0.375, 0.375; 0.0, 0.875, 0.5, 0.5, 0.5, 0.5)	(0.8, 0.5)
9	(0.5, 0.5, 0.375, 0.75, 0.25, 0.25; 0.0, 0.5, 0.375, 0.5, 0.625, 0.125)	(0.9, 0.9)

The number of changes (black to white or white to black) is counted and divided by 8 to standardize the features (recall that standardized features must have values between 0 and 1). Table 11e.2 displays the actual standardized feature vectors, which also shows the two-components of the output vectors whose values have been chosen arbitrarily to yield 10 identifiers (desired output vectors) that are different from each other. All input zeros must be put to 0.1 for training MLPs.

11f. Dataset 7—The Ten5Ten Feature Vectors

The seventh dataset contains the exemplar input and output vectors for the 10–5–10 encoder that maps 10 vectors, each with the single nonzero entry of 1 in a unique component, through a bottleneck of five middle neurodes, into themselves again as output vectors. Table 11f.1 displays these data. The output vectors are the same as the input vectors and thus are not repeated. The zeros and ones have been replaced by 0.1 and 0.9, respectively, in the table.

Such datasets can be used to train MLPs to perform data compression. For example, an MLP that is trained on the 10–5–10 dataset can be used to compress 10-bit codewords into 5-bit codewords as outputs of the hidden layer, while the output layer would decompress the

Table 11f.1.
Dataset 7: The 10–5–10 Encoder Data (10–5–10)

Input Vector Number	Input Vector
1	(0.9, 0.1, 0.1, 0.1, 0.1, 0.1, 0.1, 0.1, 0.1, 0.1)
2	(0.1, 0.9, 0.1, 0.1, 0.1, 0.1, 0.1, 0.1, 0.1, 0.1)
3	(0.1, 0.1, 0.9, 0.1, 0.1, 0.1, 0.1, 0.1, 0.1, 0.1)
4	(0.1, 0.1, 0.1, 0.9, 0.1, 0.1, 0.1, 0.1, 0.1, 0.1)
5	(0.1, 0.1, 0.1, 0.1, 0.9, 0.1, 0.1, 0.1, 0.1, 0.1)
6	(0.1, 0.1, 0.1, 0.1, 0.1, 0.9, 0.1, 0.1, 0.1, 0.1)
7	(0.1, 0.1, 0.1, 0.1, 0.1, 0.1, 0.9, 0.1, 0.1, 0.1)
8	(0.1, 0.1, 0.1, 0.1, 0.1, 0.1, 0.1, 0.9, 0.1, 0.1)
9	(0.1, 0.1, 0.1, 0.1, 0.1, 0.1, 0.1, 0.1, 0.9, 0.1)
10	(0.1, 0.1, 0.1, 0.1, 0.1, 0.1, 0.1, 0.1, 0.1, 0.9)

5-bit codewords back into 10-bit codewords. More practically, a 16–8–16 dataset could be used for training to achieve a compression rate of two-to-one encoding of bytes. The data compression would be *lossy* in that there would be some loss of information due to the fact that the mapping is not one-to-one. A better scheme might be to use two MLPs of $N–M–J = 16–16–8$ and $N–M–J = 8–16–16$ to do nonlinear encoding (compression) and decoding (decompression).

11g. Datasets 8 and 9—The StockMarket20 and StockMarket40 Indicators

The StockMarket20 data have 12 features, or components, in the feature vectors that represent 12 different indicators for predicting a stock market item. The architecture for this data is $N–M–J = 12–24–1$ and $Q = 20$ exemplar pairs. The data are presented in Table 11g.1.

Table 11g.1.
Dataset 8: The StockMarket20 Indicator Data (12–24–1)

12 Input Indicator Features												Identifiers
0.880567	0.45	0.35	0.37	−0.39	0.731118	−0.824561	0.18	0.43	0.76	0.90	0.32	−0.110316
0.893726	0.46	0.26	0.35	−0.41	0.732628	−0.819549	0.17	0.49	0.72	0.79	0.32	−0.120296
0.911943	0.42	0.27	0.31	−0.12	0.732628	−0.892230	0.14	0.45	0.68	0.74	0.33	−0.108878
0.913968	0.44	0.28	0.32	0.17	0.732628	−0.909774	0.15	0.49	0.69	0.82	0.33	−0.148070
0.914980	0.35	0.21	0.28	0.20	0.747734	−0.927318	0.11	0.45	0.70	0.81	0.34	−0.034326
0.912955	0.27	0.16	0.21	0.36	0.750755	−0.933584	0.06	0.37	0.67	0.66	0.37	−0.017829
0.927126	0.40	0.27	0.25	0.44	0.749245	−0.953634	0.12	0.55	0.62	0.59	0.36	0.004941
0.915992	0.47	0.32	0.34	0.40	0.756798	−0.908521	0.17	0.62	0.65	0.70	0.35	−0.005600
0.904858	0.48	0.42	0.42	0.35	0.756798	−0.899749	0.22	0.60	0.71	0.87	0.35	−0.039291
0.900810	0.45	0.27	0.39	0.07	0.758308	−0.877193	0.20	0.60	0.69	0.87	0.36	−0.149010
0.895749	0.47	0.34	0.35	−0.18	0.750755	−0.889724	0.19	0.55	0.64	0.67	0.36	−0.163683
0.902834	0.43	0.29	0.36	−0.25	0.761329	−0.863409	0.18	0.51	0.64	0.66	0.34	−0.075914
0.910931	0.35	0.26	0.31	−0.24	0.758308	−0.877193	0.12	0.42	0.66	0.77	0.35	−0.161709
0.905870	0.27	0.16	0.24	−0.04	0.783988	−0.869674	0.08	0.36	0.69	0.78	0.35	0.046758
0.915992	0.27	0.20	0.21	0.04	0.779456	−0.849624	0.06	0.38	0.68	0.72	0.38	0.047917
0.913968	0.42	0.26	0.26	0.18	0.771903	−0.880952	0.12	0.57	0.69	0.70	0.38	0.025302
0.928138	0.32	0.16	0.24	0.24	0.785498	−0.902256	0.10	0.56	0.72	0.67	0.34	−0.008383
0.933198	0.36	0.30	0.26	0.36	0.774924	−0.934837	0.14	0.59	0.67	0.67	0.32	−0.254290
0.940283	0.47	0.30	0.34	0.20	0.770393	−0.928571	0.18	0.70	0.68	0.76	0.30	−0.410796
0.930162	0.42	0.25	0.32	0.07	0.765861	−0.903509	0.14	0.52	0.65	0.73	0.28	−0.381759

Table 11g.2.
Dataset 9: The StockMarket40 Indicator Data

12 Input Indicator Features												Identifiers
0.880567	0.45	0.35	0.37	−0.39	0.731118	−0.824561	0.18	0.43	0.76	0.90	0.32	−0.110316
0.893725	0.46	0.26	0.35	−0.41	0.732628	−0.819549	0.17	0.49	0.72	0.79	0.32	−0.120296
0.911943	0.42	0.27	0.31	−0.12	0.732628	−0.892231	0.14	0.45	0.68	0.74	0.33	−0.108878
0.913968	0.44	0.28	0.32	0.17	0.732628	−0.909774	0.15	0.49	0.69	0.82	0.33	−0.148070
0.914980	0.35	0.21	0.28	0.20	0.747734	−0.927318	0.11	0.45	0.70	0.81	0.34	−0.034326
0.912955	0.27	0.16	0.21	0.36	0.750755	−0.933584	0.06	0.37	0.67	0.66	0.37	−0.017829
0.927126	0.40	0.27	0.25	0.44	0.749245	−0.953634	0.12	0.55	0.62	0.59	0.36	0.004941
0.915992	0.47	0.32	0.34	0.40	0.756798	−0.908521	0.17	0.62	0.65	0.70	0.35	−0.005600
0.904858	0.48	0.42	0.42	0.35	0.756798	−0.899749	0.22	0.60	0.71	0.87	0.35	−0.039291
0.900810	0.45	0.27	0.39	0.07	0.758308	−0.877193	0.20	0.60	0.69	0.87	0.36	−0.149010
0.895749	0.47	0.34	0.35	−0.18	0.750755	−0.889724	0.19	0.55	0.64	0.67	0.36	−0.163683
0.902834	0.43	0.29	0.36	−0.25	0.761329	−0.863408	0.18	0.51	0.64	0.66	0.34	−0.075914
0.910931	0.35	0.26	0.31	−0.24	0.758308	−0.877193	0.12	0.42	0.66	0.77	0.35	−0.161709
0.905870	0.27	0.16	0.24	−0.04	0.783988	−0.869674	0.08	0.36	0.69	0.78	0.35	0.046758
0.915992	0.27	0.20	0.21	0.04	0.779456	−0.849624	0.06	0.38	0.68	0.72	0.38	0.047917
0.913968	0.42	0.26	0.26	0.18	0.771903	−0.880952	0.12	0.57	0.69	0.70	0.38	0.025302
0.928138	0.32	0.16	0.24	0.24	0.785498	−0.902256	0.10	0.56	0.72	0.67	0.34	−0.008383
0.933198	0.36	0.30	0.26	0.36	0.774924	−0.934837	0.14	0.59	0.67	0.67	0.32	−0.254210
0.940283	0.47	0.30	0.34	0.20	0.770392	−0.928571	0.18	0.70	0.68	0.76	0.30	−0.410796
0.930162	0.42	0.25	0.32	0.07	0.765861	−0.903509	0.14	0.52	0.65	0.73	0.28	−0.381759
0.919028	0.32	0.18	0.25	0.01	0.785498	−0.901002	0.10	0.45	0.61	0.71	0.28	−0.460307
0.907895	0.19	0.08	0.15	−0.06	0.812689	−0.878446	0.03	0.28	0.63	0.67	0.27	−0.421007
0.919028	0.18	0.17	0.14	0.09	0.847432	−0.862155	0.03	0.27	0.62	0.60	0.29	−0.057650
0.950405	0.30	0.23	0.23	0.20	0.838369	−0.928571	0.09	0.56	0.61	0.57	0.36	−0.038430
0.942308	0.25	0.28	0.29	0.22	0.877644	−0.874687	0.09	0.59	0.59	0.53	0.38	0.078891
0.942308	0.15	0.15	0.25	0.14	0.904834	−0.875940	0.04	0.33	0.56	0.46	0.36	0.192626
0.926113	0.39	0.47	0.36	0.03	0.854985	−0.941103	0.28	0.82	0.62	0.52	0.40	0.060550
0.927126	0.73	0.56	0.59	−0.25	0.833837	−0.942356	0.47	0.95	0.67	0.62	0.41	0.014264
0.942308	0.41	0.29	0.49	−0.48	0.862538	−0.913534	0.25	0.52	0.67	0.62	0.33	0.062783
0.911943	0.31	0.23	0.30	−0.49	0.870091	−0.894737	0.10	0.40	0.62	0.55	0.29	0.085671
0.911943	0.47	0.33	0.32	−0.62	0.842900	−0.909774	0.18	0.52	0.60	0.57	0.33	0.086062
0.917004	0.55	0.46	0.46	−0.41	0.839879	−0.870927	0.27	0.54	0.65	0.70	0.35	0.100905
0.910931	0.43	0.39	0.49	−0.16	0.847432	−0.825814	0.23	0.50	0.63	0.67	0.34	0.095703
0.898785	0.41	0.27	0.38	−0.14	0.845921	−0.784461	0.16	0.50	0.57	0.53	0.32	0.063242
0.897773	0.55	0.38	0.37	−0.14	0.823263	−0.818296	0.24	0.60	0.58	0.50	0.33	−0.103210
0.887652	0.55	0.26	0.37	−0.14	0.818731	−0.807017	0.24	0.59	0.61	0.53	0.31	−0.140979
0.891700	0.36	0.20	0.27	0.10	0.832326	−0.824561	0.11	0.41	0.59	0.50	0.29	−0.198751
0.899798	0.31	0.17	0.21	0.35	0.842900	−0.857143	0.07	0.38	0.54	0.44	0.27	−0.314794
0.895749	0.31	0.28	0.26	0.34	0.853474	−0.872180	0.08	0.38	0.51	0.44	0.25	−0.265603
0.896761	0.32	0.22	0.29	0.34	0.853474	−0.888471	0.10	0.42	0.55	0.54	0.23	−0.094185

Notice the negative values in the features that are necessary to accurately portray the indicators and the identifiers. While the input exemplar feature vectors consist of 12 feature indicators, the identifier is the single valued criterion that is to be predicted. These data are noisy and are not guaranteed to be separable into classes, but they may allow the prediction of values for the output variable.

The StockMarket40 dataset is similar to that of the StockMarket20, except that $Q = 40$ exemplar pairs. The architecture of $N–M–J = 12–24–1$ remains the same. The data are listed in Table 11g.2. These also represent 12 indicators for 40 consecutive weeks and the values for the single output variable.

Chapter 12

Pattern Recognition Applications

This chapter explores application possibilities that may suggest approaches to yet other applications.

12.1. Decisionmaking and Regression as Recognition

Decisionmaking

Decisionmaking is a general process of mapping input information into an output that represents a course of action, a class, a control command, or an item, each of which may be called a *decision*. Figure 12.1 shows the process. We let $\{\mathbf{x}^{(q)}\}$ denote the set of input vectors, where $\mathbf{x}^{(q)} = (x_1^{(q)},..., x_N^{(q)})$, and $\{\mathbf{d}^{(k)}\}$ designates the set of decisions, where $\mathbf{d}^{(k)} = (d_1^{(k)},..., d_J^{(k)})$. The process is equivalent to pattern recognition, where the inputs are feature vectors, the outputs are class identifiers, and the decisionmaking selects an output identifier based on the input feature vector and its own learned or given parameters.

Many situations can be posed as decisionmaking problems. For example, a guided missile reads the horizontal and vertical angles of the line-of-sight from the missile body axis to the target, both of which are between 0° and 90°. Given an input vector $\boldsymbol{\theta} = (\theta_h, \theta_v)$ of these angles, the problem is to find an output decision (identifier) $\mathbf{c} = (c_h, c_v)$ that consists of two component thrust commands c_h and c_v in the horizontal and vertical directions, respectively. The commands $\mathbf{c}$ approximate the class prototype commands that zero out the rates of change in the line-of-sight angles. This is *proportional navigation*, which was known to the ancient Phoenicians in the form that two approaching ships will collide whenever the angle between their paths remains constant.

Another example is where we want to construct the boundary around a region that contains a particular crop in an aerial photograph, while the regions around it contain different types of plant growth. Humans could view the photograph and draw a boundary that would

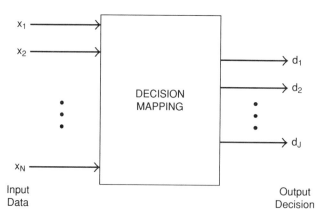

Figure 12.1. The decisionmaking process.

be sufficiently accurate most of the time, but suppose that we desire to automate the process. One approach is to process the photograph as a digital image of $N \times M$ pixels (picture elements, or dots on the screen), where each pixel takes a gray scale value from 0 (black) to 255 (white). Small rectangular blocks of pixels of fixed-size $N_1 \times M_1$ can be sampled sequentially, features of texture extracted, and a set of exemplars of feature vectors developed. Next, a feedforward artificial neural network (FANN) can be trained to recognize the texture classes to identify the crop. Once the FANN is trained to recognize the textures, a block of $N_1 \times M_1$ pixels can be passed across a row at a time and when the texture changes from one that represents the desired crop to one that does not, or from the latter to the former, a separating line segment can be drawn on the image. The block is moved across a row by advancing it two or more pixels at a time. In a similar fashion, the block is passed down each column and line segments are drawn on the image at appropriate locations.

Another example is the problem of making a decision as to whether or not to adjust interest rates by the US Federal Reserve Board to control inflation or deflation of the economy. This could be framed as a pattern classification and recognition problem. Features must be extracted from available information about the economy and a set of exemplar feature vectors $\{\mathbf{x}^{(q)}\}$ constructed. A set of output identifiers $\{\mathbf{t}^{(k(q))}\}$ must also be constructed to represent the interest rates for the various exemplar situations. The input components would be standardized to span the range from 0.0 to 1.0, exclusive of the endpoints. The identifiers must be paired with the input exemplars by means of historical and knowledge-based data. This must be done very carefully to arrive at an appropriate set of exemplar pairs that represent typical situations that worked properly historically to slow or accelerate economic growth. A FANN is then trained and tested so that it can put out the desired interest rate when an economic feature vector is put into it. This is an example of controlling a system by recognizing the state of the system from feature vectors and associating it with a corrective command to change it to a desired state.

Regression

Regression analysis is a process of determining the parameters of a mathematical function (model) so it can approximately map a set of given exemplar input points into a given set of output points. This association process is equivalent to recognition. The model is often a linear combination of basis functions so the parameters appear linearly. When a neural network is trained and tested on a good set of exemplar data that is sufficiently large to determine a solution set of weights, then it becomes a valid nonlinear model of a system that maps the given inputs to the desired outputs. Thus FANNs are tools for nonlinear regression analysis.

12.2. Texture Classification and Recognition

Texture and Features

Texture is a rather regular variation in gray levels of pixels that forms a repetitive pattern over a region of an image. The patterns that repeat are not necessarily identical for at least two reasons. First, there may be some randomness in the variation, and second, the pattern itself may be undergoing a change over space due to random or deterministic factors in the process that created the pattern. The changing texture may blend into a different texture. We discuss here some useful texture features.

A sample $N_1 \times M_1$ block of N_1 columns and M_1 rows gives rise to a histogram of the block pixels and its statistical moments that can be used as features. These features, however, provide no information about their spatial variation: Any remapping of those same gray level pixels to different pixel positions within the block would yield the same histogram (see Section 10.4, Example 10.2). Thus a large number of different block arrangements that represent different textures have the same histogram. Nonetheless, there is a need for a feature that describes the gray level distribution in a relative sense. The average squared deviation of gray levels g_l from the mean—that is, the mean-squared error—is one such feature. To that end we first take the block sample histogram mean

$$m = \sum_{(l=1, L)} g_l h(g_l) \tag{12.1}$$

where g_l is the *l*th gray level and $h(g_l)$ is the proportion of pixels at gray level g_l. The sample mean is then used to compute the sample histogram mean-squared error (variance), which is

$$s^2 = \sum_{(l=1, L)} (g_l - m)^2 h(g_l) \tag{12.2}$$

We can use s^2 to compute the *relative smoothness* feature of the $N_1 \times M_1$ block (Gonzales and Woods, 1992) via

$$R = 1 - 1/(1 + s^2) \tag{12.3}$$

For a constant gray level over the block, $s^2 = 0$ and so $R = 0$. As s^2 increases sufficiently, R approaches the asymptotic value of 1. It can be seen that any rearrangement within the block of the same pixel values of gray levels produces the same histogram and variance, and thus the same relative smoothness value, even though the local variation, and thus texture, are changed. Therefore the relative smoothness R is *invariant under rotation*; that is, if an image is rotated through an angle θ, then the block still has the same R value.

At each pixel in an $N_1 \times M_1$ block of pixels, there are eight directional derivatives, or differences, as shown in Figure 12.2. These are defined below in a counterclockwise order from angle $0°$ as differences between a fixed pixel $p(n, m)$ and its eight contiguous neighbors. Recalling that n is the column number along the horizontal x-axis and m is the row along the vertical y-axis, we have

$$d_1 = p(n + 1, m) - p(n, m)$$
$$d_2 = p(n + 1, m - 1) - p(n, m)$$
$$d_3 = p(n, m - 1) - p(n, m)$$
$$d_4 = p(n - 1, m - 1) - p(n, m)$$
$$d_5 = p(n - 1, m) - p(n, m)$$
$$d_6 = p(n - 1, m + 1) - p(n, m)$$
$$d_7 = p(n, m + 1) - p(n, m)$$
$$d_8 = p(n + 1, m + 1) - p(n, m) \tag{12.4}$$

We define the *mean-squared pixel variation* at any fixed pixel $p(n, m)$ to be

$$v_{nm}^2 = (1/8)\sum_{(j=1, 8)} d_j^2 \tag{12.5}$$

If a pixel is a boundary pixel of an image, then some of these differences do not exist, in which case the differences that exist are used and the factor $1/8$ is replaced by the appro-

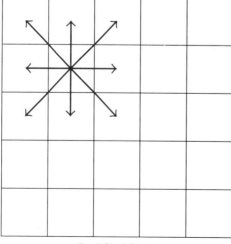

5 × 5 Pixel Block

Figure 12.2. The eight directions for pixel derivatives.

priate one in Equation (12.5). Thus for an $N_1 \times M_1$ block, we obtain an $N_1 \times M_1$ matrix of mean square pixel variational values $\{v_{nm}^2\}$ (one for each pixel). To combine this matrix into a single feature value that is rotation invariant, we compute the *blockwise total mean pixel variation*

$$m_{bv}^2 = (1/(N_1 M_1)) \sum_{(n=1, N)} \sum_{(m=1, M)} v_{nm}^2 \qquad (12.6)$$

The mean-squared error of the mean-squared pixel variation over the entire block is

$$s_{bv}^2 = (1/m_{bv}^2) \sum_{(n=1, N)} \sum_{(m=1, M)} (v_{nm}^2 - m_{bv}^2)^2 \qquad (12.7)$$

The blockwise total-mean squared pixel variation and mean-squared error are invariant to rotation of the image because a rotation does not change the set of directional derivatives. Similarly, the mean-squared error is also rotation-invariant. These features (Li, 1995) depend upon the *local* relative locations of gray levels and must change when there is a nonrotational redistribution of the pixel values within the block. They are also invariant under darkening or lightening of the entire image because they depend upon the differences of pixel values.

Image Block Moments as Texture Features

The moments of an $N \times M$ image provide texture features that are invariant under rotation, translation, and scaling (Hu, 1962). We can also apply these moments to any subimage, or $N_1 \times M_1$ block. Let $\{g(n, m)\}$ be the block of pixel gray level values. Then the pqth moments of order $p + q$ are

$$m_{pq} = \sum_{(n=1, N)} \sum_{(m=1, M)} n^p m^q g(n, m) \qquad (12.8)$$

The central pqth moments of order $p + q$ are

$$\mu_{pq} = \sum_{(n=1, N)} \sum_{(m=1, M)} (n - m_{10}/m_{00})^p (m - m_{01}/m_{00})^q g(n, m) \qquad (12.9)$$

The *normalized* central pqth moments are

$$\nu_{pq} = \mu_{pq}/(\mu_{00})^r \qquad (12.10)$$

where $r = 1 + (p + q)/2$ and $p + q \geq 2$. A set of five parameters that serve as texture features are

$$\phi_1 = \nu_{20} + \nu_{02} \qquad (12.11)$$

$$\phi_2 = (\nu_{20} - \nu_{02})^2 + 4\nu_{11}^2 \qquad (12.12)$$

$$\phi_3 = (\nu_{30} - 3\nu_{12})^2 + (3\nu_{21} - \nu_{03})^2 \qquad (12.13)$$

$$\phi_4 = (\nu_{30} + \nu_{12})^2 + (\nu_{21} - \nu_{03})^2 \qquad (12.14)$$

$$\phi_5 = (\nu_{30} - 3\nu_{12})(\nu_{30} + \nu_{12})[(\nu_{30} + \nu_{12})^2 - 3(\nu_{21} + \nu_{03})^2]$$
$$+ (3\nu_{21} - \nu_{03})(\nu_{21} + \nu_{03})[3(\nu_{30} + \nu_{12})^2 - (\nu_{21} + \nu_{03})^2] \qquad (12.15)$$

These are the first five of seven such moments due to Hu (1962) that are listed in Gonzales and Woods (1992, p. 516). They are defined in terms of the same normalized central moments up to order 3.

Growing Regions via Texture Recognition

The approach taken here was developed in Chen (1995). It extracts texture features from $N_1 \times N_1$ blocks of image pixels to form a fairly large sample $\{\mathbf{x}^{(p)}\}_{p=1, P}$ of feature vectors. This sample may contain feature vectors from blocks that overlap regions of different textures. Therefore we must do a preliminary clustering of the feature vectors into a large number of small subclasses by means of the *dog–rabbit* (see Section 7.3), the *k-means* (see Section 1.2), or other self-organizing algorithm. We select a prototype $\mathbf{x}^{(q)}$ from each qth subcluster to form the set $\{\mathbf{x}^{(q)}\}_{q=1, Q}$ of exemplar feature vectors. The output layer of a radial basis function network (RBFN) joins (ORs) the subclasses together into the required classes.

If we use an RBFN, then each of the exemplar feature vectors in $\{\mathbf{x}^{(q)}\}$ may be used as the center of a radial basis function. The architecture for the N–M–J network is designed as follows: (i) N is given by the number of texture features being used, which may include the relative smoothness, the block mean pixel variation and mean-squared error, and perhaps the first four block moments of Equations (12.11) through (12.14); (ii) $M = Q$ is the number of clusters (subclasses) of textures; and (iii) J is taken to be $\log_2(K)$, where K is the number of classes of textures. In this case we may not know K, so a number that is greater than what is required may be used. For example, if there appears to be 10 textures in an image, then we could take $K = 16$ or $K = 32$ with $J = 4$ or $J = 5$, respectively. We also need to construct an identifier vector $\mathbf{t}^{(k(q))}$ of J components for each exemplar feature vector $\mathbf{x}^{(q)}$, $q = 1,..., Q$. Then we train the RBFN on $\{\mathbf{x}^{(q)}, \mathbf{t}^{(k(q))}\}$ to recognize textures.

Once an RBFN or RBF-RVFLN is trained with the exemplar pairs $\{(\mathbf{x}^{(q)}, \mathbf{t}^{(k(q))})\}$ and a small value of σ^2 such as $\sigma^2 = 0.01$ ($\sigma = 0.1$), then the training must be tested. When a properly trained network is ready for the region growing process, an $N_1 \times N_1$ block is then moved over the image and tests are made of the texture in regions. The region growing begins from the current block, which we call a *seed* block. An $N_1 \times N_1$ *test block* overlaps the seed block by r pixels, and its feature values are put through the RBFN to identify its texture. If the texture is the same as that of the seed block, then the $N_1 \times N_1$ test block is moved up r pixels and the new texture feature vector is identified. As long as the texture remains in the same class, the test block is moved sequentially around the seed block in a counter-clockwise motion as shown in Figure 12.3. After a circuit is completed, the test block is moved to the right r pixels more and the counterclockwise sequence is repeated again. Another strategy is to move the test block horizontally from the seed block to find a different texture class and mark it. After that, the same thing is done with vertical movements. Block size is important to capturing the features of a texture and they should not be too small.

Application to Seismic Sections

Figure 12.4 presents two images of a seismic section that is obtained by setting off explosions at surface points along a ground line and receiving the reflected shock waves at other

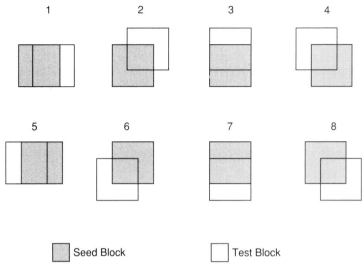

Figure 12.3. Region growing movement of test block around a seed block.

points along the line. The times of receipt of the reflected waves from different subterranean boundaries are used to adjust the depths of the boundaries so that boundary "features" are made visible. Experienced humans can look at these images and determine important boundaries where regions have been pushed up. It is these pushed-up regions where it is more likely that petroleum can be found.

Figure 12.4. An image of a seismic section. (a) Original Image (b) Image with Boundary Drawn by Human Expert.

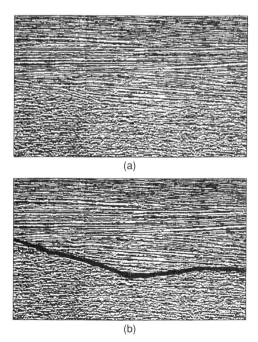

In Figure 12.4(a), the top and bottom halves of the image contain different textures. The boundary of these different textures is near mid-height on the left-hand side of the image, but curves downward as we move to the right, until a minimum is achieved about halfway across the image. Then the boundary rises upward again. In Figure 12.4(b), a human has drawn in a perceived boundary.

An open problem that has not been solved thus far is to automate the recognition of these types of boundaries and the construction of artificial lines on the important boundaries that separate the regions of different textures. Chen's observation (Chen, 1995) that features are different on the two sides of important boundaries is verified in the image shown in Figure 12.4. We have not yet tested the approach described above.

Application to Identification of Human Faces

The search for human faces in images is a difficult task based on facial features because of age, racial and gender differences, variations within these groups and locations, and variations in the sizes of the faces. Textures of skin and hair are used by Augusteijn and Skufca (1993) to either find human faces in an image or determine that none exist. They use second-order statistics of gray levels defined in Haralick et al. (1973) and Weszka et al. (1976) as texture features. They trained a *cascade correlation* FANN (see Chapter 5 and Appendix 5b) to recognize texture feature vectors. In such networks, the initial architecture contains only the input nodes and a layer of output neurodes that are trained first on the exemplar pairs. Then an extra hidden layer of only one neurode is adjoined and trained, and this is repeated until the network has learned sufficiently accurately. Appendix 5b describes the process. This has some advantages over *backpropagation*.

Their study used eight of the 14 features derived in Haralick et al. (1973), which are: (i) *angular second moment* to measure the homogeneity of the texture; (ii) *contrast*, to measure the local variation in the texture; (iii) *correlation* to measure the linear dependence; (iv) *inverse difference moment* to further measure contrast; (v) *entropy* to measure the quantity of texture randomness; (vi) *sum entropy* to also measure randomness; (vii) *difference entropy* to further measure randomness properties; and (viii) *sum average*. The feature vectors also contained the gray level mean and standard deviation of pixels for a total of 10 features. The size of the test blocks were 16×16 pixels.

A set of photographs of 45 people were used in the training with three poses taken for each person. The group of people included 28 males and 17 females of various ages, hair color, and skin tone. Image blocks of 16×16 pixels were selected from the photographs. They contained hair, skin, and other textures. Anything other than skin or hair was classified as "other" in a default class.

In the first experiment, the network was trained on blocks from a single photograph and tested on a set of different photographs of the same person. The correct recognition rate was from 83.3% to 100%, with an average of 94.4%. The second experiment used sets of photographs of four different people. The average correct rate for the first group of all brunette females was 82.4%. For the second and third groups of combined brunettes and blondes, and male and female, the average correct rates were 80.7% and 77.3%, respectively. A third experiment used combined groups of four, eight, and twelve people in three separate runs that yielded average correct rates of 82.4%, 83.6% and 84.4%, respectively.

12.3. An Experiment in Learning a Chaotic Sequence

A *chaotic* sequence of real numbers is a sequence that appears to be a random sequence from a probability distribution, but it is actually generated by a deterministic function. The pseudo-random number generators that are used in computer compilers are examples. They generate cyclic sequences of a large length (at least several millions). We use here the simple generator

$$r_{k+1} = cr_k(1 - r_k) \tag{12.16}$$

where the initial value r_0 that starts the sequence satisfies $0 < r_0 < 1$. From

$$f(r) = r(1 - r) = r - r^2$$
$$f'(r) = 1 - 2r = 0$$

we obtain the maximum at $r = 0.5$ ($f''(r) = -2 < 0$). Thus $r_k(1 - r_k)$ takes its maximum of $(0.5)(1 - 0.5) = 0.25$ at $r_k = 0.5$. We can take the constant c to be anywhere strictly between 1 and 4 to keep the sequence strictly between 0 and 1. With $c = 2.0$ we cannot let r_0 be 0.5 because $2(0.5)(1 - 0.5) = 0.5$, and this would generate a constant sequence (0.5 is a *fixed point*).

Figures 12.5 through 12.10 show plots of six sequences where c and r_0 take the respective values shown under the captions. The horizontal axis represents time over 636 iterates, while the vertical axis goes from 0.0 to 1.0 for the values of the sequence. Some of the graphs appear to have multiple lines, but these graphs only plot the sequence points rather than the lines connecting them. Thus the plots of the sequence values appear to form multi-

Figure 12.5. Chaotic sequence 1 ($r_0 = 0.1$, $c = 3.0$).

Figure 12.6. Chaotic sequence 2 ($r_0 = 0.1$, $c = 3.5$).

ple horizontal lines as they jump up and down. In Figure 12.7, two bands of pseudorandom values appear, which spread out into a single large band in Figure 12.10.

Table 12.1 presents 460 consecutive values of the initial segment of the chaotic sequence shown in Figure 12.10, which appear to be the most difficult to learn. We break the data into segments of 12 consecutive values where each segment is taken to be an exemplar input vector. The output value associated with an input exemplar vector is the next value in the chaotic sequence after the twelfth input of the sequential segment.

We would normally use a multiple-layered perceptron (MLP) network to learn the chaotic data by approximating $f(r)$ on the range 0 to 1 with a single input and single output on, say,

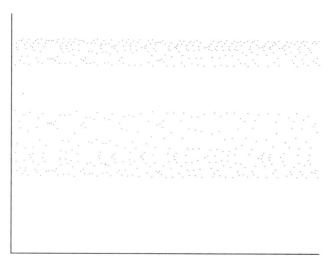

Figure 12.7. Chaotic sequence 3 ($r_0 = 0.1$, $c = 3.6$).

Figure 12.8. Chaotic sequence
4 ($r_0 = 0.1$, $c = 3.56$).

0.04, 0.08, 0.12,..., 0.96. But we decided to make the task difficult by using a radial basis
function network (RBFN) to predict the next output given the previous 12 outputs. RBFNs
are not as good for approximating functions because they require too many hidden neurodes
to obtain reasonable accuracy.

The training was done on 32 exemplars taken from a sliding window as follows: The
first 12 values in the chaotic sequence were taken as the input window, and the next value
in the sequence, the thirteenth, was taken as the output value. Then the window was moved
one value to the right to obtain the second input exemplar input vector, and so forth. After
the training, we tested some randomly selected contiguous segments of length 12 as input

Figure 12.9. Chaotic sequence
5 ($r_0 = 0.25$, $c = 3.56$).

Figure 12.10. Chaotic sequence 6 ($r_0 = 0.1$, $c = 3.68$).

vectors and compared the predicted outputs against the actual outputs of the chaotic sequence. Table 12.2 shows the results. The last four sequential values shown in Table 12.2 were well past the data upon which the network trained. The problem was, in effect, to predict the next (the thirteenth) pseudorandom number after having been given the previous 12 sequential numbers. A larger network could have learned more accurately.

12.4. Picking Winners of Football Games

A study to predict the outcomes of football games appeared in Walczak and Krause (1993) and used six input components ($N = 6$), a single output neurode ($J = 1$), and two hidden layers of six and two neurodes, respectively ($L = 6$, $M = 2$). The 6–6–2–1 MLP used the following input components: (i) Associated Press rank of Team A; (ii) a motivation factor; (iii) the point spread given by bookmakers; (iv) the AP ranking of Team B (the opponent); and (v) the two win/lose ratios of Teams A and B to date in the current season. The single output predicts the point spread. The motivation factor is determined by heuristic rules based on such conditions as a team playing a team that is ranked higher, losing the previous week, playing after three or more losses, homecoming event, and so on. All inputs are normalized to fall inside the interval [0,1].

For each team, a neural network is trained from its history to date in the current season. Because of this, no reliable predictions can be made on (at least) the first three games of the season. After that, however, the networks can be trained to predict the point spreads of upcoming games. Walczak and Krause note that because the exemplar dataset is small, the network architecture must be small (so as not to be too underdetermined by the small dataset). They use the strategy of waiting until a time in the season where enough data have been generated to train the MLPs. They then predict the point spread for each game and compare it with the point spread given by bookmakers. If the point spread predicted by the MLP is low and the point spread given by the bookmakers is high, then they bet on the team expected

Table 12.1.
A Table of Sequential Values

0.100000	0.331200	0.815144	0.554518	0.909062	0.304218	0.778944	0.633661	0.854256	0.458170
0.913561	0.290600	0.758638	0.673832	0.808799	0.569087	0.902435	0.324008	0.806019	0.575377
0.899091	0.333872	0.818438	0.546830	0.911927	0.295565	0.766199	0.659229	0.826698	0.527228
0.917272	0.279254	0.740678	0.706832	0.762572	0.666287	0.818244	0.547294	0.911769	0.296042
0.766917	0.657820	0.828341	0.523267	0.918008	0.276991	0.736983	0.713328	0.752528	0.685325
0.793609	0.602760	0.881140	0.385414	0.871682	0.411618	0.891254	0.356666	0.844395	0.483522
0.919001	0.273933	0.731929	0.722049	0.738555	0.710577	0.756819	0.677282	0.804341	0.579145
0.896949	0.340148	0.825967	0.528985	0.916908	0.280369	0.742486	0.703618	0.767426	0.656820
0.829500	0.520461	0.918459	0.275602	0.734695	0.717299	0.746235	0.696876	0.777363	0.636898
0.851033	0.466534	0.915879	0.283526	0.747551	0.694484	0.780807	0.629822	0.857978	0.448414
0.910207	0.300767	0.773926	0.643869	0.843831	0.484952	0.919167	0.273421	0.731077	0.723501
0.736174	0.714737	0.750309	0.689432	0.787946	0.614881	0.871432	0.412300	0.891696	0.355393
0.843047	0.486934	0.919372	0.272789	0.730020	0.725294	0.733213	0.719851	0.742128	0.704256
0.766469	0.658699	0.827318	0.525735	0.917563	0.278360	0.739222	0.709403	0.758633	0.673841
0.808788	0.569112	0.902423	0.324046	0.806068	0.575266	0.899153	0.333692	0.818217	0.547355
0.911748	0.296107	0.767014	0.657628	0.828564	0.522727	0.918099	0.276710	0.736522	0.714132
0.751263	0.687670	0.790391	0.609677	0.875733	0.400475	0.883549	0.378636	0.865796	0.427591
0.900706	0.329121	0.812545	0.560521	0.906521	0.311846	0.789720	0.611108	0.874570	0.403686
0.885863	0.372084	0.859786	0.443638	0.908310	0.306481	0.782186	0.626966	0.860677	0.441276
0.907310	0.309484	0.786429	0.618086	0.868685	0.419783	0.896320	0.341984	0.828113	0.523817
0.917913	0.277285	0.737464	0.712487	0.753845	0.682871	0.796934	0.595536	0.886413	0.370522
0.858307	0.447548	0.909876	0.301767	0.775390	0.640910	0.846931	0.477071	0.918065	0.276815
0.736693	0.713833	0.751734	0.686799	0.791591	0.607108	0.877783	0.394790	0.879266	0.390659
0.876004	0.399725	0.882997	0.380192	0.867177	0.423866	0.898669	0.335111	0.819947	0.543293
0.913103	0.291994	0.760779	0.669739	0.813974	0.557227	0.907948	0.307568	0.783729	0.623753
0.863642	0.433374	0.903665	0.320362	0.801247	0.586040	0.892757	0.352329	0.839752	0.495213
0.919916	0.271109	0.727200	0.730039	0.725262	0.733265	0.719761	0.742274	0.703996	0.766859
0.657933	0.828210	0.523584	0.917953	0.277159	0.737259	0.712846	0.753283	0.683919	0.795519
0.598619	0.884209	0.376770	0.864117	0.432100	0.903034	0.322234	0.803710	0.580559	0.896118
0.342573	0.828798	0.522163	0.918193	0.276423	0.736050	0.714953	0.749967	0.690061	0.787067
0.616741	0.869847	0.416624	0.894418	0.347518	0.834437	0.508398	0.919740	0.271650	0.728111
0.728512	0.727839	0.728970	0.727068	0.730259	0.724889	0.733884	0.718697	0.743991	0.700924
0.771437	0.648864	0.838449	0.498463	0.919991	0.270875	0.726806	0.730697	0.724146	0.735111
0.716580	0.747382	0.694791	0.780368	0.630730	0.857108	0.450705	0.911057	0.298197	0.770134
0.651462	0.835578	0.505586	0.919885	0.271203	0.727359	0.729773	0.725711	0.732520	0.721038
0.740203	0.707674	0.761288	0.668761	0.815192	0.554407	0.909107	0.304084	0.778750	0.634058
0.853865	0.459188	0.913871	0.289657	0.757181	0.676597	0.805234	0.577142	0.898100	0.336779
0.821961	0.538536	0.914535	0.287631	0.754030	0.682525	0.797400	0.594517	0.887125	0.368494
0.856359	0.452672	0.911757	0.296079	0.766972	0.657712	0.828467	0.522963	0.918059	0.276833
0.736723	0.713782	0.751815	0.686649	0.791797	0.606666	0.878131	0.393824	0.878514	0.392756
0.877676	0.395089	0.879497	0.390015	0.875484	0.401163	0.884051	0.377217	0.864522	0.431015
0.902487	0.323854	0.805820	0.575826	0.898842	0.334605	0.819332	0.544740	0.912634	0.293418
0.762952	0.665550	0.819142	0.545185	0.912487	0.293866	0.763632	0.664233	0.820741	0.541421
0.913686	0.290218	0.758049	0.674952	0.807362	0.572346	0.900739	0.329022	0.812421	0.560807
0.906393	0.312228	0.790250	0.609979	0.875489	0.401150	0.884042	0.377245	0.864546	0.430950
0.902454	0.323953	0.805948	0.575537	0.899002	0.334133	0.818757	0.546090	0.912183	0.294788

to lose. In case the point spread predicted by the MLP is high and the bookmaker point spread is low, then they bet on the favored team.

Figure 12.11 shows the MLP used. Table 12.3 presents the predictions for the 1993–1994 Penn State football season. It can be seen that the predictions for the first three games were based on insufficient data and would have resulted in losses if they had been bet on (the dash denotes that bets are not made on the first three games). For the following seven games,

Table 12.2.
Results of Random Testing of the Trained RBF Network

Output of Chaotic Sequence	Output of RBF Network
0.826698	0.791651
0.736983	0.768928
0.756819	0.829606
0.734695	0.740747
0.843947	0.842645
0.758633	0.790691
0.918099	0.908469
0.786429	0.808448
0.801247	0.802564
0.416019	0.453336
0.501565	0.450843
0.727466	0.771799

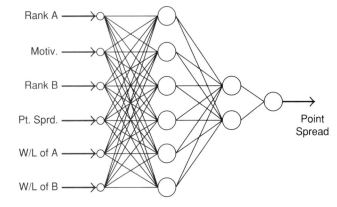

Figure 12.11. A 6–6–2–1 MLP for football game point spreads.

Table 12.3.
Results for the 1993–1994 Penn State Season

Bookmaker Spread	MLP Predicted Spread	Point Spread of Actual Game	Bet Result
5.5	17.0	1	Lose (no play)
5.5	5.0	31	Lose (no play)
14.0	9.0	24	Lose (no play)
17.5	34.5	63	Win
5.5	69.5	−8	Lose
−3.5	−26.5	−18	Win
11.0	−11.5	7	Win
10.0	27.0	14	Win
17.5	17.0	22	Lose (too close to bet)
4.5	3.0	1	Win (too close to bet)

however, the MLP predicted correctly five times out of seven, which could have yielded a considerable profit. In practice, no bets would have been placed on the last two games because there are not sufficient differences between the bookmaker point spreads and those predicted by the MLP. Note that the networks must be retrained after the results from each week of games are available.

12.5. Neural Processing of Digital Images

Edges and Images Smooth and Sharp

An *image* is an $N \times M$ array of *pixels* (picture elements) that we take here to be gray levels that vary between 0 (black, or zero intensity) and 255 (white, or full intensity). *Edges* in an image are contiguous regions where the gray levels change strongly when moving between pixels in a particular direction. Figure 12.12 shows an image block where there is an edge caused by a sharp change of gray levels in the pixels when moving horizontally, vertically, or diagonally. A *sharp* image is one that has rather strong changes in gray levels in the eight directions (see Figure 12.2). A *smooth* image has more gradual changes in the gray levels in the various directions. Figure 12.13 shows a smoother version of the image block of Figure 12.12. Its changes around the "edge" region are more gradual.

The process of *smoothing* an image or image block is to make the changes required to convert Figure 12.12 into Figure 12.13. The process of *sharpening* an image is to convert in the opposite direction—that is, from Figure 12.13 to Figure 12.12. The process of *edge detection* in an image block is (i) to recognize edges in one or more of the eight directions $\{0°, 45°, 90°, 135°, 180°, 225°, 270°, 315°\}$ and (ii) to change the edge pixels to white (0) and to darken all other pixels (or the reverse).

Figure 12.12. Sharp image block (to be smoothed).

Figure 12.13. Smooth image block (to be sharpened).

Neural Recognition of Edges

A neural network approach to edge detection was taken by Etemad and Chellappa (1993). The motivation was to develop a method that is fast, simple, nonlinear, independent of edge strength, and robust, extends to corner detection and line detection, and incorporates a degree of context without going to lower resolution. Additionally, the method can be efficiently implemented in parallel processors.

The problem is broken into two parts: (i) For any primitive block (such as 3×3 or 5×5) of pixels, associate it with a block of the same size that distinguishes the most likely edges; and (ii) combine the information of neighboring blocks into a consistent pattern that is more global. Some primitive (exemplar) blocks and their associated output exemplar blocks are shown in Figure 12.14. There must be sufficiently many exemplar pairs for proper training, so they use eight levels of gray pixels between 0 to 255 in the primitive blocks. The MLP interpolates between these.

Each pixel gray level in a 3×3 primitive block is input as a component of a nine-dimensional feature vector to an MLP type of neural network. The input feature values are normalized to fall strictly between 0 and 1. The network architecture is $N\text{--}M\text{--}J = 9\text{--}12\text{--}10$. The reason that there is an extra output neurode is that the tenth output neurode is a linear neurode that denotes the *strength* of the edge (between 0 and 1). Weak and parasitic edges are to have strength values near zero, while strong edges should have strength values near unity.

In the processing of an image, the first 3×3 block is chosen from the image starting at the upper left. After that block is processed via the trained MLP, a second block is selected by shifting one pixel to the right and that block is put through the network. When the last block on the right side of this first row has been fed through the network, the next block is obtained by moving all the way back to the left and down a single pixel. All rows are

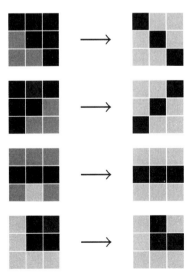

Figure 12.14.   Primitive block examples and their associated output blocks.

processed similarly until the entire image has been processed. This completes the first part of the problem solution.

To do the second part, Etemad and Chellappa (1993) use a special technique for combining the information from the local blocks into global edges. Each interior pixel (not on an image boundary) appears in nine different 3×3 blocks (or in 25 different 5×5 blocks). In one block it is the center pixel, but it occupies other positions in the other blocks. If a pixel is recognized as being an edge pixel when it is not the center block pixel, then it gets one "yes" vote, or otherwise it gets one "no" vote. When it is a center pixel, it gets two "yes" or "no" votes, respectively, which reflects the importance of the center position. A majority vote wins and either makes the pixel an edge or nonedge pixel. Edge pixels are given the black gray level by Etemad and Chellappa, while nonedge pixels are converted to white, so that the final image is white with black lines that compose a drawing. They note that Moura and Martin (1991) used neural networks for edge enhancement, but not for detection, which is what their above-described process does.

Neural Smoothing and Sharpening

Fuzzy rules were used in Russo and Ramponi (1992) to sharpen images while simultaneously suppressing noise. To illustrate sharpening, we assume gray levels from 0 to 255 and a block size of 3×3 pixels. One block at a time is selected from the image, starting from the top left. After the first block is processed, the block is moved one pixel to the right, and so on, until that row of pixels has been processed. The block is then moved back to the left side of the image and down one pixel, and that new row is processed similarly. Each pixel, unless it is on the image boundary (in which case it need not be processed), is processed as the center of a block in this manner. The center pixel of the current block is processed based on information contained in the neighboring (adjacent) pixels.

To process the center pixel of a 3×3 block, Russo and Ramponi (1992) first compute the differences of the block pixels from the center pixel at position (n, m) via

$$\delta(j, k) = p(n + j, m + k) - p(n, m) \tag{12.17}$$

for $j = -1, 0, 1$ and $k = -1, 0, 1$. Thus the gray level differences are defined via

$$\delta(-1,-1) = p(n - 1, m - 1) - p(n, m); \qquad \delta(0,-1) = p(n, m - 1) - p(n, m);$$

$$\delta(1, -1) = p(n + 1, m - 1) - p(n, m)$$

$$\delta(-1,0) = p(n - 1, m) - p(n, m); \qquad \delta(0,0) = p(n, m) - p(n, m);$$

$$\delta(1, 0) = p(n + 1, m) - p(n, m)$$

$$\delta(-1,1) = p(n - 1, m + 1) - p(n, m); \qquad \delta(0,1) = p(n, m + 1) - p(n, m);$$

$$\delta(1, 1) = p(n + 1, m + 1) - p(n, m)$$

We note that n is along the x-axis (columns) and m is along the y-axis (rows). For each (n,m)th pixel with gray level $p(n, m)$, its gray level difference matrix is

$$\begin{array}{ccc} \delta(-1,-1) & \delta(0,-1) & \delta(1,-1) \\ \delta(-1,0) & \delta(0,0) & \delta(1,0) \\ \delta(-1,1) & \delta(0,1) & \delta(1,1) \end{array} \qquad (12.18)$$

Eight matrix entries (all except the center one that is zero) are the inputs to fuzzy rules, each of which is to yield a single output difference

$$\Delta(n, m) = g(n, m) - p(n, m) \qquad (12.19)$$

where $g(n, m)$ is the processed (new) pixel value and $p(n, m)$ is the original one. In other words, $\Delta(n, m)$ is the difference between the desired new output pixel value and the old one, so we can add it to the old value to obtain

$$p(n, m) + \Delta(n, m) = p(n, m) + [g(n, m) - p(n, m)] = g(n, m) \qquad (12.20)$$

For each fixed (n, m)th pixel not on the boundary and with gray level $p(n, m)$ at the center of a block, there is an associated block of eight gray level differences $\{ \delta(j, k) : j, k = -1, 0, 1; (j, k) \neq (0,0) \}$. Russo and Ramponi (1992) put each of these gray level differences through the five fuzzy set membership functions for the respective linguistic variables shown in Figure 12.15, which are LARGE_NEGATIVE, SMALL_NEGATIVE, ZERO, SMALL_POSITIVE, LARGE_POSITIVE.

Each fuzzy rule is a conjunction (ANDing) of eight conditions: one for each of the eight block differences $\delta(j, k)$ (except the center one, $\delta(0, 0)$, which is always zero). Thus the fuzzy rules have a format such as

IF $[(\delta(-1, -1)$ is SMALL POSITIVE) AND $(\delta(0, -1)$ is ZERO) AND $(\delta(1, -1)$ is LARGE NEGATIVE)
   AND $(\delta(-1, 0)$ is SMALL NEGATIVE) AND ... AND $(\delta(1,1)$ is LARGE POSITIVE)]
THEN $[\Delta(n, m)$ is SMALL NEGATIVE] $\qquad (12.21)$

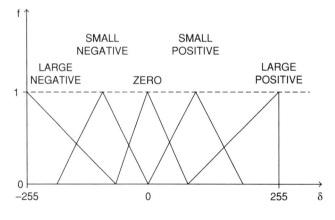

Figure 12.15. The fuzzy set membership functions for pixel differences δ.

Russo and Ramponi simplify the notation by using $=, -, 0, +, +$ in place of LARGE NEGATIVE, SMALL NEGATIVE, ZERO, SMALL POSITIVE, and LARGE POSITIVE, respectively. Thus Rule (12.21) given above may be represented by

$$\begin{matrix} + & 0 & = \\ - & x & \\ x & x & + \end{matrix} \rightarrow -$$

Here x represents an unknown linguistic variable (not specified in the exemplar rule given above). Because each difference $\delta(j, k)$ may have nonnegligible fuzzy truths for multiple linguistic variables, multiple sets of conditions may be activated with fuzzy truths. Thus r rules are invoked and each yields an output difference $\Delta_r(n, m)$. To arrive at a single output difference $\Delta(n, m)$ to add onto the old value $p(n, m)$, defuzzification must be done on the multiple output differences $\{\Delta_r(n, m)\}$. Figure 12.16 presents the output fuzzy set membership functions for $\Delta(n, m)$. When the defuzzified difference $\Delta(n, m)$ is obtained, we compute the new pixel value via $g(n, m) = p(n, m) + \Delta(n, m)$.

Russo and Ramponi sharpen images via two fuzzy rules that are appropriate whenever the gray level differences are reasonably large. For example, if a pixel $p(n, m)$ is darker than its neighboring pixels in a 3×3 block centered on $p(n, m)$, then the differences are positive. If we take the output difference $\Delta(n, m)$ to be negative in this case, then the new pixel $g(n, m) = p(n, m) + \Delta(n, m)$ becomes darker. This enhances the contrast and therefore sharpens the image. These two rules apply only when the differences are LARGE POSITIVE or LARGE NEGATIVE; in either of these cases, the difference is LARGE NEGATIVE or LARGE POSITIVE, respectively, as defined by

Rule 1   *Rule 2*

$$\begin{matrix} + & + & + \\ + & & + \\ + & + & + \end{matrix} \rightarrow = \qquad\qquad \begin{matrix} = & = & = \\ = & & = \\ = & = & = \end{matrix} \rightarrow +$$

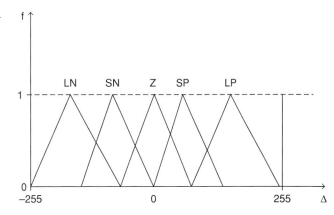

Figure 12.16. Output difference fuzzy sets.

Because these rules are equivalent to a high pass filter, they amplify high frequency noise such as "salt and pepper" noise. To avoid this, Russo and Ramponi use 10 other smoothing rules to reduce the difference in gray level of a pixel $p(n, m)$ from its neighbors in a 5×5 block when the differences were originally fairly small. This smooths the image. An example of one of these rules contains all "+" (SMALL POSITIVE) values and another contains all "−" (SMALL NEGATIVE) values. Others may have mostly all "+" or "−" values. The ones used by Russo and Ramponi are

	Rule 3								*Rule 4*					
+	+	+	+	+				−	−	−	−	−		
+	+	+	+	+				−	−	−	−	−		
+	+		+	+	→	+		−	−		−	−	→	−
+	+	+	+	+				−	−	−	−	−		
+	+	+	+	+				−	−	−	−	−		

	Rule 5								*Rule 6*					
+	+	+	−	−				−	−	−	+	+		
+	+	+	−	−				−	−	−	+	+		
+	+		−	−	→	+		−	−		+	+	→	−
+	+	+	−	−				−	−	−	+	+		
+	+	+	−	−				−	−	−	+	+		

In addition to smoothing Rules 3, 4, 5, and 6, the three other rotations of each of Rules 5 and 6 are used, so that there are a total of 10 smoothing rules. An extension of the smoothing rules to a set of 34 rules appears in Russo and Ramponi (1995). An example is Rule 11, while Rule 12 is the entrywise complement of Rule 11. All rotations of both of these rules are included in the set.

	Rule 11					
+	+	+	+	+		
+	+	+	+	−		
+	+		−	−	→	+
+	+	−	−	−		
+	−	−	−	−		

In related research, Russo (1993) uses fuzzy rules for smoothing images. We observe that the representation of these rules is highly suggestive of a neural network application. Figure 12.17 presents one such set of rules, where each 5×5 neighborhood block on the left maps into the single center pixel output on the right. Additionally, all rotations and complements of these are also rules. There are two other rules: All dark (light) noncentral pixels in a block imply a dark (respectively, light) center pixel. If none of these rules apply, then the output pixel is set at medium gray level. An MLP architecture that seems appropriate is $N–M–J = 25–8–1$.

In related research by Henson-Mack (1996), a special type of fuzzy histogram equalization was done on an image as a first pass to equalize the distribution of the gray level pix-

Figure 12.17. Rules for smoothing an image.

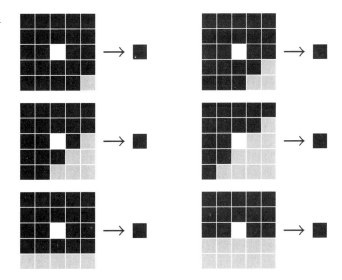

els. She used the clustering fuzzy expected value in the equalization. Regular equalization redistributes the gray levels of the $N \times M$ pixels of an image so that each gray level occurs approximately the same number of times (equal frequency). Fuzzy equalizations where the fuzzy average is used do not work well sometimes. Other types of fuzzy expected values work better. The differences between the gray levels and fuzzy type of expected value are mapped to new gray levels using fuzzy logic.

12.6. Image Compression as Recognition

The Image Compression Problem

Given an $N_x \times M_y$ image of N_x columns (x-axis) and M_y rows (y-axis) of pixels, the image compression problem is to encode groups of N contiguous pixels into K class identifiers. When N pixel values each requires b_N total bits for representation, and the number K requires b_K bits, then each b_N-bit data block is converted to a b_K-bit datum, or *codeword*, for storage. Such conversion is called data *compression* when $b_N > b_K$. The *compression ratio* is $b_N/(b_K + \alpha)$, where α is the average number of other bits of information per pixel (overhead) required for the decoding. The overhead accounts for the *codebook*, a table of blocks and their codewords that must also be stored as part of the compressed image file. We often omit the α bits to obtain an approximation b_N/b_K of the compression ratio. The inverse conversion of the class identifiers (codewords) 0 to $K - 1$ back into their associated pixel values is called *decompression*. Compression is used increasingly often to reduce the amount of storage required for files of images, audio data, and text. It allows quicker transmission of files on computer networks, especially on NSF's Internet, and can reduce the required bandwidth for high-density TV broadcast.

The compression and decompression mappings for image blocks are shown in Figure 12.18. The input blocks from an image are the feature vectors that are converted to the compressed block that is the binary class number k that represents one of the K classes. When the compression–decompression composition of mappings is a one-to-one mapping, the compression is called *lossless*, but otherwise it is called *lossy*. In the latter case, information is lost, which results in loss of resolution for decompressed images (and also for audio and other data streams as well). Lossy compression yields higher compression ratios and is thus more desirable whenever the loss can be kept small and small losses are tolerable. Certain medical images cannot tolerate loss, but most images can.

A common method of compression for still images is *run length encoding* (RLE), where image data are compressed wherever a pixel value is repeated one or more times contiguously in a fixed row. The encoded pixel datum contains a bit that indicates whether or not the next pixel value is to be repeated, followed by the number of times that value appears and then the pixel value. On typical images, RLE may yield a compression ratio of from about 1.1 to 1.5. Thus there is a need for more efficient schemes.

The Lempel–Ziv–Welsh (LZW) algorithm (used by Compuserve for *.GIF image files) constructs a code table on the fly. It checks a block of pixel values and if it has previously been assigned a codeword, then that codeword is used to represent the block. If a block has not previously appeared, then the algorithm assigns it a new (usually 12-bit) codeword and puts that new codeword and block in its temporary codebook. When the 12 bits are exhausted for codewords, then a new codebook is developed on the fly from that point forward. The inverse process also decodes on the fly to decompress so that no codebook need be stored.

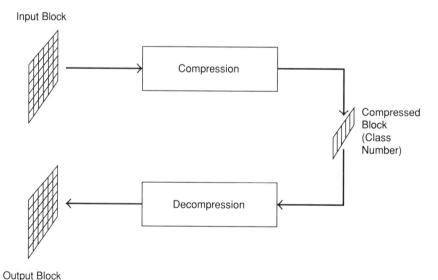

Figure 12.18.   The compression/decompression scheme.

LZW compression ratios are usually about 1.2 to 2, but may be higher or lower depending on the image. These compression schemes are lossless.

The process of building a codebook is called *vector quantization*. An $N_x \times M_y$ image can be partitioned into Q disjoint pxp blocks of pixels that cover the entire image. Letting $N = p \times p$, we use each block of N pixel values as an N-dimensional feature vector $\mathbf{x}^{(q)}$. This provides a sample of Q feature vectors $\{\mathbf{x}^{(q)}: q = 1,..., Q\}$ to be used in training a self-organizing (clustering) type of network, where $\mathbf{x}^{(q)} = (x_1^{(q)},..., x_N^{(q)})$. With 256 gray scale levels, for example, each pixel value is represented by eight bits from 00000000 to 11111111. Blocks of size 4×4 contain 16 pixel values of eight bits each. Each pixel value in the block is taken to be a component in a 16-dimensional feature vector. Suppose that we partition a 512×512 image into $Q = 128 \times 128 = 16,384$ blocks of 4×4 pixels each. Table 12.4 shows the approximate compression ratio for different numbers K of classes, where it takes $\log_2 K$ bits to represent the class numbers from 0 to $K - 1$. Q is the number of blocks (sample feature vectors) to be used in the training, and K is the size of the *codebook* (K different blocks and their associated codewords).

The Chang–Soliman–Chung Method

A very efficient lossy approach is to use a Kohonen Self-Organizing Feature Map (SOFM) or similar type of clustering algorithm on blocks of pixels (see Section 3.12). We describe here a method due to Chang et al. (1994). Let $\{\mathbf{x}^{(q)}: q = 1,..., Q\}$ be the sample of disjoint blocks from a particular image of 256 gray levels, where $\mathbf{x}^{(q)} = (x_1^{(q)},..., x_N^{(q)})$. Figure 12.19 shows the row-wise sequence of image blocks used in the processing. The component pixel values are normalized via $p(n, m) \rightarrow p(n, m)/256$.

Chang et al. use a *learning vector quantization* network (see Chapter 7) to cluster (self-organize) the Q feature vectors into K classes. The number K is not known a priori nor is the block size $N = p \times p$, but they must be selected to determine the number Q of exemplar vectors to be used in the training. There is a tradeoff in that large N yields a higher compression ratio and fewer exemplar feature vectors, but causes lower resolution and a blockier appearance in the decompressed image. The self-organizing algorithm is given below.

Table 12.4.
Approximate Compression Ratios on a 512 × 512 Image with 256 Gray Levels

K	$\log_2 K$	Block Size	Q	Compression Ratio
256	8	16 (4 × 4)	16,384	$(16 \times 8)/8 = 16.0$
1024	10	16	16,384	$(16 \times 8)/10 = 12.8$
4096	12	16	16,384	$(16 \times 8)/12 = 10.7$
1024	10	36 (6 × 6)	7,225	$(36 \times 8)/10 = 28.8$
256	8	9 (3 × 3)	29,241	$(9 \times 8)/8 = 9.0$
1024	10	4 (2 × 2)	65,536	$(4 \times 8)/10 = 3.2$
4096	12	4	65,536	$(4 \times 8)/12 = 2.7$

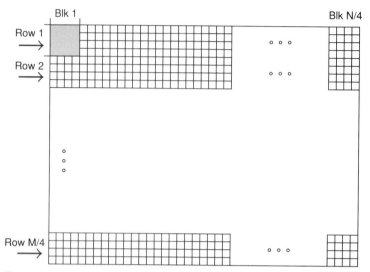

Figure 12.19. The sequence of 4×4 blocks processed in compression.

Step 1. for $k = 1$ to K do
    for $n = 1$ to N do   /set initial neurodal centers/
        $\mathbf{w}^{(k)} \leftarrow \text{random}(0,1)$;   (12.22)

Step 2. $\eta(0) \leftarrow 0.8$;   /initial learning rate, $0 < \eta(0) < 1$/
    $r \leftarrow 1$;   /initial iteration number/

Step 3. for $q = 1$ to Q do   /present each qth exemplar to the/
                               /network/
    for $k = 1$ to K do   /get distance to each kth neurode/
      $d_{kq} \leftarrow \sum_{(n=1,\,N)}[x_n^{(q)} - w_n^{(k)}(r)]^2$;   (12.23)
    $d_{q,k_{\min}} \leftarrow \min\{d_{kq}\colon k = 1,...,K\}$;   /find minimum distance, update winner/
    $\mathbf{w}^{(k_{\min})}(r+1) \leftarrow \mathbf{w}^{(k_{\min})}(r) + \eta(r)[\mathbf{x}^{(q)} - \mathbf{w}^k(r)]$;   (12.24)
    $r \leftarrow r + 1$;   /update iteration number/
    $\eta(r) \leftarrow \eta(r-1) - \Delta$;   /update with $\Delta = \eta(r-1)/8$/   (12.25)
    if $\eta(r) < 0.01$, then $\eta(r) \leftarrow 0.01$;   /limit learning rate away from zero/

Step 4. if $r \leq I$, then goto Step 3
    else stop;   /$I = sQ$, sampling frequency $s = 12$ is
                                good/

Chang et al. iterate the training until the clusters do not change further, which usually takes about 12 epochs, or $12Q$ iterations. They feel that a setting of 16 epochs is very safe. To reduce the number K of classes (codewords), and thus achieve higher compression ratios, they implement neurodal center adjustments and neurodal replenishment. First, the neurodal centers are adapted by replacing them by the centroids of their respective clusters. Neurodal replenishment is described by Nasrabadi and King (1988). The neurodal center selected for replenishment is either the least used or unused in that it did not win on any presentations of the input exemplar vectors. It is moved into the cluster of the neurode that has the largest intraset mean-squared error (see Chapter 2). The component that has the largest maximum–minus–minimum difference within that cluster is determined and the current center vector is assigned on that axis away from the mean vector of that class by use of a random number. Then that cluster is broken into two clusters with the new center for a new neurode.

The *advantages* of this method over the Kohonen SOFM and the counterpropagation network are: (i) it does not leave a large number of underutilized neurodes; (ii) it requires fewer neurodes; and (iii) the training is faster. We note that Chang et al also employ a method that uses 5×5 blocks that overlap 4×4 blocks by one pixel on all sides and the results are good.

The method of Chang et al. is similar in results to the Dog–Rabbit clustering algorithm (see Section 7.3) that also self-organizes as a type of learning vector quantization algorithm. The Dog–Rabbit algorithm uses only the neurodes that it needs and leaves the others unused, so that unused ones can be eliminated after training and before the operational mode is entered.

The decompression process needs no neural network. Once the compression training of the network is complete, the input/output exemplars are saved in the codebook. When decompressing, the next codeword k is read from the compressed file and the associated pxp block it indexes is inserted into the image matrix in the next unfilled block position. The block size N and number K of classes that determine the compression ratio are dependent on the particular image's local dispersions. An image with several large dark regions would compress much more than one with locally widely fluctuating pixel values.

Chang et al. use the *normalized mean-squared error* (NMSE) and *normalized signal-to-noise ratio* (NSNR) as measures of the similarity of the decompressed image to the original one, defined by

$$\text{NMSE} = \sum_{(n=1, N_x)}\sum_{(m=1, M_y)}[p(n, m) - p^\sim(n, m)]^2 / \sum_{(n=1, N_x)}\sum_{(m=1, M_y)}[p(n, m)]^2 \tag{12.26}$$

$$\text{NSNR} = 10 \log_{10}[1/\text{NMSE}] = -10 \log_{10}[\text{NMSE}] \tag{12.27}$$

where $p(n, m)$ is the original pixel value and $p^\sim(n, m)$ is the decompressed pixel value in position (n, m).

The *peak signal-to-noise ratio* (PSNR) is also used as a measure (Setiono and Lu, 1994) of the quality of the decompressed image. It is defined by

$$\text{PNSR} = 10 \log_{10}[Q_x N_x (256)^2 / \sum_{(m=1, M)}\sum_{(n=1, N)}(p(n, m) - p^\sim(n, m))^2] \tag{12.28}$$

In studies on compression of two thumb fingerprints, Chang et al., who call their method (described above) the *sampling-frequency self-organizing network* (SSN), obtained the results presented in Table 12.5. The LZ method used the Lempel–Ziv algorithm. JPEG is the standard method of the *Joint Photographic Experts Group* for still images that compresses via the discrete cosine transform (DCT, the real part of the DFT) followed by filtering off the low frequencies that have low energy (and thus do not affect the image appreciably). WSQ is the wavelet transform method.

12.7. Automatic Speech Recognition

The Speech Recognition Problem

Speaker independent *automatic speech recognition* (ASR) in real time is the elusive goal of past and present research. Some commercial systems are available (for example, International Business Machines showed one at COMDEX 1995 in Las Vegas), but they require considerable training time and learn to recognize an individual speaker with stopping required between words. The problem is especially difficult because different speakers have vocal tracts with variations in shape, size and movements of the parts (glottis, epiglottis, soft palate, tongue, and teeth, for example). They also have different accents, rates and styles. The satisfactory and practical solution of this problem will bring a new age where writing by hand and typing at a keyboard are no longer necessary except for special tasks.

Speech recognizers are divided into two classes: i) *isolated word recognizers*, which requires the speaker to stop between words; and ii) *continuous speech recognizers*, that operate on fluent speech. Speech is composed of: i) multiple vocal tones at natural (resonant) frequencies generated by the vocal chords; and ii) the modulation of the tones by the voice tract that extends from the vocal chords through the teeth and lips and the nostrils. The voice tract acts as a shaping filter. Both the vocal chord generator and the vocal tract filter vary over time. During continuous speech, the sounds of both vowels and consonants at different points are different because they run together and the speaker may anticipate the next syllable so that the vocal tract organs do not function exactly the same. This is called *coarticulation* and

Table 12.5.
Comparative Results of Compression of Two Thumb Fingerprints

Thumb Fingerprint	Compression Method	NMSE	NSNR (dB)	Compression Ratio
1	LZ	N/A (lossless)	N/A	1.17
1	JPEG	0.00069	31.6	12.00
1	WSQ	0.00119	29.2	13.33
1	SSN	0.00115	29.4	11.88 (22.16[a])
2	LZ	N/A (lossless)	N/A	1.23
2	JPEG	0.00061	32.2	12.00
2	WSQ	0.00070	31.6	13.33
2	SSN	0.00049	33.1	11.88 (19.48[a])

[a]On minimizing the clustering error $\sum_k \sum_q (\mathbf{x}^{(q(k))} - \mathbf{w}^{(k)})^2$, where $\mathbf{x}^{(q(k))}$ belongs to cluster with center $\mathbf{w}^{(k)}$.

includes the phenomenon that different neighboring sound units cause a sound unit to be pronounced differently.

Figure 12.20 displays a speech recognition system based on vector quantization of feature vectors into codewords that represent the basic sound units. The analog-to-digital (A/D) converter operates on the audio-frequency speech signal $s(t)$ and samples it at discrete sampling times $0, \Delta t, 2\Delta t, \ldots, r\Delta t$ into digital (binary) values. The sampling that yields discrete values of b bits degrades the information in the signal to an extent that depends upon the time and bit resolution.

The *signal-to-noise ratio* (SNR) due to the *quantization error* is σ_s^2/σ_e^2, where the mean-squared error (variance) subscripts denote "signal" and "error," respectively. Let s_{max} be the maximum amplitude of a bipolar analog signal and let b be the number of bits used in the quantized values. The errors in the values are uniformly distributed over $\Delta = 2s_{max}/2^b$, so that

$$\sigma_e^2 = \Delta^2/12 = (1/12)[2s_{max}/2^b]^2 = (s_{max})^2/[3(2^{2b})] \qquad (12.29)$$

where Δ is the error of digitization determined by the value of the least significant bit. The SNR (Furui, 1989) is thus

$$\text{SNR} = \sigma_s^2/\sigma_e^2 = \{\sigma_s^2/[(s_{max})^2/3(2^{2b})]\} = 3(2^{2b})/[s_{max}/\sigma_s]^2 \qquad (12.30)$$

To increase the SNR, the sampled signal $\{s(r\Delta t)\}_r$ can be preprocessed (Furui, 1989) to preemphasize the higher frequencies by application of the first-order filter:

$$H(z) = 1 - \alpha z^{-1} \qquad (12.31)$$

where α is close to unity.

Letting $s(t)$ now be the preemphasized speech signal, we can write

$$s(t) = v(t)*h(t) \qquad (12.32)$$

Figure 12.20.   A learning vector quantization speech recognition system.

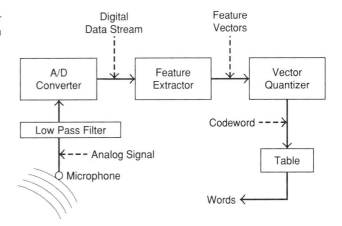

where $v(t)$ is the vocal tonal signal, $h(t)$ is the voice tract filter response and * denotes the convolution operation. In the frequency domain, this becomes

$$S(f) = V(f)H(f) \tag{12.33}$$

where $S(f)$, $V(f)$, and $H(f)$ are respectively the Fourier transforms of $s(t)$, $v(t)$, and $h(t)$ and f is the frequency argument.

The human speaking voice ranges from about 100 to 3300 Hz, so the Bell T1 (digital telephone) sampling rate is taken to be 8000 samples per second to satisfy the Nyquist theorem (to avoid aliasing). The human ear perceives speech from the power spectral information with phase information being of lesser importance (Furui, 1989).

The discrete Fourier transform (DFT) on the discrete sample $\{s(0), s(\Delta t),..., s(r\Delta t)\}$ supplies the spectral information. Researchers usually assume that short time windows of 10 to 30 milliseconds separate the time invariant segments. Each window contains R samples. The *short-time* DFT (STDFT) for each frequency $f = 0,..., R - 1$ over the sampling window of times $r = 0,..., R - 1$ is

$$S(f) = (1/R)\textstyle\sum_{(r=0, R-1)}s(r)\exp(-j2\pi fr/R) \tag{12.34}$$

A short-time rectangular window cuts off the signal sharply at each end and thus introduces high frequencies and aliasing in the spectrum, so we multiply by a cosine window such as the Hamming or Hanning windows, denoted by $\{w_{Ha\_}(r)\}$, where

$$w_{Ham}(r) = 0.54 - 0.46\cos(\pi r/(R - 1)) \tag{12.35}$$

$$w_{Han}(r) = 0.50 - 0.50\cos(\pi r/(R - 1)) \tag{12.36}$$

Note that the Hamming window does not quite reach zero at the endpoints of the windows, whereas the Hanning window does. Figure 12.21 displays rectangular and Hanning windows.

As an example, let the sampling interval be $\Delta t = 0.125$ ms, which provides $8000 = 1/\Delta t$ samples per second. For $R = 256$ (a commonly used value), the rectangular window has

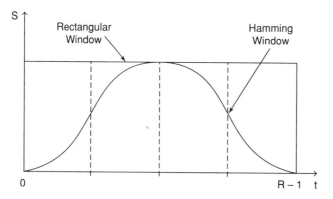

Figure 12.21. Rectangular and Hamming windows.

width of 32 ms. The frequency resolution is $\Delta f = 1/(R\Delta t) = 1/(256 \times 0.125 \times 10^{-3}) = 31$ Hz. If the rectangular window were doubled in size to 512 points, then Δf would be 15.5 Hz.

The cosine window reduces the effective length of the window by 40% (Furui, 1989) by compressing the waveforms on each end of the window, which causes the frequency resolution Δf to be coarser. The reduced window is called a *frame*. The frame is shifted across the signal sample and the STDFT is computed for each frame. For example, for a rectangular window of 256 points and a Hamming window of the same size, the window may be shifted 128 points in time for each new STDFT. With 10-kHz sampling frequency, the speech signal is assumed to be invariant over 20-ms intervals. A 10-kHz sampling rate would suffice to capture the lower frequencies, but could not capture all of the unvoiced energy (for example, the phoneme "s" could sound like "f"). A 20-kHz sampling rate provides for high-quality speech because the Nyquist frequency of 10 kHz is near the limit of human perception.

Features for Speech Recognition

The STDFT can be regarded as the product of (i) the spectral envelope (shaping filter of the vocal tract) and (ii) the spectral fine structure due to the *voiced* frequencies (an "f," "p," "s," or "t" is an *unvoiced* sound) that contains periodic patterns from the voice box generator. In order to determine the frequencies at each sampling instant $r\Delta t$, the received speech signal is fed through a bank of bandpass filters where each filter passes only a small band of frequencies. All together the bands cover the voice frequency range. Thus at $t = r\Delta t$, there are multiple intensity (or amplitude or power) values sampled, one for each frequency band.

Figure 12.22 presents a coarse voice "image," or *spectrogram*, of a speech signal for illustrative purposes. It is produced by a *spectrograph* machine. The horizontal axis represents

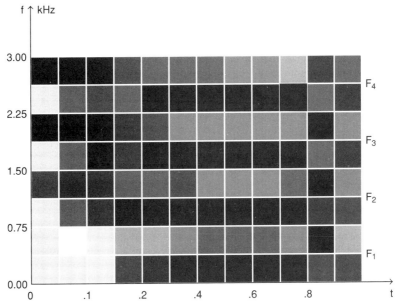

Figure 12.22. A time-frequency image of a speech signal.

the discrete time t in seconds, and the vertical axis represents the frequency f in kHz. Each axis is digitized, so there results an array of "audels" (audio elements). The four horizontal strips of the spectogram shown in the figure are called *formants*, denoted by $F_1,..., F_4$ (each consists of two rows here). The lower three formants (low frequencies) are the most important in speech recognition.

The ear does not hear tones linearly, but logarithmic, as the frequencies increase (Morgan and Scofield, 1991). Therefore, the frequency axis is often scaled nonlinearly per the mel scale given in Furui (1989) as

$$\text{mel} = 1000 \log_2(1 + f) \tag{12.37}$$

where f is the actual frequency in kHz and mel is the perceived frequency. Table 12.6 presents the mel frequency bands (Fissore et al., 1990). According to Davis and Mermelstein (1980), spectrograms that use the mel scale for the frequency axis yield higher recognition rates of basic sound units.

The process described below is called *homomorphic filtering*. The logarithm of the magnitude spectrum $|S(f)|$ of the speech signal $s(t) = v(t)h(t)$ is

$$\log(|S(f)|) = \log(|V(f)H(f)|) = \log(|V(f)||H(f)|) = \log(|V(f)|) + \log(|H(f)|) = V^{\sim}(f) + + H^{\sim}(f) \tag{12.38}$$

This separates the vocal signal from the shaping filter. The *cepstrum* $s^{\sim}(\tau)$ of $s(t)$ is the inverse Fourier transform of $S^{\sim}(f) = \log(|S(f)|)$, which yields

$$s^{\sim}(\tau) = v^{\sim}(\tau) + h^{\sim}(\tau) \tag{12.39}$$

where $v^{\sim}(\tau)$ is the inverse Fourier transform of $V^{\sim}(f) = \log(|V(f)|)$ and $h^{\sim}(\tau)$ is the inverse Fourier transform of $H^{\sim}(f) = \log(|H(f)|)$. The homomorphically filtered signal is $s^{\sim}(\tau)$, where τ is not the actual time, but is a nonlinearly warped time called *quefrency*.

A spoken sentence is composed of words and a word is composed of syllables. A syllable is made up of *phonemes*, or basic sound units referred to above. For example, "baby"

Table 12.6.
The Frequency Bands of the Mel Scale

Band Number:	1	2	3	4	5	6
Band (Hz):	187–280	280–374	374–476	476–588	588–710	710–850
Center (Hz):	229	324	422	529	646	777
Band Number:	7	8	9	10	11	12
Band (Hz):	850–1009	1009–1186	1186–1382	1382–1606	1606–1868	1868–2167
Center (Hz):	929	1094	1281	1490	1732	2012
Band Number:	13	14	15	16	17	18
Band (Hz):	2167–2522	2522–2942	2942–3456	3456–4110	4110–4950	4950–6071
Center (Hz):	2338	2724	3189	3769	4510	5482

Table 12.7.
The Phonemes Used in English

Phoneme:	i	I	e	ae	a	$\tilde{\mathfrak{z}}$	Λ	o	u	U	O
Example:	b<u>ea</u>t	b<u>i</u>t	b<u>e</u>t	b<u>a</u>t	B<u>o</u>b	b<u>ir</u>d	b<u>u</u>t	b<u>ough</u>t	b<u>oo</u>t	b<u>oo</u>k	<u>a</u>bout
Phoneme:	ɨ	aI	oI	au	eI	oU	ju	m	n	η	p
Example:	ros<u>e</u>s	b<u>uy</u>	b<u>oy</u>	d<u>ow</u>n	b<u>ai</u>t	b<u>oa</u>t	<u>you</u>	<u>m</u>et	<u>n</u>et	si<u>ng</u>	<u>p</u>et
Phoneme:	t	k	b	d	g	f	θ	s	sh	v	∂
Example:	<u>t</u>en	<u>k</u>it	<u>b</u>et	<u>d</u>ebt	<u>g</u>et	<u>f</u>at	<u>th</u>ing	<u>s</u>at	<u>sh</u>ut	<u>v</u>at	<u>th</u>at
Phoneme:	z	zh	h	j	tsh	w	l	r	y		
Example:	<u>z</u>oo	a<u>z</u>ure	<u>h</u>at	<u>j</u>udge	<u>ch</u>urch	<u>w</u>it	<u>l</u>et	<u>r</u>ent	<u>y</u>oung		

contains the two syllables "ba" and "by," each of which contains a consonant phoneme and one or more vowel phonemes. A spectrogram can be considered to contain vertical strips, or time bands across the frequencies, that represent phonemes. These strips may be used as rectangular blocks that are vectors of features in the same way as blocks of image pixels. A great difficulty is to find the points in time where one word ends and another begins. The phonemes themselves differ with different speakers and even with the same speaker, depending upon stress, rate, the neighboring phonemes, and coarticulation (the change in sound caused by the changing of the vocal tract shaping filter between and during phoneme enunciation).

Of the very large number of possible combinations of phonemes, only a relatively few are used in speech. The number of frequently used words is between 2000 and 3000, which limits the practical problem to a manageable size. Table 12.7 lists the 42 phonemes used in American English (Morgan and Scofield, 1991, p. 99).

Other blocks of features are adjacent groups of phoneme strips that form words. The difficulty here also is to find where the words end and begin in continuous speech. A popular approach is to use the cepstrum coefficients (recall that these separate out the power at the vocal resonant frequencies from the lower frequencies of the shaping filter as features). Successive frames of cepstrum coefficients can also be subtracted to obtain the *differenced cepstral coefficients* (Morgan and Scofield, 1991).

The Kondo–Kamata–Ishida Experiments

The experiments described here appear in Kondo et al. (1994). They trained a learning vector quantization (LVQ) network (see Chapter 7) to recognize a small set of words rather than the usual phonemes from which the spoken words are constructed. The words used were the Japanese names of the digits 0, 1, ..., 9. The difficult task of marking off the beginning and ending of words was done by humans based on spectral energy rather than being automated. Words were chosen rather than phonemes because the latter have the coarticulation problem. Tests were run on both isolated words and on continuous speech with rates between one and three words per second. The spoken digits are provided in Table 12.8.

The speech signals were converted to 12-bit samples (4096 different values). The sampling rate was 10 kilosamples per second. Each spoken digit signal was broken into 16 sec-

Table 12.8.
The Digits in Spoken Japanese

"zero"	(0)	"ichi"	(1)	"ni"	(2)	"san"	(3)	"yon"	(4)
"go"	(5)	"roku"	(6)	"nana"	(7)	"hachi"	(8)	"kyu"	(9)

tions between the beginning and ending points of a word and multiplied by a 256-point Hamming window. The input features are 16×16-dimensional vectors of mel-cepstrum coefficients that are normalized on each section of 16 points. Ten reference vectors, one for each spoken digit, were selected at random from those generated by five male speakers. The reference vectors provided the initial neurodal center vectors.

During the supervised training, the sample feature vectors $\{\mathbf{x}^{(q)}: q = 1,..., Q\}$ were input to the LVQ network one at a time, where the sample used 10 different speakers. An input $\mathbf{x}^{(q)}$ was compared to each reference (neurodal center) vector $\mathbf{w}^{(k)}$, $k = 0,..., 9$ to determine the closest one (the *winner*) $\mathbf{w}^{(k*)}$. The reference center vectors were updated on each qth presentation via

$$\mathbf{w}^{(k*)}(r + 1) = \mathbf{w}^{(k*)}(r) + \eta(r)[\mathbf{x}^{(q)} - \mathbf{w}^{(k*)}(r)] \tag{12.40}$$

For each $k \neq k*$ (the *losers*), the updating was done by

$$\mathbf{w}^{(k)}(r + 1) = \mathbf{w}^{(k)}(r) - \eta(r)[\mathbf{x}^{(q)} - \mathbf{w}^{(k)}(r)] \tag{12.41}$$

The sample of input feature vectors were presented to the LVQ network 1000 times (1000 epochs). Then the trained network was tested with 126 samples and achieved the accuracy rates given in Table 12.9. Kondo et al. note that the Japanese word "roku" for 6 is often spoken with the beginning and ending phonemes being unvoiced and the word suffers the effects of coarticulation. For continuous speech, a change of that word (such as "toku" in place of "roku") could help.

Table 12.9.
Recognition Accuracy on Spoken Japanese Digits

Spoken Digit	Isolated Word Rate	Continuous Speech Rate
0	100	100
1	100	100
2	100	100
3	100	100
4	100	100
5	100	100
6	92.9	72.7
7	100	100
8	100	100
9	100	91.7
	Average Rate: 99.2	Average Rate: 95.4

12.8. Optical Character Recognition of Hand-Printed Characters

Hand-Printed Characters as Textures

Optical character recognition (OCR) is widespread nowadays, and many products are on the market that recognize characters in scanned pages. Images of pages of text are converted to ASCII character files for editing, combining with other files, and so on. But these systems operate on typed fonts. For hand-printed alphanumeric characters (that include the digits), the problem is much more difficult. There are many different styles of printing, but within a given style there are also many variations. Any given person prints rather differently at different times, depending on the pen or pencil, the width of the lines, the slight rotation of the paper, the type of paper or digitizer pad, and the mood and stress level of the person. For example, there may be a loop in a character one time and not another time. The line endings may have unintentional serifs.

There are also similarities between certain characters. A "2" may appear to be a "Z" or vice versa. An "a" may appear as a "9," an "h" may appear as an "n," a "B" may appear as an "8," and so on. If the recognition features are invariant under rotation, then a "d" and "p" will have the same features and "3" and "E" may be very similar. Thus there must be some features that are not rotation-invariant to distinguish these characters. Figure 12.23 displays some hand-printed characters.

The method outlined here treats each character as a texture and extracts texture features for use in an RBF network. We note that each character is primarily determined by broad strokes rather than by serifs or loops or other more minor differences. It is the global relationship of the groups of pixels in a character block that determines the character. Thus we need a method that accounts for this.

Figure 12.23. Some hand-printed characters.

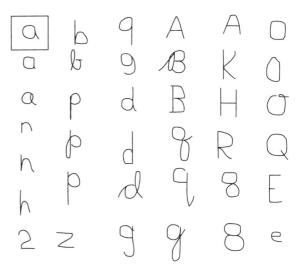

Outline of a Simple Method

The first step is to capture the characters in blocks of pixels. Next, the pixels $\{g(n, m)\}$ in the block are thresholded so as to be white (0) and black (1), which is an inversion of the usual binary pixels. This is for the purpose of finding the center of mass (c.m.) of the black pixels that form the character on a white background. Let N_x be the number of columns and M_y be the number of rows in a minimal $N_x \times M_y$ block containing the character. The c.m. is a two-dimensional vector $\mathbf{c} = (c_x, c_y)$ where

$$c_x = (1/N_x)\sum_{(n=1, Nx)}n\{\sum_{(m=1, My)}g(n, m)\} \tag{12.42}$$

$$c_y = (1/M_y)\sum_{(m=1, My)}m\{\sum_{(n=1, Nx)}g(n, m)\} \tag{12.43}$$

In Equation (12.42), for a fixed column, the pixel values are summed over all rows to obtain the total mass in the column, and this is then multiplied by the column number n (distance from the origin, where the leftmost column is number one and the rightmost is number N_x). These are then averaged over the columns. The situation is analogous for Equation (12.43). For white pixels, $g(n, m) = 1$, or else $g(n, m) = 0$ for black.

We use the c.m. location (c_x, c_y) in the pixel block as the point about which to compute moments via

$$\mu_{pq} = \sum_m\sum_n (n - c_x)^p(m - c_y)^q g(n, m) \tag{12.44}$$

The second-order moments μ_{11}, μ_{20}, and μ_{02} provide variational measures about the c.m., while the third-order moments μ_{30}, μ_{03}, μ_{21}, and μ_{12} provide a measure of the skewness of the distributions of black pixel values about the c.m. These features need to be normalized by dividing each by the appropriate powers of the c.m. They are invariant under rotation, so we also need some features that not invariant.

We partition the character block into "quarter" sections above and below and to the left and right of the c.m. The proportion of black pixels in each of these quarters provides a rotation variant set of features that can distinguish between a "d" and a "p," for example. Figure 12.24 presents the character "K" drawn with a pencil and shows the c.m. and the four sections ("quarters").

12.9. A Video Camera Tracking System

The Camera Tracking Problem

Suppose that a video camera is to be equipped with an automated system to track a moving object that is distinguishable (detectable) from its background. Given a sequence of images $\{I_r\}$ over time $r = 0, 1,...$, the images are to be processed in real time to find the approximate center of the target object relative to the center of the video image (intersection of cross-hairs). A real-time method is desired for recognizing, or associating, the camera aiming commands with the feedback input differences between the target center and the video image center. The exemplar pairs of inputs and outputs must be chosen such that the commands for the current input differences drive the differences to zero. Figure 12.25 shows the video

Figure 12.24. The character "K" and quarters.

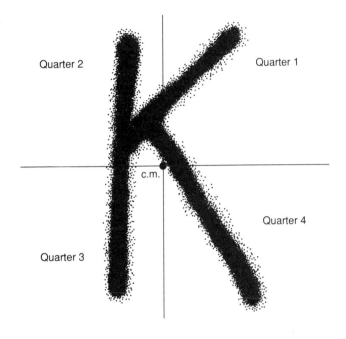

Quarter 2

Quarter 1

c.m.

Quarter 4

Quarter 3

Figure 12.25. The video camera tracking screen.

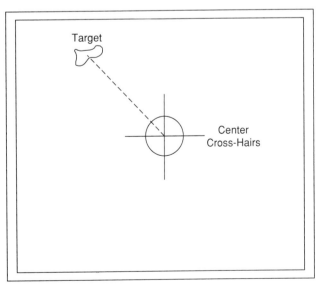

Target

Center
Cross-Hairs

Video Screen

image with a target. The video camera is mounted on a motorized base such that it can be pointed radially both horizontally and vertically.

Tracking with Radial Basis Function Networks

We cover the screen with Gaussian fuzzy set membership functions with nine balls of radius σ as shown in the *field of view* (FoV) in Figure 12.26. When the target's coordinates in the image are determined and the differences d_x and d_y computed, then (d_x, d_y) is the target's position relative to the xy-coordinate system with origin at the center of the image. Then $\mathbf{d} = (d_x, d_y)$ is an input feature vector that is fed into each mth hidden neurode's Gaussian radial basis function to obtain

$$y_m = f(d_x, d_y) = \exp[-\|\mathbf{d} - \mathbf{w}^{(m)}\|^2/(2\sigma^2)] \tag{12.45}$$

for $m = 1,..., M$. The output is $\mathbf{c} = (c_h, c_e)$ that is a pair of commands to the horizontal and elevation motors, respectively. Actually, more than two inputs were used in (Looney, 1996), as given below.

Tracking is implemented with a planar video display that shows the object being tracked. The FoV is a rectangular screen with cross-hairs at the center. The idea is to drive the current errors dx and dy of the target position (dx, dy) to zero using the input vector of feedback errors $\mathbf{e} = (dx^{(r)}, dy^{(r)}, dx^{(r-1)}, dy^{(r-1)}, dx^{(r-2)}, dy^{(r-2)})$ on iteration r. The outputs c_x and c_y are the respective x and y commands for the camera positioning motors.

An input positional error vector $\mathbf{e}$ activates one or more RBFs to put out higher y_m values ($1 \leq m \leq M$). The combination of outputs is fed into each of the two output neurodes, where the values are multiplied by the weights $\{u_{mj}\}$ ($j = 1, 2$) and summed to yield the

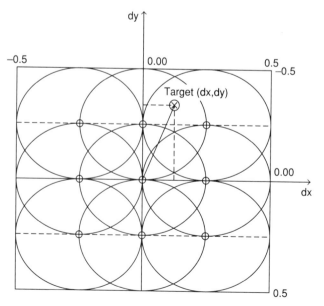

Figure 12.26. The field of view with RBF σ-contours.

Figure 12.27. The CCW target path (no control).

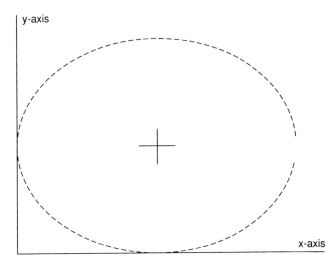

control commands, c_x and c_y. The network is trained to map the input error vector **e** into the commands c_x and c_y that are proportions of maximum turns $\theta_{x\max}$ and $\theta_{y\max}$ that the camera's gimbal motors can make.

A simulated high-speed target was run on the counterclockwise (CCW) path shown in Figure 12.27. A clockwise (CW) path (not shown) is the reflection of the path of Figure 12.27 about the vertical axis. The RBF network controlled the camera after training. The centers of the nine circles shown in Figure 12.26 were taken as the initial center vectors of the hidden neurodes. The initial output weights were selected randomly between −1 and 1.

Figure 12.28. CCW path after Training 1.

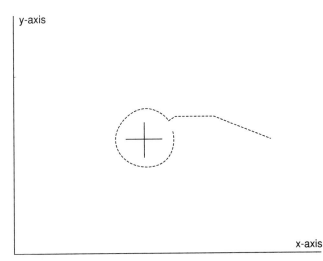

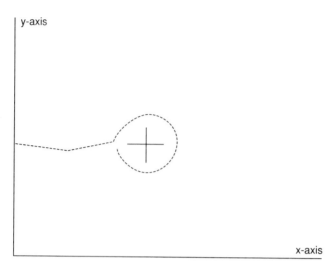

Figure 12.29. CW path after Training 1.

The network was trained by adjusting both the hidden neurode centers and output weights, one at a time, to minimize the sum-squared error (SSE) over the paths (sum of dx^2 and dy^2 over the updates of an entire path). The camera tracking system was modeled simply so that the commands c_x and c_y moved the camera through the angles θ_x and θ_y that are proportions of $\theta_{x\text{max}}$ and $\theta_{y\text{max}}$.

We trained for 20 iterations, where a single iteration adjusted each of the hidden and output weights in turn over a complete target path flyout to determine the sum-squared error. The spread parameter value $\sigma = 0.4$ yielded stable results. The CCW target path starts on the right, but the CW target path starts on the left. Figures 12.28 and 12.29 show the tar-

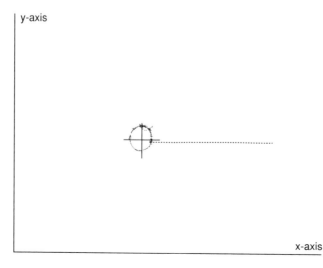

Figure 12.30. CCW path after Training 2.

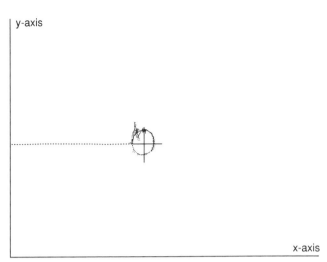

Figure 12.31. CW path after Training 2.

get position relative to the controlled camera on the respective CCW and CW paths under Training 1 runs that used only the two error inputs $dx^{(r)}$ and $dy^{(r)}$.

Figures 12.30 and 12.31 show the results of Training 2 runs that used the error inputs and previous error inputs $dx^{(r)}$, $dy^{(r)}$, $dx^{(r-1)}$, and $dy^{(r-1)}$. The Training 2 errors here are much smaller. We did not use six inputs, but we expect that the use of $dx^{(r-2)}$ and $dy^{(r-2)}$ additionally would result in an even better performance.

Exercises

12.1. Project 1: Determine the economic features that are important for predicting the economy. Construct feature vectors for an economy growing at a healthy and sustainable rate and also construct a set of feature vectors for an unhealthy economy. Train a neural network to output the adjustments to the prime interest rate to drive the economy toward a healthy sustainable state. Add a tax and train again.

12.2. Project 2: Obtain some textures (about four) and put them together into an image. Construct a set of features that can discriminate between textures. Obtain feature values from blocks (subimages) and train a neural network to recognize the textures. Now develop an algorithm so that the neural network can be used to construct boundary lines between the sections of the different features.

12.3. Project 3: Train a neural network to accurately approximate a pseudorandom number generator that generates uniform random numbers between 0 and 1 exclusively. Test the FANN by graphing consecutive pairs in the plane and examine the graph for uniformity. Retrain until uniformity is achieved.

12.4. Project 4: Obtain an image with 256 gray levels that has lots of detail. Use a neural network to sharpen the original image. Use another neural network to smooth the original image. [Option A: Use fuzzy logic to combine the sharpened and smoothed images into a new image that is both sharp and smooth. Option B: Use another neural network to detect edges of the sharpened image and draw a picture of black edges on a white background.]

12.5. Project 5: Obtain an image with 256 shades of gray that has considerable detail. Use a neural network to compress the data. Try to achieve a high compression ratio, accounting for the overhead also, and yet do not let the loss be significant. Compare the decompressed image with the original (use a measure of difference).

12.6. Project 6: Obtain files of digitized recordings of which one is human speech, another contains music (of whatever type you like), another contains various background noise. Each file contains a data stream. Construct files of differences of consecutive data values. Use blocks of differences as features and train a neural network to recognize human speech from music and background noise.

12.7. Project 7: Obtain a set of images of several signatures. Using texture features, train a network to recognize the signatures. Use a codebook so that each recognized signature can be associated with the correct name.

12.8. Project 8: Use a kinematic simulation of a moving target in the air that is approaching. Assuming that a missile can sense only the line-of-sight angles from its long body axis to the target and that it knows the approximate distance on each sensing feedback loop, train a neural network to guide the missile to intercept the target. List all assumptions. For example, you need to assume that the missile is launched in the general direction of the target at $t = 0$. Assume maximum thrust controls that the missile can exert on itself in the horizontal and vertical directions.

References

Augusteijn, M., and Skufca, T. (1993), Identification of human faces through texture-based feature recognition and neural network technology, *IEEE 1993 Int. Conf. Neural Networks*, vol. 1, 392–398.

Chang, W., Soliman, H. S., and Sung, A. H. (1994), A vector quantization neural network to compress still monochromatic images, *Proc. IEEE 1994 Int. Conf. on Neural Networks*, vol. 6, 4163–4168.

Chen, H. (1995), conversations at the University of Alabama, Tuscaloosa (September).

Davis, S. B., and Mermelstein, P. (1980), Comparison of parametric representations of monosyllabic word recognition in continuously spoken sentences, *IEEE Trans. ASSP*, vol. 28, no. 4, 357–366.

Etemad, K., and Chellappa, R. (1993), A neural network based edge detector, *IEEE 1993 Int. Conf. Neural Networks*, vol. 1, 132–137.

Fissore, L., Laface, P., and Pieraccini, R. (1990), The recognition algorithms, in *Advanced Algorithms and Architectures for Speech Understanding*, edited by G. Pirani, Springer-Verlag, Berlin.

Furui, S. (1989), *Digital Speech Processing, Synthesis and Recognition*, Marcel Dekker, New York.

Gonzales, R. C., and Woods, R. E. (1992), *Digital Image Processing*, Addison-Wesley, Reading, MA.

Haralick, R. M., Shanmugam, K., and Dinstein, I. (1973), Texture features for image classification, *IEEE Trans. Syst. Man Cybernet.*, vol. 3, 610–621.

Henson-Mack, K. (1996), *Neuro-fuzzy Block Mappings for Image Enhancement*, Ph.D. dissertation, College of Engineering, University of Alabama, Tuscaloosa.

Hu, M. K. (1962), Visual pattern recognition by moment invariants, *IRE Trans. Inf. Theory*, vol. 8, 179–187.

Kondo, K., Kamata, H., and Ishida, Y. (1994), Speaker independent spoken digit recognition using LVQ, *Proc. IEEE 1994 Int. Conf. Neural Networks*, vol. 7, 4448–4451.

Li, W. H. (1995), conversations at the University of Alabama, Tuscaloosa (September).

Looney, C. (1996), A radial basis function neurotracker, *Proceedings of the 1996 International Symposium on Artificial Life and Robotics*, Beppu, Japan.

Morgan, D. P., and Scofield, C. L. (1991), *Neural Networks and Speech Processing*, Kluwer Academic Press, Boston.

Moura, L., and Martin, F. (1991), Edge detection through cooperation and competition, *Proc. IJCNN 1991*, Singapore, vol. 3, 2588–2593.

Nasrabadi, N. N., and King, R. A. (1988), Image coding using vector quantization: a review, *IEEE Trans. Commun.*, vol. 36, no. 8, 957–971.

Russo, F. (1993), A new class of fuzzy operators for image processing: design and implementation, *Proc. IEEE 1993 Int. Conf. Neural Networks*, vol. 1, 815–820.

Russo, F., and Ramponi, G. (1992), Fuzzy operator for sharpening of noisy images, *Electron. Lett.*, vol. 29, no. 18, 1715–1716.

Russo, F., and Ramponi, G. (1995), A fuzzy operator for the enhancement of blurred and noisy images, *IEEE Trans. Image Processing*, vol. 4, no. 8, 1169–1174.

Setiono, R., and Lu, G. (1994), Image compression using a feedforward neural network, *Proc. IEEE 1994 Int. Conf. Neural Networks*, vol. 7, 4761–4765.

Walczak, S., and Krause, J. (1993), Chaos, neural networks and gaming, in *Intelligent Systems*, Third Golden West International Conference on Intelligent Systems, edited by A. Yfantis, Kluwer Academic Press, Boston, pp. 457–466.

Weszka, J. S., Dyer, C. R., and Rosenfeld, A. (1976), A comparative study of texture measures for terrain classification, *IEEE Trans. Syst. Man Cybern.*, vol. 6, no. 4, 269–285.

Index